Date Due

Library Bureau Cat. no. 1137

*

AMERICAN WRITERS SERIES
*

HARRY HAYDEN CLARK
General Editor

*

★ AMERICAN WRITERS SERIES ★

Volumes of representative selections, prepared by American scholars under the general editorship of Harry Hayden Clark, University of Wisconsin. Volumes now ready are starred.

AMERICAN TRANSCENDENTALISTS, *Raymond Adams, University of North Carolina*

*WILLIAM CULLEN BRYANT, *Tremaine McDowell, University of Minnesota*

*JAMES FENIMORE COOPER, *Robert E. Spiller, Swarthmore College*

*JONATHAN EDWARDS, *Clarence H. Faust, University of Chicago, and Thomas H. Johnson, Lawrenceville School*

*RALPH WALDO EMERSON, *Frederic I. Carpenter, Harvard University*

*BENJAMIN FRANKLIN, *Frank Luther Mott, University of Iowa, and Chester E. Jorgenson, Wayne University*

*ALEXANDER HAMILTON AND THOMAS JEFFERSON, *Frederick C. Prescott, Cornell University*

BRET HARTE, *Joseph B. Harrison, University of Washington*

*NATHANIEL HAWTHORNE, *Austin Warren, Boston University*

*OLIVER WENDELL HOLMES, *S. I. Hayakawa, University of Wisconsin, and Howard Mumford Jones, Harvard University*

*WASHINGTON IRVING, *Henry A. Pochmann, Mississippi State College*

HENRY JAMES, *Lyon Richardson, Western Reserve University*

*HENRY WADSWORTH LONGFELLOW, *Odell Shepard, Trinity College*

JAMES RUSSELL LOWELL, *Norman Foerster, University of Iowa, and Harry H. Clark, University of Wisconsin*

*HERMAN MELVILLE, *Willard Thorp, Princeton University*

*JOHN LOTHROP MOTLEY, *Chester P. Higby and B. T. Schantz, University of Wisconsin*

THOMAS PAINE, *Harry H. Clark, University of Wisconsin*

*FRANCIS PARKMAN, *Wilbur L. Schramm, University of Iowa*

*EDGAR ALLAN POE, *Margaret Alterton, University of Iowa, and Hardin Craig, Stanford University*

WILLIAM HICKLING PRESCOTT, *Michael Kraus, College of the City of New York, and William Charvat, New York University*

*SOUTHERN POETS, *Edd Winfield Parks, University of Georgia*

SOUTHERN PROSE, *Gregory Paine, University of North Carolina*

*HENRY DAVID THOREAU, *Bartholow Crawford, University of Iowa*

*MARK TWAIN, *Fred Lewis Pattee, Rollins College*

*WALT WHITMAN, *Floyd Stovall, University of Texas*

JOHN GREENLEAF WHITTIER, *Harry H. Clark, University of Wisconsin, and Bertha M. Stearns, Wellesley College*

*Pen drawing by Kerr Eby, after
a contemporary portrait*

JOHN LOTHROP MOTLEY

ÆT. CA. 50

John Lothrop Motley

REPRESENTATIVE SELECTIONS, WITH
INTRODUCTION, BIBLIOGRAPHY, AND NOTES

BY

CHESTER PENN HIGBY

Professor of History
University of Wisconsin

AND

B. T. SCHANTZ

Instructor in English
Colgate University

AMERICAN BOOK COMPANY
New York · Cincinnati · Chicago
Boston · Atlanta

MADE IN U. S. A.

PREFACE

As John Lothrop Motley is properly placed in the category of "literary" historians—that is, those writers whose work has value both for the student of belles-lettres and for the student of history—the general editor felt obliged to draft the services of two editors in the preparation of this volume, one from the field of history, the other from the field of American literature. To Professor Higby was assigned the responsibility of making the selections from Motley's three major historical works and of writing that portion of the Introduction which treats of Motley's work as a historian and as a diplomat. It was the province of Mr. Schantz to make the selections from the correspondence, the novels, and the other minor works, as well as to write those sections of the Introduction which deal with the literary apprenticeship, the literary theory, and the political and social views of Motley.

It has been the purpose of the editors, in the critical introduction, to explain Motley in terms of the genetic interrelations of his political, social, religious, and literary theories, and of his work as a diplomat and historian; to demonstrate that the various phases of his activity form coherent parts of a consistent whole. The task has been the more difficult because the writings of Motley have been subjected to but little critical examination of a close scholarly nature. The definitive biography remains to be written.

In determining the choice of representative selections from the writings of Motley, the editors perforce laid the principal emphasis upon the three major historical works, *The Rise of the Dutch Republic*, *History of the United Netherlands*, and *The Life and Death of John of Barneveld*. But they were guided in part by the fact that many of the minor works are not easily accessible to the student. These minor works have not been included in the collected edition of the *Writings*, and they are now, for the most part, out of print. This is true of the review articles, the two speeches which have been preserved, the novels, and other items of less importance. In some instances at least, these works do not deserve the obscurity into which they have been cast by the larger reputation of Motley as a historian. What is more, some of them assume a genuine significance in illustrating the growth of Motley's mind. For these reasons it has been thought proper to represent rather completely, in this text, *Historic Progress and American Democracy*, to reprint a typical group of letters, and to provide generous selections from the novels, *Morton's Hope* and *Merry-Mount*. The selections from each novel have been connected by passages which sum up the intervening text so that the reader may, in each instance, gain a fair conception of the whole novel.

Selections from *The Correspondence of John Lothrop Motley*, edited by G. W. Curtis, have been reprinted by the courtesy of the publishers, Harper & Brothers.

The editors are extremely grateful to Professor Harry Hayden Clark for helpful advice and valuable criticism, and to Professor Chester E. Jorgenson for useful suggestions.

C. P. H.

B. T. S.

CONTENTS

vii

V. Motley as a Diplomat
  A. Manuscript Sources, clvi
  B. Printed Sources: Primary, clvi
  C. Printed Sources: Secondary, clvi

VI. General American Backgrounds, clx

Selections

Letters

JOHN LOTHROP MOTLEY

John Lothrop Motley is now mainly remembered as the author of three colorful works of history dealing with the formative period of the United Netherlands. At the present time he would be classed as a historian with an unusual gift for literary expression. At the full tide of his success he undoubtedly had a somewhat different conception of himself. He had tried his apprentice hand without great success at the novel and had then turned to the writing of history. He would almost certainly have thought himself a literary man who had won success in the writing of historical works and who, as a reward for his acquaintance with Europe and his achievements in literature, had been given an opportunity to serve his country in important diplomatic posts.

In any attempt to judge his contribution to literature or history, consideration must be given to the time and place in which he wrote and worked. By birth he was an American, a New Englander of the middle years of the nineteenth century. By inheritance and training he was an heir of the European tradition. He was a member of a new society that had in the main been engrossed with the conquest and utilization of a new and somewhat raw continent, but which sprang from and in a measure kept in touch with the older society of Europe, with its more ancient and more highly developed culture and institutions. His interpreter must, in consequence, make some study of both his American environment and his European heritage.

I. LITERARY APPRENTICESHIP AND LITERARY THEORY

Motley was like Prescott in being a son of Massachusetts and "born with a silver spoon of Boston metal in his mouth."[1]

[1] *Cambridge History of American Literature*, II, 131.

The New England heritage and environment must be reckoned one of the most important factors in forming Motley's mind and determining his career. He was born in 1814 at Dorchester, now part of Boston, the son of a well-to-do merchant, and had as boyhood playmates Tom Appleton and Wendell Phillips. The finest education which New England had to offer was afforded to the future historian. He received his preparatory work at Round Hill (Northampton) under the tutelage of Joseph S. Cogswell and George Bancroft, and he attended Harvard from 1827 to 1831. The professor of rhetoric and oratory at Harvard during these years was Edward Tyrrell Channing,[2] who trained Edward Everett Hale, Emerson, Holmes, Sumner, Clarke, Bellows, and Lowell in English composition. Though Motley did not earn extraordinary distinction as a student,[3] he did evince a desire for further education, and, like Ticknor, Everett, Cogswell, Bancroft, and Longfellow, he went abroad to continue his studies in German universities.[4]

Returning to this country in 1835 after three years of study and travel on the Continent and in England, Motley took his place naturally in the most select circle of great New England figures, being essentially a member of the Brahmin caste. That

[2] *Dictionary of American Biography*, IV, 3. Professor Channing was a brother of the better-known William Ellery Channing, the Unitarian clergyman.

[3] He was third in his class at Harvard as a freshman, but he did not study diligently or consistently. In fact, he was somewhat irresponsible and for a time so negligent of assignments that he was rusticated; later, however, he so far mended his ways that the rules of the Phi Beta Kappa Society were stretched somewhat to permit his election to that fraternity. See Holmes's *John Lothrop Motley, A Memoir*, in *The Writings of Oliver Wendell Holmes* (Riverside Edition, 14 vols., Boston, 1878), XI, 329–526. This work is hereafter referred to simply as *Life*.

[4] Orie W. Long's *Literary Pioneers* (Cambridge, 1935) is a study of the first group of New Englanders who, impelled by a romantic impulse, went to Germany to study her language and literature at first hand. Motley is the latest of the group of pioneers included in Mr. Long's study.

his temperament was typical of the intellectual aristocracy composing this class is evidenced by his complaint in 1833 at finding it impossible to persuade a member of the German nobility "that in the United States anything exists but democracy and demagogues." [5] Motley's most intimate friendship among the prominent New England literary figures was that with Holmes, begun in 1835 and continuing until Motley's death in 1877.[6] The famous Saturday Club included Motley in a membership which boasted the names of Holmes, Emerson, Hawthorne, Longfellow, Lowell, Whipple, Whittier, Appleton, Dana, Agassiz, Peirce, John S. Dwight, Governor Andrew, and Charles Sumner. He was associated with the group who in 1857 founded the *Atlantic Monthly* with the serious aim of encouraging the growth of American literature, and he contributed an article entitled "Florentine Mosaics" to the first two numbers of the new periodical.[7] Lowell was so favorably impressed by the literary skill of the historian that he later begged him to contribute articles on any subject whatsoever to the *North American Review*, but without success.[8] Longfellow was one of the first to wish to encourage Motley in the days of the latter's literary apprenticeship; he wrote to Samuel Ward in May, 1839:

[5] *The Correspondence of John Lothrop Motley*, ed. by G. W. Curtis (New York, 1889), I, 32.

[6] Holmes tells us that, being two years ahead of Motley at Harvard, he had known the younger man only slightly as a student (*Life*, 515). A strong kinship in temperament, in literary taste, in respect for natural science, in political views, and in social taste served to cement a friendship which gave origin to a series of letters constituting the most delightful part of the published correspondence of Motley.

[7] Longfellow's journal contains the following entry for May 5, 1857: "Dined in town at Parker's, with Emerson, Lowell, Motley, Holmes, Cabot, Underwood, and the publisher Phillips, to talk about the new Magazine the last wishes to establish" (Samuel Longfellow, *Life of Henry Wadsworth Longfellow*, Boston, 1886, II, 298).

[8] *Correspondence*, II, 167–169, 196. See also *ibid.*, II, 29, 67, 337, for further evidence of the Lowell-Motley friendship.

When does Morton of Morton Hope[9] make its appearance?
Do you know, I have this design: if I can get the sheets of the
book, to write a notice for the July North American, provided
the book is to appear *before* July, and provided, likewise, I can
praise it heartily and warmly; . . . I am on very friendly terms
with the author, and like him, and wish to do all I can to give
him a fair start in the field.[10]

Motley was also on terms of friendship with Hawthorne, whose
work he admired,[11] and other New England acquaintances included Prescott, George Curtis, Ticknor, Everett, Felton,
Cabot, and Lodge.

A young man of intellect, nourished in the culture and refinement of this New England environment, could scarcely fail to
make a name for himself either in the field of letters or in the
public service; Motley achieved distinction in literature and, to a
less degree, in the diplomatic service as well. A second factor
to be considered in a study of his literary apprenticeship is the
impact of German culture upon his mind. An interest in German language and literature, originating under the tutelage of
Bancroft at the Round Hill School in 1824, carried over into
the college years and resulted in a translation of Goethe's "The
Ghost-Seer" for the Harvard *Collegian* and the composition of
an essay on Goethe, delivered at the college exhibition in 1831.[12]

[9] Referring to Motley's first novel, *Morton's Hope*, published in
1839.

[10] Longfellow, *op. cit.*, I, 323-324. Either the proof sheets were not
available in time, or the novel did not please Longfellow, for the proposed notice did not appear in the *North American Review*.

[11] In a letter to his father, Motley speaks in 1859 of "my friend,
Hawthorne" and mentions an acquaintance which had developed in
Rome in the winter of 1858-59 (*Correspondence*, I, 332). Hawthorne
in 1860 urged the Motleys to return to America (*ibid.*, I, 339-340).

[12] So excellent was the essay that Mr. Joseph Cogswell sent it to
Madam Goethe, who, after reading it, said, "I wish to see the first
book that young man will write" (*Life*, 340). When Motley met
her at Weimar in 1842, she was curious about his first novel (*Morton's
Hope*), but he, ashamed of his amateurish effort, would not even re-

Two years of study in Germany, at the University of Göttingen (1832–33) and the University of Berlin (1833–34), served to strengthen the German influence.[13] Motley worked harder than did most of the German students, confining his effort at Göttingen mainly to the language and at Berlin to the study of law. But it was not the specific content of the university curricula that was most valuable to him; it was the immersion in the intellectual atmosphere of Germany, the contact at first hand with German literature, at that time still pretty much dominated by the influence of Goethe. At Dresden he met Tieck, then occupied in the translation of Shakespeare, and among German scholars he learned the painstaking process of minute research which he was later to combine with the dramatic literary method in the writing of history.[14] While still a student in Germany he translated *Faust*,[15] at least in part; later he translated Tieck's *Blue Beard*[16] and wrote two review articles on Goethe.[17] Of the importance of German culture he said in 1868: "Ever since the great rising for freedom against the Roman empire, down

veal to her its title (*Correspondence*, I, 103). The most complete account of Motley's contact with German literature and culture is found in Long, *op. cit.*, 199–224.

[13] Motley met Bismarck at Göttingen, and the two students became fellow-lodgers at Berlin, thus inaugurating a lifelong friendship which survived in spite of profound differences in political opinion. The course of the friendship may be traced in the *Correspondence* (particularly, I, 174–175, 218, 220–221; II, 125–127, 159–160, 166–167, 171, 223, 309–316, 339–352) and in Mildmay (ed.), *John Lothrop Motley and His Family* (London, 1910), pp. 63–70, 133–138, 199–203, 245–249, 279–293, 299–300.

[14] Cf. *Cambridge History of American Literature*, II, 133.

[15] *Life*, 343.

[16] *New World*, I, 449–452, 478–483 (December 19, 1840).

[17] "Goethe," *New York Review*, III, 397–442 (October, 1838); "Goethe's Works," *ibid.*, V, 1–48 (July, 1839). Motley also translated Schiller's "The Diver" (*New Yorker*, January 19, 1839) and the "Wine Song" from Novalis's *Heinrich von Ofterdingen* (*ibid.*, January 26, 1839). His experiences as a student in Germany are reflected in his first novel, *Morton's Hope* (1839).

to this hour, Germany has been the main source of European and American culture." [18]

In 1835, at the age of twenty-one, Motley returned home, faced with the necessity of choosing a career. For a time he studied law, but he never became seriously engaged in the profession. In 1841 he was appointed Secretary of Legation under Mr. Todd, at that time the American Minister to Russia, but a few months in the severe winter climate of St. Petersburg caused him to resign and return to his family, for whom he had been homesick. In the meantime, he had been trying his hand at literature, a natural profession for one of his temperament, training, and experience. His first review articles, "Goethe" and "Goethe's Works," appeared in the *New York Review* in 1838 and 1839 respectively,[19] the first being, to all intents and purposes, a sketch of Goethe's life, the second a critical survey of the great poet's works, with most attention devoted to *Wilhelm Meister*, *Wahlverwandschaften*, and *Faust*. In 1839, too, appeared Motley's first novel, *Morton's Hope*, which attempts rather unsuccessfully to combine the romantic adventures of a young American provincial, pictures of German student life, scenes on the American frontier at the time of the French and Indian War, and historical episodes from the Revolutionary days.[20] The diction is bombastic and strained, the plot is awkwardly handled, and the novel is a "compound of Byronism, Bulwerism, and Vivian Greyism." [21] The chief interest for the present-day reader is autobiographical, as the book reveals much of the romantic, impetuous nature of its young author.[22] Receiving very little public notice, this novel soon

[18] *Historic Progress and American Democracy* (New York, 1869), 39.

[19] See footnote 17, above.

[20] For a summary of the narrative, see the selections in this text, pp. 32 ff.

[21] E. P. Whipple, *Recollections of Eminent Men* (Boston, 1887), 164. Holmes finds the same faults in the novel (*Life*, 372–373).

[22] An additional interest for some readers may lie in the fact that Bismarck has been identified as the original of the German student

lapsed into obscurity; its failure nearly convinced its author that fiction was not his proper realm.

Not entirely daunted, however, Motley tried once more to achieve success in the field of the novel, relying this time almost exclusively upon historical material, but weaving into it a romantic love story. *Merry-Mount*, probably completed by 1846 but not published until 1849, tells the story of the conflict between the early Puritan settlers of Massachusetts and the ribald crew of Thomas Morton.[23] Whereas *Morton's Hope* had failed largely because of an utter lack of skill in the handling of plot, *Merry-Mount* shows some improvement in this important element of long prose fiction but still no mastery. There is, on the other hand, a display of considerable ability in the handling of detached episodes, in the delineation of historical characters, and in the painting of vivid scenes. There is some truth in the judgment of one critic,[24] who says that the book "introduces adventurers of somewhat dime-novel calibre to shock Puritan sentiments and to impress Indians by aristocratic hauteur," but to say that the story is dull is to condemn it somewhat too harshly. More valid is the judgment of Holmes, to the effect that Motley could not divest himself of his personality and lose his individual character in that of his own creations, and that he was therefore better fitted for history than for the writing of fiction.[25] On its publication in 1849, *Merry-Mount* received much more favorable notice than had the first novel, and deservedly so, but it could hardly be called a successful

---

Rabenmark and that certain others of Motley's Göttingen friends also figure in the story under thin disguises. See James P. Grund, "Bismarck and Motley," *North American Review*, CLXVII, 360–376 (September, 1898).

[23] For a summary, see pp. 66 ff. The story is in most particulars faithful to history, Motley acknowledging his indebtedness to Morton's *New English Canaan* (1637) but denying an acquaintanceship with Hawthorne's "The May-Pole of Merry Mount."

[24] Ruth Putnam, in *Cambridge History of American Literature*, II, 134. [25] *Life*, 518.

novel, and the very hesitancy of the author in withholding it from publication for three years indicates that he was not satisfied that his forte lay in the writing of prose fiction.

But in 1845 Motley, attempting something in a different vein, achieved a success which was to mark the turning point in his literary career. In that year, in the October number of the *North American Review*,[26] appeared an article which purported to be a review of the Marquis de Custine's *La Russie en 1839* and John Barrow's *A Memoir of the Life of Peter the Great*, but which was actually a brilliant sketch of the career of the famous Russian ruler. Here Motley had hit his stride: relieved of the necessity of inventing plot, he wrote a rapid, interesting, almost dramatic narrative which, as Holmes points out,[27] shows in epitome his qualities as a historian and a biographer. "The style of the whole article is rich, fluent, picturesque, with light touches of humor here and there, and perhaps a trace or two of youthful jauntiness, not quite as yet outgrown." [28] Well received by the reading public, the article drew immediate attention to Motley and convinced his friends that history or biography was the field in which he must seek literary distinction. Doubtless the lukewarm reception accorded to *Merry-Mount* in 1849 demonstrated to the author the validity of this judgment.[29]

After the success of "Peter the Great" in 1845, and while the second novel was being written and offered to the public, Motley completed his literary apprenticeship with two additional

[26] "Peter the Great," *North American Review*, LXI, 269–319 (October, 1845).

[27] *Life*, 363.

[28] *Ibid.*, 364.

[29] Edmund Quincy advised him, soon after the publication of *Merry-Mount*, to turn to history (*Life*, 521). When Motley learned in 1861 that Holmes was writing his first novel (*Elsie Venner*), he wrote from London: "Did I not have two novels killed under me (as Balzac phrases it) before I found that my place was among the sappers and miners and not the lancers?" (*Correspondence*, I, 368).

articles contributed to the *North American Review*.[30] The first
of these, "The Novels of Balzac" (1847), is a twenty-three-page
review of *Les Œuvres de M. de Balzac*, a balanced, discriminating bit of criticism which finds Balzac to be an artist and only an
artist, a writer neither moral nor immoral.[31] In the second of
these articles, "Polity of the Puritans" (1849), we find a historical disquisition on the principles of self-government evolved
in New England, a refutation of the thesis of Mrs. Robinson[32]
and of Bancroft, who treat the colonization of New England as
a *democratic* movement. A democracy has indeed been the
result of that colonization, says Motley, and the seeds of political
liberty were unconsciously contained and concealed in the
principle of resistance to (or flight from) religious oppression,
"but the real reason why the democratic principle prevailed was
because it is a true principle, and because it never before had so
fair a chance to develop itself." [33] The aristocratic element in
the early government of Massachusetts naturally died out of
the system in due course of time because of the fortunate
circumstances which surrounded the colony on the frontier and
because, with all their faults, the Puritans were lovers of liberty
as well as sticklers for authority. But the Puritan colony was
not the only source of the democratic principle on the American
continent: "A great many shuttles have woven the mingled

---

[30] "The Novels of Balzac," *North American Review*, LXV, 85–108
(July, 1847); "Polity of the Puritans," *ibid.*, LXIX, 470–498 (October, 1849).

[31] The significance of this article as a statement of Motley's literary theory and critical principles will be considered in succeeding
pages.

[32] "Polity of the Puritans" is nominally a review of *Geschichte der
Colonisation von Neu-England* (1847), by Talvj (Mrs. Robinson).

[33] "Polity of the Puritans," *op. cit.*, 477. In his first major work,
Motley declares that the Dutch Republic tracks its source "to the
same high, religious origin as that of our own commonwealth" (*The
Rise of the Dutch Republic*, New York, 1856, I, 261). See also *ibid.*, I,
485, for a comparison of the Dutch Puritans with the New England
Puritans.

woof of American liberty." [34]   Motley had here found a topic
dear to his heart: a historical subject which dealt with the evolution of self-government and the principle of freedom, the sort of
subject which was to occupy his attention throughout his three
major works.   With this article and the publication of *Merry-
Mount* (both, significantly, touching upon one phase of early
American history) the period of literary apprenticeship came
to a close.   By 1850 Motley had decided to write on the early
history of the Dutch Republic, and the following year found him
in Europe, busily engaged in research for his first major production.   The years of apprenticeship in the writing of novels and
review articles had served not only to determine the choice of
history as the proper field for his literary endeavor, but to
develop "a clear and picturesque style, the flow of humor and
the eloquence which characterized his later historical writings." [35]

A study of the apprenticeship years brings the critic inevitably
to a consideration of Motley's literary theory, for it was chiefly
in these years that his ideas on style and literary form were
evolved, and to these years belong the review articles, which
contain most of his literary criticism, and the novels in which he
tried out some of his theories. [36]   Style was, in his estimation,

[34] "Polity of the Puritans," *op. cit.*, 480.

[35] *Dictionary of American Biography*, XIII, 283

[36] A detailed study of Motley's reading, as the most important
source of his literary theory, would be desirable here. Limitations
of space, however, forbid anything but the briefest sort of summary.
Even as a young boy, Motley was a constant reader, most often in
poetry or in the novels of Scott or Cooper. At the age of eleven he
found Hume's *History of England* interesting; through the preparatory and college years he kept abreast of current fiction, remark-
ing once that he liked Miss C. M. Sedgwick's *Hope Leslie* "a great
deal better" than *The Prairie*, better, in fact, than any other new
novel in two or three years excepting Scott's. In his sophomore
year at Harvard, his tutor once remonstrated with him upon the
heaps of novels on his study table. "Yes," said Motley, "I am reading historically, and have come to the novels of the nineteenth century. Taken in the lump, they are very hard reading." Shelley was,
in the Harvard days and throughout life, a favorite poet. In 1833 at

one of the most important qualities of good literature, for it is style which "above all other qualities seems to embalm for posterity." [37] A "very vicious" style, he thought, would keep Balzac out of the hall of fame, whereas Goethe added to other merits an unusually graceful and perspicuous style, a quality almost invariably wanting in German narrative prose. A good prose style combines "the flowing, the ornate, the fanciful, with the accurate, the condensed, the aphoristical." [38] It employs phraseology which is concrete and accurate in the presentation of sensory images[39] but avoids euphuistic affectations[40] and stale

---

Berlin, Motley was an enthusiastic admirer of Shakespeare, Byron, and Goethe. *Morton's Hope,* autobiographic as it undoubtedly is, furnishes an interesting account of courses of reading adopted and pursued by Motley in his youth. (See the chapter from *Morton's Hope,* I, 43–54, reprinted in this text, pp. 32 ff.). If one may judge by the authors whom Motley alludes to and quotes, his taste was catholic. They include Homer, Aristotle, Plato, Ovid, Cicero, Seneca, Juvenal, Catullus, and Horace (the unquestionable favorite among the ancients); Petrarch, Boccaccio, Machiavelli, and Dante (with whom Motley was well acquainted); Rabelais, Voltaire, Montaigne, Sue, Sand, Scudéry, Dumas, and Balzac; Schiller, Tieck, Lessing, Jean Paul, Hauf, Herder, and Goethe (on whom Motley wrote two long review articles); English poets from Milton to Tennyson, dramatists from Marlowe to Sheridan, novelists from Defoe to Dickens, essayists from Bacon to Macaulay. Favorites among the English writers were Shakespeare, Milton, Sterne ("that most delightful and original of writers"), Lamb, and Carlyle; Gibbon, Grote, and Froude. Burke, De Tocqueville, Lecky, Adam Smith, John Stuart Mill, Sir Charles Lyell, and John Bright seem to have exerted the greatest influence upon Motley in the field of political, economic, and natural sciences. He once called Mill "the acknowledged chief of English thinkers." Among American writers, Motley evidently preferred Cooper, Irving, Lowell, Hawthorne, and Holmes, with Emerson, Longfellow, Jefferson, Bancroft, and Prescott receiving occasional mention. In the field of European history he was, of course, well read; not only did he consult all the authorities, but he spent years of painstaking research in the original documents at the British State Paper Office and various European archives.

[37] "The Novels of Balzac," *op. cit.,* 108.

[38] "Goethe's Works," *op. cit.,* 18.

[39] "The Novels of Balzac," *op. cit.,* 90.

[40] *Ibid.,* 95. One of Balzac's novels is condemned for "the ponder-

metaphors.[41] It must avoid tediousness and should be direct and straightforward, not given to prolixity and involution.[42] A historian's power depends to a large extent upon his style. Motley especially admired the style of the historian Bancroft, who had been his teacher in his formative years. "The secret of Bancroft's success is, that by aid of a vigorous imagination, and a crisp, nervous style, he has been enabled, by a few sudden strokes, to reveal startling and brilliant pictures, over which the dust had collected and hardened, as it seemed, forever. It is a work rather of genius than of laborious detail."[43] "The power to sink the shaft, to explore and exhaust the mines of history," Motley said, "is rarely united with the art of coining the ore into the polished and ornamental shape which shall circulate through the civilized world."[44] How aptly he characterizes what was later to prove his own peculiar power as a historian.

Not only did Motley reach maturity at a time frequently referred to as the culmination of the romantic movement in America, and in a circle of New England writers who reflected many of the tendencies of the English romantic movement which marked the first third of the nineteenth century, but he was by nature and temperament largely romantic. He did not

---

ous pleasantry of its style, in which the manner of Sterne is most unsuccessfully copied. Even the typographical capers of this most delightful author, whom Balzac seems intensely to admire without thoroughly comprehending him, are imitated in the *Physiologie du Mariage . . .*"

[41] In 1858 Motley suggested that Holmes use as a topic for his breakfast table discussion the subject of stale metaphors (*Correspondence*, I, 225).

[42] German prose, Motley charged, is particularly faulty in its lack of directness; in general, it "drags itself in close convolutions along, parenthesis within parenthesis, coil within coil, till the sense is strangled to death, or the reader's power and patience to apprehend it, which comes to the same thing" ("Polity of the Puritans," *op. cit.*, 473). For this reason, German is a "disagreeable" language for storytelling, whether of truth or fiction.

[43] *Ibid.*, 475.   [44] *Ibid.*, 473.

share the equalitarian and humanitarian aspects of Shelleyan romanticism. Rather, his romanticism is characterized by a longing and an admiration for the romantic past. The letters recording the impressions of his first trip to Europe (1832–35) are filled with expressions of delight at castles and ruins in Germany, the constant reminders of the Middle Ages, the "poetic associations" of Continental scenery, and the rich collections of classic art so easily accessible in many European cities.[45] *Morton's Hope*, written soon after the author's return to America, devotes an entire chapter to a rhapsody on the tradition, the Gothic architecture, and the romantic association of Prague.[46] In 1842 the "cobweb tracery" of the architecture, the "colossal filigree" of the town halls, and the "transparent and fantastic lace work" of the cathedrals in Brussels, Antwerp, Ghent, and Bruges enchanted the young diplomat on his return from St. Petersburg. The Rhine in 1851, when contrasted with "our own beautiful but deaf and dumb rivers," elicited the same sort of admiration from the man of thirty-seven.[47] The following passage, written in 1849, might well have come from the pen of Washington Irving:

Who can describe the emotion produced upon his mind by the first sight of a ruined castle, by an old, gray, battered, shattered relic of the feudal age, even if it be enriched by no special memory and hallowed by no familiar name? Who can gauge

[45] See particularly *Correspondence*, I, 25–26, 31, 35–61.

[46] Book III, chapter I (*Morton's Hope*, II, 77–83). The novel is entirely romantic in its conception; it reflects the extravagant, ambitious yearnings of the young author who is reported to have adopted the Byronic affectation of turning his shirt collar down over his coat. Lady Byron once declared that she had never known anyone who looked more like her husband than did young Motley.

[47] *Correspondence*, I, 124–125. See *ibid.*, II, 271, and *passim* for evidence that Motley's response to scenes of romantic beauty was in 1867 and later years essentially unchanged. A glowing, almost poetic, description of Nôtre Dame cathedral at Antwerp may be found in *The Rise of the Dutch Republic*, I, 554–555.

the exact effect produced upon national character, the strength of the conservative feeling nourished by the constant presence of such memorials in lands where every hill-top is crowned with its ruined tower, where every valley embosoms its ivy-mantled abbey, where fable and romantic legend have lent a name and a charm to every forest, mountain, rock, and river?[48]

By contrast, America appears "naked and impoverished," but this absence of romantic past is a guarantee of the security of our democratic institutions and therefore is not to be regretted.[49]

With so romantic a cast of mind, Motley could not whole-heartedly sympathize with the brand of realism which was already making its appearance in European literature at the time of his literary apprenticeship. Yet he sought to justify the novels of Balzac as "truthful copies from human nature," for Balzac was "essentially an artist" and "not responsible for the disorders which he depicts." The audacity of modern French literature gave an author an advantage denied by the squeamishness and prudery of the English, and enabled him to "anatomize society more boldly and scientifically."[50] Balzac was a realistic artist who observed nature objectively in his search for literary material; Goethe, a great naturalist who sought the living principles of truth beneath its external manifestations, transcended the method of Balzac and brought upon himself the unjust charge of immorality.[51] In spite of his justification of the realistic method, however, Motley found his strict New England taste offended by the "rank, Old Baileyish, cheese-and-sausage odor," the "reeking and somewhat filthy character" of modern fictitious literature. Even Balzac, the most artistic of the Parisian school, was guilty of corrupt taste, for he belonged to the *blasé*

[48] "Polity of the Puritans," *op. cit.*, 493–494.
[49] We sense here the conflict between two elements in Motley's nature, which will be called to the reader's attention in the next section of this Introduction.
[50] "The Novels of Balzac," *op. cit.*, 86–88.   [51] *Ibid.*, 88–89.

school "which, in its morbid and depraved appetite for the original and the fresh, is constantly feeding upon the monstrous." [52]

The question of taste was intimately associated, in Motley's mind, with the problem of didacticism. The didactic element, when it becomes too obvious, is objectionable, for "we read novels, first of all, to be amused; and we feel rebellious at an over-dose of the didactic smuggled into them against our will." [53] The proletarian novel, then becoming popular in France, with its radical tendency to arouse class hatred, was not to be recommended for consumption in America.[54] This does not mean that works of an immoral tendency are not to be reprobated, or that art has no moral purpose. But what is the moral of the Farnese Hercules or the Venus de Medici? "The beautiful in the true we consider to be the object of all the fine arts." [55] In the preface to his second novel, *Merry-Mount*, Motley avowed a didactic purpose,[56] and at the end of the story affixed

[52] *Ibid.*, 97. Motley's friend Holmes was even more hostile to realism (as practised by Flaubert and Zola), though as a scientist he loved truth. See Holmes's *Over the Teacups* (Riverside Edition of *Writings*, IV), 105–110. For the contemporary American view of realism, consult Herbert Edwards, "Zola and the American Critics," *American Literature*, IV, 114–129 (May, 1932).

[53] "The Novels of Balzac," *op. cit.*, 91.

[54] For this type of novel, Motley conceded, there might be some justification in the European countries where the lower classes were ground under the heel of the privileged caste, but not in America, "where there are neither Brahmins nor Pariahs, no castes and no classes, no top and no bottom . . ." (*ibid.*).

[55] *Ibid.*, 92. In 1838 Motley had taken a similar stand on didacticism, holding that morals and aesthetics constitute two distinct provinces: "A work of art is perfect, when it perfectly conforms to the rules of art. . . . It may, nay, *must*, if it is true to the principles of aesthetics, exert an ennobling and refining influence; and that is all we have a right to require" ("Goethe," *op. cit.*, 438). He was hesitant, at this time, to pronounce an opinion on the question of immorality in Goethe's work, but ten years later he condemned *Wahlverwandschaften* (a story of adultery) as "extremely pernicious," an example of mental rather than moral obliquity ("Goethe's Works," *op. cit.*, 30).   [56] *Merry-Mount*, preface, 6.

this statement: "And now, patient reader, if haply a spark of
sympathy for the heroic souls [the Puritans], who in sorrow and
self-denial laid the foundation of this fair inheritance of ours,
hath been awakened in thy bosom . . . my humble end will
have been answered." [57]

In his own practice in the writing of the novel, Motley was
unmistakably romantic. *Morton's Hope* mingled autobiographic
material of a Byronic sort with romantic episodes on the frontier
and romantic scenes from the American Revolution; and *Merry-
Mount* was distinctly in the genre of the historical romance.[58]

[57] *Merry-Mount*, II, 249.

[58] The employment of the native scene in both of these novels
suggests the question of Motley's stand in the controversy over literary nationalism. *Morton's Hope* (1839) is distinctly nationalistic
in tone. Its impulsive young hero, desiring to escape the provincial
scene and find a wider scope for his ambition in Europe, is soberly
advised by Vassal Deane to remain at home, to study his age and
country, and to work upon native materials. "The sin is, that we
are not national. Our thoughts from childhood cross the ocean every
instant" (*Morton's Hope*, I, 69). But he goes on to say that this is
not altogether a matter for regret; though America is destined to
become a distinct nation politically, she will continue to be European
socially and morally. Motley was always interested in the work of
American writers, and he helped to found the *Atlantic Monthly*, devoted to the encouragement of native letters; but he was also deeply
interested in European literature, particularly that of England and
Germany. In his first review article on Goethe, he put the seal of
approval on the universal aim in literature: "He [Goethe] would not
labor for temporary or local ends, but for 'all time'; he would conse-
crate himself, not to the particular, the limited, and the one-sided,
but to the universal and permanent. . . . In creating that which
will never die while art lives, he did more for Germany, as well as
for the world, than he could have done by devoting himself to her
service in any other way" ("Goethe," *op. cit.*, 416). There was,
then, no inconsistency in the fact that Motley himself went abroad
in 1851 to work in the field of Dutch history, where he traced the
universal theme of human progress in the evolution of political and
religious freedom. For a treatment of the problem of literary nationalism, see B. T. Spencer, "A National Literature, 1837-1855," *American Literature*, VIII, 125-159 (May, 1936), and H. H. Clark, "Nationalism in American Literature," *University of Toronto Quarterly*,
II, 492-519 (July, 1933).

In the preface to the latter novel, "the crepuscular period" which immediately preceded the rise of the Massachusetts colony is said to possess "more of the elements of romance than any subsequent period," with characters "flitting like phantoms" in striking contrast to the general aspect of the place and the age, the charm of the subject lying in a certain "wild improbability" in spite of historic accuracy.[59] In 1867, writing to Holmes about the latter's novel, *The Guardian Angel*, Motley declared that "the more you take your readers into cloudland and away from the prosaic every day, which has been rather overdone by great masters of the positive and materialistic schools of novel writing, the better I as one of the faithfullest of your readers and admirers shall be pleased." [60]

In his definition of original genius and of the function of the imagination, Motley seems to take his lead from the romantic school of Coleridge, but it is interesting to observe that the emphasis is placed on the imagination controlled by *reason* and on the universality and balance of genius rather than its eccentricity. Goethe elicited Motley's admiration because he exemplified the "symmetrical development of the faculties" and because he possessed "a strong imagination, (in Coleridge's sense,) a power which always unifies." [61] The interplay of the

---

[59] *Merry-Mount*, preface, 3–4.

[60] *Correspondence*, II, 256–257. It seems odd that Motley should have overlooked entirely the underlying theme of scientific determinism in Holmes's *Elsie Venner* and regarded the book simply as a romantic novel: "As to the mother-thought of the book, it is to me original, poetical, and striking. I knew that there was no resemblance to 'Christabel'; but I had not read 'Lamia' since college days. So after finishing 'Elsie' I took up Keats and read the poem, but found no resemblance whatever" (*ibid.*, I, 368; letter to Holmes, April 19, 1861).

[61] "Goethe," *op. cit.*, 441. Motley's familiarity with the critical theories of Coleridge is indicated not only by the passage here quoted, but also by his reference to Coleridge's definition of genius (*ibid.*, 437). The probable influence of Goethe and other German romanticists must not, of course, be discounted. A good brief survey of the

imagination and the critical faculty leads eventually to a
fusion of the two faculties in the mind of a man of genius:

It is impossible that the creative impulse can be felt and
obeyed for any considerable time, without occasioning an inquiry after some principle, some regulative standard. Periods
of spontaneous production, and of critical examination alternate
with each other in the history of a man of genius, as the imagination or the critical faculty gains the ascendency. At each
transition the lines of demarcation become fainter, the two
faculties become more nearly incorporated, until the *freedom
of law* takes the place of license without law, and the imagination
works as unconstrainedly in obedience to the highest principles
of composition, as it had done in its first irregular and un-
directed efforts.[62]

Genius blends the creative impulse and the critical faculty; it
controls the imagination with reason and gains freedom *within
the law*. Genius, moreover, is catholic in its taste, is characterized by many-sidedness rather than one-sidedness, is universal
rather than idiosyncratic.[63] This idea of balance and rational
control must have been in the author's mind when he criticized
the Transcendentalists in *Morton's Hope:*

This [madness, or imbecility] is apt to be the misfortune of
those who have become enamoured and perplexed with the
singular vagaries of the German transcendentalists; a misfortune
seldom happening to the Germans, but often to their foreign
disciples. A few philosophers of subtlety, and of strong nerves,

---

literary theories of the English romanticists may be found in R. M.
Alden's introduction to his edition of *Critical Essays of the Early
Nineteenth Century* (New York, 1921).

[62] "Goethe," *op. cit.*, 427–428. There is a striking correlation between this theory of the "freedom of law" in literary creation and
Motley's doctrine of political freedom, namely, that liberty is not
license but freedom subject to the restraint of law and authority.
See page xxxix of this Introduction.

[63] "Goethe," *op. cit.*, 440–441.

have contrived an ingenious and striking theory of words and ideas. They forget to inform their apostles (what they themselves are well aware of,) that the whole science is in reality built beyond the range of the human intellect. The unhappy students imbibe greedily the draught that is set before them, and then they begin to babble. Witness in proof the witless productions that have in latter days been given to the world by a set of authors, whose ambition is to envelope common-place in a grotesque and childish garb.[64]

Uncas Morton (the hero of *Morton's Hope*) comes to the conclusion that he will seek to achieve a more rational balance through the study of natural science.[65] Physics will serve as a balance wheel to metaphysics. Similarly, in Motley's literary theory, romanticism may be said to be tempered by the emphasis on reason, balance, and universality.

One more item in Motley's literary theory must be listed because of its importance in determining his conception of history, namely, his ideas on the delineation of character. The essay on "Goethe" (1838) quotes Carlyle: "To seize a character, even that of one man, in its life and secret mechanism, requires a philosopher; to delineate it is work for a poet."[66] The highest order of biography, "the very ideal of the art," requires in its author an exceptional sort of talent. There is, indeed, a second-rate type of biographical writing which is less exacting. "If a writer has not sufficient power to give us the perspective of his subject, he may give us the parts to combine for ourselves. If he cannot get at the unity, let him give us the multiplicity from

---

[64] II, 97.

[65] Motley's interest in natural science is touched upon at greater length in Section II of this Introduction.

[66] "Goethe," *op. cit.*, 402. For Carlyle's literary theories and aims, consult F. W. Roe, *Thomas Carlyle as a Critic of Literature* (New York, 1910). Carlyle was very popular in America in the Transcendentalist Era. See F. L. Mott, "Carlyle's American Public," *Philological Quarterly*, IV, 245-264 (July, 1925).

which we may extract it. Boswell has done this, and done it in a manner which will never be excelled." [67] The same kind, if not the same degree, of talent is required to constitute a good biographer as is demanded in a good dramatist. Each must have the power to look through the "motley and confused mass of particulars" and discover the harmonizing principle, to "see *the one* in *the many*"; each must possess also "the art of perspective, by which he may reproduce for his reader, that which he sees himself." [68] The successful creation of fictitious characters, too, is a difficult task. The typical hero in Balzac's novels is not entirely convincing, for he depends too much upon externals (upon physical beauty and a facile skill in any sort of action) and is too little a creature of mind and spirit. "We fear . . . that there is a little too much outside about them for Carlyle." [69] Again Motley refers to Carlyle, whom he later met, and whose works he seems to have read diligently,[70] as the authority, the master in the art of characterization. It is a logical assumption that Carlyle's method and Carlyle's superman conception of the hero served as a standard for Motley in his own delineation of historical figures. For, like Carlyle, he conceived of history as revolving about the persons of great heroes. In 1852, when

[67] "Goethe," *op. cit.*, 402–403. For backgrounds of the theory and practice of biography, the reader may consult Harold Nicolson, *Development of English Biography* (London, 1927) and Edward H. O'Neill, *History of American Biography* (Philadelphia, 1935).

[68] "Goethe," *op. cit.*, 402. Goethe possessed the qualities of a good biographer, for he "was able to comprehend the characters of individuals most unlike himself. He went over to their standpoint, and looked through their eyes" (*ibid.*, 434). It was on just this point that Motley, in his novels, displayed a weakness in character portrayal, for he could not divest himself of his own personality and create imaginary persons that were lifelike.

[69] "The Novels of Balzac," *op. cit.*, 97.

[70] He considered Carlyle's earlier works "magnificent, wonderful monuments of poetry and imagination, profound research, and most original humour"; but in *Frederick the Great* he thought the great Scotchman displayed too much reverence for brute force (*Correspondence*, II, 105–106).

engaged in research for *The Rise of the Dutch Republic*, he wrote
to his father: "I flatter myself that I have found one great,
virtuous and heroic character, William the First of Orange,
founder of the Dutch Republic." [71] Six years later, now busy
with his second major work, the *History of the United Netherlands*, he wrote:

> The great cause of regret that I have . . . admits of no remedy.
> There is no great hero. It is difficult to scare up another
> William of Orange, and whatever success or virtue my other
> book may have had, is owing to my having discovered one of
> the great men of the world's history, who was, I think, not
> generally known or appreciated.[72]

Motley's interest in drama and the fine arts must be recognized
as supplementary to his literary interest in formulating his conception of history. In his early boyhood the future dramatist
of a nation's life history demonstrated a lively enthusiasm for
dramatic production. He and his playmates would often amuse
themselves by staging amateur theatrical performances, often
impromptu melodramas, in an attic or in the loft of a barn.[73]
In *Morton's Hope* (which, it will be remembered, is to a large
extent autobiographic) the youthful Uncas Morton writes, di-
rects, and produces his own dramatic compositions. Shakespeare was an enduring favorite with Motley, and the most
frequent source of his quotations and allusions. Even more
than the drama, the pictorial and plastic arts appealed to
Motley's aesthetic nature. Frequent references to the art

---

[71] *Ibid.*, I, 146–147.   [72] *Ibid.*, I, 318.

[73] See *Life*, 331–332. Akin to this interest in dramatic performance
is the interest in declamation. The elder Motley would have the
boys read aloud to him and would criticize their way of reading.
Motley, when a boy at Mr. Greene's school, proudly reported taking
third prize in a speaking contest (*Correspondence*, I, 1, May 13, 1824);
at the Round Hill School, several years later, he delivered Antony's
Funeral Oration in an "exhibition" (*ibid.*, I, 9); and at Harvard in
1831 he read an essay on Goethe.

treasures of Europe occur in his letters, which are often aglow with enthusiasm for particular paintings or statues, and his critical comments give evidence of a more than superficial acquaintance with the works of the great masters.[74] One letter mentions his "most sincere and unlimited love for the fine arts, and particularly for painting."[75] Van Eyck, Rubens, Rembrandt, Vandyke, Ruysdael, Holbein, Leonardo da Vinci, Raphael, Perugino, and Caravaggio are among the artists most frequently alluded to. In the novel *Merry-Mount*, a Puritan maiden is likened to Raphael's madonnas, and a scene at Merry Mount is described as "worthy of a Caravaggio's pencil."[76] Motley's contribution to the newly organized *Atlantic Monthly* in 1857 was a long critical article on the art and architecture of Florence.[77] The interrelationship of the dramatic and the pictorial arts is expressed in a letter to Holmes in 1853, when Motley had been profoundly impressed by Rubens's "Descent from the Cross": "Never was the grand tragedy represented in so profound and dramatic a manner. . . . He [Rubens] is certainly the Shakespeare of painting."[78] At another place, Motley refers to Rubens as the "most profound of colorists, most dramatic of artists."[79] It must be regarded as more than coincidence that this historian, who painted vivid scenes on a broad canvas, was fond of drawing analogies with the work of great painters and of alluding, in his histories, to the actors in his drama, to the setting of the stage, and to the tragedy being enacted before the reader's eyes.

Finally, how did Motley's period of literary apprenticeship

[74]See, for example, *ibid.*, I, 107, 111, 119, 126–127, 135–140, 164–165, 182, 188–189, 280, 282; II, 274, 327; Mildmay, *op. cit.*, 16–19.
[75]*Correspondence*, I, 135.
[76]*Merry-Mount*, I, 35, 49.
[77]"Florentine Mosaics," *Atlantic Monthly*, I, 12–22 (November, 1857); 129–138 (December, 1857).
[78]*Correspondence*, I, 164–165 (Brussels, November 20, 1853).
[79]*The Rise of the Dutch Republic*, I, 565.

fit him for his major work as a historian? How did his literary
theory and his interest in the fine arts combine to produce the
author of *The Rise of the Dutch Republic*, the *History of the
United Netherlands*, and *The Life and Death of John of Barneveld?* We have seen that the New England environment and the
German training which were Motley's furnished him with a
rich background, a select circle of acquaintances, and an intellectual training equal to the best. Turning naturally, in his
search for a career, to literary expression, he experimented in
the field of long prose fiction and in the critical review article.
This period of experimentation proved that his special capacities
were those of the historian rather than of the novelist. Somewhat lacking in the ability to handle plot and the power to
create imaginary characters, he nevertheless displayed a marked
facility in the presentation of the actual persons and events of
history; and he developed a fascinating narrative style which
brought the past to life and imparted to it the glow of reality.
In literary theory a romanticist who placed a high value upon
the restraint of reason, Motley was destined to become a
"literary" historian; perhaps as a direct result of the German
influence, he adopted the modern method of painstaking,
methodical research, but his enthusiasm did not permit him to
present his material with entire objectivity. Unable perfectly
to blend the creative impulse and the critical faculty in accordance with his own definition of genius, he wrote as a partisan, in accordance with his theory of the didactic purpose of
history.

If great literature is, by definition, universal in its aim, and
not required to serve merely the narrow and local purposes of a
limited time and a particular country, then Motley could justify
his choice of the early history of the Dutch Republic. He
looked upon the struggles of Holland and Zeeland in the sixteenth, of Holland and England united in the seventeenth, and
of the American colonies in the eighteenth centuries as forming

"but a single chapter in the great volume of human fate." [80] Furthermore, though he frowned upon too obvious a didacticism in fiction, he conceived of all great art as fundamentally moral, and of history as properly didactic. "If ten people in the world," he wrote while still engaged upon the first of his three major works, "hate despotism a little more and love civil and religious liberty a little better in consequence of what I have written, I shall be satisfied." [81]

In Motley's choice of literary method to be employed in the writing of history, we have observed two determining factors, both of which point to Carlyle as the master. First is the biographical conception of history as a record of events revolving about and influenced by the personality of a superman or heroic figure. Second, Motley's interest in drama and in painting, and his apprehension of the dramatic power of great painting, led him to the employment of the dramatic and pictorial method in the presentation of the actors, scenes, and events of history.

Thus Motley the historian emerges from the period of literary apprenticeship. From his boyhood days to the year 1850 he was, though of course not consciously, fitting himself for the work that was to bring him fame. In choice of subject for that work,[82] he was governed by his bias for religious and political freedom, his hatred of tyranny and oppression. Herein lies the connection between Motley's literary work and his interest in public questions of his own day. "To discover the great intellectual law prescribed by the Creator is the science of history. To induce mankind to conform to that law is the science of politics." [83]

[80] *The Rise of the Dutch Republic*, I, iv.

[81] Brussels, January 4, 1854; to Miss Christina Forbes (Mildmay, *op. cit.*, 42). A similar statement is found in the Preface to *The Rise of the Dutch Republic*, I, viii. See also *Correspondence*, I, 146.

[82] See below, pp. lxxx ff.

[83] *Historic Progress and American Democracy*, 28.

II. POLITICAL AND SOCIAL IDEAS

Motley's attitude toward political and social issues may best be described as that of a conservative liberal. His thinking on public questions was conditioned by several factors: his New England heritage and environment, his reading, his foreign travel and contact with European culture, his concept of political freedom as essentially connected with religious liberty, his acceptance of the findings of natural science, and his belief in human progress.[84] One or another of these factors, or a combination of more than one of them, served to determine his theory of government, his relationship to political issues both domestic and foreign, and his stand on social problems of his day. Throughout life Motley was keenly interested in contemporary questions of importance; he was in some instances in direct personal contact with current problems, and in others he expressed his ideas clearly and unmistakably. An examination of his reactions to some of the specific problems will reveal the fact that he was, by temperament and taste, a late representative of the Federalist spirit in American life; by reasoned conviction, in theory and practice, a liberal.

Let us examine first Motley's theory of government. Essentially, he believed that sovereignty rests in the people, that government should be adjusted to the needs of the people, that history reveals the progress of the human race toward liberty and freedom, that democracy is the climax of political progress, and that American democracy, though far from perfection, marks the highest point of achievement up to the present time. "Practically and philosophically," he wrote in 1849, "the foundation of government is popular consent." [85] And in 1861 in a letter to the London *Times*, which attempted to define the

[84] Some of these factors, because of their close bearing upon Motley's literary development, have been treated in the preceding section.
[85] "Polity of the Puritans," *op. cit.*, 477.

nature of the American government, he maintained that the only intelligible source of power in a country beginning its history *de novo* after a revolution, in a land never subjected to military or feudal conquest, is "the will of the people of the whole land as expressed by a majority." [86] The sovereignty of the people, Motley was certain, lay at the basis of all good government. That principle received its most severe test in America at the time of the Civil War, which to him was a revolt of the slaveholders "against the natural and legal and constitutional authority of the sovereign people." [87] Motley, who during the period of the War was the American Minister to Austria, felt keenly the European skepticism of American principles and rejoiced that now the soundness of those principles was to be demonstrated. He wrote to his mother:

Hitherto the "sovereignty of the people" has been heard of in Europe, and smiled at as a fiction, very much as we smile on our side of the water at that other little fiction, the divine right of kings. But now here comes rebellion against our idea of sovereignty, and fact on a large scale is illustrating our theoretic fiction. Privilege rebels, and the sovereign people orders an army of half a million to smash the revolt.[88]

Thus in 1862; and in 1868, in a speech made in support of Grant's campaign for the Presidency, Motley asserted his belief that the Civil War had firmly established the principle of popular sovereignty.[89]

[86] *Causes of the American Civil War* (New York, 1861), 8. This pamphlet is a reprint of Motley's letter to the London *Times*, May 23 and 24, 1861.

[87] Letter to his mother, Vienna, June 30, 1862 (*Correspondence*, II, 79–80).

[88] *Ibid.*, II, 79.

[89] *Four Questions for the People, at the Presidential Election* (Boston, 1868), 7–8: "No man outside a mad-house hopes or wishes, since the war, to upset the American Republic. The thing cannot be done; the Union is indissoluble. So much at least has been proved. And it is worth the precious price we have paid for it, to know that what

This whole-hearted acceptance of the doctrine of popular sovereignty might be expected to predicate a belief in the correlated doctrines of natural rights and natural goodness. But here the conservative element in Motley's nature seems to assert itself; at least, he does not accept these doctrines with the enthusiasm of their eighteenth-century advocates. True, he spoke of July 4, 1776, as "a day on which equal rights were proclaimed as the heritage of mankind," [90] a day which marked the commencement of a noble era. But he does not speak of *natural* rights, nor is there very strong evidence to indicate a belief in *natural* goodness, a belief that might be inferred from his enthusiasm for democratic principles. In his first novel (*Morton's Hope*, 1839), in a discussion of the weakness of the American confederation at the time of the Revolutionary War, there is an oblique reference to natural goodness:

The mob will not learn that although it is a sovereign and an absolute one, it is not beneath its dignity to confide its powers to trustworthy ministers and servants. . . . But there is no need of enlarging on the weakness of the government, for it seems that

was once believed by millions in this country, and almost universally outside of it, to be the vainest of delusions, is now an established axiom. Let the world make the most of it and govern itself accordingly. Treason has done its worst, but this government has not fallen, for it was founded on the rock of equal rights. We can read the Declaration of Independence at last, with its solemn and majestic opening clause, which peals through the world like a choral strain, proclaiming a new birth to the nations—'that this truth is self-evident, that all men are created equal; that they are endowed by their Creator with inalienable rights; that among these are life, liberty, and the pursuit of happiness,'—without a blush or a sneer or a feeble sophism, once the sole response." This campaign address is naturally grandiloquent, almost rhapsodic, in style; but it is a sincere expression of Motley's convictions, as is evident upon comparison with the expression of his opinions elsewhere.

[90] *Historic Progress and American Democracy*, 21. See also the quotation from *Four Questions for the People*, footnote 89 above, for his endorsement of the principle of equality as set forth in the Declaration of Independence.

we shall never grow wiser, and that we are still determined to neutralize our institutions by our hesitation to subscribe to that belief in human virtue which dictated their organization.[91]

Curiously enough, natural goodness is not suggested here as a justification of popular suffrage; instead, Motley castigates the unwillingness of the people to delegate their authority to elected representatives.

A suggestion is found, in the passage just quoted, of the moderation which always qualified Motley's liberalism. In spite of his belief in popular sovereignty, in spite of his apparent acquiescence in the doctrines of natural rights and natural goodness, he was far from being a radical in the European sense of the term. True, he was capable of writing to his old friend Holmes and recommending "radicalism" for the latter's son:

I am sure that he [Oliver Wendell Holmes, Jr.] will become a better American and a deeper Radical—every year of his life. He is one of the fellows who have got to prove to the world that America means Radicalism—that America came out of chaos in order to uproot, not to conserve the dead and polished productions of former ages. Not that I think there is much sense in applying European party politics to our own system. . . . But if we cannot go ahead in America without caring how much we uproot in our upward progress—we had better have left the country to the sachems and their squaws.[92]

But even here he is careful to indicate that he does not "think there is much sense in applying European party politics to our own system." In an article written nearly twenty years earlier, in which he defined democratic government as typically represented in the State of Massachusetts, he suggested that "our republican friends across the water" might learn a lesson from

[91] *Morton's Hope*, II, 184.
[92] Letter to Holmes, Vienna, March 12, 1867 (*Correspondence*, II, 255). The career of the late Mr. Justice Holmes, of the United States Supreme Court, was a noteworthy fulfillment of Motley's prophecy.

the New England character. "Their republican progress," he suggested, "would be facilitated by the study. . . . The inhabitants of Massachusetts . . . do not cut each other's throats and burn each other's houses to establish the principle of fraternity among men, after the French manner." [93]

Indeed, so strong was the conservative element in Motley's New England nature that law and order appeared to him the essential elements of good government, even in its most liberal form. Liberty did not mean license, but freedom under the control of law, a freedom which he could best define by quoting the Puritan Winthrop: "There is a freedom of doing what we list, without regard to law or justice; this liberty is indeed inconsistent with authority; but civil, moral, and federal liberty consists in every man's enjoying his property and having the benefits of the laws of his country; which is very consistent with a due subjection to the civil magistrate." [94] Massachusetts, he declared, was as absolute a democracy as ever existed. "But it is a government of law, under which life and property are

[93] "Polity of the Puritans," *op. cit.*, 498. The blending of liberalism and conservatism which defined Motley's political theory is made evident by the juxtaposition of two letters written in 1862 and 1867 respectively. With reference to Carlyle's *Frederick the Great*, he wrote in 1862 to his mother: "I said that Carlyle's other works seemed to me magnificent, wonderful monuments of poetry and imagination, profound research, and most original humour. But that I thought him a most immoral writer, from his exaggerated reverence for brute force, which he was so apt to confound with wisdom and genius. A world governed *à la* Carlyle would be a pandemonium" (Vienna, December 22, 1862; *Correspondence*, II, 105–106). Five years later, after reading Hepworth Dixon's *New America*, Motley commented in a letter to his wife: "It is readable enough—amusing; only the Mormons are to me the most insufferable of bores and beasts, and I shall be glad when the advancing tide of civilization sweeps their filthy little commonwealth out of existence" (England, August 20, 1867; *Correspondence*, II, 284). Motley distrusted equally the two extremes, aristocracy and communism; he saw safety as lying in the mean—republican democracy.

[94] "Polity of the Puritans," *op. cit.*, 490–491.

secure." [95]. This concept of liberty conditioned by law as the basis of liberal government is embodied in "Polity of the Puritans," published in 1849; more than twenty years later, in a letter to the Duchess of Argyll, Motley gave expression to a higher conception of the law which underlies good government. "After all," he wrote, "the success of Government, as the world progresses, is more and more seen to depend upon its conformity to the great elemental laws, to the simplest moral precepts. In short, Justice, Truth, and Faith are immutable, and the ship steered by that compass rarely gets among the breakers." [96] In the ideal government, then, the freedom of the individual is to be restrained by law, the law of constituted authority; but the government, founded on the immutable moral law, will insure to the individual the freedom that depends upon justice. [97]

Dominated though he was by the love of political liberty and admiration for the republican form of government, Motley did not think that this form could be imposed upon all peoples without modification. "Physical, historical, and geographical conditions," Motley wrote to Holmes, "make our democratic commonwealth a possibility, while they are nearly all wanting in England." [98] He realized that a nation must achieve a certain stage of development before it could adopt a democratic form of government. The principles of freedom he found to be embodied to varying degrees in the several European states, but particularly in the government of England, for which he had a very considerable degree of respect. In spite of her aristocratic

[95] "Polity of the Puritans," op. cit., 498.

[96] London, January 25, 1870 (Correspondence, II, 317).

[97] Motley's friend Lowell furnishes an interesting parallel to this conception of government resting upon immutable moral law in the poem "Washers of the Shroud" (1861), in which temporal law is seen as sanctioned by moral law; America's doom is conceived of as depending on an intelligent obedience to "the Law before all time": "Three roots bear up Dominion: Knowledge, Will—These twain are strong, but stronger yet the third,—Obedience."

[98] Vienna, February 26, 1862 (Correspondence, II, 63).

social order, England stood for a large measure of self-government and for freedom of thought and speech.[99]   Government,
then, according to Motley's theory, is to be adapted to the
condition of the people to be governed[100]; but that government
is best which embodies most completely the principles of freedom and of popular self-government.   That government fails
which neglects the interests of the people.   Thus a fundamental
error made the otherwise admirable labors of Peter the Great
meaningless: "A despot by birth, education, and temperament,
he had never the most glimmering notion of the existence of a
people. . . .   A people may be humanized, cultivated, brought
to any degree of perfection in arts, and arms, and sciences; but
he undertook to civilize a state in which there was but one man,
and that man himself." [101]

In his theorizing on the nature of American political institutions, Motley was concerned mainly with a problem that had
been a central one from Revolutionary days, a problem that
had divided the country in the days of Hamilton and Jefferson
into two great parties, a problem which, in the minds of many,
was the principal issue in the days of the Civil War; namely,
the question of states' rights versus strong centralized federal
authority.   On this question Motley took no uncertain stand:

[99] See, for example, the letter of January 4, 1854, in Mildmay,
op. cit., 42–43.
[100] The only touchstone applicable to governments, Motley said,
is "their capacity to insure the highest welfare of the governed" (*The
Rise of the Dutch Republic*, I, 121).   He admitted that "There may
be possible good in despotisms as there is often much tyranny in
democracy" (*ibid.*).   This conception of government is in keeping
with the historic relativism of Montesquieu and Burke, according to
whose theory political institutions must be modified to fit the age,
the geographic situation, and the character of the people to be governed.   It is in sharp contrast to the *a priori* logical abstractions of
theorists like Rousseau and Paine, who believed that the perfect
political constitution would meet the needs of any people, at any
time, in any place.
[101] "Peter the Great," *op. cit.*, 316.

he was always, without hesitation, in favor of a strong federal government and opposed to the advocates of decentralization. In the "Polity of the Puritans" (1849), after painting a glowing picture of America's future development, he warned his readers that *disunion* was the only thing which might prevent the realization of his vision of America's future grandeur.[102] With the advent of secession and the Civil War, this prophecy seemed to be on the verge of fulfillment. The war was, to Motley, a test of the fundamental principles of the American polity. In a letter to the London *Times* (May 23 and 24, 1861), intended to convert English sympathy from the Southern cause to that of the North, he defined the nature of the American government and declared that secession constituted a revolt against constituted authority:

The body politic known for seventy years as the United States of America *is not a confederacy, not a compact of sovereign states, not a copartnership; it is a commonwealth*, of which the constitution . . . is the organic, fundamental law. . . . The states were distinctly prohibited from opposing its decrees, or from exercising any of the great functions of sovereignty. . . . *Secession is, in brief, the return to chaos from which we emerged three-quarters of a century since.*[103]

[102] "Polity of the Puritans," *op. cit.*, 495–497.

[103] (The italics are Motley's.) *Causes of the American Civil War*, 6–12. Lowell held a similar view; in the essay *E Pluribus Unum* (1861) he envisaged the Civil War as a conflict for nationality and not for abolition. "The matter now in hand," he declared in that essay, "is the reëstablishment of order, the reaffirmation of national unity." The faith of a nation in its own manhood is threatened with "the formless void of anarchy." For a careful analysis of Lowell's attitude toward national problems, see H. H. Clark's "Lowell—Humanitarian, Nationalist, or Humanist?" *Studies in Philology*, XXVII, 411–441 (July, 1930).

Motley's position as outlined in his letter to the London *Times* (*Causes of the American Civil War*) was made the subject of a violent and abusive contemporary attack in Henry B. Dawson's "The Motley Letter," *Historical Magazine*, XIX, 157–201 (March, 1871). Mr. Dawson (whose article was written in 1861, immediately after

The Northern victory and the conclusion of the Civil War apparently closed the question of state sovereignty by establishing the power of the central government. In the next few years, however, problems of reconstruction brought up once more the issue of states' rights. Campaigning for Grant in the presidential election of 1868, Motley delivered an address in Boston in which he again sounded a warning of danger to the Union and reasserted his conviction that the basic principle in American government is centralization and not state sovereignty.[104] He was not, however, blind to the function of the states and municipalities in local self-government. An analogy based upon natural science defines beautifully his conception of the relationship between state and national governments:

The combination in our system of self-governed States, revolving around a central government, seems to us, who have known no other, as natural as the planetary system, and to be governed by as inevitable laws. The manner in which self-government is diffused throughout, the regularity with which each State revolves upon its own axis, and yet moves in its orbit around the centre of the system, the great natural law of reproduction within itself, under which there seems a constant scaling off of material from the organized part into the distance, to revolve in the nebulous condition of territories for a time, until agglomerating to States, it forms recognized and inhabitable portions of the system, the harmonious discord by which the centripetal and centrifugal forces keep all nature's peace,— all these elementary characteristics of our polity, are wanting in Europe, and are indigenous to our world.[105]

---

the appearance of Motley's letter, but was withheld from publication for ten years) charged that Motley "had disregarded the authenticated history of the United States" (p. 157) and that the "chaos" of which Motley spoke was "a fabrication of your own fancy" (p. 175).

[104] *Four Questions for the People*, 9–23.

[105] "Polity of the Puritans," *op. cit.*, 497. One is here reminded of the figure employed by Madison when he discussed the problem of

The functions of states and municipalities in local government, always subject to the "universal law" which governs the whole nation, are recognized also in the election speech alluded to above.[106]

For this American political system which he described in such glowing terms, Motley had a considerable amount of pride, evident not only in the ardor of a campaign speech but also in the more sober utterances of private correspondence. A letter to his parents during his student days at Berlin in 1833 reveals a certain amount of impatience because Germans will not be persuaded concerning the true character of American institutions.[107] During the months of his attachment to the American legation at St. Petersburg, Motley had an opportunity to study the political and social system of despotic Russia; he made the following entry in his diary: "The more I see of other countries, the more I like America."[108] The petty bickerings of party strife, so likely to disturb a man of aesthetic temperament and highly refined tastes, did not detract from his faith in the American system. On the contrary, he saw party spirit as essential to the endurance of democratic government:

To those who reflect upon the means and ends of popular government, nothing seems more stupid than in grand generalities to deprecate the party spirit. Why, government by parties and through party machinery is the only possible method by which a free republic can accomplish the purpose of its existence. The old republics of the Past may be said to have fallen, not

---

delegated authority: "This prerogative of the General Govt. is the great pervading principle that must controul the centrifugal tendency of the States; which, without it, will continually fly out of their proper orbits and destroy the order & harmony of the political system" (*The Records of the Federal Convention of 1787*, ed. by Max Farrand, New Haven, 1911, I, 47).

[106] *Four Questions for the People*, 10–15.
[107] Berlin, November 4, 1833 (*Correspondence*, I, 32).
[108] December 7, 1841 (*Correspondence*, I, 113).

because of party spirit, but because there was no adequate machinery by which party spirit could develop itself with facility and regularity. . . . And a free government may cease to be free, even although all the forms and appliances for energetic action are present, if the party spirit, the potent expansive vapor which moves all things, is absent or insufficient.[109]

It will be remembered that a considerable portion of Motley's mature life (all of it, with the exception of brief visits to America, from 1851 to his death in 1877) was spent in Europe, and he was therefore enabled to view the American scene with an objectivity and detachment not possible to the person who is engaged in the midst of political strife. But he always maintained a keen interest in American affairs and kept himself closely informed of events at home. Though he was an expatriate, he was an unwilling one, forced to remain in Europe both by his diplomatic appointments and by the necessity of carrying on historical research in the archives where his source documents were stored.[110]

There remains only one more item to be considered in this summary of Motley's theory of government, namely, his concept of human progress and of democracy as the climax of political progress. It will be seen that this concept rested upon two bases: first, the evidence of recorded history; second, the

[109] *Four Questions for the People,* 4–5.

[110] From time to time, Motley's letters express his regret at not being able to return to America. For example, he wrote to his mother (June 15, 1864) from the Legation at Vienna: "If I were not in Europe at a post of duty and utterly unable to leave it, I should not remain an hour longer on this side of the water. Europe has long since ceased to have attractions for me, and I have perpetually regretted that my literary profession, and subsequently, my present occupation, have made me and my children exiles" (*Correspondence,* II, 163). In June, 1861, his anxiety over the crisis in America caused him to lay aside his literary work and go suddenly to Boston. He expected to have his family follow him and take up residence in America; only his diplomatic appointment to Austria caused a change of plan.

findings of natural science. The fullest exposition of the
theory is to be found in an address which Motley delivered
before the New York Historical Society on December 16,
1868,[111] but its essence is also to be found elsewhere, particularly
in certain letters.[112] The law of progress, according to this
theory, operates steadily in the development of human civilization, though its operation may be so slow and tortuous as not
to be evident at any given point of time. "After all," Motley
wrote to Holmes in 1862, "it seems to be a law of Providence
that progress should be by a spiral movement, so that when we
seem most tortuous we may perhaps be going ahead." [113] The
same sentiment appears in the address referred to above: "And
I believe it possible to discover a law out of all this apparently
chaotic whirl and bustle; this tangled skein of human affairs as
it spins itself through the centuries. That law is progress—
slow, confused, contradictory, but ceaseless development, intellectual and moral, of the human race." [114] Because the operation of the law is slow, an individual may be able to see only in
part the general scheme by which the "Supreme Disposer"
governs the universe, for "men are short lived, while man is
immortal even on the earth." [115] A short-sighted view of the
history of human affairs is likely to lead to an erroneous conclusion: "Unless we hold fast to the fact, that in human as in
physical history, Nature is ever patiently producing her effects
through long lapses of time, by causes which have been in
operation since the beginning, History is but another word for
despair. But history is never hysterical, never proceeds by

[111] *Historic Progress and American Democracy.* This essay was
published in both New York and London in 1869; a second issue appeared with the title *Democracy, the Climax of Political Progress, and
the Destiny of Advanced Races* (London, 1869).
[112] *Correspondence,* II, 65, 76–77, 201. See also *Four Questions for
the People,* 5–6, 16–20.
[113] Vienna, February 26, 1862 (*Correspondence,* II, 65).
[114] *Historic Progress and American Democracy,* 6.
[115] *Correspondence,* II, 76.

catastrophes and cataclysms; and it is only by remembering this that we can comprehend its higher meaning." [116]

The long-range view of history, then, will reveal the slow, and at times uncertain, operation of the law of progress. It will discover the movement of civilization from East to West, one nation rising to power, then falling before another culture, always with some evidence of progress. [117] The landmarks of human motion are: "Speech, the Alphabet, Mount Sinai, Egypt, Greece, Rome, Nazareth, the wandering of the nations, the feudal system, Magna Charta, gunpowder, printing, the Reformation, the mariner's compass," and finally the discovery of America, "the chief event thus far recorded in human progress." [118]

The testimony of history to the progress of the human race is supplemented by the evidence of natural science. Motley speaks of the law of progress as "the law governing all bodies political as inexorably as Kepler's law controls the motions of the planets." [119] This law of progress has been steadily operating toward the achievement of democracy and political freedom. The evolutionary theory provides evidence of progress in the natural world which is analogous to progress in the moral sphere: "To be created at once in likeness to the Omnipotent and to a fantastic brute; to be compounded thus of the bestial and the angelic, alternately dragged upward and downward by conflicting forces, presses upon us the conviction, even without divine revelation, that this world is a place of trial and of progress towards some higher sphere." [120] The progress displayed in jumping the gap from primitive man to modern man

[116] *Historic Progress and American Democracy*, 28.

[117] *Ibid.*, 20–24.   [118] *Ibid.*, 29.   [119] *Ibid.*, 6.

[120] *Ibid.*, 14. The idea of progress was of course widely prevalent in the nineteenth century. See especially the oration by Motley's teacher and early idol, George Bancroft, on "The Necessity, the Reality, and the Promise of the Progress of the Human Race" (*Literary and Historical Miscellanies*, 1855, 481–517); the essay by his

(a much narrower gap than that between brute and man)—this progress alone should encourage faith in the eternal law.[121]

Progress to Motley meant the achievement of freedom, whether political or religious, on the part of the people. Freedom of worship is an essential corollary of political freedom: not only is this evident in the "Polity of the Puritans" and *Historic Progress and American Democracy*,[122] but it was a determining factor in Motley's choice of historic subject.[123]

---

friend and patron, Charles Sumner, on "The Law of Human Progress," 1848 (*Works of Charles Sumner*, Boston, 1875, II, 91–146); and James Russell Lowell's "The Progress of the World" (published as an introduction to *The World's Progress*, Boston, 1887). On the earlier history of the concept, see J. B. Bury's *The Idea of Progress* (New York, 1932)—a new edition with an introduction by Charles A. Beard summing up the modern, less optimistic view.

[121] *Historic Progress and American Democracy*, 15. Motley indicates (p. 13) that he relies for scientific evidence largely on Sir Charles Lyell's *Geological Evidences of the Antiquity of Man* (1863).

[122] It is the thesis of "Polity of the Puritans" that the Puritans came to America, not to set up a democratic state, but to guarantee to themselves the freedom of worship. Intolerant and autocratic as they were, the principle of freedom is so strong, and the circumstances on the frontier were so favorable, that the intolerant Puritan theocracy became eventually the foundation of the liberal democracy known as the United States. In *Historic Progress and American Democracy*, see especially pp. 26–27.

[123] See Section III of this Introduction. In all of his histories he wrote constantly as "a partisan on the side of freedom in politics and religion, of human nature as against every form of tyranny, secular or priestly" (*Life*, 434–435). Motley, in the "Polity of the Puritans" conceived of the germ of political liberty as unconsciously concealed in the Puritans' struggle against (or flight from) religious oppression in England. Though the Puritans came to America with no thought of founding a democratic state, yet this germinal principle was so powerful that, under favorable conditions in a new country, it eventually developed such strength that it crowded out the aristocratic elements of the Puritan theocracy. Similarly, in the struggle of the Dutch provinces, Protestantism and democracy fought hand in hand against the absolutism of Catholic Spain: "For the history of the United Provinces is not at all a provincial history. It is the history of European liberty. Without the struggle of Holland and England against Spain, all Europe might have been Catholic

American democracy represented to him the highest achievement in historic progress up to his time. Fortunate in point of physical advantages, in being able to profit by the experience of the Old World, in not being obliged to combat a feudal system or the theory of sovereignty by divine right, in having religion free of entanglement with political power, and in being able to establish universal education, America found herself at the most advanced point of civilization and human progress.[124] Not that she had achieved perfection, but she was at the point toward which other nations were moving—the starting point on the road to perfection.

We have seen that Motley believed, at least hesitantly, in natural rights and natural goodness and firmly in the sovereignty of the people, but that he rejected the Jeffersonian doctrine of states' rights in favor of the Federalistic doctrine of centralized power. His "radicalism" was of a very temperate variety which put the emphasis on law and order, on conformity to universal principle. The teachings of history and the evidence of modern science convinced him that the human race is making slow but steady progress and that this progress is identified with political and religious freedom, the most advanced form of which is embodied in the institutions of republican America. Let us now trace the course of his activity in connection with the political questions of his day.

Throughout his life, whether at home or abroad, Motley always took a keen interest in American public affairs. Born as he was into a wealthy New England family, accustomed to move in the best circles socially, and endowed with a temperament which preferred the artistic and the aesthetic, Motley

---

and Spanish. It was Holland that saved England in the sixteenth century, and, by so doing, secured the triumph of the Reformation, and placed the independence of the various states of Europe upon a sure foundation" (*Life*, 394; from a letter to F. H. Underwood, March 4, 1859, not included in the *Correspondence*).

[124] *Historic Progress and American Democracy*, 31.

was naturally a Federalist in spirit, though he came to maturity at an era when the party which bore that name had ceased to be a force in American politics.[125] Yet he was in political theory, as we have seen, a liberal, a believer in democracy, and an ardent supporter of American republicanism. These two tendencies may be observed in operation as we follow Motley's political career. After completing a course of study at the Universities of Berlin and Göttingen, he returned to America in 1835 to study law. Never actively engaged in the practice of law, he spent the next six years in literary pursuits, manifesting little interest in politics, until in 1841 he went to St. Petersburg as Secretary of Legation. At this time his only concern about American politics seems to have been a fear that the "locofocos" might have carried the state of Massachusetts as they had carried other states in recent elections.[126]

We have more specific evidence of his political opinions in 1844, in a letter addressed to Park Benjamin:

And the way in which it [Polk's election] has been done—the outrageous frauds, the Polk and tariff cry in Pennsylvania, Polk and free trade in Carolina, and, more atrocious than all, the infernal lies about Clay's private character . . . all these things taken together, I think must disgust any man with popular institutions, and with the very dirty politics which are their result. . . .

Before dropping the subject, and to show the perfect purity of my motives, I will only add that I am not at all anxious about the legislation under the new government. I desired the election of Clay as a moral triumph, and because the *administration* of the country, at this moment of ten thousand times more importance than its legislation, would have been placed in pure,

[125] The influence of this Federalistic temper upon his social theories and the conflict between this temper and Motley's liberal theories are dealt with below, pp. lx–lxix.

[126] See letter of December 25, 1841, to his wife (*Correspondence*, I, 89).

strong, and determined hands. It is now in the hands of the lowest of the low. The administration of Polk will be even worse and more low-lived than that of Tyler. That seems impossible now, but I believe every body will agree to it before it is over. As to the tariff, I am not afraid of them. As to Texas, if it be annexed, the result will inevitably be a separation of the Free States from the Slave States—a dissolution of the Union, which will, I think, ensue much sooner than we have been accustomed to believe. This is, perhaps, a result not very much to be deprecated; so that, so far as we of the North are concerned, it does not matter much whether Texas is annexed or not. The abolitionists now avow that they promoted the election of Polk in order to hasten the dissolution of the Union. . . . They are the dissolution party. . . . There is no attachment to the Union, no loyalty any where. The sentiment of loyalty is impossible under our institutions. Loyalty implies both respect and love; and who can respect or love institutions of which the result is four years of Tyler followed by four years of Polk?[127]

It is interesting to note here a distrust of popular institutions not at all in keeping with Motley's later utterances, the early prediction of secession which must result from annexation of slave territory, and a concern for the Union which is evident in spite of the heated language which the writer employs. Motley at this time was taking an active part in local politics, for he made two stump speeches during the 1844 campaign,[128] and in 1849 he served one term in the Massachusetts House of Representatives,[129] an experience which he found so little to his liking that he gave up all thought of a further career in local politics.

In the eighteen-fifties Motley, now pursuing his historical research in Europe, manifested a deep interest in the slavery

[127] Letter of December 17, 1844, included in Park Benjamin's "Waifs from Motley's Pen," *Harper's Magazine*, LV, 613–614 (September, 1877), but not included in the *Correspondence* or in Mildmay, *op. cit.;* discussed in *Life*, 359–362.

[128] Park Benjamin, *op. cit.*, 614.   [129] *Life*, 370–371.

issue in America. In the fall of 1852, in a letter to his mother,[130]
he expressed the fear that the November election would be a
victory "in a canter" for Pierce, from whom he once remarked
that he differed in politics "as far as it is perhaps possible for two
persons to differ."[131] Later in the same year he voiced the
opinion that the slave states could and should abolish slavery.
He thought that the power to accomplish this desired end
resided only in the states and not in the federal government. A
solution was inevitable: "The coming generation in each of the
fifteen Slave States are the people who must grapple with this
question; but the question won't be staved off for a third."[132]
A letter written two years later betrays impatience with America
for tolerating the abuse and declares that she is "a great machine
for constantly extending the growth of cotton and expanding
the area of negro slavery."[133] By 1858 Motley felt that a crisis
was at hand; the residents of the Free States, he asserted, must
"choose between an act of political suicide or connivance at the
steady expansion of the slavery system,"[134] between dissolution
of the Union or acquisition of slave territory.

In 1860 Motley counted himself a Republican,[135] and hoped
that through the efforts of his party the United States might be

[130] *Correspondence*, I, 134–135 (Dresden, September 13, 1852).

[131] *Ibid.*, I, 332 (1859).

[132] *Ibid.*, I, 148 (Dresden, December 25, 1852).

[133] *Ibid.*, I, 170–171 (May, 1854).

[134] *Ibid.*, I, 267–268 (London, June 17, 1858).

[135] The Republican Party came into being in 1854; the first actual
meeting was possibly the one at Ripon, Wis., February 28, 1854. The
Compromise Measures of 1850 had led directly to the destruction of
the old Whig Party, which committed itself in 1852 to an acceptance
of the laws regulating slavery as final. Intense opposition in non-
slave states to the further extension of the slavery system, and the
breakdown of the compromise policy of Clay, with the Kansas-
Nebraska bill and repeal of the Missouri Compromise as the incidental
causes, brought the Republican Party into existence. Its first presidential candidate, Gen. John C. Frémont, was defeated, but in 1860
Abraham Lincoln was elected to office under the banner of the new
party.

"rescued from the Government which now oppresses us."[136]
After the Republican victory at the polls in November, he
rejoiced in "the triumph of freedom over slavery"[137]; but early
in the next year he was concerned for the existence of the Union,
"for the great conspiracy to establish the Southern Republic,
concocted for twenty years, and brought to maturity by Mr.
Buchanan's Cabinet Ministers, has, by that wretched creature's
connivance and vacillation, obtained such consistency . . . as to
make it formidable."[138] He vented his wrath upon the secessionists[139] and at the outbreak of the Civil War declared it to be
a revolt on the part of the slaveholders against constituted
authority:

The existence of this government consists in its unity. Once
admit the principle of secession, and it has ceased to be; there is
no authority then left either to prevent the extension of slavery,
or to protect the life or property of a single individual on our
share of the continent. . . . This great struggle is one between
law and anarchy. The slaveholders mutiny against all government on this continent, because it has been irrevocably decided
no further to extend slavery.[140]

As the Civil War continued, Motley became an advocate of
emancipation, his sentiments on slavery still being governed by
his passion for the preservation of the Union:

The very reason which always prevented me from being an
abolitionist before the war, in spite of my anti-slavery sentiments
and opinions, now forces me to be an emancipationist. I did not

---

[136] *Correspondence*, I, 338.   [137] *Ibid.*, I, 355.   [138] *Ibid.*, I, 364.
[139] See particularly the letter of February 9, 1861, to his mother
and the long letter of June 14, 1861, to his wife (*ibid.*, I, 357–359,
371–377).
[140] *Ibid.*, II, 25. For backgrounds, consult Chapter VI, "Par-
ticularism versus Nationalism," pp. 408–496, in J. M. Jacobson's
*The Development of American Political Thought. A Documentary His-
tory* (New York, 1932); also R. G. Gettell's *History of American Political Thought* (New York, 1928), 279–375.

wish to see the Government destroyed, which was the avowed purpose of the abolitionists. When this became the avowed purpose of the slaveholders, when they made war upon us, the whole case was turned upside down.[141]

By 1862 he saw emancipation as the best way to stave off foreign interference in the civil struggle, and he was willing to throw aside any constitutional scruples which might earlier have made the measure an undesirable one.[142] He was aware, however, that a premature edict of emancipation might prove to be strategically disastrous. One year later (1863) he had a definite policy to suggest: "To offer and urge compensated emancipation on the loyal Slave States, and to proclaim, by the war power, abolition in the rebellious ones, is the legitimate and necessary result, thus far, of the war." [143] When emancipation was finally made an actuality,[144] Motley felt that a great step had been taken in the direction of human progress.

[141] Vienna, September 21, 1862; to his daughter Mary (*Correspondence*, II, 94). For backgrounds, consult, in addition to Jacobson and Gettell above, W. S. Jenkins's *Pro-Slavery Thought in the Old South* (Chapel Hill, N. C., 1935). Though Motley regarded slavery as morally wrong and a violation of human freedom, his hostility to slavery was not based on sentimental pity. Instead, it was subordinated to a passion for the Union as the basis of enduring law and order, as in the case of Bryant and (after 1850) of Lowell.

[142] Vienna, February 26, 1862; to O. W. Holmes (*Correspondence*, II, 64–65).

[143] Vienna, February 9, 1863; to Tom Hughes (Mildmay, *op. cit.*, 155). Emerson also urged that the Federal government buy the slaves and emancipate them. It is interesting to note that Motley's political views at this time differed so sharply from those held by his father that he "could never exchange written or spoken words with him on the great subject of the age and of the world" (Vienna, May 25, 1864, to his mother; *Correspondence*, II, 161).

[144] In 1862 slavery in the territories was abolished by Congress; on September 22, 1862, Lincoln issued the preliminary emancipation proclamation, followed on January 1, 1863, by the emancipation of all slaves in the states in arms against the Union; in December, 1865, a constitutional amendment was ratified abolishing slavery throughout the United States.

Motley spent nearly the whole of the Civil War period in Europe[145] and was therefore in an excellent position to observe the reactions of the European nations to the American crisis. The possibility of foreign intervention in behalf of the Southern cause, particularly the danger of British intervention, gave him great concern. Upon the outbreak of hostilities in America he wrote a long letter to the London *Times*[146] in which he tried to explain to England and to Europe the nature and conditions of the American system of government, the real cause of the strife, and the mighty issues at stake. He early appointed himself "a peace commissioner between the two countries,"[147] for he had set his heart upon "the *entente cordiale* between England and America."[148] During his brief visit to America in 1861, he spoke to President Lincoln, Seward, Chase, Blair, Bates, and others about the English attitude; and in England he took advantage of his wide acquaintance in the best social circles to bring the Northern cause to the attention of prominent people.[149] The *Trent* affair caused him much anxiety,[150] as did the Alabama

[145] He had returned to America immediately after the outbreak of the War so as to be near the scene of action during the crisis, but in the summer of 1861 he was appointed Minister to Austria, a post which he occupied for six years. His work as a diplomat is treated below, pp. cxii ff.

[146] Published in the *Times* in two installments, May 23 and 24, 1861; reprinted as a pamphlet, *The Causes of the American Civil War* (London, 1861).

[147] Boston, July 1, 1861 (*Correspondence*, II, 2).

[148] *Ibid.*, II, 4.

[149] Among others, Motley conversed with Lord John Russell and Palmerston and corresponded with the Duke of Argyll, John Bright, J. S. Mill, and the Hon. W. E. Forster, M. P., on the subject of Anglo-American relations. (See *Correspondence*, I, 366–367, 370; II, 1, 31–32, 34–35, 37, 43, 51–54, 91, 119–122.)

[150] On December 16, 1861, he wrote to his mother from Vienna about the *Trent* incident: "I do not enter into the law or the history. I simply feel that if a war is to take place *now* between England and America, I shall be in danger of losing my reason. . . . It is mere brag and fustian to talk about fighting England and the South at once . . ." (*ibid.*, II, 45; see also *ibid.*, II, 49–50; *Life*, 410–411).

claims.[151]   The possibility of intervention by France was also a
cause of some concern,[152] but the principal threat was that England might embrace the cause of the South.   Motley, like Lowell,
developed an increasing respect for Lincoln, whose wisdom,
courage, devotion to duty, and simplicity of character he
admired,[153] and he desired a victory for Lincoln over McClellan
in the election of 1864 as a victory for emancipation over
slavery.   In 1868, having returned to America for a brief visit,
he continued to support the Republican cause by making a
campaign speech for Grant, whom he admired as a fine type of
the popular military hero.   This address, *Four Questions for the
People, at the Presidential Election,* urged that the reconstruction
laws be upheld and the emancipated Negroes be guaranteed the
suffrage and that the national debt be paid rather than "repu-
diated" by making payment in depreciated greenbacks legal.[154]

[151]*Correspondence*, II, 111, 121.

[152]In 1861, stopping in Paris for a chat with Thouvenel, Minister
of Foreign Affairs, Motley said he "hammered the Northern view
into him as soundly as I could" (*ibid.*, II, 43); in 1862 he requested
Bismarck to let him know of any intrigue on the part of Louis Napoleon to interfere in America (Mildmay, *op. cit.*, 136).   In 1863 Bright
assured Motley that there was no danger of French intervention
(*Correspondence*, II, 122).

[153]*Ibid.*, II, 78 (Vienna, June 22, 1862).   In 1864 Motley wrote to
his mother: "I venerate Abraham Lincoln exactly because he is the
true honest type of American Democracy.   There is nothing of the
shabby genteel, the would-be-but-couldn't-be fine gentleman; he is
the great American Demos, honest, shrewd, homely, wise, humorous,
cheerful, brave, blundering occasionally, but through blunders
struggling onward towards what he believes the right" (*ibid.*, II,
170).

[154]The four questions were: (1) "Whether the will of the American
People, constitutionally expressed, is the law of the land?"   (2)
"Whether, in the United States, all men are endowed with equal
rights?"   (3) "Whether it is just and reasonable to pay our debts,
or to repudiate them?"   (4) "Whether economy and constitutional
purity of administration will, on the whole, be best secured by the
election of Mr. Seymour or of General Grant?"   (*Four Questions for
the People*, 24).

Partly perhaps as a reward for his party loyalty, partly in recognition of his excellent qualifications for the post, and partly as the result of the urging of so powerful a political figure as Senator Sumner, President Grant in 1869 appointed Motley to represent the United States at the Court of St. James, from which post he was recalled in November of the following year.[155] As he felt that the action of the administration in connection with this episode had been very unjust, it is no more than natural that Motley should have looked with disapproval upon the American political scene in the early eighteen-seventies. Perhaps, too, Grant the military hero had not displayed the sagacity in the White House which Motley had anticipated. However that may be, he wrote to Holmes in 1871:

Events at home fill me with disgust unfathomable. I am now amusing myself with the intrigues and the hatreds and personal and political jealousies and lyings and backbitings of the seventeenth century in the dusty archives here, as a relief to the same sort of commodities in the nineteenth.[156]

It was hardly with any great degree of satisfaction that he learned of Grant's re-election in 1872.[157] That there was more than personal animus behind his criticism of American politics

[155] For an account of Motley's diplomatic mission to England and his recall therefrom, see below, pp. cxxi–cxxv.

[156] The Hague, April 8, 1871 (*Correspondence*, II, 321). Motley was at this time engaged in research for *The Life and Death of John of Barneveld*, destined to be his last literary work.

[157] In October, 1872, Motley met Sumner at the Hague and learned that Grant's re-election was nearly certain. He mentions this fact in a tone which leads the reader to believe that he was not altogether pleased (*Correspondence*, II, 355). Two years later he heard of the death of Sumner, whom he had always considered a great public figure (*ibid.*, II, 377). Sumner seems to have been Motley's guiding star in the realm of American politics. See, for example, Motley's comment upon Sumner's article on American politics written for the anniversary number of the *North American Review* of January, 1876, in Henry Cabot Lodge's "Some Early Memories," *Scribner's Magazine*, LIII, 727 (June, 1913).

becomes evident in a letter written to Henry Cabot Lodge on March 11, 1876, in which Motley speaks of "this very putrid administration" and hopes that a gale "may blow away some of the vile effluvia by which the political atmosphere has become almost too poisonous for human existence," and in a second letter to Lodge dated June 2, 1876, which speaks of "the present shameful condition of our politics." [158]   The particular objects of Motley's ire, it appears in these two letters, are the paper currency, the corrupt condition of Civil Service, the spoils system, "rotation in office," and "that most vulgar and dangerous tyrant King Caucus."   It is noteworthy that, in these very letters in which he pours out his bitterest vitupera- tions upon the corruption of American politics, Motley reasserts his faith in the American people and the democratic principle. "But I believe in the American people nevertheless as I always have done," he says in the first letter; and in the second he assures Lodge that he does not despair, for "the people are better and braver than the politicians." [159]   It is pleasant to ob- serve a more cheerful note in his last recorded words on the state of American politics, written just a few months before his death in 1877:

> Our own political affairs look better.   Even the *Tribune* seems inclined to think it bad for the Republican party if Hayes should be "counted in" against the general sense of the country. The people themselves are behaving with a magnificent calm, and one can't help feeling proud of them.[160]

Here again is echoed Motley's abiding faith in the people and in the stability of republican institutions.

Just as Motley's interest in American politics was dominated by a bias for freedom, so a brief survey will disclose the fact

---

[158] Lodge, *op. cit.*, quotes two letters written to him by Motley on March 11, 1876, and June 2, 1876, respectively, neither of which is included in the *Correspondence* or in Mildmay.

[159] *Ibid.*   [160] *Correspondence*, II, 399 (January 11, 1877).

that his interest in the European political questions of his day was also governed by his love for the popular cause in any controversy, by his conception of democracy as the goal toward which human progress was moving. In 1854 he indicated that his sympathies in the dispute between England and Russia were entirely with England, as representing the principles of self-government and freedom of speech and thought.[161] That the democratic principle was making progress in England was demonstrated later by the reforms which transferred power from the landed aristocracy to the people by the extension of the suffrage.[162] Similarly, the disestablishment of the Irish Church met with Motley's approval in 1870, but he saw that other reforms were necessary to complete the revolution.[163] In 1876–77, however, he rejected the English point of view on the Russia-Turkey dispute and favored the Russians; the proposal for "autonomous" states between Turkey and Russia he labeled "the most preposterous notion the mind of man ever conceived." [164] In 1859, writing to his mother about the Italian war which forced the Motleys to leave Rome, he indicated that his sympathies were warmly with Sardinia: "It seems to me that no man deserves to mention the word liberty, who does not feel the warmest admiration and sympathy with so noble a cause." [165] Similarly, in 1862 and 1863, we find Motley's sympathy with the Poles in their struggle against the despotism

[161] Mildmay, *op. cit.*, 42–43 (January 4, 1854). Motley in this letter also expresses the fear that if England goes to war she may once more bully American merchant vessels, and such action might lead to war between England and America.

[162] *Historic Progress and American Democracy*, 61–63.

[163] *Correspondence*, II, 316–317. To Motley's mind the complete severance of church and state was a prerequisite of both political and religious liberty.

[164] *Ibid.*, II, 409; see also *ibid.*, II, 395, 401, 407.

[165] *Ibid.*, I, 323. See also Mildmay, *op. cit.*, 80, and *ibid.*, 103, Mrs. Motley's letter of June 8, 1861, which indicates that the Motleys regretted the death of Cavour as a blow to the right cause in Italy.

of Russia.[166] The triumph of democracy, even in Europe, was at hand; the day of dynasties and despotism had passed. Hence the Archduke Maximilian, who thought it was his "divine mission to destroy the dragon of democracy and re-establish the true Church, the Right Divine, and all sorts of games,"[167] was the object of Motley's whimsical scorn; and Louis Napoleon, unsympathetic to democracy, was "the Prince of Darkness," the Mephistopheles of the European situation.[168] Throughout 1866 the letters are full of discussion of the European situation, which for the time crowded other interests into the background. Motley hoped for the dissolution of the old German Confederation, or Bund, and the unification of Germany under the leadership of Bismarck,[169] which unification he regarded as a step toward the liberation of the people. In 1872 he declared that the German movement "must unquestionably lead to liberty and a higher civilization" because it embodied "intellect, science, nationality, popular enthusiasm."[170] In every political question, then, foreign as well as domestic, Motley was a partisan of the side which to him seemed to represent freedom and democracy.

Having examined his theory of government and his relation to political questions in America and Europe, let us turn now to Motley's ideas on certain social problems. Slavery, the one

[166] *Correspondence*, II, 78, 119, 132.

[167] *Ibid.*, II, 143 (September 22, 1863); see also *ibid.*, II, 154.

[168] *Ibid.*, II, 144, 156, 224–225, 242–243.

[169] *Ibid.*, II, 214–252.

[170] *Ibid.*, II, 352. See also *Historic Progress and American Democracy*, where the German unification is described as a movement toward popular freedom (39–45) and the progress of the democratic principle is also noted in Austria-Hungary (46–58). Motley's views of German politics were doubtless colored somewhat by his intimate friendship with Bismarck, which originated when the two were fellow students at Göttingen and Berlin and continued unshaken throughout life in spite of radical differences in political opinion. Motley was confident that under Bismarck the German consolidation must lead eventually to freedom, not despotism.

which occupied his attention more than any other, has already
been considered in connection with his political activity. We
have seen that Motley entertained strong anti-slavery sentiments before the outbreak of the Civil War but was not an
abolitionist because he saw abolition as threatening disruption
to the Union, and that soon after the beginning of the war he
looked upon emancipation both as a means of preserving the
Union and as a method of ending a great moral injustice. His
ideas on other social problems can, for the most part, be very
briefly stated; they will show him again to be a liberal—but in
one instance at least, that of his stand on class distinctions in
society, a liberal tinged with an ingrained conservatism of
breeding and temperament.

Motley's interest in the subject of education was first displayed in a public fashion in the year 1849, when, as Chairman
of the Committee on Education in the Massachusetts House of
Representatives, he presented an elaborate and, as he thought, a
masterly report. His proposal was to divide a portion of the
proceeds of the Maine lands among the three colleges of the
state. These funds had theretofore been added to the common
school fund. The report was ignominiously demolished by the
speech of Representative George S. Boutwell, a man of a
common school education from a small country town. As
Mr. Boutwell later expressed it, "Failure was inevitable. Neither
Webster nor Choate could have carried the bill." [171] It is interesting to observe that in 1873 Motley proudly told the
Baroness Meyer de Rothschild that the annual expenditure for
education in Massachusetts was about one million pounds

---

[171] *Life*, 370–371. See also George S. Boutwell's *Reminiscences of
Sixty Years in Public Affairs* (New York, 1902), I, 95. Motley, Boston bred and trained in an excellent private school at Round Hill,
Massachusetts, was graduated from Harvard in 1831 and studied at the
Universities of Göttingen and Berlin in 1832–1834. It is perhaps only
natural that in 1849 he should be more interested in securing appro-
priations for the colleges than for the common schools.

sterling.[172] His theory of democracy included universal education as an essential basis for self-government. In *Historic Progress and American Democracy* (1868) he spoke of universal suffrage as "the only possible foundation of human freedom," [173] and in the campaign speech delivered in 1868 he said: "The right to cast a vote should entail upon its possessor the corresponding duty of understanding the subject voted upon, and an educational suffrage for a whole population, whatever its colors, would perhaps be the most reasonable condition." [174] He encouraged the education of the Negro by contributing to the support of Fisk University.[175]

That Motley was interested in the sort of humanitarian protection which society must afford to its unfortunate members is evidenced by the fact that in St. Petersburg in 1842 he inspected carefully the very efficient orphan asylum he found there and described it with approval in his diary.[176] But only five years later we may detect the typical conservative attitude of distrust for external reform in an article written for the *North American Review*, in which the author takes exception to the sort of sociological-treatise novel which aimed at reform:

Slavery must be abolished, intemperance must be annihilated, the prisons, the schools, the hospitals must all be overhauled; Congress must be purged, the White House swept clean; the

[172] *Correspondence*, II, 365 (March 2, 1873). Motley sent the Baroness a copy of the annual address of the governor of Massachusetts, marking the pages relating to education.

[173] *Historic Progress and American Democracy*, 31. In the same speech (56–57) Motley highly approved of the removal of education from the control of the Catholic Church in Austria-Hungary and its establishment under the jurisdiction of the state.

[174] *Four Questions for the People*, 36. Motley objected to unfair discrimination against the Negro in the form of an educational requirement which would deprive him of the ballot and so of his civil rights.   [175] *Correspondence*, II, 373.

[176] *Ibid.*, I, 119–121. The diary jottings for January, 1842, reveal a keen interest in Russian social institutions.

press, the pulpit, and the court-house looked after; our agriculture, which in New England is three centuries behind the age, must be remodelled, and the farmers impressed with the virtues of soda and electricity; pigs must be placed in their true position; that animal, which the benevolence of the present age has discovered to be cleanly, must be redeemed from his filth and sent up stairs to bed like a Christian; . . . No doubt the country needs reformation, the world needs it. Reform every thing, and as reformation, like charity, should begin at home, take the advice of a respectable colored gentleman who drives about the streets of Boston in a cart inscribed with letters of gold,—take his advice, and "reform your tailors' bills." [177]

Humanitarian reform, in other words, is not to be substituted for the inner control and self-reform. Here Motley—like his great contemporary and fellow New Englander, Emerson—subscribes to the doctrine of "centrality" (evil lies within the individual and not without, in institutions). A most interesting statement is found in *The Rise of the Dutch Republic*. Having commented on the beauty of church architecture in Antwerp, the author observes that the age for building and decorating great cathedrals is past. He continues:

Certainly, our own age, practical and benevolent, if less poetical, should occupy itself with the present, and project itself into the future. It should render glory to God rather by causing wealth to fertilize the lowest valleys of humanity, than by rearing gorgeous temples where paupers are to kneel. To clothe the naked, redeem the criminal, feed the hungry, less by alms and homilies than by preventive institutions and beneficent legislation; above all, by the diffusion of national education, to

---

[177] "The Novels of Balzac," *op. cit.*, 92–93. Something very like a tone of contempt for the ardent reformers may be detected in these words: "For ourselves, we have arrived at the conclusion, that all the 'natural nobility' is not monopolized by the almshouse, nor all the temperance by the reformed drunkards, nor all the chastity by the penitent Magdalens. There is a sprinkling of virtue and vice throughout all the strata of society" (*ibid.*, 93).

lift a race upon a level of culture hardly attained by a class in
earlier times, is as lofty a task as to accumulate piles of ecclesiastical splendor.[178]

We observe, in this pronouncement of Motley's mature years,
a sympathy with the cause of the poor and a willingness to
employ legislation to ameliorate their condition. But it is
significant that the emphasis is placed upon education as the
most important means of obtaining improvement.[179] As to his
interest in specific reforms, it will be remembered that Motley
did not join the abolitionist movement (in spite of his hearty
disapproval of slavery) but, up to the time when secession
opened the way to war-time emancipation, recommended that
the slavery problem be left in the control of the individual
states. In 1876, it will also be recalled, he hoped that a change
in administration at Washington would bring a reform of Civil
Service and abolishment of the spoils system.

Though not a rabid advocate of narrow patriotism,[180] Motley
was, as we have seen, always vitally interested in his country
and its welfare. As early as 1852 he was alarmed at the rapidity
with which Europe was pouring emigrants into America.[181]
A letter written to Bismarck in 1862 shows that he approved of
the American policy of isolation:

The cardinal principle of American diplomacy has always
been to abstain from all intervention or participation in European affairs. This has always seemed to me the most en-

---

[178]*The Rise of the Dutch Republic*, I, 553.

[179]We have already seen that Motley's acceptance of the doctrine
of natural goodness was not a very hearty one, that he did not subscribe to the *a priori* logical abstractions of the eighteenth-century
theorists such as Rousseau, Paine, and Jefferson. His belief in progress, however, predicates a belief in human perfectibility. His
humanitarianism, we may say, is in the conservative tradition of
Christian charity.

[180]For his stand on literary nationalism, see *ante*, footnote 58.

[181]*Correspondence*, I, 147.

lightened view to take of our exceptional and therefore fortunate, political, and geographical position.[182]

In spite of his love for the refinements of European civilization, in spite of his regret, occasionally expressed, at the American lack of libraries, art galleries, and the poetic associations which a man of aesthetic taste felt to be important, Motley was not critical of the crudeness and materialism that characterized American civilization. He wrote to his mother in 1862: "The tendency of the age everywhere, and the strongest instinct of the American people, is to consolidation, unification. It is the tendency of all the great scientific discoveries and improvements which make the age of utilitarianism at which we have arrived."[183] Indeed, he recognized the essential part played by material improvement in the growth of America: without steam, electricity, and labor-saving machinery, he declared, "such a widely extended republic would be impossible."[184]

In economics Motley was, typically, a liberal conservative, his diary as early as 1841 giving evidence that he favored free trade as opposed to a protective tariff.[185] He became a disciple of Adam Smith and John Stuart Mill in political economy; with the latter he was personally acquainted, as he was with Bright and Cobden.[186] Trade and commerce, he believed, would fare best when subject to least interference in the form of governmental regulation. He was a consistent foe of the greenback and its use as legal tender, particularly in the payment of the

[182] Mildmay, *op. cit.*, 135 (Vienna, August 29, 1862).

[183] *Correspondence*, II, 76. Even the idealist Emerson saw in such material improvements as the locomotive and the steamboat a beneficent tendency, in that they would, "like enormous shuttles, shoot every day across the thousand various threads of national descent and employment and bind them fast in one web" ("The Young American," *Works of Ralph Waldo Emerson*, Standard Library Edition, Boston and New York, 1855, I, 344).

[184] *Four Questions for the People*, 17.

[185] *Correspondence*, I, 114 (Diary, December 7, 1841).

[186] *Ibid.*, II, 176 ff., 204, 206, 219–220.

national debt. As a remedy for the embarrassed finances of the American government in 1864, he advised strict economy which would permit private citizens to extend loans to the national treasury.[187] The campaign speech of 1868 warned the voters against "repudiation" of the national debt, which must follow if the Democrats came into power and authorized payment in a depreciated paper currency.[188] And in 1876, at the time of another presidential election, he expressed the hope that the people would "smash paper money as they smashed slavery." [189] This distrust of the greenback and the advocacy of strict economy as a national policy may be regarded as the conservative element in Motley's economic theory, whereas his approval of free trade and laissez-faire places him in the more liberal contemporary school of political thought.[190]

The blending of conservatism and liberalism in Motley's social thinking is even more evident in his attitude toward class distinctions and the social structure. Scion of a wealthy family

---

[187] Motley's consistent adherence to principle is illustrated here: in the interest of strict economy he advised Americans to buy in foreign markets when they were cheaper than domestic, even though most of his own fortune was invested in American manufactories. As a member of the moneyed classes whose interests were in manufacture and commerce, he might have been expected to be an exponent of the protective tariff.

[188] *Four Questions for the People*, 42–66.

[189] Lodge, *op. cit.*, 727.

[190] Motley was not unaware of the economic and social significance of the frontier in American life. In *Historic Progress and American Democracy* (66–67) he pointed to the enormous undeveloped resources on the frontier and the opportunity they afforded for future expansion. He also pointed to the South as a region only partially developed because the Mason-Dixon line had, up to the Civil War, proved an impassable barrier to the migration of labor from the crowded industrial areas of the North. The frontier, moreover, was a factor in American democracy: "In America is a landed democracy. Every man votes, and every man may be a landholder who is willing to go West for a homestead" (*ibid.*, 64). "The Polity of the Puritans," too, recognized frontier conditions as one of the factors favorable to the development of democracy on the American continent.

and a member of the Brahmin caste in Boston, he was endowed with a temperament which appreciated the luxury and refinement of an established social order. Particularly, his Federalistic approval of the aesthetic by-products of an aristocratic culture is evident from time to time in his letters. A letter to his mother in 1833 suggested that America excelled European countries in things utilitarian—railroads, warehouses, and ships—but was deplorably inferior in art galleries and libraries.[191] Another letter at a later date voices approval of the English social order: "I cannot help forming a favourable idea of English civilization when I see the position accorded in this country to those who cultivate art, science, and literature, as if those things were worth something, and were entitled to some consideration . . ."[192] After the publication of *The Rise of the Dutch Republic* in 1856, English polite society received the distinguished-looking and charming American author with open arms and showered lavish attentions upon him. Much as he enjoyed the comfort, grace, and urbanity of aristocratic England, however, Motley felt that the social structure which created them was also responsible for a distinct injustice to the masses of the population. "Unfortunately," he wrote to his youngest daughter in 1867, "the luxury, both intellectual and physical, of a few thousands, is in awful contrast to the dismal condition of many millions."[193] He found that week-ending on beautiful English country estates was "very perverting to the moral and the politico-economical sense" and, true to his democratic principles, felt that that type of life must "pass away, one of these centuries, in the general progress of humanity."[194] No desire was further removed from his thoughts than that America should evolve an aristocratic class:

[191] Berlin, September, 1833 (*Correspondence*, I, 29-30; see also *ibid.*, I, 140).

[192] *Ibid.*, I, 327 (August 18, 1859).

[193] *Ibid.*, II, 276.

[194] *Ibid.*, II, 280 (August 12, 1867).

I am most sincere when I say that I should never wish America to be Anglicised, in the aristocratic sense. Much as I can appreciate and enjoy aesthetically, sentimentally, and sensuously the infinite charm, refinement, and grace of English life, especially country life, yet I feel too keenly what a fearful price is paid by the English people in order that this splendid aristocracy, with their parks and castles, and shootings and fishings and fox-huntings, their stately and unlimited hospitality, their lettered ease and learned leisure, may grow fat, ever to be in danger of finding my judgment corrupted by it.[195]

Thus Motley wrote to his wife in 1867. Another letter, addressed to his daughter, sets forth even more explicitly his point of view on the subject of class distinctions:

For one, I like democracy. I don't say that it is pretty or genteel or jolly. But it has a reason for existing, and is a fact in America, and is founded on the immutable principle of reason and justice. Aristocracy certainly presents more brilliant social phenomena, more luxurious social enjoyments. Such a system is very cheerful for a few thousand select specimens out of the few hundred millions of the human race. It has been my lot and yours to see how much splendour, how much intellectual and physical refinement, how much enjoyment of the highest character has been created by the English aristocracy; but what a price is paid for it. Think of a human being working all day long, from six in the morning till seven at night, for fifteen or twenty kreutzers a day in Moravia or Bohemia, Ireland or Yorkshire, for forty or fifty years, to die in the workhouse at last! This is the lot of the great majority all over Europe; and yet they are of the same flesh and blood, the *natural* equals in every way of the Howards and Stanleys, Esterhazys and Liechtensteins.[196]

The conflict between Motley's aristocratic temperament and his democratic belief is admirably expressed by his daughter,

Lady Harcourt, in a letter written to Holmes some time after her father's death. "As no one knows better than you do," she said, "his belief in his own country and in its institutions at their best was so passionate and intense that it was a part of his nature, yet his refined and fastidious tastes were deeply gratified by the influences of his life in England . . ." [197]

In summary, Motley was, in governmental theory, in his relationship to politics both domestic and foreign, and in his stand on social problems, a liberal tinged with a conservatism of temperament. Accepting (though perhaps with reservations) the doctrines of natural rights, natural goodness, and the sovereignty of the people, he was nevertheless opposed to radicalism or extremes of any sort. Flatly denying the sovereignty of the states, he was Federalistic in his love of centralized power and his desire to preserve the integrity of the Union. Human progress, he held, was affirmed both by the findings of natural science and by the testimony of recorded history; and the climax of human progress was marked by democracy, the achievement of religious and political freedom. The record of Motley's participation in American politics shows perhaps the conservative rather than the liberal side of his nature, yet it shows him always on what appeared to him the side of justice and human right. In European political questions he was invariably to be found on the liberal or the popular side. His social ideas—his stand on education, reform, nationalism, economics, and the structure of society—reveal again a liberalism in theory and practice, tempered by a conservatism which sought to avoid extremes. He advocated universal education in a democracy, distrusted external reform of the more radical variety, favored a restricted nationalism and a policy of American isolation, was a believer in free trade and laissez-faire in commerce but distrusted paper currency, and above all he recommended a democratic social order in spite of his instinctive

[197] *Life*, 391

preference for the refinement and culture of aristocracy. Motley was a conservative liberal.

III. MOTLEY AS A HISTORIAN

1. *The European Heritage of History Writing*[198]

The European historical heritage from which Motley drew his models had its roots far in the past. From earliest times men had kept some record, at first oral and later written, of the events and activities of the world and the society in which they lived. As their culture developed the Greeks and Romans began to tell the story of their past in literary prose. In their historical narratives, in the main, they wrote of events which they had witnessed or known about or which were still fresh in the minds of their contemporaries. Though they invented speeches and often took sides they increasingly recognized the need for accuracy of data, the selection of relevant material,

---

[198] See on this subject: Lord Acton, "German Schools of History" in *English Historical Review* (1886), I, 7–42; Harry Elmer Barnes, "History, Its Rise and Development," in *Encyclopaedia Americana* (New York, 1936), and *A History of Historical Writing* (Norman, Okla., 1937); G. Below, *Die deutsche Geschichtschreibung* (Munich, 1924); J. B. Black, *The Art of History* (London, 1926); J. B. Bury, *Ancient Greek Historians* (New York, 1909); B. Croce, *Storia della storiografia italiana nel secolo decimonovo* (Bari, 1921); E. Fueter, *Geschichte der neuern Historiographie* (2nd edition, Munich and Berlin, 1901), and *Histoire de l'historiographie moderne* (Paris, 1904); G. P. Gooch, *History and Historians in the Nineteenth Century* (London, 1913); A. Guilland, *L'Allemagne nouvelle et ses historiens* (Paris, 1899), and *Modern Germany and Her Historians* (London, 1915); T. P. Peardon, *The Transition in English Historical Writing* (New York, 1935); J. T. Shotwell, *Introduction to the History of History* (New York, 1922); F. X. Wegele, *Geschichte der deutschen Historiographie* (Munich, 1885); G. Wolf, D. Schäfer, et H. Debruck, *Nationale Ziele der deutschen Geschichtschreibung seit der französischen Revolution* (Gotha, 1918); *Histoire et Historiens depuis cinquante ans*. (This last book is the work of many collaborators. It was written to mark the fiftieth anniversary of the appearance of the *Revue historique*.)

and the impartial treatment of men and events. Before the ancient gave way for the medieval world they had produced works of a high order both as history and as literature.

With the acceptance of Christianity by the Roman world the scope and content of history changed. In the pagan world writers of history had been local and secular in their point of view. In the Christian world they had radically changed their conception of man and the world in which he lived. They had adopted the chronology and point of view of the sacred books of the Hebrews. They had taken as their task the narration of the story of the revelation of the divine plan in human history. They had given a subordinate place to the chief nations of ancient times and emphasized the supposed ways of God, the life and death of Christ, and the spread and final acceptance of Christianity. Their attention had shifted from the facts of history to its interpretation.

The irruption of the Barbarians into the newly Christianized Roman world had again modified the historical tradition in Europe. The men of the early Middle Ages retained the Christian conception of history but lost much of the culture of the ancient world. They declined in education. They lacked the tools and the opportunity for research. They ceased to have a critical sense. They lacked perspective. They emphasized the local, the personal, the trivial, and the marvelous. They forgot the art of expressing themselves in literary form. The clerical historians of the time, in consequence, seldom rose above the level of annalists and chroniclers. They usually combined into a single narrative the biblical account of the Christian epic, the reports of earlier annalists and chroniclers, and a record of what they themselves had seen and heard.

The Renaissance gave a new direction and stimulus to historical writing. The scholars of this period ceased to be so wholly absorbed with religious and ecclesiastical matters and became more secular in their point of view and their interests.

They devoted more attention to the historians of the classical period. They became interested in the finding, comparison, criticism, and improvement of texts. They had less faith in the miraculous, criticized the sources more, and proved the falsity of many accepted documents. They wrote, in the main, of their own time and place but they again gave a literary form to the writing of history.

The Renaissance led to the Reformation. This movement turned the European historical tradition again toward religion and ecclesiastical affairs. Christendom lost its unity. The former adherents of the medieval church became divided into Roman Catholics, Lutherans, Calvinists, Anglicans, and Anabaptists. Each religious faction was at war with those who differed from it in organization, service, and theology. All seized upon history as a weapon to prove their own claims and to disprove those of their adversaries. These struggles, however, stimulated the search for documents and sharpened the critical faculties of the warring scholars.

The struggles of these religious factions, in the end, made scholars more conscious of the inadequacy of their weapons and the weak spots in their armor. After the close of the period of the Reformation, in consequence, they gradually forged the tools of external criticism. Most of them were the work of members of the congregation of St. Maur. In 1678 a layman, Charles du Fresne Du Cange, founded modern lexicography through his great work, the _Glossarium ad scriptores mediae et infimae latinitatis._ In 1681 Jean Mabillon, in his _De re diplomatica_, put on a scientific foundation the determination of the age and authenticity of documents. In 1790 three scholars—Dantine, Durance, and Dom Clément—created the art of verifying dates. This school of scholars cited sources exactly and discovered correct methods for establishing the genuineness of documents. These methods constituted a great advance in the art of writing history. The historians of the period,

however, still failed to test the credibility of witnesses sufficiently and still lacked the modern skeptical attitude toward
sources and the sense of development.

In the eighteenth century the writers of history increased its
scope. They ceased to write about their own place and time
and began to write the history of more remote periods and more
distant regions. Beginning with Voltaire, they no longer
confined themselves to war, politics, and diplomacy, but described, as well, economic, social, and cultural conditions.[199]
Hume published his *History of England* (1754–1759). Robertson wrote his *History of Scotland* (1759). Abbé Raynal produced
his declamatory *L'Histoire philosophique des établissements et
du commerce des Européens dans les Indes* (1770). Gibbon gave
to the public his *Rise and Fall of the Roman Empire* (1776–1788).

This broadening and deepening of the scope of history made
historical workers more acutely conscious of their need of
access to the sources. Under the pressure of their demand
books and manuscripts ceased to be the closely guarded monopoly of governments and the rich and powerful. Royal libraries
gradually became public institutions. Governments, with great
reluctance, began to open their archives to scholars. The
treasured books and manuscripts of private collectors commenced to find their way into these public institutions. In
1759, for example, the British Museum opened its doors. In
1795, the Bibliothèque Nationale, enriched by the spoils taken
from the king, the nobility, and the Church, was established.
In the same year, in the Belgian provinces, the Library of the
Dukes of Burgundy became a state institution. Three years
later, at the Hague, the Koninklyke Bibliotheek was opened to

---

[199] See, especially, *Le siècle de Louis XIV* (1751), and *Essai sur
l'histoire générale et sur les mœurs et l'esprit des nations depuis Charlemagne jusqu'à nos jours* (7 vols., 1756). For discussion of eighteenth-
century historians, see Carl Becker, "The New History: Philosophy
Teaching by Example," in *The Heavenly City of the Eighteenth Century Philosophers* (1932).

the public. In the years that succeeded other states followed the example of France, Great Britain, and the Netherlands.

The revolutionary period, however, affected the European historical tradition in other ways. In France it had stimulated the French people to unparalleled military efforts. French armies marched victoriously over half of Europe. This impact of French nationalism on other peoples accentuated movements already in motion. Before the revolution grammarians, literary men, and romantic historians had begun to stir into action the latent nationalism of surrounding peoples. French encroachments accelerated and strengthened the rising national feeling. This new force affected all phases of national activity.

In the historical field these movements gave rise to a new interest in the national past. The historians of the newly aroused nationalities were no longer satisfied to depend for their material on the documents that happened to be available— unreliable memoirs and old histories. They brought pressure on reluctant sovereigns to make their archives available to scholars. The British government opened the old State Paper Office, later known as the Public Record Office; the French government established the institution now called the Archives Nationales, and other governments grudgingly followed their example. In these collections scholars found the political and private papers of half legendary rulers and ministers, accurate records of ancient events and movements, and even intimate pictures of the daily life of former centuries. As a result they inaugurated movements for the printing and publication of what they had found and a search for new historical sources.

After the close of the Napoleonic period the work of finding, selecting, and printing the sources of the national history promptly got under way. Under the influence and leadership of Stein, the famous minister, a group of German scholars planned and began the publication on a large scale of the sources for the history of medieval Germany. The result of their work is the great series known as the *Monumenta Germaniae Historica* (1819 ff.).

This movement was soon followed by the establishment in Germany of a new historical school. The founder of this new school of scientific historians was the celebrated Leopold von Ranke. As a young teacher of the classics in the Gymnasium at Frankfort on the Oder he became interested in the ancient and medieval historians. As he read he was increasingly struck with the need of subjecting the sources of history to a severe criticism. He realized more and more the necessity of investigating the familiarity of their authors with events and personalities and their freedom from individual, party, religious, and political bias. In his *Zur Kritik neuerer Geschichtschreiber*, a sort of supplement to his first important historical work, *History of the Latin and Teutonic Peoples, 1494–1514*,[200] he set forth these principles and thereby laid the foundations of internal criticism of the sources of history. By the time Motley began his work as historian, von Ranke had already sent out from his seminar at the University of Berlin a group of gifted students imbued with the new ideals, and had illustrated the principles of the new school of history in a series of brilliant historical works.

In France the new movement found leadership in Guizot. In 1812 this professor and political leader began his brilliant lectures on history at the University of Paris. In them he increasingly displayed a power of analysis of past periods and an ability to discern the significance of events. His lectures reached their culmination in the years 1828 to 1830 when he lectured on the history of civilization in France and in Europe. Out of his lectures developed a series of important historical works on the struggle of crown and parliament in the seventeenth century[201] and on the history of civilization in France

[200] *Geschichte der romanischen und germanischen Völker, 1494–1514* (1824).

[201] *Histoire de la révolution d'Angleterre depuis Charles Ier à Charles*

and in Europe.[202] Under his leadership, too, began an important movement for the publication of the sources of English and French history. In 1823 there began to appear under his editorship *La collection des mémoires relatifs à l'histoire de France jusqu'à XIII siècle*, which ran to thirty-one volumes. In the same year he commenced to publish *La collection des mémoires relatifs à la révolution d'Angleterre*, which extended to twenty-six volumes. In 1833 as a minister of education under Louis Philippe, he took the initial steps toward the publication of the fundamental sources of French history known as *La collection des documents inédits*. In 1819 Petitot began to bring out his collection of French memoirs.[203] In 1829 the "Société de l'École des Chartres" was founded and commenced to train competent archivists.

In the Netherlands the new interest in national history had two centers. In Belgium the movement found leadership in Gachard, the famous archivist. Under his direction a Belgian commission, modelled after that of Guizot in France, published the *Correspondance de Guillaume le Taciturne, prince d'Orange*[204] and the *Correspondance de Philippe II*.[205]

In the Dutch Netherlands, too, pioneer work was done in the publishing of the sources of national history. About 1835 Groen van Prinsterer, the archivist and secretary of the King, began the publication of the *Archives et correspondance inédites de la maison d'Orange-Nassau*.[206] In 1836 there began the publication of *Bijdragen voor vaderlandsche geschiedenis en*

II (Paris, 1826–1827, 2 vols.), *Histoire de la république d'Angleterre et de Cromwell* (Paris, 1854, 2 vols.), and *Histoire de Protectorat de Cromwell et du rétablissement du Stuarts* (Paris, 1856, 2 vols.).

[202]*Histoire de la civilisation en France* (Paris, 1830, 4 vols.) and *Histoire de la civilisation en Europe* (Paris, 1828).

[203]*Collection complète des mémoires relatifs à l'histoire de France* (1st series, Paris, 1819–1826, 52 vols.; 2nd series, Paris, 1820–1829, 44 vols.).   [204]Brussels, 1847–1860. 6 vols.

[205]Brussels, 1848–1879. 5 vols.

[206]First Series (1552–1584), Leyden, 1835–1847. 9 vols.; Second

oudheidkunde. In 1846 the first modern manual of Dutch history appeared.[207] It was thirteen years after Motley first sailed for Europe, however, before the University of Leyden established a chair in Dutch history.

By 1851, the year that Motley sailed to begin work in Europe on his *Rise of the Dutch Republic*, the indispensable preparatory work for a study of the Dutch struggle for independence from the Spanish monarchy had been largely done. The libraries and the archives of Europe had made available to scholars their treasures of books and manuscripts. Much of the documentary material had been printed. Conditions were ready for some well equipped scholar to make a brilliant synthesis.

2. *The American Heritage of History Writing*[208]

In America the annals of the art of historical writing were much shorter than in Europe. In the seventeenth century a few of the leaders in the work of founding colonies felt the importance of what they were doing and wrote accounts of the events in which they participated. Then for a century the muse of history was practically silent. Again in the eighteenth century worthy examples of historical writing appeared in the American colonies, but only sporadically. In the colonial period, in the main, the struggle to found a new society on a new continent absorbed the attention of the population.

After the close of the American Revolution, however, the historian of historiography in America finds the beginnings of a permanent and vigorous development of the art of writing

---

Series (1584–1688), Utrecht, 1857–1862. 5 vols.; Third and Fourth Series carry the work to 1789.

[207] G. Groen van Prinsterer, *Handboek der Geschiedenis van het vaderland*, Leyden, 1846.

[208] See J. F. Jameson, *The History of Historical Writing in America* (Cambridge, 1891); J. S. Bassett, *The Middle Group of American Historians* (New York, 1917); *The Cambridge History of American Literature*, II, Chaps. XVII and XVIII.

history on American soil. From time to time histories of the various states of the new union appeared. In 1791 the famous Massachusetts Historical Society was organized. In the years from 1804 to 1807 John Marshall's *Life of George Washington* was published in five volumes. In 1811 the New York Historical Society was started.

It was not until somewhat later than this, however, that the works of the brilliant school, that has been dubbed the Middle Group of American Historians, began to appear. Most of its members came from in or near Boston. In this region conditions seem to have been somewhat more favorable to the development of literature and history than elsewhere in the country. By 1828 a period of economic prosperity had produced an urban society, a prosperous merchant and professional class able to send its sons to the Universities of Europe, the oldest and best University in America, and such institutions as the Boston Athenaeum and the Harvard Library. Within a few years this environment developed a brilliant group of collectors, editors, and literary and historical writers.

Washington Irving, the first writer of this group worthy of mention, stood somewhat apart from the others by reason of his birth in New York. In rapid succession he published three historical works, all products of his visits to Spain. In 1828 appeared his three volumes entitled *History of the Life and Voyages of Columbus;* in 1829, his *Conquest of Granada;* and in 1831, his *Voyages of the Companions of Columbus.* They were the result of considerable work in Spanish books and libraries and represented popular history at its best.

In the year 1834 a noteworthy figure in American historiography began his contribution to the historical tradition in America. In that year the first volume of George Bancroft's *History of the United States from the Discovery of the American Continent* was published. The author was master of a lively, ornate style, used the striking figures of speech so popular at the time, and wrote with partisan fire a volume filled with the dominant political ideas of the time. As a result the first and succeeding volumes sprang into an almost instant popularity which ultimately brought their author political and diplomatic offices of prominence.

In 1829 Jared Sparks began his work as an editor of important collections of historical materials. In comparatively rapid succession he published *The Diplomatic Correspondence of the American Revolution* (12 vols., 1829–1830); *The Life and Writings of George Washington* (12 vols., 1834–1837); *The Works of Benjamin Franklin* (10 vols., 1836–1840); and he directed *The Library of American Biography* (2 series, 25 vols., 1834–1847). His editorial work brought him immediate fame and finally academic preferment. In 1838 he was offered and accepted the first chair of history in America at Harvard. In 1849 he became president of Harvard College.

A little later William Hickling Prescott, in spite of poor eyesight that was close to blindness, began a series of historical works that soon became classics. Before Motley had started on his historical career, Prescott had published his *Ferdinand and Isabella* (1836), *Conquest of Mexico* (1843), and *Conquest of Peru* (1847), and was at work on his *History of Philip II*. These works brought him fame not only in the United States and Great Britain but in France, Germany, Spain, and Holland.

Yet another Bostonian preceded Motley in the field of historical writing. Francis Parkman (who, like Prescott, labored under a severe physical handicap) had published his *Oregon Trail* in 1849. In 1851 his *Conspiracy of Pontiac* inaugurated a long series of brilliant historical works, concerned with the colonial period of American history, which was concluded in 1892 with *A Half-Century of Conflict*.

The work of these forerunners naturally influenced the career of Motley. After he had failed at the writing of the novel, the success of these men inevitably suggested and stimulated an endeavor to succeed in another branch of literature—the writing of history. Their books served as models for his own. Their rewards were an incentive to ambition. In 1851, accordingly, Motley definitely took the path of history.

3. Motley's Choice of a Subject

The first task of a prospective historian is the difficult and important one of choosing a subject. In selecting a subject writers of history are, of course, influenced by such factors as their time and place of origin, their political and religious affiliations, their social outlook, and the accessibility of source material. In the case of Motley no one can with certainty explain his interest in the struggle of the Dutch people against Philip II and his successor. Like other members of the group of historical writers known as the Middle Historians he had the interest of the literary man in the dramatic and the picturesque, especially after having studied Carlyle. As soon as he definitely turned from writing novels to writing history he seems to have been gripped by the subject of the struggle of the people of the Netherlands against Philip II and the resources of Spain.

The period naturally appealed to the interests and sympathies of one born in Protestant Massachusetts and republican America. Motley had already written an essay on the American Pilgrims who came from Holland. As a Unitarian he naturally sympathized with religious liberalism and disliked bigotry. At the time of his first interview with Groen van Prinsterer, the archivist of the House of Orange-Nassau and the editor of the long series of volumes containing its correspondence, Motley told this distinguished Dutch scholar that he had been struck by the similarity between the work and character of Washington and William of Orange and between the struggles for independence of the thirteen English colonies in America and the seven Dutch provinces in the Netherlands. In the eyes of their countrymen and many others the two leaders were men of heroic mold. Both displayed unusual courage, patience, self-sacrifice, and military ability in long-drawn-out conflicts. Both led relatively small, Protestant, democratic peoples, engaged in a struggle for independence against strong, tyrannical rulers with the resources of great empires at their command.[209]

From his ancestors Charles V had inherited a great, far-flung empire which included territories in Spain, the Netherlands, Italy, and the Danube Valley. The accumulation of so many kingdoms and provinces in the hands of one man threatened the destruction of local independence within his dominions and the upsetting of the balance of power in Europe. In 1555 Charles V handed the rule over most of his great collection of widely scattered territories to his beloved son, Philip II. During the reign of this sovereign all the dangers menacing the empire of Charles V and Europe became accentuated. Philip II used his great wealth and power to advance his own political ambitions and the supposed interests of the Church. His policy led to the subordination of local interests, privileges, and leaders in Spain, Italy, and the Netherlands to imperial interests and to his interference in the domestic affairs of England, France, and Germany.

These policies of Philip II gradually aroused the peoples and states of Europe to resistance. Lutherans, Calvinists, and Anglicans, the Dutch, Flemish, and Walloons, Frenchmen and Englishmen felt that the plans of the king of Spain threatened their property, religion, and lives. In 1567, as a consequence, the inhabitants of the Netherlands revolted. They rebelled against Philip's neglect of their local leaders, against innovations in Church and State, and against the introduction of Spanish garrisons. Threatened by the same danger, Protestant England and the French Huguenots also began to oppose the king of

[209] G. Groen van Prinsterer, *Maurice et Barneveld* (The Hague, 1876), p. xxxiv.

Spain. Quickly sensing the interrelation of events, Philip II aided the Catholic factions in France and England, and the Protestant parties in these states in turn fitfully and half-heartedly supported each other. This gave a certain unity for the time being to the history of the period. The peoples and governors of France, England, Spain, Germany, and the Netherlands became actors in a moving drama that had the whole of Western Europe for its stage.

This subject thus fitted in with Motley's conception of history. It dealt with figures and peoples of heroic mold engaged in an epic struggle. William the Silent, Maurice of Nassau, John of Barneveld, Henry IV and Queen Elizabeth, Philip II, the Duke of Alva, Don Juan, the Duke of Parma, and Spinola seemed equal to or even superior to their roles. The struggle of the Dutch for independence seemed to be the story of the fight of a few small provinces against a great empire, of a handful of subjects against the powerful master of millions, of liberty against despotism, of Protestantism against Catholicism, of right against wrong. Such a subject could well be the theme of a great history.

In 1850, after Motley, with a reputation still to make, had decided to write about the Dutch struggle for independence, he learned to his great dismay that his older and already famous American contemporary, William H. Prescott, was at work on the same general subject. The discovery led to a conference between the two men. With the same generosity that he had been shown at an earlier date by Washington Irving, Prescott encouraged Motley to continue his work. The two men decided that the field was large enough for both of them. They agreed that Prescott should continue his work on the history of Philip II and that Motley should devote himself to the struggle of the people of the Netherlands against Philip II. The younger man could thereafter feel secure against intrusion upon his chosen subject.

4. The Three Principal Historical Works of Motley

As has already been stated, the fame of Motley as a historian is based on three works. The first and probably the best known of these histories, *The Rise of the Dutch Republic* (1856), is a work in three volumes. It tells the story of the Netherlands from 1555, the date of the abdication of Charles V, to 1584, the year of the assassination of William of Orange. The language and organization of his three volumes clearly reveal that Motley felt he was writing a great and tragic drama. This tragedy is concerned with the struggle of liberty against religious and political tyranny. In a lengthy introduction the author first summarizes the history of the Netherlands and sets forth the thesis that its people had always striven for liberty and had gradually embodied this ideal in free institutions won at the price of many a hard-fought battle.

A long prologue then traces the efforts of Philip II, the heir of Charles V and the symbol and embodiment of regal and sacerdotal despotism, to destroy the freedom of the Netherlands and the gradual arousal of its inhabitants to armed resistance against his tyranny. The increasing tension caused the gradual development of the hero of the drama. The stresses and strains of the conflict changed a natural leader of the Netherlands, William of Orange, a man who had started life as a rather typical courtier, luxurious in his habits, something of a spendthrift, indifferent in religion, and none too scrupulous in regard to moral principles, into a pious, conscientious, self-sacrificing, far-seeing champion of civil and religious liberty.

With the coming of the Duke of Alva in 1567 the drama proper begins. The arrival of this famous adviser of the king of Spain, with instructions to put down rebellion and enforce the royal will, precipitated a military conflict between the two great protagonists, Philip II and William of Orange, the latter misleadingly known in history as "The Silent." The limits of the successive acts of the tragedy are marked by the entry upon and withdrawal from the scene of the struggle of the representatives of Philip II in the Netherlands. In turn the cruel, determined, impassive Duke of Alva, the more skilful and tactful Requesens, the imaginative but unfortunate Don Juan of Austria, half brother of Philip II, and the gifted Alexander Farnese, Duke of Parma, succeeded each other and attempted to carry out the royal orders forwarded from Madrid.

At the beginning of the armed struggle the slender military resources of William of Orange seemed completely unequal to the task of challenging the vast power of Philip II. These resources consisted of a few mercenaries, raised on German soil, and some privateers, fitted out in the friendly Huguenot port of La Rochelle. After many discouraging episodes, however, some of the Dutch seamen succeeded in getting a foothold on land. Encouraged by this news the cities of the two provinces of Holland and Zeeland, one after the other, rose in revolt. Their action gave William of Orange a base for his military operations. For a time after the unpaid Spanish soldiers sacked the great port of Antwerp, all the seventeen provinces of the Netherlands were in rebellion against Spanish rule. As the struggle progressed the leaders of the Huguenot party in France and Queen Elizabeth and her advisers in England became increasingly conscious of the important issues at stake and from self-interest extended some assistance to the struggling people of the Netherlands. The revolt thus finally involved all of Western Europe. After a few years, however, the ten southern provinces became reconciled to their sovereign and withdrew from the war. Their action left the seven Dutch northern provinces to continue the fight for independence alone. In 1584, however, after repeated attempts, Philip II succeeded in ridding himself of the head of the revolt. At the instigation of the Spanish king William of Orange was despicably assassinated. This treacherous deed deprived the Dutch of their leader, and Motley's drama thus ended in tragedy.

The second of the major historical writings of Motley, the *History of the United Netherlands*[210] in four volumes, continues the story of the Dutch fight for independence. It begins at the year 1584, the point where the inhabitants of the seven northern provinces took up the struggle against Philip II without the aid of William of Orange, and follows the ebb and flow of war and diplomacy in the Netherlands and Western Europe down to 1609, the date of the truce and the practical recognition of Dutch independence. The new period lent itself far less than the preceding one to dramatic treatment. It had less unity. The chief actors were more numerous and of less heroic mold. In 1598 Philip II passed off the stage and left no successor equal to the task of playing his role in international affairs. The mantle of the dying William of Orange fell on the shoulders of Maurice of Nassau, his seventeen-year-old son, and John of Oldenbarneveld. In addition Spinola, Queen Elizabeth and her favorite, Leicester, the unworthy sons of Catherine de Medici, Henry IV, and the Dutch merchants and navigators, Ernest and Albert, divide the attention of the reader. The action of the story is no longer confined, as in the earlier work, mainly to the Netherlands. The author had to follow the confusing and tortuous negotiations of the chancelleries of Spain, France, England, and the United Netherlands, the fortunes of the contending armies on the widely separated battlefields of Western Europe, and the courses of bold navigators on epoch-making voyages, as well as the weary story of the capture and storming of Dutch and Flemish cities, and the marching and counter-marching of little armies in the Netherlands. As a consequence the narrative is less simple than that of the earlier work, the outline of the play is not so clear, the acts of the drama are not so distinctly differentiated. The stage is larger and more crowded, and the scenes are more confused.

At first the despairing inhabitants of the seven northern

[210] London, 1860, 1867; New York, 1861, 1868.

provinces felt unequal to the task of winning their independence without William of Orange and they sought leadership and assistance in France and England. Their representatives asked for annexation to France and besought Queen Elizabeth to take them under her protection. These long negotiations ended in almost complete failure. The Dutch suspected the intentions of the French. They found the Queen of England wary about encouraging subjects of other rulers to rebel. They discovered the German Protestants to be completely apathetic. The sole result of their negotiations was the sending of Leicester with a small force to aid the Dutch provinces.

In the end the Dutch were forced to depend on their own resources. They found competent political and diplomatic guidance in John of Oldenbarneveld and able military leadership in Maurice of Nassau. Spain, on the other hand, divided its attention and its resources between the struggle in the Netherlands, the Wars of Religion in France, and the course of politics and military affairs in England, Scotland, and on the Seven Seas. Events finally proved that Philip II had attempted too much. Maurice of Nassau and John of Oldenbarneveld held the seven northern provinces against all the efforts of Spinola. Henry IV triumphed in France. The seamen of England destroyed the Spanish Armada and harried the coasts of Spain. While these events fruitlessly exhausted the resources of Spain, Dutch seamen increased the wealth of the United Netherlands by the plundering of Spanish shipping and the discovery and exploitation of new lands. By 1609 the course of events inexorably pointed to an admission of failure and Spain concluded the twelve years' truce which for the time being ended the war. The narrative closes, consequently, with a description of the public and private rejoicing over the coming of peace.

The third of the important histories of Motley, *The Life and Death of John of Barneveld*,[211] is a work in two volumes. It

[211] London and New York, 1874.

is not a biography of the ordinary type as its title suggests but an account of events in the United Netherlands from the conclusion of the truce of 1609 to about the year 1623. During this period of nominal peace the new state of the United Netherlands felt threatened by ominous developments in foreign affairs. The Dutch saw the peoples of Europe girding themselves for the coming struggle of France with the Hapsburgs and of the Catholics of Western Europe with the Calvinists and Lutherans of Germany and Scandinavia. In the face of these dangers the Dutch continued to look for guidance to John of Oldenbarneveld and Maurice of Nassau. At first the leaders managed to work together as in former years. The period of co-operation, however, did not last long. The United Netherlands itself became divided into bitterly hostile factions over questions of theology. The two leaders of the country were drawn by the religious strife and personal tension on opposite sides. Motley represents John of Barneveld as championing the side of religious tolerance and relying for protection on the historic privileges of the provinces; and Prince Maurice, spurred on by personal ambition, as taking the side of intolerance. Given the temper of the parties there could be only one end to the conflict. Prince Maurice, though really a soldier and not a theologian, had placed himself at the head of the more popular cause. John of Oldenbarneveld, as a consequence, was defeated, brought to trial, and executed.

This contest of two great personalities gave Motley opportunity again for a dramatic treatment of history. He makes the struggle a tragic and inevitable conflict. He pictures the great politician and diplomat as a heroic and appealing figure leading a righteous but losing cause. He represents Prince Maurice as a gifted leader with a character marred by ingratitude and frustrated ambition. The rivalry of the two men is thus given something of the grandeur and inevitability of a Greek tragedy.

5. *Motley as an Historical Investigator*

The historical works of Motley reveal clearly that he possessed much of the spirit and many of the methods of the pioneer members of the modern school of scientific historians. Like them he was not satisfied, as many of the older writers of history had been, to repeat what earlier historians had said and to depend on the reports of entertaining but unreliable memoirs. He felt the need of going to the primary sources. In consequence, as his footnotes plainly reveal, he worked long years in the books and manuscripts which he found in the libraries and archives at Dresden, Brussels, the Hague, Paris, and London.

For using the materials which he found in these institutions Motley possessed many of the necessary tools. From his school days he had shown an interest in languages. By the time he began to write on the history of the Netherlands he had a good working knowledge of most of the languages of Western Europe. The footnotes of his historical works indicate that he knew and used frequently and correctly Latin, English, French, German, Spanish, Italian, and Dutch. These languages gave him the key to the sources.

Upon his arrival in Europe, armed with these linguistic tools, Motley seems to have done what any intelligent and well-recommended investigator from America, who proposed to work on a European subject, would naturally do. He put himself in touch with the scholars, librarians, and archivists who had been doing the indispensable preparatory work of discovering, arranging, and printing the treasures of their libraries and archives. In the prefaces of his three principal historical works he expresses his gratitude to Dr. Klemm, the chief librarian at Dresden, Herr von Weber, the head of the Royal Archives of Saxony, Mr. Campbell, the assistant librarian at the Hague, Bakhuysen van den Brink, chief archivist of the Kingdom of the Netherlands, and M. Gachard, the distinguished archivist of Belgium. Soon after the arrival of Motley in Holland from Dresden he called upon Groen van Prinsterer, the archivist of the royal house and the editor of the *Archives et Correspondance de la maison du Orange-Nassau.* We know from this scholar's own account[212] of this interview that he was delighted with Motley's knowledge of the Dutch sources. Evidently these men generously put their treasured books and manuscripts at the disposal of the American historian. He apparently used to a large extent the material which they called to his attention.

The modern scholar who should attempt to retrace the steps taken by Motley would find it difficult. He lacked some of the technical devices of the modern historical seminar. The libraries and archives in which he worked had undoubtedly not yet been provided with public catalogues, indexes, and repertoires. Motley refers, in consequence, rather vaguely sometimes to the documents which he used. He frequently gives only the name of the manuscript and the archive in which he found it. In referring to books, also, he is often too cryptic. He never gives the initials of the authors which he employed as sources. He often successfully conceals their identity by giving their Latin rather than their real names. He gives, likewise, no bibliographies, either critical or uncritical.

In his first major historical work, *The Rise of the Dutch Republic,* Motley made use of only a few manuscripts. He depended in the main on printed sources. One class of these might be described as the great collections of historical documents which had been making their appearance from time to time in the quarter of a century before Motley set to work at the writing of history. These included the *Papiers d'État'*[213] of Cardinal Granvelle, the chief minister of Philip II in the Netherlands from 1559 to 1664, which he found in the great

---

[212] Groen van Prinsterer, *Maurice et Barneveld*. The Hague, 1876. *Passim.*   [213] Paris, 1841–1852. 9 vols.

French series, published as a result of the initiative of Guizot, known as *La collection des documents inédits*, *La correspondance du Guillaume, le Taciturne*, and *La correspondance de Philippe II sur les affaires des Pays-Bas*, both a result of the work of the famous Belgian archivist, Gachard; the *Archives et correspondance de la maison du Orange-Nassau*, which was just being edited and published under the supervision of Groen van Prinsterer, the archivist of the royal house of the Kingdom of the Netherlands; and the *Colección de documentos ineditos para la historia de España*,[214] which had begun to appear in 1843.

Motley depended, too, on the fundamental Dutch sources which had long been known and used by scholars of the Netherlands and which will always serve as the raw material for histories of the efforts of the people of the Netherlands to gain their independence. These works were written either by contemporaries of the Dutch war for freedom from Spanish rule or by men of the succeeding generation who wrote while events were still fresh in the popular mind. In either case they sympathized with the struggle of William of Orange and his followers. These writers, too, had already done much of the work of gathering the raw materials and interpreting their significance. This group of sources included the histories of Pieter Bor, Everhard van Reyd, Emmanuel van Meteren, and Pieter Hooft. Their works constituted the principal part of the foundation on which Motley erected his own structure.

The first of this group of contemporary historians, Pieter Bor, was born at Utrecht in 1579. He lived, consequently, through much of the period of which he wrote. In 1595, at a time when the war for independence was still in progress, he began to publish his *Oorsprongk, Begin, en Vervolgh der Nederlandsche Oorlogen*. He finally carried his story of the conflict down to the year 1600. He lacked the literary style so highly prized at the time but he wrote with sincerity and was imbued

[214] Madrid, 1842–1895. 112 vols.

to a large measure with the historical spirit. He had the advantage of having had access to many of the primary sources. He knew many who took part in the conflict and in 1602 the Estates of Utrecht opened their archives to him. As a result of these advantages he gives in his great folio volumes many documents and many analyses of documentary material. In addition, though he does not seem to have known those languages himself, he had many of the Spanish and Italian sources translated for his work. In 1615, as a reward for his achievement, he was appointed historian of the provinces of Holland and West Friesland.

Less seems to be known about Everhard van Reyd, the author of the *Oorspronck ende Voortrank van de Nederlandsche Oorlogen* (1626). He was born in 1550 and died in 1602. He was not merely a contemporary, however, of the events which he records. He was as well in a position to obtain authoritative information about much of which he wrote. He was attached in an official capacity first to John of Nassau, Stadtholder of Gelderland, and later to William Lewis, Stadtholder of Friesland and one of the chief participants in the war. His history covers events in the Netherlands from 1566 to 1601 and treats the period after 1583 in great detail.

Emmanuel van Meteren was somewhat older than Bor and van Reyd. He was born in 1535. He was a Protestant merchant of Antwerp and Amsterdam. In 1583 he became consul at London. He died in 1612. His *Belgica, Historie der Neder-Landscher ende haerder Naburen Oorlogen ende Geschiedenissen tot den Jare MVI°XII* (1635) is the indispensable complement of the work of Bor. It is characterized by research, good faith, and a wealth of statistics. It was to this history that John of Oldenbarneveld turned to refresh his memory of the events in which he had taken part when he was put on trial for his life by Prince Maurice and the Counter-Remonstrant party.

Pieter Hooft only lived through the later years of the Dutch fight for independence but his father had been burgomaster of Amsterdam during much of the period of the war. He was not born until 1581. As a consequence he did not begin his *Nederlandsche Historien* (1642) until 1628. He began his narrative with the year 1555 but never got beyond the events of 1587. He was more of a literary man than the other three contemporary historians named. By the men of his own day he was considered a model of style. He gloried in the title of the Tacitus of Holland. Hooft gave accurate information and wrote with vigor and conciseness.

Besides the great collections and the fundamental Dutch works, Motley made much use, too, of what might be called the Catholic sources. Some of these were written by inhabitants of the Netherlands, particularly of the southern provinces. Others, though written by foreigners, were the work of writers who had seen something of the events or of the actors in the Dutch war for independence. Still others had written of the struggle in the Netherlands without having been in position to see anything of the movement concerning which they wrote. This class of sources included the works of such writers as L. Guicciardini, Dom Prosper l'Evesque, Famiano Strada, Luis Cabrera de Cordova, Nicolas de Bourgogne, and Cardinal Bentivoglia. They wrote, naturally, with something of a bias against William of Orange and his cause.

About some of the authors in this group little information is to be found in the usual works of reference.[215] Dom Prosper

---

[215] *Dictionnaire de biographie française* (Paris, 1933); *Biographie nationale Belge* (24 vols., Bruxelles, 1866–1931); Kok, Pieter, *Woordenboek* (35 vols., Amsterdam, 1780–1799); Molhuysen, P. C., and Blok, P. J., *Biographisch Woordenboek* (8 vols., 1911–1930); *Der Grosse Brockhaus* (20 vols., Leipzig, 1928–1935); *The Dictionary of National Biography* (63 vols., London, 1885–1903); *Enciclopedia Italiana* (Milan-Rome, 1929 ff.); *Enciclopedia Universal Ilustrada* (70 vols., Barcelona, n.d.); *Meyers' Lexikon* (12 vols. plus 4, 7th edition, Leipzig, 1924–1930); *Allgemeine Deutsche Biographie* (56 vols., Leipzig, 1875–1912); *Nouvelle Biographie Générale* (40 vols., Paris, 1855–

l'Evesque was born at Besançon in 1713 and died in 1781. He joined the Benedictine order and was finally appointed Conservateur of the Library of St. Vincent in his native city. While in this position he rescued the neglected papers of his famous compatriot and published them under the title of *Mémoires pour servir à l'histoire du Cardinal Granvelle* (1753). For knowledge of the geography of the Netherlands at the time of the Dutch war for independence Motley depended to a large extent on the interesting Italian work, *Descrittione di Lodovici Guicciardini patrioto fiorentino di tutti i Passi Bassi, altrimente dette Germania inferiore* (1581). In this volume he found a full and systematic description of cities and provinces about which he wrote. Motley made some use, too, of the *Historia Belgica* of Nicolas Bourgogne, known also as Burgundius, a professor at the academy at Ingostadt, who was born in 1586 and died in 1649 and whose history of the revolt in the Netherlands appeared in 1629.

The American historian also referred very frequently to the work of Famiano Strada, who was born in and passed his life at Rome. In 1591 he became a Jesuit. He prepared his *De Bello Belgico* with the greatest care. In the years 1632 to 1647 two volumes of this history of the Dutch war for independence appeared. Subsequently he wrote a third volume which was never printed because of the opposition of the Spanish government. The work of Strada has serious faults although this humble, modest author did not deserve the epithet "infamiano" which his bitter critic, Cardinal Bentivoglio, hurled at him. He did digress, lacked method, and favored the house of Farnese.

1866); *Nouveau Larousse Illustré* (7 vols., Paris, n.d.); Winkler Prins, *Algemeene Encyclopædie* (Amsterdam, 1932 ff.); *Historisch Biographisches Lexikon der Schweiz* (Neuenburg, 1921 ff.); *Brockhaus' Konversations-Lexikon* (17 vols. plus 4, 14th edition, Berlin and Wien, 1901–1904); *The Catholic Encyclopedia* (15 vols., New York, 1907–1912); *La Grande Encyclopédie* (31 vols., Paris, n.d.); *Encyclopædia Britannica* (24 vols., London and New York, 1929).

With this one exception, however, he wrote with a laudable measure of impartiality.

The churchman who has just been described as a bitter critic of Strada, Cardinal Bentivoglio, was born in 1579. He was in a position to obtain full and authoritative information about the conflict in the Netherlands. From 1607 to 1616 he was Papal Nuncio in Flanders. As a result of this mission he published, during his lifetime, several works throwing light on the war. These include, besides the *Della Guerra di Fiandra* (1633–1639) which Motley used, his *Memorie* (1642), *Raccolta di Lettere scritte in tempe delle nunziature di Fiandra* (1631) and *Relazione di G. Bentivoglio in tempe delle sue nunziature di Fiandra e di Francia* (1629).

For information about Philip II Motley relied to a large extent on the biography of this sovereign written by Luis Cabrera de Cordova. The author was born in 1559. In 1585 he was sent to Flanders. Subsequently he took service at court where he was in a position to observe his master at first hand. In 1598 he became secretary of the Queen. In 1619 he published the first volume of his *Historia de Rey Felipe II* (1619). This work is well written and is characterized by the abundance and exactitude of its facts.

In writing *The Rise of the Dutch Republic* Motley made frequent use of a small number of manuscript sources. He cites repeatedly several relations of Venetian ambassadors which he found in the archives in which he worked in the Netherlands. These sources, however, were undoubtedly ready for publication at the time Motley used them, for in 1855, the year before he published *The Rise of the Dutch Republic*, Gachard brought out his *Relations des Ambassadeurs Venitiens sur Charles-Quint et Philippe II*. Two of the most important of these relations, furthermore, had appeared two years earlier in the eighth volume of the *Relazioni degli ambassiatori Veneti al senato*.[216] He also

---

[216] Edited by Alberi, 15 vols. (Florence, 1840–1863). There are several supplementary series.

used a number of manuscript memoirs.[217]   Several of these sources were published soon after Motley's work appeared in print.

Motley made considerable use of secondary as well as primary sources.   He based his statements over and over again on the *Nederlandsche Historie* of Jan Wagenaar, a work in twenty-one stout volumes, which appeared first in the years 1752 to 1760 and which presents the point of view of the anti-stadholder party.   For the facts about the Inquisition Motley depended on the *Historia crítica de España*, a work in ten volumes, which was published in 1822 by Juan Antonio Llorente, one of the last secretaries of the Spanish Inquisition.   For information about other phases of the religious situation in the Netherlands Motley used the *Historie der Reformatie in en omtrent de Neder-landen* (1677–1704) of Gerard Brandt, a famous Remonstrant preacher of the seventeenth century.   For his knowledge of the lives and characteristics of quite a number of the individuals who appeared in the pages of his history, he depended very largely on two eighteenth century works of collected biography —the *Levensbeschryving van beroemde en geleerde mannen,* a

---

[217] The manuscript memoirs used by Motley in *The Rise of the Dutch Republic* include: "Recueil, par forme de Mémoires . . ." of Pasquier de la Barre; Badovaro MSS; Michele MS; Suriano MS; Pontus Payem MS; "Histoire des causes de la désunion, révoltes et alterations des Pays-Bas" of Renom de France; "Histoire des choses les plus mémorables qui sont passées en la ville et le Compté de Valenciennes; "Troubles des Pays-Bas" of Jean de Grutere; "Registre des Condamnés et Bannis à cause des Troubles des Pays-Bas"; "Chronike oft Journal van het gene in de Nederlanden . . . 1566–1593" of N. de Weert.   Badovaro and Suriano were Venetian ambassadors.   The authors of the other MSS were residents of the Netherlands.   The MSS of Suriano, Badovaro, Pontus Payem, and Renom de France have been published.   See L. P. Gachard, *Relations des ambassadeurs Venitiens sur Charles-Quint et Philippe II* (Bruxelles, 1855); *Relazioni degli ambasciatori Veneti al senato* (Florence, 1853), VIII; *Mémoires de Pontus Payem* (Bruxelles, 1861); Renom de France, *Histoire des troubles des Pays-Bas* (Bruxelles, 1886–1891).

publication in fifteen volumes, printed in Amsterdam in 1731, and the *Levensbeschryving van eenige vorname Mannen en Vrouen*, a work which appeared in Haarlem in 1794. At times, too, Motley even fell back on that last refuge of the historian, the encyclopedia, for he referred several times in his footnotes to the *Woordenboek* of Pieter Kok, which was published in the years 1780 to 1799.

For information about affairs outside of the Netherlands Motley drew on a comparatively small number of works. To throw light on events and individuals in France he made much use of the *Historia sui temporis* of Jacques Auguste de Thou, a councillor of state of both Henry III and Henry IV. This celebrated work, which appeared in the years 1604 to 1608, was based on the rich library which its author had collected and was marked by exact research and an elegant and animated style. He obtained, also, many a colorful detail of his narrative from *Les vies des grands capitaines* of Pierre de Bourdeille, abbé et seigneur de Brantôme, a work filled with stories of battles and gallantry, which was first published at Leyden in the years 1665–1666. Motley, however, made even less use of the available materials for English history.

In his second important historical work, the *History of the United Netherlands*, Motley used to a large extent the printed sources which have already been described. He continued to refer with great frequency to the great series of collected correspondence and to the fundamental Dutch and Catholic sources for the revolt of the Netherlands against the Spanish monarchy. He made much greater use, however, of manuscript sources. He refers repeatedly to material in the Archives de l'Empire at Paris, the Royal Archives at the Hague, and the old State Paper Office at London, an institution which was merged in 1854 with the newer Public Record Office. This increased use of manuscript materials is in all probability to be ascribed in part to progress in his craft and in part to the somewhat greater role played by diplomatic negotiations in the years after the death of William of Orange.

In Motley's third important historical work, *The Life and Death of John of Barneveld*, many of the old titles disappear from his footnotes and are replaced by new ones. His references to printed sources, though, are far fewer than in his two earlier works. To the great wrath of the learned Dutch editor he failed for some reason to use one important, available printed source, namely, the appropriate volumes of the great series, *Archives et correspondance de la maison du Orange-Nassau*, which had just been published. His failure to make use of these volumes brought down on his head the critical work of Groen van Prinsterer entitled *Maurice et Barneveld*. In the main Motley based his work on archival material.

Motley by no means, however, used all of the available sources. The scholar who leafs over any modern bibliography of Dutch history can find many titles which Motley failed to cite.[218] Some were primary sources which were published soon after the close of the Dutch war for independence. Some were secondary works which appeared in the years just prior to the publication of Motley's works. Many of the Spanish and English officers left accounts of military operations. Motley made little use of the proceedings and ordinances of the Estates. These omissions were not serious. They might be classed as minor sources which would not in any case have changed the general course of Motley's narrative. Such omissions were, in addition, understandable and excusable. The aids at the disposal of the modern scholar were yet to be created.

The extent to which Motley subjected his sources to criticism

[218] See bibliographies in J. P. Blok, *History of the People of the Netherlands* (London, 1898–1907), III and IV; *The Cambridge Modern History* (New York, 1905), III, 771–774, 798–809, 816–824; *Histoire générale* (Paris, 1895), V, 203–204; and Martinus Nijhoff, *History of the Netherlands, a Catalogue of Old and Modern Books* (The Hague. 1932).

can hardly be estimated, even approximately. The narrative of a historian reveals the results of his work rather than the process by which the result was obtained. Something about his methods of work, nevertheless, can be gained from the wording of his narrative and from his learned apparatus.

He certainly used more discrimination in the choice of sources than most literary men. He avoided the venomous slanders of the ex-secretary of Philip II, Antonio Perez, and the misinformed and irresponsible gossip of St. Real. He seems, too, to have used with a due amount of caution the *Apology* of William of Orange, a document written at a time the leader of the revolt of the Netherlands had just escaped assassination and was far from being in a judicial mood on the subject of Philip II, the instigator of the attempt. From these sources literary men from the sixteenth century to the present day have been creating an imaginary Philip II and Don Carlos that never really lived on land or sea.

On the contrary Motley used to a large extent, as we have already seen, the materials recommended to him by well-informed librarians and expert archivists. The authors of these sources had already done much of the work of criticism. It is probable, however, that, like most members of the historical craft, he had a somewhat too great faith in interesting and colorful accounts of events. His smoothly flowing narrative seems to make little differentiation between the possible, the probable, and the well-established. In his glowing pages there is little indication of the relative certainty of his statements. While he may have trusted his authorities somewhat too much he obviously realized that the writers of his sources were swayed by passions and prone to make mistakes. In consequence, he discounted the adulation of Spanish court biographers and used memoirs with some caution.

6. *Motley and the Selection of Facts*

The writer of history can never record all the facts about the actors, the events, and the scene of which he writes. He must select the typical, the distinctive, and the significant and omit the irrelevant, the trivial, and the unimportant. In part his choice depends on his subject. He chooses the facts which will make stand out the events, personalities, and movements logically connected with his theme. In part he is limited in the selection of facts by his sources. Many facts of the past concerning which he writes have disappeared and left no trace. The historian cannot write of them if he would. In part, however, his choice of facts is the result of his own conception of the task of the historian.

The three historical works of Motley bear within the unmistakable impress of the author. He wrote of a period that was rich in events and personalities. He had at his disposal a wealth of source material. He was free to shape his narrative according to his own conception of history. He looked upon history, as we have found, as a drama. He strove, in consequence, to represent, as far as he could, the past as a series of moving and colorful spectacles. He chose from the facts at his disposal, the striking, the dramatic, and the picturesque. From this material he painted a long succession of pen pictures.

The Rise of the Dutch Republic is especially rich in such word pictures. The work opens with a scene that has since become famous. Its author devotes an entire chapter to the abdication by Charles V of the Burgundian crown in favor of his son, Philip II.[219] He describes in great detail the stage on which the scene was enacted, the appearance and character of the principal actors, and successive events in which they took part. Scattered throughout the work are minute descriptions of the

---

[219] *The Rise of the Dutch Republic* (New York, 1856), I, 95–132. See post, pp. 121 ff.

frequent battles—St. Quentin,[220] Gravelines,[221] the first military effort of William of Orange,[222] the capture of Brill,[223] and Mook Heath,[224] and of the innumerable sieges—Valenciennes,[225] Mons,[226] Tergoes,[227] Naarden,[228] Haarlem,[229] Alkmaar,[230] and Oudenarde.[231]   Many other events—such as the obsequies of Charles V at Brussels,[232] the farewell of Philip II to the Netherlands,[233] his return to Spain,[234] the marriage of William of Orange to Anne of Saxony,[235] the working of the Inquisition,[236] the withdrawal of Cardinal Granvelle,[237] the religious persecutions,[238] the betrothal and wedding of Prince Alexander,[239] the petition of the "Beggars," [240] the religious services in the open fields,[241] the wrecking of the Cathedral of Antwerp by the mob,[242] the coming of Alva and his army,[243] the operations of the Council of Blood,[244] the kidnapping of the Count of Buren,[245] the trials and executions of the counts of Horn and

[220] *The Rise of the Dutch Republic* (New York, 1856), I, 174–182.
[221] *Ibid.*, I, 194–199.   [222] *Ibid.*, II, 248–259.
[223] *Ibid.*, II, 351–356. See post, pp. 219 ff.
[224] *Ibid.*, II, 533–540.   [225] *Ibid.*, II, 75–80.
[226] *Ibid.*, II, 369–372. See post, pp. 223 ff.
[227] *Ibid.*, II, 413–416.
[228] *Ibid.*, II, 420–423.
[229] *Ibid.*, II, 427–455.
[230] *Ibid.*, II, 463–472.
[231] *Ibid.*, III, 555–556.
[232] *Ibid.*, I, 205–206.
[233] *Ibid.*, I, 211–221.
[234] *Ibid.*, I, 221–223.
[235] *Ibid.*, I, 295–320.
[236] *Ibid.*, I, 321–347. See post, pp. 158 ff.
[237] *Ibid.*, I, 405–414.
[238] *Ibid.*, I, 333–337.
[239] *Ibid.*, I, 487–490.
[240] *Ibid.*, I, 509–525. See post, pp. 179 ff.
[241] *Ibid.*, I, 532–539.
[242] *Ibid.*, I, 551–565. See post, pp. 185 ff.
[243] *Ibid.*, II, 109–119.
[244] *Ibid.*, 135–146. See post, pp. 199 ff.
[245] *Ibid.*, 155–157. See post, pp. 206 ff.

Egmont and Baron Montigny,[246] the Massacre of St. Bartholomew,[247] the "Spanish Fury," [248] the reception of William of Orange at Brussels,[249] and the attempt of the Duke of Anjou to seize Antwerp[250]—all gave Motley an opportunity to paint a succession of historical pageants. In a final chapter he closed his work with a dramatic account of the assassination of William of Orange.[251]

The period dealt with in *History of the United Netherlands* was less adapted to dramatic treatment. Deprived of their great leader by assassination, the Dutch people sought guidance and assistance in France and England. The tedious diplomatic negotiations gave little opportunity for colorful descriptions or striking narratives. Leicester and the small body of troops finally obtained from Queen Elizabeth quarreled with the Dutch authorities and accomplished little. The actors and events of the Wars of Religion in France seemed largely futile and meaningless. Wherever he could, however, Motley gave his narrative a dramatic touch. He made the most of the long succession of sieges that constituted a large part of the war. He described in great detail such events as the attack of Drake on the coast of Spain,[252] the fight of the English seamen against the Spanish Armada,[253] the various voyages of discovery and for commerce made by Dutch navigators,[254] the last illness and the death of Philip II,[255] and the demonstrations over the conclusion of a truce in 1609.[256]

In *The Life and Death of John of Barneveld*, Motley again found a period which could be given dramatic treatment. After a somewhat prosaic introduction dealing with the foreign rela-

---

[246] *Ibid.*, 119–129, 160–179.   [247] *Ibid.*, 387–389.
[248] *Ibid.*, III, 116–122. See post, pp. 245 ff.   [249] *Ibid.*, 266–272.
[250] *Ibid.*, 560–572.   [251] *Ibid.*, 596–614. See post, pp. 278 ff.
[252] *History of the United Netherlands* (New York, 1874), II, 281–285.
[253] *Ibid.*, II, 462–508.
[254] *Ibid.*, III, 544–580; IV, 243–250, 417–425.
[255] *Ibid.*, III, 503–512.   [256] *Ibid.*, IV, 429–432.

tions of the seven Dutch provinces, the work traces the division
of the Northern provinces of the Netherlands into two hostile
religious factions. This religious dispute gradually drew into
the struggle on opposite sides the two principal leaders of the
United Netherlands. As a result the greater part of the book
traces the growing personal and partisan tension between the
men which ultimately ended in the dramatic trial and execution
of John of Oldenbarneveld.

As a result of his conception of history Motley devoted, too,
more than the usual amount of space to the actors in his drama.
He described in great detail the personal appearance of the chief
personalities of the period concerning which he wrote, their
supposed habits and characteristics, their part in events, and the
influence of their actions and policies. The result is a gallery of
portraits which includes Charles V,[257] Philip II,[258] William of
Orange[259] and the various members of his family,[260] the successive representatives of the Spanish government in the Netherlands and their principal advisers,[261] the leading nobles of the

[257] *The Rise of the Dutch Republic*, I, 102–103, 111–124.

[258] *Ibid.*, I, 103–104, 133–146; *History of the United Netherlands*, II,
303, 458–469.

[259] *The Rise of the Dutch Republic*, I, 233–247; II, 241–246, 327–328,
486–490; III, 61–62, 615–627.

[260] See especially portraits of Louis of Nassau in *The Rise of the
Dutch Republic*, I, 496, and II, 540–542; Charlotte of Bourbon in
The Rise of the Dutch Republic, III, 21–27; Maurice in *The Life and
Death of John of Barneveld*, I, 23–24, 27–29; and Louise of Coligny in
History of the United Netherlands, I, 15–17.

[261] See especially the portraits of Mary of Hungary in *The Rise of the
Dutch Republic*, I, 150; Margaret of Parma in *ibid.*, I, 233–247; the
Duke of Alva in *ibid.*, II, 103–109, 496–505; Requesens in *ibid.*, II,
511–513, and in *ibid.*, III, 50–51; Don John in *ibid.*, III, 131–147,
362–363; Alexander Farnese, Duke of Parma in *ibid.*, III, 367–375,
and in *History of the United Netherlands*, I, 135–138; Spinola in *ibid.*,
IV, 181–184. For portraits of Berlaymont, Vigilius, Arras, and
Egmont, all members of the Council of Margaret of Parma, see *The
Rise of the Dutch Republic*, I, 231–252. For portraits of Cardinal
Granvelle, see *The Rise of the Dutch Republic*, I, 247–252, 421–438.

seventeen provinces,[262] and the rulers,[263] ministers,[264] and generals[265] of the neighboring states. Besides his full length portraits of the leading figures of the period he presents numerous miniatures of minor actors in the drama.

While he was not under their spell to the same extent as present day historians, Motley was well aware of the significance of economic forces. In his volumes he repeatedly pointed out the crippling effect of the empty exchequer of Philip II on the execution of his policies.[266] He noted the economic development of England at the expense of the ten southern provinces as a result of the emigration of religious refugees.[267] He recognized the disastrous consequences of the financial policy of the Duke of Alva.[268] He does not, however, consider every historical fact as an economic phenomenon.

In his efforts to make the past seem real Motley used one obvious but very legitimate device. He made much use of the traces left by the period of which he wrote. In narrating the abdication of Charles V, for example, he endeavored to make his readers first see Brussels with its principal buildings rising above a wide expanse of fields, gardens, groves, and forests, then mount its steep streets to the grounds and palace of the

---

[262] See especially portraits of the Count of Egmont in *The Rise of the Dutch Republic*, I, 170–175, and II, 209–210; the Count of Horn in *The Rise of the Dutch Republic*, II, 210–211; Count Brederode in *The Rise of the Dutch Republic*, I, 510–511; and Philip Marnix, Lord of St. Aldegonde in *ibid.*, I, 494–496, and in *History of the United Netherlands*, I, 145–149.

[263] See especially the portraits of Mary Tudor in *The Rise of the Dutch Republic*, I, 137–139; Paul IV in *ibid.*, 157–159; Henry III in *History of the United Netherlands*, I, 37–41; Henry IV in *ibid.*, I, 45–52; and Philip III in *ibid.*, IV, 353–361.

[264] See especially the portraits of the Duke of Lerma in *History of the United Netherlands*, IV, 344–353; Robert Dudley, Earl of Leicester, in *ibid.*, II, 366–371; and Ruy Gomez de Silva in *The Rise of the Dutch Republic*, I, 148–150.

[265] For a portrait of the Duke of Guise see *ibid.*, 41–43.

[266] *The Rise of the Dutch Republic*, I, 291–294.

[267] *Ibid.*, I, 504–505.   [268] *Ibid.*, II, 282–293, 517–518.

Dukes of Brabant, next enter the spacious hall where the chapter meetings of the Order of the Golden Fleece were held, and lastly examine the principal features of the interior.[269] He prefaced his account of the image-breaking at Antwerp with a minute description of the still standing cathedral.[270] He made the tyranny of the Duke of Alva more vivid by giving a careful description of the symbol of his autocratic rule, the citadel erected at Antwerp.[271] With these surviving landmarks he created again the past of which he wrote.

Motley, too, selected facts that made the period concerning which he wrote seem alive. He represented Charles V as still following from his cloistered retreat the events of the world in which he once played such a conspicuous role.[272] He caused his readers to mingle with the throngs at Amsterdam rejoicing over the conclusion of peace,[273] and to see the wine flowing in the streets, the oxen roasting in the open air, and men and women climbing poles for prizes, hunting pigs blindfolded, and racing in sacks. He took them as unseen guests to autos-da-fé,[274] banquets,[275] and weddings.[276] They are given an opportunity to read the speeches of the principal characters, public edicts, proclamations, and documents of various kinds, and letters that shaped the course of events. He made his readers watch the unfolding of interesting plots, participate in the sacking of cities, overhear crucial conferences, and witness picturesque and interesting episodes.

7. *Motley as an Interpreter of Historical Facts*

In one important respect Motley was far behind many of his historical contemporaries. In Germany for a quarter of a

---

[269] *The Rise of the Dutch Republic*, I, 96–99.
[270] *Ibid.*, I, 551–555.
[271] *Ibid.*, II, 150–151.
[272] *Ibid.*, I, 131–132.
[273] *Ibid.*, 206–207.
[274] *Ibid.*, 221–223, 324–326.
[275] *Ibid.*, I, 519–524; III, 229–230.
[276] *Ibid.*, I, 485–490; III, 114–115.

century there had been developing a new school of scientific historians, led and trained by Leopold von Ranke, which had as its ideal the writing of history objectively. As the leader of this school phrased it they attempted merely to write history as it actually happened. By the time Motley began to write history some of the most famous of the works of von Ranke and his students had been published. In practice, of course, the members of this school often fell far short of attaining their ideal. Being human they allowed their writings to be colored by the ideas and points of view of their time, their place, and their personalities, but at least they consciously endeavored to realize the goal of objectivity.

Motley, in contrast, never tried to be objective. He never doubted the validity of the political and religious ideas of his democratic America and Protestantism. For him they were the most important of historical facts. He thought that they should be used as standards for the measurement of events, personalities, institutions, and movements. They colored, consequently, all of his historical work. He is always an advocate of a point of view. He is a stern judge as well as a colorful painter of scenes, portraits, and conditions, and a skillful narrator of actions, events, and movements.

From his time and place Motley adopted two fundamental principles. From the political theories and the institutions of his country he absorbed a profound sympathy with democracy and liberalism. From the religious theories and institutions of New England he adopted and made part of himself an intense Protestantism. As a consequence, the warp and woof of his pages are shot through with these two principles.

In the first place they caused him to take sides in the long struggle of the Netherlands for independence which constituted the theme of *The Rise of the Dutch Republic* and *History of the United Netherlands*. In both works he was on the side of the forces which in his judgment were fighting in behalf of democracy and Protestantism. He sympathized, accordingly, with England, with the Huguenot party in France, and above all with the Dutch. He opposed Spain and the Catholic parties in France and England. He condemned the Protestant princes of Germany for their inaction and the people of the ten southern provinces of the Netherlands for their defection from the good cause. He judged all the actors, parties, and peoples of the period about which he wrote by their loyalty to and effectiveness in behalf of the side of democracy and Protestantism.

Like most of his contemporaries he thought that the chosen people of America, England, and the Northern Netherlands were bound together by the tie of racial unity. He believed that their democratic and Protestant institutions had their origin beyond the limits of the Roman World in the forests of the freedom-loving Germans. From this as a center free institutions had spread and developed. Throughout their history the descendants of these early Germans in the Netherlands, England, and America had fought to obtain freedom and to preserve and develop free institutions. The Dutch war for independence was merely the last and greatest chapter in this long story.[277]

The avowed partisanship of Motley had a greater or less effect too on the long gallery of portraits which he attempted to paint with his facile pen. He sketched first a full length picture of Charles V. In the opening chapter of *The Rise of the Dutch Republic* this ruler stands out as crippled, prematurely aged, almost deformed, a scrupulous observer of the forms of religion, somewhat hypocritical, polylingual, adaptable, a good general, avaricious, autocratic, and able to read the minds and hearts of those around him.[278]

Motley painted many portraits of Philip II, the villain of his drama. In these he most often pictures him as seated at his

[277] See especially the introduction to *The Rise of the Dutch Republic*.
[278] *Ibid.*, I, 102–103, 111–124.

desk in his bare apartment in the Escorial, striving to bend the
peoples of Western Europe to his will. In mature life Motley
represents Philip II as small, meagre, cold, proud, dignified, and
cruel; a Fleming in appearance, a Spaniard in dress, bearing and
character; mentally mediocre, industrious but indecisive, bigoted
and conscientious in matters of religion, licentious in conduct, a
dissembling tyrant in affairs of state, and an oppressor and
persecutor of peoples who differed from him.[279] He gives no
hint that Philip II was the most loved and admired of Spanish
sovereigns. In describing his last sickness and death, however,
Motley was stirred to a feeling akin to admiration by Philip's
imperturbable calm in the face of great disasters, by his struggle
with disabling gout and the ills incident to advancing years,
and by his heroic bearing in his last days and hours.[280]

In the main, too, Motley judged the subordinates who served
the Spanish king in the Netherlands by the same standard of
measurement that he used in the case of their master. His pen
portraits of them, in consequence, are usually none too flattering.
He depicted Margaret of Parma, for example, as proud, imperious, energetic, talented, masculine in appearance, an enthusiastic Catholic, and versed in dissimulation[281]; and Cardinal
Granvelle as deferential, adaptable, naturally quick and dexterous, an adroit flatterer, suave and tactful, greedy, profound and
varied in his learning, possessed of literary accomplishments,
extravagant, luxurious, and a master of innuendo.[282] He
described the Duke of Alva as a tall, thin, erect, stern, haughty,
long-visaged man of sixty, difficult of access, overbearing,
vindictive, avaricious, indifferent to calumny, without virtues

[279] See especially *The Rise of the Dutch Republic*, I, 103–104, 133–
146, and *History of the United Netherlands*, II, 303, 458–462. See
post, pp. 126, 130 ff., and 331 ff.
[280] *History of the United Netherlands*, III, 503–512. See *post*, pp.
368–375.
[281] *The Rise of the Dutch Republic*, I, 227–229. See *post*, pp. 139 f.
[282] *Ibid.*, I, 247–252, 427–438. See *post*, pp. 164 ff.

but possessed by a few colossal vices, and an experienced and successful general but bloodthirsty and without political experience.[283]

He represented the Grand Commander, Requesens, as a puppet of mediocre ability, faithless, and undeserving of his reputation for moderation and sagacity,[284] and Don Juan of Austria as possessed of exceptional personal beauty, renowned for his military exploits, susceptible to feminine charm, and spurred on by personal ambition to fantastic dreams of conquest and power.[285] The American historian, though, painted a much more flattering portrait of Spinola.[286]

The championship of the side of local freedom and Protestantism by William of Orange caused Motley to make the great Dutch leader the hero of his drama. Though Motley readily admits that in early life William of Orange was predisposed to an easy, joyous, luxurious, princely life,[287] the Dutch leader became, for him, in the course of the war for Dutch independence the central personage about whom the events and characters of the epoch most naturally grouped themselves, a great man struggling upward and onward against a host of enemies and obstacles almost beyond human strength. William of Orange came to be characterized by patience, caution, a subtle, broad intellect, an even temper, fertility in expedients, eloquence, adroitness, freedom from corruption, piety, unfaltering fortitude, devotion to duty, hopefulness in defeat, and an advocacy of political and religious freedom in an age of bigotry and intolerance.[288] He is the hero of Motley as well as of the Dutch.

---

[283] *The Rise of the Dutch Republic.* II, 103–109, 497–505. See *post,* pp. 198 f.

[284] *Ibid.,* II, 511–513; III, 50–51. See *post,* pp. 244 ff.

[285] *Ibid.,* III, 131–147, 362–363.

[286] *History of the United Netherlands,* IV, 181–184.

[287] *The Rise of the Dutch Republic,* I, 233–247.

[288] *Ibid.,* II, 241–246, 327–328, 486–490; III, 61–62, 615–627.

Motley is again an avowed partisan in the struggle of personalities and principles which forms the theme of the two
volumes entitled *The Life and Death of John of Barneveld*.
In the conflict of the Remonstrants and Contra-Remonstrants
he felt that the two great principles of religious toleration and
local freedom were involved. His advocacy of these two principles strongly colored, accordingly, his conception of the two
leaders of the period. He favored John of Oldenbarneveld
because he thought that the Dutch leader stood for local
freedom and religious toleration. He opposed Maurice of
Nassau because he believed that the Prince put himself at the
head of the more intolerant religious faction and represented
the monarchical principle. Motley, in consequence, is too
ready to believe ill of the Dutch military leader.[289]

In one respect the descriptions of Motley are misleading.
When he describes minutely the Inquisition, the dissembling
diplomacy of Philip II, or the dastardly and in the end the successful attempts on the life of William of Orange he gives the
facts correctly. He fails, however, to put them in their setting.
His pages do not reveal that the Inquisition was, it is true, a
cruel and terrible tribunal but also very similar in its procedure
and punishments to other courts of the period. They give no
hint that dissembling was the usual diplomatic practice of the
time. They do not inform the reader that assassination was a
common method of getting rid of a troublesome opponent.
They arouse the righteous indignation of the reader by com-
paring the conditions of the past with the present.

8. *Motley in the Light of Modern Scholarship*

Motley, it must be remembered, was a pioneer in the field of
history. He wrote at a time when the modern school of history

---

[289] *The Life and Death of John of Barneveld*, I, 276–280, 327–330;
II, 388–393.

had just begun its work. It was to be expected, therefore, that after the volumes of Motley appeared the work of discovering, publishing, and interpreting the sources would go on. This process ultimately always makes the best of historical scholarship obsolete.

Since Motley wrote his famous histories much scholarly work has actually been done in his chosen field. The correspondence of most of the principal historical characters has been published [290] and many of them have been the subject of one or more scholarly monographs.[291] In addition two monumental

[290] *Karel V. Correspondenz* (*1513–1556*). *a. d. Kön. Archiv u. d. Bibliothèque der Bourgogne zu Brüssel*, edited by K. Lauz (Leipzig, 1844–1846); *Correspondance de la Cour d'Espagne sur les affaires des Pays-Bas au XVIIe* (Bruxelles, 1923, 1927); Cardinal de Granvelle, *Correspondance, 1565–1586* (Bruxelles, 1877–1896); L. P. Gachard, *Actes des états généraux des Pays-Bas, 1576–1585* (Brussels, 1861–1866); L. P. Gachard, *Lettres de Philippe II à ses filles* (Paris, 1884); *Calendar of State Papers*, Foreign Series Elizabeth, 1863–1901; Lodewijk van Nassau, *Correspondentie van en betreff Lodewijk van Nassau*, edited by P. J. Blok (Utrecht, 1887); *Colección de documentos ineditos para la historia de España*, IV, VII, VIII, XIV, XXXII, and XXXV; *Correspondentie van Willem den Eerste, Prins van Oranje*, edited by N. Japikse (The Hague, 1934–   ); M. Le Baron Kervyn de Letterhove, *Relations politiques des Pays-Bas et de l'Angleterre sous le règne de Philippe II* (Bruxelles, 1882); Louise de Coligny, *Correspondance* (*1598–1620*), (Paris, 1887); Luis de Requesens, *Lettres inédites* (Utrecht, 1859); L. P. Gachard, *Correspondance d'Alexandre Farnese . . . avec Philippe II, 1578–1581* (Brussels, 1850); *Calendar of State Papers*, Foreign Series, XVII (1913); Leycester, Robert Dudley, Earl of, *Correspondentie e. a. documenten betr. zijn gouvernement-generaal in de Nederlanden, 1585–1588*, edited by H. Brugmans (Utrecht, 1931).

[291] E. Armstrong, *The Emperor Charles V*, 2nd Edition (London, 1910); H. Baumgarten, *Geschichte Karl V*, (Stuttgart, 1885–1892); L. P. Gachard, *Rétrait et Mort de Charles-quint au monastère de Yuste* (Brussels, 1854–1855); C. Hare, *A Great Emperor, Charles V, 1519–1558* (London, 1917); P. Meijia, *Historia del Emperador Carlos V* (1918); M. Philippson, *Ein Ministerium unter Philipp II* (Berlin, 1895); C. Hare, *The High and Puissant Princess Marguerite of Austria* (London, 1917); M. Bruchet, *Marguerite d'Autriche* (Lille, 1927); F. Rachfahl, *Margareta von Parma* (Monaco, 1898); F. P. R. Minguez,

works dealing with the history of the Netherlands have appeared.[292] The new primary sources, however, confirm and supplement the material used by Motley rather than modify his work. The primary sources cited by the American pioneer continue to constitute the principal foundation upon which histories of the Dutch war for independence are built.

The changes wrought by modern scholarship in the writing of history are in part in the realm of the conception of the task of the historian. The works of Motley give a historical pageant. Their author painted with his pen a succession of pictures and portraits. He put undue emphasis on the striking, the dramatic, and the picturesque. He slighted what he could not describe.

The successors of Motley gradually came to have a different conception of history. They came to see the danger of treating history as a dramatic pageant. They realized that much that is important in history cannot be photographed. They sought instead merely to reconstruct the past correctly. They subjected their sources to the severest criticism and strove to divest their interpretations of facts of all that might color and distort their conclusions. They endeavored to show the influence of

---

Psicología de Felipe II (1925); P. J. Blok, *Willem de Eerste* (Amsterdam, 1919–1920); P. J. Blok, *Lodewijk von Nassau, 1538–1574* (The Hague, 1889); V. Herwerden, *Het Verblijf van Lodewijk von Nassau in Frankrijk, 1568–1572* (1932); Fr. Barado y Font, *D. Luis de Requesens y la política española en los Paises Bajos* (Madrid, 1906); B. Poreno, *Historia del serenisimo señor don Juan de Austria* (1899); Sir W. Stirling Maxwell, *Don John of Austria, 1547–1575* (1883); M. Nutting, *The Days of Prince Maurice* (1894); J. H. Wijn, *Het krijgswezen in den tijd van Prins Maurits* (1934); P. Fea, *Alessandro Farnese duca di Parma* (1886); L. van der Essen, *Alex. Farnese* (Brussels, 1933); A. Rodriguez Villa, *Ambrosio Spinola* (Madrid, 1905); Bishop Creighton, *Queen Elizabeth* (1896).

[292] P. J. Blok, *Geschiedenes van het Nederlandsche volk* (Leyden, 1923–1926. An earlier edition has been translated by O. A. Bierstadt and H. Putnam under the title of *History of the People of the Netherlands*); Henri Pirenne, *Histoire de Belgique* (1923–1932).

personalities and events on the development of movements. As a result they give a fuller and better proportioned but more prosaic and less colorful account of the period.

As a consequence of their different ideals, historical successors of Motley have modified to a certain extent his conclusions. They are less partisan. They have put some of his characters in a more favorable light. They have grasped more firmly the idea of development. They have marked more clearly the threads which make up the tangled skein of the diplomacy of the period. They have mapped more plainly the fluctuating tide of battle.

In spite of these developments in the field of historical scholarship, however, the works of Motley still stand out as monuments of historiography. They will always have a place in the history of historical writing for their contribution to Dutch and American scholarship. They will always be read for their literary qualities.

IV. MOTLEY AS A DIPLOMAT

To a president such as Lincoln or Grant, harassed by swarms of unsuitable office seekers, Motley must have seemed ideally prepared for the work of a diplomat in Europe. He was better acquainted with European conditions than most Americans. He was fitted by birth and breeding to take a place in diplomatic circles. He spoke German so well, as a result of his study and residence in Germany, that Emperor Francis Joseph, at the time of his presentation at the Austrian court, asked Motley whether he was not a German or at least of German ancestry.[293] He was likewise equipped, as his dispatches show, to carry on diplomatic conversations in idiomatic French.

He served his country, as we have already seen, three times

[293] *Foreign Relations of the United States* (1861), p. 553, Motley to Seward (November 3, 1861).

as a diplomatic agent. His first service was short and comparatively unimportant. In 1841 he acted for a short time as secretary of the legation at St. Petersburg. He found the climate unpleasant, his duties uninteresting, and living expensive. Abandoning the idea of bringing his wife and children to Russia, he soon resigned his post and came back to the United States.[294]

His first diplomatic post of importance was as minister to Austria. Motley owed his appointment to his friend and senator, Charles Sumner, at that time an influential figure in administrative circles. He served in this capacity from August 12, 1861, to June, 1867. Like every diplomat from time immemorial he had the task of presenting his country, and especially the point of view of his government, in the best possible light to the government to which he was accredited, and also the duty of faithfully and correctly reporting to his government all events and conditions in Europe, and particularly in Austria, that might be of interest to the government of the United States.

At the time of his mission to Austria the United States was not very well known in Europe. To monarchical Europe democracy seemed a radical, even a dangerous, experiment, with which the ruling classes naturally had little sympathy. During the greater part of his mission, furthermore, the United States was in the throes of a civil war which absorbed the energy and resources of its government for over four years and which prevented it from facing Europe boldly and vigorously. In this struggle the influential classes of Europe tended to side with the Confederacy. The landed aristocrats of the South stirred their sympathies. The shutting off by the federal blockade of Southern ports of their usual supplies of raw cotton injured

---

[294] *Correspondence*, I, 62–121. A product of this stay in Russia was Motley's early essay, "Peter the Great," in the *North American Review*, October, 1845.

their material interests.[295]   Only the humanitarians and the lower classes sympathized with the North.

Motley's dispatches[296] indicate that he performed well the task of representing the point of view of his country.   He maintained harmonious relations with Count Rechberg, the Austrian minister of Foreign Affairs, and with the diplomatic representatives of other countries, and presented the American point of view forcefully and cogently.   He presented the war in the United States as a rebellion of a minority against the lawfully constituted authorities, a conflict between a slaveholding aristocracy and the champions of human freedom, a struggle of the forces of unrighteousness against the right.

His task was made easier by a number of factors.   The Austrian government, because of its own peculiar internal problems arising from the composition of its population, was always inclined to look with disfavor upon rebellion against the constituted authorities.   In addition to this the interests of Austria and the United States touched very slightly.   Geography and the tariff policy of Austria tended to prevent trade or a conflict of interests.[297]

During the war only three questions arose calculated to disturb relations between the two countries—the federal blockade of Southern ports, the scarcity of cotton, and the offer of the Mexican crown to Archduke Maximilian, the brother of the Austrian Emperor.   After the opening of the war the Austrian government asked for a recognition by the government of the United States of the three principles of the declaration of Paris

[295] *Foreign Relations of the United States*, 1863.   Motley to Seward, No. 17 (January 27, 1863), II, 1919–1921; *ibid.*, 1862.   Motley to Seward (August 25, 1862), 565–566.

[296] These are to be found in the Archives of the State Department at Washington, just recently moved to the National Archives Building.   The investigator should ask for Dispatches, Austria, Vols. V, VI, VII.   Selections from them are published as part of *Foreign Relations of the United States*, 1861–1867.

[297] *Ibid.*, 1861.   Jones to Seward (April 15, 1861), p. 188.

of 1853 that a neutral flag covers enemy goods with the exception of contraband of war, that neutral goods, except contraband, are not liable to capture under enemy flag, and that blockades must be effective.[298] To this demand the government of the United States readily agreed.[299] Throughout the war the scarcity of cotton continued to hamper industry in Austria but the Austrian government seems to have recognized the situation as inevitable and unavoidable. The Mexican problem was of a nature to cause more serious trouble. During the whole episode, however, the Imperial government took the attitude that the problem was purely the personal problem of the Archduke and that it neither abetted nor favored the project of making Maximilian Emperor of Mexico.[300] Throughout the entire struggle the dispatches of Motley indicate that the attitude of the Austrian government was punctiliously correct and even sympathetic, and that that of the press and the people of the empire tended to reflect, as far as they gave any thought to the matter, the attitude of the government.[301]

During the war he felt himself at a disadvantage in representing the point of view of his government because of his inability to combat misleading rumors with authoritative information.[302] The hostile ruling classes of Europe readily believed the misinformation about Northern defeats and disasters which spread over Europe by design or accident. For the existence of this situation Motley was inclined to blame the new telegraph which flashed from the ports of Europe to Vienna fragmentary, sensational, and contradictory reports which the better informed

[298] *Ibid.*, Jones to Seward, No. 22 (July 20, 1861), p. 188.

[299] *Ibid.*, Seward to Jones (August 12, 1861), pp. 191–192; *ibid.*, Seward to Hulsemann (August 22, 1861), pp. 190–191.

[300] *Ibid.*, 1862. Motley to Seward, No. 3 (January 20, 1862), 559–561.

[301] *Ibid.*, 1862. Seward to Motley, No. 22 (November 18, 1862), 567.

[302] *Ibid.*, 1863. Motley to Seward (June 1, 1863), II, 922–926.

but slower moving post never succeeded in overtaking. As a remedy for this situation Motley vainly urged the sending semi-weekly by messenger and steamship of dispatches dealing with conditions in the United States.[303]

At the time Motley arrived at Vienna the Austrian empire was in the midst of a constitutional crisis that naturally absorbed most of the attention of the Austrian government.[304] The state gradually put together through the centuries by the Hapsburgs had from the beginning been a polyglot empire. With the awakening of nationalism among its subject peoples it was threatened by the disruption which eventually took place as a result of the World War. Until 1859 the Austrian government had attempted successfully to solve the problem of holding the empire together by a policy of absolutism and repression. Upon the defeat of Austria by France and the Kingdom of Sardinia in the struggle for the unification of Italy a continuance of this policy became impossible. The Austrian government found itself forced to make concessions to the demands of its peoples for autonomy and self-government.

The Austrian problem, however, was almost insoluble. No solution of the problem could leave sufficient power in the hands of the central government to enable it to maintain the unity of the empire and at the same time satisfy the demands of all the important peoples of the empire. The state found its subjects divided into two parties—one favoring a strong cen-

---

[303] These are to be found in the Archives of the State Department at Washington, just recently moved to the National Archives Building. The investigator should ask for Dispatches, Austria, Vols. V, VI, VII. Selections from them are published as part of *Foreign Relations of the United States*, 1864. Part IV, No. 68. Motley to Seward (July 26, 1864), 153–154.

[304] The following books will be helpful on the Austrian constitutional crisis: C. P. Higby, *Modern History* (New York, 1932); V. Bibl, *Der Zerfall Oesterreiches* (Vienna, 1922); R. Charmatz, *Oesterreichs innere Geschichte von 1848 bis 1895* (Leipzig, 1918); J. Redlich, *Das Oesterreichische Staats- und Reichsproblem* (Leipzig, 1920, 1926).

tralized government able to maintain the supremacy of the German element in the population and defend the weaker peoples, and one composed of the stronger peoples of the empire, which demanded a large measure of autonomy or almost complete independence for their nationalities.

In October, 1860, the emperor had attempted to solve the problem by a diploma designed to maintain a unitary realm in a federal form. The document aimed to recognize the individuality of the historic provinces of the empire by re-establishing the parliament of Hungary which had been suspended since the failure of the revolution of 1848 and by setting up seventeen provincial diets in the rest of the empire. These concessions gave back to the Magyar aristocracy much of its former political power and placed the new diets largely under the control of the German nobility; but the plan met with the determined opposition of the Magyar people and the German middle classes. In the face of their opposition the new constitution could not be worked.

In the hope of conciliating the opponents of the October Diploma the emperor had just promulgated a new constitution. In February, 1861, a few months before the arrival of Motley at Vienna, Francis Joseph had issued a constitutional document which provided for a parliament of two houses—one composed of members of the royal family, dignitaries of state and church, and representatives of the nobility, and one made up of deputies elected by the provincial diets. The new parliament might include or exclude representatives of Hungary and the dependent kingdoms of Croatia and Transylvania. In the first case it legislated for the whole empire. In the second it passed legislation only for the non-Hungarian portion of the state.

A number of the peoples of the Empire adopted a policy of resistance to the new constitution. The Magyars refused to send representatives to the new imperial parliament, declared its decrees of no force in Hungary, demanded the Hungarian constitution of 1848, and the restoration of Croatia, the port of

Fiume, the Serbian military frontier, and Transylvania. The Croats of Croatia followed the example of the Magyars and demanded union with Slavonia, Dalmatia, and the district occupied by the Slovenes, and a large measure of autonomy from both the Imperial and Hungarian governments. The Czechs of Bohemia and Moravia asked for autonomy and equality with the Germans and in 1863 they ceased to participate in the work of the Austrian parliament. The Poles of Galicia and the Italians of Venetia, likewise, followed a policy of passive resistance.

The Austrian government struggled for four years without success to make the constitution of 1861 work. The new parliament never had more than half of the three hundred members called for by the constitution. The policies of the government, in consequence, never had the moral support of the peoples of Austria. After waging a losing fight in behalf of the constitution of 1861 the Austrian government abandoned its efforts, in 1865 suspended the constitution, and began to negotiate with the Magyars, the strongest of its opponents.

The ensuing negotiations led to the Compromise of 1867 which established the Dual Monarchy. This document divided the empire into two states—one under control of the Germans and one dominated by the Magyars. For common affairs it created unique political machinery with very restricted powers. In Hungary the agreement re-established the constitution of 1848 with slight modifications. In the rest of the empire, henceforth known as Austria, it adapted the constitution of 1861 to meet the needs of the new situation.

Simultaneously with this constitutional crisis the government at Vienna was engaged in a great struggle with Prussia for supremacy in the German Confederation.[305] Until 1862 Prussia had pursued the policy of following the leadership of Austria.

---

[305] The following books will be helpful on the struggle of Austria and Prussia for domination over Germany: H. von Sybel, *Die Be-*

Upon the accession of Bismarck to office in the Prussian ministry, however, Prussia adopted a new course. From this date onward the Prussian state pursued a policy that within a decade led to the exclusion of Austria from Germany and the formation of the remaining German states into a federal empire dominated by Prussia. During the time he was accredited to Vienna, Motley witnessed two important steps toward this goal—the war of Prussia and Austria against Denmark over Schleswig-Holstein and the war between Prussia and Austria in 1866. The first of these struggles resulted in the separation of Schleswig-Holstein from Denmark and the establishment of a temporary and unsatisfactory joint control by Prussia and Austria over the two duchies. The second brought about the exclusion of Austria from German affairs, the annexation of Schleswig-Holstein, Hanover, Hesse-Cassel, Nassau, and Frankfort to Prussia, and the organization of all the German states except those south of the Main into a North German Confederation dominated by Prussia.

Of these events Motley's dispatches give a good picture. The reader is able to follow domestic and foreign developments step by step. For his fidelity in recording the course of the constitutional crisis and the struggle with Prussia Seward, his Secretary of State, obviously was grateful. He had told the predecessor of Motley that most United States ministers did little or nothing.[306] He repeatedly indicated, however, his satisfaction with Motley's dispatches. From time to time he speaks of

---

gründung des Deutschen Reiches durch Wilhelm I (Munisch & Leipzig, 1889, 1890); C. P. Higby, *Modern History* (New York, 1932); A. Rapp, *Grossdeutsch und kleindeutsch* (München, 1922); E. Denis, *La fondation de l'Empire Allemand, 1852–1871* (Paris, 1906); H. Friedjung, *Der Kampf um die Vorherrschaft in Deutschland* (1897); J. W. Headlam, *Bismarck and the Foundation of the German Empire* (New York, 1901); J. Ziekursch, *Politische Geschichte des neuen Deutschen Kaiserreiches* (Frankfort, 1925), I.

[306] *Foreign Relations of the United States,* 1861. Seward to Burlingame, No. 2 (April 13, 1861), 183–188.

his "able and conclusive reasoning," his "interesting despatch," his "careful and lucid exposition," his temperate survey, his "singularly graphic and comprehensive" account.[307] In his dispatches, furthermore, he showed none of the bias to which he was only too prone in his histories. He gave no indication that his observations were colored either by his personal friendship with Bismarck or from his long residence in Germany. He was, however, a little vain of his linguistic ability, a little afraid that his merits would not be sufficiently recognized, and entirely too sensitive to criticism.

These traits are well illustrated by the episode which terminated his pleasant relations with his government and his representation of his government at the Austrian court. Quite unexpectedly a dispatch from the Department of State, dated November 21, 1866, informed Motley that a citizen of the United States, who proved to be a certain George W. Mc-Crackin, had written the department from Paris charging that the ministers and consuls of the United States were for the most part bitterly hostile to President Johnson and that Motley in particular had expressed his disgust for the President's conduct, had asserted that Seward, the Secretary of State, was hopelessly degraded, and had shown a general contempt for American democracy. The Secretary asked Motley to confirm or deny the charge. In reply Motley wrote at length on his views concerning reconstruction, characterized the charge as a vile calumny, and resigned from office. In a letter dated January 5, 1867, Mr. Seward gave Motley his choice of resigning or continuing in office but the President insisted on the recall of the dispatch. This action was followed on April 18, 1867, by a brusque acceptance of Motley's resignation.[308]

[307] See *Foreign Relations of the United States*, 1862, No. 8 (October, 1862); *ibid.*, 1863. Seward to Motley, No. 30 (February 2, 1863), 922; *ibid.*, 1864. Seward to Motley, No. 52 (December 18, 1863), 107–108; *ibid.*, No. 53 (January 7, 1864), 108.

[308] See *Senate Executive Document*, Nos. 8 and 9, 39th Congress,

The second important diplomatic post held by Motley, as we have seen, was the position of minister and envoy extraordinary to Great Britain. Although he owed his appointment to his friend, Senator Sumner of Massachusetts, who was chairman of the Senate committee for foreign affairs, he seemed peculiarly fitted for this mission. For ten years he had known Lord Clarendon, Secretary of State for Foreign Affairs in Gladstone's first cabinet, and was well acquainted with many other prominent men in the country.

At the time he took office in April, 1869, the tension between the two countries was very great and their relations needed delicate handling. To these strained relations a number of important questions had contributed.[309] Probably the most serious was a heritage from the period of the Civil War. Promptly after that struggle opened the British government had accorded the Confederate States belligerent rights and subsequently it had permitted privateers, particularly the Alabama, to be built in British shipyards. Upon completion these ships wrought great damage to the commerce of the Northern States. The action of the British government caused a profound resentment in the United States which lasted for years after the close of the Civil War.

Another question at issue between the two governments was the San Juan water boundary between the island of Vancouver and the mainland. The dividing line had been so indefinitely stated in the treaty of 1846 that there was doubt as to whether it followed the channel to the east or to the west of San Juan Island. With public opinion already inflamed over

---

2nd Session; *ibid.*, No. 1, 40th Congress, 2nd Session; and John Bigelow, "Mr. Seward and Mr. Motley" in *International Review* (July–August, 1878).

[309] The series known as *Foreign Relations of the United States* has comparatively little material on the period of Motley's mission to Great Britain. The archives of the State Department must be consulted.

the Alabama problem this boundary dispute tended to make the situation still more critical.

A great deal of the tension between the two countries likewise grew out of the Fenian movement. The Fenians aimed at the freeing of Ireland from British rule. In order to attain this end some thousand Fenians undertook in 1866 to invade Canada, and other Irishmen who had been naturalized as American citizens returned to Ireland to aid in the struggle against the British government. Many of these were captured and thrown into prison as British subjects. They, in turn, appealed to the American government for assistance.

Under the predecessors of Motley serious efforts had been made to effect a settlement of the differences between the two governments. In 1868 their representatives signed a protocol by which Great Britain agreed to recognize and treat naturalized American citizens of British origin "as in all respects and for all purposes citizens of the United States." At the time Motley arrived in England this agreement had not yet been embodied in a treaty because of the delay of the British Parliament in passing the necessary preliminary legislation.[310] In the following year, after years of bickering and fruitless negotiation Reverdy Johnson of Maryland, the predecessor of Motley, had signed a convention with Lord Clarendon, designed to settle most of the outstanding disputes. This agreement, however, owing to the inflamed state of public opinion in the United States was rejected by the Senate.[311]

To be of much assistance in solving these problems Motley was hardly long enough in office. He is usually accused of having started off his mission by seriously bungling the Alabama negotiations, and he was requested and finally ordered to resign his post before he could do much toward redeeming himself.

[310] Archives of the Department of State, Great Britain, Instructions, No. 21. Fish to Motley, No. 10 (June 15, 1869).

[311] *Ibid.*, No. 3 (May 15, 1869).

According to the traditional story Motley followed the opinion of Sumner rather than his instructions in his presentation of the claims of the United States, condemning Great Britain strongly both for its grant of belligerent rights to the Confederacy and for the great damage wrought on American commerce by privateers built in British shipyards. As a punishment for emphasizing the former as well as the latter cause of complaint, Hamilton Fish, the American Secretary of State, transferred the Alabama negotiations to Washington.[312] While in all probability the situation can never be exactly reconstructed a careful reading of the instructions[313] and dispatches[314] in the archives of the State Department does throw a somewhat different light on the subject. There are discrepancies between the statements made from week to week and those emerging from the heat of controversy. In his long dispatch[315] defending his conduct of his post Motley makes the unchallenged assertion that it was understood from the beginning that the negotiations were to be conducted in the United States. Furthermore at the time Motley ran counter to his instructions by condemning Great Britain for granting belligerent rights to the Confederacy, Fish wrote Motley that he had indeed erred by putting the case of the United States too strongly but that he had erred on the right side. Only after, as a friend of Sumner, he had been ordered to resign, was he roundly condemned for this handling of the problem.

[312] For the traditional account with references to the literature of the subject see J. H. Latané, *A History of American Foreign Policy* (New York, 1927), 442–445.

[313] These are to be found in the Archives of the State Department. The investigator should ask for "Instructions," Great Britain, Vols. XXI, XXII.

[314] These are to be found in the Archives of the State Department. The investigator should ask for "Despatches, Great Britain," Vols. XCIX to CVI. These are printed in part in *Foreign Relations of the United States*, 1870. No volume of the latter was published for 1869.

[315] Archives of the Department of State, Great Britain, Despatches, Vol. CVI. Motley to Fish, No. 529 (December 7, 1870).

In consequence of his short and troubled tenure of office, Motley only really cleared up one piece of pending business. In May, 1870, the Naturalization Agreement was embodied in a treaty.[316] In the task of keeping his government informed of the course of events in the British Isles and in Europe his pen did as good work as in Austria. He gave his superior excellent pictures of Gladstone, the situation in Ireland, the course of legislation in Great Britain, and the course of the Franco-Prussian War. In the latter affair his friendship with Bismarck seems to have proved useful in facilitating communication between Washburne, the American minister besieged in Paris, and the Washington government.

The ending of Motley's diplomatic career was an unhappy and embittering episode. In June, 1870, he read a report in an English newspaper that he was about to be recalled, but he seems to have discounted it as an idle rumor.[317] On June 30th, however, the plans of Grant for the annexation of Santo Domingo were defeated in the United States Senate with the aid of Motley's friend and sponsor, Senator Sumner. The next day the State Department dispatched a telegram of which there is no copy in its archives, asking for the resignation of the American minister to Great Britain. On July 14, the department, which had received no answer to its demand, wired for a reply. Unwilling to admit that his mission was a failure and possibly hoping to take advantage of the Tenure of Office Act, Motley both wired and wrote his refusal to resign.[318] Until November he attempted to continue the performance of the duties of his office in defiance of the wishes of the President and the State Department. On the tenth of that month he received a dispatch which enclosed a letter to the Queen

---

[316] Archives of the Department of State, Great Britain, Despatches, Vol. CVI. Motley to Fish, No. 529 (December 7, 1870).

[317] *Ibid.*

[318] *Ibid.* See also Telegram of same date.

announcing his recall and instructed him to hand over the
business and property of the legation to the secretary of the
embassy.[319]   Hurt and angered at the treatment which he had
received, Motley lingered on at London for nearly a month.
Finally, on December 7, he reviewed his stewardship of his
office in a long dispatch to the State Department.[320]   A study of
the episode leads inescapably to the conclusion that President
Grant, who had never been enthusiastic about his appointment
and who had been receiving hostile reports about the minister
from the legation staff at London, sacrificed a capable and
intelligent minister out of political spite.

V. MOTLEY AS A SPOKESMAN OF HIS AGE

To what extent is Motley a spokesman of America and
American ideals?   There is a tendency today among a considerable number of literary historians to ignore him entirely
or to dismiss him briefly, in a sentence or two, presumably as
being aloof from the main current of American thought.   This
is true, for instance, in the work of such diverse scholars as
Blankenship, Boynton, Calverton, Hicks, Leisy, Pattee, and
Taylor.[321]   The distinguished V. L. Parrington, in his thirteen-
hundred-page survey of *Main Currents in American Thought*,
devotes to Motley less than one page.   "Motley," he declares,
"turned away from the partisanships of America, and while
Jacksonianism was in full swing . . . wrote his *Rise of the Dutch*

[319] *Ibid.*, Instructions, No. 22.   Fish to Motley, No. 285 (November
10, 1870).
[320] Archives of the Department of State, Great Britain, Dispatches,
No. 106.   Motley to Fish (December 7, 1870).
[321] Russell Blankenship, *American Literature* (New York, 1931);
Percy Boynton, *Literature and American Life* (Boston, 1936); V. F.
Calverton, *The Liberation of American Literature* (New York, 1932);
Granville Hicks, *The Great Tradition* (New York, 1932); E. E. Leisy,
American Literature (New York, 1929); F. L. Pattee, *The First Century of American Literature, 1770–1870* (New York, 1935); W. F. Tay-
lor, *A History of American Letters* (New York, 1936).

Republic." [322]   Motley's work, Mr. Parrington goes on to say, suggests "that aloofness from the sordid realities of America so characteristic of the Brahmin mind." [323]

That Motley was neither aloof from the spirit of his age nor unconcerned with the vital problems of his countrymen—that he was, on the contrary, thoroughly representative of many of the main currents of American thought—will be evident upon a consideration of the following facts:

(1) Motley's early interest in the Puritans and their ideals (as manifested particularly in "Polity of the Puritans" and the novel, *Merry-Mount*) was shared by such eminent New Englanders as Longfellow,[324] Hawthorne,[325] Lowell,[326] Whittier,[327] Bancroft,[328] and Fiske.[329]

(2) It is true that Motley wrote, in his major works, the life story of a foreign nation, but he was led to deal with the revolt against European feudal tyranny by his democratic Americanism. To him, the rise of political liberalism and religious tolerance in the Netherlands in the sixteenth and seventeenth

---

[322] V. L. Parrington, *The Romantic Revolution in America, 1800–1860* (New York, 1927), 438.   [323] *Ibid.*, 438–439.

[324] "The Courtship of Miles Standish" (1858); "The Birds of Killingworth" (1863); "The New England Tragedies" (1868).

[325] Particularly in *Twice-Told Tales* (1837); *Mosses from an Old Manse* (1846); *The Scarlet Letter* (1850); *The House of the Seven Gables* (1851).

[326] *New England Two Centuries Ago* (1865).

[327] *Margaret Smith's Journal* (1849); "The Pilgrims of Plymouth" (1870).

[328] Vol. I of *History of the United States* (New York, 1891). Motley in his "Polity of the Puritans" (1849) took issue with Bancroft on the question whether the Puritans were the founders of American democracy.

[329] Fiske was especially full in his treatment of the Puritans and their political ideas. See *The Beginnings of New England, or the Puritan Theocracy in Its Relation to Civil and Religious Liberty* (1889); *Civil Government in the United States* (1890); *New France and New England* (1902); *Colonization of the New World* (1905); *American Political Ideas* (1911).

centuries was a part of one great theme which found its final expression in American history in the seventeenth and eighteenth centuries.[330]   In fact, a frequent contemporary criticism of Motley's historical work was based on the charge that it displayed the author's bias for Protestantism and for democracy; in short, he was accused of being too thoroughly indoctrinated with the beliefs and the dogmas of his own country to be able to write an account of the Dutch struggle for liberty with complete objectivity.

(3) Motley represented, to be sure, the Federalistic rather than the equalitarian spirit of extreme Jacksonian democracy; but it should be borne in mind that nearly half of the leading literary spokesmen of the period in America were imbued with the Federalist spirit.   Federalism, as defined by an eminent critic, was "a government by the best, the ideal to which all philosophic statesmen have aspired . . . an aristocracy, not of birth or of privilege, but of achievement."[331]   Among those who were advocates of this ideal of government may be listed John Adams,[332] Hamilton,[333] Irving,[334] Paulding,[335]

[330] Preface to *The Rise of the Dutch Republic*, I, iv.

[331] H. S. Canby, *Classic Americans* (New York, 1931), 82.   Mr. Canby's is the most adequate and appreciative definition of the Federalistic temper as displayed in American belletristic writing.

[332] Adams's *A Defence of the Constitutions of Government of the United States of America* (1786–1787) was the most distinguished defence, before the *Federalist* papers, of the American system in opposition to the unicameral ideas of the French *philosophes*.   For a full analysis see C. M. Walsh's *The Political Science of John Adams* (New York, 1915); G. Chinard's *Honest John Adams* (Boston, 1933).

[333] Hamilton's political ideas in *The Federalist* and other writings will be found admirably discussed in F. S. Oliver's *Alexander Hamilton* (New York, 1921).

[334] Irving's Federalism is most obvious in *Salmagundi* (1807–1808) and *Knickerbocker's History of New York* (1809), but it is implicit in most of his writings.   For a concise account see Canby, *op. cit.*, 67–96. See also H. A. Pochmann's introduction to *Irving* (New York, 1934), in American Writers Series, xlii–lx.

[335] Paulding collaborated with William and Washington Irving in

Cooper,[336] Bryant[337] (at least in his earlier years), Lowell[338] (after 1850), Poe,[339] Holmes,[340] Parkman,[341] and Prescott.[342]

(4) Motley was like his fellow Federalists in his endeavor to reconcile the conflicting ideals of democratic equality and aristocratic excellence. "For Federalism was essentially an aristocratic ideal struggling to adapt itself to the conditions of a republic and the equalities of a new country."[343] His admiration for European art, culture, urbanity, and refinement did not

Salmagundi. Though Paulding was a Knickerbocker, his sympathies in later years proved to be largely Jeffersonian. See Parrington, *op. cit.*, 212–221; and Amos L. Herold, *James Kirke Paulding, Versatile American* (New York, 1926).

[336] Cooper's political and social views may be found in *Notions of the Americans* (1828), *A Letter to His Countrymen* (1834), and especially in *The American Democrat* (1838). Consult R. E. Spiller's introduction to *Cooper* (New York, 1936), in American Writers Series, pp. xi ff.

[337] For an exposition of Bryant's early political views, see Parke Godwin's *Biography* (New York, 1883), I, 128 ff.; Tremaine McDowell's introduction to *Bryant* (New York, 1935) in American Writers Series, xiii ff.

[338] See H. H. Clark's "Lowell—Humanitarian, Nationalist, or Humanist?" *Studies in Philology*, XXVII, 411–441 (July, 1930).

[339] Poe was influenced considerably by the aristocratic tradition of the South. For summaries of his political and social ideas, see Ernest Marchand's "Poe as a Social Critic," *American Literature*, VI, 28–43 (March, 1934); and Alterton and Craig's introduction to *Poe* (New York, 1935) in American Writers Series, lxvi–lxxvi.

[340] Like Irving, whom he admired, Holmes had an instinctive preference for the "social distillations" of Federalism. A Brahmin of Brahmins, he argued that society cannot long maintain a dead level; he favored paternalism, social solidarity, and an aristocracy of natural ability. (See "The Brahmin Caste," *Elsie Venner*, Ch. I.) His *Autocrat of the Breakfast Table* (1858) is liberally sprinkled with political and social allusions.

[341] For Parkman's political and social ideas, see Wilbur L. Schramm's introduction to *Parkman* (New York, 1938) in American Writers Series, lx–lxxvii.

[342] For Prescott's political and social views, see Michael Kraus and William Charvat's introduction to the forthcoming volume in American Writers Series.

[343] Canby, *op. cit.*, 77.

lessen his love for America or his respect for her republican institutions. In his recognition of the excellencies of European culture and his receptive attitude toward the best that has been thought and said in other times and lands, Motley was like his fellow travelers, Irving, Longfellow, Lowell, Ticknor, Everett, Bancroft, Cogswell, and Emerson.[344]

(5) Like Bryant, Whittier, Thoreau, and Lowell, Motley was a violent opponent of slavery. As we have observed, he was not an early abolitionist, though he regarded slavery as a moral wrong. But when the Civil War broke out, he saw in secession and rebellion an excellent excuse for emancipating the Negroes and in that way eradicating a blot upon the national character.[345]

(6) The charge that Motley stood aloof from the realities of American life is refuted by his passionate espousal of Unionism at the time of the Civil War and his considerable services in counteracting the tendency among the upper classes in England to sympathize with the Southern cause. Early in the conflict, his thirty-six-page letter to the London *Times* (May 23 and 24, 1861) analyzed the conflicting political philosophies which were pitted against each other in America and demonstrated that the secessionists were in rebellion against constituted authority. Having appointed himself an unofficial "peace commissioner" between England and America, he re-

---

[344] For an account of the influence of German culture upon Ticknor, Everett, Cogswell, Bancroft, Longfellow, and Motley, see Long, *Literary Pioneers* (1935). The transcendentalist Emerson, like the Federalists, desired a culture which could produce men of a superior mold. He declared that "the triumph of culture is to overpower nationality, by imparting the flower of each country's genius into the humanity of a gentleman" (*Journals*, VIII, 417). Again, he called for "men of original perception and original action, who can open their eyes wider than to a nationality, namely, to considerations of benefit to the human race, can act in the interest of civilization" (*Works*, IX, 302).

[345] See L. D. Turner, *Anti-Slavery Sentiment in American Literature Prior to 1865* (Washington, D. C., 1929).

turned to his native land in 1861, intending to remain near the scene of action and to observe closely what was to him a conflict of absorbing interest. A diplomatic appointment to Austria, however, took him back to Europe, where he continued in his attempt to influence public opinion in England. His position on Unionism was parallel to that of Bryant, Lowell, Holmes, Longfellow, and Webster.[346]

(7) Like Irving, Lowell, Bancroft, Hawthorne, and Howells, who established an American tradition in Europe, Motley served his country in important diplomatic posts. These distinguished men of letters, who did much to elevate America in the esteem of the Old World, were ambassadors of good will and of spiritual ideals which transcended mere political issues.

(8) Motley's faith in progress was typical of the optimistic America of his day.[347] His address[348] before the New York Historical Society in 1868 elaborated the theory that history records the tortuous but nevertheless certain evolution of political freedom, and that American democracy marked the climax of progress to that date.

In conclusion, Motley deserves a more just interpretation and a more sympathetic evaluation in the hands of future literary historians: (1) as a literary man whose novels and early review articles have been cast into an unwarranted obscurity; (2) as a diplomat who earned a better reward than the ignominy heaped upon him near the close of his career; (3) as a distinguished historian who combined the "literature of knowledge" and the

---

[346] Bryant's position is best stated in his editorial, "Peaceable Secession an Absurdity" (*The Post*, November 12, 1860); see Allan Nevins's *The Evening Post* (New York, 1922), 145 ff. Compare Lowell's poem, "Washers of the Shroud" (1861), and his essay, *E Pluribus Unum* (1861); Holmes's address on "The Inevitable Trial" (1855); Longfellow's "The Building of the Ship" (1849); Webster's "Seventh of March Speech" (1850). See Dorothy L. Werner's *The Idea of Union in American Verse (1776–1876)* (Philadelphia, 1932).

[347] See footnote 120, above.

[348] *Historic Progress and American Democracy.*

"literature of power" [349]; and (4) as a spokesman of many ideas which represent the essential traditions of American thought in his age.

[349] In an able essay, "History as Literature" (*History as Literature and Other Essays*, 1913), Theodore Roosevelt refuses to accept the thesis that history, like science, must be divorced from literature.

CHRONOLOGICAL TABLE

1814. John Lothrop Motley born at Dorchester (now part of Boston), April 15.

1824. One summer at the school of Charles W. Greene, near Boston.

1824–27. Attended the school conducted at Round Hill, Northampton, by Joseph S. Cogswell and George Bancroft. In addition to the usual subjects, he studied the German language under Bancroft (at that time one of the few thorough German scholars in the country) and made some acquaintance with German literature. Displayed a facility at languages and a great interest in reading. Somewhat spoiled; a quick but not a diligent student.

1827. Entered Harvard. Stood third in his class as a freshman. Irresponsible, negligent of his studies, he was rusticated; worked more soberly after his return to the campus, but with no effort to attain college rank. Handsome and well dressed, he appeared haughty in manner and cynical in mood to those in whom he felt no special interest. Elected to Phi Beta Kappa by an extension of the rules of the society.

1831. Graduated from Harvard. Read an essay on Goethe at the senior exhibition.

1832–33. At the University of Göttingen. Met Bismarck. Improved his knowledge of the German language and attended lectures on law.

1833. In the autumn, transferred with Bismarck to the University of Berlin, where the two became fellow lodgers. Motley translated *Faust*, at least in part, and composed verses in German. Studied law, applying himself more diligently to his studies than did most of the German students.

1834–35. Traveled on the continent and in England.

1835. Returned to America. Studied law, but never seriously engaged in the profession.

1837. March 2, at Boston, married Mary, sister of Park Benjamin.

1838. Article on "Goethe" in *New York Review* for October.

1839. *Morton's Hope* published. Review of "Goethe's Works" in *New York Review* for July.

1840. Translation of Tieck's *Blue Beard* in *New World*, December 19.

1841–42. Secretary of United States legation at St. Petersburg. Finding the climate too severe, and his income too small to permit moving his family to Russia, Motley resigned after a few months of service and returned to America.

1845. "Peter the Great," an article in the *North American Review* for October.

1846. Probably started collecting materials for a history of Holland. The second novel (*Merry-Mount*) probably written in this year.

1847. Article on "The Novels of Balzac" in the *North American Review* for July.

1849. *Merry-Mount* published. An article, "Polity of the Puritans," in the *North American Review* for October. Motley served one term in the Massachusetts house of representatives; chairman of the committee on education.

1850. Having definitely decided to write the history of the early Dutch Republic, Motley discovered that Prescott was writing a *History of Philip II*. He went to Prescott, as the latter had gone to Irving, and offered to withdraw from a field already occupied; Prescott encouraged him to go ahead with his projected work.

1851–56. Historical research at Berlin, Dresden, The Hague, and Brussels.

1855–56. Winter at Florence.

1856. *The Rise of the Dutch Republic* published.

1856–57. Winter at Boston.

1857. Helped to found the *Atlantic Monthly*, contributing a

long article ("Florentine Mosaics") to the first two numbers, November and December.

1858. Revisited England. Very popular socially. Commenced
research for second historical work.

1858–59. Winter at Rome.

1859–61. Residence in England.

1860. Vols. I and II of *History of the United Netherlands*
published.

1861. May 23 and 24, letter to the London *Times* (*Causes of the
American Civil War*). Return to America. Appointed
minister to Austria.

1861–67. U.S. Minister at Vienna. Resignation (1867) as a
result of the infamous McCrackin incident.

1868. Vols. III and IV of *History of the United Netherlands*
published. In June, Motley returned with his family to
Boston. October 20, a campaign speech for Grant: *Four
Questions for the People, at the Presidential Election* (published as a pamphlet, 1868). December 16, address before
the New York Historical Society: *Historic Progress and
American Democracy* (published as a pamphlet, 1869).

1869–70. U.S. Minister to England. Recalled, November,
1870, evidently to satisfy Grant's spleen against Sumner.

1871–72. Residence at The Hague. Research resumed.

1872–73. Residence in England. First signs of the illness that
was to prove fatal.

1873–74. Winter at Cannes, by physician's order.

1874. *The Life and Death of John of Barneveld* published.
December 31, death of Mrs. Motley.

1875. Summer and autumn, last visit to America.

1875–77. Life in England. Failing strength made literary
work impossible.

1877. May 29, died near Dorchester (England), of an apoplectic
stroke.

SELECTED BIBLIOGRAPHY

I. COLLECTED WORKS

Writings (Netherlands Edition). 17 vols. New York and London: 1900. (Vols. I–V: *The Rise of the Dutch Republic;* Vols. VI–XI: *History of the United Netherlands;* Vols. XII–XIV: *The Life and Death of John of Barneveld;* Vols. XV–XVII: *The Correspondence of John Lothrop Motley*, ed. by G. W. Curtis. This edition omits a number of titles, for which see Section II, below. Particularly important for the student are the novels, *Morton's Hope* and *Merry-Mount;* the review articles, "Goethe," "Goethe's Works," "Peter the Great," "The Novels of Balzac," and "Polity of the Puritans"; *Causes of the American Civil War; Four Questions for the People, at the Presidential Election;* and *Historic Progress and American Democracy.*)

II. SEPARATE WORKS

The Genius and Character of Goethe. An essay delivered by Motley at the Harvard Exhibition, May 3, 1831; preserved in MS at the Harvard Library. Published in Orie W. Long's *Literary Pioneers* (Cambridge: 1935), 200–203.

"Cupid Hath Been a God." A poem composed in 1831 (?), published for the first time in *Harper's Magazine*, LV, 465 (August, 1877).

"Goethe," *New York Review*, III, 397–442 (October, 1838). (Nominally a review of Goethe's *Aus meinem Leben, Dichtung und Wahrheit, Werke*, and *Memoirs*, and of Sarah Austin's *Characteristics of Goethe.* Mainly a biographic sketch of Goethe.)

Translation of Schiller's "The Diver," *New Yorker*, January 19, 1839.

Translation of "Wine Song," from Novalis's *Heinrich von Ofterdingen*, *New Yorker*, January 26, 1839.

"Goethe's Works," *New York Review*, V, 1–48 (July, 1839). (A review of Goethe's *Werke und nachgelassene Werke*.)

Morton's Hope: or The Memoirs of a Provincial. 2 vols. New York: 1839. London: 1839.

"Lines Written at Syracuse." A poem written before 1840 (?), reprinted in Park Benjamin's "Waifs from Motley's Pen," *Harper's Magazine*, LV, 610–614 (September, 1877).

Translation of Tieck's *Blue Beard*, in *New World*, I, 449–452, 478–483 (December 19, 1840).

"Peter the Great," *North American Review*, LXI, 269–319 (October, 1845). Separately printed: New York: 1877, 1893. Louisville, Ky.: 1881. London: 1887. (Nominally a review of the Marquis de Custine's *La Russie en 1839* and of John Barrow's *A Memoir of the Life of Peter the Great;* actually a brilliant biographic essay.)

"The Novels of Balzac," *North American Review*, LXV, 85–108 (July, 1847). (A discriminating review of *Les Œuvres de M. de Balzac*.)

"Polity of the Puritans," *North American Review*, LXIX, 470–498 (October, 1849). (A review of Mrs. Robinson's *Geschichte der Colonisation von Neu-England*.)

Merry-Mount; A Romance of the Massachusetts Colony. 2 vols. Boston and Cambridge: 1849.

The Rise of the Dutch Republic. 3 vols. London: 1856, 1858, 1859, 1882, 1886, 1889 (2 editions), 1909. Edinburgh: 1859. New York: 1855, 1856, 1862, 1864, 1883, 1898. Philadelphia: 1898. New York and London: 1883, 1900, 1901, 1902, 1903, 1913. 2 vols. New York: 1898, 1901. 4 vols. in 2. Philadelphia: 1898. Abridged editions: London: 1878. Utrecht:

1860. The Hague: 1868. New York: 1898 (with continuation, 1584–1897, by W. E. Griffis), 1900, 1902. New York and London: 1908 (with continuation by W. E. Griffis). Translations: Dutch, Bakhuizen van der Brink, R. C. 3 vols. The Hague: 1857–62. French, with introduction by Guizot, F. P. G. 4 vols. Paris: 1859–60. Brussels and Leipzig: 1859–60.

"Florentine Mosaics," *Atlantic Monthly*, I, 12–22 (November, 1857); *ibid.*, I, 129–138 (December, 1857).

History of the United Netherlands, from the Death of William the Silent, to the Synod of Dort. 4 vols. London: 1860–67, 1869, 1901–19. The Hague: 1860–67. New York: 1861–68, 1868, 1870–71, 1888, 1895, 1909. London and New York: 1900, 1909. Translations: French, Paris: 1859–60. Dutch, 6 vols. The Hague: 1861–69.

Causes of the American Civil War. (A letter to the London *Times*, May 23 and 24, 1861.) New York: 1861 (2 editions). Published with title, *Causes of the Civil War in America.* London: 1861.

Four Questions for the People, at the Presidential Election. (Address before the Parker Fraternity, October 20, 1868.) Boston: 1868.

Historic Progress and American Democracy. (Address delivered before the New York Historical Society, December 16, 1868.) New York: 1869. London: 1869. The second English edition (London: 1869) was entitled *Democracy, the Climax of Political Progress, and the Destiny of Advanced Races; an Historical Essay.*

"Tribute to Dean Milman," *Proceedings of the Massachusetts Historical Society*, X, 344–346. Boston: 1869.

The Life and Death of John of Barneveld, Advocate of Holland; with a View of the Primary Causes and Movements of the Thirty Years' War. 2 vols. London: 1874, 1875. New York: 1874. The Hague: 1874. 3 vols. New York and London: 1900, 1902, 1904.

For Motley's correspondence, see Section III below, entries under Curtis, G. W.; Mildmay, Susan and Herbert St. John; Benjamin, Park; Holmes, O. W.; Lodge, Henry Cabot; Wolcott, Roger; and *Proceedings of the Massachusetts Historical Society*.

III. BIOGRAPHY AND CRITICISM

(Starred items are of primary importance)

Adams, C. F., Jr. "Sir Christopher Gardiner," *Proceedings of the Massachusetts Historical Society*, 1st s., XX, 60–88 (Boston: 1884). (Sifts out the actual historical details surrounding the figures of Sir Christopher Gardiner and Mary Grove; points to the varying employment of this material for literary purposes by Motley in *Merry-Mount*, by Catherine M. Sedgwick in *Hope Leslie*, by Whittier in *Margaret Smith's Journal*, by John T. Adams in *The Knight of the Golden Melice*, and by Longfellow in *Tales of a Wayside Inn*.)

Anon. "The Rise of the Dutch Republic," *Democratic Review*, XXXVIII, 71–79 (August, 1856). (Stresses the debt of American republicanism and religious liberty to the Dutch.)

Appleton, William S. "The Whigs of Massachusetts," *Proceedings of the Massachusetts Historical Society*, 2nd series, XI, 278–282 (1896–1897). (Motley in 1840 was one of a group of younger Whigs, including Adams, Winthrop, Hillard, Curtis, and Sumner.)

Arnold, Arthur. "The Correspondence of John Lothrop Motley," *Academy*, XXXV, 177–178 (March 16, 1889). (A very brief, laudatory review of the *Correspondence*.)

"Assassination and Characteristics of William the Silent," *Chautauquan*, LII, 85–99 (September, 1908). (Selections from *The Rise of the Dutch Republic*, with a brief, uncritical introduction.)

Barnes, Harry Elmer. *A History of Historical Writing*. University of Oklahoma Press: 1937. (Brief reference to Motley as the most distinguished American representative of the school of Carlyle and Froude.)

Bassett, John Spencer. *The Middle Group of American Historians*. New York: 1917. ("John Lothrop Motley," 223–232, is an eminently fair though brief summary appraisal of the work of Motley, who is classed with Prescott as "a literary historian." Thus considered, Motley is "the last prominent historian of the early school," yet he may also be regarded as "the first of the newer school of scientific research." He lacks, however, the modern historian's sense of detachment; he is partisan to Protestantism and political liberalism.)

*Benjamin, Park, Jr. "Waifs from Motley's Pen," *Harper's Magazine*, LV, 610–614 (September, 1877). (Mr. Benjamin reprints three of Motley's translations of German poems, one from the Spanish, and an original poetic composition. He also prints a portion of a letter written by Motley shortly after the election of Polk to the presidency, setting forth Motley's political views at that time. This letter is not included in the *Correspondence* or in Mildmay.)

Bismarck, Prince Otto von. *Die gesammelten Werke*. 15 vols. Berlin: 1924–35. Vol. XIV, Parts I and II, *Briefe*. (Includes six letters to Motley, also available in the *Correspondence* of Motley, and incidental reference to Motley in other letters.)

Blok, P. J. "A Tribute from Holland," *Nation*, XCVIII, 427–428 (April 16, 1914). (A modern Dutch historian pays a brief tribute on the centenary of Motley's birth.)

Boutwell, George S. *Reminiscences of Sixty Years in Public Affairs*. 2 vols. New York: 1902. (Vol. I, pp. 94–95: Mr. Boutwell recalls Motley's brief experience in the Massachusetts Legislature.)

Bowen, Francis. "Merry-Mount," *North American Review*, LXVIII, 203–220 (January, 1849). ("The writer certainly needs practice in elaborating the details of a consistent and interesting novel; but in many respects he is well qualified for the task, and we shall be glad to meet him again on the half-historical ground that he has chosen.")

Brooks, Van Wyck. *The Flowering of New England, 1815–1865*. New York: 1936. (Pages 334–342, an interesting and, in the main, accurate account of Motley and his work. One of the few critical surveys which take into account Motley's early review articles.)

Bruce, H. Addington. "John Lothrop Motley—American," *Outlook*, XCV, 891–894 (August 20, 1910). (A review of the Mildmays' volume of letters—emphasizes Motley's patriotism.)

Bryant, William Cullen. "In Memory of John Lothrop Motley" (Sonnet), *International Review*, IV, 729 (November, 1877). Also in Holmes's *Memoir*, 526.

Caldwell, Alexander. "Some Charming Correspondence," *Dial*, X, 73–76 (August, 1889). (An insignificant review of the *Correspondence* which delights in the format of the volumes and recommends the letters for week-end reading.)

Chadwick, John W. "Motley's Correspondence," *Unitarian Review*, XXXII, 30–38 (July, 1889). (A contemporary reviewer regrets the omission of certain letters from the *Correspondence*, particularly that of letters concerning the resignation at Vienna and the recall from England.)

Chamberlain, D. H. "John Lothrop Motley," *New Englander*, LIII, 297–330 (October, 1890). (A review of the *Correspondence* and of Holmes's *Memoir*, lauds Motley as a product of American rather than of European culture.)

*Cheyney, E. P. "John Lothrop Motley," *Dictionary of American Biography*. 20 vols. New York: 1928–36. XIII, 282–287. (A concise, accurate biographic sketch, with a brief bibliography.)

Colton, Delia M. "John Lothrop Motley," *Continental Monthly*, I, 309–320 (March, 1862).

Conway, Moncure D. Biographic introduction to *The Rise of the Dutch Republic*. New York and London: 1896.

Cooke, George Willis. "Unitarianism in America," *New England Magazine*, n. s. XXII, 317–337 (May, 1900). (Lists Motley among the Unitarians who have produced scholarly work.)

"Correspondence of John Lothrop Motley," *Athenaeum*, No. 3201, 271–272 (March 2, 1889). (A brief review of the *Correspondence* in the form of a biographic sketch.)

"Correspondence of John Lothrop Motley," *Blackwood's*, CXLV, 561–566 (April, 1889). (This review is reprinted in *Littell's Living Age*, CLXXXI, 242–246 [April 27, 1889].)

"The Correspondence of John Lothrop Motley," *Spectator*, LXII, 404 (March 23, 1889). (A review of the *Correspondence*, with the interest centered in the Motley-Bismarck friendship.)

Crossley, James. "Motley's 'Life of John of Barneveld' and Gaspar Scioppius," *Notes and Queries*, 5th series, II, 445–446 (December 5, 1874). (Charges that Motley errs in calling Scioppius a Jesuit.)

Curtis, George William. "Motley's Letters," *Harper's Magazine*, LXXVIII, 611–618 (March, 1889). (The editor of the *Correspondence* demonstrates briefly how the career of Motley may be traced through the letters; calls attention to the fact that Motley, by winning the admiration of the world for the Hollander, discharged America's debt to Holland, incurred when Irving burlesqued the Dutchman in *Knickerbocker's History of New York*.)

*Curtis, George William, ed. *The Correspondence of John Lothrop Motley*. 2 vols. New York: 1889. (These volumes constitute an invaluable supplement to Holmes's *Memoir* in the study of Motley's life and work. They are, however, incomplete, many letters having been omitted because persons mentioned were still living and issues discussed were still controversial. Some of these letters may be found in *John*

Lothrop Motley and His Family, edited by Motley's daughter and her husband, Herbert St. John Mildmay.)

Dawson, Henry B. "The Motley Letter," *Historical Magazine*, XIX, 157–201 (March, 1871). (This elaborately documented letter of July 5, 1861, addressed to Motley but not transmitted to him, takes issue with the latter on his letter to the London *Times*, May 23–24, 1861; charges Motley with being untrue to the facts of American history.)

De Mille, George E. *Literary Criticism in America*. New York: 1931. (Lists Motley as a radical critic because of his daring early approval of Balzac.)

Dicey, A. V. "Motley's Life of Barneveld," *Nation*, XVIII, 300–302 (May 7, 1874). (Criticizes the work for not constituting a coherent biography of Barneveld.)

Dowe, W. "John Lothrop Motley," *National Quarterly Review*, XXXVI, 149–164 (January, 1878). (A review of the historical works of Motley, with brief biographic notes.)

Ebstein, Erich. "John Lothrop Motley und Otto von Bismarck als Göttinger Studenten," *Die Gegenwart*, XLV, 392–396 (June 18, 1904).

Falconer, A. "Motley's *John of Barneveld*," *Fraser's Magazine*, n. s. X, 223–245 (August, 1874). (Praises Motley for his lofty moral tone. "*The Life and Death of John of Barneveld* will rank with the best historical monographs in the language. It is a great drama . . .")

Fiske, John. *The Unseen World, and Other Essays*. Boston: 1876. ("Spain and the Netherlands," pp. 211–236, is an essay based on Vols. III and IV of *History of the United Netherlands*.)

Froude, J. Anthony. "The Rise of the Dutch Republic," *Westminster Review*, LXV, 173–187 (April, 1856). (Froude declares that the book will take its place among historical classics, and that in dramatic description no modern historian, except perhaps Carlyle, surpasses Motley.)

Fruin, Robert. *Verspreide Geschriften*. 11 vols. The Hague: 1900–1905. (For reference to Motley, see I, 264, 279, 328,

364, 429; II, 6, 26, 212; III, 74, 118, 224; VII, 414, 456; VIII, 331, 406; IX, 48, 93, 96, 102, 357, 453.)

Gardiner, Samuel R. "The Late Mr. J. L. Motley," *Academy*, XI, 509–510 (June 9, 1877). (An obituary notice which points out briefly the faults as well as the merits of Motley's histories.)

Gardiner, Samuel R. "The Life and Death of John of Barneveld," *Academy*, V, 161–163 (February 14, 1874); *ibid.*, V, 192–194 (February 21, 1874). (Regrets that Motley has left his own proper sphere to enter upon a phase of history with which he cannot deal adequately.)

Gooch, G. P. *History and Historians of the Nineteenth Century.* London: 1913. (Pages 416–419 are devoted to Motley. "No American historian approaches him in intensity of conviction and expression . . .")

Groen van Prinsterer, Guillaume. *Étude historique. Maurice et Barneveld.* Utrecht: 1875. (Criticism of Motley's *John of Barneveld.*)

Grund, James Pemberton. "Bismarck and Motley—With Correspondence Till Now Unpublished," *North American Review*, CLXVII, 360–376 (September, 1898); *ibid.*, 481–496 (October, 1898); *ibid.*, 569–572 (November, 1898). (Traces carefully the Bismarck-Motley friendship; indicates that Bismarck sat for the portrait of Rabenmark in Motley's first novel, *Morton's Hope.* The letters here published for the first time were later included in Mildmay, *John Lothrop Motley and His Family.*)

Guernsey, A. H. "Motley's History of the Netherlands," *Harper's Magazine*, XXXVI, 328–336 (February, 1868). (A contemporary review.)

Guernsey, A. H. "Motley's History of the United Netherlands," *Harper's Magazine*, XXII, 639–649 (April, 1861). (A contemporary review. See also the notice in the "Editor's Easy Chair," *ibid.*, 701.)

Guizot, F. P. G. *Mélanges biographiques et littéraires*. Paris: 1868. (Includes "Philippe II et ses nouveaux historiens.")

Guizot, F. P. G. "Philip II and his Times: Prescott and Motley," *Edinburgh Review*, CV, 1–45 (January, 1857). (A contemporary review of Prescott's *Philip the Second* and Motley's *The Rise of the Dutch Republic*. Motley's "strong and ardent convictions on the subject of his work have also affected its style and literary character; his narrative sometimes lacks proportion and forbearance . . .")

Hart, A. B. "The American School of Historians," *International Monthly*, II, 294–322 (September, 1900). (Motley "was really not an historian, but a describer of mighty historic deeds.")

Hawthorne, Nathaniel. *The Marble Faun*, Vol. VI in the Riverside Edition of *The Complete Works*. 12 vols. Boston: 1883. (In the introduction, Hawthorne quotes from a letter by Motley expressing a very keen appreciation of the novel.)

"History of the United Netherlands," *Atlantic Monthly*, VII, 377–381 (March, 1861). (A laudatory review of Vols. I and II.) *Ibid.*, XXI, 632–638 (May, 1868). (A review of Vols. III and IV.)

*Holmes, Oliver Wendell. *John Lothrop Motley, A Memoir*. Vol. XI, 329–526, of *The Writings of Oliver Wendell Holmes* (Riverside Edition). 14 vols. Boston: 1878. Separately published. Boston: 1879. (This sketch by an intimate personal friend is the most complete biography of Motley; no definitive life has appeared. It must be supplemented by a reading of the two volumes of *Correspondence*, edited by Curtis, and of the additional volume of letters, *John Lothrop Motley and His Family*, edited by the Mildmays.)

Holmes, Oliver Wendell. Poem of tribute to Parkman. *Proceedings of the Massachusetts Historical Society*, 2nd series, VIII, 360–361 (1894). (The poem has three beautiful stanzas which refer to Motley.)

Hook, Theodore. "Morton of Morton's Hope," *New Monthly Magazine*, LVII, 134–137 (September, 1839). (An enthusiastic review of *"Morton of Morton's Hope: an Autobiography. 3 vols."* Very justly notes the influence of Sterne in the characterization of Uncle Joshua.)

Howells, William D. *Literary Friends and Acquaintance.* New York and London: 1902. (Recollections of Motley, pp. 93–97, when Howells was consul at Venice and Motley was his official chief at Vienna.)

Irving, Leonard. "The Historian Motley at Work," *National Magazine*, XVI, 59–72 (May, 1892). (Mr. Irving arrives at the conclusion that Motley was attracted to Dutch history by the analogy between the Dutch struggle for liberty and that of the American colonies; he traces Motley's work as a historian. Based upon Holmes's *Memoir* and the *Correspondence*, this article adds no information to what is contained in those sources.)

Jameson, J. Franklin. *History of Historical Writing in America.* Boston and New York: 1891. (Pages 117–121 are devoted to the work of Motley, with which Professor Jameson finds fault only for its partisanship. "Motley," he says, "had the intense zeal of the born investigator. . . . He had likewise in full possession those qualities which engage the reader. No American has ever written a history more brilliant and dramatic.")

Jameson, J. Franklin. "John Lothrop Motley," an introduction to selections from Motley's histories in *The Warner Library* (University Edition). 30 vols. New York: 1917. XVII, 10, 373–380. (Professor Jameson concludes his biographic sketch by observing that "it is difficult to imagine that any changes of fashion can seriously diminish either Motley's general popularity or the force of his appeal to cultivated minds. His books, while nowise lacking in most of the highest qualities of scholarship, are also literature,—eloquent, glowing, and powerful,—and have, one must think, that

permanent value which belongs to every finished product of
fine art.")

"John Lothrop Motley," *Appleton's Journal*, II, 528–530
(December 11, 1869). (A brief biographic sketch; includes
the letter of February 26, 1859, about the Prescott incident.)

"John Lothrop Motley, LL.D.," *Eclectic Magazine*, LIV, 277–278
(October, 1861). (A brief biographic sketch, with a portrait.)

"John Lothrop Motley," *Every Saturday*, X, 218–219 (March 11,
1871). (A biographic note.)

"John Lothrop Motley," *Magazine of American History*, I,
458–460 (July, 1877). (A biographic sketch in the form of
an obituary notice.)

Lamson, A. "Merry-Mount," *Christian Examiner*, XLVI, 95–
107 (January, 1849). (A highly laudatory review, which in
conclusion suggests that Motley try his hand at history.)

Lancaster, Henry H. *Essays and Reviews*. Edinburgh: 1876.
("Motley's United Netherlands," 141–177, reprinted from
North British Review, No. 68, May, 1861.)

*Lodge, Henry Cabot. "Some Early Memories," *Scribner's
Magazine*, LIII, 714–729 (June, 1913). (Pages 724–728, devoted to Motley, contain interesting reminiscences of a personal friend, and two valuable letters [Motley to Lodge,
March 11, 1876, and June 2, 1876] not elsewhere published.)

Long, Orie William. *Literary Pioneers; Early American Explorers of European Culture*. Cambridge: 1935. (The essay
on Motley, 199–224, is a painstaking, accurate account of
Motley's contact with German culture and his interest in
German literature. Mr. Long lists Motley with Ticknor,
Everett, Cogswell, Bancroft, and Longfellow, men who early
brought to American intellectual life the stimulus of European
culture, but fails to show that he contributed much in this
intellectual and cultural movement.)

Longfellow, Samuel. *Life of Henry Wadsworth Longfellow*.
2 vols. Boston: 1886. (Vol. II, pp. 278–279, a letter from

Motley to Longfellow dated May 13, 1856, praising the latter's poetry, especially *Evangeline*. See also Vol. I, p. 326, for Longfellow's praise of Motley's review article on Faust, and Vol. I, p. 324, for Longfellow's letter expressing his desire to help the young novelist in 1839.)

Ludwig, Emil. *Bismarck*. Translated by Eden and Cedar Paul. London: 1927. (Traces the Bismarck-Motley friendship.)

Marcks, Erich. *Bismarck*. *Eine Biographie*. Stuttgart and Berlin: 1909. (I, 83–130: Bismarck's student days at Berlin and Göttingen.)

*Mildmay, Susan and Herbert St. John, eds. *John Lothrop Motley and His Family*. London: 1910. (This volume, a valuable supplement to the *Correspondence*, includes many letters written by Motley's wife and daughters, several additions to the Motley-Bismarck correspondence, and a number of other letters of less importance.)

"Mr. Motley's Historical Works," *Dublin Review*, n. s. XXX, 359–397 (April, 1878); XXXI, 349–380 (October, 1878). (A review of *The Rise of the Dutch Republic* and the *History of the United Netherlands*.)

"Mr. Motley's New Historical Work," *British Quarterly Review*, LX, 208–226 (October, 1874). (A review of *John of Barneveld*.)

Moore, John. "Motley's United Netherlands," *New Englander*, XIX, 386–400 (April, 1861). (A review of Vols. I and II of *History of the United Netherlands*.)

Morison, J. H. "John Lothrop Motley," *Unitarian Review*, VIII, 181–188 (August, 1877). (A tribute to Motley, in the form of an obituary notice, stresses his hatred of tyranny and his love of freedom.)

Morse, John T. "John Lothrop Motley. Centenary of the Historian," *Nation*, XCVIII, 425–427 (April 16, 1914). (This brief biographic sketch by the editor of the American Statesmen Series adds little to the body of information about Motley.)

Morse, John T. *Life and Letters of Oliver Wendell Holmes.* 2 vols. Boston and New York: 1896. (Vol. II, pp. 153–222, contains letters to Motley, most of them not included in the Motley *Correspondence.* See also the index for frequent allusions to Motley.)

"Morton's Hope," *New York Review,* V, 518–519 (October, 1839). (A brief contemporary notice of Motley's first novel which finds evidence of youthful literary promise: "The story is a tissue of wild and extravagant adventures, drawn with boldness and vigor by a masterly and facile pen . . .")

"Motley's Correspondence," *Nation,* XLVIII, 409–411 (May 16, 1889).

"Motley's Correspondence," *Quarterly Review,* CLXVIII, 297–331 (April, 1889). Reprinted in *Littell's Living Age,* CLXXXI, 451–469 (May 25, 1889).

"Motley's Correspondence," *Westminster Review,* CXXXII, 26–43 (July, 1889). (The *Correspondence* reviewed by an English Liberal, obviously in close sympathy with Motley's political views.)

"Motley's History of the Netherlands," *Blackwood's Magazine,* LXXXIX, 555–571 (May, 1861). (A review of Vols. I and II of *History of the United Netherlands,* which recognizes Motley's kinship to Carlyle in historical method.) *Ibid.,* CIV, 83–97 (July, 1868). (A review of Vols. III and IV, which finds them not quite equal to the first two volumes.)

"Motley's History of the United Netherlands," *Edinburgh Review,* CXIII, 182–220 (January, 1861). (A review of Vols. I and II.)

"Motley's History of the United Netherlands," *North American Review,* XCII, 583–584 (April, 1861). (A critical notice of Vols. I and II.) *Ibid.,* CVII, 267–280 (July, 1868). (A review of Vols. III and IV, mainly laudatory.)

"Motley's John of Barneveld," *North American Review*, CXIX, 459–471 (October, 1874). (A review which points to Motley's dramatic power, his vivid landscape painting, and his interest in all the great political problems of the past as a source of guidance to the future.)

"Motley's John of Barneveld and Sixteenth-century Diplomacy," *Quarterly Review*, CXXXVII, 131–153 (July, 1874). (A contemporary review.)

"Motley's Life and Death of John of Barneveld," *Edinburgh Review*, CXL, 55–74 (July, 1874). (A contemporary review.)

"Motley's Netherlands," *Nation*, VI, 170–172 (February 27, 1868). (Review of Vols. III and IV of *History of the United Netherlands*.)

Moulton, C. W., ed. *The Library of Literary Criticism of English and American Authors*. Buffalo: 1904. VII, 85–96. (Includes a chronological table, selections from letters and biographic sketches, and extracts from various critical estimates of Motley and his writings. Useful in tracing Motley's literary reputation.)

Nevins, Allan. "Prescott, Motley, Parkman," pp. 226–242 in *American Writers on American Literature*, ed. John Macy. New York: 1931. ("Prescott, Motley, and Parkman, all products of New England Congregationalism, united in celebrating the triumphs of the Protestant faith over Spanish and French Catholicism." Motley was weak in analytical talent and marked by strong prejudices, but he painted "a noble canvas, treated with sweep, color, and general correctness.")

Nichol, John. *American Literature*. Edinburgh: 1885. (A professor of English literature at the University of Glasgow accords high praise to Motley, pp. 150–155.)

Palfrey, Francis W. "Motley's Rise of the Dutch Republic," *North American Review*, LXXXIII, 182–217 (July, 1856). (A contemporary review.)

Peck, Harry T. *William Hickling Prescott.* New York: 1905.
(Pages 165–166, a letter from Motley, praising Prescott's
Philip II. Prescott and Motley compared, pp. 176–180:
Motley is unsurpassed in the glow and fervor of his narrative;
he excels Prescott in the power of drawing character; unlike
Prescott, "he understands the philosophy of history"; but he
lacks the poise, judgment, and objectivity of Prescott.)

Perry, Bliss. "John Lothrop Motley," pp. 82–95 in *The Early
Years of the Saturday Club,* ed. by E. W. Emerson. Boston
and New York: 1918. See also *ibid.,* 185–186, 416–418, 449,
452–453, 456–459, 479–480. (Professor Perry says of Motley
that "none of the original members of the Club made a
more vivid personal impression upon their contemporaries.")

Piñeyro, Enrique. *Hombres y Glorias de America.* Paris: 1903.
(One chapter, pp. 247–261, devoted to Motley.)

Proceedings of the Massachusetts Historical Society. Boston:
1879–1932. (Consult the indexes of the 1st, 2nd, and 3rd
series for frequent references to Motley.)

*Putnam, Ruth. "Prescott and Motley," *Cambridge History of
American Literature.* New York: 1918. II, 123–147. (Pages
131–147, devoted to Motley, constitute a concise sketch of
his life and work, with brief critical appraisal and an account
of contemporary reviews and estimates.) Bibliography:
ibid., II, 501–503.

Review of Vols. I and II of *History of the United Netherlands.*
In "History and Biography," *Westminster Review,* LXXV,
148–150 (January, 1861). Review of Vols. III and IV: *ibid.,*
LXXXIX, 124–125 (January, 1868). Review of *John of
Barneveld: ibid.,* CI, 271–272 (April, 1874).

Richardson, C. F. *American Literature, 1607–1885.* 2 vols.
New York: 1893. (Notable for an able defence against the
charge of partisanship so often brought against Motley.)

Schantz, B. T. "Sir Christopher Gardiner in Nineteenth Century American Fiction," *New England Quarterly,* XI, 807–

817 (December, 1938). (*Merry-Mount* employs a historical episode used also by Miss Sedgwick, Whittier, J. T. Adams, and Longfellow.)

Scudder, H. E. "Mr. Motley's Correspondence," *Atlantic Monthly*, LXIII, 706–711 (May, 1889). (A review of the *Correspondence*.)

"Siege and Relief of Leyden," *Chatauquan*, LII, 260–272 (October, 1908). (Selections from *The Rise of the Dutch Republic*, with a very brief, uncritical introduction.)

Snyder, Louis Leo. "Bismarck und Motley, eine Studentenfreundschaft," *Hochschule und Ausland*, 11–16 (March, 1930).

Stone, Candace. *Dana and the Sun*. New York: 1938. (At the time of his mission to England, the New York *Sun* was distinctly hostile to Motley.)

Story, W. W. "In Memoriam—John Lothrop Motley" (Poem), in Holmes's *Memoir*, 524–526.

Swift, Lindsay. "John Lothrop Motley," *Book Buyer*, XXI, 41–44 (August, 1900). (A brief biographic sketch, in "Our Literary Diplomats.")

Tribute of the Massachusetts Historical Society to the Memory of Edmund Quincy and John Lothrop Motley. Boston: 1877. (This pamphlet includes the addresses of tribute to Motley by Robert C. Winthrop, William Amory, O. W. Holmes, Rev. R. C. Waterston, and William Everett. It furnishes some biographic details not elsewhere available.) The same material is to be found in *Proceedings of the Massachusetts Historical Society*, XV, 280–299 (1876–77).

"The United Netherlands," *Quarterly Review*, CIX, 64–105 (January, 1861). (A review of *The Rise of the Dutch Republic* and Vols. I and II of *History of the United Netherlands*.)

Vincent, L. H. *American Literary Masters*. Boston: 1906. (Chapter XIII, 359–376, is devoted to the life and works of Motley.)

Waltz, John A. *German Influence in American Education and Culture.* Philadelphia: 1936. (Includes a brief discussion of the interest manifested by New Englanders in German literature of the nineteenth century, with incidental reference to Motley.)

Weiss, J. "Motley's Dutch Republic," *Christian Examiner*, LXI, 99–126 (July, 1856).

*Whipple, E. P. "Motley, the Historian," pp. 155–203, in *Recollections of Eminent Men.* Boston: 1887. (Originally published in *Harper's Magazine*, May, 1879. A delightful essay; adds some personal anecdotes to a biographic sketch based largely on Holmes's *Memoir;* evaluates Motley's historical work with the warmth of an admirer.)

Whitman, Sidney. *Personal Reminiscences of Prince Bismarck.* New York: 1903. (Bismarck's impression of Motley briefly recounted.)

Wister, S. B. "Correspondence of John Lothrop Motley," *Lippincott's Monthly Magazine*, XLIV, 564–572 (October, 1889).

Wolcott, Roger, ed. *The Correspondence of William Hickling Prescott.* Boston and New York: 1925. (Includes [p. 429] a letter to Prescott, written by Motley in 1843.)

Wolf, Gustav. *Bismarcks Lehrjahre.* Leipzig: 1907.

Additional biographic references of considerable importance are listed in Section V, "Motley as Diplomat," below.

IV. HISTORICAL BACKGROUNDS

A. General

Cambridge Modern History, ed. by A. W. Ward, G. W. Prothero, and Stanley Leathes. 13 vols. New York: 1902–12. London: 1907–24. Vols. II and III. (The principal co-operative work in English on the general history of Europe. Contains bibliographies.)

Histoire générale, ed. by Ernest Lavisse and Alfred Rambaud. 12 vols. Paris: 1893–1901. Vols. IV and V. (The principal co-operative work in French on the general history of Europe. Contains valuable bibliographic notes.)

B. England

Black, John Bennett. *The Reign of Elizabeth, 1558–1603*. Oxford: 1936. (Vol. VIII in the *Oxford History of England*, the most recent co-operative work. Bibliography, pp. 412–430.)

Davies, Godfrey. *The Early Stuarts, 1603–1660*. (To be issued as Vol. IX in the *Oxford History of England*, the most recent co-operative work.)

Hume, Martin Andrew Sharp. *Two English Queens and Philip*. New York: 1908. (Hume was the leading authority a generation ago on the history of Spain.)

Innes, Arthur D. *England under the Tudors*. New York: 1929. (Vol. IV of the 7-vol. *History of England*, ed. by Sir Charles Oman.)

Montague, Francis Charles. *The History of England, from the Accession of James I to the Restoration (1603–1660)*. London: 1929. (Vol. VII of *The Political History of England*, ed. by William Hunt and R. L. Poole.)

Pollard, Albert F. *The History of England, from the Accession of Edward VI to the Death of Elizabeth (1547–1603)*. London: 1934. (Vol. VI of *The Political History of England*, ed. by William Hunt and R. L. Poole.)

Trevelyan, G. M. *England under the Stuarts*. London: 1904. (Vol. V of the 7-vol. *History of England*, ed. by Sir Charles Oman.)

C. France

Hanotaux, Gabriel, ed. *Histoire de la nation française*. 15 vols. Paris: 1920–1929. Vol. IV, *Histoire politique (de 1515 à*

1804), par Louis Madelin. Paris: 1924. (One of the standard histories of France, arranged topically.)

Lavisse, Ernest, ed. *Histoire de France depuis les origines jusqu'à la Révolution.* 9 vols. Paris: 1900–10. (The principal co-operative work on the history of France in French.)

Zeller, B., ed. *L'Histoire de France racontée par les contemporains.* 65 vols. in 16. Paris: 1880–90. Vols. L–LXV.

D. Netherlands

Blok, Petrus Johannes. *Geschiedenis van het Nederlandsche volk.* 8 vols. Groningen: 1892–1908. (The standard history of the Netherlands on a large scale.)

Blok, Petrus Johannes. *History of the People of the Netherlands.* Translated by O. A. Bierstadt and Ruth Putnam. 5 vols. New York: 1898–1912.

Brugmans, H. *Geschiedenis van Nederland.* 8 vols. Amsterdam: 1935–1938.

Gachard, L. P. *Actes des états généraux des Pays-Bas, 1576–1585.* Brussels: 1861–66.

Geyl, Pieter. *The Revolt of the Netherlands (1555–1609).* London: 1932. (By a Dutch authority on the history of the Netherlands.)

Pirenne, Henri. *Histoire de Belgique.* 7 vols. Brussels: 1923–32. (The principal large-scale history of Belgium.)

E. Spain

Altamira y Crevea, Rafael. *Historia de España.* 4 vols. Barcelona: 1900–11. A fifth volume (in two parts) by Pio Zabala y Lera was added in 1930. (A famous history of Spain by a Spanish authority.)

Ballesteros y Beretta, D. Antonio. *Historia de España y su influencia en la historia universal.* 8 vols. Barcelona: 1919–36. (The most recent large-scale history of Spain.)

Prescott, William Hickling. *History of the Reign of Philip II, King of Spain.* Revised edition, edited by J. F. Kirk. 3 vols. Philadelphia: 1874. (A classic life of Philip II written by the most famous member of the middle school of American historians.)

F. Principal Characters in Motley's Histories

Armstrong, Edward. *The Emperor Charles V.* 2 vols. London: 1902. (A standard biography by an English authority.)

Bratli, Carl Georg Valdemar. *Philippe II, roi d'Espagne; étude sur sa vie et son caractère.* Paris: 1912. (An interesting study of the growth of a historical legend in non-Spanish countries.)

Fernández Montaña, José. *Felipe II el prudente, y su política.* Madrid: 1914. (A recent Spanish biography.)

Forneron, Henri. *Histoire de Philippe II.* 2 vols. Paris: 1887. (One of the standard biographies.)

Harrison, Frederic. *William the Silent.* London: 1897. (A classic biography.)

Hume, Martin Andrew Sharp. *Philip II of Spain.* London: 1897. (The biographer was, a generation ago, the leading authority on the history of Spain.)

Mariéjol, Jean Hippolyte. *Philip II, the First Modern King.* New York: 1933. (A recent biography by a French authority.)

Prescott, William Hickling. *The Life of Charles the Fifth after His Abdication.* (In Robertson, William. *History of the Reign of the Emperor Charles the Fifth.* III, 325–510.) Boston: 1857.

Putnam, Ruth. *William the Silent.* 2 vols. New York and London: 1898. (A standard biography by a competent American scholar.)

V. MOTLEY AS DIPLOMAT

A. Manuscript Sources

Archives, Department of State, Washington, D. C., Despatches, Austria, Vols. 5–7.

Archives, Department of State, Washington, D. C., Despatches, Great Britain, Vols. 99–106.

Archives, Department of State, Washington, D. C., Instructions, Great Britain, Vols. 21–22.

Moran, Benjamin. *Diary.* (The unpublished diary of Moran, Motley's subordinate in the American Legation at London, is available in the Manuscript Division of the Library of Congress.)

B. Printed Sources: Primary

Foreign Relations of the United States, 1861–1867. Washington, D. C.

Foreign Relations of the United States, 1870. Washington, D. C.

Senate Executive Document No. 8, 39 Congress, 2 Session; *No. 9, ibid.; No. 1*, 40 Congress, 2 Session. (For the circumstances attendant upon Motley's resignation from the Austrian mission.)

Senate Executive Document No. 11, 41 Congress, 3 Session. (For the circumstances connected with Motley's recall from the English mission.)

C. Printed Sources: Secondary

Adams, Charles Francis. "The Treaty of Washington: Before and After," pp. 31–225, in *Lee at Appomattox and Other Papers*. Boston and New York: 1902.

Adams, Randolph Greenfield. *A History of the Foreign Policy of the United States*. New York: 1924.

Badeau, Adam. *Grant in Peace*. Hartford: 1887. (Chapter XXIII, "Grant and Motley," pp. 197–209, reviews the story of Motley's mission to England and his recall. Badeau, intimate friend of Grant and Assistant Secretary of Legation under Motley, declares that Motley "was in small things as well as great utterly lacking in the diplomatic character." Accuses Motley of undue sympathy with the aristocratic ideals of English social life.)

Bemis, Samuel Flagg, ed. *The American Secretaries of State and Their Diplomacy*. 10 vols. New York: 1927–29. (Vol. VII, pp. 133, 135, 157–160: Motley's mission to England under Secretary of State Hamilton Fish.)

Bemis, Samuel Flagg. *A Diplomatic History of the United States*. New York: 1936. (The most recent and elaborate study of American foreign relations by a competent scholar.)

Bemis, Samuel Flagg, and Griffin, Grace Gardner. *Guide to the Diplomatic History of the United States, 1775–1921*. Washington: 1935.

Bigelow, John. "Mr. Seward and Mr. Motley," *International Review*, V, 544–556 (July, 1878). (An analysis of the circumstances surrounding Motley's resignation from the Austrian mission, including the pertinent portion of the McCrackin letter, Secretary Seward's letter to Motley, and Motley's reply.)

Bowers, Claude G. *The Tragic Era*. Cambridge, Massachusetts: 1929. (A famous journalist gives an interesting account, in Chapter XIV, of the conflict between Sumner and Grant, which led to the recall of Motley from the British mission.)

Cortissoz, Royal. *The Life of Whitelaw Reid*. 2 vols. New York: 1921. (Vol. I, pp. 192–193: Motley's recall from London was an act of petty malice on the part of Grant.)

Cox, Jacob D. "How Judge Hoar Ceased To Be Attorney-General," *Atlantic Monthly*, LXXVI, 162–173 (August, 1895). (Includes a discussion of the San Domingo controversy and its bearing on the recall of Motley from the English mission.)

Davis, J. C. Bancroft. *Mr. Fish and the Alabama Claims*. Boston and New York: 1893. (A detailed discussion of a perplexing problem; hostile to Motley and Sumner. Includes Davis's letter to the New York *Herald*, below.)

Davis, J. C. Bancroft. *Mr. Sumner, the Alabama Claims, and Their Settlement*. New York: 1878. (Originally published as a letter to the New York *Herald*, January 4, 1878. Charges that Motley violated his instructions; asserts that he was not the victim of political intrigue.)

Fish, Carl Russell. *American Diplomacy*. 5th ed. New York: 1929. (Contains bibliography.)

Haynes, George H. *Charles Sumner*. Philadelphia: 1909. (Holds that Motley disregarded his instructions at the Court of St. James but that his removal from the mission was due primarily to Grant's resentment toward Sumner. See index for references to the relationship between Motley and Sumner.)

Hesseltine, William Best. *Ulysses S. Grant, Politician*. New York: 1935. (Well written; an important contribution to our knowledge of the political career of Grant. Includes an able, succinct statement of Motley's appointment to the British mission, and of the unpleasant circumstances attendant upon his recall, with the parts played by Grant, Fish, and Badeau.)

Jay, John. "Motley's Appeal to History," *International Review*, IV, 838–854 (November, 1877). Separately published, New York: 1877. (Reviews the facts in Motley's recall from the Court of St. James and finds Motley blameless.)

Latané, John Holladay. *From Isolation to Leadership. A Review of American Foreign Policy*. New York: 1922. (A very brief survey, pp. 112–114, of the Anglo-American relations and the negotiations in which Motley participated.)

Latané, John Holladay. *A History of American Foreign Policy*. Garden City, New York: 1927. ("Notes on Sources," ix–xiv.)

Latané, John Holladay. *A History of American Foreign Policy*. Revised and enlarged by D. W. Wainhouse. Garden City, New York: 1934.

Nevins, Allan. *Hamilton Fish. The Inner History of the Grant Administration.* New York: 1936. (The episode of Motley's mission to the Court of St. James, and the unpleasant circumstances attendant upon his recall therefrom, are reinterpreted by an unsympathetic critic. See pp. 156–399, 451–465.)

Pierce, Edward L. *Memoir and Letters of Charles Sumner.* 4 vols. Boston: 1894. (Valuable in a study of Motley's appointment to the English mission and his recall therefrom. See particularly Vol. IV, pp. 380–381, 395–397, 403–411, 445–449. Mr. Pierce maintains that Sumner had little to do with Motley's appointment, that Badeau betrayed Motley's confidence, and that the defeat of the San Domingo treaty was the reason for the recall.)

Rhodes, James Ford. *History of the United States.* 9 vols. New York: 1893–1928. (A standard history. See Vol. VI, Chapter XXXVIII, for foreign affairs in Grant's administration.)

Sears, Louis Martin. *A History of American Foreign Relations.* New York: 1927. (Bibliography: pp. 589–611.)

Sensabaugh, Leon F. "Motley's Vienna Mission," *Southwestern Social Science Quarterly*, XVI, 29–44 (December, 1935). (A carefully documented study.)

Stuart, Graham H. *American Diplomatic and Consular Practice.* New York: 1936. (Has a brief, misleading statement [p. 327] about the recall of Motley from the English mission.)

"The *Trent* Affair," *Proceedings of the Massachusetts Historical Society*, XLV, 35–148 (1911–1912). (Includes two letters written by Motley at Vienna to C. F. Adams, U. S. Minister to Great Britain. These letters are not in the *Correspondence*.)

Tuckerman, Charles K. "Personal Recollections of William H. Seward," *Magazine of American History*, XIX, 499–503 (June, 1888). (Seward had wished to persuade Motley not to resign at Vienna, but his message was intercepted and recalled by the President's order.)

Wilson, Beckles. *America's Ambassadors to England, 1785–1929.* New York: 1929. (A popular account.)

"A Wrong or a Mistake, Certainly a Lesson," *Every Saturday,* IX, 546 (August 27, 1870). (An editorial criticizing sharply the recall of Motley from the mission to England.) See also brief comment, *ibid.,* X, 74 (January 28, 1871).

VI. GENERAL AMERICAN BACKGROUNDS

Cole, Arthur Charles. *The Irrepressible Conflict, 1850–1865.* New York: 1934.

Fish, Carl Russell. *The Rise of the Common Man, 1830–1850.* New York: 1929.

Nevins, Allan. *The Emergence of Modern America, 1865–1878.* New York: 1928.

The three works listed above, Vols. VI, VII, and VIII in *A History of American Life,* ed. by A. M. Schlesinger and D. R. Fox, are useful for the background of social history in the United States in Motley's time. Each volume has a valuable "Critical Essay on Authorities."

Clark, Harry Hayden (general editor). *American Writers Series.* New York: 1934–   . For the background in American literature, the student should consult the critical introductions and annotated bibliographies of the several volumes, completed and forthcoming. See particularly *Parkman,* ed. by Wilbur L. Schramm; and *Prescott,* ed. by Michael Kraus and William Charvat. (Parkman, Prescott, and Motley are the three most significant members of the middle group of American historians.)

Parrington, Vernon Louis. *Main Currents in American Thought.* 3 vols. New York: 1927–30. (Dismisses Motley laconically as a "Federalist expositor" and a "representative of the Brahmin spirit," whose work suggests an "aloofness from the sordid realities of America." Parrington's work, though marked by the bias of economic determinism, is nevertheless significant as the most complete treatment of the social and intellectual backgrounds of American literature from a consistent point of view.)

Riley, I. Woodbridge. *American Thought from Puritanism to Pragmatism and Beyond.* New York: 1923.

Townsend, Harvey G. *Philosophical Ideas in the United States.* New York: 1934. (Excellent bibliography.)

The works of Riley and Townsend are useful to the student who wishes to place Motley against the background of intellectual and philosophical ideas in America.

Foerster, Norman. *American Criticism.* Boston and New York: 1928. (An incisive, judicious study of the aesthetic theory and literary criticism of the major American figures.)

Quinn, Arthur Hobson. *American Fiction.* New York: 1936. (Though Motley's novels receive brief and not altogether satisfactory treatment, they are seen here in the broad stream of development of American fiction.)

For current articles the student should consult especially Grace G. Griffin's annual bibliography, *Writings on American History;* the annual bibliography of *The New England Quarterly;* bibliographical bulletins of the Modern Humanities Research Association; and bibliographies in *American Literature* and *Publications of the Modern Language Association* (American literature section).

★

Selections from

JOHN LOTHROP MOTLEY

★

LETTERS

[The letters reprinted here are all taken from *The Correspondence of John Lothrop Motley*, in two volumes, edited by George William Curtis (New York: 1889). These two volumes, which constitute an invaluable supplement to Holmes's *Memoir*, furnish an entertaining and instructive survey of Motley's activities from the time of his school days in 1824 to the date of his death in 1877. They have been scored by certain critics on the ground that they include too many letters which represent little more than Motley's delight in the polished social life of England and the Continent; but this was an important phase of his experience, and it is a factor which must not be overlooked in any attempt to estimate his mind and character. An additional volume of letters has been edited by Motley's daughter and her husband, Herbert St. John Mildmay: *John Lothrop Motley and His Family* (London: 1910). It includes a number of letters written by Motley's wife and daughters, some additions to the Bismarck-Motley correspondence, and several other letters of some importance. A few letters, published but uncollected, are available (see Bibliography, pp. cxxxix, cxlvi, and clvii). Others, however, have been withheld from publication by members of the family and friends, for personal reasons.]

[TO HIS MOTHER][1]

Göttingen,
July 1st, 1832.

MY DEAR MOTHER,—
... There is nothing here to mark out the University, except the Library and the students that you meet in the streets, for

---

[1] This letter is one of seven in the *Correspondence* (I, 14–34) which depict Motley's life at the Universities of Göttingen and Berlin in 1832–34. A comparison of these letters with Book Two of *Morton's Hope* (1839), Motley's first novel, will reveal the fashion in which the young author employed autobiographical material in his first creative effort.

there are no University buildings for the students, as with us, but the Professors lecture in their own houses, and the students lodge with the *Philisters* (tradesmen) of the town.

The Library is an immense collection of books, and all have been purchased in one hundred years; the precise number is not known, but it is thought about 400,000. It contains, however, few rare books and manuscripts, and but few splendid editions of books. Everything is for use, and the students may have almost as many books out at a time as they wish by obtaining a number of cards from a Professor.

I got here, as I told you in my last letter, in the Pentecost holidays, and had to wait a few days before I could be matriculated, which matriculation is simply this: I was summoned before the Senate of the University, and then wrote my name and whences and whats, etc., etc., in a great book. I then gave the member of the Senate who officiated three rix-dollars for his trouble, and put another into the poor-box. I have signed an immense list of promises (which are, I believe, never in the slightest degree kept by any of the students, and, consequently, a very improper exaction), the principal of which were, to obey the laws *in toto*, to join no *Landsmannschaft*, drink no beer, fight no duels, etc., etc., etc. The next day I went to the Pro-Rector of the University (Herr Hofrath Goeschen), who gave me my matricle and legitimation *cartes*, observed that the laws were binding, and, shaking my hand, informed me that I was a member of the University. The next day I was introduced to Professor Hugo, who has been a very celebrated lawyer and professor, but is now "a noble wreck in ruinous perfection." His lectures now are dull and stupid, and his titles of Aulic Counsellor, Guelphic Knight, Hofrath, Professor, etc., etc., cannot bring more than three or four students into his class-room. He still lectures, however, on the Law, but his great peculiarity is an unbounded passion for thermometers. He has four or five hanging in every room of his house, and two on each side of his head in the lecture-room; the window opposite him is raised and lowered by a cord which crosses the room, and is hitched just over his head, by means of which he very

carefully regulates the temperature of the room at the conclusion of each paragraph of his lecture. He presented me with
a book which had been lately published in England and dedicated to him, and I presented him with a louis d'or for a course
of lectures on Roman Law.

But I have said nothing yet of the students because I am
afraid of attacking such a boundless and inexhaustible subject.
The German students are certainly an original and peculiar
race of beings, and can be compared to nothing.

The University towns are the homes of "*outré-ness*," or rather,
they are places where it is impossible to be *outré*, except by
dressing or behaving like "a Christian or an ordinary man."
You can hardly meet a student in the streets whose dress would
not collect a mob anywhere else, and, at the same time, you
hardly meet two in a day who are dressed alike, every man
consulting his own taste, and fashioning himself according to
his *beau ideal*.

The most common outer garment is a red plaid or a blue
velvet frock-coat, twenty of which you find to one of cloth.
The head is covered with a very small cap with the colors of
Landsmannschaft to which the individual may belong. The
boots are garnished with spurs universally, albeit innocent of
horseflesh; the forefinger of the left hand always with an
immense seal ring (often of iron or brass); and the upper lip
and chin fortified with an immense moustachio and beard (in
fact, I have seen several students with a depending beard more
than four inches long, and there is hardly one who does not
wear moustachios). A long pipe in the mouth, a portfolio under
the arm, a stick in the hand, and one or two bulldogs at the
heels, complete a picture not in the slightest degree exaggerated
of a Göttingen student! The most promising article in the
formation of a German student's room is the pipe. There are
generally about twenty or thirty of different kinds hanging in
his room—of porcelain, meerschaum, and stone, all ornamented
with tassels, combining the colors of his *Landsmannschaft;*
and you have no idea how beautifully some of the pipes are
painted with landscapes, portraits (there are often beautiful

miniatures painted on them), or coats of arms. Pipes are a favorite present among the students (and you have anything you wish painted on one when you wish to give it away). Every one smokes, and smokes at all times, and in all occupations (except that they are not allowed to smoke in the streets), reading, writing, talking, or riding. I prefer a pipe now to a cigar, and I am hardly ever without one in my mouth (for instance, I have been smoking a great meerschaum all the time I have been writing this), and I always breakfast at half-past five o'clock (!) on a cup of coffee and a pipe, and continue the "cloud compelling" occupation through the day. I find I grow fat on it, for I never was in such health in my life. I find that I have said nothing as yet about the German duels. These things are such a common and everyday occurrence that I have ceased to think at all about them. I must, in the first place, tell you that the accounts you have read in Dwight, etc., of the frequency of these things are not in the slightest degree exaggerated, in fact it is entirely impossible to exaggerate them. I have been here now about three weeks, and during that time as many as forty have been fought *to my knowledge*, and I know of as many as one hundred and fifty more that are to take place directly.

I have seen a few of them, and though you have read accounts of them in Dwight's 'Travels in Germany,' I suppose you will be willing to hear a short description of them. The duels are not allowed to be fought in the town, and accordingly an inn, called the "Kaiser," just outside one of the gates, is a very celebrated rendezvous. As they generally take place between members of different *Landsmannschafts* (*Landsmannschaft* means countrymen-club, or society; there are as many of these as there are sets of students from the different States of Germany. The most prominent are the "Hanoverian," the "Lünenburger," the "Bremensen," and "Westphalian" Landsmannschaften. Besides which there is a club called the "Börsenschafte," which is composed in reality of the refuse of the whole University), the arms offensive and defensive required in the duel are provided for the duellists by their respective *Landsmannschafts*. These arms are a *Schläger* (or saber) about four feet in length, blunt at the point, but very sharp-edged, and a suit of stuffed leather to protect all the vital parts, leaving only the face and breast exposed. The last time I was at the "Kaiser," about sixteen duels were fought in the course of the day, ten of which I saw; and they are on the whole stupid affairs, and I think could exist nowhere but in Germany. It is not, however, a perfect trifle to fight one of these duels, although it is very seldom that any lives are lost, or even important wounds received. But the face is often most barbarously mangled, and indeed it is almost an impossibility to meet a student who has not at least one or two large scars in his visage.

In the two that I saw the other day, one man was cut, not very severely, in the breast, and the other received a wound that laid his face open from the left eye to the mouth, and will probably enhance the beauty of his countenance for the rest of his life.

Both these affairs were *Landsmannschaft* duels; the Hanoverians and the Bremensers and the Lünenburgers and the Westphalians being "los"—that is to say, at variance; in which case each Lünenburger has to fight with a Westphalian, each Hanoverian with a Bremenser, till every member of each *Landsmannschaft* has fought. In these four *Landsmannschaften*, I suppose there are from eighty to one hundred students. So here, you see, are a pretty number of duels to be fought directly. Besides this, a single Westphalian has challenged every one of the Lünenburgers to fight him (which challenge has been accepted), and a single Lünenburger has challenged every one of the Westphalians. Here, you see, are two men, each of whom has about twenty-five duels to fight this term. This Lünenburger who has challenged all the Westphalians is somewhat noted for the number of his duels. He has already fought seventy-five, and has been second in about two hundred, and he has here twenty more to fight. Besides which he has yesterday challenged another student, who had insulted his *Landsmannschaft*, to pistols at ten paces, to be reloaded till one is hit. This same fellow who is thus challenged is also challenged by each member of the insulted *Landsmannschaft* to one "gang" of sabers. The meaning of this term is, a duel to be continued till one of the parties falls, or confesses himself unable to fight longer. These duels arise in every sort of way; a very common one is the one which you have read in Dwight, of pushing or being pushed into the gutter.

There is also a regular code by which the different offenses are meted, and the degree of saber satisfaction determined. The most common and slightest insult is the "Dummer Junge" (stupid boy), which demands a duel of twelve Gangs. (A "Gang" I cannot exactly describe. It is the closing of the two combatants and a certain number of blows and parries.) The parties have each a second at his side to strike up the swords the moment a wound is received. The doctor then steps in, examines the wound, and if it proves to be "*Anschiess*" (a wound of a certain length and depth), the duel is discontinued.

A more gross insult demands twenty-four Gangs, and a still more important one, forty-eight. But the most severe duel is that of one "Gang," in which, as I have said, the duel continues until one drops.

You need be under no apprehension about my returning with a disfigured visage, for as a foreigner is seldom or never insulted, and if he be, has the right of choosing his own weapons (which in my case would be pistols or rifles, and the Germans have an aversion to gunpowder), in which event the offender generally makes an apology and backs out of the business. I assure you I have not at all exaggerated this duelling business. . . .

Your affectionate son,
J. L. M.

[TO HIS MOTHER][1]

Vienna,
June 2nd, 1834.

MY DEAR MOTHER,—
. . . Madame de Goethe, of whom I spoke in my last letter, gave me a letter to a Countess Finkenstein of Dresden, an old

---

[1] In 1834 and 1835 Motley toured the Continent and the British Isles. This letter reflects his early interest in German literature,

lady who lives in Tieck's family, and by whom I was introduced to this author. I had been very much disappointed, as you know, in not having been in Germany before Goethe's death, that I might have seen that Nestor of literature, and this has been in some sort a compensation. I do not know if many of Tieck's works have been translated into English. If they have, you will get them at the Athenæum. Inquire for "Fantasus" or "Puss in Boots" or the "World Upside Down," or Tieck's novels (which last are a set of exquisite little tales, novels in the original meaning of the word), full of old German legends and superstitions, and the authorship of which will entitle him to the title of German Boccaccio. The other works are the old nursery tales of "Fortunatus," "Puss in Boots," "Blue Beard," etc., etc., done into plays (not for the stage), and as full of playful and sharp satire, poetry and plain sense, as they can hold. If they have not been translated we shall have a chance of reading them together one of these days. I was invited by Tieck to tea on Sunday evening, when there was a small party. He is at present just about finishing his translation of Shakespeare (in company with Schlegel), and is in the habit of reading a play aloud to a party of select auditors. I did not hear him, and rather regret it, because he seems to be rather vain of his elocution. His head and bust are fine, and it was not till he got up from his chair that I observed he was slightly deformed (humpbacked). His conversation was like his books, playful, full of *bonhomie*, good-natured sort of satire, and perhaps a little childish vanity. He spoke of Cooper, Irving (whom he knew in Dresden, and whom he admired very much), steam-

which originated under the tutelage of George Bancroft at the Round Hill School. At Harvard in 1831, Motley composed an essay on "The Genius and Character of Goethe." While he was a student in Germany, he translated Goethe's *Faust*, at least in part, and tried his hand at the composition of original verses in German. In 1838 and 1839, he published two articles on Goethe in the *New York Review;* in 1839, translations of Schiller's "The Diver" and Novalis's "Wine Song" (from *Heinrich von Ofterdingen*) in the *New Yorker;* in 1840, a translation of Tieck's drama, *Blue Beard*, in the *New World*.

boats, homœopathism, himself, elocution, with Shakespeare and the musical glasses. His conversation was pleasing and quiet, but without any great show or brilliancy; "and so much for Buckingham."

[TO DR. O. W. HOLMES][1]

London,
May 16th, 1858.

MY DEAR WENDELL,—Your most agreeable and affectionate letter ought not to have remained so long unanswered. That such has been the case is not the fault of my heart, but my head. You, whose reservoir is always filled from the perennial fountains thousands of feet above the heads of *nous autres*, so that you have only to turn the plug to get a perpendicular jet straight into the clouds, must have compassion on those condemned to the forcing-pump. I do not mean, God forbid, that I have not written because I despaired of being witty or amusing. Certainly I do not look upon a friendship such as ours as requiring any demonstrations beyond those of sincerity and steadfastness. At the same time, I have got of late to be affected—"but why I know not," as Hamlet says—with such a constant and chronic blue deviltry, that I am ashamed to write to any one. Unfortunately, the disease with me takes the form of pure and unmitigated stupidity, so that it is not in the least interesting or romantic. *You* do not know what it is to re-echo daily poor Sir Andrew Aguecheek's pathetic complaint, "Sometimes I have no more wit than a Christian or an ordinary man."

---

[1] Motley was, in 1858, engaged in research for his second historical work, *History of the United Netherlands*. The success of his first history, *The Rise of the Dutch Republic*, had brought him instant recognition and had put him on terms of easy familiarity in the best social and literary circles in England. His correspondence with Holmes constitutes the most entertaining and the most instructive portion of the published letters. It reveals many sides of Motley's mind and character: his interest in literature, politics, and social life; his methods of research; his opinions of prominent figures of the day; in short, all the elements of his personality.

All this is intended, not as an apology for my silence, but an explanation thereof. I have been doing my best. I bought six months ago a memorandum-book, as big as a ledger, to take notes of my own conversation, in the manner recommended by the original autocrat who reigned over us, *consule Planco*, and I have been patiently hoping to catch myself saying or even thinking a good thing, in which case down it would have gone in black and white for your benefit. In vain I have placed myself in the attitude of Sterne's portraits, with my forefinger on the bump of ideality, in which attitude, he says, he verily believes he has often intercepted ideas which were intended for somebody else's brain. It is all no go.

By the way, your letter had various adventures before reaching me. I was then in Brussels. My address was, and always is, Baring Brothers and Co., London. You had the original conception of addressing me to the care of *Brown* Brothers and Co., London. Now it is rather a remarkable fact, that although there are several persons rejoicing in that name in London, the only Browns who have anything fraternal about them in the whole town are some chairmakers in Piccadilly. They declined receiving your letter, and then it somehow went back to Liverpool. Some weeks later I heard from home that you had sent the letter, and I wrote to Russell Sturgis (of the Barings) to help me if possible to it. He very kindly wrote to the General Post Office, and also to Brown, Shipley and Co., Liverpool, and eventually the letter was extricated and sent to me, covered all over with very funny hieroglyphics illustrating its various adventures. I might have used this as an excuse for my delay in answering, had I not preferred making a confession rather than an apology. Your letters, fortunately, are not like eggs, telegrams, and things of that nature, good for nothing except fresh, and therefore I enjoyed it the more in consequence of the difficulty in getting it. I was much obliged for your kindness in mentioning the favorable opinion concerning me expressed by Mr. Dorsheimer, and the fact gave me great pleasure. I regret to say that I have seen of the *Atlantic Magazine* only the first two numbers. The reason for this is that I have been for the last six months, with hardly an interval, in very out-of-the-way and obscure places, where light never comes that comes at all. Nice at first, and Brussels afterwards. I took my family in November to the former place on account of Lily, whose health was very delicate, but I rejoice to say she has very much improved, and after establishing them there, I departed to spend the most solitary winter I ever spent in my life in Brussels. I was all day in the Archives, and nearly all night in my chamber. I hardly ever spoke except to exchange a few brief signals with my fellow worms, who were feeding like myself on the carcase of the buried centuries, and the consequences of such a solitary and Ghoul-like existence, was to subdue my nature to the condition of the carrion I had been consuming.

I find your "Autocrat" (the first two numbers of which, as stated, are all I have yet seen) as fresh and poignant in flavor as those of twenty years since, which is sufficiently high praise as to manner. As to matter, the substance is unquestionably stronger, sterner stuff than in those days, and will endure long. You must always have an eye to their subsequent appearance in volumes by themselves, when of course you can leave out what you think of transitory interest, and give them the last polish. I have but just arrived in London, but as this is Sunday and I shall be immersed in hard work from tomorrow forward, in the State Paper Office and British Museum, I thought I had better sit down and have a little talk with you when I was sure of perfect solitude. Tomorrow I shall get all the numbers of the *Atlantic* and devour with immense greediness first the "Autocrats," and then Lowell and Emerson and Longfellow and others, as doubtless I shall know them all by the "twinkling of their eyes." If I meet any literary men, I shall not fail to call their attention to it, as unquestionably the best magazine in the language. I hope when I next write I may have something amusing to tell you. As I said before, I have but just arrived. A young friend of mine who is in Parliament is going to take me to his club tonight, where I hope to hear not logic chopped but politics discussed, as they are at the very culminating point of a crisis; the debate of Friday having been adjourned over till tomorrow.

À propos of the Atlantic, not the magazine, but the ocean, I happened to find this paragraph the other day in the commencement of articles on some subject, I forget what, in the *Allgemeine Zeitung*, and since you have become a German scholar, I hope you will laugh at it as heartily as I did. "Seit der Entdeckung Amerikas ist die Geschichte nicht mehr thalassisch sondern oceanisch." I could read no more of the article. I was already washed out of existence by such a world of water. I suppose you sometimes are glad of a suggestion or two of topics for your ukases at the breakfast table. I think you might handle the subject of stale metaphors for a page or two with much effect. Take for example the ship of state from the time of Horace's "navis referent in mare," etc., down to the last speech of the member for Milwaukee, there has perhaps never been an oration delivered, or a poem perpetrated, without some reference to that unlucky ship of state, which always *will* be getting on breakers, and to the pilot who always *will* be weathering the storm as freshly as if no such allusion had ever been made. The best of it is the satisfaction with which these metaphors are produced as if perfectly fresh and choice, and the conscientious manner in which they are polished up for exhibition. Then there is the deadly upas tree, which has so long poisoned everybody's young existence, the phœnix, the dying dolphin, and many such fools and fishes, and do say something about that unpleasant Spartan boy, who has been following us about, with the fox biting away his nether integuments from time immortal. Then you may write an imaginary puff on somebody's hair dye, or still better get some living barber to pay you handsomely for it by merely changing a few words in Goldsmith's "When lovely woman stoops to folly," ending of course with "is to dye."

There, I consider I have given you at least $20, for if you cannot beat those golden thoughts into a platitude of two magazine pages, you are not the goldbeater I took you for. Pray take all the credit and all the money yourself. I do not ask a commission. Do not say, "An eminent historian, now running to seed in a foreign land, has suggested the following very brilliant, and at the same time profound thoughts." If you should ever hint at my existence again in the magazine, I will never forgive you. I prefer to rest upon the verses in the first number, of which both for the affection, and the generous over-appreciation revealed, I shall be proud all the days of my life, and my children after me, and I do not wish anything to disturb that impression. I have been running on with a most intolerable skimble-skamble. I wish I had anything better to say. Pray forgive my dulness, and prove it by writing to me very soon. Give my kindest regards to your wife and children. Also remember me particularly to Lowell, Longfellow, Agassiz, Felton, Whipple, and others who may remember me, and believe me always,

Most sincerely your friend,
J. L. M.

P.S.—This letter was written yesterday, but was not sent. Meantime, last evening, I dined with a small party at the Mackintoshes. Thackeray was there, and suddenly in the middle of dinner he made the following observation, not to me, but to his neighbor on the other side of the table: "Have you read the "Autocrat of the Breakfast Table," by Holmes, in the new *Atlantic Magazine?*" He then went on to observe that no man in England could now write with that charming mixture of wit, pathos, and imagination, that your papers were better by far than anything in their magazines. I expressed my delight at his warm language, and told him I knew you would be pleased to hear that he had thus spoken of you. He said that he had been so much interested, that he had been about to write to you, and I begged him urgently to do so. The opening observation had been made by Thackeray, entirely *à propos des bottes*. Not a word had been said by me, or any one else at table, of the magazine, or of you. After dinner I had a good deal of talk with him about you, and he spoke with much warmth and appreciation of your poems; he praised particularly "The Last

Leaf" and "The Punch Bowl." I cannot help thinking that it will please you to hear this, so I have gone to the expense of a new envelope (price one penny), in order to mention it, my letter having been already sealed and directed before I went to dinner.

Always affectionately yours,

J. L. M.

[TO HIS MOTHER][1]

31, Hertford Street,
February 9th, 1861.

MY DEAREST MOTHER, . . . I wrote you a long letter of eight pages yesterday, and then tossed it into the fire, because I found I had been talking of nothing but American politics. Although this is a subject which, as you may suppose, occupies my mind almost exclusively for the time being, yet you have enough of it at home, as before this letter reaches you it will perhaps be decided whether there is to be civil war, peaceable dissolution, or a patch-up; it is idle for me to express any opinions on the subject. I do little else but read American newspapers, and we wait with extreme anxiety to know whether the pro-slavery party will be able to break up the whole compact at its own caprice, to seize Washington, and prevent by force of arms the inauguration of Lincoln. That event must necessarily be followed by civil war, I should think. Otherwise, I suppose it may be avoided. But whatever be the result, it is now proved beyond all possibility of dispute that we never have had a government, and that the much eulogized constitution of the United States never was a constitution at all, for the triumphant secession of the Southern States shows that we have only had a league of treaty among two or three dozen petty sovereignties, each of them insignificant in itself, but each having the power to break up the whole compact at its own caprice. Whether the separation takes place now, or whether there is a patch-

[1] This letter is typical of Motley's absorbing interest in the American situation at the approach of the Civil War. Throughout the duration of the War, from his home at the American Legation in Vienna, he followed the course of events with great anxiety.

up, there is no escaping the conclusion that a government proved to be incapable of protecting its own property and the honor of its own flag is no government at all, and may fall to pieces at any moment. The pretense of a people governing itself, without the need of central force and a powerful army, is an exploded fallacy which can never be revived. If there is a compromise now, which seems possible enough, because the Northern States are likely to give way, as they invariably have done, to the bluster of the South, it will perhaps be the North which will next try the secession dodge, when we find ourselves engaged in a war with Spain for the possession of Cuba, or with England on account of the reopened African slave trade, either of which events are in the immediate future.

But I find myself getting constantly into this maelstrom of American politics and must break off short. . . .

I am most affectionately your son,

J. L. M.

[TO HIS WIFE][1]

Woodland Hill,
June 23rd, 1861.

My dearest Mary,—

. . . As I told you before, there is no lack of good officers. The great cause of future trouble may be in neglecting to make proper use of them, through this detestable system of appointing politicians and militia men to be brigadiers and major-generals. General Mansfield, who commands in Washington, seems to me a first-class man in every respect, and so do McDowell and Colonel Heintzelman. McClellan, who commands in the West, is said to be equal to Scott in talent, and thirty years his junior; while General Lyon, a Connecticut man and a West Pointer, seems to be carrying all before him in Missouri, and is rather the favorite of the hour. I do not go quite into military de-

[1] Immediately after the outbreak of hostilities, Motley's anxiety in the crisis led him to return to America. His family was expected to follow him, but his appointment to the post of U. S. Minister to Austria, which became vacant after his return, changed the plan.

tails, because you get them, true or false, in the papers. I have already ordered you the *Daily Advertiser*, and tomorrow I shall see that you get the *New York Times* regularly. Up to this time nothing of importance has happened, and I think that you will derive from my letters as much information to be relied upon as you could get anywhere. With regard to Missouri, there is not the slightest possibility of her getting out of the Union. The Governor is a Secessionist and a fugitive, and his following is comparatively small. I had a long conversation last evening with the Attorney-General of the United States, Mr. Bates, who is himself of Missouri, and he tells me that secession there is simply an impossibility. General Lyon with his United States forces has already nearly put down secession there; but should the insurrection be protracted much longer, the State would be entered on three sides at once (for it is surrounded by Free States) and 150,000 slaves liberated. There is no child's play intended any longer, and the word compromise, which has been the country's curse for so long, has been expunged from the dictionary. Bates has been the champion of freedom for many years, and he has lived to sit in a cabinet with men of his own faith. He is a plain man, shrewd, intelligent.

Sumner, who arrived Wednesday night, told me that Montgomery Blair, the Postmaster-General, was desirous of making my acquaintance. Friday morning I was engaged to breakfast with Mr. Chase. The conversation was very pleasant and instructive to me, turning on the topics already mentioned, and as I walked down with him to the Treasury Department, he insisted on my going with him into his office to finish the subject, "the purport of which," he said, "I have already given you." Afterwards I went with Sumner to Mr. Blair's. He is a Virginian by birth and education, and it is therefore the more to his credit that, like General Scott, he is of the warmest among Unionists, and perhaps the most go-ahead, uncompromising enemy to the rebels in the cabinet, not even excepting Mr. Chase. While we were talking, he asked me what I thought of the President's views. I told him that I had only passed half an hour with him a few evenings before, when I had been introduced to him by Mr. Seward, and that since then it had been advertised conspicuously in all the papers that the President would receive no visitors, being engaged in preparing his message to Congress. "But you must see him; it is indispensable that you should see him, and tell him about English affairs," said Blair. I told him that I was leaving Washington that afternoon. He asked if I could not defer my departure. I said no, for my arrangements were already made.

The truth is, I had resolved not to force myself upon the President. If he did not care to converse with me, it was indifferent to me whether I saw him or not. But Mr. Blair begged me to stop a moment in his library, and incontinently rushed forth into the street to the White House, which was near, and presently came back, saying that the President would be much obliged if I would pay him a visit.

I went and had an hour's talk with Mr. Lincoln. I am very glad of it, for had I not done so, I should have left Washington with a very inaccurate impression of the President. I am now satisfied that he is a man of very considerable native sagacity; and that he has an ingenuous, unsophisticated, frank, and noble character. I believe him to be as true as steel, and as courageous as true. At the same time there is doubtless an ignorance about State matters, and particularly about foreign affairs, which he does not affect to conceal, but which we must of necessity regret in a man placed in such a position at such a crisis. Nevertheless his very modesty in this respect disarms criticism.

Our conversation was, of course, on English matters, and I poured into his not unwilling ear everything which my experience, my knowledge, and my heart, could suggest to me, in order to produce a favorable impression in his mind as to England, the English Government, and the English people. There is no need of my repeating what I said, for it is sufficiently manifest throughout this letter. And I believe that I was not entirely unsuccessful, for he told me that he thought that I was right, that he was much inclined to agree with me, but he added, "It does not so much signify what I think, you must persuade Seward to think as you do." I told him that I found the secretary much mitigated in his feelings compared with what I had expected. He expressed his satisfaction. I do not quote any of his conversation because he was entirely a listener in this part of the interview. Afterwards he took up his message, which was lying in loose sheets upon the writing-table, and read me nearly the whole of it, so far as it was written. On the whole, the document impressed me very favorably. With the exception of a few expressions, it was not only highly commendable in spirit, but written with considerable untaught grace and power. These were my first impressions, which I hope will not be changed when the document comes before the world. It consists mainly of a narrative of events from the 4th of March up to the present hour. Nothing had yet been written as to foreign relations, but I understand from Seward that they are all to be dismissed in a brief paragraph, such as will create neither criticism nor attention anywhere.

We parted very affectionately, and perhaps I shall never set eyes on him again, but I feel that so far as perfect integrity and directness of purpose go, the country will be safe in his hands. With regard to the great issue, we have good generals, good soldiers, good financiers, twenty-three millions of good people "whose bosoms are one," a good cause, and endless tin.

The weather has been beautiful ever since I landed, magnificent sunshine and delicious heat. Just now there is a heavy shower. When it is over I am going to drive over to Camp Andrew, to see the Massachusetts 2nd.

Ten more regiments have been ordered from Massachusetts, and seven, including Gordon's, will soon be ready to take the field at once. This will make 15,000 men from Massachusetts alone. New York has already sent 20,000 and has a reserve of 20,000 ready. Pennsylvania about the same, and so on. The only struggle is who shall get the number accepted.

Give my love to all my English friends. Kiss my three darlings 3000 times, and believe me,

Most lovingly,
J. L. M.

[TO DR. O. W. HOLMES]

Legation of the U. S. America, Vienna,
February 26th, 1862.

MY DEAR HOLMES,—You are the most generous and delightful of correspondents and friends. I have two long and most interesting letters of yours to acknowledge. The first of 7th January, the second of 3rd February. They are exactly the kind of letters which I most value. I want running commentaries on men and events produced on such a mind as yours by the rapidly developing history of our country at its most momentous crisis. I take great pleasure in reading your prophecies, and intend to be just as free in hazarding my own, for, as you so well say, our mortal life is but a string of guesses at the future, and no one but an idiot would be discouraged at finding himself sometimes far out in his calculations. If I find you signally right in any of your predictions, be sure that I will congratulate and applaud. If you make mistakes, you shall never hear of them again, and I promise to forget them. Let me ask the same indulgence from you in return. This is what makes letter-writing a comfort and journalism dangerous. For this reason, especially as I am now in an official position, I have the greatest horror lest any of my crudities should get into print. I have also to acknowledge the receipt of a few lines by Wendell. They gave me very great pleasure. I am delighted to hear of his entire recovery, and I suppose you do not object, so much as he does, to his being detained for a time from camp by recruiting service. I shall watch his career with deep interest. Just now we are intensely anxious about the Burnside expedition, of which, as you know, my nephew Lewis Stackpole is one. He is almost like my son. I feel very proud of his fine intellectual and manly qualities, and although it is a sore trial to his mother to part with him, yet I am sure that she would in future days have regretted his enrolment in the "stay-at-home rangers."

That put me in mind to acknowledge the receipt of "Songs in Many Keys." It lies on our drawing-room table, and is constantly in our hands. I cannot tell you how much pleasure I derived from it. Many of the newer pieces I already know by heart, and admire them as much as you know I have always done their predecessors. The "Ballad" is in a new vein for you, and is I think most successful. If I might venture to mention the separate poems by name which most please me, I should certainly begin with "Iris, Her Book," "Under the Violets," "The Voiceless," which are full of tenderness and music. Then the clarion ring of the verses for the centennial celebration of Burns has an immense charm for me, and so the trumpet tones of the "Voice of the Loyal North"; but I should go on a long time if I tried to express my honest and hearty admiration for the volume as fully as it deserves. I thank you most sincerely for it, and I assure you that you increase in fulness and power and artistic finish without losing any of your youthful freshness of imagination. I am glad that the Emperor had the sense to appreciate your "Vive la France." I agree with him that it is *plein d'inspiration* and exceedingly happy." I admire it the more because for the moment it communicated to me the illusion under the spell of which you wrote it. For of course France hates us as much as England does, and Louis Napoleon is capable of playing us a trick at any moment.

I am obliged to reason like a Cosmopolite. The English have a right to hate America if they instinctively feel that the existence of a great, powerful, prosperous, democratic republic is a standing menace to the tenure of their own privileges. I think the instinct false, however, to a certain extent. Physical, historical, and geographical conditions make our democratic commonwealth a possibility, while they are nearly all wanting in England. I do not think the power or glory or prosperity of the English monarchy any menace to our institutions. I think it an unlucky and unreasoning perverseness which has led the English aristocracy to fear our advance in national importance. I do not mean that, on the whole, the Government has behaved ill to us. Especially international dealings with us have been courteous and conciliatory. I like personally English ways, English character, Englishmen and Englishwomen. It is a great empire in arts and arms, and their hospitalities are very pleasant. Nevertheless I love my own country never so much as at this moment. Never did I feel so strong a faith in her destiny as now. Of John Bright we have already spoken, and of the daily and noble battle waged for us by the *Daily News* (which I hope you read); and now how must we all rejoice at the magnificent essay in *Fraser's Magazine* by the acknowledged chief of Engish thinkers, John Stuart Mill!

It is awful to reflect that the crisis of our fate is so rapidly approaching. The ides of March will be upon us before this letter reaches you. We have got to squash the rebellion soon, or be squashed for ever as a nation—*aut fer, aut feri*. I do not pretend to judge military plans or the capacity of generals; but, as you suggest, perhaps I can take a more just view of the whole picture of this eventful struggle at this great distance than do those absolutely acting and suffering in the scene. Nor can I resist the desire to prophesy any more than you do, knowing that I may prove utterly mistaken. I say, then, our great danger comes from foreign interference. What will prevent that?—Our utterly defeating the Confederates in some *great* and *conclusive* battle, or our possession of the cotton ports and opening them to European trade, or a most *unequivocal policy* of slave emancipation. Any one of these three conditions would stave off recognition by foreign Powers until we had ourselves abandoned the attempt to reduce the South to obedience.

The last measure is to my mind the most important. The South has, by going to war with the United States Government, *thrust into our hands against our will* the invincible weapon which constitutional reasons had hitherto forbidden us to employ. At the same time, it has given us the power to remedy a great wrong to four millions of the human race, in which we had hitherto been obliged to acquiesce. We are threatened with national annihilation, and defied to use the only means of national preservation. The question is distinctly proposed to us, Shall slavery die or the Great Republic? It is most astounding to me that there can be two opinions in the Free States as to the answer. If we do fall, we deserve our fate. At the beginning of the contest, constitutional scruples might be respectable.

But now we are fighting to subjugate the South, that is, slavery. We are fighting for the Union. Who wishes to destroy the Union? The slaveholders. Nobody else. Are we to spend 1200 millions and raise 600,000 soldiers in order to *protect* slavery?

It really does seem to me too simple for argument. I am anxiously waiting for the coming Columbus who will set this egg of ours on end by smashing in the slavery end. We shall be rolling about in every direction until that is done. I do not know that it is to be done by proclamation. Rather perhaps by facts. Well, I console myself by thinking that the people, the American people at least, is about as wise collectively as less numerous collections of individuals, and that the people has really decreed emancipation and is only puzzling how to carry it into effect. After all it seems to be a law of Providence that progress should be by a spiral movement, so that when we seem most tortuous we may perhaps be going ahead. I am firm in the faith that slavery is now wriggling itself to death. With slavery in its primitive vigor I should think the restored Union neither possible nor desirable. Do not understand me as not taking fully into account all the strategical considerations against premature governmental utterances on this great subject.

But are there any trustworthy friends of the Union among the slaveholders? Should we lose many Kentuckians and Virginians who are now with us if we boldly confiscated the slaves of all rebels? And a confiscation of property which has legs and so confiscates itself at command, is not only a legal, but would prove a very practical, measure in time of war. In brief, the time is fast approaching, I think, when "Thorough" should be written on all our banners. Slavery will never accept a subordinate position. The Great Republic and slavery cannot both survive. We have been defied to mortal combat, and yet we hesitate to strike. These are my poor thoughts on this great subject. Perhaps you will think them crude.

I was much struck with what you quote from Mr. Conway, that if emancipation was proclaimed on the Upper Mississippi it would be known to the negroes of Louisiana in advance of the telegraph. And if once the blacks had leave to run, how many whites would have to stay at home to guard their dissolving property?

You have had enough of my maunderings. But before I conclude them, may I ask you to give all our kindest regards to Lowell, and to express our admiration for the "Yankee Idyll"? I am afraid of using too extravagant language if I say all I think about it. Was there ever anything more stinging, more concentrated, more vigorous, more just? He has condensed into those few pages the essence of a hundred diplomatic papers and historical disquisitions and 4th July orations. I have very pleasant relations with all the "J. B.'s" here. They are all friendly and well disposed to the North. I speak of the Embassy, which, with the Ambassador and dress, numbers eight or ten souls, some of them very intellectual ones.

Shall I say anything of Austria? What can I say that would interest you? That is the reason why I hate to write. All my thoughts are in America. Do you care to know about the Archduke Ferdinand Maximilian (if L. N. has his way). He is next brother to the Emperor; but although I have had the honor of private audience of many archdukes here, this one is a resident of Trieste. He is about thirty, has an adventurous disposition, some imagination, a turn for poetry—has voyaged a good deal about the world in the Austrian ship of war, for in one respect he much resembles that unfortunate but anonymous ancestor of his, the King of Bohemia, with the seven castles, who, according to Corporal Trim, had such a passion for navigation and sea affairs, "with never a seaport in all his dominions." But now the present King of Bohemia has got the sway of Trieste, and Ferdinand Maximilian has been resident there, and is Lord High Admiral and chief of the Marine Department. He has been much in Spain and also in South America. I have read some travels—"Reise Skizzen"—of his, printed, not published. They are not without talent, and he ever and anon relieves his prose jog-trot by breaking into a canter of poetry. He adores bull-fights, rather regrets the Inquisition, and considers the Duke of Alva everything noble and chivalrous and the most abused of men. It would do your heart good to hear his invocations to that deeply injured shade, his denunciations of the ignorant and vulgar Protestants who have defamed him. "Du armer Alva! weil du dem Willen deines Herren unerschütterlich treu warst, weil die fest bestimmten Grundsätze der Regierung," etc., etc., etc. You can imagine the rest. (N.B.— Let me observe that the D. R. was not published until long after the "Reise Skizzen" were written.)

Dear me, I wish I could get back to the 16th and 17th centuries! If once we had the "rebels licked, Jeff. Davis hanged, and all," I might shunt myself back to my old rails. But alas! the events of the 19th century are too engrossing. If Lowell cares to read this letter, will you allow me to make it over to him jointly, as Captain Cuttle says? I wished to write to him, but I am afraid only you would tolerate my writing so much when I have nothing to say. If he would ever send me a line I should be infinitely obliged, and would quickly respond. We read the "Washers of the Shroud" with fervent admiration. Always remember me most sincerely to the Club, one and all. It touches me nearly when you assure me that I am not forgotten by them. Tomorrow is *Saturday*, and *last of the month*. We are going to dine with our Spanish colleague. But the first bumper of the Don's champagne I shall drain to the health of the Parker House friends. Mary and Lily join me in kindest regards to you and all yours; and I am as always,

Sincerely your friend,
J. L. M.

[TO HIS MOTHER]

Marien Villa, Vöslau,
August 18th, 1862.

MY DEAREST MOTHER,—It seems to me at times as if I could not sit out this war in exile. I console myself with reflecting that I could be of little use were I at home, and that I may occasionally be of some service abroad. The men whom I most envy are those who are thirty years of age and who were educated at West Point, or rather that portion of them who did not imbibe a love for the noble institution of slavery together with their other acquirements at that college.

There is no doubt, I believe, that Louis Napoleon passes most of his time in urging the English Government to unite with him in interfering on behalf of the slave-dealing, negro-breeding confederacy, and that the agents of that concern have offered to go down and worship him in any way he likes, even to the promising of some kind of bogus abolition scheme, to take effect this time next century, in case he will help them cut the throat of the United States Government. Thus far the English Government have resisted his importunities. But their resistance will not last long. The only thing that saves us as yet from a war with the slaveholders, allied with both France and England, is the anti-slavery feeling of a very considerable portion of the British public. Infinite pains are taken by the agents of the slaveholders to convince the world that the North is as much in favor of slavery as the South, but the anti-slavery acts of the present Congress have given the lie to these assertions. Nevertheless, I am entirely convinced, not as a matter of theory but as fact, that nothing but a proclamation of emancipation to every negro in the country will save us from war with England and France combined.

I began this note determined not to say a single word on the subject of the war, as if it were possible to detach one's thoughts from it for a moment. I continue to believe in McClellan's military capacity as on the whole equal to that of any of his opponents. I do not think that this war has developed any very great military genius as yet. But it is not a military war, if such a contradiction can be used. It is a great political and moral revolution, and we are in the first stage of it. The coming man, whoever he may be, must have military genius united with intense faith in something. In the old civil wars of Holland, France, and England, the men who did the work were the men who either believed intensely in the Pope and the Inquisition, or who intensely hated those institutions; who either believed in the Crown or in the people; who either adored or detested civil and religious liberty. And in our war, supposing other nations let us fight it out, which they are not likely to do, the coming man is some tremendous negro-seller with vast military capacity, or some John Brown with ditto. I have an abiding faith in the American people; in its courage, love of duty, and determination to pursue the right when it has made up its mind. So I believe this conspiracy of the slaveholders will yet be squashed, but it will not be till the people has made a longer stride than it has yet made. Pardon me for this effusion. Out of the fulness of the heart the mouth speaketh. And these are times when every man not only has a right, but is urged by the most sacred duty to speak his mind. We are very tranquil externally, speaking here in Vöslau, where we shall remain till the middle of October. God bless you, my dear mother. All send love to you and the governor, and I remain,

Most affectionately, your son,

J. L. M.

[TO HIS ELDEST DAUGHTER]

Vienna,
November 23rd, 1864.

My dearest Lily,—

... Throughout this great war of principle I have been sustained by one great faith, my belief in democracy. The American people has never known a feudal superior, in perfect good faith and simplicity has always felt itself to be sovereign over its whole territory, and because for a long period it allowed itself to be led by the nose, without observing it, by a kind of sham aristocracy, which had developed itself out of the slave-dealing system of the South, it was thought to have lost all its virtue, all its energy, and all its valor. The People did not fairly realize for a long time that this doughty aristocracy of the cotton planters intended to revolt against the sovereignty of the People. The People were wonderfully *naïf*, good-humored, astonished, and placable, for it took them a long time to understand that the rebellion was actually against popular sovereignty.

But when the object of the great conspiracy was fairly revealed, I suppose that no despotic monarch that ever lived, not

Charles V nor Louis XIV nor the Czar Nicholas, was ever more thoroughly imbued with the necessity of putting down the insurrection of serfs or subjects than was the American Demos. As to doubting its power to do this, such a sentiment has never entered my head. The democratic principle is potent even in Europe, where it only exists in solution and in hidden and mutually neutralizing combinations with other elements. In America it is omnipotent, and I have always felt that the slave power has undertaken a task which is not difficult but impossible. I don't use this as a figure of speech; I firmly believe that the democratic principle is as immovable and absolute a fact upon our soil (not to change its appearance until after some long processes of cause and effect, the beginnings of which for centuries to come cannot even be imagined) as any of its most marked geological and geographical features, and that is as much a necessary historical and philosophical result as they are.

For one, I like democracy. I don't say that it is pretty or genteel or jolly. But it has a reason for existing, and is a fact in America, and is founded on the immutable principle of reason and justice. Aristocracy certainly presents more brilliant social phenomena, more luxurious social enjoyments. Such a system is very cheerful for a few thousand select specimens out of the few hundred millions of the human race. It has been my lot and yours to see how much splendor, how much intellectual and physical refinement, how much enjoyment of the highest character has been created by the English aristocracy; but what a price is paid for it! Think of a human being working all day long, from six in the morning to seven at night, for fifteen or twenty kreutzers a day in Moravia or Bohemia, Ireland or Yorkshire, for forty or fifty years, to die in the workhouse at last! This is the lot of the great majority all over Europe; and yet they are of the same flesh and blood, the *natural* equals in every way of the Howards and Stanleys, Esterhazys and Liechtensteins. . . .

> Ever, my dear child,
> Your affectionate
> PAPA.

[TO HIS ELDEST DAUGHTER]

Vienna,
August 14th, 1866.

MY DEAREST LILY,—

... It is melancholy to see the breakdown of this House of Hapsburg. They seem to be suffering, as is always the case, for the sins of former centuries, to say nothing of the early part of this one. There are no real catastrophes in history.

Sap—sap—sap, gnaw—gnaw—gnaw, nibble—nibble—nibble. A million insects and mildews, and rats and mice, do their work for ages, and at last a huge fabric goes down in a smash, and the foolish chroniclers of the day wonder why it tumbles. The wonder was that the hollow thing stood. I don't mean that Austria has disappeared, but the traditional German Empire or Confederation with a Hapsburg word to it, the Austrian prestige, the great imperial, military, dictatorial power, this is as far off as the empire of Cyrus.

Well, I shan't go into philosophical discussions in this letter. You know Austrian "society" as well as I do, and society so-called governs Austria. It is the last aristocracy extant. England is a plutocratical oligarchy, not an aristocracy of birth. In Austria, birth is everything; wit, wisdom, valor, science, comparatively nothing. Fancy going about in a fashionable salon in Vienna to look for the Lyells, Murchisons, Gladstones, Disraelis, Tennysons, Landseers, Macaulays of Austria, if such there be. Fancy a London house where they would not be welcome guests. Well, thereby hangs a tale. Dancing well, driving well, a charming manner, and thirty-two quarterings, can't be got to govern the world in these degenerate days, and so you have Königgrätz and the Peace of Prague.

Did any one tell you that the only man who ever found out Benedek's "plan" was the old ex-Emperor Ferdinand? He found it out three weeks before the war opened (they say), and immediately left Prague and established himself triumphantly

at Innspruck! By the way, we are getting a curious collection
of ancient relics here in Vienna. It will soon rival the Ambras
museum of old armor. The King of Saxony, the King of
Hanover, and Crown Prince the Duke of Nassau and Hesse,
and a lot of other discrowned potentates are thronging hither.
There is a faint scent in the atmosphere of mildly decaying
royalty. May not that dread epidemic Democracy burst out
some day in consequence? I forgot to tell you in my last that
the King of Hanover wished to see our dear diplomatic body.
So we all turned out in full fig the other day. The King is
living quietly at Knesebeck's, his envoy having declined Schön-
brunn, where Saxony lives. The apartment is the same where
Count Waldstein once dwelt, in the Wallner Gasse. You remember dining there in his time. The King is very tall, per-
sonable, stately, handsome, but blind. There was something
pathetic in seeing the earnestness and satisfaction with which
he went round the circle.

It lasted longer than any one at the Burg. He paid the expenses of the conversation with each dip. When he came to
me he could not ask about the President's grandmother or
brothers-in-law, not knowing them personally, but he had got
himself up a little, even for me, with Knesebeck's coaching.
Referred to the civil war happily terminated; and then to his
own troubles and those of Germany.

Not knowing what to say, I mumbled something about sympathy, which I could not help feeling at the sight of this blind,
grey, discrowned Guelph, who had at least put himself at the
head of his battalions and done his best to fight his way through
for a cause, which as it was that of crowned heads and the
existing order of things, he believed to be identical with that
of the human race. How should he think otherwise? He caught
at my expressions of sympathy, said he felt much obliged to
me for what I said, and that he had tried to do his duty as he
understood it. And so he did.

All France is furious at the Emperor's loss of prestige, that
very subtle article, so potent, but liable to evaporate so suddenly. I don't think with Prussia going it so easy in Europe

that Louis Napoleon will try to pick up his drowning prestige by the locks in the Gulf of Mexico. He must assert himself somewhat nearer home.

Your ever affectionate
P.

From MORTON'S HOPE: OR THE MEMOIRS OF A PROVINCIAL[1]

[The story opens in the fall of 1760 in the villa of Joshua
Morton (uncle of the narrator), ten miles from Boston. Morton's Hope is the fantastic and grotesque cottage of the eccentric
bachelor, Uncle Joshua, who has adopted the infant Uncas,
half-breed son of his brother Maurice. The latter lives on the
frontier among the Indians. In a theatrical scene at the opening
of the story, he appears suddenly at the Hope and begs to be
allowed to take young Uncas with him. But Joshua, deeming
the father unfit to take care of his own son, refuses the request.
Uncas grows up, goes away to college, and then returns to the
Hope; here he indulges a passion for reading and study as
described in the chapter which follows.]

BOOK I, CHAPTER VII

STUDIES AND READING[2]

For the next two years I remained at the Hope. Joshua had
become more full of projects than ever. The resolutions passed

[1] Motley's first novel, published in 1839, was unsuccessful. Compounded of heterogeneous elements, marked by faulty plot construction and weak characterization, and couched in strained and bombastic diction, it gave little promise of the literary power to be displayed later. Its chief interest lies in its autobiographic quality,
for the portrait of the author is unmistakable. Uncas Morton's
boyhood interest in dramatic performances, the Byronic passion
and cynicism and fantastic dreams of his youth, and many of his
experiences at Göttingen and Berlin—these are direct transcriptions
from Motley's own life. In no other of his writings, says Holmes,
do we get such an inside view of his character "with its varied im-
pulses, its capricious appetites, its unregulated forces, its impatient
grasp for all kinds of knowledge" (*Life*, 352). The novel attracted
very little critical notice, and that little not very favorable. For
discussion, see Introduction, pp. xvi–xvii, xxvi, xxviii–xxix.

[2] This chapter, doubtless the most completely autobiographic in
the novel, reveals something of Motley's boyhood reading habits,

32

in Boston a year or two previous, recommending, in consequence of the imposition of extravagant duties on imported
articles, the attention of the colonists to domestic manufacture
had had their effect upon him. He devoted himself assiduously
to his cotton-mill, and he had besides already instituted a soap-
boiling establishment and a starch manufactory. As for me,
I heard or heeded nothing of the events that were going on
around me. The air was already murky with the gathering
clouds of the revolution; but retired within my own childish
egotism, I was unconscious of the coming storm.

I was always a huge reader; my mind was essentially craving
and insatiable. Its appetite was enormous, and it devoured
too greedily for its health. I rejected all guidance in my studies.
I already fancied myself a misanthrope. I had taken a step
very common for boys of my age, and strove with all my
might to become a cynic.

I read furiously. To poetry, like most infants, I devoted
most of my time. I had already revelled in the copious flood
of modern poetry, and I now thirsted for the fountains whence
the torrent had gone forth. I was imbued with the common
passion for studying, as I called it, systematically, and my next
step was antiquarianism. From Spencer [*sic*] and the dramatists, I got back to Chaucer and Gower. If I had stopped here,
it would have been well enough; but these, though rude, I found
already artists. From Chaucer and Gower I ascended through
a mass of ballads, becoming ruder and more unintelligible at
every step, to the first beginning of English vernacular poetry,
and still determined to thread the river to its source. I mounted
to the Anglo-Norman, and was proceeding still farther, when I
found myself already lost in a dismal swamp of barbarous
romances and lying Latin chronicles. This Slough of Despond
I mistook for the parent lake, and here I determined to fix. I
read the wild fables of Jeoffrey of Monmouth with real delight,
and the worthy friar introduced me to a whole fraternity of

his unbounded thirst for knowledge, his unfixed, restless ambition.
For this reason it has been deemed worthy of inclusion in the selections in this text, in spite of its lack of narrative value.

monks. I forced or fancied myself into admiring such grotesque barbarians as Robert of Gloucester, Benevil, and Robert Mannyng, and quoted some hideous couplets from the "Prickke of Conscience" by the Hermit of Hampole, as the very prosopopeia of a graceful lyric. I got hold of the Bibliotheca Monastica, containing a copious account of Anglo-Norman authors, with notices of their works, and set seriously to reading every one of them. I fell into the common error of boyish antiquaries, and admired as venerable that which was only old, and persuaded myself into considering that as quaint and beautiful, which was merely grotesque and rude. I had not learned that art, in its earlier stages, is interesting as matter of history, but its monuments useless in themselves; and that to consume time and labor in mastering the monastic and fossil remains of the barbarous age of poetry, was as absurd as for an amateur of the fine arts to fill his museum with wooden statues in the manner of Dedalus, or of paintings in the style of the early Pisans.

One profit of my antiquarianism was, however, an attention to foreign languages. Having mounted, in my literary inquiries, to the confluence of the English and French languages, —to the fork where the two rivers flow into each other, I found myself obliged to master the French before I could get any farther. As I was on the subject, I applied myself to several others; but my literary studies in other languages were as falsely directed as in my own. In French I occupied myself only with the works of the earlier Trouveurs; in Spanish, with the oldest ballad-mongers; in Germany, neglecting the wonderful and stupendous fabric of a single century which comprised most that is brilliant in that literature, I confined myself to the Heldenbuch and the Niebelungen Lied, and to the farcical productions of the ancient tinkers and tailors. As for the Italian literature, it was too classic and too finished for my taste, and I returned from them all to the barbarians I loved.

After floundering for a time in this stagnant pool of literature, I had at last the good sense to extricate myself, and with my wings all clogged as they were, I set off upon a higher and more daring flight. From the modern poets I ascended to the ancients, and from Latin I got to Greek. It was a blessed transition! When I read the odes of Pindar, and the immortal dramas of Aeschylus, Euripides, and Sophocles, I felt as if I had ascended to the iced mountain-tops of poetry, and felt in a purer and sublimer atmosphere. I found that the perfection of poetry was in the perfection of art. It seemed strange to me that these were *ancients*. I could hardly realize that the men, from whose clutches I had just rescued myself, had lived centuries after the Greeks, and Greece itself had died. I could not understand that a nation had so nearly reached perfection in literature and art, and then expired. I saw the magnificent mausoleum which art and poetry had reared upon the grave of Greece; but I was bewildered with the reflection that it covered a mouldering corpse. I read the name and the glorious epitaph, and could not realize that all below were only bones and dust. The mortifying truth, that a bound was set to human intellect, now forced itself for the first time upon my mind. I saw that Greece had been born, and had illumined the world, and then had died and been buried; and that, centuries after, other nations had arisen only to do the same. I felt, as I occupied myself with the study of Greece and her literature, as if I had been transplanted to a deserted planet, filled with cities and temples, and palaces indeed, but whose inhabitants had all died—which still revolved and shone in the universal system, but in which there was no life.

I could have revelled in Grecian poetry for ever, but I had become possessed with the ridiculous desire of arriving at the beginning or the source of poetry. I forgot that its source was the human heart, just as the source of heat, in all climates and all ages, is the sun. I sought for the beginning of poetry. I might as well have sought for the beginning of the circle. From Greece I got to Asia. I studied the history of the Oriental languages, and became convinced of the necessity of examining them for myself. I already fancied myself learned, and in the course of a breakfast conversation, in which I already manifested considerable contempt for my Aunt Fortitude's intellect,

I announced to Joshua my intention of studying Hebrew and Chinese, and requested a tutor. My uncle, being a little startled at this index to the copiousness of my studies, saw fit to catechize me a little, and finding me as deplorably ignorant on all necessary subjects as I was intensely learned on matters, in his estimation, not worth a half-penny, begged me seriously to turn my attention to history.

The groundwork of my early character was plasticity and fickleness. I was mortified by this exposure of my ignorance, and disgusted with my former course of reading. I now set myself violently to the study of history. With my turn of mind, and with the preposterous habits which I had been daily acquiring, I could not fail to make as gross mistakes in the pursuit of this as of other branches of knowledge. I imagined, on setting out, a system of strict and impartial investigation of the sources of history. I was inspired with the absurd ambition, not uncommon to youthful students, of knowing as much as their masters. I imagined it necessary for me, stripling as I was, to study the authorities; and, imbued with the strict necessity of judging for myself, I turned from the limpid pages of the modern historians, to the notes and authorities at the bottom of the page. These, of course, sent me back to my monastic acquaintances, and I again found myself in such congenial company to a youthful and ardent mind, as Florence of Worcester, and Simeon of Durham, the venerable Bede, and Matthew Paris; and so on to Gregory and Fredegarius, down to the more modern and elegant pages of Froissart, Hollinshed, Hooker, and Stowe. Infant as I was, I presumed to grapple with masses of learning almost beyond the strength of the giants of history. A spendthrift of my time and labor, I went out of my way to collect materials, and to build for myself, when I should have known that older and abler architects had already appropriated all that was worth preserving; that the edifice was built, the quarry exhausted, and that I was, consequently, only delving amidst rubbish.

This course of study was not absolutely without its advantages. The mind gained a certain proportion of vigor by even this exercise of its faculties, just as my bodily health would have been improved by transporting the refuse ore of a mine from one pit to another, instead of coining the ingots which lay heaped before my eyes. Still, however, my time was squandered. There was a constant want of fitness and concentration of my energies. My dreams of education were boundless, brilliant, indefinite; but, alas! they were only dreams. There was nothing accurate and defined in my future course of life. I was ambitious and conceited, but my aspirations were vague and shapeless. I had crowded together the most gorgeous, and even some of the most useful and durable materials for my woof, but I had no pattern, and, consequently, never began to weave.

I had not made the discovery that an individual cannot learn, nor be, everything; that the world is a factory in which each individual must perform his portion of work:—happy enough if he can choose it according to his taste and talent, but must renounce the desire of observing or superintending the whole operation.

My passion for self-instruction was carried to an enormous and unwholesome excess.—From scorning all assistance and inquisition from the friends about me, I even dared to deride the learning and the labor of the master minds of literature. From studying and investigating the sources of history with my own eyes, I went a step further; I refused the guidance of modern writers; and proceeding from one point of presumption to another, I came to the magnanimous conviction that I could not know history as I ought to know it, unless I *wrote* it for myself. I knew now where the stores lay, and I could select and arrange according to my own judgment. I abjured allegiance, accordingly, to the graceful moderns, to immerse myself in the barbarous learning of the darker ages. I voluntarily dashed down the lantern, for no other purpose but that I might grope by myself in the dark. It would be tedious and useless to enlarge upon my various attempts and various failures. I forbear to comment upon mistakes which I was in time wise enough to retrieve. Pushing out, as I did, without compass and without experience, on the boundless ocean of learning, what could I expect but an utter and a hopeless shipwreck?

Thus I went on, becoming more learned, and therefore more ignorant, more confused in my brain, and more awkward in my habits, from day to day. I was ever at my studies, and could hardly be prevailed upon to allot a moment to exercise or recreation. I breakfasted with a pen behind my ear, and dined in company with a folio bigger than the table. I became solitary and morose, the necessary consequence of reckless study; talked impatiently of the value of my time, and the immensity of my labors; spoke contemptuously of the learning and acquirements of the whole world, and threw out mysterious hints of the magnitude and importance of my own projects. In a word, the youth, who at fifteen, confessed himself a sated libertine, was, at seventeen, transformed into a most intolerable pedant.

In the midst of all this study, and this infant authorship, the perusal of such masses of poetry could not fail to produce their effect. Of a youth whose mind, like mine at that period, possessed some general capability, without perhaps a single prominent and marked talent, a proneness to imitation is sure to be the besetting sin. I consequently, for a large portion of my earlier life, never read a work which struck my fancy, without planning a better one upon its model; for my ambition, like my vanity, knew no bounds. It was a matter of course that I should be attacked by the poetic mania. I took the infection at the usual time, went through its various stages, and recovered as soon as could be expected. I discovered soon enough that emulation is not capability, and he is fortunate to whom is soonest revealed the relative extent of his ambition and his powers.

My ambition was boundless; my dreams of glory were not confined to authorship and literature alone; but every sphere in which the intellect of man exerts itself, revolved in a blaze of light before me. And there I sat in my solitude, and dreamed such wondrous dreams! Events were thickening around me which were soon to shake the world,—but they were unmarked by me. The country was changing to a mighty theatre, on whose stage, those who were as great as I fancied myself to be, were to enact a stupendous drama in which I had no part. I saw it not; I knew it not; and yet how infinitely beautiful were the imaginations of my solitude! Fancy shook her kaleidoscope each moment as chance directed, and lo! what new, fantastic, brilliant, but what unmeaning visions! My ambitious anticipations were as boundless as they were various and conflicting. There was not a path which leads to glory, in which I was not destined to gather laurels. As a warrior, I would conquer and over-run the world. As a statesman, I would reorganize and govern it. As a historian, I would consign it all to immortality; and in my leisure moments, I would be a great poet and a man of the world.

In short, I was already enrolled in that large category of what are called young men of genius,—men who are the pride of their sisters, and the glory of their grandmothers,—men of whom unheard-of things are expected, till after long preparation, comes a portentous failure, and then they are forgotten; subsiding into indifferent apprentices and attorneys' clerks.

Alas! for the golden imaginations of our youth. They are all disappointments. They are bright and beautiful; but they fade. They glitter brightly enough to deceive the wisest and most cautious, and we garner them up in the most secret caskets of our hearts; but are they not like the coins which the Dervise gave the merchant in the story? When we look for them the next morning, do we not find them withered leaves?

MORTON'S FELLOW STUDENTS[1]

[In 1769, Uncas meets and falls violently in love with Mayflower Vane. "Mafy" for a short time thinks that she returns Morton's love, but she soon deserts him for Vassal Deane, a

[1]Fox Rabenmark, whose portrait is sketched partially here and at greater length in Book II, Chapter IV, is very probably a fictitious representation of Prince Bismarck, who was a fellow student with Motley at Göttingen and Berlin. Their friendship was an enduring one, as is evident to the reader of the many letters which have been preserved.

young patriot who has been participating in demonstrations
against unjust British taxation. Uncas romantically contem-
plates suicide. Immediately after his marriage to Mafy, Deane
is killed in the Boston Massacre, and Uncas exultantly carries
the news to the young widow.

Book II is devoted to Uncas' student life in Germany. Un-
interested in the approaching conflict between the colonies and
Great Britain, Uncas seeks a more congenial atmosphere in
Europe. He has his first glimpse of German students in Auer-
bach's Cellar at Leipzig, where he meets a group who are just
concluding a "beer journey."]

Sansterre Lackland was about ten years older than myself,
and, consequently, a little nearer thirty than twenty; he was of
high descent, and small property—the youngest son of the
youngest brother of the Earl of Agincourt. The features of
Antinous were not more accurately moulded, nor more beautiful than his; and his tall figure and distinguished address were
worthy of his nation and his race.

With him I was sitting a little apart from the rest of the company, with most of whom he was tolerably well acquainted.
There were six students from Göttingen, and half-a-dozen others
of Leipzig who had been making what is technically called a
"beer journey," during the Pentecost holidays, and as the osten-
sible and only object of such a pilgrimage (which usually con-
ducts the party from one university to another) is to drink as
great a quantity of beer and Rhenish at each stopping place, as
human beings are capable of, they had not unwisely made
Leipzig the last stage of their journey, where they had been
revelling in the most glorious intoxication, till it was time for
them to return.

These journeys are always made on foot. A knapsack contains a change of linen; and as at each university town they are
accustomed, according to universal usage, to quarter themselves
upon their respective friends among the students there, the
only use to which their scanty supply of Fredericks-d'or is
applied, is to pay for the wine and beer which form the objects
of the journey.

As their Fredericks had nearly all flown, they were to take their departure next day; and as both Lackland and myself were idle men, without aim or object, we had agreed to study a phenomenon of human nature that was new to us, and had determined to return with this party to Göttingen.

Among these students, there were two who are connected with certain adventures, which I propose to relate. These were Otto Von Rabenmark, and Hermann Leopold Caspar Bernard Adolph Ulrich Count Trump Von Toggenburg-Hohenstaufer.

Rabenmark was the "fox" (the slang term for a student in his first year) who had just been challenging the veteran student to drink. He was very young, even for a fox; for at the time I write of, he was not yet quite seventeen; but in precocity of character, in every respect, he went immeasurably beyond any person I have ever known. As to his figure, I certainly have seldom seen a more unprepossessing person at first sight, though on better acquaintance, after I had become warmly attached to him, I began to think him rather well-looking. He had coarse scrubby hair, of a mixed color, something between a red and a whity-brown. His face was peppered all over with freckles, and his eyes were colorless in the centre, and looked as if edged with red tape. An enormous scar, the relic of a recent duel, in which like a thorough fox, he was constantly engaged, extended from the tip of his nose to the edge of his right ear, and had been sewed up with fourteen stitches, every one of which (as the "Pauk Doctor" had been a botcher at his trade) was distinctly and grotesquely visible. As every one of the students present was tattooed and scarified in the same way, like so many New Zealand chiefs, his decoration of itself hardly excited attention; but as, to heighten the charms of his physiognomy, he had recently shaved off one of his eyebrows, his face certainly might lay claim to a bizarre and very unique character. His figure was slender, and not yet mature, but already of a tolerable height. His dress was in the extreme of the then Göttingen fashion. He wore a chaotic coat, without collar or buttons, and as destitute of color as of shape; enormously wide trowsers, and boots with iron heels and portentous spurs. His shirt-collar, unconscious of cravat, was doubled over his shoulders, and his hair hung down about his ears and neck. A faint attempt at moustachios, of an indefinite color, completed the equipment of his face, and a huge sabre strapped round his waist, that of his habiliments. As he wrote Von before his name, and was descended of a Bohemian family, who had been baronized before Charlemagne's time, he wore an enormous seal ring on his forefinger, with his armorial bearing. Such was Otto Von Rabenmark, a youth, who, in a more fortunate sphere, would have won himself name and fame. He was gifted with talents and acquirements immeasurably beyond his years. He spoke half a dozen languages—Heaven knows when he had picked them up—was an excellent classical scholar, and well read in history; played well on the violin and piano; and if not a dexterous was at least a desperate and daring swordsman. He was of undoubted courage, and a little of a renomist, (or swaggerer,) a defect which his extreme youth excused, and from which he very soon recovered.

GÖTTINGEN

[Uncas and Sansterre Lackland join the group of students and accompany them to Göttingen. Uncas's picture of that famous old university town follows.]

Göttingen is rather a well built and handsome looking town, with a decided look of the Middle Ages about it. Although the college is new, the town is ancient, and like the rest of the German university towns, has nothing external, with the exception of a plain-looking building in brick for the library, and one or two others for natural collections, to remind you that you are at the seat of an institution for education. The professors lecture, each on his own account, at his own house, of which the basement floor is generally made use of as an auditorium. The town is walled in, like most of the continental cities of that date, although the ramparts, planted with linden-trees, have since been converted into a pleasant promenade, which reaches quite round the town, and is furnished with a gate and guard at the end of each principal avenue. It is this careful fortification, combined with the nine-story houses, and the narrow streets, which imparts the compact, secure look peculiar to all the German towns. The effect is forcibly to remind you of the days when the inhabitants were huddled snugly together, like sheep in a sheepcote, and locked up safe from the wolfish attacks of the gentlemen highwaymen, the ruins of whose castles frown down from the neighboring hills.

The houses are generally tall and gaunt, consisting of a skeleton of framework, filled in with brick, with the original rafters, embrowned by time, projecting like ribs through the yellowish stucco, which covers the surface. They are full of little windows, which are filled with little panes, and as they are built to save room, one upon another, and consequently rise generally to eight or nine stories, the inhabitants invariably live as it were in layers. Hence it is not uncommon, to find a professor occupying the lower stories or strata, a tailor above the professor, a student upon the tailor, a beer seller conveniently upon the student, a washerwoman upon the beer-merchant, and perhaps a poet upon the top; a pyramid with a poet for its apex, and a professor for the base.

The solid and permanent look of all these edifices, in which, from the composite and varying style of architecture, you might read the history of half a dozen centuries in a single house, and which looked as if built before the memory of man, and like to last for ever, reminded me, by the association of contrast, of the straggling towns and villages of America, where the houses are wooden boxes, worn out and renewed every fifty years; where the cities seem only temporary encampments, and where, till people learn to build for the future as well as the present, there will be no history, except in pen and ink, of the changing centuries in the country.

As I passed up the street, I saw on the lower story of a sombre-looking house, the whole legend of Samson and Delilah rudely carved in the brown freestone, which formed the abutments of the house opposite; a fantastic sign over a portentous shop with an awning ostentatiously extended over the sidewalk,

announced the cafe and ice-shop: overhead, from the gutters
of each of the red-tiled roofs, were thrust into mid-air the grim
heads of dragons with long twisted necks, portentous teeth,
and goggle eyes, serving, as I learned the first rainy day, the
peaceful purpose of a water spout; while on the sidewalks, and
at every turn, I saw enough to convince me I was in an university
town, although there were none of the usual architectural indications. As we passed the old gothic church of St. Nicholas,
I observed through the open windows of the next house, a
party of students smoking, and playing billiards, and I recognized some of the faces of my Leipzig acquaintance. In the
street were plenty of others of all varieties. Some, with plain
caps and clothes, and a meek demeanor, sneaked quietly
through the streets, with portfolios under their arms. I observed the care with which they turned out to the left, and
avoided collision with every one they met. These were camels
"or studious students" returning from lecture—others swag-
gered along the sidewalk, turning out for no one, with clubs
in their hands, and bulldogs at their heels—these were dressed
in marvellously fine caps, and polonaise coats, covered with
cords and tassels, and invariably had pipes in their mouths,
and were fitted out with the proper allowance of spurs and
moustachios. These were "Renomists," who were always
ready for a row.

At almost every corner of the street was to be seen a solitary
individual of this latter class, in a ferocious fencing attitude,
brandishing his club in the air, and cutting quart and tierce in
the most alarming manner, till you were reminded of the truculent Gregory's advice to his companion; "Remember thy swash-
ing blow."

All along the street, I saw, on looking up, the heads and
shoulders of students projecting from every window. They
were arrayed in tawdry smoking caps, and heterogeneous-
looking dressing gowns with the long pipes and flash tassels
depending from their mouths. At his master's side, and looking
out of the same window, I observed, in many instances, a grave
and philosophical-looking poodle, with equally grim mousta-

chios, his head reposing contemplatively on his fore-paws, and engaged apparently, like his master, in ogling the ponderous housemaids who were drawing water from the street pumps.

BOOK II, CHAPTER IV

FOX RABENMARK

[One of the most interesting of Uncas's fellow-students at Göttingen is Fox Rabenmark. He illustrates the method employed in finding a pretext for fighting a duel, the most popular sport in the German university of those days.]

The next morning I lounged up the Weender Strasse. The day was fine, and the streets were thronged with more than the usual number of Students and Philistines. As I got near the end of the street, I saw one or two small boys, and half-a-dozen housemaids, looking with wonder at a strange figure, preceded by a strange dog, that was passing along the side walk.

On looking at him at first, at a short distance, I took him for a maniac, escaped from the lunatic asylum. He wore a cap embroidered in crimson and gold, shaped like a shaving-bason, and of the sort usually denominated beer-caps,* a dressing-gown of many colours, strapped tightly about his loins with a leathern girdle, in which were thrust two horse-pistols, and a long basket-hilted "schläger," or duelling-sword, and on his feet a pair of red Turkish slippers. His neck was open, and his legs bare from the ankle to the knees. In one hand he brandished an oaken cudgel, and in the other he held a small memorandum-book. He was preceded by a small dog of the comical breed called "Deckel," a kind of terrier, which considerably resembles the English turnspit. The individual one which now presented itself, was, like all its class, as ugly as a dog can well be. His body was very long, and his legs very short; his color was a mixture of black and a dirty red; his tail curled itself as gracefully as a pig's, his knees were bowed parenthetically outwards, and he turned out his toes like a country dancing-master. In order

* Cerevis-mütze. [*Motley's note.*]

to heighten the effects of these personal charms, his master
had tied a wreath of artificial flowers round his neck, and decorated his tail with fancy-colored ribbons.

Attired in this guise, the dog and his master proceeded gravely
down the street, apparently without heeding the laughter of the
admiring spectators. There seemed to be no students in the
immediate vicinity, and the Philistines were beneath his notice.
As I approached him, I observed something familiar in his
countenance, and, immediately afterwards, the singular individual caught me by the hand, and kissed me affectionately on
both cheeks. It was Rabenmark, my Leipzig acquaintance.
He invited me to accompany him to his rooms, and smoke a
pipe. I complied, and turned about with him; and we continued
our walk down the street. I was not sufficiently intimate with
him to expostulate with, or to interrogate him with regard to
the peculiar costume in which he had thought proper to array
himself, and I accordingly took his arm as gravely as if he had
been the burgomaster of the town, in his holiday suit. We
had not gone far, before I perceived a group of students approaching. I was curious to observe if he would treat their
animadversions with the same indifference as he had done those
of the town's-men. The terrier was about a rod in advance of
us, and on his passing the students, there was an universal
laugh. Rabenmark hastened toward them. They were four
stout fellows, in blue-and-silver caps, and on observing the
absurd appearance of my companion, they all began to laugh the
louder.

"What the devil are you laughing at?" said Rabenmark,
ferociously, with his arms a-kimbo; "I see nothing to laugh at!"

"I was laughing at your dog," said the first student.

"I was laughing at his master," said the second.

"And I—" "And I—" said the third and fourth.

"Have the kindness to tell me your names?" said Rabenmark
to the second, third, and fourth.

"Pott,"—"Kopp,"—"Fizzleberg," answered the three, con-
secutively.

"Your addresses?" continued Rabenmark.

The addresses were given, and Rabenmark wrote them all carefully down in his note-book.

"Now," said he, "allow me to observe, Messieurs Pott, Kopp, and Fizzleberg, that you are all three stupid boobies (dumme Jungen)!"

This epithet, "dumme Jungen," like the "drole," in French, is an insult, or a "touché," and requires a duel of twelve rounds (Gänge) to revenge it. There is, however, another insult, which is a grade beyond it, and which is about equivalent to the pleasing epithet, in English, of "infamous scoundrel." This may be retorted, and the consequence is a challenge of twenty-four "gangs," from the opposite party.

"*Your* name?" demanded the second student.

"Von Rabenmark," answered my companion.

"You are an infamous Hundsfott!" said Pott.

"You are an infamous Hundsfott!" said Kopp.

"You are an infamous Hundsfott!" said Fizzleberg.

"Very well, gentlemen," said Rabenmark: "very well, indeed: all perfectly in order.—You shall hear from me this afternoon, or tomorrow morning," and he politely touched his cap, as if it was the most agreeable thing in the world to be called an infamous Hundsfott.

"As for you, sir," continued Rabenmark, turning to the first student; "our quarrel is not so easily settled. I care not much for insult to myself, because I can defend myself: but an insult to my dog, to little Fritz, is cowardly; for Fritz, according to the 'Comment,' cannot resent the injury. Fritz, sir, as you perceive, bears the name of the immortal hero of Prussia, 'Frederick *the only*,'—a monarch for whom I have the most profound respect, and I request you instantly to apologise to Fritz."

The student laughed in his face.

"Your name?" said Rabenmark.

"Weissbier," said the student.

"Well, Mr. Weissbier, I request you instantly to repair with me to my apartment. Choose either of your three friends for your second; here is mine," said he, pointing to me; "and we will settle Fritz's quarrel with these instruments, at three paces, and no barrier," he concluded, touching his pistols.

Weissbier began to look serious.

"What a devil of a renomist," said Pott, shaking his head.

"Shocking!" said Kopp and Fizzleberg, shaking theirs.

"I shall accept no challenge," said Weissbier; "I do not feel myself bound thereto by any code of honor. I will fight you with sabres, without caps or duelling-breeches, if you choose. I will accept no other challenge."

"Ah, you are not fond of gunpowder. I am sorry you met Fritz this morning. He is, perhaps, foolishly strict on this point. I am not near so exacting myself; but Fritz is inexorable. I am sorry, sir, but I shall be obliged to post you publicly: you will be expelled from your club"; and Rabenmark was moving away.

"Stay—" said Weissbier, looking very pale and very foolish, "if there is no alternative—but how am I to apologise to your cursed dog?"

"Ah,—now you are beginning to be reasonable; and I shall be very happy to assist you in your endeavor to appease Fritz's wounded honor. You will readily understand that it would be of little consequence to apologise to him in words, because he would not understand you. There is, however, a very simple method. Fritz is fond of jumping—he is fond of a companion in his sports; and if you will have the kindness to afford him your company, his anger will be extinguished at once.—Here, Fritz—Fritz!" cried he, calling to the terrier.

The dog came to his whistle, and Rabenmark held his stick, a foot's distance from the ground.

"Hopp, hopp!" said Rabenmark, and the dog jumped over the stick.

"Now sir," he continued, "if you will have the kindness to place yourself on all fours, and jump over the stick in like manner, I pledge my honor to you that Fritz will be perfectly satisfied."

"Thousand Donner Wetter!" roared Mr. Weissbier, in a rage, "what upon earth do you take me for, Mr. Von Rabenmark?"

"A coward, sir—only a coward! If you are willing, however, to prove I am mistaken, I shall be very happy to show you the way to my rooms; but really I must request you to hasten your decision, for time presses, and I have many things to attend to."

I believe that Weissbier thought he had really got hold of the devil. He had become very pale, and his teeth began to chatter.

"In the name of God, is there no way of getting out of this infernal scrape?" said he, looking round in despair.

His companions turned their backs upon him.

"Well—well, I cannot have my brains blown out for this miserable dog. Hold out your stick, Mr. Von Rabenmark, if it be Heaven's will."

So Mr. Von Rabenmark, as it was Heaven's will, held out his stick—down plumped the miserable Weissbier on his hands and knees.

"Hopp—hopp!" said Rabenmark,—over jumped the detected bully—and, jumping up again, fled rapidly up a narrow lane.

"Good morning, Mr. Weissbier," said Rabenmark:—"good morning, Messieurs Kopp, Pott, and Fizzleberg. You shall hear from me this afternoon"; and so saying, he gravely continued his promenade.

BOOK II, CHAPTER XXI

THE COUNTER PLOT

[Morton and Lackland assist their friends, Count Trump von Toggenburg and Pappenheim, in an unsuccessful attempt at elopement. Rabenmark kills his opponent in a duel, and secretly marries Bertha Wallenstein at the cottage of Skamp, a rogue of many illegal occupations. When Rabenmark flees the town to escape the police, he is accompanied by Morton, Lackland, Trump, and others.]

A week or two had passed since the events recorded in the last chapter. I now found myself established in a cavern in one of the most savage and secluded forests of the Hartz.

Rabenmark, Pappenheim, Trump von Toggenburg, Lackland, and myself, with a score or two of others, whom we had persuaded to be our companions, had made our escape from Göttingen. We had more or less violated the laws—we were all reckless and dissipated young men. All were panting for an unrestrained and lawless existence. It is exactly under such circumstances, and by such wild spirits, that a band of outlaws was not unfrequently formed in these regions. Our pioneer and principal captain was the versatile Skamp. It was not the first time that he had exercised the profession to which we now devoted ourselves. As for Pappenheim and Trump, they had both been reduced to despair by the frustration of their plans on the occasion which I have recorded, and by a rather serious quarrel which their subsequent dissolute conduct had occasioned between themselves and their mistresses.

Rabenmark had remained a day or two concealed in the town, at the imminent risk of his life. Although he had on one or two occasions miraculously escaped discovery, yet it was impossible for him to hope for such success any longer. It was necessary to separate for a time from Bertha. She was left to take the important step she had so long meditated. She returned to her father. Rabenmark hovered for a few days in the suburbs of the town. He heard nothing from her.

At last he reluctantly submitted to the solicitations of Pappenheim and myself, and together we all retired to the Hartz mountains. Very soon after this we made an incursion into a neighboring village for the necessaries of life. We had no money to buy, and so we committed depredations. It was found such capital sport, that we commenced hostilities on all the villages for miles round. I have no intention to dilate upon adventures, which, although true, are of a hackneyed description. Suffice, that we went from one indiscretion to another. From nightly forays against granaries and farmhouses, we proceeded to direct attacks upon passengers on the road. In a word, we became robbers. It is true, that we were faithful to the creed of all romantic highwaymen. We only robbed the rich, that we might give unto the poor. It was our chief delight to surround a parcel of peasants and poor devils, and take them off with many threats to our retreat; after which, we would present them with the total spoils of some rich hunks whom we had rifled the day before, and send them away rejoicing. We most certainly never earned a groschen by our fatiguing and hazardous profession. We were only footpads for fun. I will not, however, vouch for Skamp. He was too much of a man of business to be contented long as an amateur; but it was, of course, impossible for us to be rid of him, and he was allowed to follow his own course.

It was customary for some of us to penetrate, in disguise, into the very heart of the villages which had been the scene of our rogueries. It was amusing to join in the conversation of the peasants, and be entertained by the exaggerated accounts of our own achievements. On one occasion, Rabenmark and I had advanced far beyond the usual limit of such masquerading excursions. We were so successful, that we resolved, in spite of every thing, to effect a journey to Göttingen. He hoped to have an interview with Bertha, and thus to relieve the anguish in his mind. After a little dissuasion, I found that his purpose was not to be shaken. I agreed to accompany him. Lackland was to be associated in the enterprise.

We reached Göttingen in a few days, without much difficulty. We were all disguised as peasants. We entered an obscure pot-house on the outskirts of the town. A long deal table was in the middle of the dirty-looking public room. A number of persons were seated at it. Some were drinking schnapps; some were eating an offensive kind of cheese, much beloved by the lower classes; some were smoking a filthy sort of tobacco; some were drinking beer.

We seated ourselves, and ordered portions of the villanous cheese, beer, and tobacco. We entered into conversation with the worthies who were assembled there. I recognised several of the faces. The town-crier was present. A barber's boy asked him the contents of a paper he had with him. The crier opened, and read it in a pompous voice. It was a proclamation describing the person of the Baron Otto von Rabenmark, and offering a thousand rix-dollars for his apprehension. It was signed "Wallenstein." The fox turned pale for a moment, but recovering himself suddenly, he began a colloquy with his next neighbor. It was the postillion Schnobb. Little by little, Rabenmark led him on to a description of the Robbery on Baron Poodleberg's carriage. Schnobb congratulated himself that he had been indisposed on that occasion, and that another postillion had been substituted for him.

"By whom do you think the robbery was committed?" asked Rabenmark.

"Who knows?" said Schnobb. "Perhaps by the same devil that dwells now up there in the Hartz."

"What devil?"

"Sacrament! have you not heard of the fiend of the Hartz? He has appeared in the mountains after an absence of fifty years. The cottages of the peasants, and the castles of the nobles, are all pillaged by him."

"Then the story that a gang of robbers had taken up their abode in those regions, is not true?"

"Donnerwetter,—no! I tell you it is by the Hartz devil. He has a tail more than seven yards long, and lives on the top of the Brocken."

"Truly an interesting personage. Has any one seen him?"

"Yes; there is a friend of mine who has been making a peddling expedition to Gosslar; he was met by this devil. He was, however, a religious man, and held a crucifix towards him. The devil uttered a yell, and disappeared into the earth."

"Who is your friend?"

"There he is; he is just coming into the room. It is Mr. Skamp, the coffin-maker."

All three of us gave an involuntary start. Luckily it was not observed by any of the company. We directed our eyes to the door, and the coffin-maker stood indeed before us.

He walked into the room with the utmost coolness. He had a pack on his back, and a staff in his hand.

He saluted the company, with most of whom he seemed familiarly acquainted; nodded carelessly to us, and then very quietly opened his pack, and exposed his wares to the company.

"Here, Schnobb," said he, "here is a silver mouthpiece for your bugle. I bought it for you on purpose; the price is two gulden. Buy it; the elector will never give you one for your skill in melody."

"Here, Gottlob," he continued, to the red-headed son of the executioner; "here is a pair of braces to tie up your breeches, when you get a pair; and here is a silver buckle which I bought as a present for your father. Here is a tin trumpet for you, Mr. Crier; and here is a paper of pins that your wife told you to buy for her at the fair, Mr. Farmer."

With these last words, he tossed a package to Rabenmark, which his quick eye instantly told him was a letter.

"The price is six groschen," said he.

The fox adroitly haggled a moment about the price. He at last paid him five groschen. Soon afterwards he slipped out of the room, whispering to us that he would soon return.

In the meantime, after Skamp had disposed of most of his merchandise, he entered into conversation with the postillion.

"Well, brother-in-law!" said he, "you have not thanked me for my company on a certain evening last month. But for me on that occasion, you would have been indubitably eaten up by that Hartz devil. It was he, I have since discovered, who made the attack on Poodleberg's carriage. God alone knows what has become of the unfortunate postillions who drove that carriage!" said Skamp, piously lifting his hands and eyes to heaven.

Lackland and I left the room; we made a sign to Skamp, and in about half an hour he joined us. It was dusk. We all walked together, and conferred. We took care, however, to keep in the neighborhood of the tavern, that we might meet Rabenmark.

"In the name of wonder, old Skamp," said Lackland, "how the devil came you here?"

"Why, your excellency, when I found that three of my most promising disciples had engaged in so hazardous an expedition, it behoved me to be watchful, and to keep them, if possible, out of the danger into which their youth and inexperience might hurry them. I instantly assumed this disguise that I might follow you and protect you. Oh my dear children! (if your excellencies will permit me the endearing expression) you have no conception of the agitation of mind into which I was thrown. Unmindful of all dangers, I determined to watch over you as a hen over an infant brood."

"But are you not afraid of discovery?" I asked.

"Lord bless you! no. Now that I am here, I affect no disguise; every body here knows, and, I may add, respects pious Skamp the coffin-maker."

"Yes; but I have heard people speak disparagingly of a certain 'Crooked Skamp the smuggler,' and 'poaching Skamp,' and a gentleman who bears a variety of other nicknames. Is he no relation of yours?" I asked.

"Oh your excellency!" said the rogue, with a grin, "I cannot deny that I have heard of such a person, and that I take a deep interest in his welfare. But, jesting apart, I assure you I am in no sort of danger; they would as soon suspect Count Wallenstein of a share in a conspiracy as me."

"Apropos of Count Wallenstein! what has become of the fox?" said Lackland.

"Happier than any of us, I suspect," said the smuggler.

"On arriving here, I was happy enough, by the merest accident, to convey a letter from the Baron Rabenmark to the Countess Bertha. He entrusted me with it some days ago, and I promised to use all exertions to get it to her as soon as possible. I did not think, then, that I should take it to this town in person. I found this afternoon a washerwoman who was going to the Commandant's house with a basket. She was an old gossip of mine. I gave her the letter. It was not a very sentimental method; but it proved a very efficient one, as I gave Baron Rabenmark an answer just now. But enough of this at present. Now give me all your attention. I have just formed a plan which shall be both pleasant and profitable. You know, Mr. Lackland, and I dare say you too, Mr. Morton, that I have been engaged with the Jew Potiphar in certain mercantile transactions. These were of a character which the law unfortunately does not look upon with the same indulgence that I do. I have always observed that legislators have very contracted views of life. Suffice, that if these doings of ours were revealed, and Mein Herr Potiphar brought to trial, he would suffer a certain imprisonment, to say nothing of a confiscation of the greater part of his immense property, which, of course, he would do any thing to save. I owe old Potiphar a grudge. I am, besides, particularly incensed against him for his appearance at Wolfenbüttel so inopportunely. No matter, I shall yet have my revenge. I shall also have the pleasure of serving most effectually Count Trump von Toggenburg, in whom I take a great interest. There is, in fact, no one of my protégés in whose welfare I am more interested than in his. I have no doubt also, that if the plan, which I am about to mention to you, succeeds, he will reward me liberally. Count Trump von Toggenburg is a generous young nobleman. Now the matter I have in hand, is this: I have just heard that Potiphar is to set out the day after tomorrow night, alone, on a journey to Hamburg. As he wishes to visit a relation in Gosslar, he must pass directly through the Hartz. His carriage must pass within a dozen miles of our retreat. We will be prepared. We will attack him. We will drag him up into our retreat. We will threaten him with disclosures of his doings, and we will be so minute, that he shall be frightened, although we will take good care to keep ourselves disguised. We will thus force him to sign a paper, giving his consent to Count von Trump's marriage with his daughter. The Count shall receive this paper, and hasten to his sweetheart. After that, perhaps I may induce the old gentleman to confer a small gratuity upon me."

The virtuous coffin-maker concluded. Lackland and I assured him that we gave him all due credit for his ingenuity, and would do our best to serve Trump's interest and his own.

To do this effectually, however, it was necessary to hasten our departure for our retreat. Rabenmark had not yet returned. What were we to do? After waiting as long as was prudent,

we at last followed the advice of Skamp. He represented to us
that we could do nothing for Rabenmark; that our waiting only
endangered ourselves, without assisting him, and that the best
thing we had to do, was to beat a retreat as soon as possible.
He promised for his own part, to wait for Rabenmark, and to
meet us all at the cavern in three days.

We were convinced by his reasoning, shook hands with him,
and departed.

[Rabenmark rejoins the band of amateur outlaws, and the
attack on Potiphar's carriage is successfully concluded. Rabenmark returns to Göttingen, hoping to rejoin his young wife;
instead, he kills Count Wallenstein in a duel, is tried for murder,
and sentenced to death. In the courtroom he melodramatically
kills Commandant Wallenstein and then commits suicide by
taking poison.

Book III, after a lapse of six years (1777), finds Uncas Morton
at Prague, a very serious student of the natural sciences.

In Book IV he has an affair with an eighteen-year-old opera
singer who, when he tires of her, attempts to kill him. A letter
from his father informs Uncas that the latter has inherited the
fortune of his Uncle Joshua and begs him to return to America
and fight for her freedom.

Book V finds Uncas back in America, where he organizes
and equips a regiment of volunteers at his own expense. He
meets Colonel Waldron and a young Captain Eliot, who hands
him a bulky letter one evening just before they part for the
night. This letter (which occupies seven chapters in the text
of the novel) details the earlier adventures of Uncas' father,
who has been known on the frontier under the name of Patanko
Morris. At one time Patanko was captured by a tribe of
Canadian Indians whose chief, White-cat, took a liking to the
prisoner and tried to induce him to join the tribe. Patanko's
account of his escape from White-cat follows.]

BOOK V, CHAPTER VII

THE ADVENTURES OF PATANKO[1]

"Having now satisfactorily accomplished this corollary to his grand undertaking, White-cat determined to make up for lost time. By dint of forced marches, we soon reached the upper part of the great Connecticut valley, and were soon joined by two or three of the other detachments.

"The work of destruction now commenced. The atrocities practised upon their Indian brethren, of which I have already given a sketch, were trivial in comparison with the butcheries to which the New England provinces were now exposed.

"Village after village was attacked—the houses burned, and the inhabitants massacred.

"During the continuance of the whole expedition, I was compelled to be a spectator of the miseries of my countrymen. I was led by a rope fastened around my neck; while my arms were pinioned by another.

"Fortunately for the English, there had been latterly some defalcation on the part of the Southern allies of the Canadian Indians. Repeated quarrels had taken place, and threats had passed so often between the different tribes who were united in this expedition, that it was more than probable that their arms would soon be turned against each other.

"In consequence of this, White-cat called a council of the chiefs upon whom he could most depend; and it having been decided that it was dangerous to proceed any farther at present, he resolved that the village of T——, from which we were then ten miles distant, should be the extreme point of their expedition.

---

[1] The adventures of Patanko, recorded in a letter which occupies Chapters III–IX of Book Five, are, in the main, antecedent to the opening of the story proper, which is the account of Uncas Morton's adventures. The awkward device by which this episode is introduced into the story is only one of many bits of evidence which betray the author's inability to handle plot. The employment of the Indian and of the backwoodsman reflects Motley's early familiarity with Cooper's novels.

"Accordingly the destruction of the devoted village was resolved upon, as the finale to the whole business.

"It was decided that as soon as they had accomplished it, they would immediately retrace their steps, and return to their own habitations.

"We assaulted the village about noon in five strong parties, and at five points.

"The inhabitants assembled at the sound of the terrific Indian yell, and a desperate resistance was made.

"The party which was headed by White-cat, fought its way up the principal street of the place, and the ground was covered with the mangled bodies of the victims.

"Their numbers were so inconsiderable in comparison with ours, that they were soon obliged to yield. The work of plunder and of massacre now succeeded.

"Old White-cat who was the most whimsical of Indians, had throughout the expedition, insisted upon my remaining continually at his side. I was, he facetiously observed, an exceedingly useful aid-de-camp, and as my labors were lightened by the two Indians who held me by the ropes, it was hardly possible that I could be much fatigued. All this I received as indisputable; and I believed that the old scoundrel, from some unnatural freak, had in reality conceived an affection for me, and I began to think it possible eventually to escape with life.

"The whites had now nearly all surrendered. A feeble firing was kept up from windows of a single house at a distant corner of the village, but as White-cat had despatched a half-dozen warriors to reduce the occupants to submission, he troubled himself no more about the matter.

"I observed that the Indians had one and all a passion for masquerading. Upon this occasion, as soon as their more truculent appetites were satisfied, I saw a large number of them disappear into some of the houses.

"Presently afterwards they reappeared, having decked themselves out in the most preposterous manner.

"Some wore white hats; and some woolen night-caps; some had endued themselves in bombazine petticoats, and several of them strutted about decked in the finery of old militia uniforms. Six of them had rigged themselves out in flannel shirts and bandanna handkerchiefs of the favorite scarlet color, and now marched gravely forward, beating time upon an iron kettle; while one tall fellow with a woman's bonnet on his head, a ponderous pair of boots upon his legs, and otherwise in complete nudity, capered about with much agility, and excited universal admiration.

"Captain White-cat looked upon these playful warriors, and grunted from time to time with great satisfaction. While he was thus employed, one of the principal inhabitants of the village, and its earliest settler, was brought before him. He had been taken captive after having destroyed four Indians with his own hand—he was well aware of his fate—but when he was confronted with Wahquimacutt who was endeavoring to assume a commanding demeanor, he regarded him with an expression of perfect indifference and contempt.

"The old hypocrite advanced towards him, and seized him by both hands, which he shook heartily.

"'I salute thee, my brother!' said he; 'Am I not your uncle and your brother?'

"With this he commanded two of his adherents to hold the prisoner fast, and then, without more ado, he stripped his shirt from his back, and his boots from his legs, and proceeded to array himself therein.

"When he had completed his toilet, he knocked the captive's brains out, without farther ceremony; and then making an incision in his breast, scooped out a handful of blood, and drank it off with much relish.

"'I am a great man!' said the old braggadocio, turning to me; 'I am the son of the Great Spirit. I drink the heart's blood of my foes, and it makes me fat.'

"Having finished this pretty speech, he strutted up and down the street for a few minutes, and then ordered a council of his most eminent warriors.

"This he informed me, was his 'general court,' (a term which he had learned in his intercourse with the white men,) and assured me that the wisdom of its deliberations was unequalled in the world.

"Accordingly the bare-legged legislators squatted themselves on their hams before the council fire, and began smoking and grunting with admirable solemnity.

"While they were thus employed, the deputation which had been sent against the still-resisting party above-mentioned, returned with their prisoners. The house had been demolished, and its garrison, consisting of two white men and an aged negro, were now placed before the conclave.

"Although the assembly were deliberating upon other and weighty matters, yet White-cat requested them to assist him with their advice concerning the disposal of these prisoners.

"A great many violent speeches were accordingly made; but as they could arrive at no conclusion, it was determined to defer the matter till the next day. The prisoners were placed in strict confinement, and left for the present in ignorance of their fate.

"The next morning the prisoners requested to know, if possible, the punishment that was to be awarded to them; they were informed that Wahquimacutt intended to give a grand entertainment that afternoon, and that their fate would be then decided.

"In the afternoon, accordingly, a very solemn council was again assembled; the prisoners were made to sit upon the ground in the centre of the circle, and the proceedings were conducted in a business-like manner.

"They were of course condemned to immediate death, and three or four set immediately about the execution.

"Their clothes were torn from their bodies and thrown into the fire; stakes were then driven into the ground, to which they were secured.

"A number of the savages then proceeded to draw a circle around them, which they fancifully decorated with flowers.

"A couple of conjurors then commenced a series of ridiculous antics, which were supposed to give an additional solemnity to the scene.

"As soon as this was finished, all the Indians present, sachems, counsellors, spectators, and all, commenced dancing and jumping violently to the music of two drums, beaten by a couple of half-breeds, who composed the band of the tribe.

"When this was over, three individuals, painted and adorned in a fantastic and terrible manner, and who I found were the executioners, now brought the brushwood, and other combustible materials, and kindled a fire around the stakes. The captives were burned; and the next day the Indians commenced their retreat.

"After we had been two days on our homeward march, Wahquimacutt summoned me to his presence. He told me that I had now had sufficient opportunity to become acquainted with his merits, and requested my consent to join his tribe.

"I replied in the negative. He then told me the only alternative was death. I assured him that I expected it, and that I was wearied and disgusted with my life; that death was the greatest favor he could bestow upon me, and the sooner he set about it the better.

"I suppose it was the constant contempt with which I treated him that excited the liking to which I have referred. It was evident that he was unwilling to order my execution, and that he was anxious to secure me to his person.

"He seemed, however, decided on this occasion, and bade me prepare for death on the following day. I lay awake the whole night, devising means of escape. Early the next morning our march was resumed.

"Very fortunately the company were a good deal dispersed in search of game, and my two faithful guardians and myself were left considerably behind.

"During the night I had contrived to free one of my hands from the noose which confined them, although the manner in which the savages had attached themselves to my person while asleep, prevented me from profiting by that circumstance to make my escape.

"About nine in the morning our course lay across a deep and rapid brook. As soon as my companions reached its edge they both stooped down to drink.

"In the twinkling of an eye I seized the lucky moment, sprang upon the nearest like a tiger, succeeded in wresting his knife from its sheath, and drove it through his heart.

"The other had slipped into the water, but he rose and grappled with me. The contest was for life; but I was the stronger of the two. We were now in the centre of the stream, and the water reached to our waists. With a desperate effort I threw him down, and succeeded in holding him under the water. In a few seconds his struggles grew fainter and fainter—they ceased. I possessed myself of his knife, and the gun which was lying on the bank.

"I was now free from my immediate keepers, but surrounded by my enemies.

"The morning was foggy, and I was entirely uncertain of the direction which the savages had taken, and was entirely ignorant of the points of the compass.

"It seemed to me therefore that my wisest course was to conceal myself, if possible, in the neighborhood of this very place.

"It was probable that the Indians would proceed on their day's journey in the same irregular manner in which they had commenced, and that consequently my escape would not be discovered before the evening.

"In this way, the Indians would have probably proceeded thirty or forty miles beyond my present position; and that distance being once placed between us, it would not be difficult for me to profit by the night, and eventually to effect my escape.

"On the contrary, if I endeavored to make my way through the mist which prevented me from discovering any object at a rod's distance, it was highly probable that I should stumble upon some of my enemies before I had advanced a quarter of a mile.

"I selected, therefore, a pile of drift wood, which the force of the water had heaped up in a marshy angle of the brook. Under this cover I contrived to secrete myself and my gun so completely that it was not likely that I should accidentally be discovered, and I trusted that not being missed I should probably not become the object of a direct search.

"I lay snug in my hiding-place for nearly an hour, during which time I had the satisfaction of hearing the voices of my enemies, the crack of their rifles, and their imitations of the different cries of the game which they were pursuing with hardly a moment's cessation.

"At last the cries seemed to grow fainter, the shots became less frequent, and I began to console myself with the belief that they had at last proceeded on their journey.

"I felt comparatively so tranquil, and had been so much exhausted with excitement, and with my watching the whole of the previous night, that I was already sinking into a doze.

"Hardly, however, were my eyes closed, than I was startled by the shrill whoop of a savage, which sounded within a yard of my ear.

"I felt certain that I was discovered, and that this was a yell of exultation at my discovery. I grasped my knife and determined to sell my life as dearly as possible.

"Still, however, I lay motionless in my hiding-place.

"In a few moments the whoop was repeated, still more savagely than before. A pause—and then it was answered by the faint halloos of several others in the distance. The cries grew stronger—the voices sounded nearer—and in a few moments, a wild and unearthly shriek—a yell from many voices—rose directly above the place where I lay.

"My blood curdled—my fate was evidently sealed; and death, which I had been for many days expecting with composure, seemed doubly bitter, now that I had a glimpse of freedom.

"It was unaccountable why I had not been immediately dragged from my hiding-place, for now several minutes had slipped since I had first heard the yell of the savages.

"There was a chink in the pile of wood which concealed me. I contrived stealthily to change my position, and to look out.

"I saw, with a feeling of relief, that I had not been discovered. The first savage had discovered the bodies of my victims, whom the current had washed ashore not far from my hiding-place, and had given the alarm to his companions. There were now nearly a dozen of them collected around the bodies, yelling, chattering, gesticulating, and testifying by their voices and gestures their rage and astonishment.

"I lay in an agony of suspense. It seemed impossible that I could now escape. Although my lurking-place was not yet discovered, yet it seemed impossible that it could remain so long.

"After indulging themselves in a few more howls of mingled anger and lamentations, they commenced their search.

"They shook the trees—beat the bushes—traversed the place in all directions. I heard their voices distinctly, and several of them were often so near me that I could have touched them.

"At last one of them observed that it was probable I had already advanced a little way, and proposed searching for me farther off.

"A ray of hope gleamed through my heart. The savages seemed to assent to the proposition. One of them, however, before departing took up a stick from the pile which concealed me, and began scattering the heap. Presently, another followed his example, and of course I gave up myself for lost.

"They pitched off and threw away half a dozen bits of wood, and during the process, they touched me repeatedly. The morning, however, was so misty, and the color of my garments was so similar to that of the bark of the wood, that I remained without discovery.

"After a short time they uttered an exclamation or two of disappointment, and then apparently gave over their search.

"With a beating heart I listened to their retreating footsteps.

"At last all was quiet."

[Patanko falls in with a band of friendly Mohawks, joins the tribe, and marries the chief's daughter. Later their son Uncas is seized by White-cat and delivered to Joshua Morton, who adopts the child. Their daughter Neida likewise is kidnapped, presumably also by White-cat. At the outbreak of the Revolutionary War, Patanko enlists a band of Indians to fight on the side of the colonists, is commissioned Colonel Waldron, and uses the letter narrating his life story as a means of introducing himself to his son. Uncas is overjoyed at the reunion.

In the engagement with the British troops at Saratoga, Uncas and Captain Eliot (who proves to be Mayflower Vane) are made prisoners. The nurse who dresses Uncas' wounds is none other than his long-lost sister, Neida. These three escape to the American lines, where one of the prisoners of war is Captain Sansterre Lackland, who promptly falls in love with Neida. They all go to Morton's Hope, where Uncas marries Mayflower and Lackland marries Neida.]

From MERRY–MOUNT[1]

A Romance of the Massachusetts Colony

A RESCUE IN THE FOREST

[Thomas Morton, an educated man of some classical attainment, is in 1628 lord of Merry-Mount, refuge for straggling survivors of a number of early unsuccessful trading posts in New England, and a thorn in the side of the Puritans at Plymouth, who object to the unholy mode of life tolerated at Merry-Mount. Sir Christopher Gardiner, who is scheming to establish a colony on the Gorges patent and eventually to become the governor of Massachusetts, moves freely in both communities, known at Plymouth as a saintly Puritan but at Merry-Mount as a worldly plotter. Walter Ludlow and his sister Esther, both devout Puritans, live at Naumkeak. Esther has left behind her in England a lover, Henry Maudsley, whom she pretends to scorn as a worldling.]

Esther sat musing long and deeply upon the rustic seat, formed upon the stump of a gigantic oak, where she had been conversing with her brother. It seemed a strange effect of destiny, that so beautiful a creature, well born, accomplished, and gifted with higher and stronger intellectual powers than often falls to the lot of woman, should thus be seated musing alone in that wild forest. Esther was beautiful. Her features, although distinguished by an extreme purity of outline, possessed great mobility and variety of expression; her fair hair was

---

[1] Motley's second novel was probably completed as early as 1846, but it did not appear in print until 1849. It received much more favorable critical notice than had its predecessor (*Morton's Hope*), and deservedly so, but it was not a very successful novel. It served to demonstrate once more that Motley had no great skill in plot manipulation or the delineation of imaginary character; but at the same time it showed his increasing power in the depiction of scenes, the re-creation of historic characters, and the rapid narration of actual events. For discussion, see pp. xvii–xviii, xxv–xxvii.

smoothed placidly from a forehead, which, as in all classic faces, was rather low, but of madonna-like breadth and pensiveness; her eyes were long and full, and thoughtful rather than passionate. Her sad-colored garments, of the unadorned simplicity affected by the Puritan women of England, were not unbecoming to a figure slightly exceeding middle height, and possessing the robust, healthful, but eminently feminine development characteristic of English beauty, and heightened her resemblance to those types of virgin grace and purity, the early madonnas, painted by Raphael, while something of Perrugino's severity still lingered around his pencil.

Wearied with her solitary reflections, she at last arose and wandered through the open glade which stretched from the edge of the pine forest near their residence, and was ornamented with magnificent oaks of many a century's growth, and covered with strong coarse grass, springing in wild luxuriance from the virgin soil. She amused herself with gathering a few violets, almost buried in the rank verdure, and sighed as she compared their almost scentless petals with the delicious fragrance of their sister flowers at home.

The oaks which studded the waving sea of turf around her, brought to her remembrance the bosky parks and ancestral trees of England, and the early birds of spring, filling the air with their clamorous melody, as they darted from the ground, or made the leafless spray vocal with their love songs, soothed her thoughts, and bore them far away to softer and fondly remembered scenes.

She had wandered insensibly farther from her palisaded home than she intended, and was approaching a thickly wooded and swampy forest of maples and birches, in which the glade was terminated, when she was suddenly startled from her reverie, by a low, suppressed noise, which strangely resembled the angry growling of a dog. What was her horror upon looking up, to behold a large wolf upon the verge of the thicket, standing motionless with eyes glaring full upon her, twenty paces from the spot where she stood.

The animal was as large as the largest sized dog, and might

have been mistaken for one, but for his small erect ears, pointed snout, and long bushy tail, resembling that of a fox. Grisly grey in color, broad breasted, lean paunched, with yellow green eyes flashing savage fire upon her, he sat upon his haunches, motionless, as if carved in stone, and fascinating the lonely girl by his fixed and terrible stare.

The American wolf is a ferocious, but comparatively a cowardly animal, and except impelled by famine is slow to attack the human race. The winter had, however, been long and stern, and these savage creatures had often hunted in droves about the neighborhood, preying upon the few domestic animals, which the planters had brought with them, and filling the air at midnight with their howlings. Esther was aware that the courageous men, who inhabited that lonely wilderness, were accustomed to encounter these brutes, single-handed, without fear, and she had often been told that the animal would shrink like a whipped cur from the attack of man. But thus, solitary, and far from help, to be confronted with a ferocious beast of the forest, was a fearful thing for a maiden nurtured all her life in the security of a civilized land. Frozen almost to a statue with terror, with marble cheek, rigid lips, suppressed breath, and eyes almost starting from their sockets, she instinctively, and as if impelled by an irresistible fascination, gazed full into the eyes of her ferocious antagonist. The lion is fabled to crouch submissively at a virgin's feet, but the wolf who cowers before the strong man was never thought to be generous to the helpless. Was it then the mysterious power of the human eye, which seemed to exert its subtle and unfathomable influence upon that compact mass of savage sinew, bone, and muscle, subjugating the will which they should have instinctively obeyed, and checking the wild impulse which would have driven the brute, with one savage bound, upon its prey? Could it be fear that kept the monster motionless, crouching, but glaring still with those eyeballs of fire? Was it all real, or was her fearful foe but a phantom of her heated imagination?

Her brain reeled, the vast and leafless oaks seemed to whirl and dance around her; the mighty forest, swaying before the rising wind, seemed to rush through the air, sweeping and shifting from earth to heaven, as in the mad and bewildering changes of a dream. The incessant and shrill notes of a thousand singing birds thrilled in her ears like the warning cry of invisible spirits. Everything seemed to move and change around her; there was a rushing in her ears, as of a mighty wind, and then all seemed growing black as a funeral pall. She roused herself from the swoon which she felt was coming over her. It was no dream, the woods had ceased to move, save to the gentle impulse of the morning breeze; she was alone in the wilderness, and there stood the gaunt wolf, with his glittering teeth and fearful stare, motionless and threatening as before.

She roused herself at last, and became perfectly calm. She reflected that the beast who shrunk from the conflict with a man, might even cower before the attack of a determined woman.

She had a slight branch in her hand, which she had accidentally picked from the ground in her walk—a dried, leafless, last year's shoot, feeble as a rush, and held in the weak hand of a woman. But she had aroused her spirit now; her heart throbbed high with excitement, and the blood which had been chilled bounded like impetuous fire through her veins. She advanced a step forward, brandishing the weapon above her head, with her eyes flashing full upon her adversary. The wolf sprang to his feet, glared fixedly upon her, but stood motionless as before. He seemed irresolute, whether to advance upon his antagonist, or to retreat into the forest. She moved a step nearer, her nerves quivering with strange excitement. It was a contest not of strength, but of nerve; not of muscle, but of spirit. Her foe remained motionless upon his feet. She advanced another step. She was near enough to hear his suppressed breathing. Another, and the wolf with a furious glare opened his armed jaws, and uttered a long, dismal howl, which resounded fearfully through the forest, and struck renewed terror to the heart of the unprotected girl.

She paused again, as if paralyzed, and stood unable to advance or to retreat, within ten yards of the ferocious brute who remained still glaring, and motionless, but seeming less in-

timidated than enraged. Esther's strength began to fail her—
her prayers froze upon her lips—her eyes grew dim—but, even
as they glazed, she saw the wolf springing towards her. Suddenly the bushes of a remote thicket cracked beneath an
advancing step; the report of a firearm rang through the wood,
and the furious beast, bounding high in air, fell stone dead at
her feet.

Exhausted by emotion, overwhelmed by the sudden change
from imminent and fearful death, to life and safety again,
Esther sank insensible upon the ground. The hunter, to whose
sure but distant aim her preservation was owing, struggled
slowly through the tangled and swampy thicket through which
he had plunged to her rescue, when suddenly a tall form, in a
short, dark cloak, and steeple-crowned hat, strode down the
glade from the opposite quarter, lifted the unconscious maiden
in his arms, and bore her towards her residence. That man
was Sir Christopher Gardiner.

A moment afterwards, a young man, in hunting attire,
emerged breathless from the thicket, and stood upon the spot
where Esther Ludlow had for a few moments endured such
speechless agony, and where, but for his prompt assistance, she
must have died a fearful death.

The youth was tall and slender, but active and muscular.
His chestnut lovelocks, long enough to distract the whole
congregation at Plymouth, his clear, hazel eye, and regular features, proclaimed his Anglo-Saxon blood, which his bronzed
cheek and wild attire might have almost rendered doubtful.

Esther was gone, and there was nothing upon the sward
save the bleeding carcass of the wolf. The hunter spurned it
contemptuously with his foot, and then leaned, lost in thought,
upon his fowling-piece.

MAY–DAY AT MERRY–MOUNT

[Henry Maudsley, recently arrived in America, had fired
the shot which saved Esther Ludlow's life but was ignorant
of the fact that it was Esther. While a guest of Morton at

Merry-Mount, he chances to befriend a Puritan messenger carrying dispatches to Esther and offers to deliver the letters himself. Failing to persuade her to give up her "bigoted" religion, he warns her against the wiles of Gardiner. Not long afterward, he erroneously supposes that the knight has gained some favor with Esther and, overcome by jealousy, determines to attack Gardiner but is prevented by a mysterious youth (Jaspar, supposed cousin of Gardiner). Maudsley is a disapproving spectator at the May-day revels at Merry-Mount, which begin on April 30th and continue through the next day.]

In a few moments the whole wild crew, who had passed the night in the forest, had entered upon the open field, and after a short pause formed a procession and moved slowly towards the mount. They were bringing home the May-pole, which was a vast pine nearly a hundred feet in length. The tree had been stripped of its bark and branches, ornamented with garlands of wintergreen and forest-tree blossoms, and placed upon rudely constructed wheels. In place of oxen, some fifty savages were yoked together, each wearing May garlands upon their swarthy brows, and evidently taking a grave satisfaction in thus assisting at a solemn ceremony, which Bootefish had assured them was an initiatory step towards their conversion from paganism, and which was sure to require copious besprinklings of the strong water, which they worshipped as the white man's God.

Thus harnessed, the savages drew the mighty May-pole slowly along, with the Lord of Merry-Mount seated upon it in solemn state. The rest of the company thronged around him in his triumphal progress, marching in unison to the braying of trumpets and the thump of drums, whose rude music sounded strangely among those ancient woods. After a time, and with great efforts, the May-pole was at last brought to the top of the Merry-Mount, where, after a pair of elk antlers had been fastened to its top, and the red cross banner of England, with a variety of other pennons, added to its other decorations, it was triumphantly erected upon the summit. Many shouts of congratulation now rent the air, and then the company, a little wearied with their exertions, threw themselves upon the ground for a few moments' repose. Morton and several of his adherents now withdrew for a time from the mount, leaving the company under the charge of his lieutenant and grand master of the ceremonies; who, after serving out to them what he considered a sufficient quantity of liquor, soon after retired himself. A grand arbor was now constructed of green branches upon the hill, not far from the May-pole, and another of lesser dimensions near it. A considerable time had thus been spent, and the sun was already approaching the zenith, when suddenly the music again was heard advancing from the neighborhood of the palace, and presently a fantastically attired company were seen advancing gravely toward the mount. The procession was led by the sovereign of Merry-Mount himself, who, as Lord of the May, was attired according to immemorial custom in the green forest garb of Robin Hood. He wore moreover upon his head a gilt and glittering crown, and held a gilded staff in his hand, as symbols of his supremacy. Hanging upon his arm, came a dark-eyed, dusky daughter of the forest, who, for lack of a fairer representative, was arrayed as Maid Marian, the May Lord's favorite dame. She too, as Queen of the May, wore a gilded crown upon her swarthy brows, with her glossy black tresses floating almost to her feet, and was arrayed in gaily colored robes of purple and crimson cloth. They were followed by Cakebread, who had recovered from the effects of the flagellation received at Mishawum, and who now figured as court jester. The respectable buffoon wore a fool's-cap and bells, a motley coat, with tight-fitting Venetian pantaloons, whereof one leg was of flame color and the other of purple. He held a bauble or fool's baton in his hand, and his dress was hung with little bells, which jingled merrily as he danced along, occasionally refreshing himself and the spectators with one of his favorite somersets. Next came the grave and dignified Bootefish as Friar Tuck, his short but portly person arrayed in a monkish robe bound about his ample waist with a cord from which hung a rosary and cross, and his rubicund physiognomy looking particularly effulgent, as it broke out like a rising sun from the dark and cloud-like cowl which covered his venerable head. Rednape followed as the lover of Maid Marian, wearing a tawdry cap, ornamented with a wreath of violets, fastened securely to the right side of his head, and a sky-blue jacket; while his long legs were daintily incased in scarlet breeches and hose, cross gartered, and with countless ribbons and true lover's knots streaming from every portion of his dress. Next came the Spanish gentleman and the Morisco, personated by less distinguished members of the company, and wearing immoderately loose breeches, curling shoes of a yard's dimension, and enormous, empty sleeves hanging from their gaily colored jerkins. The principal musical performer followed, with a drum hanging from his neck, a tamborine in his hand, and a lathe sword at his side. Next came a creature with a wolf's head and a fox's tail, with half a dozen green and golden snakes wreathed round his waist; after him, a kind of goblin wearing the grim head and portentous teeth of a shark, with a dragon's tail; then several palmers masqued and cloaked; then a jack-in-the-green, or living pyramid of blossoming branches, dancing grotesquely along to the wild music which accompanied the procession. Last of all came the merry Bernaby Doryfall, riding the hobby-horse, the animal's head and shoulders artistically contrived of pasteboard, while an ample housing, or rather petticoat of parti-colored cloth, descended to the ground, and effectually concealed the rider's legs. The amiable Centaur wore a pumpkin helmet of formidable appearance, and flourished a wooden dagger in his right hand, while with the other he reined in his restive steed as he gaily pranced and capered about, bringing up the rear of the pageant in a very effective style.

The procession ascended the mount in an orderly manner, and arranged themselves about the May-pole, while the rest of the revellers arose from their recumbent positions and stood, awaiting the orders of their sovereign. That potentate now took a roll of paper from his bosom, upon which he had inscribed a short poem, setting forth, in very high flown and classical doggerel, an allegorical description of the ceremony, combined with many enigmatical allusions to the present and prospective condition of the nascent empire of the Massachusetts. This, after he had read it in a sonorous and impressive voice, he gravely affixed to the May-pole, that it might serve for the edification of his guests, whenever they felt inclined for literary relaxation. Then, with an indescribable air of majesty, he again extended his hand to the dusky Queen of the Revels, and conducted her with stately step to the great arbor, where he seated her upon a rustic throne. Then advancing once more in front of the verdant tent, he exclaimed,—

"With gilded staff and crossed scarf, the May Lord, here I stand. Know ye, therefore, my faithful subjects, that your sports are to be conducted in an orderly and reputable guise, so as in no wise to cast discredit upon the court of your sovereign, or to invoke a blush upon the tender cheek of our loving queen,—

> 'Music, awake! ye lieges all advance,
> And circling join in merry Morrice dance.'"

Thus having spoken, the merry monarch seated himself at the side of his queen, while the whole of the company, Christians and heathens, friars and dragons, palmers, masquers and mummers all joined hand in hand, and danced madly about the May-pole. Round and round they frisked, their brains, already heated with draughts stronger than May-dew, whirling faster than their heels, and their many voices, frantic with unbridled excitement, ringing forth upon the solemn wilderness around them so wildly and discordantly, that the very beasts which peopled the forests might have shrunk to their caves in dismay. Round and round they whirled, shouting, laughing, yelling; now some of them rolling by dozens upon the earth, and dragged about by their companions till they found their feet again; now the more active of them leaping and curvetting over each other's heads, or frisking about upon each other's shoulders, the riders hallooing in triumph and the victims staggering blindly about, but all yelling and leaping as if the wild and stunning music which still played more and more furiously had maddened their senses or transformed them into goblins. Faster and faster flew their heels, louder and louder sounded the diabolical strains of the music, more fierce and frantic rose the piercing shouts; startling the echoes of the stern and savage hills around them, which seemed to reverberate an indignant response to their demoniacal merriment.

Suddenly Cakebread, the jester, broke from the circle and frisked forth into the centre of the group, shaking his bauble, and commanding silence. The whirling vortex paused for a moment in its mad career, and the revellers, knowing scarcely if they stood upon heads or heels, became stationary for a moment, to listen to his communication.

"Look ye, my masters," he cried, "this is indeed the music of the spheres, though something cracked and discordant it may be, and this the circling of the starry hosts around the sun. Beshrew me, though, but these whirls be faster than befitteth some of the planets. As for me, I am a comet, bound to no orbit, and dance but for my own pleasure. If ye will that I execute a hornpipe, such as my virtuous dam, whom the Lord assoilzie, was wont to delight the world withal, so—if not, may the devil blow his trumpet, and set ye all whirling again— but the comet shall break loose from your influences."

Peter, it should be observed, was fond of stating confidentially to his friends that his parents had both been rope-dancers and fire-eaters by profession, and that he had been brought up from earliest childhood to their respectable calling. Furthermore, he was apt to mention that his destiny in life had been perverted by a pious and charitable schoolmaster, who had attempted to save him, like a brand from the burning, and had instructed him in Latin and the humanities, but had thrown him away again afterwards. By this process he had acquired an enlightened education, but had lost his ancestral calling, and had become neither flesh nor fish, and only fitted for a buffoon. This may serve to explain his vein of conversation, occasionally more ambitious than that of his confederates.

The company signified their approbation of his intentions, and accordingly Peter Cakebread came forward, his eyes glittering with merriment, and executed his promised hornpipe with wonderful zeal and agility, and in a manner to do credit to his parentage and education. Never before, at least in that wilderness, were seen such prodigious caperings, such impossible pigeon wings, such a breathless profusion of miraculous somersets, such a hopeless confusion and entanglement of head, heels, arms, and legs, in one rapid and bewildering contortion. Merrily jingled the jester's bells upon foolscap, jerkin, and bauble, as he span and gambolled about, and merrily did the company applaud, as they gazed with open mouths and staring eyes upon this exhibition of his dexterity, and swore that he must have made a compact with the evil one, and exchanged his soul for a skeleton of whalebone, so superhuman did his pranks appear. In short, Peter Cakebread outdid himself, and seemed to have combined and embodied within himself, at least for that occasion, all the extraordinary and necromantic qualities of his departed and illustrious parents. As he finished his dance, by standing stock-still upon the point of one toe, in the most graceful and preternatural manner, he was greeted with noisy plaudits, in which the sovereign of the revels heartily joined, as he sat there upon his rustic throne.

"Excellent well, Master Cakebread," he cried; "of a truth thou hast surpassed thyself. A merrier buffoon, a nimbler morrice-dancer, 'choreis aptior et jocis,' it could hardly have been my lot to meet with in this savage wilderness. Thy sovereign drinks to thy health, and the gentle Marian likewise," he concluded, after touching with his lips the tankard presented officiously by Bootefish, and then extending it to the dusky sharer of his throne, who, nothing loth, did due honor to the toast, or at least to the tankard, which she seemed better to understand.

After Cakebread had finished his dance, and had meekly and modestly returned thanks for the applause so generously bestowed upon his exertions, the master of ceremonies came forward with an important air, and conferred gravely with his sovereign.

"Thou art right, worthy Robin," answered that potentate,

upon receiving this communication; "truly the chariot of Phoebus is already wheeling from its zenith, and the day will yet prove too short for our sports if we use not better diligence. Let the pyramid of tankards and trinkets be erected, that the rosy milkmaids, according to immemorial custom, may dance for their simple prizes about it."

Bootefish accordingly beckoned two or three of the revellers to his assistance, while the rest remained recumbent upon the grass, pledging each other in the fiery liquor, and laughing uproariously at the jibes of Cakebread, who, stimulated by the applause which he had received, and the copious draughts which he had imbibed, exerted his utmost powers worthily to discharge the high functions of court jester, which had been conferred upon him by his sovereign.

Presently Bootefish and his assistants had erected upon the mount, about half way between the May-pole and Robin Hood's arbor, a tall pyramid of tankards, pewter plates, and flagons, which were to be used at the ensuing banquet, and garnished it with ribbons, small looking-glasses, strings of gaudy beads, gaily-colored strips of cloth, and a profusion of such cheap and trifling finery, as was most pleasing to savage eyes. He then apprized the lord of the revels that the pyramid was ready.

"Be it known to ye, my lieges," said Morton, rising to address his subjects, "that the milkmaid's dance is one of the most ancient and time-honored customs of the May-day, and that no festivity in honor of our sovereign lady could be esteemed complete, where this most graceful and becoming ceremony was wanting. Rings, chains, gooches, ribbons, and such simple bravery, are the appropriate rewards for the gentle contenders. It were a burning shame, if this custom, thus honored throughout the Christian land of our birth, should be omitted in this our first festivity in this benighted wilderness. The dance of the rosy milkmaids, pleasing and pretty as it is, can in no wise be dispensed with. Rosy milkmaids, come forth!"

At this concluding exclamation of Morton, his faithful master of the ceremonies gravely led forth a band of savage maidens, who had easily been prevailed upon, by promises of liberal reward, and for the sake of the glittering gewgaws which were conspicuously displayed upon the pyramid, to agree to take share in the pageant.

The rosy milkmaids, accordingly, as the Lord of Merry-Mount facetiously designated these dusky daughters of the forest, came forward, hand in hand. Though differing widely from the buxom lasses of England, their prototypes upon this occasion, yet there was something far from disagreeable in these lithe and graceful creatures, with their bright, savage eyes, supple limbs, and elastic movements. They joined hand in hand, and executed gracefully one of their own wild dances, ever and anon, accompanying their airy bounds with sudden, shrill, but not unmusical snatches of rude vocal music. Their countrymen, mingled with their paler-faced confederates, looked on with dignified composure, occasionally applauding their vigorous whirls with a deep grunt of approval. When the dance was finished, they stood stock-still, and received at the hands of the master of ceremonies, the prizes which were suspended from the pyramid, with a composure and dignity which might have befitted princesses. There was no struggling, no snatching, no exultation of manner, but they quietly adorned their swarthy, but exquisitely moulded persons, with the various petty decorations which they received, and then gracefully and silently withdrew towards the principal group of revellers.

The company were now refreshed with a slight repast of dried venison and bear's meat, of which they partook as they reclined together upon the grass, and when the meal was concluded the sports were resumed. There were now many games of skill and strength exhibited. A mark was set up at the extremity of the mound, and the savages and Christians contested with each other with the bow and arrow, in which, as was observed with considerable satisfaction by the sovereign, the palm of superiority was by no means always to be awarded to the Indians, but was fully as often due to his more immediate subjects, who manfully contended for victory with their swarthy allies. The savage was foiled at his own weapons. Perhaps it was the fire-water which dimmed his eye and rendered his nerves unsteady, while it left comparatively unaffected the more practised organizations of the English. Games of wrestling, Indian hug and trip and twitch succeeded, in which the savages, with their slippery skins, almost naked persons, and pliable limbs, were almost constantly victorious. Then there were merry bouts with the quarterstaff, in which the hardy Saxon regained his lost supremacy, while many a broken head and bloody coxcomb dealt liberally among the heathen champions, attested the prowess of the English at their own national game. Late and long were the games protracted, and long and loud continued the uproar and the merriment. The sun was now fast approaching the horizon, and the hardy frames both of pagan and Christian would have been well nigh exhausted, but for the liberal circulation of the butler's flagon, which still flew gaily around, wherever a feeling of lassitude seemed creeping over the revellers. As the subtle influence mounted to their brains, again their spirits kindled, again their frames became instinct with renovated vigor, as if the wand of an enchanter had been waved above their heads.

To the games of wrestling and quarterstaff, which had been conducted with orderly precision, now succeeded a general pell-mell, in which all parties, old and young, male and female, Saxon and savage, mingled in desperate and bewildering confusion, hugging, tumbling, knocking, thumping, tripping, twitching, pulling, leaping, dancing, singing, whooping and hallooing, as if they had all gone mad.

At last the Lord of Merry-Mount extended his hand to his savage queen, and led her forth with majestic grace towards the May-pole. Both, wearing their golden crowns upon their heads and decked in royal robes, now danced a slow and stately measure, and then, with agreeable condescension, joining hand in hand with the whole group of revellers, they commenced once more the merry Morrice dance, the sovereign accompanying his steps by singing in a clear, melodious voice the initiatory verses of the song to which he had alluded. The whole assembly pealed out the chorus, making a din loud enough as they did so, to shame the howling of the forest wolves. When the song was concluded, the monarch and his queen slipped out from the throng, while the rest continued leaping and frisking about the May-pole, in a rapidly revolving circle, which increased every instant in its dizzy speed, till one after another, overpowered by his exertions, was sucked into the merry whirlpool and sank overcome upon the ground. The revellers, thus fairly danced off their legs, remained reposing upon the sward for a few minutes, till the master of ceremonies again sounded his trumpet, when all, suddenly inspired with renewed vigor, sprang to their feet again, and marshaled by the indefatigable Bootefish, formed again into solemn procession and marched down the mount towards the palace.

THE DUEL

[Morton is seized by a small band of Puritans under the leadership of Captain Standish and sent to England for trial. Esther, lost in the forest one day, is rescued from death at the hands of a savage by two friendly Indians and the mysterious Jaspar, who advises her to beware of Gardiner and to sport no longer with her own happiness and Maudsley's. Gardiner and Maudsley meet at Shawmut and fight a duel.]

Gardiner watched its motions, supposing that it was probably the solitary inhabitant of the promontory returning to his domain. As the boat neared him, however, his keen eye at once recognized the boat and its occupant, and a dark and singular expression shot across his features. He stood motionless, looking towards the little skiff, as it slowly drifted before the faint summer breeze. In a few moments the keel grated upon the pebbly beach within a few yards of the spot where he stood, and a man sprang hastily out, paused an instant to moor his boat, and then strode directly towards him. The new comer was Henry Maudsley.

"Good morrow, Master Maudsley," said the knight, with unperturbed visage; "if you are bent upon a visit to the hermit of Shawmut this afternoon, I fear, like myself, you are come but upon a fool's errand."

"I thank you, Sir Christopher, for your information, which is doubly agreeable to me," answered Maudsley, whose voice was low and husky. "I did indeed purpose a visit to Master Blaxton today, but I am fortunate, both in finding him absent, and in finding yourself as his substitute."

"Indeed," said Gardiner, calmly, "and in what manner can I serve you, Master Maudsley? In what way can I act as the representative of the holy clerk of Shawmut?"

"My affair," answered Maudsley, with rising passion, "my affair with Master Blaxton can be deferred; that with Sir Christopher Gardiner brooks no delay."

"Indeed," said Gardiner, with a sneering affectation of curiosity, "have we such pressing business to settle? Pray, let me remain no longer ignorant of such weighty matters. Let us proceed to business at once."

"With all my heart," said Maudsley, unsheathing his sword with a sudden movement.

"Hey-day, hey-day, Master Maudsley!" said the knight, in an accent of astonishment, unbaring his own rapier, however, with lightning-like rapidity; "was your voyage to Shawmut this morning made for the special purpose of my assassination? If it be not presumptuous, I would fain ask your cause of quarrel."

"I have no inclination to waste these precious moments in idle brawling," answered Maudsley. "Your own hypocritical heart will tell you in clearer tones than mine, our cause of quarrel. You have escaped me once, through, I could almost believe, supernatural agency. Should I fail a second time to chastise your villany, the fault would be mine."

"These be bold and bitter words," returned Gardiner, who seemed for some mysterious reason to be singularly averse to an encounter with Maudsley. "But stay, the days are long at this particular season, and I am a searcher after truth. Enlighten me, for by St. John, you shall take nothing by your braggadocio humor, and shall lose nothing by a more perspicuous course of conduct."

Maudsley stared at the knight in profound astonishment. He was utterly at a loss to understand what possible motives could restrain him from accepting a combat thus fiercely urged upon him. Of his courage and skill at every weapon he entertained no doubt, and his imperturbable coolness at this particular juncture, proved that he was acting deliberately. Maudsley, as we know, before the particular cause for his hatred had occurred, had already conceived a peculiar and unaccountable detestation of Gardiner, which the knight had upon all occasions appeared very cordially to reciprocate. There had always seemed something more than caprice in Maudsley's aversion, and Gardiner's conduct had always been apparently dictated by some secret, but decided motive. In short, it seemed that Maudsley was governed either by interest, or presentiment, or by both, while Gardiner's hatred was the result of actual, although concealed, knowledge.

As for Sir Christopher, he seemed to have an especial motive for self-control, and he stood in a careless attitude of defence, like a reposing gladiator, calmly, but fixedly, regarding his antagonist in the eye, and silently awaiting his response.

"I came not here to play the fool," said Maudsley at last, "nor to answer to any catechism. Neither am I disposed to enter upon a detail of grievances of which you are as well instructed as myself. If you must have reasons, let this suffice," and, as he spoke, the impetuous youth endeavored to strike his antagonist with the flat of his sword.

"Fairly and softly," answered the knight, coolly, but adroitly, recoiling a few paces to avoid the proffered insult. "If there be really so many and such weighty reasons already existing, why invent fictitious and imaginary ones? Tell me frankly and nobly, as befits the dignity of this imposing solitude, tell me plainly your wrongs, and if there be no redress, I swear to you, you shall have vengeance."

Maudsley was more and more irritated, and yet more and more perplexed. An impetuous, passionate man, particularly if he be very young, is very apt to be worsted in an altercation with a cool, adroit man of maturer years, and he is the more likely to be worsted if he happens to be entirely in the right. Feeling sure to be baffled in argument, because he felt himself too angry to utter an intelligible syllable, he took refuge for the moment in silence.

"Then you persist in denying me your catalogue of grievances," continued Gardiner, after a pause. "'Tis strange, but one would have even expected eloquence from your lips upon such a subject. Since, however, you will not speak, and since I have no more desire than yourself for prolonging this interview, I shall myself state your cause of quarrel. It lies in an almond shell, good Master Maudsley, even in the soft eyes of a certain Puritan maiden——"

Maudsley started, and made a fierce, quick gesture of assent.

"Jealousy is a common passion," continued Gardiner, "a common cause of quarrel. I will not say that in some respects there may not be foundation for your jealousy. But, good Master Maudsley, where many strive but one can be chosen."

"In one word," cried Maudsley, boiling over with his hitherto painfully repressed wrath, "I pronounce you a hypocrite and a villain. Whence and wherefore sprang the hatred which I have borne you since your dark shadow first fell across my path, I ask not. There may be hatred at first sight, it seems, as ardent as first love. That you are a hypocrite, I know. Your object is the perdition of one who, in her saintly purity, is as far above your sphere as heaven from hell. I know that your designs are all artful and base, and that your whole existence in this wilderness, of which you prate so loftily, is one long lie."

"And think you," answered Sir Christopher, still preserving the same careless attitude, in spite of Maudsley's violent language, "and think you to arrogate to yourself a monopoly of jealousy? Think you that the dark passion finds its only home in your bosom? Think you that I, even I," continued he, with an ominous expression upon his dark brow, and with a voice of rising passion, "am a stranger to your sweet and stolen interviews with a certain gentle, blue-eyed, mysterious youth? Think you that I am your laughing-stock and your dupe? Hath your effrontery grown to such a height that you defy me to

the teeth, with your saintly heroics touching the fair Puritan?
Shame on you, shame, Master Maudsley!"

A sudden light broke upon Maudsley's mind as the knight
gave utterance to these taunts. He stood for an instant bewildered, and hardly knowing what to reply, or whither this strange
interview was tending. He was far from suspecting the real
cause of Gardiner's singular forbearance even now, although
so suddenly enlightened as to a part of the mysteries which had
enveloped him. He replied not immediately, but stood leaning
upon his sword, and reflecting for an instant upon his course.

"Fool, fool," muttered the knight to himself—"Are my projects, after all, to be foiled by the rash temper of this hot-headed
boy? I thought him already in my power. Hath the charm
failed? By heavens! it shall be decided, and at once. Hark
you, my gentle master, I have a word for your most secret
ear," said he aloud.

"And fear you," said Maudsley, "that yonder crows will
prate of your secret, that it must be whispered in the silent
wilderness?"

"Nay, nay, my quick-tempered friend," replied the knight,
"but there be many words and many matters which sound more
becomingly in a whisper, even though there be no lurking ear
in the whole universe, save those for whom they are meant.
Hark you, I say——!"

With this, the knight strode hastily forward to Maudsley,
and whispered in his ear for half a minute.

Maudsley started, as if a serpent had stung him.

"Liar and villain!" he cried, almost beside himself with fury.
—"It needed but this to set my soul on fire. Defend yourself;
for nothing human shall restrain me longer."

With this Maudsley threw himself madly upon Sir Christopher, who now entirely upon his guard, received his onset with
perfect calmness and precision. Maudsley, by profession a
soldier, was daring and skilful with his weapon, but he was
inflamed by passion. Gardiner was a consummate swordsman,
and besides, was wary and collected. Finding that his project
of making Maudsley useful to him had failed, the knight was

now desirous of being relieved of the embarrassment caused by his presence in New England. The combat proved desperate but brief. Maudsley, after a few fierce passes, which were skilfully parried by Sir Christopher, at last by a lucky feint, pushed within his adversary's guard. His rapier's point was upon the knight's breast, and it seemed that his last and desperate thrust must necessarily, at that instant, terminate the adventurer's career, when, to his astonishment and rage, the treacherous blade, encountering some hidden obstacle, shivered at the hilt. At the same moment as he stood disconcerted and defenceless, the knight sprang nimbly forward and passed his rapier through his body. Maudsley glared at his foe with a last look of defiance and fell to the earth without uttering a sound.

Sir Christopher stood stock-still for a few moments, gazing upon his prostrate adversary, while a thousand dark emotions chased each other across his brow.

"'Twas thy destiny," he hoarsely muttered, "thy destiny and mine. I swear, I sought to spare thee, but thou shouldest not have crossed my path. Have I not avoided thee as my evil genius? My God!" exclaimed the knight in a still more husky tone, as he bent over the fallen Maudsley, "what a terrible resemblance, closer and more fearful even than in life! The same haughty features, the same chestnut locks. My God! that icy look, that ghastly resemblance will haunt me to my grave!"

Muttering thus incoherently, Gardiner stood musing in that terrible companionship, till the cloudless midsummer's sun was nearly set. His level beams poured full across the glassy cove, and rained a flood of light upon the spot where Maudsley lay. It was a fearful contrast,—that virgin wilderness, that golden summer sunset, and that scene of blood. Sir Christopher Gardiner had been familiar with scenes of violence even from his boyhood, but there was something appalling to him in the solitude which had been just profaned by the desperate affray. It seemed to his heated imagination, as he gazed around him, as if the world had suddenly renewed its infancy, and that the first murder had at that instant been enacted. His brother's blood seemed to cry to him from the ground. He sprang to his feet, as if he felt the hot brand searing his forehead, and fled from the spot like the guilty and conscience-stricken Cain.

[The hermit Blaxton comes upon Maudsley, discovers that he is not quite dead, and nurses him back to health and strength in the seclusion of his cottage. By this time a second Puritan colony has been established at Naumkeak (Salem). Maudsley, convinced by certain discoveries of Gardiner's knavery, returns to England for corroborative evidence. He and Esther come to an understanding by correspondence, his attitude toward her religion having changed. Meanwhile, Morton has returned to Merry-Mount, where he indulges in the sport of hawking and enrages the Salem Puritans by other unseemly conduct as well. Once more he is arrested, this time by Winthrop's men.

Esther is abducted by Sir Christopher, who reveals his expectation of becoming master of all Massachusetts and demands that she become either his wife or his slave. At the propitious moment, Maudsley (just returned from England) arrives with armed retainers at Merry-Mount, burns the "Palace" (now the residence of Gardiner), and rescues Esther but carelessly allows the villain to escape. The mysterious Jaspar proves to be Gardiner's mistress, disguised as a youth. Maudsley and Esther Ludlow are married. Morton, after a second banishment to England, returns to America once more in 1643, only to die two years later.]

From HISTORIC PROGRESS AND AMERICAN DEMOCRACY[1]

. . . But neither fools nor sages; neither individuals nor nations; have any other light to guide them along the track which all must tread, save that long glimmering vista of yesterdays which grows so swiftly fainter and fainter as the present fades off into the past.

And I believe it possible to discover a law out of all this apparently chaotic whirl and bustle; this tangled skein of human affairs as it spins itself through the centuries. That law is progress—slow, confused, contradictory, but ceaseless development, intellectual and moral, of the human race.

It is of Human Progress that I speak tonight. It is of Progress that I find a startling result when I survey the spectacle which the American Present displays.

This nation stands on the point towards which other peoples are moving—the starting-point, not the goal. It has put itself —or rather Destiny has placed it—more immediately than other nations in subordination to the law governing all bodies political as inexorably as Kepler's law controls the motions of the planets.

The law is Progress; the result Democracy. Nearly forty

[1] An address delivered before the New York Historical Society, December 16, 1868; published in pamphlet form in both New York and London in 1869. The second London edition (1869) was entitled *Democracy, the Climax of Political Progress, and the Destiny of Advanced Races; an Historical Essay.* Having completed the third and fourth volumes of *History of the United Netherlands* early in 1868, Motley returned with his family to Boston in June. On October 20, he made a campaign speech for Grant ("Four Questions for the People, at the Presidential Election"), and in December addressed the New York Historical Society. In 1869 he returned once more to Europe, having been appointed U. S. Minister to England by the Grant administration. *Historic Progress and American Democracy*, in its relation to the body of Motley's political thought, is considered in Section II of the Introduction, "Political and Social Ideas" (pp. xlv–xlix).

years ago the clear, philosophical mind of De Tocqueville was so impressed by this comparatively infant Republic, the phenomena of which he had examined with microscopic minuteness and with statesman-like breadth of vision, that he exhorted his countrymen and Europe in general to accept the fact that democracy was the preordained condition of the human race— a condition to which the world was steadily tending—and to seek happiness in conforming to the divine command instead of wearing themselves out in futile struggles with the Inevitable.

Circumstances, mainly due to now very obvious phenomena in the policy of this country to which the philosopher did not pay sufficient heed, have retarded the result; but it is again signalling its approach with swiftly augmenting speed.

Whether it be a bane or a blessing, it is all-important for us to accept and make the best of it. No man more thoroughly believes and rejoices in the fundamental truth on which our system is founded than I do; but it is not to flatter nor exult that I allude to this foremost position which we occupy; not entirely through our merits but mainly from the bounty of heaven.

Sydney Smith once alluded, if I remember rightly, to a person who allowed himself to speak disrespectfully of the equator. I have a strong objection to be suspected of flattering the equator. Yet were it not for that little angle of 23°, 27′, 26″, which it is good enough to make with the plane of the ecliptic, the history of this earth and of "all which it inherit" would have been essentially modified, even if it had not been altogether a blank.

> "Some say he bid his angels turn askance
> The poles of earth twice ten degrees and more
> From the sun's axle; they with labor pushed
> Oblique the central globe . . . .
> . . . . . . to bring in change
> Of seasons to each clime, else had the spring
> Perpetual smiled on earth with verdant flowers
> Equal in days and nights, except to those
> Beyond the polar circles."

Out of the obliquity of the equator has come forth our civilization. It was long ago observed by one of the most thoughtful writers that ever dealt with human history, John von Herder, that it was to the gradual shading away of zones and alternation of seasons that the vigor and variety of mankind were attributable. Nothing good or great could ever come out of the eternal spring or midsummer of the tropics, nor from the thick-ribbed winter of the poles. From the temperate zone, with its healthful and stimulating succession of seasons, have come civilization and progress.* . . .

I asked where and when were the good old times? This earth of ours has been spinning about in space, great philosophers tell us, some few hundred millions of years. We are not very familiar with our predecessors on this continent. For the present, the oldest inhabitant must be represented here by the man of Natchez, whose bones were unearthed not long ago under the Mississippi bluffs in strata which were said to argue him to be at least one hundred thousand years old. Yet he is a mere modern, a *parvenu* on this planet, if we are to trust illustrious teachers of science, compared with the man whose bones and whose implements have been found in high mountain valleys and gravel-pits of Europe; while these again are thought by the same authorities to be descendants of races which flourished many year-thousands before, and whose relics Science is confidently expecting to discover, although the icy sea had once engulfed them and their dwelling-places.

We of today have no filial interest in the man of Natchez. He was no ancestor of ours, nor have he and his descendants left traces along the dreary track of their existence to induce a desire to claim relationship with them.

We are Americans—but yesterday we were Europeans—Netherlanders, Saxons, Normans, Swabians, Celts—and the day before yesterday, Asiatics, Mongolians, what you will. Go to the ancestral home of many of us. Strike into the busy heart of London with pickaxe and spade. Sink a shaft in the central

* See *Ideen zur Geschichte der Menschheit*. 1ter Theil, 1tes Buch, S. iv. Herder's Sämmtliche Werke, 28ter Band. [*Motley's note.*]

ganglion of confused and thickly-crammed streets about Tower Hill and Thames Street, along which the ever accumulating mass of traffic has been rolling for a dozen centuries. And if you go deep enough, and excavate widely enough, you will find beautiful statues, tesselated pavements, mosaic pictures, pagan shrines —relics of that puissant Roman people who governed what they thought the world, when Britons were painted savages. Yet they never dreamed of the existence of that great American continent where the man of Natchez and his race had been roaming hundreds of year-thousands before, but never producing temples nor pictures, statues nor fountains.

For what are Roman antiquities in England or anywhere else? Many of us trace back our ancestry to Bedfordshire and Suffolk, and are never weary of tracking the footsteps of our pilgrim fathers in quiet villages and peaceful English scenery of two or three hundred years ago. Go back two or three hundred thousand years, and saunter on the margin of the Ouse, or through the primitive valleys of Bedford, and find your ancestors, as great naturalists inform us you will, contemporaries and companions of the mammoth and the woolly rhinoceros, the lion and the hyena.*

Yet we talk of history because we can grope backwards dimly and vaguely for a matter of thirty centuries, while those rude forefathers of ours have faded for ever from our chronicles.

Men through all ages—other than those accepting the revelations of Holy Writ—have solaced or distressed themselves with shadowy or whimsical fancies of a great beginning of the Universe and of themselves; but perhaps they had better pause in their theorizing until the modern dauntless investigators shall find in full fruition of their hopes, among the fossils of the pre-glacial period, some connecting anthropo-simial links, some precious relics of the ancient ancestral ape, and

> "Madly play with that great kinsman's bone
> As with a club,"

* Sir Charles Lyell. *Geological Evidences of the Antiquity of Man.* 2d edition. Murray, 1863. Pages 375–376. [*Motley's note.*]

to smite all other theories to the earth. But even then we shall probably arrive at the same conclusion with the venerable Ephraim Jenkinson, in the "Vicar of Wakefield," who sold Moses a gross of green spectacles with copper rims, and told him at the same time "that the cosmogony or creation of the world had puzzled the philosophers of all ages."

One thing is certain. Man is here. And another thing is equally certain: he has arrived at his present condition through a long series of improvements and developments. Placed on "this isthmus of a middle state," between two eternities, he looks backward with a curiosity half-exultant, half-loathing, and forward with a hope which is often akin to despair. To be created at once in likeness to the Omnipotent and to a fantastic brute; to be compounded thus of the bestial and the angelic, alternately dragged upward and downward by conflicting forces, presses upon us the conviction, even without divine revelation, that this world is a place of trial and of progress towards some higher sphere.

But let the gorilla stand erect in frightful caricature of humanity. Weigh his brain and a Hottentot's together in the same balance, if you choose, and find less difference between the two than between Hannibal's and a more southern African's. Until you can find a dumb animal endowed with the religious faculty; who worships the Eternal Father on his knees; who has treasured in his heart the hope of an immortal future; who "looks before and after, and pines for what is not"; you may be sure that the interval between Man and the angels will be crossed at a single leap sooner than the infinite space between the brute and Man will be diminished by a hair's-breath. All the inconceivable time since primeval Man before the glacial flood is but an hour's span compared to that which the brute must traverse before he can crawl even to the threshold of humanity. Nothing can betoken a weaker faith in Omnipotent love than to "sag with doubt" before the grand generalizations of science, for fear of forfeiting the grasp on immortality. If to survey the enormous progress already made does not encourage faith in that eternal law, I know not of what element hope can be compounded.

There is something in man alone which has weighed the heavenly bodies, measured their inconceivable distances, marked the spot where lost worlds after year-thousands must reappear, prescribed the course in which the planets wheel, expounded the laws which the universe obeys; something which has guided the almost divine finger of the sculptor, the pencil of the painter to create visions more beautiful than Nature's self has revealed; something which has inspired the poet to raise his less gifted brethren into spheres of thought and emotion far above the visible world; something which has produced from shapeless matter the Grecian temple, the Gothic cathedral, the Pacific Railroad; something which has nerved heroes to despise luxury and welcome death in the sacred cause of country; something which ties the great sailor to the main-top, above the smoke of the conflict, that he may control his fleet and guide the battle, nor fall, even though he die, till victory is won; something which chains the great soldier, despite of danger, opposition, or censure, to one line, even if it takes all summer, ay, and all winter too, when Duty commands; something which has enabled the scientific adventurer to confront for years, alone and almost forgotten, the perils of torrid, barbarous Africa, or the barriers which guard the frozen mysteries of the Pole; something which has sustained thousands of obscure men and feeble women, as they were consuming by slow fire at the stake, when a word against what they believed religious truth would have saved them. So long as history garners such proofs of progress out of the lower depths, Man needs not to tremble lest the angelic part of him should be imperilled by his likeness to the brute.

Language makes Man. The beast can chatter, roar, or bellow, but man can speak. The child talks in fragments, and earlier languages are monosyllabic. A Chinese Dr. Johnson would be impossible. He would perish for want of polysyllables.

If it had not been for the tower of Babel, we should have been spared much superfluous trouble; for although we are all speaking very choice Aryan at bottom, we find it difficult to converse fluently with each other in that tongue, or even in the more modern Sanscrit, which we are told by great scholars—no doubt with accuracy—is essentially English, French, German, or Greek.

It is also an awful thought that languages perhaps cannot live unless they are stone dead. Cicero or Demosthenes might take his stand on any platform today and be reported in the papers for a classically educated public; but should King Alfred come from his tomb, like the elder Hamlet, to reveal important secrets, he would find no living soul, save a professor or two, throughout his ancient realms, to comprehend his warnings.

The great German of all, from whom the race is fancied to derive its name—Herman, Arminius, War-Man, Ger-Man—the patriot who smote Varus in the Frisian swamps, and caused Augustus to shriek through his marble halls for his legions, would be unintelligible to his Fatherland should he come forth to make a speech on the Schleswig-Holstein question, to the National, Patriotic, German Union of to-day.*

We celebrated Shakespeare's third century four years ago. Let another half a dozen centuries go by, and perhaps there will be none to philosophize with Hamlet, or weep over the sorrows of Lear. Shakespeare himself may become as mythical as either of those princes whom he seems to have endowed with immortality, and some future Wolf may divide him into a score of ballad-mongers. It is a dreary possibility, at least, that unless the Anglo-Saxon race dies out after a few centuries, the accretions and transmutations of language may make those wonderful dramas as obsolete as the odes of the Kymri, or the lays of Llewellyn.

If a Somersetshire peasant needs but three hundred words out of the hundred and fifty million now perhaps in use on this planet, how much of human vocabulary can be saved by poets, philosophers, and men of business from desuetude, as Time rolls remorselessly away?

Man, as far back as we know or imagine him, could speak, but it was long before he learned his letters, without which accomplishment erudition is apt to be limited. At last school-

* See Lyell. *Antiquity of Man*. Chap. xxiii. Pp. 454–470. [*Motley's note.*]

master Cadmus came out of the East—as is the habit of school-masters—and brought sixteen counters in his pocket, which he had picked up among the Pelasgians.

The schoolmaster being abroad at last, progress became rapid enough. For in truth what human invention can compare with that of the Alphabet? It is no wonder that Cadmus was pronounced not only a king's son, but allied to the immortals. "Founders of states and lawgivers," says Lord Bacon, "were honored with the titles of demigods; but inventors were ever consecrated among the gods themselves." And if heathen mythology still prevailed, what a Pantheon we should have in the Patent Office at Washington!

After the almost infinite space already traversed by Mankind, at last something like Tradition, Record, Monumental History began. The civilization of Egypt is a parenthesis between two barbarisms; the present wandering tribes of the Delta having inherited no more culture from the Pharaohs and the Ptolemies than did those royal lines from the savages who preceded them.

And contemporaneous with the epoch of Egyptian and Hebrew grandeur there was a siege—so men say—of a city in Asia Minor, and it chanced that a blind man, if he was a man and was blind, sang some songs about it. Wonderful power of poetic genius! The leading personages in that war, their passions and sentiments, the minute details of their costume, the color of their hair and eyes, the names of their soldiers and their ships, their habits of social life, the scenery surrounding them, the daily military and household events of that insignificant quarrel, are almost as familiar in this remote hemisphere today as the siege of Vicksburg, with all its heroic, picturesque, and passionate circumstance, and its momentous consequences for all time.

And out of the confusion of songs, monuments, and records, there comes at last a glimmer of chronology. There was once a cook in Athens. Whether he was skilful or not in the kitchen is unknown, but he was swift of foot. He ran a race at the Olympic Games; his name was the first to be recorded victor on the archives of those festivals; and accordingly the subsequent history of Greece, with all her heroes, poets, sages, is registered from the Olympiad in which Coroebus won his race. Truly, says Sir Thomas Browne, "the iniquity of oblivion blindly scattereth her poppies, and deals with the memories of men without regard to merit of perpetuity."

Strangely enough, too, the date of this first registered Olympiad has a sacred but familiar sound in our ears. It was 776 before Christ; 1776 years after Christ another epoch was established, from which this great Republic dates its records; a day on which equal rights were proclaimed as the heritage of mankind; a nobler era for the world than any that cooks or racers are ever likely to establish.

At exactly the same period with Coroebus—as chronologists have settled it among themselves—there was a certain she-wolf in an Italian swamp, with a pair of promising foster-children; and, as we all have read in the story-books, the foster-children founded a city, which has had much influence for good and evil upon the cause of human progress.

The orbit of civilization—so far as our perishing records enable us to trace it—seems preordained from East to West. China, India, Palestine, Egypt, Greece, Rome, are successively lighted up as the majestic orb of day moves over them; and as he advances still further through his storied and mysterious zodiac, we behold the shadows of evening as surely falling on the lands which he leaves behind him. Religion, poetry, aesthetic art, have already ennobled the progress of Man. What would the world have been without Palestine? What present idea of human civilization would be possible without the poetry, sculpture, architecture, the magnificent drama, the subtle, lofty, almost divine philosophy of Greece; without the imperious and cruel nationalism, the all-surpassing military art, the colossal self-esteem, the cynic materialism, the massive, sharply-chiselled jurisprudence, which made Rome the mistress of the world?

Dead Athens shines there for ever—not a constellation, but a whole universe of lustre—with the milky way of her exquisite, half nebulous fables; with the pure starry light of her fixed and unchanging truth—illuminating vast spaces of obscurity before and since her brief mortal existence.

Rome, both in her military and legal glory, and in her shameful and crapulous decrepitude, remains a perpetual memory to encourage human progress, and to warn from the dangers of luxury, ambition, and ineffable disdain of human rights by which she justly perished.

And then came the wandering of the nations; the northern deluge. Rome sank miserably beneath the glacial flood, which like that in early geological ages, had become necessary in the grand scheme of civilization. Surely the Roman world had need of submergence and of ice. And at last as the deluge subsided, Germany had conquered Rome, and the new civilization began. But a low civilization at best. The passionate rising for freedom, the great mutiny against Rome, resulted only in new and heterogeneous forms of despotism. Man made progress still, for he had been born again out of death into life, but the People did not exist, nor were there indications of its birth. Europe became a camp on conquered territory. The iron-clad man on horseback divided the whole soil among his captains and corporals; the multitudes were throttled and made to wear the collar of serfdom, marked with their owners' names; land-robbers and filibusters became kings and princes by grace of God—which meant the steel-gloved fist; the feudal system was established, and poetry, romance, grovelling legend and sycophantic chronicle have spread a halo around the perpetual crime even unto our own days. Do what you will, even in this distant land and age, you can not entirely remove, as yet, the tenacious fibres from that foreign root which are twisted into our law, history, literature, into our social and political being.

Man still reeled on—falling, rising again, staggering forward with hue and cry at his heels—a wounded felon daring to escape from the prison to which grace of God had inexorably doomed him. And still there was progress. Besides the sword, two other instruments grew every day more potent—the pen and the purse.

The power of the pen soon created a stupendous monopoly. Clerks obtained privilege of murder because of their learning; a Norman king gloried in the appellation of "fine clerk" because he could spell; the sons of serfs and washerwomen became high pontiffs, put their feet on the neck of emperors, through the might of education, and appalled the souls of tyrants with their weird anathemas. Naturally, the priests kept the talisman of learning to themselves. How should education help them to power and pelf if the people could participate in the mystic spell? The icy Dead-hand of the Church, ever extended, was filled to overflowing by trembling baron and superstitious hind. The fairest valleys, the richest plains, the noblest forests of Europe were clutched by the comfortable friars in perpetual mortmain.

But there was another power steadily augmenting—the magic purse of Fortunatus with its clink of perennial gold. Commerce changed clusters of hovels, cowering for protection under feudal castles, into powerful cities. Burghers wrested or purchased liberties from their lords and masters. And at last there were leagues of municipalities, chains of commercial republics in all but name, stretched across Christendom, and tripping up tyranny at every turn. Liberties in the plural, not liberty of man; concessions to corporations from the iron fist, from grace of God, in exchange for coin or in reparation of buffets.

And still Man struggled on. An experimenting friar, fond of chemistry, in one corner of Europe, put nitre, sulphur, and charcoal together; a sexton or doctor, in another obscure nook, carved letters on blocks of wood; and lo! there were explosions shaking the solid earth, and causing the iron-clad man on horseback to reel in his saddle.

It was no wonder that Dr. Faustus was supposed to have sold his soul to the fiend. Whence but from devilish alliance could he have derived such power to strike down grace of God?

The military encampment had secured all territory to the crown; the pen had given control of the human mind to the Church; floating capital was locked up in the strong-box of corporations. Man had made progress, but everywhere the People was submerged; pursuing its monotonous and darkened course, destined to gloomy servitude almost beneath the reach of hope; with encampments, establishments, corporations, piled upon it mountains high.

But Sacerdotalism, political Priesthood, reigned too long and went too far. Auction sales of indulgences, for every possible and imaginable crime, had been too audacious; Christian temples had grown too gorgeous on the proceeds of remitted sin; the baleful splendor which had grown out of the putrescence of the traffic had become too noisome an exhalation for the human mind to endure.

There was a reformation. But it was only a leap into the light. It was not a mere difference of creed and dogma. Good Catholics and virtuous men were as much offended at heart by Borgianism, as Luther or Calvin had been. It was not an uprising against the Church, but against the prostitution of the Church to temporal purposes. Much good was accomplished, both in the ancient and the new establishments, but freedom of religion was scarcely dreamed of; mutual toleration was accounted a crime. Priesthood was triumphant after all, for Church and State maintained their incestuous union. The people obtained new creeds if their masters professed one, or remained with the ball and chain of ancient dogma rivetted to their limbs, if their masters remained faithful to that.

Whoever governs you, his religion shall be yours! *Cujus regio, ejus religio.* Were ever more blasphemous and insulting words hurled in the face of mankind?

Yet this was accepted as the net result of the Reformation, so far as priests and princes could settle the account. This was the ingenious compromise by which it was thought possible to remove the troublesome question of religion for ever from the sphere of politics.

Cujus regio, ejus religio! Could it be doubted that the ancient Church would seize this weapon from the Protestant hands which had forged it, and smite every people with it that struggled for emancipation? Not freedom of religion, but freedom of princes to prescribe religion to their slaves—for this so many tens of thousands had died on the battlefield, or been burned, and buried alive!

And it was sincerely hoped and believed that humanity could be thus remanded to its dungeon, buffeted, flouted, jeered out of its rights, and the padlock placed for ever on the immortal mind. And truly to those who reckon history by the year, who find the record of man's progress only in political annals, how dreary must seem our fate! What can be more monotonous than the dull catalogue of kings, princes, and priestly or courtly politicians, with their palace revolutions, insipid ceremonials, and ghastly chronicles of murderous wars for petty questions, as whether Charles or Ferdinand, Louis or Peter, shall sit on this throne, restore that province, or espouse this princess?

Unless we hold fast to the fact, that in human as in physical history, Nature is ever patiently producing her effects through long lapses of time, by causes which have been in operation since the beginning, History is but another word for despair. But history is never hysterical, never proceeds by catastrophes and cataclysms; and it is only by remembering this that we can comprehend its higher meaning.

To discover the great intellectual law prescribed by the Creator is the science of history. To induce mankind to conform to that law is the science of politics.

The great mutiny against sacerdotal Rome, which we call the Reformation, even like the universal revolt against imperial Rome a thousand years before, which we call the wandering of the nations, had been balked of its logical result.

The first mutiny established the Feudal system over the people; the second strengthened Church and military government by confirming instead of dissolving the connection between the two.

But now another talisman was to change the face of the world; for the great discoveries are apt to leap from the highly electrified brain of Man at identical epochs. Christopher Columbus, confiding in his own stout heart and the mariner's compass, sailed forth on unknown seas, and behold America! Here was the chief event thus far recorded in human progress, as Time, in its deliberate patience, was one day to prove.

Speech, the Alphabet, Mount Sinai, Egypt, Greece, Rome, Nazareth, the wandering of the nations, the feudal system, Magna Charta, gunpowder, printing, the Reformation, the mariner's compass, America—here are some of the great landmarks of human motion.

As we pause for a moment's rest, after our rapid sweep through the eons and the centuries, have we not the right to record proof of man's progress since the days of the rhinoceros-eaters of Bedfordshire, of the man of Natchez?

And for details and detached scenes in the general phantasmagoria, which has been ever shifting before us, we may seek for illustration, instruction, or comfort, in any age or land where authentic record can be found. We may take a calm survey of passionate, democratic Greece in her great civil war through the terse, judicial narrative of Thucydides; we may learn to loathe despotism in that marvellous portrait-gallery of crime which the sombre and terrible Tacitus has bequeathed; we may cross the yawning abysses and dreary deserts which lie between two civilizations over that stately viaduct of a thousand arches which the great hand of Gibbon has constructed; we may penetrate to the inmost political and social heart of England, during a period of nine years, by help of the magic wand of Macaulay; we may linger in the stately portico to the unbuilt dome which the daring genius of Buckle consumed his life in devising; we may yield to the sweet fascinations which ever dwell in the picturesque pages of Prescott; we may investigate rules, apply and ponder examples; but the detail of history is essentially a blank, and nothing could be more dismal than its pursuit unless the mind be filled by a broad view of its general scheme.

But what concerns us most nearly at present is the actual civilization of Europe and America. Europe and America—twin sisters—the one long hidden in entranced sleep within primeval forests, while the other was slowly groping its way along the path of progress; yet both indissolubly connected by an ever palpitating bond.

In the fulness of time, after so many errors, crimes, and disappointments, civilization seemed to find a fresh field for its endeavors, as the discovery of this continent revealed a virgin world.

It is impossible to imagine a more fortunate position than that occupied by this Republic. Nature has done its best, and it is not for physical advantages alone that she should be ever grateful.

All the experience of the old world, all its acquisitions, all its sufferings, all its beacons of warning are for our benefit. Feudal System, Divine Right, are essentially as dead figments here as the laws of Lycurgus or Draco. Religion can be honestly and ardently cherished because priesthood is deprived of political power. Universal education, the only possible foundation of human freedom, is the easiest duty, because the Church is powerless to arrogate a function which it can never discharge.

To be rid of the cumbrous machinery of military conquest, to have escaped from all the grand Lamas into whom the soul of the great Schaka successively passes, enduing them with infallibility and omniscience, to have forgotten many of these worn-out traditions of Europe and Asia, is a boon for which America ought to be daily upon her knees.

The great inventions making democracy on an imperial scale possible; representation by rule of three, the steam-engine, the telegraph, the free school, and that immense instrument of civilization, the daily press, had been waiting to be perfected until she could show their value on a colossal scale.

For in time a new term would have to be invented for what men call civilization and polity. From *civitas*—city, civilization, civility; from *polis*—politics, politician, polity—always from the city had grown empire as in antiquity, or by the city had been wrested liberties as in mediaeval times. Culture was ever of the town, townish. But here a vast empire had been waiting for its empty spaces to be peopled, three millions of miles with never a town on its surface. Clearly the phenomenon was a new one and culture here could only mean Democracy.

But to the solemn birthday of the infant America, around

whose cradle, obscure as it was, so many good spirits had invisibly clustered, one malignant fairy had not been bidden, and her name was Privilege. And even as in the story-book she sent a curse to avenge the slight. Almost on that natal day—we know the tale too well, and have had cause to ponder it bitterly—came the accursed bark with its freight of victims from unhappy Africa, and Privilege had silently planted in this virgin soil the seeds of her future sway.

It was an accident—if any thing can be called accidental in the grand scheme of Creation—yet out of that grain of mustard-seed was one day to sprout an evil to overshadow this land; to poison with its deadly exhalations the vigorous atmosphere of freedom. Oligarchy grew up and held its own, side by side with Democracy—until the time came for deciding whether the one principle or the other was in conformity with the eternal law.

Chemistry resolves the universe into a few ingredients. What, for example, is a man? Take a little hydrogen and oxygen, nitrogen and carbon, potash, lime, and sulphur, with a pinch or two of salt; and there is your hero or your prize-fighter; your Plato or your Washington. And political chemistry is no less subtle and rapid in its analysis. Oligarchy is resolved into the same gaseous vapors on one side the ocean and the other. So soon as it was demonstrated that the Slave power rested on Divine Right; so soon as it was ascertained on authority that the Bible ordained not negro slavery merely, but human slavery without distinction of color; so soon as it had been proclaimed that "the Bible argument in favor of slavery was its sheet-anchor"; so soon as it had been categorically stated at the South, "that slavery is just, natural, and necessary, and that it does not depend on difference of color"; so soon as the new Evangel had announced that "the experiment of universal liberty had failed, that the evils of free society are insufferable, and that policy and humanity alike forbade the extension of its evils to new peoples and coming generations," and that "there was no solution of the great problem of reconciling the interests of capital and labor so simple and effective as to make the laborer himself capital"—in all which statements I am only quoting literally from eminent slave-power authority—it became obvious that the identity of Privilege, whether cis- or trans-Atlantic, was perfect. Grace of God, Right Divine, property in mankind claimed by human creatures superior to mankind, military dominion, political priesthood—what are all these but the nitrogen, hydrogen, carbon, lime, and potash out of which Privilege is always compounded?

Yet this great, innocent, ingenuous American Demos rubbed its eyes with astonishment—as its great fight with Oligarchy began—to find no tears running down the iron cheek of Privilege. Why, Privilege would have been an idiot if it had wept in sympathy with the Demos. Nothing but the *sancta simplicitas* of perfect confidence in the right, nothing but the conviction that the Declaration of Independence reaffirmed the statutes of the Omnipotent could have explained the popular delusion. Slavery and serfdom have been abolished throughout Europe, but so long as the soil of many great empires belongs to an exquisitely small minority of the inhabitants, are not Wamba the Witless and Gurth the Swineherd almost as much born thralls to their master as if his collar were still upon their necks?

"Patriotism," said Samuel Johnson, at the epoch of our war of Independence, "is the last refuge of a scoundrel." His parents believed, you remember, in the right divine of a queen's finger to cure the scrofula. And there has been a series of Dr. Johnsons from his day to ours, all over Europe, to denounce patriots and republicans, especially when they are causing interruptions to trade. So close an electric chain unites America and Europe, so instantaneous are their action and retroaction, that the American civil war, at least in Western Europe, became as much an affair of passionate party feeling as if it were raging on that side the Atlantic. "I had no idea," said a very eminent statesman to John Bright, on two different occasions, "how much influence the example of that Republic was having upon public opinion in England until I discovered the universal congratulation that the Republic was likely to be broken up."

And yet, strange to say, in spite of the breathless interest with which the result and the daily details were watched for, it would be difficult to exaggerate the ignorance enwrapping the general mind of Europe as to the merits and meaning of the conflict.

In popular periodicals and lectures of today you may learn much of bays, rivers, inlets, oceans, and continents of the planet Mars; and if inclined for a vacation excursion, and could you find a conveyance thither, you might easily arrange a tour in that planet, starting from Huggin's Inlet and sailing thirty thousand miles along one of its very convenient estuaries without ever losing sight of land. I know not whether the Martians have accepted the nomenclature of Dawes Continent, Table-Leg Bay, and the other designations laid down on their planet by the spirited geographers of ours; but at least they might be flattered did they know of the interest they excite on this earth.

Perhaps, however, if they knew what was said of them here, they might be almost as much amazed as we used to be in America at the wonderful discoveries made by Europe concerning our politics, geography, history, statistics, national character, constitution, and condition during the late civil war.

It was not that light was impossible. The thinkers and the workers were never misled; the brains and the bone and muscle of Europe were in the right place.

Without mentioning other illustrious names which might be cited, I will remind you but of this. There was one man in England—greatest and truest of all—who made our cause his own through good report and bad report, whose voice found an echo in every patriotic heart in this country, and whose intellect shone like the sun through the mists of passion and prejudice obscuring the cause of liberty; a statesman whose public speeches will be always treasured on either side the ocean as models of eloquence; and whose simple Anglo-Saxon name will be always dear to lovers of liberty in future times as in the present. You know already that I mean John Bright.

And the great conflict went on while the world stood wondering. Never in human history has there been such a battle with such a stake. It was not for territory, empire, power. It was not merely for the integrity of this vast republican heritage. These things, though precious, are of little worth compared to the sacred principle concerned in the struggle. For it was to be decided whether the great law of history which we have been tracing was a truth or a lie; whether the human race has been steadily although slowly progressing or whether we have been fatally drifting back to Chaos. For surely if freedom is an evil from which society, new or old, is to be saved and slavery the great remedy and the great hope for the world, the only solution of political problems, then is the science of history the most contemptible of all imaginable studies. It was not a question for America but for the world. The toiling multitudes of the earth are interested in the fate of this great republic of refuge, which receives and protects the oppressed of every race. "My countrymen who work for your living," said John Bright, at Birmingham, in 1863, "remember this, there will be one wild shriek of freedom to startle all mankind if that Republic should be overthrown." But the game was fought out, and both winners and losers are the gainers. The South, while deeming itself to have lost all save honor, will be more prosperous than it ever dreamed of ere a generation of mankind shall have passed away. Let its "bruised arms be hung up for monuments," along with the trophies of the triumphant North; for the valor, the endurance, and self-sacrifice were equal on both sides, and the defeated party was vanquished because neither pride of color nor immortal hate can successfully struggle against the inexorable law of Freedom and Progress.

I have spoken much of America. The political affairs of its sister Europe are at this moment in a more fluid state than usual. The effect of the triumph of freedom in this country on the cause of progress in Europe is plain; but it would be impossible in the limits of this address to take a survey of the whole field. It seems natural, however, to glance at that political and social heart of Europe—Germany. Ever since the great rising for freedom against the Roman empire, down to this hour, Germany has been the main source of European and American culture.

The common mother of nations and empires—*alma mater felix prole*—she still rules the thought of her vast brood of children; Franks, Goths, Saxons, Lombards, Normans, Netherlanders, Americans—Germans all. Her Gothic branches in the fifth and sixth centuries sweeping to and fro over the extinct Roman empire from the Ultima Thule of Britain to the confines of Asia, overlaying and controlling the Latin, Celtic, Sclavonic provinces and tribes; her energetic Norman branch of pirates, seating themselves afterwards with such happy audacity on every throne in Europe, from the Williams and Henrys of the North to the Rogers, Tancreds, Godfreys, and Baldwins of the South and East, from the Rurics of Russia to the Roderics of Spain; everywhere in high places and low, all-conquering Germany has stamped our civilization with her impress and bequeathed to modern languages the treasures of her ample and varied dialects.

Europe, essentially homogeneous in its upper strata, might have been a united nation a thousand years ago, had Science been sufficiently advanced to make Union and Democracy possible or even conceivable.

But disintegration was the preliminary process by which the ground was prepared for new culture. Everywhere separation into small national groupings was the initial characteristic of European history. Seven German kingdoms in what we now call England; as many independent dukes and sovereigns in present France; a dozen kings in Spain; in Italy; hundreds of them in Germany proper; a plurality of sovereignties, in short, in all the districts of Christendom; thus was Europe broken into hostile and discordant fragments. And the tendency to unite these jarring sovereignties into a few solid masses has marked her later history. . . .

Such was "the holy Roman empire"—an appellation which, as Voltaire remarked, was open to criticism on three points. It was not holy, was not Roman, and was not an empire. With those exceptions, the description was perfect. The people were ground to powder and kept in microscopic divisions of territory which had neither the dignity of monarchy nor the freedom of republicanism. A net-work of sovereign and independent custom-houses and forts at every turn as thick as mile-stones, an intolerable confusion of debased and detestable currencies, strangled commerce and impeded circulation, while the great German heart, yearning for union and nationality, and for freedom, the legitimate child of both, grew sick with hope deferred.

After nearly two centuries more had passed away, the Congress of Vienna, as part of the little good that it accomplished for humanity, at least much diminished the catalogue of petty princes in Germany. Three hundred and odd of them went up to that political guillotine, and only thirty-five escaped with life. The Germanic Confederation, a league of sovereigns called in the vernacular the Bund, was set up in place of the defunct empire, and conducted itself with much pomp until its power of standing alone should be tested. Magnificent in its deportment towards the lesser powers of Germany, and especially towards the people, whose existence it never recognized, it was on its knees whenever the great empire or the great kingdom—Austria or Prussia—wore a frowning face.

Meantime the German Demos, striving after union and strength, had partially achieved, under the lead of Prussia, a Customs' Union. The National league, filled with larger ideas of union, resolved, as an exemplification of a principle, to free the German inhabitants of Schleswig-Holstein from the Danish crown. The two great powers took the war into their own hands. Else had Democracy taken the bit into its teeth. The Schleswig-Holstein war was soon over. The provinces were taken from Denmark. Then followed the dispute for the booty.

The rest of the story is familiar. The seven weeks war and the peace of Prague—which passed all understanding—for behold, when the smoke was cleared away, not only was Austria excluded from Germany, but even her allies in the defunct Bund—the southern states—had accepted, by treaty, the military and commercial supremacy of Prussia. Thus another immense stride had been made toward German unity. In 1648, more than three hundred sovereignties. In 1815, three dozen.

In 1866, with exception of the Germanic possessions of Austria, essentially and practically one.

How much has liberty gained by this progress? Time will show that progress and liberty are identical. It is impossible that the success of Prussia is to end in the establishment of one great military empire the more. The example and the retro-action of America; the success here of freedom and progress—forbid that result. The great statesman of Prussia is distinguished for courage, insight, breadth of vision, iron will, and a warm and steadfast heart. His genius consists in the instinctive power of governing by conforming to the spirit of the age. No man knows better than Bismarck, to read the signs of the times. Small is the chance of Despotism in these latter days to stem the Rapids. She may utter dismal shrieks, but shoot Niagara she must.

The present government of Austria has nobly placed itself on the right road out of great perplexities. Numerous individual deeds of knightly valor worthy of the age of chivalry; loyal devotion to antique but sacred ideals; above all, a spontaneous and signal benevolence manifested by all classes, after the war; from highest to humblest—converting the palaces of great nobles, the mansions of burghers and cottages of the peasant, into hospitals, where the sick and wounded were tenderly ministered to by fair and loving hands—could not arrest the inexorable march of events. The brief history of constitutionalism in that empire is full of instruction. . . .

The problem of fusing nationalities into a nation is always hard to solve. In Austria, the leading three are the German, Hungarian, and Sclavonic. The Magyars, the last direct emigration out of Asia into Europe, have held the wide, fruitful plains on the borders of Turkey and Russia for a thousand years, wedging themselves firmly between the more ancient settlers of the Sclavonic family. At this moment there are about five million Magyars, nine million Germans, and fifteen million Sclavonians, out of thirty-two millions of the whole population of the empire.

But there has been no single dominant, national language to

absorb into itself those various tongues. And difference of speech has kept nationalities distinct, and of course promoted disunion. So soon as the pressure of absolutism was removed, each nationality began to assert its own rights, its own independence, its own dialect, and to separate its aspirations and traditions from those of its sisters. Subjects which would seem more appropriate to antiquarian societies or debating clubs than to the realm of politics became popular themes for statesmen and legislators. The Magyars—a proud, chivalrous people, with much aptitude for politics—had for centuries governed twice their number of Sclavonians, controlling not only the whole of Hungary, but the annexed provinces of Transylvania and Croatia. In those remote, and, to the general American public, obscure regions, lie the seeds of many future convulsions in Europe, to which I shall not allude on this occasion. . . .

The imperial arch may be said, therefore, to rest on the two columns of Germanism and Magyarism; upon the two dominant nationalities in which the Chancellor Baron Beust expects firmest support. Some of the most progressive and eloquent German representatives in the old Reichsrath have seats in the West Cabinet.

Still more significant are the abolition of the Concordat and the liberation of education and marriage from the exclusive control of the Catholic priesthood or of any priesthood.

"The law of last December establishes free liberty for all opinions, liberty of marriage, liberty of education, liberty of the press, liberty of faith, no matter of what confession or doctrine. It grants to the members of each confession the rights of establishing public schools and colleges, and members of every confession are allowed to be admitted on the same footing with the sanction of the state." *

On the 25th of May of the present year, a law on education was passed, "which suppresses all the influence of the Catholic Church or of any church over education, decreeing that the whole superior supervision of education, literature, and science,

---

* The quotation is from the Papal allocution, in which the measures are described in order to be denounced. [*Motley's note.*]

as also the inspection of schools, belongs to the state, which finally decrees that religious teaching in the public schools must be placed in the hands of members of each separate confession; that any religious society may open private or special schools for the youth of its faith; that these schools shall also be subject to the supreme inspection of the state, and that the school-books shall be subject to the approval of the civil authorities, with the exception, however, of such books as are meant for religious instruction, which must be submitted to the approval of the competent authorities of each confession." *

More just, enlightened, progressive legislation than this, on such vital subjects, could not be expected in our own land— in New-York, Ohio, Massachusetts—where you will.

An ecclesiastical convention has been held in the Tyrol for the avowed purpose of "restoring the Lord God to his rights," invaded by this legislation of the Reichsrath on education and marriage. The twenty-five bishops of the empire addressed a passionate appeal to the emperor on the subject of the Concordat and of these new laws, and received from his Majesty a stern reply that such matters were in the hands of his responsible advisers, and that the duty of the church was to assist government in this grave national crisis rather than to add to its difficulties by inflammatory and seditious language.

This autograph letter of the emperor was read in the Reichsrath amid tumultuous cheers; the whole assembly rising to their feet.

E pluribus duo is established. The attempt to square the political circle has a fair prospect of success. To assist the separate nationalities in moving off from each other in all directions, to cultivate separation of language, literature, tradition, costume, habit, law—disintegration, in short—would be to remand the empire into Absolutism or Chaos. The cause of human progress is benefited by the experiment now making in Austria, and the friends of civilization and freedom should wish it Godspeed. A double ministry, out of which a third one is evolved for imperial purposes only—such a scheme seems

*From the Papal allocution. [*Motley's note.*]

delicate and complicated for rough work. But Dualism, combined with personal union under one sovereign, is rather a phrase than a fact; the two halves of the empire being practically conjoined and dependent on each other, especially on the two great departments of war and foreign affairs.

Thus do we find signs of healthful progress in many parts of Europe toward free institutions. So far has the democratic principle, ever glowing amid heaps of scoriae, forced itself above the superincumbent crust.

Happy this single great nation on earth, where that principle is recognized as the legitimate source of life and heat, not dreaded as flame from the lowest pit to devastate and consume!

But alas! progress must be fettered and halting everywhere, under the military rule prevailing over continental Europe.

Reflect upon these little figures in simple arithmetic:

> France has 1,200,000 soldiers.
> Italy has 500,000.
> Prussia about one million.
> Austria, 800,000.
> Russia nearly a million.

Thus merely the Pentarchy of the continent, its five leading powers alone—not counting the middle and lesser powers, of which almost the least have larger armies than the present forces of the United States—keep nearly five millions of men perpetually on foot, while this great Republic has about 40,000 men.

No epigram could be terser. We know from recent experience how much it costs to keep up great armies. And we have proved to the world that where great principles or where the national existence is at stake, every citizen becomes a soldier, that immortal commanders start out of obscurity into fame, and that great armies resolve themselves again into the mass of the people, becoming ennobled by their military experience, and even better citizens than before.

But here is the heart of life taken systematically out of all these citizens in every monarchy. For a period varying from fifteen to nine years—the whole of youth and the cream of middle age—these men lose their family, their home, their country; becoming citizens only of that dangerous military commonwealth which holds potentates and subjects alike in its iron grasp.

Is it really the final result of European civilization to decide which nation shall have the most populous armies and the biggest guns?

Before the infinity of the universe and the great laws of motion were known, historical disquisition was but a meagre and discomforting pursuit. But now—standing on this bank and shoal of time—we are able at least to hazard dim glances into those infinite spaces which we call the Past and the Future, and to guess at some of those laws of intellectual motion which we call Progress.

Nor is a contemplation of the conditions of any nation inspiring or suggestive, unless the presence of that electric chain is felt by which all humanity is darkly bound. It is impossible for one nation to acquire without acquiring for all—for one great member of the human family to advance or to retrograde without hastening or retarding the general march of humanity. And it is for this reason that I have called your attention tonight to a superficial and most inadequate view of human progress through innumerable ages, and especially to the influence exerted upon that progress and upon the fortunes of man by the example and the fate of this Republic.

I have dwelt long, by way of illustration, on recent events in Central Europe. I should have liked to say something of Spain, of Italy, of France, but time fails me, and perhaps one or two examples are as useful as a score.

It is impossible, however, not to make a passing allusion to the presidential election which has just occurred in Great Britain almost simultaneously with our own. I say presidential election—because on the vote just taken it has been decided that Mr. Gladstone, and not Mr. Disraeli, is to preside over affairs in England for the next political term, be it long or short— as conclusively as if their names had been voted for on general ticket. There the First Lord of the Treasury is Prime Minister for Her Majesty the Queen. Here the President is Prime Minister for His Majesty the People.

Who can doubt that among the indirect results of the success of the Union in the late war was the passage of a reform bill by a Tory government, establishing something nearly approaching to universal suffrage in England? A vast revolution has been accomplished in that great country, which is destined to place her—where she ought ever to be—side by side, in full friendship and in generous rivalry of freedom and the arts of peace with this Republic—both children of the ancient German mother.

The British Parliament, which governs thirty millions of citizens, and one hundred and fifty millions of subjects, which by a statute passed at any moment can change the constitution, alter the succession to the crown, convert the monarchy into a commonwealth or a despotism, prescribe the creed of the Church—has been hitherto a representative of land, and not of man. The best club in London, exclusive, full of distinguished and eloquent gentlemen; delightfully situated on the Thames, with charming terraces and bay-windows on the river; an excellent library, within five minutes' walk of all the public offices, and with the privilege of governing a splendid empire into the bargain, it is no wonder that men were willing to pay well in times past for seats in the House of Commons; and it is a sure mark of progress that the average expense of seats has been steadily diminishing. The good old times are gone for ever when boroughs comfortably advertised themselves for sale in the public journals, and when a working majority of the House held their seats on the nomination and at the pleasure of less than two hundred landholders—about two members on an average for each landholder. It is certainly to the credit of the British people, and proof of their indomitable love of liberty, that they have moved steadily forward, and, without civil war, have achieved such triumphs as Catholic emancipation, the corn law repeal, the reform bill of 1830, and the reform bill just coming into operation.

After all, the English household suffrage bill is the fruit of the Appomattox apple-tree. Who imagined in 1862 that power would be transferred, in England, so soon from land to people, without bloodshed, and that it would be done by Tories?

Meantime Land is likely to hold its own for a season longer in its race against Man; but Man must be the winner at last, and will soon learn the meaning of the revolution which has been accomplished.

England is a landed aristocracy. Twenty million men live in England, thirty thousand men own England. The pyramid stands on its apex.

In America is a landed democracy. Every man votes, and every man may be a landholder who is willing to go West for a homestead. Our experiment has often been pronounced a new and a bold one. It is an experiment, but scarcely a bold one. It is simply to see if the pyramid can be made to stand on its base. Thus far it has stood, although Privilege was amazed the other day that it was not toppled over, feeling that no other government could have resisted such a shock as was dealt to our fabric.

Over the whole surface of Europe there are symptoms of human progress. There are few people so benighted as to be incapable of imagining light; as in caverns where the sun never shone, naturalists tell us of organized beings, insects, reptiles, fishes, with at least the rudiments of eyes and wings.

There is movement all over Europe, as I hope to have proved by pregnant examples. Through the long Past there have been political lullabies for the infant Man; Divine right, Infallibility, charters to the people instead of charters from the people; universal suffrage combined with universal bayonets; above all, the magnificent platitude that government always exists with full consent of the governed.

America stands upon the firm land toward which other nations are slowly making their way through revolutions or without them. If she does not now start on an upward progress, intellectual and moral, such as was never known before, she commits a crime against mankind.

The European emigrant, the forlorn outcast it may be of older civilizations, finds already accomplished here the revolution which he has "dreaded but dwelt upon" as the darkest of crimes. But that emigration, amounting to three millions of Europeans every ten or twelve years, has been always in one direction and on a comparatively limited scale.

Two centuries before the Christian era, many millions of men were occupied—as we have all read in the School Books—ten years long in building a wall. That wall, although decaying, stands to this day. It is fifteen hundred miles in length; it is twenty-five feet high, and so broad that six cavalrymen can ride abreast upon it. It is sometimes carried over mountains of a mile's perpendicular height. Its masonry is so conscientious that it is said to be impossible to thrust a nail between the massive stones of which it is composed. There are towers and bastions for armed men at regular intervals through all its prodigious length.

This wall was built—as we all know—by Tsin-Shee-Hwang-Tee, founder of the dynasty of Tsin, as protection against the incursions of the Tartars.

But what is this stupendous piece of mason work, bristling with armed men, which has done its best for two thousand years to protect one third of the human race from the invasion of their fellow-creatures, compared to that air-drawn barrier, invisible, impalpable, yet until recent events impregnable, which has barred the road to emigration southward, and which we call Mason and Dixon's line?

The European wanderer, pushing westward after landing on these shores, finds an enormous plain stretching between the Rocky and the Appalachian mountains—from the gulf to the Arctic, and containing, below the forty-fifth parallel, a surface of unexampled fertility of a million and a half square miles in extent. There are coal-fields, too, larger than the whole surface of Great Britain. Farther on, there are gold mines which in twenty years have produced more of the precious metal than had the mines of Mexico and Peru, after they had trebled the prices of commodities and revolutionized the commerce of the world. There is no feudal system, no state church to prescribe or proscribe his religious creed and prohibit the education of his children. The most commodious building in every town is usually the school-house, in which his children are gratuitously educated in common with those of the richest citizens, and where all are converted into Americans together; not taught to harp upon nationalities or to wrangle of creeds. He finds Catholics, Protestants, Hebrews side by side in mutual respect and affection; illustrious men not more admired and beloved by those of their own faith than by those of a different church.

But the most tempting, semi-tropical region, producing the great staple on which so large a part of the world's industry depends, has not cultivated much more than one per cent of the soil—a region three times as large as France—which might yield that precious plant in profusion, feed and clothe untold millions and maintain empires. The cotton crop has languished far behind its possibilities because, while there was no limit to the demand, an increase to the supply of labor was sternly forbidden; few emigrants daring to cross that awful barrier.

We stand on the threshold of great events. A change in the conditions of mankind is impending;

> "A multitude like which the populous North
> Poured never from her frozen loins to pass
> Rhene or the Danaw when her barbarous sons
> Came like a deluge on the South,"

is gradually collecting in distant regions. Is it possible that those vast and fruitful plains, which have so long been panting in vain for culture are to lie fallow still when the famishing labor of the world is anxious for a summons?

No country ever prospered long where labor was dishonored. Look at Spain, where, two and a half centuries ago, the most effective population in the land—five hundred thousand full-grown men and women—were expelled from the country, at the dictate of the archbishop of Toledo, because they were industrious and because they were Moors—an achievement of such stupendous idiocy that a wiser churchman, Cardinal Richelieu, afterwards declared it to be the most audacious and barbarous ever recorded by history—and think of Spanish misfortunes from that day to this. On remote Bohemian, Moravian, Swabian, Swedish mountains and plains human creatures are toiling life long, from squalid cradle to pauper grave, for a daily wage of ten cents each. Down among dismal coal-mines in various parts of Europe, men, women, and children are banished, weeks and months long, from "the warm precincts of the cheerful day," from home affections, from education, from civilization; companions of the fossilized reptiles which perished hundreds of thousand-years ago, overshadowed and begrimed by the charred and carbonized forests of the primeval world; moiling from childhood to old age for a pittance barely sufficient to support life, that they may pile up still higher the magnificent fabric of feudal pomp which has so long doomed them and their fellows to a living burial. Is it to be imagined that such stepchildren of European civilization would not be wooed from their dismal caves into the genial climate, the virgin forests, the exuberant savannahs of the South, and be converted from gnomes and cobolds into men, so soon as the long trance has been broken there, labor raised from degradation, and the great law of Democracy accepted?

The inestimable blessing of the abolition of slavery to the cause of progress, above all to the South itself, can never be exaggerated. The fetters have fallen not from the black alone, but from the white, from all mankind. The standing reproach to Democracy is removed at last, the basis of our national institutions has become an everlasting truth.

Thus far I have trespassed on your patience, while dimly endeavoring to trace from what we know or imagine of history, proofs of that law of progress to the disbelievers in which history can teach nothing. My faith in that law and in the welfare of this Republic, in proportion to her conformity to that law, is absolute. That all mankind are capable of progress I as devoutly believe. None can be debarred from the inalienable right to intellectual and moral development, which is the true meaning of the pursuit of happiness, as proclaimed in our great statute. And hope may come to all. In some of the Western portions of this country, amidst the profusion of nearly all the gifts of Heaven, there is a deficiency of pure water. But American energy is not to be balked by dissembling Nature of that first necessity of life. Artesian wells are sunk through the sod of the prairies, through the loam, through the gravel, through the hard-pan which is almost granite, until at last, one thousand or fifteen hundred feet beneath the surface, the hand of man reveals a deep and rapid river coursing through those solitary, sunless depths at a speed of ten miles the hour, swifter than Ohio, or Mississippi, or Hudson, or any of the bountiful and imperial streams of this country, flowing as they do through picturesque mountain scenery, stately forest or enamelled meadow, amid towered cities or cultivated fields. And when the shaft has reached that imprisoned river, and the rent for the first time has been made through its dungeon wall, the waters, remembering the august source on far distant mountain tops whence ages ago they fell, leap upward to the light with terrible energy, rising in an instant far above the surface of the earth and pouring forth their healthful and fertilizing current to delight and refresh Mankind. And with even such an awakening are we gladdened when half-forgotten Humanity bursts from time to time out of the depths in which it has pursued its joyless, sunless course, moaning and murmuring through long centuries but never quite forgetting its divine and distant origin.

Such was the upward movement out of intellectual thraldom which we call the Reformation when the shaft of Luther struck the captive stream; such an awakening but a more significant and hopeful one—has been heralded for this whole Republic, East and West, North and South, and for all humanity by the triumph of the Right in the recent four years' conflict in which all have been the conquerors.

From THE RISE OF THE DUTCH REPUBLIC

[THE TREND OF DUTCH HISTORY]

[The first of Motley's three major historical works, *The Rise of the Dutch Republic,* begins with a long introduction which analyzes and summarizes the history of the seven northern provinces of the Netherlands prior to 1555. In the two following paragraphs he gives his conclusions concerning the trend of Dutch history.]

The civil institutions of the country had assumed their last provincial form in the Burgundo-Austrian epoch. As already stated, their tendency, at a later period a vicious one, was to substitute fictitious personages for men. A chain of corporations was wound about the liberty of the Netherlands; yet that liberty had been originally sustained by the system in which it one day might be strangled. The spirit of local self-government, always the lifeblood of liberty, was often excessive in its manifestations. The centrifugal force had been too much developed, and, combining with the mutual jealousy of corporations, had often made the nation weak against a common foe. Instead of popular rights there were state rights; for the large cities, with extensive districts and villages under their government, were rather petty states than municipalities. Although the supreme legislative and executive functions belonged to the sovereign, yet each city made its bylaws, and possessed, besides, a body of statutes and regulations, made from time to time by its own authority and confirmed by the prince. Thus a large portion, at least, of the nation shared practically in the legislative functions, which, technically, it did not claim; nor had the requirements of society made constant legislation so necessary, as that to exclude the people from the work was to enslave the country. There was popular power enough to effect much good, but it was widely scattered, and, at the same time, confined in artificial forms. The guilds were vassals of the towns, the towns vassals of the feudal lord. The guild voted in the "broad council" of the city as one person; the city voted in the estates as one person. The people of the United Netherlands was the personage yet to be invented. It was a privilege, not a right, to exercise a handiwork, or to participate in the action of government. Yet the mass of privileges was so large, the shareholders so numerous, that practically the towns were republics. The government was in the hands of a large number of the people. Industry and intelligence led to wealth and power. This was great progress from the general servitude of the eleventh and twelfth centuries, an immense barrier against arbitrary rule. Loftier ideas of human rights, larger conceptions of commerce, have taught mankind, in later days, the difference between liberties and liberty, between guilds and free competition. At the same time it was the principle of mercantile association in the middle ages which protected the infant steps of human freedom and human industry against violence and wrong. Moreover, at this period, the tree of municipal life was still green and vigorous. The healthful flow of sap from the humblest roots to the most verdurous branches indicated the internal soundness of the core, and provided for the constant development of exterior strength. The road to political influence was open to all, not by right of birth, but through honorable exertion of heads and hands.[1]

Thus in this rapid sketch of the course and development of the Netherland nation during sixteen centuries, we have seen it ever marked by one prevailing characteristic, one master-passion —the love of liberty, the instinct of self-government. Largely compounded of the bravest Teutonic elements, Batavian and Frisian, the race ever battles to the death with tyranny, organizes extensive revolts in the age of Vespasian, maintains a partial independence even against the sagacious dominion of Charlemagne, refuses in Friesland to accept the papal yoke or feudal chain, and, throughout the dark ages, struggles resolutely towards the light, wresting from a series of petty sovereigns

[1] *The Rise of the Dutch Republic* (New York, 1856), I, 81–82.

a gradual and practical recognition of the claims of humanity.
With the advent of the Burgundian family, the power of the
commons has reached so high a point that it is able to measure
itself, undaunted, with the spirit of arbitrary rule, of which that
engrossing and tyrannical house is the embodiment. For more
than a century the struggle for freedom, for civic life, goes on;
Philip the Good, Charles the Bold, Mary's husband Maximilian,
Charles V, in turn, assailing or undermining the bulwarks
raised, age after age, against the despotic principle. The combat
is ever renewed. Liberty, often crushed, rises again and again
from her native earth with redoubled energy. At last, in the sixteenth century, a new and more powerful spirit, the genius of
religious freedom, comes to participate in the great conflict.
Arbitrary power, incarnated in the second Charlemagne, assails
the new combination with unscrupulous, unforgiving fierceness.
Venerable civic magistrates, haltered, grovel in sackcloth and
ashes; innocent religious reformers burn in holocausts. By the
middle of the century, the battle rages more fiercely than ever.
In the little Netherland territory, Humanity, bleeding but not
killed, still stands at bay and defies the hunters. The two great
powers have been gathering strength for centuries. They are
soon to be matched in a longer and more determined combat
than the world had ever seen. The emperor is about to leave
the stage. The provinces, so passionate for nationality, for
municipal freedom, for religious reformation, are to become the
property of an utter stranger; a prince foreign to their blood,
their tongue, their religion, their whole habits of life and
thought.[1]

[FAREWELL OF CHARLES V]

[The author commences his narrative proper with the famous
scene, the farewell of Charles V to the estates of the Netherlands.]

On the 25th day of October, 1555, the estates of the Netherlands were assembled in the great hall of the palace at Brussels.
They had been summoned to be the witnesses and the guaran-

[1] *Ibid.*, I, 91–92.

tees of the abdication which Charles V had long before resolved
upon, and which he was that day to execute. The emperor, like
many potentates before and since, was fond of great political
spectacles. He knew their influence upon the masses of mankind. Although plain, even to shabbiness, in his own costume,
and usually attired in black, no one ever understood better than
he how to arrange such exhibitions in a striking and artistic
style. We have seen the theatrical and imposing manner in
which he quelled the insurrection at Ghent, and nearly crushed
the life for ever out of that vigorous and turbulent little commonwealth. The closing scene of his long and energetic reign
he had now arranged with profound study, and with an accurate
knowledge of the manner in which the requisite effects were to
be produced. The termination of his own career, the opening
of his beloved Philip's, were to be dramatised in a manner
worthy the august character of the actors, and the importance
of the great stage where they played their parts. The eyes of
the whole world were directed upon that day towards Brussels;
for an imperial abdication was an event which had not, in the
sixteenth century, been staled by custom.[1]

At the western end [of the palace] a spacious platform or stage,
with six or seven steps, had been constructed, below which was a
range of benches for the deputies of the seventeen provinces.
Upon the stage itself there were rows of seats, covered with
tapestry, upon the right hand and upon the left. These were
respectively to accommodate the knights of the order and the
guests of high distinction. In the rear of these were other
benches, for the members of the three great councils. In the
centre of the stage was a splendid canopy, decorated with the
arms of Burgundy, beneath which were placed three gilded arm-
chairs. All the seats upon the platform were vacant, but the
benches below, assigned to the deputies of the provinces, were
already filled. Numerous representatives from all the states
but two—Gelderland and Overyssel—had already taken their
places. Grave magistrates in chain and gown, and executive

[1] *The Rise of the Dutch Republic* (New York, 1856), I, 95–96.

officers in the splendid civic uniforms for which the Netherlands were celebrated, already filled every seat within the space allotted. The remainder of the hall was crowded with the more favored portion of the multitude which had been fortunate enough to procure admission to the exhibition. The archers and hallebardiers of the bodyguard kept watch at all the doors. The theater was filled—the audience was eager with expectation—the actors were yet to arrive. As the clock struck three, the hero of the scene appeared. Caesar, as he was always designated in the classic language of the day, entered, leaning on the shoulder of William of Orange. They came from the chapel, and were immediately followed by Philip the Second and Queen Mary of Hungary. The Archduke Maximilian, the Duke of Savoy, and other great personages, came afterwards, accompanied by a glittering throng of warriors, councillors, governors, and Knights of the Fleece.

Many individuals of existing or future historic celebrity in the Netherlands, whose names are so familiar to the student of the epoch, seemed to have been grouped as if by premeditated design upon this imposing platform, where the curtain was to fall for ever upon the mightiest emperor since Charlemagne, and where the opening scene of the long and tremendous tragedy of Philip's reign was to be simultaneously enacted. There was the Bishop of Arras, soon to be known throughout Christendom by the more celebrated title of Cardinal Granvelle, the serene and smiling priest whose subtle influence over the destinies of so many then present, and over the fortunes of the whole land, was to be so extensive and so deadly. There was that flower of Flemish chivalry, the lineal descendant of ancient Frisian kings, already distinguished for his bravery in many fields, but not having yet won those two remarkable victories which were soon to make the name of Egmont like the sound of a trumpet throughout the whole country. Tall, magnificent in costume, with dark flowing hair, soft brown eye, smooth cheek, a slight moustache, and features of almost feminine delicacy; such was the gallant and ill-fated Lamoral Egmont. The Count of Horn, too, with bold, sullen face, and fanshaped beard—a brave, honest, discontented, quarrelsome, unpopular man; those other twins in doom—the Marquis Berghen and the Lord of Montigny; the Baron Berlaymont, brave, intensely royal, insatiably greedy for office and wages, but who, at least, never served but one party; the Duke of Aerschot, who was to serve all, essay to rule all, and to betray all—a splendid seignor, magnificent in cramoisy velvet, but a poor creature, who traced his pedigree from Adam, according to the family monumental inscriptions at Louvain, but who was better known as grand-nephew of the emperor's famous tutor, Chièvres; the bold, debauched Brederode, with handsome, reckless face and turbulent demeanor; the infamous Noircarmes, whose name was to be covered with eternal execration, for aping towards his own compatriots and kindred as much of Alva's atrocities and avarice as he was permitted to exercise; the distinguished soldiers, Meghen and Aremberg—these, with many others whose deeds of arms were to become celebrated throughout Europe, were all conspicuous in the brilliant crowd. There, too, was that learned Frisian, President Viglius, crafty, plausible, adroit, eloquent—a small, brisk man, with long yellow hair, glittering green eyes, round, tumid, rosy cheeks, and flowing beard. Foremost among the Spanish grandees, and close to Philip, stood the famous favorite Ruy Gomez, or as he was familiarly called "Re y Gomez" (King and Gomez), a man of meridional aspect, with coal-black hair and beard, gleaming eyes, a face pallid with intense application, and slender but handsome figure; while in immediate attendance upon the Emperor was the immortal Prince of Orange.

Such were a few only of the most prominent in that gay throng, whose fortunes, in part, it will be our duty to narrate; how many of them passing through all this glitter to a dark and mysterious doom!—some to perish on public scaffolds, some by midnight assassination; others, more fortunate, to fall on the battlefield—nearly all, sooner or later, to be laid in bloody graves!

All the company present had risen to their feet as the Emperor entered. By his command, all immediately afterwards resumed their places. The benches at either end of the platform were accordingly filled with the royal and princely personages invited with the Fleece Knights, wearing the insignia of their order, with the members of the three great councils, and with the governors. The Emperor, the King, and the Queen of Hungary, were left conspicuous in the center of the scene. As the whole object of the ceremony was to present an impressive exhibition, it is worth our while to examine minutely the appearance of the two principal characters.

Charles the Fifth was then fifty-five years and eight months old; but he was already decrepit with premature old age. He was of about the middle height, and had been athletic and well-proportioned. Broad in the shoulders, deep in the chest, thin in the flank, very muscular in the arms and legs, he had been able to match himself with all competitors in the tourney and the ring, and to vanquish the bull with his own hand in the favorite national amusement of Spain. He had been able in the field to do the duty of captain and soldier, to endure fatigue and exposure, and every privation except fasting. These personal advantages were now departed. Crippled in hands, knees, and legs, he supported himself with difficulty upon a crutch, with the aid of an attendant's shoulder. In face he had always been extremely ugly, and time had certainly not improved his physiognomy. His hair, once of a light color, was now white with age, close clipped and bristling; his beard was gray, coarse, and shaggy. His forehead was spacious and commanding; the eye was dark blue, with an expression both majestic and benignant. His nose was aquiline, but crooked. The lower part of his face was famous for its deformity. The under lip, a Burgundian inheritance, as faithfully transmitted as the duchy and county, was heavy and hanging; the lower jaw protruding so far beyond the upper that it was impossible for him to bring together the few fragments of teeth which still remained, or to speak a whole sentence in an intelligible voice. Eating and talking, occupations to which he was always much addicted, were becoming daily more arduous, in consequence of this original defect, which now seemed hardly human, but rather an original deformity.

So much for the father. The son, Philip the Second, was a small meager man, much below the middle height, with thin legs, a narrow chest, and the shrinking, timid air of an habitual invalid. He seemed so little, upon his first visit to his aunts, the Queens Eleanor and Mary, accustomed to look upon proper men in Flanders and Germany, that he was fain to win their favor by making certain attempts in the tournament, in which his success was sufficiently problematical. "His body," says his professed panegyrist, "was but a human cage, in which, however brief and narrow, dwelt a soul to whose flight the immeasurable expanse of heaven was too contracted." The same wholesale admirer adds, that "his aspect was so reverend, that rustics who met him alone in a wood, without knowing him, bowed down with instinctive veneration." In face he was the living image of his father, having the same broad forehead, and blue eye, with the same aquiline, but better proportioned, nose. In the lower part of the countenance, the remarkable Burgundian deformity was likewise reproduced. He had the same heavy, hanging lip, with a vast mouth, and monstrously protruding jaw. His complexion was fair, his hair light and thin, his beard yellow, short, and pointed. He had the aspect of a Fleming, but the loftiness of a Spaniard. His demeanor in public was still, silent, almost sepulchral. He looked habitually on the ground when he conversed, was chary of speech, embarrassed, and even suffering in manner. This was ascribed partly to a natural haughtiness, which he had occasionally endeavored to overcome, and partly to habitual pains in the stomach, occasioned by his inordinate fondness for pastry.

Such was the personal appearance of the man who was about to receive into his single hand the destinies of half the world; whose single will was, for the future, to shape the fortunes of every individual then present, of many millions more in Europe, America, and at the ends of the earth, and of countless millions yet unborn.

The three royal personages being seated upon chairs placed triangularly under the canopy, such of the audience as had seats provided for them now took their places, and the proceedings commenced. Philibert de Bruxelles, a member of the privy council of the Netherlands, arose at the Emperor's command, and made a long oration.[1]

The Emperor then rose to his feet. Leaning on his crutch, he beckoned from his seat the personage upon whose arm he had leaned as he entered the hall. A tall, handsome youth of twenty-two came forward—a man whose name from that time forward, and as long as history shall endure, has been, and will be, more familiar than any other in the mouths of Netherlanders. At that day he had rather a southern than a German or Flemish appearance. He had a Spanish cast of features, dark, well chiselled, and symmetrical. His head was small, and well placed upon his shoulders. His hair was dark brown, as were also his moustache and peaked beard. His forehead was lofty, spacious, and already prematurely engraved with the anxious lines of thought. His eyes were full, brown, well opened, and expressive of profound reflection. He was dressed in the magnificent apparel for which the Netherlanders were celebrated above all other nations, and which the ceremony rendered necessary. His presence being considered indispensable at this great ceremony, he had been summoned but recently from the camp on the frontier, where, notwithstanding his youth, the Emperor had appointed him to command his army in chief, against such antagonists as Admiral Coligny and the Duc de Nevers.

Thus supported upon his crutch and upon the shoulder of William of Orange, the Emperor proceeded to address the states, by the aid of a closely-written brief which he held in his hand. He reviewed rapidly the progress of events from his seventeenth year up to that day. He spoke of his nine expeditions into Germany, six to Spain, seven to Italy, four to France, ten to the Netherlands, two to England, as many to Africa, and of his eleven voyages by sea. He sketched his various wars, victories, and treaties of peace, assuring his hearers that the welfare of his subjects and the security of the Roman Catholic religion had ever been the leading objects of his life. As long as

[1] *The Rise of the Dutch Republic* (New York, 1856), I, 98–105.

God had granted him health, he continued, only enemies could have regretted that Charles was living and reigning; but now that his strength was but vanity, and life fast ebbing away, his love for his dominion, his affection for his subjects, and his regard for their interests, required his departure. Instead of a decrepit man with one foot in the grave, he presented them with a sovereign in the prime of life and the vigor of health. Turning toward Philip, he observed, that for a dying father to bequeath so magnificent an empire to his son was a deed worthy of gratitude, but that when the father thus descended to the grave before his time, and by an anticipated and living burial sought to provide for the welfare of his realms and the grandeur of his son, the benefit thus conferred was surely far greater. He added, that the debt would be paid to him and with usury, should Philip conduct himself in his administration of the provinces with a wise and affectionate regard to their true interests. Posterity would applaud his abdication, should his son prove worthy of his bounty; and that could only be by living in the fear of God, and by maintaining law, justice, and the Catholic religion in all their purity, as the true foundation of the realm. In conclusion, he entreated the estates, and, through them, the nation, to render obedience to their new prince, to maintain concord and to preserve inviolate the Catholic faith; begging them, at the same time, to pardon him all errors or offenses which he might have committed towards them during his reign, and assuring them that he should unceasingly remember their obedience and affection in his every prayer to that Being to whom the remainder of his life was to be dedicated.

Such brave words as these, so many vigorous asseverations of attempted performances of duty, such fervent hopes expressed of a benign administration in behalf of the son, could not but affect the sensibilities of the audience, already excited and softened by the impressive character of the whole display. Sobs were heard throughout every portion of the hall, and tears poured profusely from every eye. The Fleece Knights on the platform and the burghers in the background were all melted with the same emotion. As for the Emperor himself, he sank almost fainting upon his chair as he concluded his address. An ashy paleness overspread his countenance, and he wept like a child. Even the icy Philip was almost softened, as he rose to perform his part in the ceremony. Dropping upon his knees before his father's feet, he reverently kissed his hand. Charles placed his hands solemnly upon his son's head, made the sign of the cross, and blessed him in the name of the Holy Trinity. Then raising him in his arms, he tenderly embraced him, saying, as he did so, to the great potentates around him, that he felt a sincere compassion for the son on whose shoulders so heavy a weight had just devolved, and which only a lifelong labor would enable him to support. Philip now uttered a few words expressive of his duty to his father and his affection for his people. Turning to the orders, he signified his regret that he was unable to address them either in the French or Flemish language, and was therefore obliged to ask their attention to the Bishop of Arras, who would act as his interpreter. Anthony Perrenot accordingly arose, and in smooth, fluent, and well-turned commonplaces, expressed at great length the gratitude of Philip towards his father, with his firm determination to walk in the path of duty, and to obey his father's counsels and example in the future administration of the provinces. This long address of the prelate was responded to at equal length by Jacob Maas, member of the Council of Brabant, a man of great learning, eloquence, and prolixity, who had been selected to reply on behalf of the States-General, and who now, in the name of these bodies, accepted the abdication in an elegant and complimentary harangue. Queen Mary of Hungary, the "Christian widow" of Erasmus, and Regent of the Netherlands during the past twenty-five years, then rose to resign her office, making a brief address expressive of her affection for the people, her regrets at leaving them, and her hopes that all errors which she might have committed during her long administration would be forgiven her. Again the redundant Maas responded, asserting in terms of fresh compliment and elegance the uniform satisfaction of the provinces with her conduct during her whole career.

The orations and replies having now been brought to a close, the ceremony was terminated. The Emperor, leaning on the shoulders of the Prince of Orange and of the Count de Buren, slowly left the hall, followed by Philip, the Queen of Hungary, and the whole court; all in the same order in which they had entered, and by the same passage into the chapel.[1]

[PHILIP II]

[The description of the abdication of Charles V is followed by a discussion of various aspects of the career of Charles V. In these pages Motley interprets the significance of the rule of the emperor for the Netherlands, sets forth the reasons for his abdication, and describes his life during his years of retirement. The author then turns to the emperor's son and successor, Philip II.]

Philip the Second had received the investiture of Milan and the crown of Naples, previously to his marriage with Mary Tudor. The imperial crown he had been obliged, much against his will, to forego. The archduchy of Austria, with the hereditary German dependencies of his father's family, had been transferred by the Emperor to his brother Ferdinand, on the occasion of the marriage of that prince with Anna, only sister of King Louis of Hungary. Ten years afterwards, Ferdinand (King of Hungary and Bohemia since the death of Louis, slain in 1526 at the battle of Mohács) was elected King of the Romans, and steadily refused all the entreaties made to him in behalf of Philip, to resign his crown and his succession to the Empire in favor of his nephew. With these diminutions, Philip had now received all the dominions of his father. He was king of all the Spanish kingdoms and of both the Sicilies. He was titular King of England, France, and Jerusalem. He was "Absolute Dominator" in Asia, Africa, and America; he was Duke of Milan and of both Burgundies, and Hereditary Sovereign of the seventeen Netherlands.

Thus the provinces had received a new master. A man of foreign birth and breeding, not speaking a word of their

[1] *The Rise of the Dutch Republic* (New York, 1856), I, 106–110.

language, nor of any language which the mass of the inhabitants understood, was now placed in supreme authority over them, because he represented, through the females, the "good" Philip of Burgundy, who a century before had possessed himself by inheritance, purchase, force, or fraud, of the sovereignty in most of those provinces. It is necessary to say an introductory word or two concerning the previous history of the man to whose hands the destiny of so many millions was now intrusted.

He was born in May, 1527, and was now, therefore, twenty-eight years of age. At the age of sixteen he had been united to his cousin, Maria of Portugal, daughter of John III and of the Emperor's sister, Donna Catalina. In the following year (1544) he became father of the celebrated and ill-starred Don Carlos, and a widower.... In 1548, he had made his first appearance in the Netherlands. He came thither to receive homage in the various provinces as their future sovereign, and to exchange oaths of mutual fidelity with them all. Andrew Doria, with a fleet of fifty ships, had brought him to Genoa, whence he had passed to Milan, where he was received with great rejoicing. At Trent he was met by Duke Maurice of Saxony, who warmly begged his intercession with the Emperor in behalf of the imprisoned Landgrave of Hesse. This boon Philip was graciously pleased to promise, and to keep the pledge as sacredly as most of the vows plighted by him during this memorable year. The Duke of Aerschot met him in Germany with a regiment of cavalry and escorted him to Brussels. A summer was spent in great festivities, the cities of the Netherlands vying with each other in magnificent celebrations of the ceremonies, by which Philip successively swore allegiance to the various constitutions and charters of the provinces, and received their oaths of future fealty in return. His oath to support *all* the constitutions and privileges was without reservation, while his father and grandfather had only sworn to maintain the charters granted or confirmed by Philip and Charles of Burgundy. Suspicion was disarmed by these indiscriminate concessions, which had been resolved upon by the unscrupulous Charles to conciliate the goodwill of the people. In view of the pretensions which might be preferred by the Brederode family in Holland, and by other descendants of ancient sovereign races in other provinces, the Emperor, wishing to insure the succession to his sisters in case of the deaths of himself, Philip, and Don Carlos without issue, was unsparing in those promises which he knew to be binding only upon the weak. . . . Philip's oaths were therefore without reserve, and the lighthearted Flemings, Brabantines, and Walloons received him with open arms. In Valenciennes the festivities which attended his entrance were on a most gorgeous scale, but the "joyous entrance" arranged for him at Antwerp was of unparalleled magnificence. A cavalcade of the magistrates and notable burghers, "all attired in cramoisy velvet," attended by lackies in splendid liveries, and followed by four thousand citizen soldiers in full uniform, went forth from the gates to receive him. Twenty-eight triumphal arches, which alone, according to the thrifty chronicler, had cost 26,800 Carolus guldens, were erected in the different streets and squares, and every possible demonstration of affectionate welcome was lavished upon the Prince and the Emperor. The rich and prosperous city, unconscious of the doom which awaited it in the future, seemed to have covered itself with garlands to honor the approach of its master. Yet icy was the deportment with which Philip received these demonstrations of affection, and haughty the glance with which he looked down upon these exhibitions of civic hilarity, as from the height of a grim and inaccessible tower. The impression made upon the Netherlanders was anything but favorable, and when he had fully learned the futility of the projects on the Empire which it was so difficult both for his father and himself to resign, he returned to the more congenial soil of Spain. In 1554 he had again issued from the peninsula to marry the Queen of England, a privilege which his father had graciously resigned to him. He was united to Mary Tudor at Winchester, on the 25th July of that year, and if congeniality of tastes could have made a marriage happy, that union should have been thrice blessed. To maintain the supremacy of the Church seemed to both the main object of existence; to execute unbelievers, the most sacred duty imposed by the Deity upon anointed princes; to convert their kingdoms into a hell, the surest means of winning heaven for themselves. It was not strange that the conjunction of two such wonders of superstition in one sphere should seem portentous in the eyes of the English nation. Philip's mock efforts in favor of certain condemned reformers, and his pretended intercessions in favor of the Princess Elizabeth, failed entirely of their object. The Parliament refused to confer upon him more than a nominal authority in England. His children, should they be born, might be sovereigns; he was but husband of the Queen—of a woman who could not atone by her abject but peevish fondness for himself, and by her congenial bloodthirstiness towards her subjects, for her eleven years' seniority, her deficiency in attractions, and her incapacity to make him the father of a line of English monarchs. It almost excites compassion even for Mary Tudor, when her passionate efforts to inspire him with affection are contrasted with his impassiveness. Tyrant, bigot, murderess though she was, she was still woman, and she lavished upon her husband all that was not ferocious in her nature. Forbidding prayers to be said for the soul of her father, hating her sister and her people, burning bishops, bathing herself in the blood of heretics, to Philip she was all submissiveness and feminine devotion. It was a most singular contrast, Mary the Queen of England and Mary the wife of Philip. Small, lean, and sickly; painfully nearsighted, yet with an eye of fierceness and fire; her face wrinkled by the hands of care and evil passions still more than by time; with a big man's voice, whose harshness made those in the next room tremble, yet feminine in her tastes, skilful with her needle, fond of embroidery work, striking the lute with a touch remarkable for its science and feeling, speaking many languages, including Latin, with fluency and grace; most feminine, too, in her constitutional sufferings, hysterical of habit, shedding floods of tears daily at Philip's coldness, undisguised infidelity, and frequent absences from England—she almost awakens compassion, and causes a momentary oblivion of her identity.

Her subjects, already half-maddened by religious persecution, were exasperated still further by the pecuniary burdens which she imposed upon them to supply the King's exigencies, and she unhesitatingly confronted their frenzy, in the hope of winning a smile from him. When at last her chronic maladies had assumed the memorable form which caused Philip and Mary to unite in a letter to Cardinal Pole, announcing not *the expected* but the *actual* birth of a prince, but judiciously leaving the date in blank, the momentary satisfaction and delusion of the Queen was unbounded. The false intelligence was transmitted everywhere. Great were the joy and the festivities in the Netherlands, where people were so easily made to rejoice and keep holiday for anything. "The Regent, being in Antwerp," wrote Sir Thomas Gresham to the lords of council, "did cause the great bell to ringe to give all men to understand that the news was trewe. The Queene's highness' mere merchants caused all our Inglishe ships to shoote off with such joy and triumph, as by men's arts and pollicey coulde be devised—and the Regent sent our Inglishe maroners one hundred crownes to drynke." If bell-ringing and cannon-firing could have given England a Spanish sovereign, the devoutly-wished consummation would have been reached. When the futility of the royal hopes could no longer be concealed, Philip left the country, never to return till his war with France made him require troops, subsidies, and a declaration of hostilities from England.

The personal appearance of the new sovereign has already been described. His manner was far from conciliatory, and in this respect he was the absolute reverse of his father. Upon his first journey out of Spain, in 1548, into his various dominions, he had made a most painful impression everywhere. "He was disagreeable," says Envoy Suriano, "to the Italians, detestable to the Flemings, odious to the Germans."

The remonstrances of the Emperor, and of Queen Mary of Hungary, at the impropriety of his manners, had produced, however, some effect, so that on his wedding journey to England he manifested much "gentleness and humanity, mingled with royal gravity." Upon this occasion, says another Venetian, accredited to him, "he had divested himself of that Spanish haughtiness which, when he first came from Spain, had rendered him so odious." The famous ambassador, Badovaro, confirms the impression. "Upon his first journey," he says, "he was esteemed proud, and too greedy for the imperial succession; but now 'tis common opinion that his humanity and modesty are all which could be desired." These humane qualities, however, it must be observed, were exhibited only in the presence of ambassadors and grandees, the only representatives of "humanity" with whom he came publicly and avowedly in contact.

He was thought deficient in manly energy. He was an infirm valetudinarian, and was considered as sluggish in character, as deficient in martial enterprise, as timid of temperament, as he was fragile and sickly of frame. It is true that, on account of the disappointment which he occasioned by his contrast to his warlike father, he mingled in some tournaments in Brussels, where he was matched against Count Mansfeld, one of the most distinguished chieftains of the age, and where, says his professed panegyrist, "he broke his lances very much to the satisfaction of his father and aunts."

That learned and eloquent author, Estelle Calvete, even filled the greater part of a volume, in which he described the journey of the Prince, with a minute description of these feasts and jousts, but we may reasonably conclude that to the loyal imagination of his eulogist Philip is indebted for most of these knightly trophies. It was the universal opinion of unprejudiced contemporaries that he was without a spark of enterprise. He was even censured for a culpable want of ambition, and for being inferior to his father in this respect; as if the love of encroaching on his neighbor's dominions, and a disposition to foreign commotions and war, would have constituted additional virtues, had he happened to possess them. Those who were most disposed to think favorably of him, remembered that there was a time when even Charles the Fifth was thought weak and indolent, and were willing to ascribe Philip's pacific disposition to his habitual cholic and side-ache, and to his father's inordinate care for him in youth. They even looked forward to the time when he should blaze forth to the world as a conqueror and a hero. These, however, were views entertained by but few; the general and the correct opinion, as it proved, being that Philip hated war, would never certainly acquire any personal distinction in the field, and when engaged in hostilities would be apt to gather his laurels at the hands of his generals, rather than with his own sword. He was believed to be the reverse of the Emperor. Charles sought great enterprises; Philip would avoid them. The Emperor never recoiled before threats; the son was reserved, cautious, suspicious of all men, and capable of sacrificing a realm from hesitation and timidity. The father had a genius for action; the son a predilection for repose. Charles took "all men's opinions, but reserved his judgment," and acted on it, when matured, with irresistible energy; Philip was led by others, was vacillating in forming decisions, and irresolute in executing them when formed.

Philip, then, was not considered, in that warlike age, as likely to shine as a warrior. His mental capacity, in general, was likewise not very highly esteemed. His talents were, in truth, very much below mediocrity. His mind was incredibly small. A petty passion for contemptible details characterized him from his youth, and, as long as he lived, he could neither learn to generalize, nor understand that one man, however diligent, could not be minutely acquainted with all the public and private affairs of fifty millions of other men. He was a glutton of work. He was born to write despatches, and to scrawl comments upon those which he received. He often remained at the council-board four or five hours at a time, and he lived in his cabinet. He gave audiences to ambassadors and deputies very willingly, listening attentively to all that was said to him, and answering in monosyllables. He spoke no tongue but Spanish, and was sufficiently sparing of that, but he was indefatigable with his pen. He hated to converse, but he could write a letter eighteen pages long, when his correspondent was in the next room, and when the subject was, perhaps, one which a man of talent could have settled with six words of his tongue. The world, in his opinion, was to move upon protocols and apostilles. Events had no right to be born throughout his dominions, without a preparatory course of his obstetrical pedantry. He could never learn that the earth would not rest on its axis while he wrote a programme of the way it was to turn. He was slow in deciding, slower in communicating his decisions. He was prolix with his pen, not from affluence, but from paucity of ideas. He took refuge in a cloud of words, sometimes to conceal his meaning, often to conceal the absence of any meaning, thus mystifying not only others but himself. To one great purpose, formed early, he adhered inflexibly. This, however, was rather an instinct than an opinion; born with him, not created by him. The idea seemed to express itself through him, and to master him, rather than to form one of a stock of sentiments which a free agent might be expected to possess. Although at certain times, even this master feeling could yield to the pressure of a predominant self-interest—thus showing that even in Philip bigotry was not absolute—yet he appeared on the whole the embodiment of Spanish chivalry and Spanish religious enthusiasm, in its late and corrupted form. He was entirely a Spaniard. The Burgundian and Austrian elements of his blood seemed to have evaporated, and his veins were filled alone with the ancient ardor which in heroic centuries had animated the Gothic champions of Spain. The fierce enthusiasm for the Cross, which in the long internal warfare against the Crescent, had been the romantic and distinguishing feature of the national character, had degenerated into bigotry. That which had been a nation's glory now made the monarch's shame. The Christian heretic was to be regarded with a more intense hatred than even Moor or Jew had excited in the most Christian ages, and Philip was to be the latest and most perfect incarnation of all this traditional enthusiasm, this perpetual hate. Thus he was likely to be singlehearted in his life. It was believed that his ambition would be less to extend his dominions than to vindicate his title of the Most Catholic King. There could be little doubt entertained that he would be, at least, dutiful to his father in this respect, and that the edicts would be enforced to the letter.

He was by birth, education, and character, a Spaniard, and that so exclusively, that the circumstance would alone have made him unfit to govern a country so totally different in habits and national sentiments from his native land. He was more a foreigner in Brussels, even, than in England. The gay, babbling, energetic, noisy life of Flanders and Brabant was detestable to him. The loquacity of the Netherlanders was a continual reproach upon his taciturnity. His education had imbued him, too, with the antiquated international hatred of Spaniard and Fleming, which had been strengthening in the metropolis, while the more rapid current of life had rather tended to obliterate the sentiment in the provinces.

The flippancy and profligacy of Philip the Handsome, the extortion and insolence of his Flemish courtiers, had not been forgotten in Spain, nor had Philip the Second forgiven his grandfather for having been a foreigner. And now his mad old grandmother, Joanna, who had for years been chasing cats in the lonely tower where she had been so long imprisoned, had just died; and her funeral, celebrated with great pomp by both her sons, by Charles at Brussels and Ferdinand at Augsburg, seemed to revive a history which had begun to fade, and to recall the image of Castilian sovereignty which had been so long obscured in the blaze of imperial grandeur.

His education had been but meager. In an age when all kings and noblemen possessed many languages, he spoke not a word of any tongue but Spanish, although he had a slender knowledge of French and Italian, which he afterwards learned to read with comparative facility. He had studied a little history and geography, and he had a taste for sculpture, painting, and architecture. Certainly if he had not possessed a feeling for art, he would have been a monster. To have been born in the earlier part of the sixteenth century, to have been a king, to have had Spain, Italy, and the Netherlands as a birthright, and not to have been inspired with a spark of that fire which glowed so intensely in those favored lands and in that golden age, had indeed been difficult.

The King's personal habits were regular. His delicate health made it necessary for him to attend to his diet, although he was apt to exceed in sweetmeats and pastry. He slept much, and took little exercise habitually, but he had recently been urged by the physicians to try the effect of the chase as a corrective to his sedentary habits. He was most strict in religious observances; as regular at mass, sermons, and vespers as a monk; much more, it was thought by many good Catholics, than was becoming to his rank and age. Besides several friars who preached regularly for his instruction, he had daily discussions with others on abstruse theological points. He consulted his confessor most minutely as to all the actions of life, inquiring anxiously whether this proceeding or that were likely to burden his conscience. He was grossly licentious. It was his chief amusement to issue forth at night disguised, that he might indulge himself in the common haunts of vice. This was his solace at Brussels in the midst of the gravest affairs of state. He was not illiberal, but, on the contrary, it was thought that he would have been even generous, had he not been straitened for money at the outset of his career. During a cold winter he distributed alms to the poor of Brussels with an open hand. He was fond of jests in private, and would laugh immoderately, when with a few intimate associates, at buffooneries, which he checked in public by the icy gravity of his deportment. He dressed usually in the Spanish fashion, with close doublet, trunk hose, and short cloak, although at times he indulged in the more airy fashions of France and Burgundy, wearing buttons on his coats and feathers in his hat. He was not thought at that time to be cruel by nature, but was usually spoken of, in the conventional language appropriated to monarchs, as a prince "clement, benign, and debonnaire." Time was to shew the justice of his claims to such honorable epithets.[1]

[MARGARET OF PARMA]

[Upon assuming the crowns abdicated by his father, Philip II found himself enmeshed in the long war which had divided Europe ever since the accession of Charles V. To rule in so many states and territories threatened to upset the balance of power in

Europe. It was not until the close of the war in 1559, consequently, that Philip II felt himself in a position to retire to the state that he considered as home, namely, Spain. A considerable portion of *The Rise of the Dutch Republic*, as a result, is taken up with the closing scenes of these so-called Italian Wars. The retirement of Philip II to Spain, however, made necessary the appointment of a regent in the Netherlands. From 1559 to 1567 his representative was his natural sister, Margaret of Parma.]

She was about thirty-seven years of age when she arrived in the Netherlands, with the reputation of possessing high talents, and a proud and energetic character. She was an enthusiastic Catholic, and had sat at the feet of Loyola, who had been her confessor and spiritual guide. She felt a greater horror for heretics than for any other species of malefactors, and looked up to her father's bloody edicts as if they had been special revelations from on high. She was almost strenuous in her observance of Roman rites, and was accustomed to wash the feet of twelve virgins every Holy Week, and to endow them in marriage afterwards. Her acquirements, save that of the art of horsemanship, were not remarkable.

Carefully educated in the Machiavellian and Medicean school of politics, she was versed in that "dissimulation" to which liberal Anglo-Saxons give a shorter name, but which formed the main substance of statesmanship at the court of Charles and Philip. In other respects her accomplishments were but meager, and she had little acquaintance with any language but Italian. Her personal appearance, which was masculine, but not without a certain grand and imperial fascination, harmonized with the opinion generally entertained of her character. The famous moustache upon her upper lip was supposed to indicate authority and virility of purpose, an impression which was confirmed by the circumstance that she was liable to severe attacks of gout, a disorder usually considered more appropriate to the sterner sex.[1]

[1] *The Rise of the Dutch Republic* (New York, 1856), I, 230.

[WILLIAM OF ORANGE]

[After drawing the preceding portrait of the new regent of the Netherlands the author proceeds to describe the various members of her council. This body at that time included William of Orange, the hero of *The Rise of the Dutch Republic*.]

William of Nassau, Prince of Orange, although still young in years, is already the central personage about whom the events and the characters of the epoch most naturally group themselves; destined as he is to become more and more with each succeeding year the vivifying source of light, strength, and national life to a whole people.

The Nassau family first emerges into distinct existence in the middle of the eleventh century. It divides itself almost as soon as known into two great branches. The elder remained in Germany, ascended the imperial throne in the thirteenth century in the person of Adolph of Nassau, and gave to the country many electors, bishops, and generals. The younger and more illustrious branch retained the modest property and petty sovereignty of Nassau Dillenbourg, but at the same time transplanted itself to the Netherlands, where it attained at an early period to great power and large possessions. The ancestors of William, as Dukes of Guelders, had begun to exercise sovereignty in the provinces four centuries before the advent of the house of Burgundy. That overshadowing family afterwards numbered the Netherland Nassaus among its most staunch and powerful adherents. Engelbert the Second was distinguished in the turbulent councils and in the battlefields of Charles the Bold, and was afterwards the unwavering supporter of Maximilian in court and camp. Dying childless, he was succeeded by his brother John, whose two sons, Henry and William of Nassau, divided the great inheritance after their father's death. William succeeded to the German estates, became a convert to Protestantism, and introduced the Reformation into his dominions. Henry, the eldest son, received the family possessions and titles in Luxembourg, Brabant, Flanders, and Holland, and distinguished himself as much as his uncle Engelbert, in the service of the Burgundo-Austrian house. The confidential friend of Charles the Fifth, whose governor he had been in that Emperor's boyhood, he was ever his most efficient and reliable adherent. It was he whose influence placed the imperial crown upon the head of Charles. In 1515 he espoused Claudia de Chalons, sister of Prince Philibert of Orange, "in order," as he wrote to his father, "to be obedient to his imperial Majesty, to please the King of France, *and more particularly for the sake of his own honor and profit.*" His son René de Nassau-Chalons succeeded Philibert. The little principality of Orange, so pleasantly situated between Provence and Dauphiny, but in such dangerous proximity to the seat of the "Babylonian captivity" of the Popes at Avignon, thus passed to the family at Nassau. The title was of high antiquity. Already in the reign of Charlemagne, Guillaume au Court-Nez, or "William with the Short Nose," had defended the little town of Orange against the assaults of the Saracens. The interest and authority acquired in the demesnes thus preserved by his valor became extensive, and in process of time hereditary in his race. The principality became an absolute and free sovereignty, and had already descended, in defiance of the Salic law, through the three distinct families of Orange, Baux, and Chalons.

In 1544, Prince René died at the Emperor's feet in the trenches of Saint Dizier. Having no legitimate children, he left all his titles and estates to his cousin-german, William of Nassau, son of his father's brother William, who thus at the age of eleven years became William the Ninth of Orange. For this child, whom the future was to summon to such high destinies and such heroic sacrifices, the past and present seemed to have gathered riches and power together from many sources. He was the descendant of the Othos, the Engelberts, and the Henrys, of the Netherlands, the representative of the Philiberts and the Renés of France; the chief of a house, humbler in resources and position in Germany, but still of high rank, and which had already done good service to humanity by being among the first to embrace the great principles of the Reformation.

His father, younger brother of the Emperor's friend, Henry,

was called William the Rich—he was, however, only rich in children. Of these he had five sons and seven daughters by his wife Juliana of Stolberg. She was a person of most exemplary character and unaffected piety. She instilled into the minds of all her children the elements of that devotional sentiment which was her own striking characteristic, and it was destined that the seed sown early should increase to an abundant harvest. Nothing can be more tender or more touching than the letters which still exist from her hand, written to her illustrious sons in hours of anxiety or anguish, and to the last recommending to them with as much earnest simplicity as if they were still little children at her knee, to rely always, in the midst of the trials and dangers which were to beset their paths through life, upon the great hand of God. Among the mothers of great men, Juliana of Stolberg deserves a foremost place, and it is no slight eulogy that she was worthy to have been the mother of William of Orange and of Lewis, Adolphus, Henry, and John of Nassau.

At the age of eleven years, William having thus unexpectedly succeeded to such great possessions, was sent from his father's roof to be educated in Brussels. No destiny seemed to lie before the young prince but an education at the Emperor's court, to be followed by military adventures, embassies, viceroyalties, and a life of luxury and magnificence. At a very early age he came, accordingly, as a page into the Emperor's family. Charles recognized, with his customary quickness, the remarkable character of the boy. At fifteen, William was the intimate, almost confidential friend of the Emperor, who prided himself, above all other gifts, on his power of reading and of using men. The youth was so constant an attendant upon his imperial chief, that even when interviews with the highest personages, and upon the gravest affairs, were taking place, Charles would never suffer him to be considered superfluous or intrusive. There seemed to be no secrets which the Emperor held too high for the comprehension or discretion of his page. His perceptive and reflective faculties, naturally of remarkable keenness and depth, thus acquired a precocious and extraordinary develop-

ment. He was brought up behind the curtain of that great
stage where the world's dramas were daily enacted. The machinery and the masks which produced the grand delusions of
history had no deceptions for him. Carefully to observe men's
actions, and silently to ponder upon their motives, was the
favorite occupation of the Prince during his apprenticeship
at court. As he advanced to man's estate, he was selected by
the Emperor for the highest duties. Charles, whose only merit,
so far as the provinces were concerned, was in having been born
in Ghent, and that by an ignoble accident, was glad to employ
this representative of so many great Netherland houses in the
defense of the land. Before the Prince was twenty-one he was
appointed general-in-chief of the army on the French frontier,
in the absence of the Duke of Savoy. The post was coveted
by many most distinguished soldiers—the Counts of Buren,
Bossu, Lalain, Aremberg, Meghem, and particularly by Count
Egmont; yet Charles showed his extraordinary confidence in
the Prince of Orange by selecting him for the station, although
he had hardly reached maturity, and was, moreover, absent in
France. The young Prince acquitted himself of his high command in a manner which justified his appointment.

It was the Prince's shoulder upon which the Emperor leaned
at the abdication; the Prince's hand which bore the imperial
insignia of the discrowned monarch to Ferdinand, at Augsburg.
With these duties his relations with Charles were ended, and
those with Philip begun. He was with the army during the hostilities which were soon after resumed in Picardy; he was the
secret negotiator of the preliminary arrangement with France,
soon afterwards confirmed by the triumphant treaty of April,
1559. He had conducted these initiatory conferences with the
Constable Montmorency and Marshal de Saint André with great
sagacity, although hardly a man in years, and by so doing he
had laid Philip under deep obligations. The King was so
inexpressibly anxious for peace, that he would have been capable
of conducting a treaty upon almost any terms. He assured the
Prince that "the greatest service he could render him in this
world was to make peace, and that he desired to have it at any

price whatever, so eager was he to return to Spain." To the envoy Suriano, Philip had held the same language. "Oh, Ambassador," said he, "I wish peace on any terms, and if the King of France had not sued for it, I would have begged for it myself."

With such impatience on the part of the sovereign, it certainly manifested diplomatic abilities of a high character in the Prince, that the treaty negotiated by him amounted to a capitulation by France. He was one of the hostages selected by Henry for the due execution of the treaty, and while in France made that remarkable discovery which was to color his life. While hunting with the King in the forest of Vincennes, the Prince and Henry found themselves alone together, and separated from the rest of the company. The French monarch's mind was full of the great scheme which had just secretly been formed by Philip and himself, to extirpate Protestantism by a general extirpation of Protestants. Philip had been most anxious to conclude the public treaty with France, that he might be the sooner able to negotiate that secret convention by which he and his Most Christian Majesty were solemnly to bind themselves to massacre all the converts to the new religion in France and the Netherlands. This conspiracy of the two Kings against their subjects was the matter nearest the hearts of both. The Duke of Alva, a fellow hostage with William of Orange, was the plenipotentiary to conduct this more important arrangement. The French monarch, somewhat imprudently imagining that the Prince was also a party to the plot, opened the whole subject to him without reserve. He complained of the constantly-increasing number of sectaries in his kingdom, and protested that his conscience would never be easy, nor his state secure, until his realm should be delivered of "that accursed vermin." A civil revolution, under pretext of a religious reformation, was his constant apprehension, particularly since so many notable personages in the realm, and even princes of the blood, were already tainted with heresy. Nevertheless, with the favor of Heaven, and the assistance of his son and brother Philip, he hoped soon to be master of the rebels. The King then pro-

ceeded, with cynical minuteness, to lay before his discreet companion the particulars of the royal plot, and the manner in
which all heretics, whether high or humble, were to be discovered and massacred at the most convenient season. For the
furtherance of the scheme in the Netherlands, it was understood
that the Spanish regiments would be exceedingly efficient. The
Prince, although horror-struck and indignant at the royal revelations, held his peace, and kept his countenance. The King was
not aware that, in opening this delicate negotiation to Alva's
colleague and Philip's plenipotentiary, he had given a warning
of inestimable value to the man who had been born to resist
the machinations of Philip and of Alva. William of Orange
earned the surname of "the Silent," from the manner in which
he received these communications of Henry without revealing
to the monarch, by word or look, the enormous blunder which
he had committed. His purpose was fixed from that hour. A
few days afterwards he obtained permission to visit the Netherlands, where he took measures to excite, with all his influence,
the strongest and most general opposition to the continued
presence of the Spanish troops, of which forces, much against
his will, he had been, in conjunction with Egmont, appointed
chief. He already felt, in his own language, that "an Inquisition
for the Netherlands had been resolved upon more cruel than
that of Spain; since it would need but to look askance at an
image to be cast into the flames." Although having as yet no
spark of religious sympathy for the reformers, he could not,
he said, "but feel compassion for so many virtuous men and
women thus devoted to massacre," and he determined to save
them if he could. At the departure of Philip he had received
instructions, both patent and secret, for his guidance as stadholder of Holland, Friesland, and Utrecht. He was ordered
"most expressly to correct and extirpate the sects reprobated
by our Holy Mother Church; to execute the edicts of his Imperial Majesty, renewed by the King, with absolute rigor. He was
to see that the judges carried out the edicts, *without infraction,
alteration, or moderation*, since they were there to enforce, not to
make or to discuss, the law." In his secret instructions he was

informed that the execution of the edicts was to be with all rigor, and without any respect of persons. He was also reminded that, whereas some persons had imagined the severity of the law "to be only intended against Anabaptists, on the contrary, the edicts were to be enforced on Lutherans and all other sectaries without distinction." Moreover, in one of his last interviews with Philip, the King had given him the names of several "excellent persons suspected of the new religion," and had commanded him to have them put to death. This, however, he not only omitted to do, but, on the contrary, gave them warning, so that they might effect their escape, "thinking it more necessary to obey God than man."

William of Orange, at the departure of the King for Spain, was in his twenty-seventh year. He was a widower; his first wife, Anne of Egmont, having died in 1558, after seven years of wedlock. This lady, to whom he had been united when they were both eighteen years of age, was the daughter of the celebrated general, Count de Buren, and the greatest heiress in the Netherlands. William had been thus faithful to the family traditions, and had increased his possessions by a wealthy alliance. He had two children, Philip and Mary. The marriage had been more amicable than princely marriages arranged for convenience often prove. The letters of the Prince to his wife indicate tenderness and contentment. At the same time he was accused, at a later period, of "having murdered her with a dagger." The ridiculous tale was not even credited by those who reported it, but it is worth mentioning, as a proof that no calumny was too senseless to be invented concerning the man whose character was from that hour forth to be the mark of slander, and whose whole life was to be its signal, although often unavailing, refutation.

Yet we are not to regard William of Orange, thus on the threshold of his great career, by the light diffused from a somewhat later period. In no historical character more remarkably than in his is the law of constant development and progress illustrated. At twenty-six he is not the "*pater patriae*," the great man struggling upward and onward against a host of enemies and obstacles almost beyond human strength, and along the dark and dangerous path leading through conflict, privations, and ceaseless labor to no repose but death. On the contrary, his foot was hardly on the first step of that difficult ascent which was to rise before him all his lifetime. He was still among the primrose paths. He was rich, powerful, of sovereign rank. He had only the germs within him of what was thereafter to expand into moral and intellectual greatness. He had small sympathy for the religious reformation, of which he was to be one of the most distinguished champions. He was a Catholic, nominally, and in outward observance. With doctrines he troubled himself but little. He had given orders to enforce conformity to the ancient Church, not with bloodshed, yet with comparative strictness, in his principality of Orange. Beyond the compliance with rites and forms, thought indispensable in those days to a personage of such high degree, he did not occupy himself with theology. He was a Catholic, as Egmont and Horn, Berlaymont and Mansfeld, Montigny and even Brederode, were Catholic. It was only tanners, dyers, and apostate priests who were Protestants at that day in the Netherlands. His determination to protect a multitude of his harmless inferiors from horrible deaths did not proceed from sympathy with their religious sentiments, but merely from a generous and manly detestation of murder. He carefully averted his mind from sacred matters. If, indeed, the seed implanted by his pious parents were really the germ of his future conversion to Protestantism, it must be confessed that it lay dormant a long time. But his mind was in other pursuits. He was disposed for any easy, joyous, luxurious, princely life. Banquets, masquerades, tournaments, the chase, interspersed with the routines of official duties, civil and military, seemed likely to fill out his life. His hospitality, like his fortune, was almost regal. While the King and the foreign envoys were still in the Netherlands, his house, the splendid Nassau palace of Brussels, was ever open. He entertained for the monarch, who was, or who imagined himself to be, too poor to discharge his own duties in this respect, but he entertained at his own expense. This splendid household was still continued. Twenty-four noblemen and eighteen pages of gentle birth officiated regularly in his family. His establishment was on so extensive a scale that upon one day twenty-eight master cooks were dismissed, for the purpose of diminishing the family expenses, and there was hardly a princely house in Germany which did not send cooks to learn their business in so magnificent a kitchen. The reputation of his table remained undiminished for years. We find at a later period that Philip, in the course of one of the nominal reconciliations which took place several times between the monarch and William of Orange, wrote that, his head cook being dead, he begged the Prince to "make him a present of his chief cook, Master Herman, who was understood to be very skilful."

In this hospitable mansion the feasting continued night and day. From early morning till noon the breakfast tables were spread with wines and luxurious viands in constant succession, to all comers, and at every moment. The dinner and supper were daily banquets for a multitude of guests. The highest nobles were not those alone who were entertained. Men of lower degree were welcomed with a charming hospitality which made them feel themselves at their ease. Contemporaries of all parties unite in eulogizing the winning address and gentle manners of the Prince. "Never," says a most bitter Catholic historian, "did an arrogant or indiscreet word fall from his lips. He, upon no occasion, manifested anger to his servants, however much they might be in fault, but contented himself with admonishing them graciously, without menace or insult. He had a gentle and agreeable tongue, with which he could turn all the gentlemen at court any way he liked. He was beloved and honored by the whole community." His manner was graceful, familiar, caressing, and yet dignified. He had the good breeding which comes from the heart, refined into an inexpressible charm from his constant intercourse, almost from his cradle, with mankind of all ranks.

It may be supposed that this train of living was attended with expense. Moreover, he had various other establishments in town and country, besides his almost royal residence in Brussels.

He was ardently fond of the chase, particularly of the knightly sport of falconry. In the country he "consoled himself by taking every day a heron in the clouds." His falconers alone cost him annually fifteen hundred florins, after he had reduced their expenses to the lowest possible point. He was much in debt, even at this early period and with his princely fortune. "We come of a race," he wrote carelessly to his brother Louis, "who are somewhat bad managers in our young days, but when we grow older, we do better, like our late father: *sicut erat in principio, et nunc, et semper et in secula seculorum.* My greatest difficulty," he adds, "as usual, is on account of the falconers."

His debts already amounted, according to Granvelle's statement, to eight or nine hundred thousand florins. He had embarrassed himself, not only through his splendid extravagance, by which all the world about him were made to partake of his wealth, but by accepting the high offices to which he had been appointed. When general-in-chief on the frontier, his salary was three hundred florins monthly; "not enough," as he said, "to pay the servants in his tent," his necessary expenses being twenty-five hundred florins, as appears by a letter to his wife. His embassy to carry the crown to Ferdinand, and his subsequent residence as a hostage for the treaty in Paris, were also very onerous, and he received no salary, according to the economical system in this respect pursued by Charles and Philip. In these two embassies or missions alone, together with the entertainments offered by him to the court and to foreigners, after the peace at Brussels, the Prince spent, according to his own estimate, one million five hundred thousand florins. He was, however, although deeply, not desperately involved, and had already taken active measures to regulate and reduce his establishment. His revenues were vast, both in his own right and in that of his deceased wife. He had large claims upon the royal treasury for service and expenditure. He had, besides, ample sums to receive from the ransoms of the prisoners of St. Quentin and Gravelines, having served in both campaigns. . . .

Such, then, at the beginning of 1560, was William of Orange

—a generous, stately, magnificent, powerful grandee. As a military commander, he had acquitted himself very creditably of highly important functions at an early age. Nevertheless, it was the opinion of many persons that he was of a timid temperament. He was even accused of having manifested an unseemly panic at Philippeville, and of having only been restrained by the expostulations of his officers from abandoning both that fortress and Charlemont to Admiral Coligny, who had made his appearance in the neighborhood, merely at the head of a reconnoitering party. If the story were true, it would be chiefly important as indicating that the Prince of Orange was one of the many historical characters, originally of an excitable and even timorous physical organization, whom moral courage and a strong will have afterwards converted into dauntless heroes. Certain it is that he was destined to confront open danger in every form, that his path was to lead through perpetual ambush, yet that his cheerful confidence and tranquil courage were to become not only unquestionable, but proverbial. It may be safely asserted, however, that the story was an invention, to be classed with those fictions which made him the murderer of his first wife, a common conspirator against Philip's crown and person, and a crafty malefactor in general, without a single virtue. It must be remembered that even the terrible Alva, who lived in harness almost from the cradle to the grave, was, so late as at the period with which we are now occupied, censured for timidity, and had been accused in youth of flat cowardice. He despised the insinuation, which for him had no meaning. There is no doubt, too, that caution was a predominant characteristic of the Prince. It was one of the chief sources of his greatness. At that period, perhaps at any period, he would have been incapable of such brilliant and dashing exploits as had made the name of Egmont so famous. It had even become a proverb, "the counsel of Orange, the execution of Egmont"; yet we shall have occasion to see how far this physical promptness which had been so felicitous on the battlefield was likely to avail the hero of St. Quentin in the great political combat which was approaching.

As to the talents of the Prince, there was no difference of opinion. His enemies never contested the subtlety and breadth of his intellect, his adroitness and capacity in conducting state affairs, his knowledge of human nature, and the profoundness of his views. In many respects it must be confessed that his surname of the Silent, like many similar appellations, was a misnomer. William of Orange was neither "silent" nor "taciturn," yet these are the epithets which will be for ever associated with the name of a man who, in private, was the most affable, cheerful, and delightful of companions, and who on many great public occasions was to prove himself, both by pen and by speech, the most eloquent man of his age. His mental accomplishments were considerable. He had studied history with attention, and he spoke and wrote with facility Latin, French, German, Flemish, and Spanish.[1]

[THE NETHERLANDS IN 1559]

[The author stopped the course of his narrative many times to describe the situation in the Netherlands. He gives the following description of the country in 1559.]

The aristocracy of the Netherlands was excessively extravagant, dissipated, and already considerably embarrassed in circumstances. It had been the policy of the Emperor and of Philip to confer high offices, civil, military, and diplomatic, upon the leading nobles, by which enormous expenses were entailed upon them, without any corresponding salaries. The case of Orange has been already alluded to, and there were many other nobles less able to afford the expense, who had been indulged with these ruinous honors. During the war, there had been however, many chances of bettering broken fortunes. Victory brought immense prizes to the leading officers. The ransoms of so many illustrious prisoners as had graced the triumphs of Saint Quentin and Gravelines had been extremely profitable. These sources of wealth had now been cut off;

[1] *The Rise of the Dutch Republic* (New York, 1856), I, 233–247.

yet, on the departure of the King from the Netherlands, the luxury increased instead of diminishing. "Instead of one court," said a contemporary, "you would have said that there were fifty." Nothing could be more sumptuous than the modes of life in Brussels. The household of Orange has been already painted; that of Egmont was almost as magnificent. A rivalry in hospitality and in display began among the highest nobles, and extended to those less able to maintain themselves in the contest. During the war there had been the valiant emulation of the battlefield; gentlemen had vied with each other how best to illustrate an ancient name with deeds of desperate valor, to repair the fortunes of a ruined house with the spoils of war. They now sought to surpass each other in splendid extravagance. It was an eager competition who should build the stateliest palaces, have the greatest number of nobles, pages, and gentlemen in waiting, the most gorgeous liveries, the most hospitable tables, the most scientific cooks. There was also much depravity as well as extravagance. The morals of high society were loose. Gaming was practiced to a frightful extent. Drunkenness was a prevailing characteristic of the higher classes. Even the Prince of Orange himself, at this period, although never addicted to habitual excess, was extremely convivial in his tastes, tolerating scenes and companions not likely at a later day to find much favor in his sight. "We kept Saint Martin's joyously," he wrote at about this period to his brother, "and in the most jovial company. Brederode was one day in such a state that I thought he would certainly die, but he has now got over it." Count Brederode, soon afterwards to become so conspicuous in the early scenes of the revolt, was, in truth, most notorious for his performances in these banqueting scenes. He appeared to have vowed as uncompromising hostility to cold water as to the Inquisition, and always denounced both with the same fierce and ludicrous vehemence. Their constant connexion with Germany at that period did not improve the sobriety of the Netherland nobles. The aristocracy of that country, as is well known, were most "potent at potting." "When the German finds himself sober," said the bitter Badovaro, "he believes himself to be ill." Gladly, since the peace, they had welcomed the opportunities afforded for many a deep carouse with their Netherland cousins. The approaching marriage of the Prince of Orange with the Saxon princess—an episode which will soon engage our attention—gave rise to tremendous orgies. Count Schwartzburg, the Prince's brother-in-law, and one of the negotiators of the marriage, found many occasions to strengthen the bonds of harmony between the countries by indulgence of these common tastes. "I have had many princes and counts at my table," he wrote to Orange, "where a good deal more was drunk than eaten. The Rhinegrave's brother fell down dead after drinking too much malvoisie; but we have had him balsamed and sent home to his family." [1]

The lesser nobles emulated the grandees, and vied with each other in splendid establishments, banquets, masquerades, and equipages. Their estates, in consequence, were mortgaged, deeply and more deeply; then, after a few years, sold to the merchants, or rich advocates and other gentlemen of the robe, to whom they had been pledged. The more closely ruin stared the victims in the face, the more heedlessly did they plunge into excesses. . . . Many of the nobles being thus embarrassed, and some even desperate, in their condition, it was thought that they were desirous of creating disturbances in the common-wealth, that the payment of just debts might be avoided, that their mortgaged lands might be wrested by main force from the lowborn individuals who had become possessed of them, that, in particular, the rich abbey lands held by idle priests might be appropriated to the use of impoverished gentlemen who could turn them to so much better account. It is quite probable that interested motives such as these were not entirely inactive among a comparatively small class of gentlemen. The religious refor-mation in every land of Europe derived a portion of its strength from the opportunity it afforded to potentates and great nobles for helping themselves to Church property. No doubt many Netherlanders thought that their fortunes might be improved

[1] *The Rise of the Dutch Republic* (New York, 1856), I, 253–254.

at the expense of the monks, and for the benefit of religion. Even without apostasy from the mother Church, they looked with longing eyes on the wealth of her favored and indolent children. They thought that the King would do well to carve a round number of handsome military commanderies out of the abbey lands, whose possessors should be bound to military service after the ancient manner of fiefs, so that a splendid cavalry, headed by the gentlemen of the country, should be ever ready to mount and ride at the royal pleasure, in place of a horde of lazy epicureans, telling beads and indulging themselves in luxurious vice.[1]

For the state of the people was very different from the condition of the aristocracy. The period of martyrdom had lasted long and was to last longer; but there were symptoms that it might one day be succeeded by a more active stage of popular disease. The tumults of the Netherlands were long in ripening; when the final outbreak came, it would have been more philosophical to inquire, not why it had occurred, but how it could have been so long postponed. During the reign of Charles, the sixteenth century had been advancing steadily in strength as the once omnipotent Emperor lapsed into decrepitude. That extraordinary century had not dawned upon the earth only to increase the strength of absolutism and superstition. The new world had not been discovered, the ancient world reconquered, the printing press perfected, only that the Inquisition might reign undisturbed over the fairest portions of the earth, and chartered hypocrisy fatten upon its richest lands. It was impossible that the most energetic and quick-witted people of Europe should not feel sympathy with the great effort made by Christendom to shake off the incubus which had so long paralyzed her hands and brain. In the Netherlands, where the attachment to Rome had never been intense, where in the old times the Bishops of Utrecht had been rather Ghibelline than Guelph, where all the earliest sects of dissenters—Waldenses, Lollards, Hussites—had found numerous converts and thou-

[1] *Ibid.*, I, 255–256.

sands of martyrs, it was inevitable that there should be a response from the popular heart to the deeper agitation which
now reached to the very core of Christendom. . . .

The people were numerous, industrious, accustomed for
centuries to a state of comparative civil freedom, and to a lively
foreign trade, by which their minds were saved from the stagnation of bigotry. It was natural that they should begin to generalize, and to pass from the concrete images presented them
in the Flemish monasteries to the abstract character of Rome
itself. The Flemings, above all their other qualities, were a
commercial nation. Commerce was the mother of their freedom, so far as they had acquired it, in civil matters. It was
struggling to give birth to a larger liberty, to freedom of conscience. The provinces were situated in the very heart of
Europe. The blood of a world-wide traffic was daily coursing
through the thousand arteries of that water-inwoven territory.
There was a mutual exchange between the Netherlands and all
the world; and ideas were as liberally interchanged as goods.
Truth was imported as freely as less precious merchandise.
The psalms of Marot were as current as the drugs of Molucca
or the diamonds of Borneo. The prohibitory measures of a
despotic government could not annihilate this intellectual trade,
nor could bigotry devise an effective quarantine to exclude the
religious pest which lurked in every bale of merchandise and
was wafted on every breeze from East and West.

The edicts of the Emperor had been endured, but not accepted. The horrible persecution under which so many thousands had sunk had produced its inevitable result. Fertilized
by all this innocent blood, the soil of the Netherlands became
as a watered garden, in which liberty, civil and religious, was
to flourish perennially. The scaffold had its daily victims, but
did not make a single convert. The statistics of these crimes
will perhaps never be accurately adjusted, . . . but those who
love horrible details may find ample material. The chronicles
contain the lists of these obscure martyrs; but their names,
hardly pronounced in their lifetime, sound barbarously in our
ears, and will never ring through the trumpet of fame. Yet they

were men who dared and suffered as much as men can dare and suffer in this world, and for the noblest cause which can inspire humanity. Fanatics they certainly were not, if fanaticism consists in show without corresponding substance. For them all was terrible reality. The Emperor and his edicts were realities; the axe, the stake, were realities; and the heroism with which men took each other by the hand and walked into the flames, or with which women sang a song of triumph while the gravedigger was shovelling the earth upon their living faces, was a reality also.

Thus, the people of the Netherlands were already pervaded, throughout the whole extent of the country, with the expanding spirit of religious reformation. It was inevitable that sooner or later an explosion was to arrive. They were placed between two great countries, where the new principles had already taken root. The Lutheranism of Germany and the Calvinism of France had each its share in producing the Netherland revolt, but a mistake is often made in estimating the relative proportion of these several influences. The Reformation first entered the provinces, not through the Augsburg, but the Huguenot gate. The fiery field-preachers from the south of France first inflamed the excitable hearts of the kindred population of the south-western Netherlands. The Walloons were the first to rebel against, and the first to reconcile themselves with, papal Rome, exactly as their Celtic ancestors, fifteen centuries earlier, had been foremost in the revolt against imperial Rome, and precipitate in their submission to her overshadowing power. The Batavians, slower to be moved, but more steadfast, retained the impulse which they received from the same source which was already agitating their "Welsh" compatriots. There were already French preachers at Valenciennes and Tournay, to be followed, as we shall have occasion to see, by many others. Without undervaluing the influence of the German Churches, and particularly of the garrison-preaching of the German military chaplains in the Netherlands, it may be safely asserted that the early Reformers of the provinces were mainly Huguenots in their belief. The Dutch Church became, accordingly, not

Lutheran, but Calvinistic, and the founder of the commonwealth hardly ceased to be a nominal Catholic before he became
an adherent to the same creed.[1]

[THE INQUISITION]

[After he had described the actors in the drama and the stage
upon which they performed, Motley began to tell the story of
the struggle of the Dutch people and their leaders against
Philip II and his policies. In his narrative the author finds
the revolt to be caused by three features of the royal policy—
the edicts, the new bishoprics, and the imposition of foreign
soldiers. He considers the inquisition established by the edicts
as the main cause of the rebellion of the Netherlands against
Philip II.]

The Spanish Inquisition, strictly so called, that is to say, the
modern or later institution established by Pope Alexander the
Sixth and Ferdinand the Catholic, was doubtless invested with
a more complete apparatus for inflicting human misery and for
appalling human imagination than any of the other less artfully
arranged inquisitions, whether papal or episcopal. It had been
originally devised for Jews or Moors, whom the Christianity
of the age did not regard as human beings, but who could not
be banished without depopulating certain districts. It was
soon, however, extended from pagans to heretics. The Do-
minican Torquemada was the first Moloch to be placed upon
this pedestal of blood and fire, and from that day forward the
"Holy Office" was almost exclusively in the hands of that band
of brothers. In the eighteen years of Torquemada's administration, ten thousand two hundred and twenty individuals were
burned alive, and ninety-seven thousand three hundred and
twenty-one punished with infamy, confiscation of property, or
perpetual imprisonment, so that the total number of families
destroyed by this one friar alone amounted to one hundred
and fourteen thousand four hundred and one. In course of
time the jurisdiction of the office was extended. It taught the

[1] *The Rise of the Dutch Republic* (New York, 1856), I, 256–259.

savages of India and America to shudder at the name of Christianity. The fear of its introduction froze the earlier heretics of Italy, France, and Germany into orthodoxy. It was a court owing allegiance to no temporal authority, superior to all other tribunals. It was a bench of monks without appeal, having its familiars in every house, diving into the secrets of every fireside, judging, and executing its horrible decrees without responsibility. It condemned not deeds, but thoughts. It affected to descend into individual conscience, and to punish the crimes which it pretended to discover. Its process was reduced to a horrible simplicity. It arrested on suspicion, tortured till confession, and then punished by fire. Two witnesses, and those to separate facts, were sufficient to consign the victim to a loathsome dungeon. Here he was sparingly supplied with food, forbidden to speak, or even to sing—to which pastime it could hardly be thought he would feel much inclination—and then left to himself, till famine and misery should break his spirit. When that time was supposed to have arrived he was examined. Did he confess, and forswear his heresy, whether actually innocent or not, he might then assume the sacred shirt, and escape with confiscation of all his property. Did he persist in the avowal of his innocence, two witnesses sent him to the stake, one witness to the rack. He was informed of the testimony against him, but never confronted with the witness. That accuser might be his son, father, or the wife of his bosom, for all were enjoined, under the death-penalty, to inform the inquisitors of every suspicious word which might fall from their nearest relatives. The indictment being thus supported, the prisoner was tried by torture. The rack was the court of justice; the criminal's only advocate was his fortitude—for the nominal counsellor, who was permitted no communication with the prisoner, and was furnished neither with documents nor with power to procure evidence, was a puppet, aggravating the lawlessness of the proceedings by the mockery of legal forms. The torture took place at midnight, in a gloomy dungeon, dimly lighted by torches. The victim—whether man, matron, or tender virgin —was stripped naked and stretched upon the wooden bench.

Water, weights, fires, pulleys, screws—all the apparatus by which the sinews could be strained without cracking, the bones bruised without breaking, and the body racked exquisitely without giving up its ghost—was now put into operation. The executioner, enveloped in a black robe from head to foot, with his eyes glaring at his victim through holes cut in the hood which muffled his face, practiced successively all the forms of torture which the devilish ingenuity of the monks had invented. The imagination sickens when striving to keep pace with these dreadful realities. Those who wish to indulge their curiosity concerning the details of the system, may easily satisfy themselves at the present day. The flood of light which has been poured upon the subject more than justifies the horror and the rebellion of the Netherlanders.

The period during which torture might be inflicted from day to day was unlimited in duration. It could only be terminated by confession; so that the scaffold was the sole refuge from the rack. Individuals have borne the torture and the dungeon fifteen years, and have been burned at the stake at last.

Execution followed confessions, but the number of condemned prisoners was allowed to accumulate, that a multitude of victims might grace each great gala-day. The *auto-da-fé* was a solemn festival. The monarch, the high functionaries of the land, the reverend clergy, the populace, regarded it as an inspiring and delightful recreation. When the appointed morning arrived, the victim was taken from his dungeon. He was then attired in a yellow robe without sleeves, like a herald's coat, embroidered all over with black figures of devils. A large conical paper miter was placed upon his head, upon which was represented a human being in the midst of flames, surrounded by imps. His tongue was then painfully gagged, so that he could neither open nor shut his mouth. After he was thus accoutred, and just as he was leaving his cell, a breakfast, consisting of every delicacy, was placed before him, and he was urged, with ironical politeness, to satisfy his hunger. He was then led forth into the public square. The procession was formed with great pomp. It was headed by the little school children, who were immediately followed by the band of prisoners, each attired in the horrible yet ludicrous manner described. Then came the magistrates and nobility, the prelates and other dignitaries of the Church: the holy inquisitors, with their officials and familiars, followed, all on horseback, with the blood-red flag of the "sacred office" waving above them, blazoned upon either side with the portraits of Alexander and of Ferdinand, the pair of brothers who had established the institution. After the procession came the rabble. When all had reached the neighborhood of the scaffold, and had been arranged in order, a sermon was preached to the assembled multitude. It was filled with laudations of the inquisition, and with blasphemous revilings against the condemned prisoners. Then the sentences were read to the individual victims. Then the clergy chanted the fifty-first psalm, the whole vast throng uniting in one tremendous *miserere*. If a priest happened to be among the culprits, he was now stripped of the canonicals which he had hitherto worn, while his hands, lips, and shaven crown were scraped with a bit of glass, by which process the oil of his consecration was supposed to be removed. He was then thrown into the common herd. Those of the prisoners who were reconciled, and those whose execution was not yet appointed, were now separated from the others. The rest were compelled to mount a scaffold, where the executioner stood ready to conduct them to the fire. The inquisitors then delivered them into his hands, with an ironical request that he would deal with them tenderly, and without bloodletting or injury. Those who remained steadfast to the last were then burned at the stake; they who in the last extremity renounced their faith were strangled before being thrown into the flames. Such was the *Spanish* Inquisition—technically so called. It was, according to the biographer of Philip the Second, a "heavenly remedy, a guardian angel of Paradise, a lion's den in which Daniel and other just men could sustain no injury, but in which perverse sinners were torn to pieces." It was a tribunal superior to all human law, without appeal, and certainly owing no allegiance to the powers of earth or heaven. No rank, high or humble, was safe from its jurisdiction. The royal family were not sacred, nor the pauper's hovel. Even death afforded no protection. The Holy Office invaded the prince in his palace and the beggar in his shroud. The corpses of dead heretics were mutilated and burned. The inquisitors preyed upon carcases and rifled graves. A gorgeous festival of the Holy Office had, as we have seen, welcomed Philip to his native land. The news of these tremendous *autos-da-fé*, in which so many illustrious victims had been sacrificed before their sovereign's eyes, had reached the Netherlands almost simultaneously with the bulls creating the new bishoprics in the provinces. It was not likely that the measure would be rendered more palatable by this intelligence of the royal amusements.

The *Spanish* Inquisition had never flourished in any soil but that of the peninsula. It is possible that the King and Granvelle were sincere in their protestations of entertaining no intention of introducing it into the Netherlands, although the protestations of such men are entitled to but little weight. The truth was that the inquisition existed already in the provinces. It was the main object of the government to confirm and extend the institution. The Episcopal Inquisition, as we have already seen, had been enlarged by the enormous increase in the number of bishops, each of whom was to be head inquisitor in his diocese, with two special inquisitors under him. With this apparatus and with the edicts, as already described, it might seem that enough had already been done for the suppression of heresy. But more had been done. A regular Papal Inquisition also existed in the Netherlands. This establishment, like the edicts, was the gift of Charles the Fifth. A word of introduction is here again necessary—nor let the reader deem that too much time is devoted to this painful subject. On the contrary, no definite idea can be formed as to the character of the Netherland revolt without a thorough understanding of this great cause —the religious persecution in which the country had lived, breathed, and had its being, for half a century, and in which, had the rebellion not broken out at last, the population must have been either exterminated or entirely embruted. The few years which are immediately to occupy us in the present and succeeding chapter, present the country in a daily increasing ferment from the action of causes which had existed long before, but which received an additional stimulus as the policy of the new reign developed itself.

Previously to the accession of Charles V, it cannot be said that an inquisition had ever been established in the provinces. Isolated instances to the contrary, adduced by the canonists who gave their advice to Margaret of Parma, rather proved the absence than the existence of the system. In the reign of Philip the Good, the vicar of the inquisitor-general gave sentence against some heretics, who were burned in Lille (1448). In 1459, Pierre Troussart, a Jacobin monk, condemned many Waldenses, together with some leading citizens of Artois, accused of sorcery and heresy. He did this, however, as inquisitor for the Bishop of Arras, so that it was an act of Episcopal, and not Papal Inquisition. In general, when inquisitors were wanted in the provinces, it was necessary to borrow them from France or Germany. The exigencies of persecution making a domestic staff desirable, Charles the Fifth, in the year 1522, applied to his ancient tutor, whom he had placed on the papal throne.

Charles had, however, already, in the previous year, appointed Francis Van der Hulst to be inquisitor-general for the Netherlands. This man, whom Erasmus called a "wonderful enemy to learning," was also provided with a coadjutor, Nicholas of Egmond by name, a Carmelite monk, who was characterized by the same authority as "a madman armed with a sword." The inquisitor-general received full powers to cite, arrest, imprison, torture heretics without observing the ordinary forms of law, and to cause his sentences to be executed without appeal. He was, however, in pronouncing definite judgments, to take the advice of Laurens, president of the grand council of Mechlin, a coarse, cruel, and ignorant man, who "hated learning with a more than deadly hatred," and who might certainly be relied upon to sustain the severest judgments which the inquisitor might fulminate. Adrian accordingly commissioned Van der Hulst to be universal and general inquisitor for all the Netherlands. At the same time it was expressly stated that his functions were not to supersede those exercised by the bishops as inquisitors in their own sees. Thus the Papal Inquisition was established in the provinces. Van der Hulst, a person of infamous character, was not the man to render the institution less odious than it was by its nature. Before he had fulfilled his duties two years, however, he was degraded from his office by the Emperor for having forged a document. In 1525, Buedens, Houseau, and Coppin were confirmed by Clement the Seventh as inquisitors in the room of Van der Hulst. In 1537 Ruard Tapper and Michael Drutius were appointed by Paul the Third, on the decease of Coppin, the other two remaining in office. The powers of the papal inquisitors had been gradually extended, and they were, by 1545, not only entirely independent of the Episcopal Inquisition, but had acquired right of jurisdiction over bishops and archbishops, whom they were empowered to arrest and imprison. They had also received and exercised the privilege of appointing delegates, or sub-inquisitors, on their own authority. Much of the work was, indeed, performed by these officials, the most notorious of whom were Barbier, De Monte, Titelmann, Fabry, Campo de Zon, and Stryen. In 1545, and again in 1550, a stringent set of instructions was drawn up by the Emperor for the guidance of these papal inquisitors. A glance at their context shows that the establishment was not intended to be an empty form.[1]

[THE ADMINISTRATION OF CARDINAL GRANVELLE]

[The tension caused by the policy of Philip II in the Netherlands steadily increased. As a result the able Cardinal Granvelle, the chief instrument of the royal policy, grew more and more unpopular. In 1564, he was finally forced to give up his political office and retire to his native Franche Comté. At the end of his narrative of this struggle, accordingly, Motley gives his estimate of the great churchman's administration.]

[1] *The Rise of the Dutch Republic* (New York, 1856), I, 322–329.

In estimating the conduct of the minister, in relation to the provinces, we are met upon the threshold by a swarm of vague assertions which are of a nature to blind or distract the judgment. His character must be judged as a whole, and by its general results, with a careful allowance for contradictions and equivocations. Truth is clear and single, but the lights are parti-colored and refracted in the prism of hypocrisy. The great feature of his administration was a prolonged conflict between himself and the leading seigniors of the Netherlands. The ground of the combat was the religious question. Let the quarrel be turned or tortured in any manner that human ingenuity can devise, it still remains unquestionable that Granvelle's main object was to strengthen and to extend the Inquisition, that of his adversaries to overthrow the institution. It followed, necessarily, that the ancient charters were to be trampled in the dust before that tribunal could be triumphant. The nobles, although all Catholics, defended the cause of the poor religious martyrs, the privileges of the nation, and the rights of their order. They were conservatives, battling for the existence of certain great facts, entirely consonant to any theory of justice and divine reason—for ancient constitutions which had been purchased with blood and treasure. "I will maintain," was the motto of William of Orange. Philip, bigoted and absolute almost beyond comprehension, might perhaps have proved impervious to any representations, even of Granvelle. Nevertheless, the minister might have attempted the task, and the responsibility is heavy upon the man who shared the power and directed the career, but who never ceased to represent the generous resistance of individuals to frantic cruelty, as offenses against God and the King.

Yet extracts are drawn from his letters to prove that he considered the Spaniards as "proud and usurping," that he indignantly denied ever having been in favor of subjecting the Netherlands to the soldiers of that nation, that he recommended the withdrawal of the foreign regiments, and that he advised the King, when he came to the country, to bring with him but few Spanish troops. It should, however, be remembered that he employed, according to his own statements, every expedient which human ingenuity could suggest to keep the foreign soldiers in the provinces, that he "lamented to his inmost soul" their forced departure, and that he did not consent to that measure until the people were in a tumult, and the Zeelanders threatening to lay the country under the ocean. "You may judge of the means employed to excite the people," he wrote to Perez in 1563, "by the fact that a report is circulated that the Duke of Alva is coming hither to tyrannize the provinces." Yet it appears by the admission of Del Ryo, one of Alva's blood council, that "Cardinal Granvelle expressly advised that an army of Spaniards should be sent to the Netherlands, to maintain the obedience to his Majesty and the Catholic religion, and that the Duke of Alva was appointed chief by the advice of Cardinal Spinosa, and by that of *Cardinal Granvelle*, as appeared by many letters written at the time to his friends." By the same confessions, it appeared that the course of policy thus distinctly recommended by Granvelle "was to place the country under a system of government like that of Spain and Italy, and to reduce it entirely under the council of Spain." When the terrible Duke started on his errand of blood and fire, the Cardinal addressed him a letter of fulsome flattery, protesting "that all the world knew that no person could be found so appropriate as he, to be employed in an affair of such importance"; urging him to advance with his army as rapidly as possible upon the Netherlands; hoping that "the Duchess of Parma would not be allowed to consent that any pardon or concession should be made to the cities, by which the construction of fortresses would be interfered with, or the revocation of the charters which had been forfeited, be prevented"; and giving him much advice as to the general measures to be adopted, and the persons to be employed upon his arrival, in which number the infamous Noircarmes was especially recommended. In a document found among his papers, these same points, with others, were handled at considerable length. The incorporation of the provinces into one kingdom, of which the King was to be crowned absolute sovereign; the establishment of a universal law for the Catholic religion, care being taken not to call that law inquisition, "because there was nothing so odious to the northern nations as the word *Spanish Inquisition*, although the *thing in itself be most holy and just*"; the abolition and annihilation of the broad or general council in the cities, the only popular representation in the country; the construction of many citadels and fortresses to be garrisoned with Spaniards, Italians, and Germans. Such were the leading features in that remarkable paper.

The manly and open opposition of the nobles was stigmatized as a cabal by the offended priest. He repeatedly whispered in the royal ear that their league was a treasonable conspiracy, which the Attorney-General ought to prosecute; that the seigniors meant to subvert entirely the authority of the Sovereign; that they meant to put their King under tutelage, to compel him to obey all their commands, to choose another prince of the blood for their chief, to establish a republic by the aid of foreign troops. If such insinuations, distilled thus secretly into the ear of Philip, who, like his predecessor, Dionysius, took pleasure in listening daily to charges against his subjects and to the groans of his prisoners, were not likely to engender a dangerous gangrene in the royal mind, it would be difficult to indicate any course which would produce such a result. Yet the Cardinal maintained that he had never done the gentlemen ill service, but that "they were angry with him for wishing to sustain the authority of the master." In almost every letter he expressed vague generalities of excuse, or even approbation, while he chronicled each daily fact which occurred to their discredit. The facts he particularly implored the King to keep to himself, the vague laudation he as urgently requested him to repeat to those interested. Perpetually dropping small innuendos like pebbles into the depth of his master's suspicious soul, he knew that at last the waters of bitterness would overflow, but he turned an ever-smiling face upon those who were to be his victims. There was ever something in his irony like the bland request of the inquisitor to the executioner that he would deal with his prisoners gently. There was about the same result in regard to such a prayer to be expected from Philip as from the hangman. Even if his criticisms had been uniformly indulgent, the position of the nobles and leading citizens thus subjected to a constant but secret superintendence, would have been too galling to be tolerated. They did not know, so precisely as we have learned after three centuries, that all their idle words and careless gestures as well as their graver proceedings were kept in a noting book to be pored over and conned by rote in the recesses of the royal cabinet and the royal mind; but they suspected the espionage of the Cardinal, and they openly charged him with his secret malignity.

The men who refused to burn their fellow-creatures for a difference in religious opinion were stigmatized as demagogues; as ruined spendthrifts who wished to escape from their liabilities in the midst of revolutionary confusion; as disguised heretics who were waiting for a good opportunity to reveal their true characters. Montigny, who, as a Montmorency, was nearly allied to the Constable and Admiral of France, and was in epistolary correspondence with those relatives, was held up as a Huguenot; of course, therefore, in Philip's eye, the most monstrous of malefactors.

Although no man could strew pious reflections and holy texts more liberally, yet there was always an afterthought even in his most edifying letters. A corner of the mask is occasionally lifted and the deadly face of slow but abiding vengeance is revealed. "I know very well," he wrote, soon after his fall, to Viglius, "that vengeance is the Lord's—God is my witness that I pardon all the past." In the same letter, nevertheless, he added, "My theology, however, does not teach me that by enduring one is to enable one's enemies to commit even greater wrongs. If the royal justice is not soon put into play, I shall be obliged to right myself. This thing is going on too long— patience exhausted changes to fury. 'Tis necessary that every man should assist himself as he can, and when I choose to throw the game into confusion I shall do it perhaps more notably than the others." A few weeks afterwards, writing to the same correspondent, he observed, "We shall have to turn again, and rejoice together. Whatever the King commands I shall do, even were I to march into the fire; whatever happens, and without fear or respect for any person, I mean to remain the same man to the end. *Durate*—and I have a head that is hard enough when I do undertake anything—*nec animum despondeo.*" Here, certainly, was significant foreshadowing of the general wrath to come, and it was therefore of less consequence that the portraits painted by him of Berghen, Horn, Montigny, and others, were so rarely relieved by the more flattering tints which he occasionally mingled with the somber coloring of his other pictures.[1]

[WILLIAM OF ORANGE IN 1564]

[Motley quite correctly represents the William the Silent of history as the product of a slow development. He gives the following sketches of him in 1564.]

Orange had three great objects in view, by attaining which the country, in his opinion, might yet be saved, and the threatened convulsions averted. These were to convoke the States-General, to moderate or abolish the edicts, and to suppress the council of finance and the privy council, leaving only the council of state. The two first of these points, if gained, would, of course, subvert the whole absolute policy which Philip and Granvelle had enforced; it was, therefore, hardly probable that any impression would be made upon the secret determination of the government in these respects. As to the council of state, the limited powers of that body, under the administration of the Cardinal, had formed one of the principal complaints against that minister. The justice and finance councils were sinks of iniquity. The most barefaced depravity reigned supreme. A gangrene had spread through the whole government. The public functionaries were notoriously and outrageously venal. The administration of justice had been poisoned at the fountain, and the people were unable to slake their daily thirst at

[1] *The Rise of the Dutch Republic* (New York, 1856), 427–433.

the polluted stream. There was no law but the law of the longest purse. The highest dignitaries of Philip's appointment had become the most mercenary hucksters that ever converted the temple of justice into a den of thieves. Law was an article of merchandise, sold by judges to the highest bidder. A poor customer could obtain nothing but stripes and imprisonment, or if tainted with suspicion of heresy, the fagot or the sword; but for the rich everything was attainable. Pardons for the most atrocious crimes, passports, safe-conducts, offices of trust and honor, were disposed of at auction to the highest bidder. Against all this sea of corruption did the brave William of Orange set his breast, undaunted and unflinching. Of all the conspicuous men in the land, he was the only one whose worst enemy had never hinted, through the whole course of his public career, that his hands had known contamination. His honor was ever untarnished by even a breath of suspicion. The Cardinal could accuse him of pecuniary embarrassment, by which a large proportion of his revenues were necessarily diverted to the liquidation of his debts, but he could not suggest that the Prince had ever freed himself from difficulties by plunging his hands into the public treasury, when it might easily have been opened to him.

It was soon, however, sufficiently obvious that as desperate a struggle was to be made with the many-headed monster of corruption as with the Cardinal by whom it had been so long fed and governed. The Prince was accused of ambition and intrigue. It was said that he was determined to concentrate all the powers of government in the state-council, which was thus to become an omnipotent and irresponsible senate, while the King would be reduced to the condition of a Venetian Doge. It was, of course, suggested that it was the aim of Orange to govern the new Tribunal of Ten. No doubt the Prince was ambitious. Birth, wealth, genius, and virtue could not have been bestowed in such eminent degree on any man without carrying with them the determination to assert their value. It was not his wish so much as it was the necessary law of his being to impress himself upon his age and to rule his fellow men. But he practiced no arts to arrive at the supremacy which he felt must always belong to him, whatever might be his nominal position in the political hierarchy. He was already, although but just turned of thirty years, vastly changed from the brilliant and careless grandee, as he stood at the hour of the imperial abdication. He was becoming careworn in face, thin of figure, sleepless of habit. The wrongs of which he was the daily witness, the absolutism, the cruelty, the rottenness of the government, had marked his face with premature furrows. "They say that the Prince is very sad," wrote Morillon to Granvelle; "and 'tis easy to read as much in his face. They say *he cannot sleep.*" Truly might the monarch have taken warning that here was a man who was dangerous, and who thought too much. "Sleek-headed men, and such as slept o' nights," would have been more eligible functionaries, no doubt, in the royal estimation, but, for a brief period, the King was content to use, to watch, and to suspect the man who was one day to be his great and invincible antagonist. He continued assiduous at the council, and he did his best, by entertaining nobles and citizens at his hospitable mansion, to cultivate good relations with large numbers of his countrymen. He soon, however, had become disgusted with the court. Egmont was more lenient to the foul practices which prevailed there, and took almost a childish pleasure in dining at the table of the Duchess, dressed, as were many of the younger nobles, in short camlet doublet with the wheat-sheaf buttons.

The Prince felt more unwilling to compromise his personal dignity by countenancing the flagitious proceedings and the contemptible supremacy of Armenteros, and it was soon very obvious, therefore, that Egmont was a greater favorite at court than Orange. At the same time the Count was also diligently cultivating the good graces of the middle and lower classes in Brussels, shooting with the burghers at the popinjay, calling every man by his name, and assisting at jovial banquets in townhouse or guildhall. The Prince, although at times a necessary partaker also in these popular amusements, could find small cause for rejoicing in the aspect of affairs. When

his business led him to the palace, he was sometimes forced to
wait in the antechamber for an hour, while Secretary Armenteros was engaged in private consultation with Margaret upon
the most important matters of administration. It could not be
otherwise than galling to the pride and offensive to the patriotism of the Prince, to find great public transactions intrusted to
such hands. Thomas de Armenteros was a mere private secretary—a simple clerk. He had no right to have cognizance of
important affairs, which could only come before his Majesty's
sworn advisers. He was, moreover, an infamous peculator.
He was rolling up a fortune with great rapidity by his shame-
less traffic in benefices, charges, offices, whether of church or
state. His name of Armenteros was properly converted into
Argenteros, in order to symbolize the man who was made of
public money. His confidential intimacy with the Duchess
procured for him also the name of "Madame's barber," in allusion to the famous ornaments of Margaret's upper lip, and to
the celebrated influence enjoyed by the barbers of the Duke of
Savoy and of Louis the Eleventh. This man sold dignities and
places of high responsibility at public auction. The Regent
not only connived at these proceedings, which would have been
base enough, but she was full partner in the disgraceful commerce. Through the agency of the Secretary, she, too, was
amassing a large private fortune. "The Duchess has gone into
the business of vending places to the highest bidders," said
Morillon, "with the bit between her teeth." The spectacle presented at the council-board was often sufficiently repulsive not
only to the cardinalists, who were treated with elaborate insolence, but to all men who love honor and justice, or who
felt an interest in the prosperity of government. There was
nothing majestic in the appearance of the Duchess, as she sat
conversing apart with Armenteros, whispering, pinching, gig-
gling, or disputing, while important affairs of state were de-
bated, concerning which the Secretary had no right to be
informed. It was inevitable that Orange should be offended
to the utmost by such proceedings, although he was himself
treated with comparative respect. As for the ancient adherents

of Granvelle, the Bordeys, Baves, and Morillons, they were forbidden by the favorite even to salute him in the streets.[1]

Then, however, William the Silent opened his lips, and poured forth a long and vehement discourse, such as he rarely pronounced, but such as few except himself could utter. There was no shuffling, no disguise, no timidity in his language. He took the ground boldly that the time had arrived for speaking out. The object of sending an envoy of high rank and European reputation like the Count of Egmont, was to tell the King the truth. Let Philip know it now. Let him be unequivocally informed that this whole machinery of placards and scaffolds, of new bishops and old hangmen, of decrees, inquisitors, and informers, must once and for ever be abolished. Their day was over. The Netherlands were free provinces, they were surrounded by free countries, they were determined to vindicate their ancient privileges. Moreover, his Majesty was to be plainly informed of the frightful corruption which made the whole judicial and administrative system loathsome. The venality which notoriously existed everywhere—on the bench, in the council chamber, in all public offices, where purity was most essential—was denounced by the Prince in scathing terms. He tore the mask from individual faces, and openly charged the Chancellor of Brabant, Engelbert Maas, with knavery and corruption. He insisted that the King should be informed of the necessity of abolishing the two inferior councils, and of enlarging the council of state by the admission of ten or twelve new members selected for their patriotism, purity, and capacity. Above all, it was necessary plainly to inform his Majesty that the canons of Trent, spurned by the whole world, even by the Catholic Princes of Germany, could never be enforced in the Netherlands, and that it would be ruinous to make the attempt. He proposed and insisted that the Count of Egmont should be instructed accordingly. He avowed in conclusion that he was a Catholic himself and intended to remain in the faith, but that he could not look on with pleasure when

[1] *The Rise of the Dutch Republic* (New York, 1856), I, 440–444.

princes strove to govern the souls of men, and to take away their liberty in matters of conscience and religion.[1]

[THE RESULT OF THE ROYAL POLICY]

The uneasiness, the terror, the wrath of the people, seemed rapidly culminating to a crisis. Nothing was talked of but the edicts and the Inquisition. Nothing else entered into the minds of men. In the streets, in the shops, in the taverns, in the fields; at market, at church, at funerals, at weddings; in the noble's castle, at the farmer's fireside, in the mechanic's garret, upon the merchant's exchange, there was but one perpetual subject of shuddering conversation. It was better, men began to whisper to each other, to die at once than to live in perpetual slavery. It was better to fall with arms in hand than to be tortured and butchered by the Inquisition. Who could expect to contend with such a foe in the dark?

They reproached the municipal authorities with lending themselves as instruments to the institution. They asked magistrates and sheriffs how far they would go in their defense before God's tribunal for the slaughter of his creatures, if they could only answer the divine arraignment by appealing to the edict of 1550. On the other hand, the inquisitors were clamorous in abuse of the languor and the cowardice of the secular authorities. They wearied the ear of the Duchess with complaints of the difficulties which they encountered in the execution of their functions—of the slight alacrity on the part of the various officials to assist them in the discharge of their duties. Notwithstanding the express command of his Majesty to that effect, they experienced, they said, a constant deficiency of that cheerful co-operation which they had the right to claim, and there was perpetual discord in consequence. They had been empowered by papal and by royal decree to make use of the gaols, the constables, the whole penal machinery of each province; yet the officers often refused to act, and had even dared to close the prisons. Nevertheless, it had been intended,

[1] *The Rise of the Dutch Republic* (New York, 1856), I, 455–456.

as fully appeared by the imperial and royal instructions to the inquisitors, that their action through the medium of the provincial authorities should be unrestrained. Not satisfied with these representations to the Regent, the inquisitors had also made a direct appeal to the King. Judocus Tiletanus and Michael de Bay addressed to Philip a letter from Louvain. They represented to him that they were the only two left of the five inquisitors-general appointed by the Pope for all the Netherlands, the other three having *been recently converted into bishops*. Daily complaints, they said, were reaching them of the prodigious advance of heresy; but their own office was becoming so odious, so calumniated, and exposed to so much resistance, that they could not perform its duties without personal danger. They urgently demanded from his Majesty, therefore, additional support and assistance. Thus the Duchess, exposed at once to the rising wrath of a whole people, and to the shrill blasts of inquisitorial anger, was tossed to and fro, as upon a stormy sea. The commands of the King, too explicit to be tampered with, were obeyed. The theological assembly had met and given advice. The Council of Trent was here and there enforced. The edicts were republished and the inquisitors encouraged. Moreover, in accordance with Philip's suggestion, orders were now given that the heretics should be executed at midnight in their dungeons, by binding their heads between their knees, and then slowly suffocating them in tubs of water. Secret drowning was substituted for public burning, in order that the heretic's crown of vainglory, which was thought to console him in his agony, might never be placed upon his head.

In the course of the summer, Margaret wrote to her brother that the popular frenzy was becoming more and more intense. The people were crying aloud, she said, that the Spanish Inquisition, or a worse than Spanish Inquisition, had been established among them by means of bishops and ecclesiastics. She urged Philip to cause the instructions for the inquisitors to be revised. Egmont, she said, was vehement in expressing his dissatisfaction at the discrepancy between Philip's language to him by word of mouth, and that of the royal despatches on the religious question. The other seigniors were even more indignant.[1]

Meanwhile the pamphlets, handbills, pasquils, and other popular productions, were multiplied. To use a Flemish expression, they "snowed in the streets." They were nailed nightly on all the great houses in Brussels. Patriots were called upon to strike, speak, redress. Pungent lampoons, impassioned invectives, and earnest remonstrances, were thrust into the hands of the Duchess. The publications, as they appeared, were greedily devoured by the people. "We are willing," it was said, in a remarkable letter to the King, "to die for the Gospel, but we read therein, 'Render unto Caesar that which is Caesar's, and unto God that which is God's.' We thank God that our enemies themselves are compelled to bear witness to our piety and patience; so that it is a common saying, 'He swears not, he is a Protestant; he is neither a fornicator nor a drunkard; he is of the new sect.' Yet, notwithstanding these testimonials to our character, no manner of punishment has been forgotten by which we can possibly be chastised." This statement of the morality of the Puritans of the Netherlands was the justification of martyrs—not the self-glorification of Pharisees. The fact was incontrovertible. Their tenets were rigid, but their lives were pure. They belonged generally to the middling and lower classes. They were industrious artisans, who desired to live in the fear of God and in honor of their King. They were protected by nobles and gentlemen of high position, very many of whom came afterwards warmly to espouse the creed which at first they had only generously defended. Their whole character and position resembled, in many features, those of the English Puritans, who, three quarters of a century afterwards, fled for refuge to the Dutch Republic, and thence departed to establish the American Republic. The difference was, that the Netherlanders were exposed to a longer persecution, and a far more intense martyrdom.[2]

[1] *The Rise of the Dutch Republic* (New York, 1856), I, 473–475.
[2] *Ibid.*, I, 484–485.

The condition of the country was frightful. The most determined loyalists, such as Berlaymont, Viglius, and Hopper, advised her not to mention the name of Inquisition in a conference which she was obliged to hold with a deputation from Antwerp. She feared, all feared, to pronounce the hated word. She wrote despairing letters to Philip, describing the condition of the land and her own agony in the gloomiest colors. Since the arrival of the royal orders, she said, things had gone from bad to worse. The King had been ill-advised. It was useless to tell the people that the Inquisition had always existed in the Provinces. They maintained that it was a novelty; that the institution was a more rigorous one than the Spanish Inquisition, which, said Margaret, "was most odious, as the King knew." It was utterly impossible to carry the edicts into execution. Nearly all the governors of provinces had told her plainly that they would not help to burn fifty or sixty thousand Netherlanders. Thus bitterly did Margaret of Parma bewail the royal decree; not that she had any sympathy for the victims, but because she felt the increasing danger to the executioner. One of two things it was now necessary to decide upon,— concession or armed compulsion. Meantime, while Philip was slowly and secretly making his levies, his sister, as well as his people, was on the rack. Of all the seigniors, not one was placed in so painful a position as Egmont. His military reputation and his popularity made him too important a personage to be slighted, yet he was deeply mortified at the lamentable mistake which he had committed. He now averred that he *would never take arms against the King*, but that he would go where man should never see him more.

Such was the condition of the nobles, greater and less. That of the people could not well be worse. Famine reigned in the land. Emigration, caused not by overpopulation, but by persecution, was fast weakening the country. It was no wonder that not only foreign merchants should be scared from the great commercial cities by the approaching disorders, but that every industrious artisan who could find the means of escape should seek refuge among strangers, wherever an asylum could be found. That asylum was afforded by Protestant England, who received these intelligent and unfortunate wanderers with cordiality, and learned with eagerness the lessons in mechanical skill which they had to teach. Already there were thirty thousand emigrant Netherlanders established in Sandwich, Norwich, and other places, assigned to them by Elizabeth. It had always, however, been made a condition of the liberty granted to these foreigners for practicing their handiwork, that each house should employ at least one English apprentice. "Thus," said a Walloon historian, splenetically, "by this regulation, and by means of heavy duties on foreign manufactures, have the English built up their own fabrics and prohibited those of the Netherlands. Thus have they drawn over to their own country our skilful artisans to practice their industry, not at home but abroad, and our poor people are losing the means of earning their livelihood. Thus has clothmaking, silk-making, and the art of dyeing declined in this country, and would have been quite extinguished but by our wise countervailing edicts." The writer, who derived most of his materials and his wisdom from the papers of Councillor d'Assonleville, could hardly doubt that the persecution to which these industrious artisans, whose sufferings he affected to deplore, had been subjected, must have had something to do with their expatriation; but he preferred to ascribe it wholly to the protective system adopted by England. In this he followed the opinion of his preceptor. "For a long time," said Assonleville, "the Netherlands have been the Indies to England; and as long as she has them, she needs no other. The French try to surprise our fortresses and cities: the English make war upon our wealth and upon the purses of the people." Whatever the cause, however, the current of trade was already turned. The clothmaking of England was already gaining preponderance over that of the Provinces. Vessels now went every week from Sandwich to Antwerp, laden with silk, satin, and cloth, manufactured in England, while as many, but a few years before, had borne the Flemish fabrics of the same nature from Antwerp to England.

It might be supposed by disinterested judges that persecution was at the bottom of this change in commerce. The Prince of Orange estimated that up to this period fifty thousand persons in the Provinces had been put to death in obedience to the edicts. He was a moderate man, and accustomed to weigh his words. As a new impulse had been given to the system of butchery; as it was now sufficiently plain that "if the father had chastised his people with a scourge, the son held a whip of scorpions"; as the edicts were to be enforced with renewed vigor—it was natural that commerce and manufactures should make their escape out of a doomed land as soon as possible, whatever system of tariffs might be adopted by neighboring nations.[1]

[THE BEGGARS]

[The conditions produced in the Netherlands by the royal policy led to a formal protest by a large body of the nobles, particularly the lower nobility. Upon these scenes Motley put a great deal of emphasis.]

It was about six o'clock in the evening, on the third day of April (1566), that the long-expected cavalcade at last entered Brussels. An immense concourse of citizens of all ranks thronged around the noble confederates as soon as they made their appearance. They were about two hundred in number, all on horseback, with pistols in their holsters, and Brederode, tall, athletic, and martial in his bearing, with handsome features and fair curling locks upon his shoulders, seemed an appropriate chieftain for that band of Batavian chivalry. The procession was greeted with frequent demonstrations of applause as it wheeled slowly through the city till it reached the mansion of Orange Nassau. Here Brederode and Count Louis alighted, while the rest of the company dispersed to different quarters of the town.

"They thought that I should not come to Brussels," said Brederode, as he dismounted. "Very well, here I am; and per-

[1] *The Rise of the Dutch Republic* (New York, 1856), I, 503–506.

haps I shall depart in a different manner." In the course of the
next day, Counts Culemburg and Van den Berg entered the
city with one hundred other cavaliers.

On the morning of the 5th of April, the confederates were
assembled at the Culemburg mansion, which stood on the
square called the Sablon, within a few minutes' walk of the
palace. A straight handsome street led from the house along
the summit of the hill to the splendid residence of the ancient
Dukes of Brabant, then the abode of Duchess Margaret. At a
little before noon, the gentlemen came forth, marching on foot,
two by two, to the number of three hundred. Nearly all were
young, many of them bore the most ancient historical names of
their country, every one was arrayed in magnificent costume.
It was regarded as ominous that the man who led the processions, Philip de Bailleul, was lame. The line was closed by
Brederode and Count Louis, who came last, walking arm in
arm. An immense crowd was collected in the square in front
of the palace, to welcome the men who were looked upon as
the deliverers of the land from Spanish tyranny, from the cardinalists, and from the Inquisition. They were received with
deafening huzzas and clappings of hands by the assembled
populace. As they entered the council-chamber, passing
through the great hall, where ten years before the Emperor had
given away his crowns, they found the Emperor's daughter
seated in the chair of state, and surrounded by the highest personages of the country. The emotion of the Duchess was
evident, as the procession somewhat abruptly made its appearance; nor was her agitation diminished as she observed among
the petitioners many relatives and retainers of the Orange and
Egmont houses, and saw friendly glances of recognition exchanged between them and their chiefs.

As soon as all had entered the senate-room, Brederode advanced, made a low obeisance, and spoke a brief speech. He
said that he had come thither with his colleagues to present an
humble petition to her Highness. He alluded to the reports
which had been rife, that they had contemplated tumult, sedition, foreign conspiracies, and, what was more abominable than

all, a change of sovereign. He denounced such statements as calumnies, begged the Duchess to name the men who had thus aspersed an honorable and loyal company, and called upon her to inflict exemplary punishment upon the slanderers. With these prefatory remarks he presented the petition. The famous document was then read aloud. Its tone was sufficiently loyal, particularly in the preamble, which was filled with protestations of devotion to both King and Duchess. After this conventional introduction, however, the petitioners proceeded to state, very plainly, that the recent resolutions of his Majesty, with regard to the edicts and the Inquisition, were likely to produce a general rebellion. They had hoped, they said, that a movement would be made by the seigniors or by the estates, to remedy the evil by striking at its cause, but they had waited in vain. The danger, on the other hand, was augmenting every day, universal sedition was at the gate, and they had therefore felt obliged to delay no longer, but come forward the first and do their duty. They professed to do this with more freedom, because the danger touched them very nearly. They were the most exposed to the calamities which usually spring from civil commotion, for their houses and lands, situate in the open fields, were exposed to the pillage of all the world. Moreover, there was not one of them, whatever his condition, who was not liable at any moment to be executed under the edicts, at the false complaint of the first man who wanted to obtain his estate, and who chose to denounce him to the inquisitor, at whose mercy were the lives and property of all. They therefore begged the Duchess Regent to despatch an envoy on their behalf, who should humbly implore his Majesty to abolish the edicts. In the meantime they requested her Highness to order a general surcease of the Inquisition, and of all executions, until the King's further pleasure was made known, and until new ordinances made by his Majesty with advice and consent of the States-General duly assembled, should be established. The petition terminated, as it had commenced, with expressions of extreme respect and devoted loyalty.

The agitation of Duchess Margaret increased very perceptibly during the reading of the paper. When it was finished, she remained for a few minutes quite silent, with tears rolling down her cheeks. As soon as she could overcome her excitement, she uttered a few words to the effect that she would advise with her councillors and give the petitioners such answer as should be found suitable. The confederates then passed out from the council-chamber into the grand hall; each individual, as he took his departure, advancing towards the Duchess and making what was called the "caracole," in token of reverence. There was thus ample time to contemplate the whole company, and to count the numbers of the deputation.

After this ceremony had been concluded, there was much earnest debate in the council. The Prince of Orange addressed a few words to the Duchess, with the view of calming her irritation. He observed that the confederates were no seditious rebels, but loyal gentlemen, well-born, well-connected, and of honorable character. They had been influenced, he said, by an honest desire to save their country from impending danger—not by avarice or ambition. Egmont shrugged his shoulders, and observed that it was necessary for him to leave the court for a season, in order to make a visit to the baths of Aix, for an inflammation which he had in the leg. It was then that Berlaymont, according to the account which has been sanctioned by nearly every contemporary writer, whether Catholic or Protestant, uttered the gibe which was destined to become immortal, and to give a popular name to the confederacy. "What, Madam!" he is reported to have cried in a passion, "is it possible that your Highness can entertain fears of these beggars (*gueux*)? Is it not obvious what manner of men they are? They have not had wisdom enough to manage their own estates, and are they now to teach the King and your Highness how to govern the country? By the living God, if my advice were taken, their petition should have a cudgel for a commentary, and we would make them go down the steps of the palace a great deal faster than they mounted them."

The Count of Meghem was equally violent in his language. Aremberg was for ordering "*their reverences*, the confederates," to quit Brussels without delay. The conversation, carried on in so violent a key, might not unnaturally have been heard by such of the gentlemen as had not yet left the grand hall adjoining the council-chamber. The meeting of the council was then adjourned for an hour or two, to meet again in the afternoon, for the purpose of deciding deliberately upon the answer to be given to the Request. Meanwhile, many of the confederates were swaggering about the streets, talking very bravely of the scene which had just occurred, and it is probable, boasting not a little of the effect which their demonstration would produce. As they passed by the house of Berlaymont, that nobleman, standing at his window in company with Count Aremberg, is said to have repeated his jest. "There go our fine beggars again," said he. "Look, I pray you, with what bravado they are passing before us!" . . .

The board glittered with silver and gold. The wine circulated with more than its usual rapidity among the band of noble Bacchanals, who were never weary of drinking the healths of Brederode, of Orange, and Egmont. It was thought that the occasion imperiously demanded an extraordinary carouse, and the political events of the past three days lent an additional excitement to the wine. There was an earnest discussion as to an appropriate name to be given to their confederacy. Should they call themselves the "Society of Concord," the restorers of lost liberty, or by what other attractive title should the league be baptized? Brederode was, however, already prepared to settle the question. He knew the value of a popular and original name; he possessed the instinct by which adroit partisans in every age have been accustomed to convert the reproachful epithets of their opponents into watchwords of honor, and he had already made his preparations for a startling theatrical effect. Suddenly, amid the din of voices, he arose, with all his rhetorical powers at command. He recounted to the company the observations which the Seigneur de Berlaymont was reported to have made to the Duchess, upon the presentation of the request, and the name which he had thought fit to apply to them collectively. Most of the gentlemen then heard the memorable sarcasm for the first time. Great was the indignation of all, that the state-councillor should have dared to stigmatize as beggars a band of gentlemen with the best blood of the land in their veins. Brederode, on the contrary, smoothing their anger, assured them with good humor that nothing could be more fortunate. "They call us beggars!" said he; "let us accept the name. We will contend with the Inquisition, but remain loyal to the King, even till compelled to wear the beggar's sack."

He then beckoned to one of his pages, who brought him a leathern wallet, such as was worn at that day by professional mendicants, together with a large wooden bowl, which also formed part of their regular appurtenances. Brederode immediately hung the wallet around his neck, filled the bowl with wine, lifted it with both hands, and drained it at a draught. "Long live the beggars!" he cried, as he wiped his beard and set the bowl down. "*Vivent les gueux!*" Then for the first time, from the lips of those reckless nobles rose the famous cry, which was so often to ring over land and sea, amid blazing cities, on blood-stained decks, through the smoke and carnage of many a stricken field. The humor of Brederode was hailed with deafening shouts of applause. The Count then threw the wallet around the neck of his nearest neighbor and handed him the wooden bowl. Each guest, in turn, donned the mendicant's knapsack. Pushing aside his golden goblet, each filled the beggar's bowl to the brim, and drained it to the beggars' health. Roars of laughter and shouts of "*Vivent les gueux*," shook the walls of the stately mansion, as they were doomed never to shake again. The shibboleth was invented. The conjuration which they had been anxiously seeking was found. Their enemies had provided them with a spell, which was to prove, in afterdays, potent enough to start a spirit from palace or hovel, forest or wave, as the deeds of the "wild beggars," the "wood beggars," and the "beggars of the sea" taught Philip at last to understand the nation which he had driven to madness.

When the wallet and bowl had made the circuit of the table, they were suspended to a pillar in the hall. Each of the company in succession then threw some salt into his goblet, and, placing himself under these symbols of the brotherhood, repeated a jingling distich, produced impromptu for the occasion:

> "By this salt, by this bread, by this wallet still,
>   These beggars change not, fret who will."[1]

[IMAGE–BREAKING]

[The resentment of the lower classes toward the royal policy took the form of image-breaking.]

On the following morning there was a large crowd collected in front of the cathedral. The image, instead of standing in the centre of the church, where, upon all former occasions, it had been accustomed during the week succeeding the ceremony to receive congratulatory visits, was now ignominiously placed behind an iron railing within the choir. It had been deemed imprudent to leave it exposed to sacrilegious hands. The precaution excited derision. Many vagabonds of dangerous appearance, many idle apprentices and ragged urchins were hanging for a long time about the imprisoned image, peeping through the railings, and indulging in many a brutal jest. "Mayken! Mayken!" they cried, "art thou terrified so soon? Hast flown to thy nest so early? Dost think thyself beyond the reach of mischief? Beware, Mayken! thine hour is fast approaching!" Others thronged around the balustrade, shouting, "*Vivent les gueux!*" and hoarsely commanding the image to join in the beggars' cry. Then, leaving the spot, the mob roamed idly about the magnificent church, sneering at the idols, execrating the gorgeous ornaments, scoffing at crucifix and altar. . . .

In the morning, as it was known that no precaution had been taken, the audacity of the Reformers was naturally increased. Within the cathedral a great crowd was at an early hour collected, whose savage looks and ragged appearance denoted that the day and night were not likely to pass away so peacefully as

[1] *The Rise of the Dutch Republic* (New York, 1856), I, 511–522.

the last. The same taunts and imprecations were hurled at the image of the Virgin; the same howling of the beggars' cry resounded through the lofty arches. For a few hours, no act of violence was committed, but the crowd increased. A few trifles, drifting, as usual, before the event, seemed to indicate the approaching convulsion. A very paltry old woman excited the image-breaking of Antwerp. She had for years been accustomed to sit before the door of the cathedral with wax tapers and wafers, earning a scanty subsistence from the profits of her meager trade, and by the small coins which she sometimes received in charity. Some of the rabble began to chaffer with this ancient huckstress. They scoffed at her consecrated wares; they bandied with her ribald jests, of which her public position had furnished her with a supply; they assured her that the hour had come when her idolatrous traffic was to be for ever terminated, when she and her patroness, Mary, were to be given over to destruction together. The old woman, enraged, answered threat with threat, and gibe with gibe. Passing from words to deeds, she began to catch from the ground every offensive missile or weapon which she could find, and to lay about her in all directions. . Her tormentors defended themselves as they could. Having destroyed her whole stock-in-trade, they provoked others to appear in her defense. The passers-by thronged to the scene; the cathedral was soon filled to overflowing; a furious tumult was already in progress.

Many persons fled in alarm to the Town House, carrying information of this outbreak to the magistrates. John Van Immerzeel, margrave of Antwerp, was then holding communication with the senate, and awaiting the arrival of the ward-masters, whom it had at last been thought expedient to summon. Upon intelligence of this riot, which the militia, if previously mustered, might have prevented, the senate determined to proceed to the cathedral in a body, with the hope of quelling the mob by the dignity of their presence. The margrave, who was the high executive officer of the little commonwealth, marched down to the cathedral accordingly, attended by the two burgomasters and all the senators. At first their authority, solicitations, and personal influence, produced a good effect. Some of those outside consented to retire, and the tumult partially subsided within. As night, however, was fast approaching, many of the mob insisted upon remaining for evening service. They were informed that there would be none that night, and that for once the people could certainly dispense with their vespers.

Several persons now manifesting an intention of leaving the cathedral, it was suggested to the senators that if they should lead the way, the populace would follow in their train, and so disperse to their homes. The excellent magistrates took the advice, not caring, perhaps, to fulfil any longer the dangerous but not dignified functions of police officers. Before departing, they adopted the precaution of closing all the doors of the church, leaving a single one open, that the rabble still remaining might have an opportunity to depart. It seemed not to occur to the senators that the same gate would as conveniently afford an entrance for those without as an egress for those within. That unlooked-for event happened, however. No sooner had the magistrates retired than the rabble burst through the single door which had been left open, overpowered the margrave, who, with a few attendants, had remained behind, vainly endeavoring by threats and exhortations to appease the tumult, drove him ignominiously from the church, and threw all the other portals wide open. Then the populace flowed in like an angry sea. The whole of the cathedral was at the mercy of the rioters, who were evidently bent on mischief. The wardens and treasurers of the church, after a vain attempt to secure a few of its most precious possessions, retired. They carried the news to the senators, who, accompanied by a few halberdmen, again ventured to approach the spot. It was but for a moment, however, for appalled by the furious sounds which came from within the church, as if subterranean and invisible forces were preparing a catastrophe which no human power could withstand, the magistrates fled precipitately from the scene. Fearing that the next attack would be upon the Town House, they hastened to concentrate at that point their available forces, and left the stately cathedral to its fate.

And now, as the shadows of night were deepening the perpetual twilight of the church, the work of destruction commenced. Instead of vespers rose the fierce music of a psalm, yelled by a thousand angry voices. It seemed the preconcerted signal for a general attack. A band of marauders flew upon the image of the Virgin, dragged it forth from its receptacle, plunged daggers into its inanimate body, tore off its jewelled and embroidered garments, broke the whole figure into a thousand pieces, and scattered the fragments along the floor. A wild shout succeeded, and then the work which seemed delegated to a comparatively small number of the assembled crowd, went on with incredible celerity. Some were armed with axes, some with bludgeons, some with sledge-hammers; others brought ladders, pulleys, ropes, and levers. Every statue was hurled from its niche, every picture torn from the wall, every wonderfully painted window shivered to atoms, every ancient monument shattered, every sculptured decoration, however inaccessible in appearance, hurled to the ground. Indefatigably, audaciously, endowed, as it seemed, with preternatural strength and nimbleness, these furious iconoclasts clambered up the dizzy heights, shrieking and chattering like malignant apes, as they tore off in triumph the slowly-matured fruit of centuries. In a space of time wonderfully brief, they had accomplished their task.

A colossal and magnificent group of the Saviour crucified between two thieves adorned the principal altar. The statue of Christ was wrenched from its place with ropes and pulleys, while the malefactors, with bitter and blasphemous irony, were left on high, the only representatives of the marble crowd which had been destroyed. A very beautiful piece of architecture decorated the choir,—the "repository," as it was called, in which the body of Christ was figuratively enshrined. This much-admired work rested upon a single column, but rose, arch upon arch, pillar upon pillar, to the height of three hundred feet, till quite lost in the vault above. It was now shattered into a million pieces. The statues, images, pictures, ornaments, as they lay upon the ground, were broken with sledge hammers, hewn with axes, trampled, torn, and beaten into shreds. A troop of harlots, snatching waxen tapers from the altars, stood around the destroyers and lighted them at their work. Nothing escaped their omnivorous rage. They desecrated seventy chapels, forced open all the chests of treasure, covered their own squalid attire with the gorgeous robes of the ecclesiastics, broke the sacred bread, poured out the sacramental wine into golden chalices, quaffing huge draughts to the beggars' health; burned all the splendid missals and manuscripts, and smeared their shoes with the sacred oil, with which kings and prelates had been anointed. It seemed that each of these malicious creatures must have been endowed with the strength of a hundred giants. How else, in the few brief hours of a midsummer night, could such a monstrous desecration have been accomplished by a troop, which, according to all accounts, was not more than one hundred in number. There was a multitude of spectators, as upon all such occasions, but the actual spoilers were very few.

The noblest and richest temple of the Netherlands was a wreck, but the fury of the spoilers was excited, not appeased. Each seizing a burning torch, the whole herd rushed from the cathedral, and swept howling through the streets. "Long live the beggars!" resounded through the sultry midnight air, as the ravenous pack flew to and fro, smiting every image of the Virgin, every crucifix, every sculptured saint, every Catholic symbol which they met with upon their path. All night long, they roamed from one sacred edifice to another, thoroughly destroying as they went. Before morning they had sacked thirty churches within the city walls. They entered the monasteries, burned their invaluable libraries, destroyed their altars, statues, pictures, and descended into the cellars, broached every cask which they found there, pouring out in one great flood all the ancient wine and ale with which those holy men had been wont to solace their retirement from generation to generation. They invaded the nunneries, whence the occupants, panic-stricken, fled for refuge to the houses of their friends and kindred. The streets were filled with monks and nuns, running this way and that, shrieking and fluttering, to escape the claws of these fiendish Calvinists. The terror was imaginary, for not the least remarkable feature in these transactions was that neither insult nor injury was offered to man or woman, and that not a farthing's value of the immense amount of property destroyed was appropriated. It was a war, not against the living, but against graven images, nor was the sentiment which prompted the onslaught in the least commingled with a desire of plunder. The principal citizens of Antwerp, expecting every instant that the storm would be diverted from the ecclesiastical edifices to private dwellings, and that robbery, rape, and murder would follow sacrilege, remained all night expecting the attack, and prepared to defend their hearths, even if the altars were profaned. The precaution was needless. It was asserted by the Catholics that the confederates and other opulent Protestants had organized this company of profligates for the meager pittance of ten stivers a day. On the other hand, it was believed by many that the Catholics had themselves plotted the whole outrage in order to bring odium upon the Reformers. Both statements were equally unfounded. The task was most thoroughly performed, but it was prompted by a furious fanaticism, not by baser motives.

Two days and nights longer the havoc raged unchecked through all the churches of Antwerp and the neighboring villages. Hardly a statue or picture escaped destruction. . . . Yet the rage was directed exclusively against stocks and stones. Not a man was wounded nor a woman outraged. Prisoners, indeed, who had been languishing hopelessly in dungeons, were liberated. A monk, who had been in the prison of the Barefoot Monastery for twelve years, recovered his freedom. Art was trampled in the dust, but humanity deplored no victims.[1]

[DECISION OF WILLIAM OF ORANGE]

[These events confronted every inhabitant of the Netherlands with the necessity of taking sides in the approaching struggle. Motley, thus, describes the decision of William of Orange at this time.]

[1] *The Rise of the Dutch Republic* (New York, 1856), I, 557–565.

The Prince of Orange had, as we have seen, been exerting all his energies faithfully to accomplish the pacification of the commercial metropolis, upon the basis assented to beforehand by the Duchess. He had established a temporary religious peace, by which alone at that crisis the gathering tempest could be averted; but he had permitted the law to take its course upon certain rioters, who had been regularly condemned by courts of justice. He had worked day and night—notwithstanding immense obstacles, calumnious misstatements, and conflicting opinions—to restore order out of chaos; he had freely imperilled his own life—dashing into a tumultuous mob on one occasion, wounding several with a halberd which he snatched from one of his guard, and dispersing almost with his single arm a dangerous and threatening insurrection—and he had remained in Antwerp, at the pressing solicitations of the magistracy, who represented that the lives of not a single ecclesiastic would be safe as soon as his back was turned, and that all the merchants would forthwith depart from the city. It was nevertheless necessary that he should make a personal visit to his government of Holland, where similar disorders had been prevailing, and where men of all ranks and parties were clamoring for their stadholder.

Notwithstanding all his exertions, however, he was thoroughly aware of the position in which he stood towards the government. The sugared phrases of Margaret, the deliberate commendation of the "benign and *debonair*" Philip, produced no effect upon this statesman, who was accustomed to look through and through men's actions to the core of their hearts. In the hearts of Philip and Margaret he already saw treachery and revenge indelibly imprinted. He had been especially indignant at the insult which the Duchess Regent had put upon him by sending Duke Eric of Brunswick with an armed force into Holland in order to protect Gouda, Woerden, and other places within the Prince's own government. He was thoroughly conversant with the general tone in which the other seigniors and himself were described to their sovereign. He was already convinced that the country was to be conquered by foreign mercenaries, and that his own life, with those of many other nobles, was to be sacrificed. The moment had arrived in which he was justified in looking about him for means of defense, both for himself and his country, if the King should be so insane as to carry out the purposes which the Prince suspected. The time was fast approaching in which a statesman placed upon such an elevation before the world as that which he occupied would be obliged to choose his part for life. To be the unscrupulous tool of tyranny, a rebel, or an exile, was his necessary fate. To a man so prone to read the future, the moment for his choice seemed already arrived. Moreover, he thought it doubtful, and events were most signally to justify his doubts, whether he could be accepted as the instrument of despotism, even were he inclined to prostitute himself to such service. At this point, therefore, undoubtedly began the treasonable thoughts of William the Silent, if it be treason to attempt the protection of ancient and chartered liberties against a foreign oppressor. He despatched a private envoy to Egmont, representing the grave suspicions manifested by the Duchess in sending Duke Eric into Holland, and proposing that means should be taken into consideration for obviating the dangers with which the country was menaced. Catholics, as well as Protestants, he intimated, were to be crushed in one universal conquest as soon as Philip had completed the formidable preparations which he was making for invading the provinces. For himself, he said, he would not remain in the land to witness the utter desolation of the people, nor to fall an unresisting victim to the vengeance which he foresaw. If, however, he might rely upon the co-operation of Egmont and Horn, he was willing, with the advice of the States-General, to risk preparations against the armed invasion of Spaniards by which the country was to be reduced to slavery. It was incumbent, however, upon men placed as they were, "not to let the grass grow under their feet"; and the moment for action was fast approaching.

This was the scheme which Orange was willing to attempt. To make use of his own influence and that of his friends, to interpose between a sovereign insane with bigotry, and a people in a state of religious frenzy, to resist brutal violence if need should be by force, and to compel the sovereign to respect the charters which he had sworn to maintain, and which were far more ancient than his sovereignty; so much of treason did William of Orange already contemplate, for in no other way could he be loyal to his country and his own honor.[1]

[THE DUKE OF ALVA]

[The majority of the people of the Netherlands followed either openly or secretly the example of William of Orange. By 1567 the situation had become so serious in that province that Philip II decided to send into the Netherlands the Duke of Alva, one of his two most trusted advisers, at the head of a Spanish army, supposedly the best troops in Europe.]

It was determined at last that the Netherland heresy should be conquered by force of arms. The invasion resembled both a crusade against the infidel and a treasure-hunting foray into the auriferous Indies, achievements by which Spanish chivalry had so often illustrated itself. The banner of the cross was to be replanted upon the conquered battlements of three hundred infidel cities, and a torrent of wealth, richer than ever flowed from Mexican or Peruvian mines, was to flow into the royal treasury from the perennial fountains of confiscation. Who so fit to be the Tancred and the Pizarro of this bicolored expedition as the Duke of Alva, the man who had been devoted from his earliest childhood, and from his father's grave, to hostility against unbelievers, and who had prophesied that treasure would flow in a stream, a yard deep, from the Netherlands as soon as the heretics began to meet with their deserts? An army of chosen troops was forthwith collected, by taking the four legions, or terzios, of Naples, Sicily, Sardinia, and Lombardy, and filling their places in Italy by fresh levies. About ten thousand picked and veteran soldiers were thus obtained, of which the Duke of Alva was appointed general-in-chief.

[1] *The Rise of the Dutch Republic*, II, 29–32.

Fernando Alvarez de Toledo, Duke of Alva, was now in his sixtieth year. He was the most successful and experienced general of Spain, or of Europe. No man had studied more deeply, or practiced more constantly, the military science. In the most important of all arts at that epoch he was the most consummate artist. In the only honorable profession of the age, he was the most thorough and the most pedantic professor. Since the day of Demetrius Poliorcetes, no man had besieged so many cities. Since the days of Fabius Cunctator, no general had avoided so many battles, and no soldier, courageous as he was, ever attained to a more sublime indifference to calumny or depreciation. Having proved in his boyhood at Fontarabia, and in his maturity at Mühlberg, that he could exhibit heroism and headlong courage when necessary, he could afford to look with contempt upon the witless gibes which his enemies had occasionally perpetrated at his expense. Conscious of holding his armies in his hand, by the power of an unrivalled discipline, and the magic of a name illustrated by a hundred triumphs, he could bear with patience and benevolence the murmurs of his soldiers when their battles were denied them.

He was born in 1508, of a family which boasted imperial descent. A Palaeologus, brother of a Byzantine emperor, had conquered the city of Toledo, and transmitted its appellation as a family name. The father of Fernando, Don Garcia, had been slain on the Isle of Gerbes, in battle with the Moors, when his son was but four years of age. The child was brought up by his grandfather, Don Frederic, and trained from his tenderest infancy to arms. Hatred to the infidel, and a determination to avenge his father's blood, crying to him from a foreign grave, were the earliest of his instincts. As a youth he was distinguished for his prowess. His maiden sword was fleshed at Fontarabia, where, although but sixteen years of age, he was considered, by his constancy in hardship, by his brilliant and desperate courage, and by the example of military discipline which he afforded to the troops, to have contributed in no small degree to the success of the Spanish arms.

In 1530 he accompanied the Emperor in his campaign against the Turk. Charles, instinctively recognizing the merit of the youth who was destined to be the lifelong companion of his toils and glories, distinguished him with his favor at the opening of his career. Young, brave, and enthusiastic, Fernando de Toledo at this period was as interesting a hero as ever illustrated the pages of Castilian romance. His mad ride from Hungary to Spain and back again, accomplished in seventeen days, for the sake of a brief visit to his newly-married wife, is not the least attractive episode in the history of an existence which was destined to be so dark and sanguinary. In 1535 he accompanied the Emperor on his memorable expedition to Tunis. In 1546 and 1547 he was generalissimo in the war against the Smalcaldian league. His most brilliant feat of arms —perhaps the most brilliant exploit of the Emperor's reign— was the passage of the Elbe and the battle of Mühlberg, accomplished in spite of Maximilian's bitter and violent reproaches, and the tremendous possibilities of a defeat. That battle had finished the war. The gigantic and magnanimous John Frederic, surprised at his devotions in the church, fled in dismay, leaving his boots behind him, which, for their superhuman size, were ridiculously said afterwards to be treasured among the trophies of the Toledo house. The rout was total. "I came, I saw, and God conquered," said the Emperor, in pious parody of his immortal predecessor's epigram. Maximilian, with a thousand apologies for his previous insults, embraced the heroic Don Fernando over and over again, as, arrayed in a plain suit of blue armor, unadorned save with streaks of his enemies' blood, he returned from pursuit of the fugitives. So complete and so sudden was the victory, that it was found impossible to account for it, save on the ground of miraculous interposition. Like Joshua, in the vale of Ajalon, Don Fernando was supposed to have commanded the sun to stand still for a season, and to have been obeyed. Otherwise, how could the passage of the river, which was only concluded at six in the evening, and the complete overthrow of the Protestant forces, have all been accomplished within the narrow space of an

April twilight? The reply of the Duke to Henry the Second of France, who questioned him subsequently upon the subject, is well known: "Your Majesty, I was too much occupied that evening with what was taking place on the earth beneath, to pay much heed to the evolutions of the heavenly bodies." Spared as he had been by his good fortune from taking any part in the Algerine expedition, or in witnessing the ignominious retreat from Innspruck, he was obliged to submit to the intercalation of the disastrous siege of Metz in the long history of his successes. Doing the duty of a field-marshal and a sentinel, supporting his army by his firmness and his discipline when nothing else could have supported them, he was at last enabled, after half the hundred thousand men with whom Charles had begun the siege had been sacrificed, to induce his imperial master to raise the siege before the remaining fifty thousand had been frozen or starved to death.

The culminating career of Alva seemed to have closed in the mist which gathered around the setting star of the Empire. Having accompanied Philip to England in 1554, on his matrimonial expedition, he was destined in the following year, as viceroy and generalissimo of Italy, to be placed in a series of false positions. A great captain engaged in a little war, the champion of the cross in arms against the successor of St. Peter, he had extricated himself, at last, with his usual adroitness, but with very little glory. To him had been allotted the mortification, to another the triumph. The luster of his own name seemed to sink in the ocean, while that of a hated rival, with new-spangled ore, suddenly "flamed in the forehead of the morning sky." While he had been paltering with a dotard, whom he was forbidden to crush, Egmont had struck down the chosen troops of France, and conquered her most illustrious commanders. Here was the unpardonable crime which could only be expiated by the blood of the victor. Unfortunately for his rival, the time was now approaching when the long-deferred revenge was to be satisfied.

On the whole, the Duke of Alva was inferior to no general of his age. As a disciplinarian he was foremost in Spain, perhaps in Europe. A spendthrift of time, he was an economist of blood, and this was, perhaps, in the eye of humanity his principal virtue. "Time and myself are two," was a frequent observation of Philip, and his favorite general considered the maxim as applicable to war as to politics. Such were his qualities as a military commander. As a statesman, he had neither experience nor talent. As a man, his character was simple. He did not combine a great variety of vices, but those which he had were colossal, and he possessed no virtues. He was neither lustful nor intemperate, but his professed eulogists admitted his enormous avarice, while the world has agreed that such an amount of stealth and ferocity, of patient vindictiveness and universal bloodthirstiness, was never found in a savage beast of the forest, and but rarely in a human bosom. His history was now to show that his previous thrift of human life was not derived from any love of his kind. Personally he was stern and overbearing. As difficult of access as Philip himself, he was even more haughty to those who were admitted to his presence. He addressed every one with the depreciating second person plural. Possessing the right of being covered in the presence of the Spanish monarch, he had been with difficulty brought to renounce it before the German Emperor. He was of an illustrious family, but his territorial possessions were not extensive. His duchy was a small one, furnishing him with not more than fourteen thousand crowns of annual income, and with four hundred soldiers. He had, however, been a thrifty financier all his life, never having been without a handsome sum of ready money at interest. Ten years before his arrival in the Netherlands, he was supposed to have already increased his income to forty thousand a year by the proceeds of his investments at Antwerp. As already intimated, his military character was sometimes profoundly misunderstood. He was often considered rather a pedantic than a practical commander, more capable to discourse of battles than to gain them. Notwithstanding that his long life had been an almost unbroken campaign, the ridiculous accusation of timidity was frequently made against him. A gentleman at the court of the Emperor

Charles once addressed a letter to the Duke with the title of "General of his Majesty's armies in the Duchy of Milan in time of peace, and majordomo of the household in the time of war." It was said that the lesson did the Duke good, but that he rewarded very badly the nobleman who gave it, having subsequently caused his head to be taken off. In general, however, Alva manifested a philosophical contempt for the opinions expressed concerning his military fame, and was especially disdainful of criticism expressed by his own soldiers. "Recollect," said he, at a little later period, to Don John of Austria, "that the first foes with whom one has to contend are one's own troops, with their clamors for an engagement at this moment, and their murmurs about results at another; with their 'I thought that the battle should be fought'; or, 'it was my opinion that the occasion ought not to be lost.' Your Highness will have opportunity enough to display valor, and will never be weak enough to be conquered by the babble of soldiers."

In person he was tall, thin, erect, with a small head, a long visage, lean yellow cheeks, dark twinkling eyes, a dust complexion, black bristling hair, and a long sable-silvered beard, descending in two waving streams upon his breast.[1]

[PURPOSE OF THE DUKE OF ALVA]

[The purpose of Philip II in sending the Duke of Alva and his army into the Netherlands is thus set forth by the author.]

As already observed, the advent of Alva at the head of a foreign army was the natural consequence of all which had gone before. The delusion of the royal visit was still maintained, and the affectation of a possible clemency still displayed, while the monarch sat quietly in his cabinet without a remote intention of leaving Spain, and while the messengers of his accumulated and long-concealed wrath were already descending upon their prey. It was the deliberate intention of Philip, when the Duke was despatched to the Netherlands, that all the

---

[1] *The Rise of the Dutch Republic*, II, 102–109.

leaders of the anti-inquisition party, and all who had, at any time or in any way, implicated themselves in opposition to the government, or in censure of its proceedings, should be put to death. It was determined that the provinces should be subjugated to the absolute domination of the council of Spain, a small body of foreigners sitting at the other end of Europe, a junta in which Netherlanders were to have no voice and exercise no influence. The despotic government of the Spanish and Italian possessions was to be extended to these Flemish territories, which were thus to be converted into the helpless dependencies of a foreign and an absolute crown. There was to be a re-organisation of the inquisition, upon the same footing claimed for it before the outbreak of the troubles, together with a re-enactment and vigorous enforcement of the famous edicts against heresy.[1]

[THE COUNCIL OF BLOOD]

[One of the first steps of the Duke of Alva in the execution of this plan was the establishment of the notorious tribunal known in history as "The Council of Blood."]

In the same despatch of the 9th September, in which the Duke communicated to Philip the capture of Egmont and Horn, he announced to him his determination to establish a new court for the trial of crimes committed during the recent period of troubles. This wonderful tribunal was accordingly created with the least possible delay. It was called the Council of Troubles, but it soon acquired the terrible name, by which it will be for ever known in history, of the Blood-Council. It superseded all other institutions. Every court, from those of the municipal magistracies up to the supreme councils of the provinces, were forbidden to take cognisance in future of any cause growing out of the late troubles. The Council of State, although it was not formally disbanded, fell into complete desuetude, its members being occasionally summoned into

[1]*Ibid.*, II, 117–118.

Alva's private chambers in an irregular manner, while its principal functions were usurped by the Blood-Council. Not only citizens of every province, but the municipal bodies, and even the sovereign provincial estates themselves, were compelled to plead, like humble individuals, before this new and extraordinary tribunal. It is unnecessary to allude to the absolute violation which was thus committed of all charters, laws, and privileges, because the very creation of the council was a bold and brutal proclamation that those laws and privileges were at an end. The constitution or maternal principle of this suddenly erected court was of a twofold nature. It defined and it punished the crime of treason. The definitions, couched in eighteen articles, declared it to be treason to have delivered or signed any petition against the new bishops, the Inquisition, or the edicts; to have tolerated public preaching under any circumstances; to have omitted resistance to the image-breaking, to the field-preaching, or to the presentation of the Request by the nobles; and "either through sympathy or surprise" to have asserted that the King did not possess the right to deprive all the provinces of their liberties, or to have maintained that this present tribunal was bound to respect in any manner any laws or any charters. In these brief and simple, but comprehensive terms, was the crime of high treason defined. The punishment was still more briefly, simply, and comprehensively stated, for it was instant death in all cases. So well, too, did this new and terrible engine perform its work, that in less than three months from the time of its erection, eighteen hundred human beings had suffered death by its summary proceedings; some of the highest, the noblest, and the most virtuous in the land among the number; nor had it then manifested the slightest indication of faltering in its dread career.

Yet, strange to say, this tremendous court, thus established upon the ruins of all the ancient institutions of the country, had not been provided with even a nominal authority from any source whatever. The King had granted it no letters-patent or charter, nor had even the Duke of Alva thought it worth while to grant any commissions, either in his own name or as Captain-General, to any of the members composing the board. The Blood-Council was merely an informal club, of which the Duke was perpetual president, while the other members were all appointed by himself.

Of these subordinate councillors, two had the right of voting, subject, however, in all cases, to his final decision, while the rest of the number did not vote at all. It had not, therefore, in any sense, the character of a judicial, legislative, or executive tribunal, but was purely a board of advice, by which the bloody labors of the Duke were occasionally lightened as to detail, while not a feather's weight of power or of responsibility was removed from his shoulders. He reserved for himself the final decision upon all causes which should come before the council, and stated his motives for so doing with grim simplicity. "Two reasons," he wrote to the King, "have determined me thus to limit the power of the tribunal: the first that, not knowing its members, I might be easily deceived by them; the second, that *the men of law* only condemn *for crimes which are proved*, whereas your Majesty knows that the affairs of state are governed by very different rules from *the laws which they have here*." [1]

The Council of Blood, thus constituted, held its first session on the 20th September, at the lodgings of Alva. Springing completely grown and armed to the teeth from the head of its inventor, the new tribunal—at the very outset in possession of all its vigor—forthwith began to manifest a terrible activity in accomplishing the objects of its existence. The councillors having been sworn to "eternal secrecy as to anything which should be transacted at the board, and having likewise made oath to denounce any one of their number who should violate the pledge," the court was considered as organized. Alva worked therein seven hours daily. It may be believed that the subordinates were not spared, and that their office proved no sinecure. Their labors, however, were not encumbered by antiquated forms. As this supreme and only tribunal for all the Netherlands had no commission or authority save the will

[1] *The Rise of the Dutch Republic*, II, 135-137.

of the Captain-General, so it was also thought a matter of supererogation to establish a set of rules and orders such as might be useful in less independent courts. The forms of proceeding were brief and artless. There was a rude organization by which a crowd of commissioners, acting as inferior officers of the council, were spread over the province, whose business was to collect information concerning all persons who might be incriminated for participation in the recent troubles. The greatest crime, however, was to be rich, and one which could be expiated by no virtues, however signal. Alva was bent upon proving himself as accomplished a financier as he was indisputably a consummate commander, and he had promised his master an annual income of 500,000 ducats from the confiscations which were to accompany the executions.

It was necessary that the blood-torrent should flow at once through the Netherlands, in order that the promised golden river, a yard deep, according to his vaunt, should begin to irrigate the thirsty soil of Spain. It is obvious, from the fundamental laws which were made to define treason at the same moment in which they established the council, that any man might be at any instant summoned to the court. Every man, whether innocent or guilty, whether Papist or Protestant, felt his head shaking on his shoulders. If he were wealthy, there seemed no remedy but flight, which was now almost impossible, from the heavy penalties affixed by the new edict upon all carriers, shipmasters, and waggoners who should aid in the escape of heretics.

A certain number of these commissioners were particularly instructed to collect information as to the treason of Orange, Louis of Nassau, Brederode, Egmont, Horn, Culemburg, Van den Berg, Berghen, and Montigny. Upon such information the proceedings against those distinguished seigniors were to be summarily instituted. Particular councillors of the Court of Blood were charged with the arrangement of these important suits, but the commissioners were to report in the first instance to the Duke himself, who afterwards returned the paper into the hands of his subordinates.

With regard to the inferior and miscellaneous cases which were daily brought in incredible profusion before the tribunal, the same preliminaries were observed, by way of aping the proceedings in courts of justice. Alva sent the cartloads of information which were daily brought to him, but which neither he nor any other man had time to read, to be disposed of by the board of councillors. It was the duty of the different subalterns, who, as already stated, had no right of voting, to prepare reports upon the cases. Nothing could be more summary. Information was lodged against a man, or against a hundred men, in one document. The Duke sent the papers to the council, and the inferior councillors reported at once to Vargas. If the report concluded with a recommendation of death to the man, or the hundred men in question, Vargas instantly approved it, and execution was done upon the man, of the hundred men, within forty-eight hours. If the report *had any other conclusion*, it was immediately sent back for revision, and the reporters were overwhelmed with reproaches by the President.

Such being the method of operation, it may be supposed that the councillors were not allowed to slacken in their terrible industry. The register of every city, village, and hamlet throughout the Netherlands shewed the daily lists of men, women, and children thus sacrificed at the shrine of the demon who had obtained the mastery over this unhappy land. It was not often that an individual was of sufficient importance to be tried—if trial it could be called—by himself. It was found more expeditious to send them in batches to the furnace. Thus, for example, on the 4th of January, eighty-four inhabitants of Valenciennes were condemned; on another, day, ninety-five miscellaneous individuals, from different places in Flanders; on another, forty-six inhabitants of Malines; on another, thirty-five persons from different localities, and so on.

The evening of Shrovetide, a favorite holiday in the Netherlands, afforded an occasion for arresting and carrying off a vast number of doomed individuals at a single swoop. It was correctly supposed that the burghers, filled with wine and wassail, to which perhaps the persecution under which they lived lent an additional and horrible stimulus, might be easily taken from their beds in great numbers, and be delivered over at once to the council. The plot was ingenious, the net was spread accordingly. Many of the doomed were, however, luckily warned of the terrible termination which was impending over their festival, and bestowed themselves in safety for a season. A prize of about five hundred prisoners was all which rewarded the sagacity of the enterprise. It is needless to add that they were immediately executed. It is a wearisome and odious task to ransack the mouldy records of three centuries ago, in order to reproduce the obscure names of the thousands who were thus sacrificed. The dead have buried their dead, and are forgotten. It is likewise hardly necessary to state that the proceedings before the council were all *ex parte*, and that any information was almost inevitably followed by a death-warrant. It sometimes happened even that the zeal of the councillors outstripped the industry of the commissioners. The sentences were occasionally in advance of the docket. Thus upon one occasion a man's case was called for trial, but before the investigation was commenced it was discovered that he had been already executed. A cursory examination of the papers proved, moreover, as usual, that the culprit had committed no crime. "No matter for that," said Vargas, jocosely, "if he had died innocent, it will be all the better for him when he takes his trial in the other world."

But, however the councillors might indulge in these gentle jests among themselves, it was obvious that innocence was in reality impossible, according to the rules which had been laid down regarding treason. The practice was in accordance with the precept, and persons were daily executed with senseless pretexts, which was worse than executions with no pretexts at all. Thus Peter De Witt of Amsterdam was beheaded, because at one of the tumults in that city he had persuaded a rioter *not to fire* upon a magistrate. This was taken as sufficient proof that he was a man in authority among the rebels, and he was accordingly put to death. Madam Juriaen, who, in 1566, had struck with her slipper a little wooden image of the Virgin, together with her maidservant, who had witnessed without denouncing the crime, were both drowned by the hangman in a hogshead placed on the scaffold.

Death, even, did not in all cases place a criminal beyond the reach of the executioner. Egbert Meynartzoon, a man of high official rank, had been condemned, together with two colleagues, on an accusation of collecting money in a Lutheran church. He died in prison of dropsy. The sheriff was indignant with the physician, because, in spite of cordials and strengthening prescriptions, the culprit had slipped through his fingers before he had felt those of the hangman. He consoled himself by placing the body on a chair, and having the dead man beheaded in company with his colleagues.

Thus the whole country became a charnel-house; the death-bell tolled hourly in every village; not a family but was called to mourn for its dearest relatives, while the survivors stalked listlessly about, the ghosts of their former selves, among the wrecks of their former homes. The spirit of the nation, within a few months after the arrival of Alva, seemed hopelessly broken. The blood of its best and bravest had already stained the scaffold; the men to whom it had been accustomed to look for guidance and protection, were dead, in prison, or in exile. Submission had ceased to be of any avail, flight was impossible, and the spirit of vengeance had alighted at every fireside. The mourners went daily about the streets, for there was hardly a house which had not been made desolate. The scaffolds, the gallows, the funeral piles, which had been sufficient in ordinary times, furnished now an entirely inadequate machinery for the incessant executions. Columns and stakes in every street, the doorposts of private houses, the fences in the fields, were laden with human carcases, strangled, burned, beheaded. The orchards in the country bore on many a tree the hideous fruit of human bodies.

Thus the Netherlands were crushed, and but for the stringency of the tyranny which had now closed their gates, would have been depopulated. The grass began to grow in the streets of those cities which had recently nourished so many artisans. In all those great manufacturing and industrial marts, where the tide of human life had throbbed so vigorously, there now reigned the silence and the darkness of midnight. It was at this time that the learned Viglius wrote to his friend Hopper, that all venerated the prudence and gentleness of the Duke of Alva. Such were among the first fruits of that prudence and gentleness.[1]

[THE KIDNAPPING OF THE COUNT OF BUREN]

[Knowing himself to be menaced by the terrible new tribunal William of Orange withdrew from the Netherlands and the jurisdiction of Philip II. For some reason not now known he left his thirteen-year-old son, the Count de Buren, at school in Louvain. Of this situation the king of Spain was quick to take advantage. He ordered the seizure of the young count and his removal to Spain as a hostage.]

His character had, however, already been attacked, his property threatened with confiscation. His closest ties of family were now to be severed by the hand of the tyrant. His eldest child, the Count de Buren, torn from his protection, was to be carried into indefinite captivity in a foreign land. It was a remarkable oversight, for a person of his sagacity, that, upon his own departure from the provinces, he should leave his son, then a boy of thirteen years, to pursue his studies at the college of Louvain. Thus exposed to the power of the government, he was soon seized as a hostage for the good behavior of the father. Granvelle appears to have been the first to recommend the step in a secret letter to Philip, but Alva scarcely needed prompting. Accordingly, upon the 13th of February, 1568, the Duke sent the Seigneur de Chassy to Louvain, attended by four officers and by twelve archers. He was furnished with a letter to the Count de Buren, in which that young nobleman was requested to place implicit confidence in the bearer of the despatch, and was informed that the desire which his Majesty

[1] *The Rise of the Dutch Republic*, II, 141–147.

had to see him educated for his service, was the cause of the communication which the Seigneur de Chassy was about to make.

That gentleman was, moreover, minutely instructed as to his method of proceeding in this memorable case of kidnapping. He was to present the letter to the young Count in presence of his tutor. He was to invite him to Spain in the name of his Majesty. He was to assure him that his Majesty's commands were solely with a view to his own good, and that he was not commissioned to arrest, but only to escort him. He was to allow the Count to be accompanied only by two valets, two pages, a cook, and a keeper of accounts. He was, however, to induce his tutor to accompany him, at least, to the Spanish frontier. He was to arrange that the second day after his arrival at Louvain, the Count should set out for Antwerp, where he was to lodge with Count Lodron, after which they were to proceed to Flushing, whence they were to embark for Spain. At that city he was to deliver the young Prince to the person whom he would find there, commissioned for that purpose by the Duke. As soon as he had made the first proposition at Louvain to the Count, he was, with the assistance of his retinue, to keep the most strict watch over him day and night, but without allowing the supervision to be perceived.

The plan was carried out admirably. It was fortunate, however, for the kidnappers, that the young Prince proved favorably disposed to the plan. He accepted the invitation of his captors with alacrity. He even wrote to thank the governor for his friendly offices in his behalf. He received with boyish gratification the festivities with which Lodron enlivened his brief sojourn at Antwerp, and he set forth without reluctance for that gloomy and terrible land of Spain, whence so rarely a Flemish traveller had returned. A changeling, as it were, from his cradle, he seemed completely transformed by his Spanish tuition, for he was educated and not sacrificed by Philip. When he returned to the Netherlands, after a twenty years' residence in Spain, it was difficult to detect in his gloomy brow, saturnine character, and Jesuitical habits, a trace of the generous spirit which characterized that race of heroes, the house of Orange-Nassau.[1]

[PUNISHMENT OF THE NETHERLANDS]

[In 1568 William of Orange made his first military effort against the Spanish forces in the Netherlands. The campaign ended in failure. The provinces, in consequence, were severely punished for their participation in the attack on the Spanish authorities.]

The page which records their victorious campaign is foul with outrage and red with blood. None of the horrors which accompany the passage of hostile troops through a defenseless country were omitted. Maids and matrons were ravished in multitudes, old men butchered in cold blood. As Alva returned, with the rear-guard of his army, the whole sky was red with a constant conflagration; the very earth seemed changed to ashes. Every peasant's hovel, every farmhouse, every village upon the road had been burned to the ground. So gross and so extensive had been the outrage, that the commander-in-chief felt it due to his dignity to hang some of his own soldiers who had most distinguished themselves in this work.[2]

Having fully subdued the province, he had no occupation for such a force, but he improved the opportunity by cutting off the head of an old woman in Utrecht. The Vrouw van Diemen, eighteen months previously, had given the preacher Arendsoon a night's lodging in her house. The crime had, in fact, been committed by her son-in-law, who dwelt under her roof, and who had himself, without her participation, extended this dangerous hospitality to a heretic; but the old lady, although a devout Catholic, was rich. Her execution would strike a wholesome terror into the hearts of her neighbors. The confiscation of her estates would bring a handsome sum into the government coffers. It would be made manifest that the same hand which could destroy an army of twelve thousand rebels at

[1] *The Rise of the Dutch Republic*, II, 155–157.   [2] *Ibid.*, II, 224.

a blow could inflict as signal punishment on the small delinquencies of obscure individuals. The old lady, who was past
eighty-four years of age, was placed in a chair upon the scaffold.
She met her death with heroism, and treated her murderers with
contempt. "I understand very well," she observed, "why my
death is considered necessary. The calf is fat and must be
killed." To the executioner she expressed a hope that his sword
was sufficiently sharp, "as he was likely to find her old neck
very tough." With this grisly parody upon the dying words
of Anne Boleyn, the courageous old gentlewoman submitted
to her fate.[1]

The Duke having thus crushed the project of Count Louis,
and quelled the insurrection in Friesland, returned in triumph
to Brussels. Far from softened by the success of his arms, he
renewed with fresh energy the butchery which, for a brief
season, had been suspended during his brilliant campaign in
the north. The altars again smoked with victims; the hanging,
burning, drowning, beheading, seemed destined to be the perpetual course of his administration, so long as human bodies
remained on which his fanatical vengeance could be wreaked.
Four men of eminence were executed soon after his return to
the capital. They had previously suffered such intense punishment on the rack, that it was necessary to carry them to the
scaffold, and bind them upon chairs, that they might be beheaded. These four sufferers were a Frisian nobleman named
Galena, the secretaries of Egmont and Horn, Bakkerzeel and
La Loo, and the distinguished Burgomaster of Antwerp,
Antony van Straalen. The arrest of the three last-mentioned
individuals, simultaneously with that of the two Counts, has
been related in a previous chapter. In the case of Van Straalen,
the services rendered by him to the provinces during his long
and honorable career had been so remarkable that even the
Blood-Council, in sending his case to Alva for his sentence,
were inspired by a humane feeling. They felt so much com-
punction at the impending fate of a man who, among other

[1] *Ibid.*, II, 224–225.

meritorious acts, had furnished nearly all the funds for the brilliant campaign in Picardy, by which the opening years of Philip's reign had been illustrated, as to hint at the propriety of a pardon.   But the recommendation to mercy, though it came from the lips of tigers, dripping with human blood, fell unheeded on the tyrant's ear.   It seemed meet that the man who had supplied the nerves of war in that unforgiven series of triumphs, should share the fate of the hero who had won the laurels.[1]

[THE CHANGE IN WILLIAM OF ORANGE]

[While these events were taking place the character of William of Orange was being moulded by the movement in which he had decided to participate.]

It was about this time that a deep change came over his mind.   Hitherto, although nominally attached to the communion of the ancient Church, his course of life and habits of mind had not led him to deal very earnestly with things beyond the world.   The severe duties, the grave character of the cause to which his days were henceforth to be devoted, had already led him to a closer inspection of the essential attributes of Christianity.   He was now enrolled for life as a soldier of the Reformation.   The Reformation was henceforth his fatherland, the sphere of his duty and his affection.   The religious Reformers became his brethren, whether in France, Germany, the Netherlands, or England.   Yet his mind had taken a higher flight than that of the most eminent Reformers.   His goal was not a new doctrine, but religious liberty.   In an age when to think was a crime, and when bigotry and a persecuting spirit characterised Romanists and Lutherans, Calvinists and Zwinglians, he had dared to announce freedom of conscience as the great object for which noble natures should strive.   In an age when toleration was a vice, he had the manhood to cultivate it as a virtue.   His parting advice to the Reformers of the Netherlands, when he left them for a season in the spring of 1567, was

[1] *The Rise of the Dutch Republic*, II, 239–240.

to sink all lesser differences in religious union. Those of the Augsburg Confession and those of the Calvinistic Church, in their own opinion as incapable of commingling as oil and water, were, in his judgment, capable of friendly amalgamation. He appealed eloquently to the good and influential of all parties to unite in one common cause against oppression. Even while favoring daily more and more the cause of the purified Church, and becoming daily more alive to the corruption of Rome, he was yet willing to tolerate all forms of worship, and to leave reason to combat error.

Without a particle of cant or fanaticism, he had become a deeply religious man. Hitherto he had been only a man of the world and a statesman, but from this time forth he began calmly to rely upon God's providence in all the emergencies of his eventful life. His letters written to his most confidential friends, to be read only by themselves, and which have been gazed upon by no other eyes until after the lapse of nearly three centuries, abundantly prove his sincere and simple trust. This sentiment was not assumed for effect to delude others, but cherished as a secret support for himself. His religion was not a cloak to his designs, but a consolation in his disasters. In his letter of instruction to his most confidential agent, John Bazius, while he declared himself frankly in favor of the Protestant principles, he expressed his extreme repugnance to the persecution of Catholics. "Should we obtain power over any city or cities," he wrote, "let the communities of Papists be as much respected and protected as possible. Let them be overcome, not with violence, but with gentle-mindedness and virtuous treatment." After the terrible disaster at Jemmingen, he had written to Louis, consoling him, in the most affectionate language, for the unfortunate result of his campaign. Not a word of reproach escaped from him, although his brother had conducted the operations in Friesland, after the battle of Heiliger-Lee, in a manner quite contrary to his own advice. He had counselled against a battle, and had foretold a defeat; but after the battle had been fought, and a crushing defeat sustained, his language breathed only unwavering submission to the will of God, and continued confidence in his own courage. "You may be well assured, my brother," he wrote, "that I have never felt anything more keenly than the pitiable misfortune which has happened to you, for many reasons which you can easily imagine. Moreover, it hinders us much in the levy which we are making, and has greatly chilled the hearts of those who otherwise would have been ready to give us assistance. Nevertheless, since it has thus pleased God, it is necessary to have patience, and to lose not courage; conforming ourselves to His divine will, as for my part I have determined to do in everything which may happen, still proceeding onward in our work with his Almighty aid." *Saevis tranquillus in undis*, he was never more placid than when the storm was wildest, and the night darkest. He drew his consolations and refreshed his courage at the never-failing fountains of Divine mercy.

"I go tomorrow," he wrote to the unworthy Anna of Saxony; "but when I shall return, or when I shall see you, I cannot, on my honor, tell you with certainty. I have resolved to place myself in the hands of the Almighty, that He may guide me whither it is His good pleasure that I should go. *I see well enough that I am destined to pass this life in misery and labor, with which I am well content, since it thus pleases the Omnipotent,* for I know that I have merited still greater chastisement. I only implore Him graciously to send me strength to endure with patience." [1]

[ALVA'S PERSECUTION OF THE NETHERLANDS]

[In the meantime the inhabitants of the Netherlands continued to suffer from the measures of the Duke of Alva.]

Meantime, neither in the complacency of his triumph over William of Orange, nor in the torrent of his wrath against the English Queen, did the Duke for a moment lose sight of the chief end of his existence in the Netherlands. The gibbet and the stake were loaded with their daily victims. The records of the period are foul with the perpetually renewed barbarities

[1] *The Rise of the Dutch Republic*, II, 243–246.

exercised against the new religion. To the magistrates of the different cities were issued fresh instruction, by which all municipal officers were to be guided in the discharge of their great duty. They were especially enjoined by the Duke to take heed that Catholic midwives, and none other, should be provided for every parish, duly sworn to give notice within twenty-four hours of every birth which occurred, in order that the curate might instantly proceed to baptism. They were also ordered to appoint certain spies, who should keep watch at every administration of the sacraments, whether public or private, whether at the altar or at deathbeds, and who should report for exemplary punishment (that is to say, death by fire) all persons who made derisive or irreverential gestures, or who did not pay suitable honor to the said sacraments. Furthermore, in order that not even death itself should cheat the tyrant of his prey, the same spies were to keep watch at the couch of the dying, and to give immediate notice to the government of all persons who should dare to depart this life without previously receiving extreme unction and the holy wafer. The estates of such culprits, it was ordained, should be confiscated, and their bodies dragged to the public place of execution.

An affecting case occurred in the north of Holland, early in this year, which, for its peculiarity, deserves brief mention. A poor Anabaptist, guilty of no crime but his fellowship with a persecuted sect, had been condemned to death. He had made his escape, closely pursued by an officer of justice, across a frozen lake. It was late in the winter, and the ice had become unsound. It trembled and cracked beneath his footsteps, but he reached the shore in safety. The officer was not so fortunate. The ice gave way beneath him, and he sank into the lake, uttering a cry for succor. There was none to hear him, except the fugitive whom he had been hunting. Dirk Willemzoon, for so was the Anabaptist called, instinctively obeying the dictates of a generous nature, returned, crossed the quaking and dangerous ice, at the peril of his life, extended his hand to his enemy, and saved him from certain death. Unfortunately for human nature, it cannot be added that the generosity of the action was met by a corresponding heroism. The officer was desirous, it is true, of avoiding the responsibility of sacrificing the preserver of his life, but the burgomaster of Aspern sternly reminded him to remember his oath. He accordingly arrested the fugitive, who, on the 16th of May following, was burned to death under the most lingering tortures.

Almost at the same time four clergymen, the eldest seventy years of age, were executed at the Hague, after an imprisonment of three years. All were of blameless lives, having committed no crime save that of having favored the Reformation. As they were men of some local eminence, it was determined that they should be executed with solemnity. They were condemned to the flames; and as they were of the ecclesiastical profession, it was necessary before execution that their personal sanctity should be removed. Accordingly, on the 27th May, attired in the gorgeous robes of high mass, they were brought before the Bishop of Bois le Duc. The prelate, with a pair of scissors, cut a lock of hair from each of their heads. He then scraped their crowns and the tips of their fingers with a little silver knife very gently, and without inflicting the least injury. The mystic oil of consecration was thus supposed to be sufficiently removed. The prelate then proceeded to disrobe the victims, saying to each one as he did so, *"Eximo tibi vestem justitiae, quem volens abjecisti"*; to which the oldest pastor, Arent Dirdzoon, stoutly replied, *"Imo vestem injustitiae."* The Bishop having thus completed the solemn farce of desecration, delivered the prisoners to the Blood-Council, begging that they might be handled very gently. Three days afterwards they were all executed at the stake, having, however, received the indulgence of being strangled before being thrown into the flames.

It was precisely at this moment, while the agents of the Duke's government were thus zealously enforcing his decrees, that a special messenger arrived from the Pope, bringing as a present to Alva a jewelled hat and sword. It was a gift rarely conferred by the Church, and never save upon the highest dignitaries, or upon those who had merited her most signal rewards by the most shining exploits in her defense. The Duke was requested, in the autograph letter from his Holiness which accompanied the presents, "to remember, when he put the hat upon his head, that he was guarded with it as with a helmet of righteousness, and with the shield of God's help, indicating the heavenly crown which was ready for all princes who support the Holy Church and the Roman Catholic faith." The motto on the sword ran as follows, "*Accipe sanctum gladium, munus a Deo, in quo dejicies adversarios populi mei Israel.*" [1]

[THE TAX PLANS OF THE DUKE OF ALVA]

[One of the chief complaints against the Duke of Alva was his plan for taxing the Netherlands.]

The Duke had been dissatisfied with the results of his financial arrangements. The confiscation of banished and murdered heretics had not proved the inexhaustible mine he had boasted. The stream of gold which was to flow perennially into the Spanish coffers soon ceased to flow at all. This was inevitable. Confiscations must, of necessity, offer but a precarious supply to any treasury. It was only the frenzy of an Alva which could imagine it possible to derive a permanent revenue from such a source. It was, however, not to be expected that this man, whose tyranny amounted to insanity, could comprehend the intimate connexion between the interests of a people and those of its rulers, and he was determined to exhibit by still more fierce and ludicrous experiments, how easily a great soldier may become a very paltry financier.

He had already informed his royal master that, after a very short time, remittances would no longer be necessary from Spain to support the expenses of the army and government in the Netherlands. He promised, on the contrary, that at least two millions yearly should be furnished by the provinces, over and above the cost of their administration, to enrich the treasury at home. Another Peru had already been discovered by his

[1] *The Rise of the Dutch Republic*, II, 279–282.

ingenuity, and one which was not dependent for its golden fertility on the continuance of that heresy which it was his mission to extirpate. His boast had been much ridiculed in Madrid, where he had more enemies than friends, and he was consequently the more eager to convert it into reality. Nettled by the laughter with which all his schemes of political economy had been received at home, he was determined to show that his creative statesmanship was no less worthy of homage than his indisputable genius for destruction.

His scheme was nothing more than the substitution of an arbitrary system of taxation by the Crown, for the legal and constitutional right of the provinces to tax themselves. It was not a very original thought, but it was certainly a bold one. For although a country so prostrate might suffer the imposition of any fresh amount of tyranny, yet it was doubtful whether she had sufficient strength remaining to bear the weight after it had been imposed. It was certain, moreover, that the new system would create a more general outcry than any which had been elicited even by the religious persecution. There were many inhabitants who were earnest and sincere Catholics, and who therefore considered themselves safe from the hangman's hands, while there were none who could hope to escape the grip of the new taxgatherers. Yet the Governor was not the man to be daunted by the probable unpopularity of the measure. Courage he possessed in more than mortal proportion. He seemed to have set himself to the task of ascertaining the exact capacity of the country for wretchedness. He was resolved accurately to gauge its width and its depth; to know how much of physical and moral misery might be accumulated within its limits, before it should be full to overflowing. Every man, woman, and child in the country had been solemnly condemned to death; and arbitrary executions, in pursuance of that sentence, had been daily taking place. Millions of property had been confiscated, while the most fortunate and industrious, as well as the bravest of the Netherlanders, were wandering penniless in distant lands. Still the blows, however recklessly distributed, had not struck every head. The inhabitants had been decimated, not annihilated, and the productive energy of the country, which for centuries had possessed so much vitality, was even yet not totally extinct. In the wreck of their social happiness, in the utter overthrow of their political freedom, they had still preserved the shadow, at least, of one great bulwark against despotism. The king could impose no tax.

The *Joyeuse Entrée* of Brabant, as well as the constitutions of Flanders, Holland, Utrecht, and all the other provinces, expressly prescribed the manner in which the requisite funds for government should be raised. The sovereign or his stadholder was to appear before the estates in person, and make his request for money. It was for the estates, after consultation with their constituents, to decide whether or not this petition (*bede*) should be granted; and should a single branch decline compliance, the monarch was to wait with patience for a more favorable moment. Such had been the regular practice in the Netherlands, nor had the reigning houses often had occasion to accuse the estates of parsimony. It was, however, not wonderful that the Duke of Alva should be impatient at the continued existence of this provincial privilege. A country of condemned criminals, a nation whose universal neck might at any moment be laid upon the block without ceremony, seemed hardly fit to hold the purse-strings, and to dispense alms to its monarch. The Viceroy was impatient at this arrogant vestige of constitutional liberty. Moreover, although he had taken from the Netherlanders nearly all the attributes of freemen, he was unwilling that they should enjoy the principal privilege of slaves, that of being fed and guarded at their master's expense. He had therefore summoned a general assembly of the provincial estates in Brussels, and on the 20th of March, 1569, had caused the following decrees to be laid before them:—

A tax of the hundredth penny, or one per cent, was laid upon all property, real and personal, to be collected instantly. This impost, however, was not perpetual, but only to be paid once, unless, of course, it should suit the same arbitrary power by which it was assessed to require it a second time.

A tax of the twentieth penny, or five per cent, was laid upon every transfer of real estate. This imposition was perpetual.

Thirdly, a tax of the tenth penny, or ten per cent, was *assessed upon every article of merchandise or personal property, to be paid as often as it should be sold*. This tax was likewise to be perpetual.

The consternation in the assembly when these enormous propositions were heard can be easily imagined. People may differ about religious dogmas. In the most bigoted persecutions there will always be many who, from conscientious although misguided motives, heartily espouse the cause of the bigot. Moreover, although resistance to tyranny in matters of faith is always the most ardent of struggles, and is supported by the most sublime principle in our nature, yet all men are not of the sterner stuff of which martyrs are fashioned. In questions relating to the world above, many may be seduced from their convictions by interest, or forced into apostasy by violence. Human nature is often malleable or fusible, where religious interests are concerned; but in affairs material and financial, opposition to tyranny is apt to be unanimous.

The interests of commerce and manufacture, when brought into conflict with those of religion, had often proved victorious in the Netherlands. This new measure, however—this arbitrary and most prodigious system of taxation, struck home to every fireside. No individual, however adroit or timeserving, could parry the blow by which all were crushed.

It was most unanswerably maintained in the assembly, that this tenth and twentieth penny would utterly destroy the trade and the manufactures of the country. The hundredth penny, or the one per cent assessment on all property throughout the land, although a severe subsidy, might be borne with for once. To pay, however, a twentieth part of the full value of a house to the government as often as the house was sold, was a most intolerable imposition. A house might be sold twenty times in a year, and in the course, therefore, of the year be confiscated in its whole value. It amounted either to a prohibition of all transfers of real estate, or to an eventual surrender of its price.

As to the tenth penny upon articles of merchandise, to be paid by the vendor at every sale, the scheme was monstrous. All trade and manufactures must, of necessity, expire, at the very first attempt to put it into execution. The same articles might be sold ten times in a week, and might therefore pay one hundred per cent weekly. An article, moreover, was frequently compounded of ten different articles, each of which might pay one hundred per cent, and therefore the manufactured article, if ten times transferred, one thousand per cent weekly. Quick transfers and unfettered movements being the nerves and muscles of commerce, it was impossible for it long to survive the paralysis of such a tax. The impost could never be collected, and would only produce an entire prostration of industry. It could by no possibility enrich the government.

The King could not derive wealth from the ruin of his subjects; yet to establish such a system was the stern and absurd determination of the Governor-General. The infantine simplicity of the effort seemed incredible. The ignorance was as sublime as the tyranny. The most lucid arguments and the most earnest remonstrances were all in vain. Too opaque to be illumined by a flood of light, too hard to be melted by a nation's tears, the Viceroy held calmly to his purpose. To the keen and vivid representations of Viglius, who repeatedly exhibited all that was oppressive, and all that was impossible in the tax, he answered simply that it was nothing more nor less than the Spanish *alcabala*, and that he derived 50,000 ducats yearly from its imposition in his own city of Alva.[1]

[THE CAPTURE OF BRILL]

[The first military success of the inhabitants of the Netherlands was won at sea. In 1570 a band of Dutch privateersmen captured the town of Brill. Orange issued commissions, in his capacity of sovereign, to various seafaring persons, who were empowered to cruise against Spanish commerce.]

[1] *The Rise of the Dutch Republic*, II, 282–287.

In the latter days of March, therefore, a sentence to virtual excommunication was pronounced against De la Marck and his rovers. A peremptory order of Elizabeth forbade any of her subjects to supply them with meat, bread, or beer. The command being strictly complied with, their further stay was rendered impossible. Twenty-four vessels accordingly, of various sizes, commanded by De la Marck, Treslong, Adam van Haren, Brand, and other distinguished seamen, set sail from Dover in the very last days of March. Being almost in a state of starvation, these adventurers were naturally anxious to supply themselves with food. They determined to make a sudden foray upon the coasts of North Holland, and accordingly steered for Enkhuizen, both because it was a rich seaport and because it contained many secret partisans of the Prince. On Palm Sunday they captured two Spanish merchantmen. Soon afterwards, however, the wind becoming contrary, they were unable to double the Helder or the Texel, and on Tuesday, the 1st of April, having abandoned their original intention, they dropped down towards Zeeland, and entered the broad mouth of the river Meuse. Between the town of Brill, upon the southern lip of this estuary, and Maaslandsluis, about half a league distant, upon the opposite side, the squadron suddenly appeared at about two o'clock of an April afternoon, to the great astonishment of the inhabitants of both places. It seemed too large a fleet to be a mere collection of trading vessels, nor did they appear to be Spanish ships. Peter Koppelstok, a sagacious ferryman, informed the passengers whom he happened to be conveying across the river, that the strangers were evidently the water beggars. The dreaded name filled his hearers with consternation, and they became eager to escape from so perilous a vicinity. Having duly landed his customers, however, who hastened to spread the news of the impending invasion, and to prepare for defense or flight, the stout ferryman, who was secretly favorable to the cause of liberty, rowed boldly out to inquire the destination and purposes of the fleet.

The vessel which he first hailed was that commanded by William de Blois, Seigneur of Treslong. This adventurous noble, whose brother had been executed by the Duke of Alva in 1568, had himself fought by the side of Count Louis at Jemmingen, and, although covered with wounds, had been one of the few who escaped alive from that horrible carnage. During the intervening period he had become one of the most famous rebels on the ocean, and he had always been well known in Brill, where his father had been governor for the King. He at once recognised Koppelstok, and hastened with him on board the Admiral's ship, assuring De la Marck that the ferryman was exactly the man for their purpose. It was absolutely necessary that a landing should be affected, for the people were without the necessaries of life. Captain Martin Brand had visited the ship of Adam van Haren, as soon as they had dropped anchor in the Meuse, begging for food. "I gave him a cheese," said Adam, afterwards relating the occurrence, "and assured him that it was the last article of food to be found in the ship." The other vessels were equally destitute. Under the circumstances, it was necessary to attempt a landing. Treslong, therefore, who was really the hero of this memorable adventure, persuaded De la Marck to send a message to the city of Brill, demanding its surrender. This was a bold summons to be made by a handful of men, three or four hundred at most, who were both metaphorically and literally beggars. The city of Brill was not populous, but it was well walled and fortified. It was, moreover, a most commodious port. Treslong gave his signet ring to the fisherman, Koppelstok, and ordered him, thus accredited as an envoy, to carry their summons to the magistracy. Koppelstok, nothing loath, instantly rowed ashore, pushed through the crowd of inhabitants, who overwhelmed him with questions, and made his appearance in the town-house before the assembled magistrates. He informed them that he had been sent by the Admiral of the fleet and by Treslong, who was well known to them, to demand that two commissioners should be sent out on the part of the city to confer with the patriots. He was bidden, he said, to give assurance that the deputies would be courteously treated. The only object of those who had sent him was to free the land from the tenth penny, and to overthrow the tyranny of Alva and his Spaniards. Hereupon he was asked by the magistrates, how large a force De la Marck had under his command. To this question the ferryman carelessly replied, that there might *be some five thousand in all.* This enormous falsehood produced its effect upon the magistrates. There was now no longer any inclination to resist the invaders; the only question discussed being whether to treat with them or to fly. On the whole, it was decided to do both. With some difficulty, two deputies were found sufficiently valiant to go forth to negotiate with the beggars, while in their absence most of the leading burghers and functionaries made their preparations for flight. The envoys were assured by De la Marck and Treslong that no injury was intended to the citizens or to private property, but that the overthrow of Alva's government was to be instantly accomplished. Two hours were given to the magistrates in which to decide whether or not they would surrender the town, and accept the authority of De la Marck as Admiral of the Prince of Orange. They employed the two hours thus granted in making an ignominious escape. Their example was followed by most of the townspeople. When the invaders, at the expiration of the specified term, appeared under the walls of the city, they found a few inhabitants of the lower class gazing at them from above, but received no official communication from any source.

The whole rebel force was now divided into two parties, one of which, under Treslong, made an attack upon the southern gate, while the other, commanded by the Admiral, advanced upon the northern. Treslong after a short struggle succeeded in forcing his entrance, and arrested, in doing so, the governor of the city, just taking his departure. De la Marck and his men made a bonfire at the northern gate, and then battered down the half-burned portal with the end of an old mast. Thus rudely and rapidly did the Netherland patriots conduct their first successful siege. The two parties, not more perhaps than two hundred and fifty men in all, met before sunset in the center of the city, and the foundation of the Dutch Republic was laid. The weary spirit of freedom, so long a fugitive over earth and sea, had at last found a resting-place which rude and even ribald hands had prepared.

The panic created by the first appearance of the fleet had been so extensive, that hardly fifty citizens had remained in the town. The rest had all escaped, with as much property as they could carry away. The Admiral, in the name of the Prince of Orange, as lawful stadholder of Philip, took formal possession of an almost deserted city. No indignity was offered to the inhabitants of either sex, but as soon as the conquerors were fairly established in the best houses of the place, the inclination to plunder the churches could no longer be restrained. The altars and images were all destroyed, the rich furniture and gorgeous vestments appropriated to private use. Adam van Haren appeared on his vessel's deck attired in a magnificent high mass chasuble. Treslong thenceforth used no drinking cups in his cabin save the golden chalices of the sacrament. Unfortunately, their hatred to Popery was not confined to such demonstrations. Thirteen unfortunate monks and priests, who had been unable to effect their escape, were arrested and thrown into prison, from whence they were taken a few days later, by order of the ferocious Admiral, and executed under circumstances of great barbarity.[1]

[THE FALL OF MONS]

[The struggle in the Netherlands was inextricably interwoven with events in surrounding countries. The Massacre of St. Bartholomew in France, for example, weakened the Protestant party and caused the fall of Mons. The capture of this city illustrates well the warfare of the time.]

The city was evacuated on the 21st September. Alva entered it upon the 24th. Most of the volunteers departed with the garrison, but many who had, most unfortunately, prolonged their farewells to their families, trusting to the word of the Spanish Captain Molinos, were thrown into prison. Noircarmes, the butcher of Valenciennes, now made his appearance in Mons. As grand bailiff of Hainault, he came to the place

[1] *The Rise of the Dutch Republic*, II, 351–355.

as one in authority, and his deeds were now to complete the infamy which must for ever surround his name. In brutal violation of the terms upon which the town had surrendered, he now set about the work of massacre and pillage. A Commission of Troubles, in close imitation of the famous Blood Council at Brussels, was established, the members of the tribunal being appointed by Noircarmes, and all being inhabitants of the town. The council commenced proceedings by condemning all the volunteers, although expressly included in the capitulation. Their wives and children were all banished; their property all confiscated. On the 15th December the executions commenced. The intrepid De Leste, silk manufacturer, who had commanded a band of volunteers, and sustained during the siege the assaults of Alva's troops with remarkable courage at a very critical moment, was one of the earliest victims. In consideration "that he was a gentleman, and not among the most malicious," he was executed by sword. "In respect that he heard the mass, and made a sweet and Catholic end," it was allowed that he should be "buried in consecrated earth." Many others followed in quick succession. Some were beheaded, some were hanged, some were burned alive. All who had borne arms or worked at the fortifications were, of course, put to death. Such as refused to confess and receive the Catholic sacraments perished by fire. A poor wretch, accused of having ridiculed these mysteries, had his tongue torn out before being beheaded. A cobbler, named Blaise Bouzet, was hanged for having eaten meat-soup upon Friday. He was also accused of going to the Protestant preachings for the sake of participating in the alms distributed on these occasions, a crime for which many other paupers were executed. An old man of sixty-two was sent to the scaffold for having permitted his son to bear arms among the volunteers. At last, when all pretexts were wanting to justify executions, the council assigned as motives for its decrees an adhesion of heart on the part of the victims to the cause of the insurgents, or to the doctrines of the Reformed Church. Ten, twelve, twenty persons were often hanged, burned, or beheaded in a single day.

Gibbets laden with mutilated bodies lined the public highways, while Noircarmes, by frightful expressions of approbation, excited without ceasing the fury of his satellites. This monster would perhaps be less worthy of execration had he been governed in these foul proceedings by fanatical bigotry or by political hatred; but his motives were of the most sordid description. It was mainly to acquire gold for himself that he ordained all this carnage. With the same pen which signed the death-sentences of the richest victims, he drew orders to his own benefit on their confiscated property. The lion's share of the plunder was appropriated by himself. He desired the estate of François de Glarges, Seigneur d'Eslesmes. The gentleman had committed no offense of any kind, and, moreover, lived beyond the French frontier. Nevertheless, in contempt of international law, the neighboring territory was invaded, and d'Eslesmes dragged before the blood tribunal of Mons. Noircarmes had drawn up beforehand, in his own handwriting, both the terms of the accusation and of the sentence. The victim was innocent and a Catholic, but he was rich. He confessed to have been twice at the preaching, from curiosity, and to having omitted taking the sacrament at the previous Easter. For these offences he was beheaded, and his confiscated estate adjudged at an almost nominal price to the secretary of Noircarmes, bidding for his master. "You can do me no greater pleasure," wrote Noircarmes to the council, "than to make quick work with all these rebels, and to proceed with the confiscation of their estates, real and personal. Don't fail to put all those to the torture out of whom anything can be got." [1]

[THE SIEGE OF LEYDEN]

[The war, in fact, was to a large extent a succession of sieges. One of the most dramatic of these sieges was the investment and relief of Leyden.]

On the 26th of May, Valdez reappeared before the place, at the head of eight thousand Walloons and Germans, and

[1] *The Rise of the Dutch Republic*, II, 403-405.

Leyden was now destined to pass through a fiery ordeal. This city was one of the most beautiful in the Netherlands. Placed in the midst of broad and fruitful pastures, which had been reclaimed by the hand of industry from the bottom of the sea, it was fringed with smiling villages, blooming gardens, fruitful orchards. The ancient and, at last, decrepit Rhine, flowing languidly towards its sandy deathbed, had been multiplied into innumerable artificial currents, by which the city was completely interlaced. These watery streets were shaded by lime trees, poplars, and willows, and crossed by one hundred and forty-five bridges, mostly of hammered stone. The houses were elegant, the public edifices imposing, while the whole aspect of the place suggested thrift, industry, and comfort. Upon an artificial elevation, in the centre of the city, rose a ruined tower of unknown antiquity. By some it was considered to be of Roman origin, while others preferred to regard it as a work of the Anglo-Saxon Hengist, raised to commemorate his conquest of England. Surrounded by fruit-trees, and overgrown in the center with oaks, it afforded, from its moldering battlements, a charming prospect over a wide expanse of level country, with the spires of neighboring cities raised in every direction. It was from this commanding height, during the long and terrible summer days which were approaching, that many an eye was to be strained anxiously seaward, watching if yet the ocean had begun to roll over the land.

Valdez lost no time in securing himself in the possession of Maeslandsluis, Vlaardingen, and The Hague. Five hundred English, under command of Colonel Edward Chester, abandoned the fortress of Valkenburg, and fled towards Leyden. Refused admittance by the citizens, who now, with reason, distrusted them, they surrendered to Valdez, and were afterwards sent back to England. In the course of a few days, Leyden was thoroughly invested, no less than sixty-two redoubts, some of them having remained undestroyed from the previous siege, now girdling the city, while the besiegers already numbered nearly eight thousand, a force to be daily increased. On the other hand, there were no troops in the town, save a small corps of "freebooters," and five companies of the burgher guard. John Van der Does, Seigneur of Nordwyck, a gentleman of distinguished family, but still more distinguished for his learning, his poetical genius, and his valor, had accepted the office of military commandant.

The main reliance of the city, under God, was on the stout hearts of its inhabitants within the walls, and on the sleepless energy of William the Silent without. The Prince, hastening to comfort and encourage the citizens, although he had been justly irritated by their negligence in having omitted to provide more sufficiently against the emergency while there had yet been time, now reminded them that they were not about to contend for themselves alone, but that the fate of their country and of unborn generations would, in all human probability, depend on the issue about to be tried. Eternal glory would be their portion if they manifested a courage worthy of their race and of the sacred cause of religion and liberty. He implored them to hold out at least three months, assuring them that he would, within that time, devise the means of their deliverance. The citizens responded courageously and confidently, to these missives, and assured the Prince of their firm confidence in their own fortitude and his exertions.[1]

The city of Leyden was equally cold to the messages of mercy, which were especially addressed to its population by Valdez and his agents. Certain Netherlanders, belonging to the King's party, and familiarly called "Glippers," despatched from the camp many letters to their rebellious acquaintances in the city. In these epistles the citizens of Leyden were urgently and even pathetically exhorted to submission by their loyal brethren, and were implored "to take pity upon their poor old fathers, their daughters, and their wives." But the burghers of Leyden thought that the best pity which they could show to those poor old fathers, daughters, and wives, was to keep them from the clutches of the Spanish soldiery; so they made no answer to

---

[1] *The Rise of the Dutch Republic*, II, 552–554.

the Glippers, save by this single line, which they wrote on a sheet of paper, and forwarded, like a letter, to Valdez:—

"Fistula dulce canit, volucrem cum decipit auceps."

According to the advice early given by the Prince of Orange, the citizens had taken an account of their provisions of all kinds, including livestock. By the end of June, the city was placed on a strict allowance of food, all the provisions being purchased by the authorities at an equitable price. Half a pound of meat and half a pound of bread were allotted to a full-grown man, and to the rest a due proportion. The city being strictly invested, no communication, save by carrier pigeons, and by a few swift and skilful messengers, called jumpers, was possible. Sorties and fierce combats were, however, of daily occurrence, and a handsome bounty was offered to any man who brought into the city gates the head of a Spaniard. The reward was paid many times, but the population was becoming so excited, and so apt, that the authorities felt it dangerous to permit the continuance of these conflicts. Lest the city, little by little, should lose its few disciplined defenders, it was now proclaimed, by sound of church bell, that in future no man should leave the gates.

The Prince had his headquarters at Delft and at Rotterdam. Between those two cities, an important fortress, called Polderwaert, secured him in the control of the alluvial quadrangle, watered on two sides by the Yssel and the Meuse. On the 29th June, the Spaniards, feeling its value, had made an unsuccessful effort to carry this fort by storm. They had been beaten off, with the loss of several hundred men, the Prince remaining in possession of the position, from which alone he could hope to relieve Leyden. He still held in his hand the keys with which he could unlock the ocean gates, and let the waters in upon the land, and he had long been convinced that nothing could save the city but to break the dikes. Leyden was not upon the sea, but he could send the sea to Leyden, although an army fit to encounter the besieging force under Valdez could not be levied. The battle of Mookerheyde had, for the present, quite settled the question of land relief, but it was possible to besiege the besiegers with the waves of the ocean. The Spaniards occupied the coast from the Hague to Vlaardingen, but the dikes along the Meuse and Yssel were in possession of the Prince. He determined that these should be pierced, while, at the same time, the great sluices at Rotterdam, Schiedam, and Delftshaven should be opened. The damage to the fields, villages, and growing crops would be enormous, but he felt that no other course could rescue Leyden, and with it the whole of Holland, from destruction. His clear expositions and impassioned eloquence at last overcame all resistance. By the middle of July, the estates fully consented to his plan, and its execution was immediately undertaken. "Better a drowned land than a lost land," cried the patriots, with enthusiasm, as they devoted their fertile fields to desolation. The enterprise for restoring their territory, for a season, to the waves, from which it had been so patiently rescued, was conducted with as much regularity as if it had been a profitable undertaking. A capital was formally subscribed, for which a certain number of bonds were issued, payable at a long date. In addition to this preliminary fund, a monthly allowance of forty-five guldens was voted by the estates, until the work should be completed, and a large sum was contributed by the ladies of the land, who freely furnished their plate, jewellery, and costly furniture to the furtherance of the scheme.

Meantime, Valdez, on the 30th July, issued most urgent and ample offers of pardon to the citizens if they would consent to open their gates and accept the King's authority, but his overtures were received with silent contempt, notwithstanding that the population was already approaching the starvation point. Although not yet fully informed of the active measures taken by the Prince, yet they still chose to rely upon his energy and their own fortitude, rather than upon the honied words which had formerly been heard at the gates of Haarlem and of Naarden. On the 3d of August, the Prince, accompanied by Paul Buys, chief of the commission appointed to execute the enterprise, went in person along the Yssel, as far as Kappelle, and superintended the rupture of the dikes in sixteen places. The gates at Schiedam and Rotterdam were opened, and the ocean began to pour over the land. While waiting for the waters to rise, provisions were rapidly collected, according to an edict of the Prince, in all the principal towns of the neighborhood, and some two hundred vessels, of various sizes, had also been got ready at Rotterdam, Delftshaven, and other ports.

The citizens of Leyden were, however, already becoming impatient, for their bread was gone, and of its substitute, malt cake, they had but slender provision. On the 12th of August, they received a letter from the Prince, encouraging them to resistance, and assuring them of a speedy relief, and on the 21st they addressed a despatch to him in reply, stating that they had now fulfilled their original promise, for they had held out two months with food, and another month without food. If not soon assisted, human strength could do no more; their malt cake would last but four days, and after that was gone, there was nothing left but starvation. Upon the same day, however, they received a letter, dictated by the Prince, who now lay in bed at Rotterdam with a violent fever, assuring them that the dikes were all pierced, and that the water was rising upon the "Landscheiding," the great outer barrier which separated the city from the sea. He said nothing, however, of his own illness, which would have cast a deep shadow over the joy which now broke forth among the burghers.

The letter was read publicly in the market-place; and to increase the cheerfulness, burgomaster Van der Werf, knowing the sensibility of his countrymen to music, ordered the city musicians to perambulate the streets, playing lively melodies and martial airs. Salvos of cannon were likewise fired, and the starving city for a brief space put on the aspect of a holiday, much to the astonishment of the besieging forces, who were not yet aware of the Prince's efforts. They perceived very soon, however, as the water everywhere about Leyden had risen to the depth of ten inches, that they stood in a perilous position. It was no trifling danger to be thus attacked by the waves of the ocean, which seemed about to obey with docility the command of William the Silent. Valdez became anxious and uncomfortable at the strange aspect of affairs; for the besieging army was now in its turn beleaguered, and by a stronger power than man's. He consulted with the most experienced of his officers, with the countrypeople, with the most distinguished among the Glippers, and derived encouragement from their views concerning the Prince's plan. They pronounced it utterly futile and hopeless. The Glippers knew the country well, and ridiculed the desperate project in unmeasured terms.

Even in the city itself, a dull distrust had succeeded to the first vivid gleam of hope, while the few royalists among the population boldly taunted their fellow-citizens to their faces with the absurd vision of relief which they had so fondly welcomed. "Go up to the tower, ye Beggars," was the frequent and taunting cry, "go up to the tower, and tell us if ye can see the ocean coming over the dry land to your relief"—and day after day they did go up to the ancient tower of Hengist, with heavy heart and anxious eye, watching, hoping, praying, fearing, and at last almost despairing of relief by God or man. On the 27th they addressed a desponding letter to the estates, complaining that the city had been forgotten in its utmost need, and on the same day a prompt and warmhearted reply was received, in which the citizens were assured that every human effort was to be made for their relief. "Rather," said the estates, "will we see our whole land and all our possessions perish in the waves, than forsake thee, Leyden. We know full well, moreover, that with Leyden all Holland must perish also." They excused themselves for not having more frequently written upon the ground that the whole management of the measures for their relief had been entrusted to the Prince, by whom alone all the details had been administered, and all the correspondence conducted.

[The relief of Leyden was delayed by the sickness of William of Orange.]

The preparations for the relief of Leyden, which, notwithstanding his exertions, had grown slack during his sickness, were now vigorously resumed. On the 1st of September, Admiral

Boisot arrived out of Zeeland with a small number of vessels, and with eight hundred veteran sailors. A wild and ferocious crew were those eight hundred Zeelanders. Scarred, hacked, and even maimed, in the unceasing conflicts in which their lives had passed; wearing crescents in their caps, with the inscription "Rather Turkish than Popish"; renowned far and wide, as much for their ferocity as for their nautical skill; the appearance of these wildest of the "Sea-beggars" was both eccentric and terrific. They were known never to give nor to take quarter, for they went to *mortal* combat only, and had sworn to spare neither noble nor simple, neither king, kaiser, nor pope, should they fall into their power.

More than two hundred vessels had been now assembled, carrying generally ten pieces of cannon, with from ten to eighteen oars, and manned with twenty-five hundred veterans, experienced both on land and water. The work was now undertaken in earnest. The distance from Leyden to the outer dike, over whose ruins the ocean had already been admitted, was nearly fifteen miles. This reclaimed territory, however, was not maintained against the sea by these external barriers alone. The flotilla made its way with ease to the Land-scheiding, a strong dike within five miles of Leyden, but here its progress was arrested. The approach to the city was surrounded by many strong ramparts, one within the other, by which it was defended against its ancient enemy, the ocean, precisely like the circumvallations by means of which it was now assailed by its more recent enemy, the Spaniard. To enable the fleet, however, to sail over the land, it was necessary to break through this twofold series of defences. Between the Land-scheiding and Leyden were several dikes, which kept out the water; upon the level territory, thus encircled, were many villages, together with a chain of sixty-two forts, which completely occupied the land. All these villages and fortresses were held by the veteran troops of the King, the besieging force being about four times as strong as that which was coming to the rescue.

The Prince had given orders that the Land-scheiding, which was still one-and-a-half foot above water, should be taken

possession of at every hazard. On the night of the 10th and
11th of September this was accomplished, by surprise, and in a
masterly manner. The few Spaniards who had been stationed
upon the dike were all despatched or driven off, and the
patriots fortified themselves upon it, without the loss of a man.
As the day dawned the Spaniards saw the fatal error which they
had committed in leaving this bulwark so feebly defended, and
from two villages which stood close to the dike, the troops now
rushed in considerable force to recover what they had lost. A
hot action succeeded, but the patriots had too securely established themselves. They completely defeated the enemy, who
retired, leaving hundreds of dead on the field, and the patriots
in complete possession of the Land-scheiding. This first action
was sanguinary and desperate. It gave an earnest of what these
people, who came to relieve their brethren by sacrificing their
property and their lives, were determined to effect. It gave a
revolting proof, too, of the intense hatred which nerved their
arms. A Zeelander, having struck down a Spaniard on the dike,
knelt on his bleeding enemy, tore his heart from his bosom,
fastened his teeth in it for an instant, and then threw it to a dog,
with the exclamation, "'Tis too bitter." The Spanish heart was,
however, rescued, and kept for years, with the marks of the
soldier's teeth upon it,—a sad testimonial of the ferocity engendered by this war for national existence.

The great dike having been thus occupied, no time was lost
in breaking it through in several places, a work which was accomplished under the very eyes of the enemy. The fleet sailed
through the gaps; but, after their passage had been effected in
good order, the Admiral found, to his surprise, that it was not
the only rampart to be carried. The Prince had been informed,
by those who claimed to know the country, that, when once
the Land-scheiding had been passed, the water would flood the
country as far as Leyden, but the "Green-way," another long
dike, three quarters of a mile farther inward, now rose at least
a foot above the waters, to oppose their further progress. Fortunately, by a second and still more culpable carelessness, this
dike had been left by the Spaniards in as unprotected a state as

the first had been. Promptly and audaciously Admiral Boisot took possession of this barrier also, levelled it in many places and brought his flotilla, in triumph, over its ruins. Again, however, he was doomed to disappointment. A large mere, called the Freshwater Lake, was known to extend itself directly in his path about midway between the Land-scheiding and the city. To this piece of water, into which he expected to have instantly floated, his only passage lay through one deep canal. The sea, which had thus far borne him on, now diffusing itself over a very wide surface, and under the influence of an adverse wind, had become too shallow for his ships. The canal alone was deep enough, but it led directly towards a bridge, strongly occupied by the enemy. Hostile troops, moreover, to the amount of three thousand, occupied both sides of the canal. The bold Boisot, nevertheless, determined to force his passage, if possible. Selecting a few of his strongest vessels, his heaviest artillery, and his bravest sailors, he led the van himself, in a desperate attempt to make his way to the mere. He opened a hot fire upon the bridge, then converted into a fortress, while his men engaged in hand-to-hand combat with a succession of skirmishers from the troops along the canal. After losing a few men, and ascertaining the impregnable position of the enemy, he was obliged to withdraw, defeated, and almost despairing.

A week had elapsed since the great dike had been pierced, and the flotilla now lay motionless in shallow water, having accomplished less than two miles. The wind, too, was easterly, causing the sea rather to sink than to rise. Everything wore a gloomy aspect, when, fortunately, on the 18th, the wind shifted to the northwest, and for three days blew a gale. The waters rose rapidly, and before the second day was closed the armada was afloat again. Some fugitives from Zoetermeer village now arrived, and informed the Admiral that, by making a detour to the right, he could completely circumvent the bridge and the mere. They guided him, accordingly, to a comparatively low dike, which led between the villages of Zoetermeer and Benthuyzen. A strong force of Spaniards was stationed in each place, but seized with a panic, instead of sallying to defend the barrier, they fled inwardly towards Leyden, and halted at the village of North Aa. It was natural that they should be amazed. Nothing is more appalling to the imagination than the rising ocean tide, when man feels himself within its power; and here were the waters, hourly deepening and closing around them, devouring the earth beneath their feet, while on the waves rode a flotilla, manned by a determined race, whose courage and ferocity were known throughout the world. The Spanish soldiers, brave as they were on land, were not sailors, and in the naval contests which had taken place between them and the Hollanders had been almost invariably defeated. It was not surprising, in these amphibious skirmishes, where discipline was of little avail, and habitual audacity faltered at the vague dangers which encompassed them, that the foreign troops should lose their presence of mind.

Three barriers, one within the other, had now been passed, and the flotilla, advancing with the advancing waves, and driving the enemy steadily before it, was drawing nearer to the beleaguered city. As one circle after another was passed, the besieging army found itself compressed within a constantly contracting field. The "Ark of Delft," an enormous vessel, with shot-proof bulwarks, and moved by paddle-wheels turned by a crank, now arrived at Zoetermeer, and was soon followed by the whole fleet. After a brief delay, sufficient to allow the few remaining villagers to escape, both Zoetermeer and Benthuyzen, with the fortifications, were set on fire, and abandoned to their fate. The blaze lighted up the desolate and watery waste around, and was seen at Leyden, where it was hailed as the beacon of hope. Without further impediment, the armada proceeded to North Aa; the enemy retreating from this position also, and flying to Zoeterwoude, a strongly fortified village but a mile and three quarters from the city walls. It was now swarming with troops, for the bulk of the besieging army had gradually been driven into a narrow circle of forts within the immediate neighborhood of Leyden. Besides Zoeterwoude, the two posts where they were principally established were

Lammen and Leyderdorp, each within three hundred rods of the town. At Leyderdorp, were the headquarters of Valdez; Colonel Borgia commanded in the very strong fortress of Lammen.

The fleet was, however, delayed at North Aa by another barrier, called the "Kirk-way." The waters, too, spreading once more over a wider space, and diminishing under an east wind which had again arisen, no longer permitted their progress, so that very soon the whole armada was stranded anew. The waters fell to the depth of nine inches, while the vessels required eighteen and twenty. Day after day the fleet lay motionless upon the shallow sea. Orange, rising from his sickbed as soon as he could stand, now came on board the fleet. His presence diffused universal joy; his words inspired his desponding army with fresh hope. He rebuked the impatient spirits who, weary of their compulsory idleness, had shewn symptoms of ill-timed ferocity; and those eight hundred mad Zeelanders, so frantic in their hatred to the foreigners who had so long profaned their land, were as docile as children to the Prince. He reconnoitred the whole ground, and issued orders for the immediate destruction of the Kirk-way, the last important barrier which separated the fleet from Leyden. Then, after a long conference with Admiral Boisot, he returned to Delft.

Meantime, the besieged city was at its last gasp. The burghers had been in a state of uncertainty for many days; being aware that the fleet had set forth for their relief, but knowing full well the thousand obstacles which it had to surmount. They had guessed its progress by the illumination from the blazing villages, they had heard its salvos of artillery on its arrival at North Aa; but since then all had been dark and mournful again, hope and fear, in sickening alternation, distracting every breast. They knew that the wind was unfavorable, and, at the dawn of each day, every eye was turned wistfully to the vanes of the steeples. So long as the easterly breeze prevailed, they felt, as they anxiously stood on towers and housetops, that they must look in vain for the welcome ocean. Yet, while thus patiently waiting, they were literally starving; for even the misery endured at Haarlem had not reached that depth and intensity of agony to which Leyden was now reduced. Bread, malt cake, horseflesh, had entirely disappeared; dogs, cats, rats, and other vermin, were esteemed luxuries. A small number of cows, kept as long as possible for their milk, still remained; but a few were killed from day to day, and distributed in minute proportions, hardly sufficient to support life among the famishing population. Starving wretches swarmed daily around the shambles where these cattle were slaughtered, contending for any morsel which might fall, and lapping eagerly the blood as it ran along the pavement; while the hides, chopped and boiled, were greedily devoured. Women and children, all day long, were seen searching gutters and dunghills for morsels of food, which they disputed fiercely with the famishing dogs. The green leaves were stripped from the trees, every living herb was converted into human food, but these expedients could not avert starvation. The daily mortality was frightful—infants starved to death on the maternal breasts, which famine had parched and withered; mothers dropped dead in the streets, with their dead children in their arms. In many a house the watchmen, in their rounds, found a whole family of corpses, father, mother, and children, side by side; for a disorder called the plague, naturally engendered of hardship and famine, now came, as if in kindness, to abridge the agony of the people. The pestilence stalked at noonday through the city, and the doomed inhabitants fell like grass beneath its scythe. From six thousand to eight thousand human beings sank before this scourge alone, yet the people resolutely held out—women and men mutually encouraging each other to resist the entrance of their foreign foe—an evil more horrible than pest or famine.

The missives from Valdez, who saw more vividly than the besieged could do, the uncertainty of his own position, now poured daily into the city, the enemy becoming more prodigal of his vows, as he felt that the ocean might yet save the victims from his grasp. The inhabitants, in their ignorance, had gradually abandoned their hopes of relief, but they spurned the summons to surrender. Leyden was sublime in its despair. A few murmurs were, however, occasionally heard at the steadfastness of the magistrates, and a dead body was placed at the door of the burgomaster, as a silent witness against his inflexibility. A party of the more fainthearted even assailed the heroic Adrian Van der Werf with threats and reproaches as he passed through the streets. A crowd had gathered around him as he reached a triangular place in the center of the town, into which many of the principal streets emptied themselves, and upon one side of which stood the church of Saint Pancras, with its high brick tower surmounted by two pointed turrets, and with two ancient lime-trees at its entrance. There stood the burgomaster, a tall, haggard, imposing figure, with dark visage, and a tranquil but commanding eye. He waved his broad-leaved felt hat for silence, and then exclaimed, in language which has been almost literally preserved, "What would ye, my friends? Why do ye murmur that we do not break our vows and surrender the city to the Spaniards?—a fate more horrible than the agony which she now endures. I tell you I have made an oath to hold the city, and may God give me strength to keep my oath! I can die but once; whether by your hands, the enemy's, or by the hand of God. My own fate is indifferent to me, not so that of the city intrusted to my care. I know that we shall starve if not soon relieved; but starvation is preferable to the dishonored death which is the only alternative. Your menaces move me not; my life is at your disposal; here is my sword, plunge it into my breast, and divide my flesh among you. Take my body to appease your hunger, but expect no surrender so long as I remain alive."

The words of the stout burgomaster inspired a new courage in the hearts of those who heard him, and a shout of applause and defiance arose from the famishing but enthusiastic crowd. They left the place after exchanging new vows of fidelity with their magistrate, and again ascended tower and battlement to watch for the coming fleet. From the ramparts they hurled renewed defiance at the enemy. "Ye call us rat-eaters and dog-eaters," they cried, "and it is true. So long, then, as ye hear dog bark or cat mew within the walls, ye may know that the city holds out. And when all has perished but ourselves, be sure that we will each devour our left arms, retaining our right to defend our women, our liberty, and our religion against the foreign tyrant. Should God, in His wrath, doom us to destruction, and deny us all relief, even then will we maintain ourselves for ever against your entrance. When the last hour has come, with our own hands we will set fire to the city, and perish, men, women, and children together in the flames, rather than suffer our homes to be polluted, and our liberties to be crushed." Such words of defiance, thundered daily from the battlements, sufficiently informed Valdez as to his chance of conquering the city, either by force or fraud, but at the same time he felt comparatively relieved by the inactivity of Boisot's fleet, which still lay stranded at North Aa. "As well," shouted the Spaniards, derisively, to the citizens, "as well can the Prince of Orange pluck the stars from the sky as bring the ocean to the walls of Leyden for your relief."

On the 28th of September, a dove flew into the city, bringing a letter from Admiral Boisot. In this despatch, the position of the fleet at North Aa was described in encouraging terms, and the inhabitants were assured that, in a very few days at furthest, the long-expected relief would enter their gates. The letter was read publicly upon the market-place, and the bells were rung for joy. Nevertheless, on the morrow, the vanes pointed to the east, the waters, so far from rising, continued to sink, and Admiral Boisot was almost in despair. He wrote to the Prince, that if the spring-tide, now to be expected, should not, together with a strong and favorable wind, come immediately to their relief, it would be in vain to attempt anything further, and that the expedition would of necessity be abandoned. The tempest came to their relief. A violent equinoctial gale, on the night of the 1st and 2d of October, came storming from the northwest, shifting after a few hours full eight points, and then blowing still more violently from the southwest. The waters of the North Sea were piled in vast masses upon the southern coast of Holland, and then dashed furiously landward, the ocean rising over the earth, and sweeping with unrestrained power across the ruined dikes.

In the course of twenty-four hours, the fleet at North Aa, instead of nine inches, had more than two feet of water. No time was lost. The Kirk-way, which had been broken through, according to the Prince's instructions, was now completely overflowed, and the fleet sailed at midnight, in the midst of the storm and darkness. A few sentinel vessels of the enemy challenged them as they steadily rowed towards Zoeterwoude. The answer was a flash from Boisot's cannon, lighting up the black waste of waters. There was a fierce naval midnight battle—a strange spectacle among the branches of those quiet orchards, and with the chimney-stacks of half-submerged farmhouses rising around the contending vessels. The neighboring village of Zoeterwoude shook with the discharges of the Zeelanders' cannon, and the Spaniards assembled in that fortress knew that the rebel Admiral was at last afloat, and on his course. The enemy's vessels were soon sunk, their crews hurled into the waves. On went the fleet, sweeping over the broad waters which lay between Zoeterwoude and Zwieten. As they approached some shallows, which led into the great mere, the Zeelanders dashed into the sea, and with sheer strength shouldered every vessel through. Two obstacles lay still in their path —the forts of Zoeterwoude and Lammen, distant from the city five hundred and two hundred and fifty yards respectively. Strong redoubts, both well supplied with troops and artillery, they were likely to give a rough reception to the light flotilla; but the panic, which had hitherto driven their foes before the advancing patriots, had reached Zoeterwoude. Hardly was the fleet in sight, when the Spaniards, in the early morning, poured out from the fortress, and fled precipitately to the left, along a road which led in a westerly direction towards The Hague. Their narrow path was rapidly vanishing in the waves, and hundreds sank beneath the constantly deepening and treacherous flood. The wild Zeelanders, too, sprang from their vessels upon the crumbling dike, and drove their retreating foes into the sea. They hurled their harpoons at them with an accuracy acquired in many a polar chase; they plunged into the waves in the keen pursuit, attacking them with boat-hook and dagger. The numbers who thus fell beneath these corsairs, who neither gave nor took quarter, were never counted, but probably not less than a thousand perished. The rest effected their escape to The Hague.

The first fortress was thus seized, dismantled, set on fire, and passed, and a few strokes of the oars brought the whole fleet close to Lammen. This last obstacle rose formidable and frowning directly across their path. Swarming as it was with soldiers, and bristling with artillery, it seemed to defy the armada either to carry it by storm or to pass under its guns into the city. It appeared that the enterprise was, after all, to founder within sight of the long expecting and expected haven. Boisot anchored his fleet within a respectful distance, and spent what remained of the day in carefully reconnoitering the fort, which seemed only too strong. In conjunction with Leyderdorp, the headquarters of Valdez, a mile and a half distant on the right, and within a mile of the city, it seemed so insuperable an impediment that Boisot wrote in despondent tone to the Prince of Orange. He announced his intention of carrying the fort, if it were possible, on the following morning, but if obliged to retreat, he observed, with something like despair, that there would be nothing for it but to wait for another gale of wind. If the waters should rise sufficiently to enable them to make a wide detour, it might be possible—if, in the meantime, Leyden did not starve or surrender—to enter its gates from the opposite side.

Meantime, the citizens had grown wild with expectation. A dove had been despatched by Boisot, informing them of his precise position, and a number of citizens accompanied the burgomaster, at nightfall, toward the tower of Hengist—"Yonder," cried the magistrate, stretching out his hand towards Lammen, "yonder, behind that fort, are bread and meat, and brethren in thousands. Shall all this be destroyed by the Spanish guns, or shall we rush to the rescue of our friends?" "We will tear the fortress to fragments with our teeth and nails," was the reply, "before the relief, so long expected, shall be wrested from us." It was resolved that a sortie, in conjunction with the operations of Boisot, should be made against Lammen with the earliest dawn. Night descended upon the scene, a pitch-dark night, full of anxiety to the Spaniards, to the armada, to Leyden. Strange sights and sounds occurred at different moments to bewilder the anxious sentinels. A long procession of lights issuing from the fort was seen to flit across the black face of the waters, in the dead of night, and the whole of the city wall, between the Cow-gate and the Tower of Burgundy, fell with a loud crash. The horror-struck citizens thought that the Spaniards were upon them at last; the Spaniards imagined the noise to indicate a desperate sortie of the citizens. Everything was vague and mysterious. Day dawned at length, after the feverish night, and the Admiral prepared for the assault. Within the fortress reigned a death-like stillness, which inspired a sickening suspicion. Had the city, indeed, been carried in the night; had the massacre already commenced; had all this labor and audacity been expended in vain? Suddenly a man was descried, wading breast-high through the water from Lammen towards the fleet, while at the same time, one solitary boy was seen to wave his cap from the summit of the fort. After a moment of doubt, the happy mystery was solved. The Spaniards had fled, panic-struck, during the darkness. Their position would still have enabled them, with firmness, to frustrate the enterprise of the patriots, but the hand of God, which had sent the ocean and the tempest to the deliverance of Leyden, had struck her enemies with terror likewise. The lights which had been seen moving during the night were the lanterns of the retreating Spaniards, and the boy who was now waving his triumphant signal from the battlements had alone witnessed the spectacle. So confident was he in the conclusion to which it led him, that he had volunteered at daybreak to go thither all alone. The magistrates, fearing a trap, hesitated for a moment to believe the truth, which soon, however, became quite evident. Valdez, flying himself from Leyderdorp, had ordered Colonel Borgia to retire with all his troops from Lammen. Thus, the

Spaniards had retreated at the very moment that an extraordinary accident had laid bare a whole side of the city for their entrance. The noise of the wall, as it fell, only inspired them with fresh alarm; for they believed that the citizens had sallied forth in the darkness to aid the advancing flood in the work of destruction. All obstacles being now removed, the fleet of Boisot swept by Lammen, and entered the city on the morning of the 3d of October. Leyden was relieved.

The quays were lined with the famishing population, as the fleet rowed through the canals, every human being who could stand coming forth to greet the preservers of the city. Bread was thrown from every vessel among the crowd. The poor creatures who for two months had tasted no wholesome human food, and who had literally been living within the jaws of death, snatched eagerly the blessed gift, at last too liberally bestowed. Many choked themselves to death, in the greediness with which they devoured their bread; others became ill with the effects of plenty thus suddenly succeeding starvation;—but these were isolated cases, a repetition of which was prevented. The Admiral, stepping ashore, was welcomed by the magistracy, and a solemn procession was immediately formed. Magistrates and soldiers, women, children—nearly every living person within the walls, all repaired without delay to the great church, stout Admiral Boisot leading the way. The starving and heroic city, which had been so firm in its resistance to an earthly king, now bent itself in humble gratitude before the King of kings. After prayers, the whole vast congregation joined in the thanksgiving hymn. Thousands of voices raised the song, but few were able to carry it to its conclusion, for the universal emotion, deepened by the music, became too full for utterance. The hymn was abruptly suspended, while the multitude wept like children. This scene of honest pathos terminated, the necessary measures for distributing the food and for relieving the sick were taken by the magistracy.[1]

[1] *The Rise of the Dutch Republic*, II, 557–577.

[DON LUIS DE REQUESENS]

[In 1573 the unpopular and unsuccessful Duke of Alva was succeeded by Requesens. He attempted to rule the Netherlands for the next three years. Of this official, Motley painted an unflattering word portrait.]

It is not necessary to review elaborately his career, the chief incidents of which have been sufficiently described. Requesens was a man of high position by birth and office, but a thoroughly commonplace personage. His talents, either for war or for civil employments, were not above mediocrity. His friends disputed whether he was greater in the field or in the council, but it is certain that he was great in neither. His bigotry was equal to that of Alva, but it was impossible to rival the Duke in cruelty. Moreover, the condition of the country, after seven years of torture under his predecessor, made it difficult for him, at the time of his arrival, to imitate the severity which had made the name of Alva infamous. The Blood-Council had been retained throughout his administration, but its occupation was gone, for want of food for its ferocity. The obedient provinces had been purged of Protestants; while, crippled, too, by confiscation, they offered no field for further extortion. From Holland and Zeeland, whence Catholicism had been nearly excluded, the King of Spain was nearly excluded also. The Blood-Council, which, if set up in that country, would have executed every living creature of its population, could only gaze from a distance at those who would have been its victims. Requesens had been previously distinguished in two fields of action: the Granada massacres and the carnage of Lepanto. Upon both occasions he had been the military tutor of Don John of Austria, by whom he was soon to be succeeded in the government of the Netherlands. To the imperial bastard had been assigned the pre-eminence, but it was thought that the Grand Commander had been entitled to a more than equal share of the glory. We have seen how much additional reputation was acquired by Requesens in the provinces. The expedition against Duiveland and Schouwen, was, on the whole, the most brilliant feat of arms during the war, and its success reflects an undying luster on the hardihood and discipline of the Spanish, German, and Walloon soldiery. As an act of individual audacity in a bad cause, it has rarely been equalled. It can hardly be said, however, that the Grand Commander was entitled to any large measure of praise for the success of the expedition. The plan was laid by Zeeland traitors. It was carried into execution by the devotion of the Spanish, Walloon, and German troops, while Requesens was only a spectator of the transaction. His sudden death arrested, for a moment, the ebb-tide in the affairs of the Netherlands, which was fast leaving the country bare and desolate, and was followed by a train of unforeseen transactions, which it is now our duty to describe.[1]

[THE "SPANISH FURY"]

[One of the most striking and important episodes of the revolt of the Netherlands against Philip II was the mutiny of the unpaid Spanish troops which culminated in the sack of Antwerp. This event exactly fitted in with Motley's conception of history and he gave a great deal of space to its description.]

It was in vain that arguments and expostulations were addressed to soldiers who were suffering from want and maddened by injustice. They determined to take their cause into their own hand, as they had often done before. By the 15th of July, the mutiny was general on the isle of Schouwen. Promises were freely offered, both of pay and pardon; appeals were made to their old sense of honor and loyalty; but they had had enough of promises, of honor, and of work. What they wanted now were shoes and jerkins, bread and meat and money. Money they would have, and that at once. The King of Spain was their debtor. The Netherlands belonged to the King of Spain. They would therefore levy on the Netherlands for payment of their debt. Certainly this was a logical deduction. They knew by experience that this process had heretofore excited more indignation in the minds of the Netherland people than in that of their master. Moreover, at this juncture, they cared little for their sovereign's displeasure, and not at all for that of the Netherlanders. By the middle of July, then, the mutineers, now entirely beyond control, held their officers imprisoned within their quarters at Zierickzee. They even surrounded the house of Mondragon, who had so often led them to victory, calling upon him with threats and taunts to furnish them with money. The veteran, roused to fury by their insubordination and their taunts, sprang from his house into the midst of the throng. Baring his breast before them, he fiercely invited and dared their utmost violence. Of his lifeblood, he told them bitterly, he was no niggard, and it was at their disposal. His wealth, had he possessed any, would have been equally theirs. Shamed into temporary respect, but not turned from their purpose by the choler of their chief, they left him to himself. Soon afterwards, having swept Schouwen island bare of everything which could be consumed, the mutineers swarmed out of Zeeland into Brabant, devouring as they went.

It was their purpose to hover for a time in the neighborhood of the capital, and either to force the Council of State to pay them their long arrears, or else to seize and sack the richest city upon which they could lay their hands. The compact, disciplined mass, rolled hither and thither, with uncertainty of purpose, but with the same military precision of movement which had always characterized these remarkable mutinies. It gathered strength daily. The citizens of Brussels contemplated with dismay the eccentric and threatening apparition. They knew that rapine, murder, and all the worst evils which man can inflict on his brethren, were pent within it, and would soon descend. Yet, even with all their past experience, did they not forsee the depth of woe which was really impending. The mutineers had discarded such of their officers as they could not compel to obedience, and had, as usual, chosen their Eletto. Many straggling companies joined them as they swept to and fro. They came to Herenthals, where they were met by Count Mansfeld, who was deputed by the Council of State to treat with them, to appeal to them, to pardon them, to offer them everything but money. It may be supposed that the success of the commander-in-chief was no better than that of Mondragon and his subalterns. They laughed him to scorn when he reminded them how their conduct was tarnishing the glory which they had acquired by nine years of heroism. They answered, with their former cynicism, that glory could be put neither into pocket nor stomach. They had no use for it; they had more than enough of it. Give them money, or give them a city; these were their last terms.[1]

By the beginning of September the mutiny was general. All the Spanish army, from general to pioneer, were united. The most important German troops had taken sides with them. Sancho d'Avila held the citadel of Antwerp, vowing vengeance, and holding open communication with the soldiers at Alost. The Council of State remonstrated with him for his disloyalty. He replied by referring to his long years of service, and by reproving them for affecting an authority which their imprisonment rendered ridiculous. The Spaniards were securely established. The various citadels which had been built by Charles and Philip to curb the country now effectually did their work. With the castles of Antwerp, Valenciennes, Ghent, Utrecht, Culemburg, Vianen, Alost, in the hands of six thousand veteran Spaniards, the country seemed chained in every limb. The foreigner's foot was on its neck. Brussels was the only considerable town out of Holland and Zeeland which was even temporarily safe. The important city of Maestricht was held by a Spanish garrison, while other capital towns and stations were in the power of the Walloon and German mutineers. The depredations committed in the villages, the open country, and the cities, were incessant—the Spaniards treating every Netherlander as their foe. Gentleman and peasant, Protestant and Catholic, priest and layman, all were plundered, maltreated, outraged. The indignation became daily more general and more intense. There were frequent skirmishes between the soldiery

[1] *The Rise of the Dutch Republic*, III, 70–72.

and promiscuous bands of peasants, citizens, and students—conflicts in which the Spaniards were invariably victorious. What could such half-armed and wholly untrained partisans effect against the bravest and most experienced troops in the whole world? Such results only increased the general exasperation, while they impressed upon the whole people the necessity of some great and general effort to throw off the incubus.[1]

The Spaniards, foiled in their views upon Brussels, had recently avowed an intention of avenging themselves in the commercial capital. They had waited long enough and accumulated strength enough. Such a trifling city as Alost could no longer content their cupidity, but in Antwerp there was gold enough for the gathering. There was reason for the fears of the inhabitants, for the greedy longing of their enemy. Probably no city in Christendom could at that day vie with Antwerp in wealth and splendor. Its merchants lived in regal pomp and luxury. In its numerous massive warehouses were the treasures of every clime. Still serving as the main entrepôt of the world's traffic, the Brabantine capital was the center of that commercial system which was soon to be superseded by a larger international life. In the midst of the miseries which had so long been raining upon the Netherlands, the stately and egotistical city seemed to have taken stronger root and to flourish more freshly than ever. It was not wonderful that its palaces and its magazines, glittering with splendor, and bursting with treasure, should arouse the avidity of a reckless and famishing soldiery. Had not a handful of warriors of their own race rifled the golden Indies? Had not their fathers, few in number, strong in courage and discipline, revelled in the plunder of a new world? Here were the Indies in a single city. Here were gold and silver, pearls and diamonds, ready and portable; the precious fruit dropping, ripened, from the bough. Was it to be tolerated that base, pacific burghers should monopolize the treasure by which a band of heroes might be enriched?

A sense of coming evil diffused itself through the atmosphere.

[1] *The Rise of the Dutch Republic*, III, 80–81.

The air seemed lurid with the impending storm; for the situation was one of peculiar horror. The wealthiest city in Christendom lay at the mercy of the strongest fastness in the world; a castle which had been built to curb, not to protect the town. It was now inhabited by a band of brigands, outlawed by government, strong in discipline, furious from penury, reckless by habit, desperate in circumstance—a crew which feared not God, nor man, nor devil. The palpitating quarry lay expecting hourly the swoop of its trained and pitiless enemy; for the rebellious soldiers were now in a thorough state of discipline. Sancho d'Avila, castellan of the citadel, was recognized as the chief of the whole mutiny, the army and the mutiny being now one. The band, entrenched at Alost, were upon the best possible understanding with their brethren in the citadel, and accepted without hesitation the arrangements of their superior. On the side of the Scheldt, opposite Antwerp, a fortification had been thrown up by Don Sancho's orders, and held by Julian Romero. Lier, Breda, as well as Alost, were likewise ready to throw their reinforcements into the citadel at a moment's warning. At the signal of their chief, the united bands might sweep from their impregnable castle with a single impulse.

The city cried aloud for help, for it had become obvious that an attack might be hourly expected. Meantime an attempt, made by Don Sancho d'Avila to tamper with the German troops stationed within the walls, was more than partially successful. The forces were commanded by Colonel Van Ende and Count Oberstein. Van Ende, a crafty traitor to his country, desired no better than to join the mutiny on so promising an occasion, and his soldiers shared his sentiments. Oberstein, a brave but blundering German, was drawn into the net of treachery by the adroitness of the Spaniard and the effrontery of his comrade. On the night of the 29th of October, half-bewildered and half-drunk, he signed a treaty with Sancho d'Avila and the three colonels—Fugger, Frondsberger, and Polwiller. By this unlucky document, which was, of course, subscribed also by Van Ende, it was agreed that the Antwerp burghers should be forthwith disarmed; that their weapons should be sent into the citadel; that Oberstein should hold the city at the disposition of Sancho d'Avila; that he should refuse admittance to all troops which might be sent into the city, excepting by command of Don Sancho; and that he should decline compliance with any orders which he might receive from individuals calling themselves the council of state, the States-General, or the estates of Brabant. This treaty was signed, moreover, by Don Jeronimo de Roda, then established in the citadel, and claiming to represent exclusively his Majesty's government.

Hardly had this arrangement been concluded than the Count saw the trap into which he had fallen. Without intending to do so, he had laid the city at the mercy of its foe; but the only remedy which suggested itself to his mind was an internal resolution not to keep his promises. The burghers were suffered to retain their arms, while, on the other hand, Don Sancho lost no time in despatching messages to Alost, to Lier, to Breda, and even to Maestricht, that as large a force as possible might be assembled for the purpose of breaking immediately the treaty of peace which he had just concluded. Never was a solemn document regarded with such perfectly bad faith by all its signers as the accord of the 29th of October.

Three days afterwards a large force of Walloons and Germans was despatched from Brussels to the assistance of Antwerp. The command of these troops was entrusted to the Marquis of Havré, whose brother, the Duke of Aerschot, had been recently appointed chief superintendent of military affairs by the deputies assembled at Ghent. The miscellaneous duties comprehended under this rather vague denomination did not permit the Duke to take charge of the expedition in person, and his younger brother, a still more incompetent and unsubstantial character, was accordingly appointed to the post. A number of young men of high rank, but of lamentably low capacity, were associated with him. Foremost among them was Philip, Count of Egmont, a youth who had inherited few of his celebrated father's qualities, save personal courage and a love of personal display. In character and general talents he was beneath mediocrity. Besides these were the reckless but unstable De Héze, who had executed the *coup d'état* against the State Council, De Berselen, De Capres, D'Oyngies, and others, all vaguely desirous of achieving distinction in those turbulent times, but few of them having any political or religious convictions, and none of them possessing experience or influence enough to render them useful at the impending crisis.

On Friday morning, the 2d of November, the troops appeared under the walls of Antwerp. They consisted of twenty-three companies of infantry, and fourteen of cavalry, amounting to five thousand foot and twelve hundred horse. They were nearly all Walloons, soldiers who had already seen much active service, but unfortunately of a race warlike and fiery indeed, but upon whose steadiness not much more dependence could be placed at that day than in the age of Civilis. Champagny, brother of Granvelle, was Governor of the city. He was a sincere Catholic, but a still more sincere hater of the Spaniards. He saw in the mutiny a means of accomplishing their expulsion, and had already offered to the Prince of Orange his eager co-operation towards this result. In other matters there could be but small sympathy between William the Silent and the Cardinal's brother, but a common hatred united them, for a time at least, in a common purpose.

When the troops first made their appearance before the walls, Champagny was unwilling to grant them admittance. The addle-brained Oberstein had confessed to him the enormous blunder which he had committed in his midnight treaty, and at the same time ingenuously confessed his intention of sending it to the winds. The enemy had extorted from his dulness or his drunkenness a promise which his mature and sober reason could not consider binding. It is needless to say that Champagny rebuked him for signing, and applauded him for breaking the treaty. At the same time, its ill effects were already seen in the dissensions which existed among the German troops. Where all had been tampered with, and where the commanders had set the example of infidelity, it would have been strange if all had held firm. On the whole, however, Oberstein thought he could answer for his own troops. Upon Van Ende's division, although the crafty colonel dissembled his real intentions, very little reliance was placed. Thus there was distraction within the walls. Among those whom the burghers had been told to consider their defenders, there were probably many who were ready to join with their mortal foes at a moment's warning. Under these circumstances, Champagny hesitated about admitting these fresh troops from Brussels. He feared lest the Germans, who knew themselves doubted, might consider themselves doomed. He trembled lest an irrepressible outbreak should occur within the walls, rendering the immediate destruction of the city by the Spaniards from without inevitable. Moreover, he thought it more desirable that this auxiliary force should be disposed at different points outside, in order to intercept the passage of the numerous bodies of Spaniards and other mutineers, who, from various quarters, would soon be on their way to the citadel. Havré, however, was so peremptory, and the burghers were so importunate, that Champagny was obliged to recede from his opposition before twenty-four hours had elapsed. Unwilling to take the responsibility of a further refusal, he admitted the troops through the Burgherhout gate, on Saturday, the 3d of November, at ten o'clock in the morning.

The Marquis of Havré, as commander-in-chief, called a council of war. It assembled at Count Oberstein's quarters, and consulted at first concerning a bundle of intercepted letters which Havré had brought with him. These constituted a correspondence between Sancho d'Avila with the heads of the mutiny at Alost, and many other places. The letters were all dated subsequently to Don Sancho's treaty with Oberstein, and contained arrangements for an immediate concentration of the whole available Spanish force at the citadel.

The treachery was so manifest, that Oberstein felt all self-reproach for his own breach of faith to be superfluous. It was however evident that the attack was to be immediately expected. What was to be done? All the officers counselled the immediate erection of a bulwark on the side of the city exposed to the castle, but there were no miners or engineers. Champagny, however, recommended a skilful and experienced engineer to superintend the work in the city; and pledged himself that burghers enough would volunteer as miners. In less than an hour, ten or twelve thousand persons, including multitudes of women of all ranks, were at work upon the lines marked out by the engineer. A ditch and breastwork extending from the gate of the Beguins to the street of the Abbey Saint Michael were soon in rapid progress. Meantime, the newly arrived troops, with military insolence, claimed the privilege of quartering themselves in the best houses which they could find. They already began to insult and annoy the citizens whom they had been sent to defend; nor were they destined to atone, by their subsequent conduct in the face of the enemy, for the brutality with which they treated their friends. Champagny, however, was ill-disposed to brook their licentiousness. They had been sent to protect the city and the homes of Antwerp from invasion. They were not to establish themselves at every fireside on their first arrival. There was work enough for them out of doors and they were to do that work at once. He ordered them to prepare for a bivouac in the streets, and flew from house to house, sword in hand, driving forth the intruders at imminent peril of his life. Meantime, a number of Italian and Spanish merchants fled from the city, and took refuge in the castle. The Walloon soldiers were for immediately plundering their houses, as if plunder had been the object for which they had been sent to Antwerp. It was several hours before Champagny, with all his energy, was able to quell these disturbances.

In the course of the day, Oberstein received a letter from Don Sancho d'Avila, calling solemnly upon him to fulfil his treaty of the 29th October. The German colonels from the citadel had, on the previous afternoon, held a personal interview with Oberstein beneath the walls, which had nearly ended in blows, and they had been obliged to save themselves by flight from the anger of the Count's soldiers, enraged at the deceit by which their leader had been so nearly entrapped. This summons of ridiculous solemnity to keep a treaty which had already been torn to shreds by both parties, Oberstein answered with defiance and contempt. The reply was an immediate cannonade from the batteries of the citadel, which made the position of those erecting the ramparts excessively dangerous. The wall was strengthened with bales of merchandise, casks of earth, upturned wagons, and similar bulky objects, hastily piled together. In some places it was sixteen feet high; in others less than six. Night fell before the fortification was nearly completed. Unfortunately it was bright moonlight. The cannon from the fortress continued to play upon the half-finished works. The Walloons, and at last the citizens, feared to lift their heads above their frail rampart. The senators, whom Champagny had deputed to superintend the progress of the enterprise, finding the men so ill-disposed, deserted their posts. They promised themselves that, in the darkest hour of the following night, the work should be thoroughly completed. Alas! all hours of the coming night were destined to be dark enough, but in them was to be done no manner of work for defense. On Champagny alone seemed devolved all the labor and all the responsibility. He did his duty well, but he was but one man. Alone, with a heart full of anxiety, he wandered up and down all the night. With his own hands, assisted only by a few citizens and his own servants, he planted all the cannon with which they were provided, in the "Fencing Court," at a point where the battery might tell upon the castle. Unfortunately, the troops from Brussels had brought no artillery with them, and the means of defense against the strongest fortress in Europe were meager indeed. The rampart had been left very weak at many vital points. A single upturned wagon was placed across the entrance to the important street of the Beguins. This negligence was to cost the city dear. At daybreak, there was a council held in Oberstein's quarters. Nearly all Champagny's directions had been neglected. He had desired that strong detachments should be posted during the night at various places of security on the outskirts of the town, for the troops which were expected to arrive in small bodies at the citadel from various parts might have thus been cut off before reaching their destination. Not even scouts had been stationed in sufficient numbers to obtain information of what was occurring outside. A thick mist hung over the city that eventful morning. Through its almost impenetrable veil, bodies of men had been seen moving into the castle, and the tramp of cavalry had been distinctly heard, and the troops of Romero, Vargas, Oliveira, and Valdez, had already arrived from Lier, Breda, Maestricht, and from the forts on the Scheldt.

The whole available force in the city was mustered without delay. Havré had claimed for his post the defense of the lines opposite the citadel, the place of responsibility and honor. Here the whole body of Walloons were stationed, together with a few companies of Germans. The ramparts, as stated, were far from impregnable, but it was hoped that this living rampart of six thousand men, standing on their own soil, and in front of the firesides and altars of their own countrymen, would prove a sufficient bulwark even against Spanish fury. Unhappily, the living barrier proved more frail than the feeble breastwork which the hands of burghers and women had constructed. Six thousand men were disposed along the side of the city opposite the fortress. The bulk of the German troops was stationed at different points on the more central streets and squares. The cavalry was posted on the opposite side of the city, along the Horse-market, and fronting the "New-town." The stars were still in the sky when Champagny got on horseback and rode through the streets, calling on the burghers to arm and assemble at different points. The principal places of rendezvous were the Cattle-market and the Exchange. He rode along the lines of the Walloon regiments, conversing with the officers, Egmont, De Héze, and others, and encouraging the men, and went again to the Fencing Court, where he pointed the cannon with his own hand, and ordered their first discharge at the fortress. Thence he rode to the end of the Beguin street, where he dismounted and walked out upon the edge of the esplanade which stretched between the city and the castle. On this battleground a combat was even then occurring between a band of burghers and a reconnoitering party from the citadel. Champagny saw with satisfaction that the Antwerpers were victorious. They were skirmishing well with their disciplined foe, whom they at last beat back to the citadel. His experienced eye saw, however, that the retreat was only the signal for a general onslaught which was soon to follow; and he returned into the city to give the last directions.

At ten o'clock, a moving wood was descried, approaching the citadel from the southwest. The whole body of the mutineers from Alost, wearing green branches in their helmets, had arrived under command of their Eletto, Navarrete. Nearly three thousand in number, they rushed into the castle, having accomplished their march of twenty-four miles since three o'clock in the morning. They were received with open arms. Sancho d'Avila ordered food and refreshments to be laid before them, but they refused everything but a draught of wine. They would dine in Paradise, they said, or sup in Antwerp. Finding his allies in such spirit, Don Sancho would not balk their humor. Since early morning, his own veterans had been eagerly awaiting his signal, "straining upon the start." The troops of Romero, Vargas, Valdez, were no less impatient. At about an hour before noon, nearly every living man in the citadel was mustered for the attack, hardly men enough being left behind to guard the gates. Five thousand veteran foot soldiers, besides six hundred cavalry, armed to the teeth, sallied from the portals of Alva's citadel. In the counterscarp they fell upon their knees, to invoke, according to custom, the blessing of God upon the devil's work, which they were about to commit. The Eletto bore a standard, one side of which was emblazoned with the crucified Saviour, and the other with the Virgin Mary. The image of Him who said, "Love your enemies," and the gentle face of the Madonna, were to smile from heaven upon deeds which might cause a shudder in the depths of hell. Their brief orison concluded, they swept forward to the city. Three thousand Spaniards, under their Eletto, were to enter by the street of Saint Michael; the Germans, and the remainder of the Spanish foot, commanded by Romero, through that of Saint George. Champagny saw them coming, and spoke a last word of encouragement to the Walloons. The next moment the compact mass struck the barrier, as the thunderbolt descends from the cloud. There was scarcely a struggle. The Walloons, not waiting to look their enemy in the face, abandoned the posts which they had themselves claimed. The Spaniards crashed through the bulwark, as though it had been a wall of glass. The Eletto was the first to mount the rampart; the next instant he was shot dead, while his followers, undismayed, sprang over his body, and poured into the streets. The fatal gaps, due to timidity and carelessness, let in the destructive tide. Champagny, seeing that the enemies had all crossed the barrier, leaped over a garden wall, passed through a house into a narrow lane, and thence to the nearest station of the German troops. Hastily collecting a small force, he led them in person to the rescue. The Germans fought well, died well, but they could not reanimate the courage of the Walloons, and all were now in full retreat, pursued by the ferocious Spaniards. In vain Champagny stormed among them; in vain he strove to rally their broken ranks. With his own hand he seized a banner from a retreating ensign, and called upon the nearest soldiers to make a stand against the foe. It was to bid the flying clouds pause before the tempest. Torn, broken, aimless, the scattered troops whirled through the streets before the pursuing wrath. Champagny, not yet despairing, galloped hither and thither, calling upon the burghers everywhere to rise in defense of their homes, nor did he call in vain. They came forth from every place of rendezvous, from every alley, from every house. They fought as men fight to defend their hearths and altars; but what could individual devotion avail, against the compact, disciplined, resistless mass of their foes? The order of defense was broken, there was no system, no concert, no rallying point, no authority. So soon as it was known that the Spaniards had crossed the rampart, that its six thousand defenders were in full retreat, it was inevitable that panic should seize the city.

Their entrance once effected, the Spanish force had separated, according to previous arrangement, into two divisions, half charging up the long street of Saint Michael, the other forcing its way through the street of Saint Joris. "Santiago, Santiago!

España, España! á sangre, á carne, á fuego, á sacco!" Saint
James, Spain, blood, flesh, fire, sack!—such were the hideous
cries which rang through every quarter of the city, as the savage
cries advanced. Van Ende, with his German troops, had been
stationed by the Marquis of Havré to defend the Saint Joris
gate, but no sooner did the Spaniards under Vargas present
themselves, than he deserted to them instantly with his whole
force. United with the Spanish cavalry, these traitorous defenders of Antwerp dashed in pursuit of those who had only
been fainthearted. Thus the burghers saw themselves attacked
by many of their friends, deserted by more. Whom were they
to trust? Nevertheless, Oberstein's Germans were brave and
faithful, resisting to the last, and dying every man in his harness.
The tide of battle flowed hither and thither, through every street
and narrow lane. It poured along the magnificent Place de
Meer, where there was an obstinate contest. In front of the
famous Exchange, where, in peaceful hours, five thousand merchants met daily, to arrange the commercial affairs of Christendom, there was a determined rally, a savage slaughter. The
citizens and faithful Germans, in this broader space, made a
stand against their pursuers. The tesselated marble pavement,
the graceful, cloister-like arcades, ran red with blood. The ill-
armed burghers faced their enemies clad in complete panoply,
but they could only die for their homes. The massacre at this
point was enormous, the resistance at last overcome.

Meantime the Spanish cavalry had cleft its way through the
city. On the side farthest removed from the castle, along the
Horse-market, opposite the New-town, the states dragoons and
the light horse of Beveren had been posted, and the flying masses
of pursuers and pursued swept at last through this outer circle.
Champagny was already there. He essayed, as his last hope,
to rally the cavalry for a final stand, but the effort was fruitless.
Already seized by the panic, they had attempted to rush from
the city through the gate of Eeker. It was locked; they then
turned and fled towards the Red-gate, where they were met
face to face by Don Pedro Tassis, who charged upon them
with his dragoons. Retreat seemed hopeless. A horseman in

complete armor, with lance in rest, was seen to leap from the parapet of the outer wall into the moat below, whence, still on horseback, he escaped with life. Few were so fortunate. The confused mob of fugitives and conquerors, Spaniards, Walloons, Germans, and burghers struggling, shouting, striking, cursing, dying, swayed hither and thither like a stormy sea. Along the spacious Horse-market, the fugitives fled onwards towards the quays. Many fell beneath the swords of the Spaniards, numbers were trodden to death by the hoofs of horses, still greater multitudes were hunted into the Scheldt. Champagny, who had thought it possible, even at the last moment, to make a stand in the New-town, and to fortify the palace of the Hansa, saw himself deserted. With great daring and presence of mind, he effected his escape to the fleet of the Prince of Orange in the river. The Marquis of Havré, of whom no deeds of valor on that eventful day have been recorded, was equally successful. The unlucky Oberstein, attempting to leap into a boat, missed his footing, and, oppressed by the weight of his armor, was drowned.

Meantime, while the short November day was fast declining, the combat still raged in the interior of the city. Various currents of conflicts, forcing their separate way through many streets, had at last mingled in the *Grande Place*. Around this irregular, not very spacious square, stood the gorgeous Hôtel de Ville, and the tall, many-storied, fantastically gabled, richly decorated palaces of the guilds. Here a long struggle took place. It was terminated for a time by the cavalry of Vargas, who, arriving through the street of Saint Joris, accompanied by the traitor Van Ende, charged decisively into the mêlée. The masses were broken, but multitudes of armed men found refuge in the buildings, and every house became a fortress. From every window and balcony a hot fire was poured into the square, as, pent in a corner, the burghers stood at last at bay. It was difficult to carry the houses by storm, but they were soon set on fire. A large number of sutlers and other varlets had accompanied the Spaniards from the citadel, bringing torches and kindling materials for the express purpose of firing the town. With great dexterity these means were now applied, and in a brief interval, the City-hall and other edifices on the square were in flames. The conflagration spread with rapidity, house after house, street after street, taking fire. Nearly a thousand buildings, in the most splendid and wealthy quarter of the city, were soon in a blaze, and multitudes of human beings were burned with them. In the City-hall many were consumed, while others leaped from the windows to renew the combat below. The many tortuous streets which led down a slight descent from the rear of the Town-house to the quays were all one vast conflagration. On the other side, the magnificent cathedral, separated from the *Grande Place* by a single row of buildings, was lighted up, but not attacked by the flames. The tall spire cast its gigantic shadow across the last desperate conflict. In the street called the *Canal au Sucre*, immediately behind the Town-house, there was a fierce struggle, a horrible massacre. A crowd of burghers, grave magistrates, and such of the German soldiers as remained alive, still confronted the ferocious Spaniards. There, amid the flaming desolation, Goswyn Verreyck, the heroic margrave of the city, fought with the energy of hatred and despair. The burgomaster, Van der Meere, lay dead at his feet; senators, soldiers, citizens, fell fast around him, and he sank at last upon a heap of slain. With him effectual resistance ended. The remaining combatants were butchered, or were slowly forced downward to perish in the Scheldt. Women, children, old men, were killed in countless numbers, and still, through all this havoc, directly over the heads of the struggling throng, suspended in mid-air above the din and smoke of the conflict, there sounded, every half-quarter of every half-hour, as if in gentle mockery, from the belfry of the cathedral, the tender and melodious chimes.

Never was there a more monstrous massacre, even in the blood-stained history of the Netherlands. It was estimated that, in course of this and the two following days, not less than eight thousand human beings were murdered. The Spaniards seemed to cast off even the vizard of humanity. Hell seemed emptied of its fiends. Night fell upon the scene before the soldiers were masters of the city; but worse horrors began after the contest was ended. This army of brigands had come thither with a definite, practical purpose, for it was not blood-thirst, nor lust, nor revenge, which had impelled them, but it was avarice, greediness for gold. For gold they had waded through all this blood and fire. Never had men more simplicity of purpose, more directness in its execution. They had con-quered their India at last; its gold mines lay all before them, and every sword should open a shaft. Riot and rape might be deferred; even murder, though congenial to their taste, was only subsidiary to their business. They had come to take possession of the city's wealth, and they set themselves faithfully to ac-complish their task. For gold, infants were dashed out of existence in their mother's arms; for gold, parents were tortured in their children's presence; for gold, brides were scourged to death before their husbands' eyes. Wherever treasure was suspected, every expedient which ingenuity, sharpened by greediness, could suggest, was employed to extort it from its possessors. The fire, spreading more extensively and more rapidly than had been desired through the wealthiest quarter of the city, had unfortunately devoured a vast amount of property. Six millions, at least, had thus been swallowed; a destruction by which no one had profited. There was, however, much left. The strong boxes of the merchants, the gold, silver, and precious jewellery, the velvets, satins, brocades, laces, and similar well-concentrated and portable plunder, were rapidly appropriated. So far the course was plain and easy, but in private houses it was more difficult. The cash, plate, and other valuables were not so easily discovered. Torture was, therefore, at once em-ployed to discover the hidden treasures. After all had been given, if the sum seemed too little, the proprietors were brutally punished for their poverty or their supposed dissimulation. A gentlewoman, named Fabry, with her aged mother and other females of the family, had taken refuge in the cellar of her man-sion. As the day was drawing to a close, a band of plunderers entered, who, after ransacking the house, descended to the cellarage. Finding the door barred, they forced it open with gunpowder. The mother, who was nearest the entrance, fell dead on the threshold. Stepping across her mangled body, the brigands sprung upon her daughter, loudly demanding the property which they believed to be concealed. They likewise insisted on being informed where the master of the house had taken refuge. Protestations of ignorance as to hidden treasure, or the whereabouts of her husband, who, for aught she knew, was lying dead in the streets, were of no avail. To make her more communicative, they hanged her on a beam in the cellar, and after a few moments cut her down before life was extinct. Still receiving no satisfactory reply, where a satisfactory reply was impossible, they hanged her again. Again, after another brief interval, they gave her a second release, and a fresh interrogatory. This barbarity they repeated several times, till they were satisfied that there was nothing to be gained by it, while, on the other hand, they were losing much valuable time. Hoping to be more successful elsewhere, they left her hanging for the last time, and trooped off to fresher fields. Strange to relate, the person thus horribly tortured survived. A servant in her family, married to a Spanish soldier, providentially entered the house, in time to rescue her perishing mistress. She was restored to existence, but never to reason. Her brain was hopelessly crazed, and she passed the remainder of her life, wandering about her house, or feebly digging in her garden for the buried treasure which she had been thus fiercely solicited to reveal.

A wedding feast was rudely interrupted. Two young persons, neighbors of opulent families, had been long betrothed, and the marriage day had been fixed for Sunday, the fatal 4th of November. The guests were assembled, the ceremony concluded, the nuptial banquet in progress, when the horrible outcries in the streets proclaimed that the Spaniards had broken loose. Hour after hour of trembling expectation succeeded. At last, a thundering at the gate proclaimed the arrival of a band of brigands. Preceded by their captain, a large number of soldiers forced their way into the house, ransacking every chamber, no opposition being offered by the family and friends, too few and powerless to cope with this band of well-armed ruffians. Plate chests, wardrobes, desks, caskets of jewellery, were freely offered, eagerly accepted, but not found sufficient; and to make the luckless wretches furnish more than they possessed, the usual brutalities were employed. The soldiers began by striking the bridegroom dead. The bride fell shrieking into her mother's arms, whence she was torn by the murderers, who immediately put the mother to death, and an indiscriminate massacre then followed the fruitless attempts to obtain by threats and torture treasure which did not exist. The bride, who was of remarkable beauty, was carried off to the citadel. Maddened by this last outrage, the father, who was the only man of the party left alive, rushed upon the Spaniards. Wresting a sword from one of the crew, the old man dealt with it so fiercely that he stretched more than one enemy dead at his feet, but it is needless to add that he was soon despatched. Meantime, while the party were concluding the plunder of the mansion, the bride was left in a lonely apartment of the fortress. Without wasting time in fruitless lamentation, she resolved to quit the life which a few hours had made so desolate. She had almost succeeded in hanging herself with a massive gold chain which she wore, when her captor entered the apartment. Inflamed, not with lust, but with avarice, excited, not by her charms, but by her jewellery, he rescued her from her perilous position. He then took possession of her chain and the other trinkets with which her wedding dress was adorned, and caused her to be entirely stripped of her clothing. She was then scourged with rods till her beautiful body was all bathed in blood, and at last alone, naked, nearly mad, was sent back into the city. Here the forlorn creature wandered up and down through the blazing streets, among the heaps of dead and dying, till she was at last put out of her misery by a gang of soldiers.

Such are a few isolated instances, accidentally preserved in their details, of the general horrors inflicted on this occasion. Others innumerable have sunk into oblivion. On the morning of the 5th of November, Antwerp presented a ghastly sight. The magnificent marble Town-house, celebrated as a "world's wonder," even in that age and country, in which so much splendor was lavished on municipal palaces, stood a blackened ruin—all but the walls destroyed, while its archives, accounts, and other valuable contents had perished. The more splendid portion of the city had been consumed; at least five hundred palaces, mostly of marble or hammered stone, being a smouldering mass of destruction. The dead bodies of those fallen in the massacre were on every side, in greatest profusion around the Place de Meer, among the Gothic pillars of the Exchange, and in the streets near the Town-house. The German soldiers lay in their armor, some with their heads burned from their bodies, some with legs and arms consumed by the flames through which they had fought. The Margrave Goswyn Verreyck, the burgomaster Van der Meere, the magistrates Lancelot Van Urselen, Nicholas Van Boekholt, and other leading citizens, lay among piles of less distinguished slain. They remained unburied until the overseers of the poor, on whom the living had then more importunate claims than the dead, were compelled by Roda to bury them out of the pauper fund. The murderers were too thrifty to be at funeral charges for their victims. The ceremony was not hastily performed, for the number of corpses had not been completed. Two days longer the havoc lasted in the city. Of all the crimes which men can commit, whether from deliberate calculation, or in the frenzy of passion, hardly one was omitted, for riot, gaming, rape, which had been postponed to the more stringent claims of robbery and murder, were now rapidly added to the sum of atrocities. History has recorded the account indelibly on her brazen tablets; it can be adjusted only at the judgment-seat above.[1]

[ALEXANDER FARNESE, DUKE OF PARMA]

[From 1576 to 1578 Don John of Austria, half-brother of Philip II, tried to quell the revolt. Upon the death of Don John in 1578 his nephew Alexander Farnese took up the task of attempting to regain the Netherlands for Philip II.]

[1] *The Rise of the Dutch Republic*, III, 96–116.

A fifth governor now stood in the place which had been successively vacated by Margaret of Parma, by Alva, by the Grand Commander, and by Don John of Austria. Of all the eminent personages to whom Philip had confided the reins of that most difficult and dangerous administration, the man who was now to rule was by far the ablest and the best fitted for his post. If there were living charioteer skilful enough to guide the wheels of state, whirling now more dizzily than ever through *"confusum chaos,"* Alexander Farnese was the charioteer to guide—his hand the only one which could control. . . .

His personal appearance corresponded with his character. He had the head of a gladiator, round, compact, combative, with something alert and snake-like in its movements. The black, closely-shorn hair was erect and bristling. The forehead was lofty and narrow. The features were handsome, the nose regularly aquiline, the eyes well opened, dark, piercing, but with something dangerous and sinister in their expression. There was an habitual look askance, as of a man seeking to parry or inflict a mortal blow—the look of a swordsman and professional fighter. The lower part of the face was swallowed in a bushy beard; the mouth and chin being quite invisible. He was of middle stature, well formed, and graceful in person, princely in demeanor, sumptuous and stately in apparel. His high ruff of point lace, his badge of the Golden Fleece, his gold-inlaid Milan armor, marked him at once as one of high degree. On the field of battle he possessed the rare gift of inspiring his soldiers with his own impetuous and chivalrous courage. He ever led the way upon the most dangerous and desperate ventures, and, like his uncle and his imperial grandfather, well knew how to reward the devotion of his readiest followers with a poniard, a feather, a riband, a jewel, taken with his own hands from his own attire.

His military abilities—now for the first time to be largely called into employment—were unquestionably superior to those of Don John, whose name had been surrounded with such splendor by the world-renowned battle of Lepanto. Moreover, he possessed far greater power for governing men, whether in camp or cabinet. Less attractive and fascinating, he was more commanding than his kinsman. Decorous and self-poised, he was only passionate before the enemy, but he rarely permitted a disrespectful look or word to escape condign and deliberate chastisement. He was no schemer or dreamer. He was no knight-errant. He would not have crossed seas and mountains to rescue a captive queen, nor have sought to place her crown on his own head as a reward for his heroism. He had a single and concentrated kind of character. He knew precisely the work which Philip required, and felt himself to be precisely the workman that had so long been wanted. Cool, incisive, fearless, artful, he united the unscrupulous audacity of a *condottiere* with the wily patience of a Jesuit. He could coil unperceived through unsuspected paths, could strike suddenly, sting mortally. He came prepared, not only to smite the Netherlanders in the open field, but to cope with them in tortuous policy; to outwatch and outweary them in the game to which his impatient predecessor had fallen a baffled victim. He possessed the art and the patience—as time was to prove—not only to undermine their most impregnable cities, but to delve below the intrigues of their most accomplished politicians. To circumvent at once both their negotiators and their men-at-arms was his appointed task. Had it not been for the courage, the vigilance, and the superior intellect of a single antagonist, the whole of the Netherlands would have shared the fate which was reserved for the more southern portion. Had the life of William of Orange been prolonged, perhaps the evil genius of the Netherlands might have still been exorcised throughout the whole extent of the country.[1]

[THE DIVISION OF THE NETHERLANDS]

[By 1579 Alexander Farnese, by taking advantage of the religious differences existing among the inhabitants of the Netherlands, had succeeded in dividing the seventeen provinces. The ten southern provinces, which were predominantly Catho-

[1] *The Rise of the Dutch Republic*, III, 367-373.

lic, decided to accept again the rule of Philip II. The seven northern provinces, on the contrary, signed the Union of Utrecht and continued the struggle for independence.]

After various preliminary meetings in December and January, the deputies of Gelderland and Zutphen, with Count John, stadholder of these provinces, at their head, met with the deputies of Holland, Zeeland, and the provinces between the Ems and the Lauwers, early in January, 1579, and on the 23d of that month, without waiting longer for the deputies of the other provinces, they agreed provisionally upon a Treaty of Union which was published afterwards, on the 29th, from the Town House of Utrecht.

This memorable document—which is ever regarded as the foundation of the Netherland Republic—contained twenty-six articles.

The preamble stated the object of the union. It was to strengthen, not to forsake the Ghent Pacification, already nearly annihilated by the force of foreign soldiery. For this purpose, and in order more conveniently to defend themselves against their foes, the deputies of Gelderland, Zutphen, Holland, Zeeland, Utrecht, and the Frisian provinces, thought it desirable to form a still closer union. The contracting provinces agreed to remain eternally united, as if they were but one province. At the same time, it was understood that each was to retain its particular privileges, liberties, laudable and traditionary customs, and other laws. The cities, corporations, and inhabitants of every province were to be guaranteed as to their ancient constitutions. Disputes concerning these various statutes and customs were to be decided by the usual tribunals, by "good men," or by amicable compromise. The provinces, by virtue of the union, were to defend each other "with life, goods, and blood," against all force brought against them in the King's name or behalf. They were also to defend each other against all foreign or domestic potentates, provinces, or cities, provided such defense were controlled by the "generality" of the union. For the expense occasioned by the protection of the provinces, certain imposts and excises were to be equally assessed and collected. No truce or peace was to be concluded, no war commenced, no impost established affecting the "generality," but by unanimous advice and consent of the provinces. Upon other matters the majority was to decide; the votes being taken in the manner then customary in the assembly of the States-General. In case of difficulty in coming to a unanimous vote when required, the matter was to be referred to the stadholders then in office. In case of their inability to agree, they were to appoint arbitrators, by whose decision the parties were to be governed. None of the United Provinces, or of their cities or corporations, were to make treaties with other potentates or states, without consent of their confederates. If neighboring princes, provinces, or cities, wished to enter into this confederacy, they were to be received by the unanimous consent of the United Provinces. A common currency was to be established for the confederacy. In the matter of divine worship, Holland and Zeeland were to conduct themselves as they should think proper. The other provinces of the union, however, were either to conform to the religious peace already laid down by Archduke Matthias and his council, or to make such other arrangements as each province should for itself consider appropriate for the maintenance of its internal tranquillity—provided always that every individual should remain free in his religion, and that no man should be molested or questioned on the subject of divine worship, as had already been established by the Ghent Pacification. As a certain dispute arose concerning the meaning of this important clause, an additional paragraph was inserted a few days afterwards. In this it was stated that there was no intention of excluding from the confederacy any province or city which was wholly Catholic, or in which the number of the Reformed was not sufficiently large to entitle them, by the religious peace, to public worship. On the contrary, the intention was to admit them, provided they obeyed the articles of union, and conducted themselves as good patriots; it being intended that no province or city should interfere with another in the matter of divine service. Disputes between two provinces were to be decided by the others, or—in case the generality were concerned—by the provisions of the ninth article.

The confederates were to assemble at Utrecht whenever summoned by those commissioned for that purpose. A majority of votes was to decide on matters then brought before them, even in case of the absence of some members of the confederacy, who might, however, send written proxies. Additions or amendments to these articles could only be made by unanimous consent. The articles were to be signed by the stadholders, magistrates, and principal officers of each province and city, and by all the train-bands, fraternities, and sodalities which might exist in the cities or villages of the union.

Such were the simple provisions of that instrument which became the foundation of the powerful Commonwealth of the United Netherlands. On the day when it was concluded, there were present deputies from five provinces only. Count John of Nassau signed first, as stadholder of Gelderland and Zutphen. His signature was followed by those of four deputies from that double province; and the envoys of Holland, Zeeland, Utrecht, and the Frisian provinces, then signed the document. . . .

The Union of Utrecht was the foundation-stone of the Netherland Republic; but the framers of the confederacy did not intend the establishment of a republic, or of an independent commonwealth of any kind. They had not forsworn the Spanish monarch. It was not yet their intention to forswear him. Certainly the act of union contained no allusion to such an important step. On the contrary, in the brief preamble they expressly stated their intention to strengthen the Ghent Pacification, and the Ghent Pacification acknowledged obedience to the King. They intended no political innovation of any kind. They expressly accepted matters as they were. All statutes, charters, and privileges of provinces, cities, or corporations were to remain untouched. They intended to form neither an independent state nor an independent federal system. No doubt the formal renunciation of allegiance, which was to follow within two years, was contemplated by many as a future probability; but it could not be foreseen with certainty.

The simple act of union was not regarded as the constitution of a commonwealth. Its object was a single one—defense against a foreign oppressor. The contracting parties bound themselves together to spend all their treasure and all their blood in expelling the foreign soldiery from their soil. To accomplish this purpose, they carefully abstained from intermeddling with internal politics, and with religion. Every man was to worship God according to the dictates of his conscience. Every combination of citizens, from the provincial states down to the humblest rhetoric club, was to retain its ancient constitution. The establishment of a republic, which lasted two centuries, which threw a girdle of rich dependencies entirely round the globe, and which attained so remarkable a height of commercial prosperity and political influence, was the result of the Utrecht Union; but it was not a premeditated result. A state, single towards the rest of the world, a unit in its external relations, while permitting internally a variety of sovereignties and institutions—in many respects the prototype of our own much more extensive and powerful union—was destined to spring from the act thus signed by the envoys of five provinces. Those envoys were acting, however, under the pressure of extreme necessity, and for what was believed an evanescent purpose. The future confederacy was not to resemble the system of the German Empire, for it was to acknowledge no single head. It was to differ from the Achaian League, in the far inferior amount of power which it permitted to its general assembly, and in the consequently greater proportion of sovereign attributes which were retained by the individual states. It was, on the other hand, to furnish a closer and more intimate bond than that of the Swiss Confederacy, which was only a union for defence and external purposes, of cantons otherwise independent. It was, finally, to differ from the American federal commonwealth in the great feature that it was to be merely a confederacy of sovereignties, not a representative republic. Its foundation was a compact, not a constitution. The contracting parties were states and corporations, who considered themselves as representing small nationalities *de jure et de facto*, and as succeeding to the supreme power at the very instant in which allegiance to the Spanish monarch was renounced. The general assembly was a collection of diplomatic envoys, bound by instructions from independent states. The voting was not by heads, but by states. The deputies were not representatives of the people, but of the states; for the people of the United States of the Netherlands never assembled—as did the people of the United States of America two centuries later—to lay down a constitution by which they granted a generous amount of power to the union, while they reserved enough of sovereign attributes to secure that local self-government which is the lifeblood of liberty.

The Union of Utrecht, narrowed as it was to the nether portion of that country which, as a whole, might have formed a commonwealth so much more powerful, was in origin a proof of this lamentable want of patriotism. Could the jealousy of great nobles, the rancor of religious differences, the Catholic bigotry of the Walloon population on the one side, contending with the democratic insanity of the Ghent populace on the other, have been restrained within bounds by the moderate counsels of William of Orange, it would have been possible to unite seventeen provinces instead of seven, and to save many long and blighting years of civil war.

The Utrecht Union was, however, of inestimable value. It was time for some step to be taken, if anarchy were not to reign until the Inquisition and absolutism were restored. Already, out of Chaos and Night, the coming Republic was assuming substance and form. The union, if it created nothing else, at least constructed a league against a foreign foe whose armed masses were pouring faster and faster into the territory of the provinces. Farther than this it did not propose to go. It maintained what it found. It guaranteed religious liberty, and accepted the civil and political constitutions already in existence. Meantime, the defects of those constitutions, although visible and sensible, had not grown to the large proportions which they were destined to attain.

Thus by the Union of Utrecht on the one hand, and the fast-approaching reconciliation of the Walloon provinces on the other, the work of decomposition and of construction went hand in hand.[1]

[ASSASSINATION OF WILLIAM OF ORANGE]

[*The Rise of the Dutch Republic* closed, as it had begun, with a moving scene. In 1584 an assassin killed William of Orange, the hero of the narrative.]

Parma had long been looking for a good man to murder Orange, feeling—as Philip, Granvelle, and all former governors of the Netherlands had felt—that this was the only means of saving the royal authority in any part of the provinces. Many unsatisfactory assassins had presented themselves from time to time, and Alexander had paid money in hand to various individuals—Italians, Spaniards, Lorrainers, Scotchmen, Englishmen—who had generally spent the sums received without attempting the job. Others were supposed to be still engaged in the enterprise, and at that moment there were four persons —each unknown to the others, and of different nations—in the city of Delft, seeking to compass the death of William the Silent. Shag-eared, military, hirsute ruffians—ex-captains of free companies and such marauders—were daily offering their services; there was no lack of them, and they had done but little. How should Parma, seeing this obscure, under-sized, thin-bearded, runaway clerk before him, expect pith and energy from *him*? He thought him quite unfit for an enterprise of moment, and declared as much to his secret councillors and to the King. He soon dismissed him, after receiving his letter, and it may be supposed that the bombastic style of that epistle would not efface the unfavorable impression produced by Balthazar's exterior. The representations of Haultepenne and others induced him so far to modify his views as to send his confidential councillor, D'Assonleville, to the stranger, in order to learn the details of the scheme. Assonleville had accordingly

[1] *The Rise of the Dutch Republic*, III, 410–417.

an interview with Gérard, in which he requested the young man to draw up a statement of his plan in writing, and this was done upon the 11th of April 1584.

In this letter Gérard explained his plan of introducing himself to the notice of Orange, at Delft, as the son of an executed Calvinist; as himself warmly, though secretly, devoted to the Reformed faith, and as desirous, therefore, of placing himself in the Prince's service, in order to avoid the insolence of the Papists. Having gained the confidence of those about the Prince, he would suggest to them the great use which might be made of Mansfeld's signet in forging passports for spies and other persons whom it might be desirous to send into the territory of the royalists. "With these or similar feints and frivolities," continued Gérard, "he should soon obtain access to the person of the said Nassau," repeating his protestation that nothing had moved him to his enterprise "save the good zeal which he bore to the faith and true religion guarded by the Holy Mother Church Catholic, Apostolic, and Roman, and to the service of his Majesty." He begged pardon for having purloined the impressions of the seals—a turpitude which he would never have committed, but would sooner have suffered a thousand deaths, except for the great end in view. He particularly wished forgiveness for that crime before going to his task, "in order that he might confess, and receive the holy communion at the coming Easter, without scruples of conscience." He likewise begged the Prince of Parma to obtain for him absolution from his Holiness for this crime of pilfering—the more so "as he was about to keep company for some time with heretics and atheists, and in some sort to conform himself to their customs."

From the general tone of the letters of Gérard, he might be set down at once as a simple, religious fanatic, who felt sure that, in executing the command of Philip publicly issued to all the murderers of Europe, he was meriting well of God and his King. There is no doubt that he was an exalted enthusiast, but not purely an enthusiast. The man's character offers more than one point of interest, as a psychological phenomenon. He had convinced himself that the work which he had in hand was eminently meritorious, and he was utterly without fear of consequences. He was, however, by no means so disinterested as he chose to represent himself in letters which, as he instinctively felt, were to be of perennial interest. On the contrary, in his interviews with Assonleville, he urged that he was a poor fellow, and that he had undertaken this enterprise in order to acquire property—to make himself rich—and that he depended upon the Prince of Parma's influence in obtaining the reward promised by the ban to the individual who should put Orange to death.

This second letter decided Parma so far that he authorized Assonleville to encourage the young man in his attempt, and to promise that the reward should be given to him in case of success, and to his heirs in the event of his death. Assonleville, in the second interview, accordingly made known these assurances in the strongest manner to Gérard, warning him, at the same time, on no account, if arrested, to inculpate the Prince of Parma. The councillor, while thus exhorting the stranger, according to Alexander's commands, confined himself, however, to generalities, refusing even to advance fifty crowns, which Balthazar had begged from the Governor-General in order to provide for the necessary expenses of his project. Parma had made similar advances too often to men who had promised to assassinate the Prince and had then done little, and he was resolute in his refusal to this new adventurer, of whom he expected absolutely nothing. Gérard, notwithstanding this rebuff, was not disheartened. "I will provide myself out of my own purse," said he to Assonleville, "and within six weeks you will hear of me." "Go forth, my son," said Assonleville, paternally, upon this spirited reply, "and if you succeed in your enterprise, the King will fulfil all his promises, and you will gain an immortal name beside."

The "inveterate deliberation," thus thoroughly matured, Gérard now proceeded to carry into effect. He came to Delft, obtained a hearing of Villers, the clergyman and intimate friend of Orange, shewed him the Mansfeld seals, and was, somewhat against his will, sent to France, to exhibit them to Maréchal Biron, who, it was thought, was soon to be appointed governor of Cambray. Through Orange's recommendation, the Burgundian was received into the suite of Noël de Caron, Seigneur de Schoneval, then setting forth on a special mission to the Duke of Anjou. While in France, Gérard could rest neither by day nor night, so tormented was he by the desire of accomplishing his project, and at length he obtained permission, upon the death of the Duke, to carry this important intelligence to the Prince of Orange. The despatches having been entrusted to him, he travelled post-haste to Delft, and, to his astonishment, the letters had hardly been delivered before he was summoned in person to the chamber of the Prince. Here was an opportunity such as he had never dared to hope for. The arch-enemy to the Church and to the human race, whose death would confer upon his destroyer wealth and nobility in this world, besides a crown of glory in the next, lay unarmed, alone, in bed, before the man who had thirsted seven long years for his blood.

Balthazar could scarcely control his emotions sufficiently to answer the questions which the Prince addressed to him concerning the death of Anjou; but Orange, deeply engaged with the despatches, and with the reflections which their deeply important contents suggested, did not observe the countenance of the humble Calvinist exile, who had been recently recommended to his patronage by Villers. Gérard had, moreover, made no preparation for an interview so entirely unexpected, had come unarmed, and had formed no plan for escape. He was obliged to forego his prey when most within his reach, and after communicating all the information which the Prince required, he was dismissed from the chamber.

It was Sunday morning, and the bells were tolling for church. Upon leaving the house he loitered about the courtyard, furtively examining the premises, so that a sergeant of halberdiers asked him why he was waiting there. Balthazar meekly replied that he was desirous of attending Divine worship in the church opposite, but added, pointing to his shabby and travel-stained attire, that, without at least a new pair of shoes and stockings, he was unfit to join the congregation. Insignificant as ever, the small, pious, dusty stranger excited no suspicion in the mind of the good-natured sergeant. He forthwith spoke of the wants of Gérard to an officer, by whom they were communicated to Orange himself, and the Prince instantly ordered a sum of money to be given him. Thus Balthazar obtained from William's charity what Parma's thrift had denied—a fund for carrying out his purpose!

Next morning, with the money thus procured he purchased a pair of pistols, or small carabines, from a soldier, chaffering long about the price because the vender could not supply a particular kind of chopped bullets or slugs which he desired. Before the sunset of the following day that soldier had stabbed himself to the heart, and died despairing, on hearing for what purpose the pistols had been bought.

On Tuesday, the 10th of July, 1584, at about half-past twelve, the Prince, with his wife on his arm, and followed by the ladies and gentlemen of his family, was going to the dining-room. William the Silent was dressed upon that day, according to his usual custom, in very plain fashion. He wore a wide-leaved, loosely-shaped hat of dark felt, with a silken cord round the crown—such as had been worn by the Beggars in the early days of the revolt. A high ruff encircled his neck, from which also depended one of the Beggars' medals, with the motto, *"Fidèles au roy jusqu'à la besace,"* while a loose surcoat of gray frieze cloth, over a tawny leather doublet, with wide, slashed underclothes completed his costume. Gérard presented himself at the doorway, and demanded a passport. The Princess, struck with the pale and agitated countenance of the man, anxiously questioned her husband concerning the stranger. The Prince carelessly observed, that "it was merely a person who came for a passport," ordering, at the same time, a secretary forthwith to prepare one. The Princess, still not relieved, observed in an undertone that "she had never seen so villanous a countenance." Orange, however, not at all impressed with the appearance of Gérard, conducted himself at table with his usual cheerfulness, conversing much with the burgomaster of

Leeuwarden, the only guest present at the family dinner, concerning the political and religious aspects of Friesland. At two o'clock the company rose from table. The Prince led the way, intending to pass to his private apartments above. The dining-room, which was on the ground floor, opened into a little square vestibule, which communicated, through an arched passageway, with the main entrance into the courtyard. This vestibule was also directly at the foot of the wooden staircase leading to the next floor, and was scarcely six feet in width. Upon its left side, as one approached the stairway, was an obscure arch, sunk deep in the wall, and completely in the shadow of the door. Behind this arch a portal opened to the narrow lane at the side of the house. The stairs themselves were completely lighted by a large window, halfway up the flight. The Prince came from the dining-room, and began leisurely to ascend. He had only reached the second stair, when a man emerged from the sunken arch, and, standing within a foot or two of him, discharged a pistol full at his heart. Three balls entered his body, one of which, passing quite through him, struck with violence against the wall beyond. The Prince exclaimed in French, as he felt the wound, "O my God, have mercy upon my soul! O my God, have mercy upon this poor people!"

These were the last words he ever spoke, save that when his sister, Catharine of Schwartzburg, immediately afterwards asked him if he commended his soul to Jesus Christ, he faintly answered, "Yes." His master of the horse, Jacob van Maldere, had caught him in his arms as the fatal shot was fired. The Prince was then placed on the stairs for an instant, when he immediately began to swoon. He was afterwards laid upon a couch in the dining-room, where in a few minutes, he breathed his last in the arms of his wife and sister.

The murderer succeeded in making his escape through the side door, and sped swiftly up the narrow lane. He had almost reached the ramparts, from which he intended to spring into the moat, when he stumbled over a heap of rubbish. As he rose, he was seized by several pages and halberdiers, who had pursued him from the house. He had dropped his pistols upon the spot where he had committed the crime, and upon his person were found a couple of bladders, provided with a piece of pipe with which he had intended to assist himself across the moat, beyond which a horse was waiting for him. He made no effort to deny his identity, but boldly avowed himself and his deed. He was brought back to the house, where he immediately underwent a preliminary examination before the city magistrates. He was afterwards subjected to excruciating tortures; for the fury against the wretch who had destroyed the Father of the country was uncontrollable, and William the Silent was no longer alive to intercede—as he had often done before—in behalf of those who assailed his life.[1]

[CHARACTER AND WORK OF WILLIAM OF ORANGE]

[After describing this dramatic death of William of Orange, Motley gave a final estimate of his character and work.]

William of Orange, at the period of his death, was aged fifty-one years and sixteen days. He left twelve children. By his first wife, Anne of Egmont, he had one son, Philip, and one daughter, Mary, afterwards married to Count Hohenlo. By his second wife, Anna of Saxony, he had one son, the celebrated Maurice of Nassau, and two daughters, Anna, married afterwards to her cousin, Count William Louis, and Emilie, who espoused the Pretender of Portugal, Prince Emanuel. By Charlotte of Bourbon, his third wife, he had six daughters; and by his fourth, Louisa de Coligny, one son, Frederic William, afterwards stadholder of the Republic in her most palmy days. The Prince was entombed on the 3d of August, at Delft, amid the tears of a whole nation. Never was a more extensive, unaffected, and legitimate sorrow felt at the death of any human being.

The life and labors of Orange had established the emancipated commonwealth upon a secure foundation, but his death

[1] *The Rise of the Dutch Republic*, III, 603–610.

rendered the union of all the Netherlands into one republic hopeless. The efforts of the malcontent nobles, the religious discord, the consummate ability, both political and military, of Parma, all combined with the lamentable loss of William the Silent to separate for ever the southern and Catholic provinces from the northern confederacy. So long as the Prince remained alive, he was the Father of the whole country; the Netherlands —saving only the two Walloon provinces—constituting a whole. Notwithstanding the spirit of faction and the blight of the long civil war, there was at least one country, or the hope of a country, one strong heart, one guiding head, for the patriotic party throughout the land. Philip and Granvelle were right in their estimate of the advantage to be derived from the Prince's death; in believing that an assassin's hand could achieve more than all the wiles which Spanish or Italian statesmanship could teach, or all the armies which Spain or Italy could muster. The pistol of the insignificant Gérard destroyed the possibility of a united Netherland state, while during the life of William there was union in the policy, unity in the history of the country.

In the following year, Antwerp, hitherto the center around which all the national interests and historical events group themselves, fell before the scientific efforts of Parma. The city which had so long been the freest, as well as the most opulent capital in Europe, sunk for ever to the position of a provincial town. With its fall, combined with other circumstances, which it is not necessary to narrate in anticipation, the final separation of the Netherlands was completed. On the other hand, at the death of Orange, whose formal inauguration as sovereign Count had not yet taken place, the states of Holland and Zeeland reassumed the sovereignty. The commonwealth which William had liberated for ever from Spanish tyranny continued to exist as a great and flourishing republic during more than two centuries, under the successive stadholderates of his sons and descendants.

His life gave existence to an independent country—his death defined its limits. Had he lived twenty years longer, it is probable that the seven provinces would have been seventeen; and that the Spanish title would have been for ever extinguished both in Nether Germany and Celtic Gaul. Although there was to be the length of two human generations more of warfare ere Spain acknowledged the new government, yet before the termination of that period the united states had become the first naval power and one of the most considerable commonwealths in the world; while the civil and religious liberty, the political independence of the land, together with the total expulsion of the ancient foreign tyranny from the soil, had been achieved ere the eyes of William were closed. The Republic existed, in fact, from the moment of the abjuration in 1581.

The most important features of the polity which thus assumed a prominent organization have been already indicated. There was no revolution, no radical change. The ancient rugged tree of Netherland liberty—with its moss-grown trunk, gnarled branches, and deep-reaching roots—which had been slowly growing for ages, was still full of sap, and was to deposit for centuries longer its annual rings of consolidated and concentric strength. Though lopped of some luxuriant boughs, it was sound at the core, and destined for a still larger life than even in the healthiest moments of its medieval existence.

The history of the rise of the Netherland Republic has been at the same time the biography of William the Silent. This, while it gives unity to the narrative, renders an elaborate description of his character superfluous. That life was a noble Christian epic; inspired with one great purpose from its commencement to its close; the stream flowing ever from one fountain with expanding fullness, but retaining all its original purity. A few general observations are all which are necessary by way of conclusion.

In person, Orange was above the middle height, perfectly well-made and sinewy, but rather spare than stout. His eyes, hair, beard, and complexion were brown. His head was small, symmetrically shaped, combining the alertness and compactness characteristic of the soldier, with the capacious brow, furrowed prematurely with the horizontal lines of thought, denoting the statesman and the sage. His physical appearance was, therefore, in harmony with his organization, which was of antique model. Of his moral qualities, the most prominent was his piety. He was more than anything else a religious man. From his trust in God he ever derived support and consolation in the darkest hours. Implicitly relying upon almighty wisdom and goodness, he looked danger in the face with a constant smile, and endured incessant labors and trials with a serenity which seemed more than human. While, however, his soul was full of piety, it was tolerant of error. Sincerely and deliberately himself a convert to the Reformed Church, he was ready to extend freedom of worship to Catholics on the one hand, and to Anabaptists on the other; for no man ever felt more keenly than he that the Reformer who becomes in his turn a bigot is doubly odious.

His firmness was allied to his piety. His constancy in bearing the whole weight of struggle, as unequal as men have ever undertaken, was the theme of admiration even to his enemies. The rock in the ocean, "tranquil amid raging billows," was the favorite emblem by which his friends expressed their sense of his firmness. From the time when, as a hostage in France, he first discovered the plan of Philip to plant the Inquisition in the Netherlands, up to the last moment of his life, he never faltered in his determination to resist that iniquitous scheme. This resistance was the labor of his life. To exclude the Inquisition, to maintain the ancient liberties of his country, was the task which he appointed to himself when a youth of three-and-twenty. Never speaking a word concerning a heavenly mission, never deluding himself or others with the usual phraseology of enthusiasts, he accomplished the task, through danger, amid toils, and with sacrifices such as few men have ever been able to make on their country's altar;—for the disinterested benevolence of the man was as prominent as his fortitude. A prince of high rank and with royal revenues, he stripped himself of station, wealth, almost at times of the common necessaries of life, and became, in his country's cause, nearly a beggar as well as an outlaw. Nor was he forced into his career by an accidental impulse from which there was no recovery. Retreat was ever open to him. Not only pardon, but advancement, was urged upon him again and again. Officially and privately, directly and circuitously, his confiscated estates, together with indefinite and boundless favors in addition, were offered to him on every great occasion. On the arrival of Don John, at the Breda negotiations, at the Cologne conferences, we have seen how calmly these offers were waved aside, as if their rejection was so simple that it hardly required many words for its signification; yet he had mortgaged his estates so deeply that his heirs hesitated at accepting their inheritance, for fear it should involve them in debt. Ten years after his death, the account between his executors and his brother John amounted to one million four hundred thousand florins due to the Count, secured by various pledges of real and personal property, and it was finally settled upon this basis. He was, besides, largely indebted to every one of his powerful relatives, so that the payment of the incumbrances upon his estates very nearly justified the fears of his children. While on the one hand, therefore, he poured out these enormous sums like water, and firmly refused a hearing to the tempting offers of the royal government, upon the other hand, he proved the disinterested nature of his services by declining, year after year, the sovereignty over the provinces; and by only accepting, in the last days of his life, when refusal had become almost impossible, the limited constitutional supremacy over that portion of them which now makes the realm of his descendants. He lived and died, not for himself, but for his country. "God, pity this poor people!" were his dying words.

His intellectual faculties were various and of the highest order. He had the exact, practical, and combining qualities which make the great commander; and his friends claimed that, in military genius, he was second to no captain in Europe. This was, no doubt, an exaggeration of partial attachment, but it is certain that the Emperor Charles had an exalted opinion of his capacity for the field. His fortification of Philippeville and Charlemont in the face of the enemy—his passage of the Meuse in Alva's sight—his unfortunate but well-ordered campaign against that general—his sublime plan of relief, projected and successfully directed at last from his sickbed, for the besieged city of Leyden —will always remain monuments of his practical military skill.

Of the soldier's great virtues—constancy in disaster, devotion to duty, hopefulness in defeat—no man ever possessed a larger share. He arrived, through a series of reverses, at a perfect victory. He planted a free commonwealth under the very battery of the Inquisition, in defiance of the most powerful empire existing. He was therefore a conqueror in the loftiest sense, for he conquered liberty and a national existence for a whole people. The contest was long, and he fell in the struggle; but the victory was to the dead hero, not to the living monarch. It is to be remembered, too, that he always wrought with inferior instruments. His troops were usually mercenaries, who were but too apt to mutiny upon the eve of battle, while he was opposed by the most formidable veterans of Europe, commanded successively by the first captains of the age. That, with no lieutenant of eminent valor or experience, save only his brother Louis, and with none at all after that chieftain's death, William of Orange should succeed in baffling the efforts of Alva, Requesens, Don John of Austria, and Alexander Farnese—men whose names are among the most brilliant in the military annals of the world—is in itself sufficient evidence of his warlike ability. At the period of his death he had reduced the number of obedient provinces to two; only Artois and Hainault acknowledging Philip, while the other fifteen were in open revolt, the greater part having solemnly forsworn their sovereign.

The supremacy of his political genius was entirely beyond question. He was the first statesman of the age. The quickness of his perception was only equalled by the caution which enabled him to mature the results of his observations. His knowledge of human nature was profound. He governed the passions and sentiments of a great nation as if they had been but the keys and chords of one vast instrument; and his hand rarely failed to evoke harmony even out of the wildest storms. The turbulent city of Ghent, which could obey no other master, which even the haughty Emperor could only crush without controlling, was ever responsive to the master-hand of Orange. His presence scared away Imbize and his bat-like crew, confounded the schemes of John Casimir, frustrated the wiles of Prince Chimay, and while he lived Ghent was what it ought always to have remained, the bulwark, as it had been the cradle of popular liberty. After his death it became its tomb. . . .

This power of dealing with his fellow-men he manifested in the various ways in which it has been usually exhibited by statesmen. He possessed a ready eloquence—sometimes impassioned, oftener argumentative, always rational. His influence over his audience was unexampled in the annals of that country or age; yet he never condescended to flatter the people. He never followed the nation, but always led her in the path of duty and of honor, and was much more prone to rebuke the vices than to pander to the passions of his hearers. He never failed to administer ample chastisement to parsimony, to jealousy, to insubordination, to intolerance, to infidelity, wherever it was due, nor feared to confront the states or the people in their most angry hours, and to tell them the truth to their faces. This commanding position he alone could stand upon, for his countrymen knew the generosity which had sacrificed his all for them, the self-denial which had eluded rather than sought political advancement, whether from king or people, and the untiring devotion which had consecrated a whole life to toil and danger in the cause of the emancipation. While, therefore, he was ever ready to rebuke, and always too honest to flatter, he at the same time possessed the eloquence which could convince or persuade. He knew how to reach both the mind and the heart of his hearers. His orations, whether extemporaneous or prepared—his written messages to the States-General, to the provincial authorities, to the municipal bodies —his private correspondence with men of all ranks, from emperors and kings down to secretaries, and even children—all shew an easy flow of language, a fulness of thought, a power of expression rare in that age, a fund of historical allusion, a considerable power of imagination, warmth of sentiment, a breadth of view, a directness of purpose—a range of qualities, in short, which would in themselves have stamped him as one of the master minds of his century, had there been no other monument to his memory than the remains of his spoken or written eloquence. The bulk of his performances in this department was prodigious. Not even Philip was more industrious in the cabinet. Not even Granvelle held a more facile pen. He wrote and spoke equally well in French, German, or Flemish; and he possessed, besides, Spanish, Italian, Latin. The weight of his correspondence alone would have almost sufficed for the common industry of a lifetime, and although many volumes of his speeches and letters have been published, there remain in the various archives of the Netherlands and Germany many documents from his hand which will probably never see the light. If the capacity for unremitted intellectual labor in an honorable cause be the measure of human greatness, few minds could be compared to the "large composition" of this man. The efforts made to destroy the Netherlands by the most laborious and painstaking of tyrants were counteracted by the industry of the most indefatigable of patriots.

Thus his eloquence, oral or written, gave him almost boundless power over his countrymen. He possessed, also, a rare perception of human character, together with an iron memory which never lost a face, a place, or an event, once seen or known. He read the minds, even the faces of men, like printed books. No man could overreach him, excepting only those to whom he gave his heart. He might be mistaken where he had confided, never where he had been distrustful or indifferent. He was deceived by Renneberg, by his brother-in-law Van den Berg, by the Duke of Anjou. Had it been possible for his brother Louis, or his brother John, to have proved false, he might have been deceived by them. He was never outwitted by Philip, or Granvelle, or Don John, or Alexander of Parma. Anna of Saxony was false to him, and entered into correspondence with the royal governors and with the King of Spain; Charlotte of Bourbon or Louisa de Coligny might have done the same had it been possible for their natures also to descend to such depths of guile.

As for the Aerschots, the Havrés, the Chimays, he was never influenced either by their blandishments or their plots. He was willing to use them when their interest made them friendly, or to crush them when their intrigues against his policy rendered them dangerous. The adroitness with which he converted their schemes in behalf of Matthias, of Don John, of Anjou, into so many additional weapons for his own cause, can never be too often studied. It is instructive to observe the wiles of the Machiavellian school employed by a master of the craft, to frustrate, not to advance, a knavish purpose. This character, in a great measure, marked his whole policy. He was profoundly skilled in the subtleties of Italian statesmanship, which he had learned as a youth at the imperial court, and which he employed in his manhood in the service, not of tyranny, but of liberty. He fought the Inquisition with its own weapons. He dealt with Philip on his own ground. He excavated the earth beneath the King's feet by a more subtle process than that practiced by the most fraudulent monarch that ever governed the Spanish empire, and Philip, chain-mailed as he was in complicated wiles, was pierced to the quick by a keener policy than his own.

It is difficult to find any other characteristic deserving of grave censure, but his enemies have adopted a simpler process. They have been able to find few flaws in his nature, and therefore have denounced it in gross. It is not that his character was here and there defective, but that the eternal jewel was false. The patriotism was counterfeit; the self-abnegation and the generosity were counterfeit. He was governed only by ambition—by a desire of personal advancement. They never attempted to deny his talents, his industry, his vast sacrifices of wealth and station; but they ridiculed the idea that he could have been inspired by any but unworthy motives. God alone knows the heart of man. He alone can unweave the tangled skein of human motives, and detect the hidden springs of human action, but, as far as can be judged by a careful observation of undisputed facts, and by a diligent collation of public and private documents, it would seem that no man—not even Washington—has ever been inspired by a purer patriotism. At any rate, the charge of ambition and self-seeking can only be answered by a reference to the whole picture which these volumes have attempted to portray. The words, the deeds of the man are there. As much as possible, his inmost soul is revealed in his confidential letters, and he who looks in a right spirit will hardly fail to find what he desires.

Whether originally of a timid temperament or not, he was certainly possessed of perfect courage at last. In siege and battle—in the deadly air of pestilential cities—in the long exhaustion of mind and body which comes from unduly-protracted labor and anxiety—amid the countless conspiracies of assassins—he was daily exposed to death in every shape. Within two years, five different attempts against his life had been discovered. Rank and fortune were offered to any malefactor who would compass the murder. He had already been shot through the head and almost mortally wounded. Under such circumstances even a brave man might have seen a pitfall at every step, a dagger in every hand, and poison in every cup. On the contrary, he was ever cheerful, and hardly took more precaution than usual. "God in His mercy," said he, with unaffected simplicity, "will maintain my innocence and my honor during my life and in future ages. As to my fortune and my life, I have dedicated both, long since, to His service. He will do therewith what pleases Him for His glory and my salvation." Thus his suspicions were not even excited by the ominous face of Gérard, when he first presented himself at the dining-room door. The Prince laughed off his wife's prophetic apprehension at the sight of his murderer, and was as cheerful as usual to the last.

He possessed, too, that which to the heathen philosopher seemed the greatest good—the sound mind in the sound body. His physical frame was after death found so perfect that a long life might have been in store for him, notwithstanding all which he had endured. The desperate illness of 1574, the frightful gunshot wound inflicted by Jaureguy in 1582, had left no traces.

The physicians pronounced that his body presented an aspect of perfect health.

His temperament was cheerful. At table, the pleasures of which, in moderation, were his only relaxation, he was always animated and merry, and this jocoseness was partly natural, partly intentional. In the darkest hours of his country's trial, he affected a serenity which he was far from feeling, so that his apparent gaiety at momentous epochs was even censured by dullards, who could not comprehend its philosophy, nor applaud the flippancy of William the Silent.

He went through life bearing the load of a people's sorrows upon his shoulders with a smiling face. Their name was the last word upon his lips, save the simple affirmative, with which the soldier who had been battling for the right all his lifetime commended his soul in dying "to his great Captain, Christ." The people were grateful and affectionate, for they trusted the character of their "Father William," and not all the clouds which calumny could collect ever dimmed to their eyes the radiance of that lofty mind to which they were accustomed, in their darkest calamities, to look for light. As long as he lived, he was the guiding-star of a whole brave nation, and when he died the little children cried in the streets.[1]

[1] *The Rise of the Dutch Republic*, III, 614–627.

[EUROPE IN 1584]

[In the *History of the United Netherlands* Motley broadened
decidedly the scope of his narrative. While the course of events
in the Netherlands continued to be the center of interest he
devoted more attention to what took place in the other countries
of Western Europe. In the following passages he characterized
the situation in that region immediately after the assassination
of William of Orange.]

Yet such was the condition of Europe at that day. A small,
dull, elderly, imperfectly educated, patient, plodding invalid,
with white hair and protruding under-jaw and dreary visage,
was sitting day after day, seldom speaking, never smiling,
seven or eight hours out of every twenty-four, at a writing
table covered with heaps of interminable despatches, in a cabinet far away beyond the seas and mountains, in the very heart
of Spain. A clerk or two, noiselessly opening and shutting
the door from time to time, fetching fresh bundles of letters
and taking away others—all written and composed by secretaries or high functionaries—and all to be scrawled over in the
margin by the diligent old man in a big schoolboy's hand and
style—if ever schoolboy, even in the sixteenth century, could
write so illegibly or express himself so awkwardly; couriers in
the courtyard arriving from or departing for the uttermost
parts of earth—Asia, Africa, America, Europe—to fetch and
carry these interminable epistles which contained the irresponsible commands of this one individual, and were freighted
with the doom and destiny of countless millions of the world's
inhabitants—such was the system of government against which
the Netherlands had protested and revolted. It was a system
under which their fields had been made desolate, their cities
burned and pillaged, their men hanged, burned, drowned, or

hacked to pieces, their women subjected to every outrage; and
to put an end to which they had been devoting their treasure
and their blood for nearly the length of one generation. It
was a system, too, which, among other results, had just brought
about the death of the foremost statesman of Europe, and had
nearly effected simultaneously the murder of the most eminent
sovereign in the world. The industrious Philip, safe and
tranquil in the depths of the Escorial, saying his prayers three
times a day with exemplary regularity, had just sent three bullets
through the body of William the Silent at his dining-room
door in Delft. "Had it only been done two years earlier," observed the patient old man, "much trouble might have been
spared me; but 'tis better late than never." [1]

Invisible as the Grand Lama of Thibet, clothed with power
as extensive and absolute as had ever been wielded by the most
imperial Caesar, Philip the Prudent, as he grew older and
feebler in mind and body, seemed to become more gluttonous
of work, more ambitious to extend his scepter over lands which
he had never seen or dreamed of seeing, more fixed in his determination to annihilate that monster Protestantism, which
it had been the business of his life to combat, more eager to put
to death every human creature, whether anointed monarch or
humble artisan, that defended heresy or opposed his progress
to universal empire.

If this enormous power, this fabulous labor, had been
wielded or performed with a beneficent intention; if the man
who seriously regarded himself as the owner of a third of the
globe, with the inhabitants thereof, had attempted to deal with
these extensive estates inherited from his ancestors with the
honest intention of a thrifty landlord, an intelligent slave-
owner, it would have yet been possible for a little longer to
smile at the delusion, and endure the practice.

But there was another old man, who lived in another palace
in another remote land, who, in his capacity of representative
of Saint Peter, claimed to dispose of all the kingdoms of the

[1] *History of the United Netherlands* (New York, 1860–1867), I, 2–3.

earth—and had been willing to bestow them upon the man who would go down and worship him. Philip stood enfeoffed, by divine decree, of all America, the East Indies, the whole Spanish Peninsula, the better portion of Italy, the seventeen Netherlands, and many other possessions far and near; and he contemplated annexing to this extensive property the kingdoms of France, of England and Ireland. The Holy League, maintained by the sword of Guise, the pope's ban, Spanish ducats, Italian condottieri, and German mercenaries, was to exterminate heresy and establish the Spanish dominion in France. The same machinery, aided by the pistol or poniard of the assassin, was to substitute for English Protestantism and England's queen the Roman Catholic religion and a foreign sovereign. "The Holy League," said Duplessis-Mornay, one of the noblest characters of the age, "has destined us all to the same sacrifice. The ambition of the Spaniard, which has overleaped so many lands and seas, thinks nothing inaccessible."

The Netherland revolt had therefore assumed world-wide proportions. Had it been merely the rebellion of provinces against a sovereign, the importance of the struggle would have been more local and temporary. But the period was one in which the geographical landmarks of countries were almost removed. The dividing-line ran through every state, city, and almost every family. There was a country which believed in the absolute power of the church to dictate the relations between man and his Maker, and to utterly exterminate all who disputed that position. There was another country which protested against that doctrine, and claimed, theoretically or practically, a liberty of conscience. The territory of these countries was mapped out by no visible lines, but the inhabitants of each, whether resident in France, Germany, England, or Flanders, recognized a relationship which took its root in deeper differences than those of race or language. It was not entirely a question of doctrine or dogma. A large portion of the world had become tired of the antiquated delusion of a papal supremacy over every land, and had recorded its determination, once for all, to have done with it. The transition to freedom of conscience became a necessary step, sooner or later to be taken. To establish the principle of toleration for all religions was an inevitable consequence of the Dutch revolt; although thus far, perhaps only one conspicuous man in advance of his age had boldly announced that doctrine and had died in its defense. But a great true thought never dies—though long buried in the earth—and the day was to come, after long years, when the seed was to ripen into a harvest of civil and religious emancipation, and when the very word toleration was to sound like an insult and an absurdity.

A vast responsibility rested upon the head of a monarch, placed as Philip II found himself, at this great dividing point in modern history. To judge him, or any man in such a position, simply from his own point of view, is weak and illogical. History judges the man according to its point of view. It condemns or applauds the point of view, itself. The point of view of a malefactor is not to excuse robbery and murder. Nor is the spirit of the age to be pleaded in defense of the evildoer at a time when mortals were divided into almost equal troops. The age of Philip II was also the age of William of Orange and his four brethren, of Sainte-Aldegonde, of Olden-Barneveldt, of Duplessis-Mornay, La Noue, Coligny, of Luther, Melanchthon, and Calvin, Walsingham, Sidney, Raleigh, Queen Elizabeth, of Michel Montaigne, and William Shakespeare. It was not an age of blindness, but of glorious light. If the man whom the Maker of the Universe had permitted to be born to such boundless functions, chose to put out his own eyes that he might grope along his great pathway of duty in perpetual darkness, by his deeds he must be judged. The King perhaps firmly believed that the heretics of the Netherlands, of France, or of England, could escape eternal perdition only by being extirpated from the earth by fire and sword, and therefore, perhaps, felt it his duty to devote his life to their extermination. But he believed, still more firmly, that his own political authority, throughout his dominions, and his road to almost universal empire, lay over the bodies of those heretics. Three centuries have nearly passed since this memorable epoch; and the world knows the fate of the states which accepted the dogma which it was Philip's lifework to enforce, and of those who protested against the system. The Spanish and Italian Peninsulas have had a different history from that which records the career of France, Prussia, the Dutch Commonwealth, the British Empire, the Transatlantic Republic.

Yet the contest between those seven meager provinces upon the sandbanks of the North Sea, and the great Spanish Empire, seemed at the moment with which we are now occupied a sufficiently desperate one. Throw a glance upon the map of Europe. Look at the broad magnificent Spanish Peninsula, stretching across eight degrees of latitude and ten of longitude, commanding the Atlantic and the Mediterranean, with a genial climate, warmed in winter by the vast furnace of Africa, and protected from the scorching heats of summer by shady mountain and forest, and temperate breezes from either ocean. A generous southern territory, flowing with wine and oil, and all the richest gifts of a bountiful nature—splendid cities—the new and daily expanding Madrid, rich in the trophies of the most artistic period of the modern world—Cadiz, as populous at that day as London, seated by the straits where the ancient and modern systems of traffic were blending like the mingling of the two oceans—Granada, the ancient wealthy seat of the fallen Moors—Toledo, Valladolid, and Lisbon, chief city of the recently conquered kingdom of Portugal, counting, with its suburbs, a larger population than any city, excepting Paris, in Europe, the mother of distant colonies, and the capital of the rapidly developing traffic with both the Indies—these were some of the treasure of Spain herself. But she possessed Sicily also, the better portion of Italy, and important dependencies in Africa, while the famous maritime discoveries of the age had all inured to her aggrandizement. The world seemed suddenly to have expanded its wings from east to west, only to bear the fortunate Spanish Empire to the most dizzy heights of wealth and power. The most accomplished generals, the most disciplined and daring infantry the world has ever known, the best-equipped and most extensive navy, royal and mercantile, of the age, were at the absolute command of the sovereign. Such was Spain.

Turn now to the northwestern corner of Europe. A morsel of territory, attached by a slight sand-hook to the continent, and half-submerged by the stormy waters of the German Ocean—this was Holland. A rude climate, with long, dark, rigorous winters, and brief summers, a territory, the mere wash of three great rivers, which had fertilized happier portions of Europe only to desolate and overwhelm this less-favored land, a soil so ungrateful, that if the whole of its four hundred thousand acres of arable land had been sowed with grain, it could not feed the laborers alone, and a population largely estimated at one million of souls—these were the characteristics of the province which already had begun to give its name to the new commonwealth. The isles of Zeeland—entangled in the coils of deep slow-moving rivers, or combating the ocean without—and the ancient episcopate of Utrecht, formed the only other provinces that had quite shaken off the foreign yoke. In Friesland, the important city of Groningen was still held for the King, while Bois-le-Duc, Zutphen, besides other places in Gelderland and North Brabant, also in possession of the royalists, made the position of those provinces precarious.

The limit of the Spanish or "obedient" provinces, on the one hand, and of the United Provinces on the other, cannot, therefore, be briefly and distinctly stated. The memorable treason—or, as it was called, the "reconciliation" of the Walloon provinces in the year 1583–84—had placed the provinces of Hainault, Artois, Douai, with the flourishing cities, Arras, Valenciennes, Lille, Tournay, and others—all Celtic Flanders, in short—in the grasp of Spain. Cambray was still held by the French governor, Seigneur de Balagny, who had taken advantage of the Duke of Anjou's treachery to the States, to establish himself in an unrecognized but practical petty sovereignty, in defiance both of France and Spain; while East Flanders and South Brabant still remained a disputed territory, and the immediate field of contest. With these limitations, it may be assumed, for general purposes, that the territory of the United States was that of the modern Kingdom of the Netherlands, while the obedient provinces occupied what is now the territory of Belgium.

Such, then, were the combatants in the great Eighty Years' War for civil and religious liberty; sixteen of which had now passed away. On the one side, one of the most powerful and populous world-empires of history, then in the zenith of its prosperity; on the other hand, a slender group of cities, governed by merchants and artisans, and planted precariously upon a meager, unstable soil. A million and a half souls against the autocrat of a third part of the known world. The contest seemed as desperate as the cause was certainly sacred; but it had ceased to be a local contest. For the history which is to occupy us in these volumes is not exclusively the history of Holland. It is the story of the great combat between despotism, sacerdotal and regal, and the spirit of rational human liberty. The tragedy opened in the Netherlands, and its main scenes were long enacted there; but as the ambition of Spain expanded, and as the resistance to the principle which she represented became more general, other nations were, of necessity, involved in the struggle. There came to be one country, the citizens of which were the Leaguers; and another country, whose inhabitants were Protestants. And in this lay the distinction between freedom and absolutism. The religious question swallowed all the others. There was never a period in the early history of the Dutch revolt when the provinces would not have returned to their obedience, could they have been assured of enjoying liberty of conscience or religious peace; nor was there ever a single moment in Philip II's life in which he wavered in his fixed determination never to listen to such a claim. The quarrel was in its nature irreconcilable and eternal as the warfare between wrong and right; and the establishment of a comparative civil liberty in Europe and America was the result of the religious war of the sixteenth and seventeenth centuries. The struggle lasted eighty years, but the prize was worth the contest.

The object of the war between the Netherlands and Spain

was not, therefore, primarily, a rebellion against established authority for the maintenance of civil rights. To preserve these rights was secondary. The first cause was religion. The provinces had been fighting for years against the Inquisition. Had they not taken arms, the Inquisition would have been established in the Netherlands, and very probably in England, and England might have become in its turn a province of the Spanish Empire.[1]

[FRENCH LEADERS IN 1584]

[After the assassination of their leader, William of Orange, the seven northern provinces of the Netherlands turned to France and England for assistance. In the succeeding pages Motley characterized the most prominent personalities in the French monarchy.]

Henry III, last of the Valois line, was now thirty-three years of age. Less than king, less even than man, he was one of those unfortunate personages who seem as if born to make the idea of royalty ridiculous, and to test the capacity of mankind to eat and drink humiliation as if it were wholesome food. It proved how deeply engraved in men's minds of that century was the necessity of kingship, when the hardy Netherlanders, who had abjured one tyrant, and had been fighting a generation long rather than return to him, were now willing to accept the sovereignty of a thing like Henry of Valois.

He had not been born without natural gifts, such as Heaven rarely denies to prince or peasant; but the courage which he once possessed had been exhausted on the field of Moncontour, his manhood had been left behind him at Venice, and such wit as Heaven had endowed him withal was now expended in darting viperous epigrams at court-ladies whom he was only capable of dishonoring by calumny, and whose charms he burned to outrival in the estimation of his minions. For this monarch of France was not unfrequently pleased to attire himself like a woman and a harlot. With silken flounces, jewelled stomacher,

[1] *History of the United Netherlands* (New York, 1860–1867), I, 3–10.

and painted face, with pearls of great price adorning his bared neck and breast, and satin-slippered feet, of whose delicate shape and size he was justly vain, it was his delight to pass his days and nights in a ceaseless round of gorgeous festivals, tourneys, processions, masquerades, banquets, and balls, the cost of which glittering frivolities caused the popular burden and the popular execration to grow, from day to day, more intolerable and more audible. Surrounded by a gang of "minions," the most debauched and the most desperate of France, whose bedizened dresses exhaled perfumes throughout Paris, and whose sanguinary encounters dyed every street in blood, Henry lived a life of what he called pleasure, careless of what might come after, for he was the last of his race. The fortunes of his minions rose higher and higher, as their crimes rendered them more and more estimable in the eyes of a king who took a woman's pride in the valor of such champions to his weakness, and more odious to a people whose miserable homes were made even more miserable, that the coffers of a few court-favorites might be filled. Now sauntering, full-dressed, in the public promenades, with ghastly little death's-heads strung upon his sumptuous garments, and fragments of human bones dangling among his orders of knighthood—playing at cup and ball as he walked, and followed by a few select courtiers who gravely pursued the same exciting occupation—now presiding like a queen of beauty at a tournament to assign the prize of valor, and now, by the advice of his mother, going about the streets in robes of penitence, telling his beads as he went, that the populace might be edified by his piety, and solemnly offering up prayers in the churches that the blessing of an heir might be vouchsafed to him—Henry of Valois seemed straining every nerve in order to bring himself and his great office into contempt.

As orthodox as he was profligate, he hated the Huguenots, who sought his protection and who could have saved his throne, as cordially as he loved the Jesuits, who passed their lives in secret plottings against his authority and his person, or in fierce denunciations from the Paris pulpits against his manifold crimes. Next to an exquisite and sanguinary fop, he dearly loved a monk. The presence of a friar, he said, exerted as agreeable an effect upon his mind as the most delicate and gentle tickling could produce upon his body; and he was destined to have a fuller dose of that charming presence than he coveted.

His party—for he was but the nominal chief of a faction, *tanquam unus ex nobis*—was the party in possession—the office-holders' party; the spoilsmen, whose purpose was to rob the exchequer and to enrich themselves. His minions—for the favorites were called by no other name—were even more hated, because less despised than the King. Attired in cloth of gold—for silk and satin were grown too coarse a material for them—with their little velvet porringer-caps stuck on the sides of their heads, with their long hair stiff with pomatum, and their heads set inside a well-starched ruff a foot wide, "like St. John's head in a charger," as a splenetic contemporary observed, with a nimbus of musk and violet-powder enveloping them as they passed before vulgar mortals, these rapacious and insolent courtiers were the impersonation of extortion and oppression to the Parisian populace. They were supposed, not unjustly, to pass their lives in dancing, blasphemy, duelling, dicing, and intrigue, in following the King about like hounds, fawning at his feet, and showing their teeth to all besides; and for virtues such as these they were rewarded by the highest offices in church, camp, and state, while new taxes and imposts were invented almost daily to feed their avarice and supply their extravagance. France, doomed to feel the beak and talons of these harpies in its entrails, impoverished by a government that robbed her at home while it humiliated her abroad, struggled vainly in its misery, and was now on the verge of another series of internecine combats—civil war seeming the only alternative to a voluptuous and licentious peace.[1]

Henry with the Scar, Duke of Guise, the well-known chief of the house of Lorraine, was the chief of the extreme papistical party. He was now thirty-four years of age, tall, stately, with

[1] *History of the Netherlands* (New York, 1860–1867), I, 37–39.

a dark, martial face and dangerous eyes, which Antonio Moro loved to paint; a physiognomy made still more expressive by the arquebus-shot which had damaged his left cheek at the fight near Château-Thierry and gained him his name of Balafré. Although one of the most turbulent and restless plotters of that plotting age, he was yet thought more slow and heavy in character than subtle, Teutonic rather than Italian. He was the idol of the Parisian burghers. The grocers, the marketmen, the members of the arquebus and crossbow clubs, all doted on him. The fishwomen worshipped him as a god. He was the defender of the good old religion under which Paris and other cities of France had thriven, the uncompromising opponent of the newfangled doctrines which western clothiers, and dyers, and tapestry-workers, had adopted, and which the nobles of the mountain country, the penniless chevaliers of Béarn and Gascony and Guienne, were ceaselessly taking the field and plunging France into misery and bloodshed to support. But for the Balafré and Madam League—as the great Spanish Catholic conspiracy against the liberties of France, and of England, and of all Europe, was affectionately termed by the Paris populace—honest Catholics would fare no better in France than they did in England, where, as it was well known, they were every day subjected to fearful tortures. The shop-windows were filled with colored engravings, representing, in exaggerated fashion, the sufferings of the English Catholics under bloody Elizabeth, or Jezebel, as she was called; and as the gaping burghers stopped to ponder over these works of art, there were ever present, as if by accident, some persons of superior information who would condescendingly explain the various pictures, pointing out with a long stick the phenomena most worthy of notice. These caricatures proving highly successful, and being suppressed by order of government, they were repeated upon canvas on a larger scale, in still more conspicuous situations, as if in contempt of the royal authority, which sullied itself by compromise with Calvinism. The pulpits, meanwhile, thundered denunciations on the one hand against the weak and wicked King, who worshipped idols, and who sacrificed the dearly-earned pittance of his subjects to feed the insolent pomp of his pampered favorites; and on the other, upon the arch-heretic, the arch-apostate, the Béarnese Huguenot, who, after the death of the reigning monarch, would have the effrontery to claim his throne, and to introduce into France the persecutions and the horrors under which unhappy England was already groaning.

The scarce-concealed instigator of these assaults upon the royal and upon the Huguenot faction was, of course, the Duke of Guise,—the man whose most signal achievement had been the Massacre of St. Bartholomew—all the preliminary details of that transaction having been arranged by his skill. So long as Charles IX was living, the Balafré had created the confusion which was his element, by entertaining and fomenting the perpetual intrigues of Anjou and Alençon against their brother; while the altercations between them and the Queen-Mother and the furious madman who then sat upon the throne, had been the cause of sufficient disorder and calamity for France. On the death of Charles IX Guise had sought the intimacy of Henry of Navarre, that by his means he might frustrate the hopes of Alençon for the succession. During the early period of the Béarnese's residence at the French court the two had been inseparable, living together, going to the same festivals, tournaments, and masquerades, and even sleeping in the same bed. "My master," was ever Guise's address to Henry; "My gossip," the young King of Navarre's reply. But the crafty Béarnese had made use of the intimacy only to read the secrets of the Balafré's heart; and on Navarre's flight from the court, and his return to Huguenotism, Guise knew that he had been played upon by a subtler spirit than his own. The simulated affection was now changed into undisguised hatred. Moreover, by the death of Alençon, Navarre now stood next the throne, and Guise's plots became still more extensive and more open as his own ambition to usurp the crown on the death of the childless Henry III became more fervid.

Thus, by artfully inflaming the populace of Paris, and—through his organized bands of confederates—that of all the large towns of France, against the Huguenots and their chief, by appeals to the religious sentiment; and at the same time by stimulating the disgust and indignation of the taxpayers everywhere at the imposts and heavy burdens which the boundless extravagance of the court engendered, Guise paved the way for the advancement of the great League which he represented. The other two political divisions were ingeniously represented as mere insolent factions, while his own was the true national and patriotic party, by which alone the ancient religion and the cherished institutions of France could be preserved.

And the great chief of this national patriotic party was not Henry of Guise, but the industrious old man who sat writing despatches in the depths of the Escorial. Spanish counsels, Spanish promises, Spanish ducats—these were the real machinery by which the plots of Guise against the peace of France and of Europe were supported. Madam League was simply Philip II. Nothing was written, officially or unofficially, to the French government by the Spanish court that was not at the same time communicated to "Mucio"—as the Duke of Guise was denominated in the secret correspondence of Philip, —and Mucio was in Philip's pay, his confidential agent, spy, and confederate, long before the actual existence of the League was generally suspected.

The Queen-Mother, Catharine de' Medici, played into the Duke's hands. Throughout the whole period of her widowhood, having been accustomed to govern her sons, she had, in a certain sense, been used to govern the kingdom. By sowing dissensions among her own children, by inflaming party against party, by watching with care the oscillations of France—so that none of the great divisions should obtain preponderance—by alternately caressing and massacring the Huguenots, by cajoling or confronting Philip, by keeping, as she boasted, a spy in every family that possessed the annual income of two thousand livres, by making herself the head of an organized system of harlotry, by which the soldiers and politicians of France were inveigled, their secrets faithfully revealed to her by her well-disciplined maids of honor, by surrounding her unfortunate sons with temptation from earliest youth, and plunging them by cold calculation into deepest debauchery, that their enervated faculties might be ever forced to rely in political affairs on the maternal counsel, and to abandon the administration to the maternal will: such were the arts by which Catharine had maintained her influence, and a great country had been governed for a generation—Machiavellian statecraft blended with the more simple wiles of a procuress.

Now that Alençon was dead, and Henry III hopeless of issue, it was her determination that the children of her daughter, the Duchess of Lorraine, should succeed to the throne. The matter was discussed as if the throne were already vacant, and Guise and the Queen-Mother, if they agreed in nothing else, were both cordial in their detestation of Henry of Navarre. The Duke affected to support the schemes in favor of his relatives, the Princes of Lorraine, while he secretly informed the Spanish court that this policy was only a pretense. He was not likely, he said, to advance the interests of the younger branch of a house of which he was himself the chief, nor were their backs equal to the burden. It was necessary to amuse the old queen, but he was profoundly of opinion that the only sovereign for France, upon the death of Henry, was Philip II himself. This was the Duke's plan of arriving, by means of Spanish assistance, at the throne of France; and such was Henry of Balafré, chief of the League.

And the other Henry, the Huguenot, the Béarnese, Henry of Bourbon, Henry of Navarre, the chieftain of the Gascon chivalry, the king errant, the hope and the darling of the oppressed Protestants in every land—of him it is scarce needful to say a single word. At his very name a figure seems to leap forth from the mist of three centuries, instinct with ruddy vigorous life. Such was the intense vitality of the Béarnese prince, that even now he seems more thoroughly alive and recognizable than half the actual personages who are fretting their hour upon the stage.

We see, at once, a man of moderate stature, light, sinewy, and strong; a face browned with continual exposure; small, mirthful, yet commanding blue eyes, glittering from beneath an arching brow, and prominent cheekbones; a long hawk's nose, almost resting upon a salient chin, a pendant moustache, and a thick, brown, curly beard, prematurely grizzled; we see the mien of frank authority and magnificent good humor, we hear the ready sallies of the shrewd Gascon mother-wit, we feel the electricity which flashes out of him, and sets all hearts around him on fire, when the trumpet sounds to battle. The headlong desperate charge, the snow-white plume waving where the fire is hottest, the large capacity for enjoyment of the man, rioting without affectation in the *certaminis gaudia*, the insane gallop, after the combat, to lay its trophies at the feet of the Cynthia of the minute, and thus to forfeit its fruits; all are as familiar to us as if the seven distinct wars, the hundred pitched battles, the two hundred sieges, in which the Béarnese was personally present, had been occurrences of our own day.

He at least was both king and man, if the monarch who occupied the throne was neither. He was the man to prove, too, for the instruction of the patient letter-writer of the Escorial, that the crown of France was to be won with foot in stirrup and carbine in hand, rather than to be caught by the weaving and casting of the most intricate nets of diplomatic intrigue, though thoroughly weighted with Mexican gold.

The King of Navarre was now thirty-one years old; for the three Henrys were nearly of the same age. The first indications of his existence had been recognized amid the cannon and trumpets of a camp in Picardy, and his mother had sung a gay Béarnese song as he was coming into the world at Pau. "Thus," said his grandfather, Henry of Navarre, "thou shalt not bear to us a morose and sulky child." The good king, without a kingdom, taking the child, as soon as born, in the lapel of his dressing-gown, had brushed his infant lips with a clove of garlic, and moistened them with a drop of generous Gascon wine. "Thus," said the grandfather again, "shall the boy be both merry and bold." There was something mythologically prophetic in the incidents of his birth.[1]

[1] *History of the United Netherlands* (New York, 1860–1867), I, 41–46.

The same sensible grandfather, having different views on the subject of education from those manifested by Catharine de' Medici towards her children, had the boy taught to run about bareheaded and barefooted, like a peasant, among the mountains and rocks of Béarn, till he became as rugged as a young bear, and as nimble as a kid. Black bread, and beef, and garlic, were his simple fare; and he was taught by his mother and his grandfather to hate lies and liars, and to read the Bible.

When he was fifteen, the third religious war broke out. Both his father and grandfather were dead. His mother, who had openly professed the reformed faith, since the death of her husband, who hated it, brought her boy to the camp at Rochelle, where he was received as the chief of the Huguenots. His culture was not extensive. He had learned to speak the truth, to ride, to shoot, to do with little sleep and less food. He could also construe a little Latin, and had read a few military treatises; but the mighty hours of an eventful life were now to take him by the hand, and to teach him much good and much evil, as they bore him onward.[1]

A silken web of palace-politics, palace-diplomacy, palace-revolutions, enveloped him. Schemes and counter-schemes, stratagems and conspiracies, assassinations and poisonings; all the state-machinery which worked so exquisitely in fair ladies' chambers, to spread havoc and desolation over a kingdom, were displayed before his eyes. Now campaigning with one royal brother against Huguenots, now fighting with another on their side, now solicited by the Queen-Mother to attempt the life of her son, now implored by Henry III to assassinate his brother, the Béarnese, as fresh antagonisms, affinities, combinations, were developed, detected, neutralized almost daily, became rapidly an adept in Medicean state-chemistry. Charles IX in his grave, Henry III on the throne, Alençon in the Huguenot camp—Henry at last made his escape. The brief war and peace of Monsieur succeeded, and the King of Navarre formally

[1] *History of the United Netherlands* (New York, 1860–1867), I, 46–47.

abjured the Catholic creed. The parties were now sharply
defined. Guise mounted upon the League, Henry astride upon
the Reformation, were prepared to do battle to the death.[1]

And thus he stood the chieftain of that great austere party of
Huguenots, the men who went on their knees before the battle,
beating their breasts with their iron gauntlets, and singing in
full chorus a psalm of David, before smiting the Philistines hip
and thigh.

Their chieftain—scarcely their representative—fit to lead his
Puritans on the battlefield, was hardly a model for them elsewhere. Yet, though profligate in one respect, he was temperate
in every other. In food, wine, and sleep, he was always
moderate. Subtle and crafty in self-defense, he retained something of his old love of truth, of his hatred for liars. Hardly
generous perhaps, he was a friend of justice, while economy
in a wandering King like himself was a necessary virtue, of
which France one day was to feel the beneficent action. Reckless and headlong in appearance, he was in truth the most careful
of men. On the religious question most cautious of all, he
always left the door open behind him, disclaimed all bigotry
of opinion, and earnestly implored the Papists to seek, not his
destruction, but his instruction. Yet prudent as he was by
nature in every other regard, he was all his life the slave of one
woman or another, and it was by his good luck rather than by
sagacity that he did not repeatedly forfeit the fruits of his
courage and conduct, in obedience to his master-passion.

Always open to conviction on the subject of his faith, he re-
pudiated the appellation of heretic. A creed, he said, was not
to be changed like a shirt, but only on due deliberation, and
under special advice. In his secret heart he probably regarded
the two religions as his chargers, and was ready to mount
alternately the one or the other, as each seemed the more likely
to bear him safely in the battle. The Béarnese was no Puritan,
but he was most true to himself and to his own advancement.
His highest principle of action was to reach his goal, and to that

[1] *Ibid.,* I, 47–48.

principle he was ever loyal. Feeling, too, that it was the interest of France that he should succeed, he was even inspired—compared with others on the stage—by an almost lofty patriotism.

Amiable by nature and by habit, he had preserved the most unimpaired good-humor throughout the horrible years which succeeded St. Bartholomew, during which he carried his life in his hand, and learned not to wear his heart upon his sleeve. Without gratitude, without resentment, without fear, without remorse; entirely arbitrary, yet with capacity to use all men's judgments; without convictions, save in regard to his dynastic interests, he possessed all the qualities necessary to success. He knew how to use his enemies. He knew how to use his friends, to abuse them, and to throw them away. He refused to assassinate Francis Alençon at the bidding of Henry III, but he attempted to procure the murder of the truest of his own friends, one of the noblest characters of the age—whose breast showed twelve scars received in his service—Agrippa D'Aubigné, because the honest soldier had refused to become his pimp—a service the King had implored upon his knees.

Beneath the mask of perpetual careless good-humor, lurked the keenest eye, a subtle, restless, widely combining brain, and an iron will. Native sagacity had been tempered into consummate elasticity by the fiery atmosphere in which feebler natures had been dissolved. His wit was as flashing and as quickly unsheathed as his sword. Desperate, apparently reckless temerity on the battlefield was deliberately indulged in, that the world might be brought to recognize a hero and chieftain in a king. The do-nothings of the Merovingian line had been succeeded by the Pepins; to the effete Carlovingians had come a Capet; to the impotent Valois should come a worthier descendant of St. Louis. This was shrewd Gascon calculation, aided by constitutional fearlessness. When despatch-writing, invisible Philips, star-gazing Rudolphs, and petticoated Henrys sat upon the thrones of Europe, it was wholesome to show the world that there was a king left who could move about in the bustle and business of the age, and could charge as well as most soldiers at the head of his cavalry; that there was one more sovereign fit to reign over men, besides the glorious Virgin who governed England.

Thus courageous, crafty, far-seeing, consistent, untiring, imperturbable, he was born to command, and had a right to reign. He had need of the throne, and the throne had still more need of him.[1]

[THE APPEAL TO FRANCE AND ENGLAND]

[The reasons for the appeal of the seven northern provinces of the Netherlands to France and England are thus summarized.]

It was obvious to the Netherlanders that France, although torn by faction, was a great and powerful realm. There had now been with the brief exception of the lovers' war in 1580, a religious peace of eight years' duration. The Huguenots had enjoyed tranquil exercise of their worship during that period, and they expressed perfect confidence in the good faith of the King. That the cities were inordinately taxed to supply the luxury of the court could hardly be unknown to the Netherlanders. Nevertheless they knew that the kingdom was the richest and most populous of Christendom, after that of Spain. Its capital, already called by contemporaries the "compendium of the world," was described by travellers as "stupendous in extent and miraculous for its numbers." It was even said to contain eight hundred thousand souls, and although its actual population did not probably exceed three hundred and twenty thousand, yet this was more than double the number of London's inhabitants, and thrice as many as Antwerp could then boast, now that a great proportion of its foreign denizens had been scared away. Paris was at least by one hundred thousand more populous than any city of Europe, except perhaps the remote and barbarous Moscow, while the secondary cities of France, Rouen in the north, Lyons in the center, and Marseilles in the south, almost equalled in size, business, wealth, and numbers, the capitals of other countries. In the whole kingdom

[1] *History of the United Netherlands* (New York, 1860–1867), I, 50–52.

were probably ten or twelve millions of inhabitants, nearly as many as in Spain, without her colonies, and perhaps three times the number that dwelt in England.

In a military point of view, too, the alliance of France was most valuable to the contiguous Netherlands. A few regiments of French troops, under the command of one of their experienced marshals, could block up the Spaniards in the Walloon Provinces, effectually stop their operations against Ghent, Antwerp, and the other great cities of Flanders and Brabant, and, with the combined action of the United Provinces on the north, so surround and cripple the forces of Parma, as to reduce the power of Philip, after a few vigorous and well-concerted blows, to an absolute nullity in the Low Countries. As this result was of as vital importance to the real interests of France and of Europe, whether Protestant or Catholic, as it was to the Provinces, and as the French government had privately manifested a strong desire to oppose the progress of Spain towards universal empire, it was not surprising that the States-General, not feeling capable of standing alone, should make their application to France. This they had done with the knowledge and concurrence of the English government. What lay upon the surface the Netherland statesmen saw and pondered well. What lurked beneath, they surmised as shrewdly as they could, but it was impossible, with plummet and fathom-line ever in hand, to sound the way with perfect accuracy, where the quicksands were ever shifting, and the depth or shallowness of the course perpetually varying. It was not easy to discover the intentions of a government which did not know its own intentions, and whose changing policy was controlled by so many hidden currents.

Moreover, as already indicated, the envoys and those whom they represented had not the same means of arriving at a result as are granted to us. Thanks to the liberality of many modern governments of Europe, the archives where the state secrets of the buried centuries have so long moldered are now open to the student of history. To him who has patience and industry many mysteries are thus revealed, which no political sagacity or critical acumen could have divined. He leans over the shoulder of Philip the Second at his writing-table, as the King spells patiently out, with cipher-key in hand, the most concealed hieroglyphics of Parma or Guise or Mendoza. He reads the secret thought of "Fabius," as that cunctative Roman scrawls his marginal apostilles on each despatch; he pries into all the stratagems of Camillus, Hortensius, Mucius, Julius, Tullius, and the rest of those ancient heroes who lent their names to the diplomatic masqueraders of the 16th century; he enters the cabinet of the deeply-pondering Burghley, and takes from the most private drawer the memoranda which record that minister's unutterable doubtings; he pulls from the dressing-gown folds of the stealthy, softly-gliding Walsingham the last secret which he has picked from the Emperor's pigeonholes, or the Pope's pocket, and which, not Hatton, nor Buckhurst, nor Leicester, nor the Lord Treasurer, is to see—nobody but Elizabeth herself; he sits invisible at the most secret councils of the Nassaus and Barneveldt and Buys, or pores with Farnese over coming victories and vast schemes of universal conquest; he reads the latest bit of scandal, the minutest characteristic of king or minister, chronicled by the gossiping Venetians for the edification of the Forty; and, after all this prying and eavesdropping, having seen the cross-purposes, the bribings, the windings, the fencings in the dark, he is not surprised if those who were systematically deceived did not always arrive at correct conclusions.[1]

[THE NETHERLANDS IN 1584]

[France, however, was wary about annexing the seven northern provinces of the Netherlands and finally refused the offer of the Dutch envoys. At this point, consequently, Motley stopped the course of his narrative in order to describe the situation in the Netherlands.]

The Netherlands, by the death of Orange, had been left without a head. On the other hand, the Spanish party had never been so fortunate in their chief at any period since the destiny

[1] *History of the United Netherlands* (New York, 1860–1867), I, 52–55.

of the two nations had been blended with each other. Alexander Farnese, Prince of Parma, was a general and a politician, whose character had been steadily ripening since he came into the command of the country. He was now thirty-seven years of age—with the experience of a sexagenarian. No longer the impetuous, arbitrary, hot-headed youth, whose intelligence and courage hardly atoned for his insolent manner and stormy career, he had become pensive, modest, almost gentle. His genius was rapid in conception, patient in combination, fertile in expedients, adamantine in the endurance of suffering; for never did a heroic general and a noble army of veterans manifest more military virtue in the support of an infamous cause than did Parma and his handful of Italians and Spaniards. That which they considered to be their duty they performed. The work before them they did with all their might.

Alexander had vanquished the rebellion in the Celtic provinces, by the masterly diplomacy and liberal bribery which have been related in a former work. Artois, Hainault, Douay, Orchies, with the rich cities of Lille, Tournay, Valenciennes, Arras, and other important places, were now the property of Philip. These unhappy and misguided lands, however, were already reaping the reward of their treason. Beggared, trampled upon, plundered, despised, they were at once the prey of the Spaniards, and the cause that their sister-states, which still held out, were placed in more desperate condition than ever. They were also, even in their abject plight, made still more forlorn by the forays of Balagny, who continued in command of Cambray. Catharine de' Medici claimed that city as her property, by will of the Duke of Anjou. A strange title—founded upon the treason and cowardice of her favorite son—but one which, for a time, was made good by the possession maintained by Balagny. That usurper meantime, with a shrewd eye to his own interests, pronounced the truce of Cambray, which was soon afterwards arranged, from year to year, by permission of Philip, as a "most excellent milch-cow"; and he continued to fill his pails at the expense of the "reconciled" provinces, till they were thoroughly exhausted.

This large southwestern section of the Netherlands being thus permanently re-annexed to the Spanish crown, while Holland, Zeeland, and the other provinces, already constituting the new Dutch Republic, were more obstinate in their hatred of Philip than ever, there remained the rich and fertile territory of Flanders and Brabant as the great debatable land. Here were the royal and political capital, Brussels, the commercial capital, Antwerp, with Mechlin, Dendermonde, Vilvorde, and other places of inferior importance, all to be struggled for to the death. With the subjection of this district, the last bulwark between the new commonwealth and the old empire would be overthrown, and Spain and Holland would then meet face to face.

If there had ever been a time when every nerve in Protestant Christendom should be strained to weld all those provinces together into one great commonwealth, as a bulwark for European liberty, rather than to allow them to be broken into stepping stones, over which absolutism could stride across France and Holland into England, that moment had arrived. Every sacrifice should have been cheerfully made by all Netherlanders, the uttermost possible subsidies and auxiliaries should have been furnished by all the friends of civil and religious liberty in every land to save Flanders and Brabant from their impending fate.[1]

Alexander rose with the difficulty and responsibility of his situation. His vivid, almost poetic intellect formed its schemes with perfect distinctness. Every episode in his great and, as he himself termed it, his "heroic enterprise," was traced out beforehand with the tranquil vision of creative genius; and he was prepared to convert his conceptions into reality, with the aid of an iron nature that never knew fatigue or fear.

But the obstacles were many. Alexander's master sat in his cabinet with his head full of Mucio, Don Antonio, and Queen Elizabeth; while Alexander himself was left neglected, almost

[1] *History of the United Netherlands* (New York, 1860–1867), I, 135–137.

forgotten. His army was shrinking to a nullity. The demands upon him were enormous, his finances delusive, almost exhausted. To drain an ocean dry he had nothing but a sieve. What was his position? He could bring into the field perhaps eight or ten thousand men over and above the necessary garrisons. He had before him Brussels, Antwerp, Mechlin, Ghent, Dendermonde, and other powerful places, which he was to subjugate. Here was a problem not easy of solution. Given an army of eight thousand, more or less, to reduce therewith in the least possible time, half-a-dozen cities, each containing fifteen or twenty thousand men able to bear arms. To besiege these places in form was obviously a mere chimera. Assault, battery, and surprises—these were all out of the question.

Yet Alexander was never more truly heroic than in this position of vast entanglement. Untiring, uncomplaining, thoughtful of others, prodigal of himself, generous, modest, brave; with so much intellect and so much devotion to what he considered his duty, he deserved to be a patriot and a champion of the right, rather than an instrument of despotism.

And thus he paused for a moment—with much work already accomplished, but his hardest life-task before him; still in the noon of manhood, a fine martial figure, standing, spear in hand, full in the sunlight, though all the scene around him was wrapped in gloom—a noble, commanding shape, entitled to the admiration which the energetic display of great powers, however unscrupulous, must always command. A dark, meridional physiognomy; a quick, alert, imposing head; jet-black, close-clipped hair; a bold eagle's face, with full, bright, restless eye; a man rarely reposing, always ready, never alarmed; living in the saddle, with harness on his back—such was the Prince of Parma, matured and mellowed, but still unharmed by time.[1]

[JOHN OF OLDEN–BARNEVELD]

[Upon the assassination of William of Orange, John of Olden-Barneveld assumed the leading role in the conduct of

[1] *History of the United Netherlands* (New York, 1860–1867), I, 137–138.

the political and diplomatic affairs of the Dutch provinces. Motley, accordingly, sketched a portrait of him at the time he took up this difficult task.]

He was now in his thirty-eighth year, having been born at Amersfoort on the 14th of September, 1547. He bore an imposing name, for the Olden-Barnevelds of Gelderland were a race of unquestionable and antique nobility. His enemies, however, questioned his right to the descent which he claimed. They did not dispute that the great-grandfather, Claas van Olden-Barneveld, was of distinguished lineage and allied to many illustrious houses, but they denied that Claas was really the great-grandfather of John. John's father, Gerritt, they said, was a nameless outcast, a felon, a murderer, who had escaped the punishment due to his crimes, but had dragged out a miserable existence in the downs, burrowing like a rabbit in the sand. They had also much to say in disparagement of all John's connections. Not only was his father a murderer, but his wife, whom he had married for money, was the child of a most horrible incest, his sisters were prostitutes, his sons and brothers were debauchees and drunkards, and, in short, never had a distinguished man a more uncomfortable and discreditable family-circle than that which surrounded Barneveld, if the report of his enemies was to be believed. Yet it is agreeable to reflect that, with all the venom which they had such power of secreting, these malignant tongues had been unable to destroy the reputation of the man himself. John's character was honorable and upright, his intellectual power not disputed even by those who at a later period hated him the most bitterly. He had been a profound and indefatigable student from his earliest youth. He had read law at Leyden, in France, at Heidelberg. Here, in the headquarters of German Calvinism, his youthful mind had long pondered the dread themes of foreknowledge, judgment absolute, free will, and predestination. To believe it worth the while of a rational and intelligent Deity to create annually several millions of thinking beings, who were to struggle for a brief period on earth, and to consume in perpetual brimstone afterwards, while others were predestined to endless enjoyment, seemed to him an indifferent exchange for a faith in the purgatory and paradise of Rome. Perplexed in the extreme, the youthful John bethought himself of an inscription over the gateway of his famous but questionable great-grandfather's house at Amersfoort—*Nil scire tutissima fides*. He resolved thenceforth to adopt a system of ignorance upon matters beyond the flaming walls of the world; to do the work before him manfully and faithfully while he walked the earth, and to trust that a benevolent Creator would devote neither him nor any other man to eternal hell-fire. For this most offensive doctrine he was howled at by the strictly pious, while he earned still deeper opprobrium by daring to advocate religious toleration. In face of the endless horrors inflicted by the Spanish Inquisition upon his native land, he had the hardihood—although a determined Protestant himself—to claim for Roman Catholics the right to exercise their religion in the free states on equal terms with those of the reformed faith. "Any one," said his enemies, "could smell what that meant who had not a wooden nose." In brief, he was a liberal Christian, both in theory and practice, and he nobly confronted in consequence the wrath of bigots on both sides. At a later period the most zealous Calvinists called him Pope John, and the opinions to which he was to owe such appellations had already been formed in his mind.

After completing his very thorough legal studies, he had practiced as an advocate in Holland and Zeeland. An early defender of civil and religious freedom, he had been brought at an early day into contact with William the Silent, who recognized his ability. He had borne a snaphance on his shoulder as a volunteer in the memorable attempt to relieve Haarlem, and was one of the few survivors of that bloody night. He had stood outside the walls of Leyden in company of the Prince of Orange when that magnificent destruction of the dykes had taken place by which the city had been saved from the fate impending over it. At a still more recent period we have seen him landing from the gunboats upon the Kowenstyn, on the fatal 26th May. These military adventures were, however, but brief and accidental episodes in his career, which was that of a statesman and diplomatist. As pensionary of Rotterdam, he was constantly a member of the General Assembly, and had already begun to guide the policy of the new commonwealth. His experience was considerable, and he was now in the high noon of his vigor and his usefulness.

He was a man of noble and imposing presence, with thick hair pushed from a broad forehead rising dome-like above a square and massive face; a strong, deeply-colored physiognomy, with shaggy brow, a chill blue eye, not winning but commanding, high cheekbones, a solid, somewhat scornful nose, a firm mouth and chin, enveloped in a copious brown beard; the whole head not unfitly framed in the stiff formal ruff of the period; and the tall stately figure well draped in magisterial robes of velvet and sable—such was John of Olden-Barneveld.[1]

[ROBERT DUDLEY, EARL OF LEICESTER]

[Rebuffed by the French the Dutch leaders turned to the English government. While they found Queen Elizabeth reluctant to take part openly in the conflict against Spain, she did allow her favorite, Leicester, to go with a small body of troops to the aid of the Dutch people. Motley stopped his narrative, in consequence, to give a full-length pen portrait of this courtier.]

Robert Dudley, Earl of Leicester, was then fifty-four years of age. There are few personages in English history whose adventures, real or fictitious, have been made more familiar to the world than his have been, or whose individuality has been presented in more picturesque fashion, by chronicle, tragedy, or romance. Born in the same day of the month and hour of the day with the Queen, but two years before her birth, the supposed synastry of their destinies might partly account, in that age of astrological superstition, for the influence which he perpetually exerted. They had, moreover, been fellow-prison-

[1] *History of the United Netherlands* (New York, 1860–1867), I, 314–317.

ers together, in the commencement of the reign of Mary, and it is possible that he may have been the medium through which the indulgent expressions of Philip II were conveyed to the Princess Elizabeth.

His grandfather, John Dudley, that "caterpillar of the commonwealth," who lost his head in the first year of Henry VIII as a reward for the "grist which he brought to the mill" of Henry VII; his father, the mighty Duke of Northumberland, who rose out of the wreck of an obscure and ruined family to almost regal power, only to perish, like his predecessor, upon the scaffold, had bequeathed him nothing save rapacity, ambition, and the genius to succeed. But Elizabeth seemed to ascend the throne only to bestow gifts upon her favorite. Baronies and earldoms, stars and garters, manors and monopolies, castles and forests, church livings and college chancellorships, advowsons and sinecures, emoluments and dignities, the most copious and the most exalted, were conferred upon him in breathless succession. Wine, oil, currants, velvets, ecclesiastical benefices, university headships, licenses to preach, to teach, to ride, to sail, to pick and to steal, all brought "grist to his mill." His grandfather, "the horse leach and shearer," never filled his coffers more rapidly than did Lord Robert, the fortunate courtier. Of his early wedlock with the ill-starred Amy Robsart, of his nuptial projects with the Queen, of his subsequent marriages and mock-marriages with Douglas Sheffield and Lettice of Essex, of his plottings, poisonings, imaginary or otherwise, of his countless intrigues, amatory and political—of that luxuriant, creeping, flaunting, all-pervading existence which struck its fibers into the mold, and coiled itself through the whole fabric, of Elizabeth's life and reign—of all this the world has long known too much to render a repetition needful here. The inmost nature and the secret deeds of a man placed so high by wealth and station can be seen but darkly through the glass of contemporary record. There was no tribunal to sit upon his guilt. A grandee could be judged only when no longer a favorite, and the infatuation of Elizabeth for Leicester terminated only with his life. He stood now upon the soul of the

Netherlands in the character of a "Messiah," yet he had been charged with crimes sufficient to send twenty humbler malefactors to the gibbet. "I think," said a most malignant arraigner of the man, in a published pamphlet, "that the Earl of Leicester hath more blood lying upon his head at this day, crying for vengeance, than ever had private man before, were he never so wicked."

Certainly the mass of misdemeanors and infamies hurled at the head of the favorite by that "green-coated Jesuit," Father Parsons, under the title of "Leycester's Commonwealth," were never accepted as literal verities; yet the value of the precept to calumniate boldly, with the certainty that much of the calumny would last forever, was never better illustrated than in the case of Robert Dudley. Besides the lesser delinquencies of filling his purse by the sale of honors and dignities, by violent ejectments from land, fraudulent titles, rapacious enclosures of commons, by taking bribes for matters of justice, grace, and supplication to the royal authority, he was accused of forging various letters to the Queen, often to ruin his political adversaries, and of plottings to entrap them into conspiracies, playing first the comrade and then the informer. The list of his murders and attempts to murder was almost endless. "His lordship hath a special fortune," saith the Jesuit, "that when he desireth any woman's favor, whatsoever person standeth in his way hath the luck to die quickly." He was said to have poisoned Alice Drayton, Lady Lennox, Lord Sussex, Sir Nicholas Throgmorton, Lord Sheffield, whose widow he married and then poisoned, Lord Essex, whose widow he also married, and intended to poison, but who was said to have subsequently poisoned him—besides murders or schemes for murder of various other individuals, both French and English. "He was a rare artist in poison," said Sir Robert Naunton, and certainly not Caesar Borgia, nor his father or sister, was more accomplished in that difficult profession than was Dudley, if half the charges against him could be believed. Fortunately for his fame, many of them were proved to be false. Sir Henry Sidney, lord deputy of Ireland, at the time of the death of Lord

Essex, having caused a diligent inquiry to be made into that dark affair, wrote to the council that it was usual for the Earl to fall into a bloody flux when disturbed in his mind, and that his body when opened showed no signs of poison. It is true that Sir Henry, although an honorable man, was Leicester's brother-in-law, and that perhaps an autopsy was not conducted at that day in Ireland on very scientific principles.

His participation in the strange death of his first wife was a matter of current belief among his contemporaries. "He is infamed by the death of his wife," said Burghley, and the tale has since become so interwoven with classic and legendary fiction, as well as with more authentic history, that the phantom of the murdered Amy Robsart is sure to arise at every mention of the Earl's name. Yet a coroner's inquest—as appears from his own secret correspondence with his relative and agent at Cumnor—was immediately and persistently demanded by Dudley. A jury was impanelled—every man of them a stranger to him, and some of them enemies. Antony Forster, Appleyard, and Arthur Robsart, brother-in-law and brother of the lady, were present, according to Dudley's special request; "and if more of her friends could have been sent," said he, "I would have sent them"; but with all their minuteness of inquiry, "they could find," wrote Blount, "no presumptions of evil," although he expressed a suspicion that "some of the jurymen were sorry that they could not." That the unfortunate lady was killed by a fall downstairs was all that could be made of it by a coroner's inquest, rather hostile than otherwise, and urged to rigorous investigation by the supposed culprit himself. Nevertheless, the calumny has endured for three centuries, and is likely to survive as many more.

Whatever crimes Dudley may have committed in the course of his career, there is no doubt whatever that he was the most abused man in Europe. He had been deeply wounded by the Jesuit's artful publication, in which all the misdeeds with which he was falsely or justly charged were drawn up in awful array, in a form half colloquial, half judicial. "You had better give some contentment to my Lord Leicester," wrote the French envoy from London to his government, "on account of the bitter feelings excited in him by these villainous books lately written against him."

The Earl himself ascribed these calumnies to the Jesuits, to the Guise faction, and particularly to the Queen of Scots. He was said, in consequence, to have vowed an eternal hatred to that most unfortunate and most intriguing Princess. "Leicester has lately told a friend," wrote Charles Paget, "that he will persecute you to the uttermost, for that he supposeth your Majesty to be privy to the setting forth of the book against him." Nevertheless, calumniated or innocent, he was at least triumphant over calumny. Nothing could shake his hold upon Elizabeth's affections. The Queen scorned but resented the malignant attacks upon the reputation of her favorite. She declared "before God and in her conscience, that she knew the libels against him to be most scandalous, and such as none but an incarnate devil himself could dream to be true." His power, founded not upon genius nor virtue, but upon woman's caprice, shone serenely above the gulf where there had been so many shipwrecks. "I am now passing into another world," said Sussex, upon his deathbed, to his friends, "and I must leave you to your fortunes; but beware of the Gipsy, or he will be too hard for you. You know not the beast so well as I do."

The "Gipsy," as he had been called from his dark complexion, had been renowned in youth for the beauty of his person, being "tall and singularly well-featured, of a sweet aspect, but high-foreheaded, which was of no discommendation," according to Naunton. The Queen, who had the passion of her father for tall and proper men, was easier won by externals, from her youth even to the days of her dotage, than befitted so very sagacious a personage. Chamberlains, squires of the body, carvers, cup-bearers, gentlemen-ushers, porters, could obtain neither place nor favor at court, unless distinguished for stature, strength, or extraordinary activity. To lose a tooth had been known to cause the loss of a place, and the excellent constitution of leg which helped Sir Christopher Hatton into the chancellorship, was no more remarkable perhaps than the success of similar endowments in other contemporaries. Leicester, although stately and imposing, had passed his summer solstice. A big, bulky man, with a long red face, a bald head, a defiant, somewhat sinister eye, a high nose, and a little torrent of foam-white curly beard, he was still magnificent in costume. Rustling in satin and feathers, with jewels in his ears, and his velvet toque stuck as airily as ever upon the side of his head, he amazed the honest Hollanders, who had been used to less gorgeous chieftains. "Everybody is wondering at the great magnificence and splendor of his clothes," said the plain chronicler of Utrecht. For, not much more than a year before, Fulke Greville had met at Delft a man whose external adornments were simpler; a somewhat slip-shod personage, whom he thus portrayed:—"His uppermost garment was a gown," said the euphuistic Fulke, "yet such as, I confidently affirm, a mean-born student of our Inns of Court would not have been well disposed to walk the streets in. Unbuttoned his doublet was, and of like precious matter and form to the other. His waistcoat, which showed itself under it, not unlike the best sort of those woollen knit ones which our ordinary barge-watermen row us in. His company about him, the burgesses of that beer-brewing town. *No external sign of degree could have discovered the inequality of his worth or estate from that multitude.* Nevertheless, upon conversing with him, there *was an outward passage of inward greatness.*" [1]

[ENGLAND AND THE UNITED NETHERLANDS]

[The following passage gives in a striking way Motley's interpretation of the role of England and the United Netherlands in history.]

Those two statesmen, for eloquence, learning, readiness, administrative faculty, surpassed by few who have ever wielded the destinies of free commonwealths, were fully equal to the task thrown upon their hands by the progress of events. That

[1] *History of the United Netherlands* (New York, 1860–1867), I, 366–371.

task was no slight one, for it was to the leading statesmen of Holland and England, sustained by the indomitable resistance to despotism almost universal in the English and Dutch nations, that the liberty of Europe was entrusted at that momentous epoch. Whether united under one crown, as the Netherlands ardently desired, or closely allied for aggression and defense, the two peoples were bound indissolubly together. The clouds were rolling up from the fatal south, blacker and more portentous than ever; the artificial equilibrium of forces, by which the fate of France was kept in suspense, was obviously growing every day more uncertain; but the prolonged and awful interval before the tempest should burst over the lands of freedom and Protestantism, gave at least time for the prudent to prepare. The Armada was growing every day in the ports of Spain and Portugal, and Walsingham doubted, as little as did Buys or Barneveld, toward what shores that invasion was to be directed. England was to be conquered in order that the rebellious Netherlands might be reduced; and "Mucio" was to be let slip upon the unhappy Henry III so soon as it was thought probable that the Béarnese and the Valois had sufficiently exhausted each other. Philip was to reign in Paris, Amsterdam, London, and Edinburgh, without stirring from the Escorial. An excellent programme, had there not been some English gentlemen, some subtle secretaries of state, some Devonshire skippers, some Dutch advocates and merchants, some Zeeland flyboatsmen, and six million men, women, and children, on the two sides of the North Sea, who had the power of expressing their thoughts rather bluntly than otherwise in different dialects of old Anglo-Saxon speech.

Certainly it would be unjust and ungracious to disparage the heroism of the great Queen when the hour of danger really came, nor would it be legitimate for us, who can scan that momentous year of expectation, 1587, by the light of subsequent events and of secret contemporaneous record, to censure or even sharply to criticize the royal hankering for peace, when peace had really become impossible. But as we shall have occasion to examine rather closely the secrets of the Spanish,

French, English, and Dutch councils, during this epoch, we are likely to find, perhaps, that at least as great a debt is due to the English and Dutch people, in mass, for the preservation of European liberty at that disastrous epoch as to any sovereign, general, or statesman.

For it was in the great waters of the sixteenth century that the nations whose eyes were open, discovered the fountain of perpetual youth, while others, who were blind, passed rapidly onward to decrepitude. England was, in many respects, a despotism so far as regarded governmental forms; and no doubt the Catholics were treated with greater rigor than could be justified even by the perpetual and most dangerous machinations of the seminary priests and their instigators against the throne and life of Elizabeth. The word "liberty" was never musical in Tudor ears, yet Englishmen had blunt tongues and sharp weapons which rarely rusted for want of use. In the presence of a parliament, and the absence of a standing army, a people accustomed to read the Bible in the vernacular, to handle great questions of religion and government freely, and to bear arms at will, was most formidable to despotism. There was an advance on the olden time. A Francis Drake, a John Hawkins, a Roger Williams, might have been sold, under the Plantagenets, like an ox or an ass. A "female villain" in the reign of Henry III could have been purchased for eighteen shillings—hardly the price of a fatted pig, and not one-third the value of an ambling palfrey—and a male villain, such an one as could in Elizabeth's reign circumnavigate the globe in his own ship, or take imperial field-marshals by the beard, was worth but two or three pounds sterling in the market. Here was progress in three centuries, for the villains were now become admirals and generals in England and Holland, and constituted the main stay of these two little commonwealths, while the commanders who governed the "invincible" fleets and armies of omnipotent Spain, were all cousins of emperors, or grandees of bluest blood. Perhaps the system of the Reformation would not prove the least effective in the impending crisis.

It was most important, then, that these two nations should

be united in counsel, and should stand shoulder to shoulder as their great enemy advanced. But this was precisely what had been rendered almost impossible by the course of events during Leicester's year of administration, and by his sudden but not final retirement at its close. The two great national parties which had gradually been forming, had remained in a fluid state during the presence of the governor-general. During his absence they gradually hardened into the forms which they were destined to retain for centuries. In the history of civil liberty, these incessant contests, these oral and written disquisitions, these sharp concussions of opinion, and the still harder blows, which, unfortunately, were dealt on a few occasions by the combatants upon each other, make the year 1587 a memorable one. The great questions of the origin of government, the balance of dynastic forces, the distribution of powers, were dealt with by the ablest heads, both Dutch and English, that could be employed in the service of the kingdom and republic. It was a war of protocols, arguments, orations, rejoinders, apostilles, and pamphlets, very wholesome for the cause of free institutions and the intellectual progress of mankind. The reader may perhaps be surprised to see with how much vigor and boldness the grave questions which underlie all polity, were handled so many years before the days of Russell and Sidney, of Montesquieu and Locke, Franklin, Jefferson, Rousseau, and Voltaire; and he may be even more astonished to find exceedingly democratic doctrines propounded, if not believed in, by trained statesmen of the Elizabethan school. He will be also apt to wonder that a more fitting time could not be found for such philosophical debate than the epoch at which both the kingdom and the republic were called upon to strain every sinew against the most formidable and aggressive despotism that the world had known since the fall of the Roman Empire.[1]

[1] *History of the United Netherlands* (New York, 1860–1867), II, 112–115.

[THE TEN SOUTHERN PROVINCES]

[In the opinion of Motley the ten southern provinces of the
Netherlands made a fatal choice when they became reconciled to
Philip II. In a few pages he set forth the results of that decision
by contrasting conditions in the obedient and the rebellious
provinces.]

The condition of the Republic and of the Spanish Provinces
was, at that moment, most signally contrasted. If the effects of
despotism and of liberty could ever be exhibited at a single
glance, it was certainly only necessary to look for a moment at
the picture of the obedient and of the rebel Netherlands.

Since the fall of Antwerp, the desolation of Brabant, Flanders,
and of the Walloon territories had become complete. The
King had recovered the great commercial capital, but its commerce was gone. The Scheldt, which, till recently, had been
the chief mercantile river in the world, had become as barren
as if its fountains had suddenly dried up. It was as if it no
longer flowed to the ocean, for its mouth was controlled by
Flushing. Thus Antwerp was imprisoned and paralyzed. Its
docks and basins, where 2500 ships had once been counted,
were empty, grass was growing in its streets, its industrious
population had vanished, and the Jesuits had returned in swarms.
And the same spectacle was presented by Ghent, Bruges, Valenciennes, Tournay, and those other fair cities, which had once
been types of vigorous industry and tumultuous life. The
seacoast was in the hands of two rising commercial powers,
the great and free commonwealths of the future. Those powers
were acting in concert, and commanding the traffic of the world,
while the obedient provinces were excluded from all foreign
intercourse and all markets, as the result of their obedience.
Commerce, manufactures, agriculture, were dying lingering
deaths. The thrifty farms, orchards, and gardens, which had
been a proverb and wonder of industry, were becoming wildernesses. The demand for their produce by the opulent and
thriving cities, which had been the workshops of the world,
was gone. Foraging bands of Spanish and Italian mercenaries

had succeeded to the famous tramp of the artisans and mechanics, which had often been likened to an army, but these new customers were less profitable to the gardeners and farmers. The clothiers, the fullers, the tapestry-workers, the weavers, the cutlers, had all wandered away, and the cities of Holland, Friesland, and of England, were growing skilful and rich by the lessons and the industry of the exiles to whom they afforded a home. There were villages and small towns in the Spanish Netherlands that had been literally depopulated. Large districts of country had gone to waste, and cane-brakes and squalid morasses usurped the place of yellow harvest-fields. The fox, the wild boar, and the wolf infested the abandoned homes of the peasantry; children could not walk in safety in the neighborhood even of the larger cities; wolves littered their young in the deserted farmhouses; two hundred persons, in the winter of 1586–87, were devoured by wild beasts in the outskirts of Ghent. Such of the remaining laborers and artisans as had not been converted into soldiers, found their most profitable employment as brigands, so that the portion of the population spared by war and emigration was assisting the enemy in preying upon their native country. Brandschätzung, burglary, highway robbery, and murder, had become the chief branches of industry among the working classes. Nobles and wealthy burghers had been changed to paupers and mendicants. Many a family of ancient lineage, and once of large possessions, could be seen begging their bread, at the dusk of evening, in the streets of great cities, where they had once exercised luxurious hospitality; and they often begged in vain.

For while such was the forlorn aspect of the country—and the portrait, faithfully sketched from many contemporary pictures, has not been exaggerated in any of its dark details—a great famine smote the land with its additional scourge. The whole population, soldiers and brigands, Spaniards and Flemings, beggars and workmen, were in danger of perishing together. Where the want of employment had been so great as to cause a rapid depopulation, where the demand for labor had almost entirely ceased, it was a necessary result, that during the process, prices should be low, even in the presence of foreign soldiery, and despite the inflamed profits, which such capitalists as remained required, by way not only of profit but insurance, in such troublous times. Accordingly, for the last year or two, the price of rye at Antwerp and Brussels had been one florin for the veertel (three bushels) of one hundred and twenty pounds; that of wheat, about one-third of a florin more. Five pounds of rye, therefore, were worth one penny sterling, reckoning, as was then usual, two shillings to the florin. A pound weight of wheat was worth about one farthing. Yet this was forty-one years after the discovery of the mines of Potosí (A.D. 1545), and full sixteen years after the epoch, from which is dated that rapid fall in the value of silver, which in the course of seventy years caused the average price of corn and of all other commodities to be tripled or even quadrupled. At that very moment the average cost of wheat in England was sixty-four shillings the quarter, or about seven and sixpence sterling the bushel, and in the markets of Holland, which in truth regulated all others, the same prices prevailed. A bushel of wheat in England was equal therefore to eight bushels in Brussels. . . .

On the other hand, the prosperity of the Republic was rapidly increasing. Notwithstanding the war, which had been raging for a terrible quarter of a century without any interruption, population was increasing, property rapidly advancing in value, labor in active demand. Famine was impossible to a state which commanded the ocean. No corn grew in Holland and Zeeland, but their ports were the granary of the world. The fisheries were a mine of wealth almost equal to the famous Potosí, with which the commercial world was then ringing. Their commerce with the Baltic nations was enormous. In one month eight hundred vessels left their havens for the eastern ports alone. There was also no doubt whatever—and the circumstance was a source of constant complaint and of frequent ineffective legislation—that the rebellious provinces were driving a most profitable trade with Spain and the Spanish possessions, in spite of their revolutionary war. The mines of Peru and Mexico were as fertile for the Hollanders and Zeelanders as for the Spaniards themselves. The war paid for the war; one hundred large frigates were constantly cruising along the coasts to protect the fast-growing traffic, and an army of twenty thousand foot-soldiers and two thousand cavalry were maintained on land. There were more ships and sailors at that moment in Holland and Zeeland than in the whole kingdom of England.

While the seaports were thus rapidly increasing in importance, the towns in the interior were advancing as steadily. The woolen manufacture, the tapestry, the embroideries of Gelderland, and Friesland, and Overyssel, were becoming as famous as had been those of Tournay, Ypres, Brussels, and Valenciennes. The emigration from the obedient provinces and from other countries was very great. It was difficult to obtain lodgings in the principal cities; new houses, new streets, new towns, were rising every day. The single Province of Holland furnished regularly, for war expenses alone, two millions of florins (two hundred thousand pounds) a year, besides frequent extraordinary grants for the same purpose, yet the burden imposed upon the vigorous young commonwealth seemed only to make it the more elastic. "The coming generations may see," says a contemporary historian, "the fortifications erected at the epoch in the cities, the costly and magnificent havens, the docks, the great extension of the cities; for truly *the war had become a great benediction to the inhabitants.*" [1]

[RECALL OF LEICESTER]

[The administration of Leicester in the Netherlands was marked by lack of support from England and quarrels with the Estates-General and the Dutch leaders. In a few pages Motley describes the recall of Leicester and results of his rule.]

It had now become quite obvious that the game of Leicester was played out. His career—as it has now been fully exhibited

[1] *History of the United Netherlands* (New York, 1860–1867), II, 128–134.

—could have but one termination. He had made himself thoroughly odious to the nation whom he came to govern. He had lost for ever the authority once spontaneously bestowed, and he had attempted in vain, both by fair means and foul, to recover that power. There was nothing left him but retreat. Of this he was thoroughly convinced. He was anxious to be gone, the Republic most desirous to be rid of him, her Majesty impatient to have her favorite back again. The indulgent Queen, seeing nothing to blame in his conduct, while her indignation at the attitude maintained by the provinces was boundless, permitted him, accordingly, to return; and in her letter to the States, announcing this decision, she took a fresh opportunity of emptying her wrath upon their heads.

She told them that, notwithstanding her frequent messages to them, signifying her evil contentment with their unthankfulness for her exceeding great benefits, and with their gross violations of their contract with herself and with Leicester, whom they had, of their own accord, made absolute governor without her instigation, she had never received any good answer to move her to commit their sins to oblivion, nor had she remarked any amendment in their conduct. On the contrary, she complained that they daily increased their offenses most notoriously in the sight of the world, and in so many points that she lacked words to express them in one letter. She however thought it worth while to allude to some of their transgressions. She declared that their sinister or rather barbarous interpretation of her conduct had been notorious in perverting and falsifying her princely and Christian intentions, when she imparted to them the overtures that had been made to her for a treaty of peace for herself and for them with the King of Spain. Yet although she had required their allowance, before she would give her assent, she had been grieved that the world should see what impudent untruths had been forged upon her, not only by their sufferance, but by their special permission, for her Christian good meaning towards them. She denounced the statements as to her having concluded a treaty, not only without their knowledge, but with the sacrifice of their liberty and religion, as utterly false, either for anything done in act, or intended in thought, by her. She complained that upon this most false ground had been heaped a number of like untruths and malicious slanders against her cousin Leicester, who had hazarded his life, spent his substance, left his native country, absented himself from her, and lost his time, only for their service. It had been falsely stated among them, she said, that the Earl had come over the last time, knowing that peace had been secretly concluded. It was false that he had intended to surprise divers of their towns, and deliver them to the King of Spain. All such untruths contained matter so improbable, that it was most strange that any person, having any sense, could imagine them correct. Having thus slightly animadverted upon their wilfulness, unthankfulness, and bad government, and having, in very plain English, given them the lie, eight distinct and separate times upon a single page, she proceeded to inform them that she had recalled her cousin Leicester, having great cause to use his services in England, and not seeing how, by his tarrying there, he could either profit them or herself. Nevertheless she protested herself not void of compassion for their estate, and for the pitiful condition of the great multitude of kind and godly people, subject to the miseries which, by the States' government, were like to fall upon them, unless God should specially interpose; and she had therefore determined, for the time, to continue her subsidies, according to the covenant between them. If, meantime, she should conclude a peace with Spain, she promised to them the same care for their country as for her own.

Accordingly the Earl, after despatching an equally ill-tempered letter to the States, in which he alluded, at unmerciful length, to all the old grievances, blamed them for the loss of Sluys, for which place he protested that they had manifested no more interest than if it had been San Domingo in Hispaniola, took his departure for Flushing. After remaining there, in a very moody frame of mind, for several days, expecting that the States would, at least, send a committee to wait upon him and receive his farewells, he took leave of them by letter. "God send me shortly a wind to blow me from them all," he exclaimed —a prayer which was soon granted—and before the end of the year he was safely landed in England. "These legs of mine," said he, clapping his hands upon them as he sat in his chamber at Margate, "shall never go again into Holland. Let the States get others to serve their mercenary turn, for me they shall not have." Upon giving up the government, he caused a medal to be struck in his own honor. The device was a flock of sheep watched by an English mastiff. Two mottoes—"*Non gregem sed ingratos*," and "*Invitus desero*"—expressed his opinion of Dutch ingratitude and his own fidelity. The Hollanders, on their part, struck several medals to commemorate the same event, some of which were not destitute of invention. Upon one of them, for instance, was represented an ape smothering her young ones to death in her embrace, with the device, "*Libertas ne ita chara ut simiae catuli*"; while upon the reverse was a man avoiding smoke and falling into the fire, with the inscription, "*Fugiens fumum, incidit in ignem.*"

Leicester found the usual sunshine at Greenwich. All the efforts of Norris, Wilkes, and Buckhurst, had been insufficient to raise even a doubt in Elizabeth's mind as to the wisdom and integrity by which his administration of the provinces had been characterized from beginning to end. Those who had appealed from his hatred to the justice of their sovereign, had met with disgrace and chastisement. But for the great Earl the Queen's favor was a rock of adamant. At a private interview he threw himself at her feet, and with tears and sobs implored her not to receive him in disgrace whom she had sent forth in honor. His blandishments prevailed, as they had always done. Instead, therefore, of appearing before the council, kneeling, to answer such inquiries as ought surely to have been instituted, he took his seat boldly among his colleagues, replying haughtily to all murmurs by a reference to her Majesty's secret instructions.

The unhappy English soldiers, who had gone forth under his banner in midsummer, had been returning, as they best might, in winter, starving, half-naked wretches, to beg a morsel of bread at the gates of Greenwich palace, and to be driven away as vagabonds, with threats of the stocks. This was not the fault of the Earl, for he had fed them with his own generous hand in the Netherlands, week after week, when no money for their necessities could be obtained from the paymasters. Two thousand pounds had been sent by Elizabeth to her soldiers when sixty-four thousand pounds of arrearage were due, and no language could exaggerate the misery to which these outcasts, according to eyewitnesses of their own nation, were reduced.

Lord Willoughby was appointed to the command of what remained of these unfortunate troops, upon the Earl's departure. The sovereignty of the Netherlands remained undisputed with the States. Leicester resigned his commission by an instrument dated 17 December, which, however, never reached the Netherlands till April of the following year. From that time forth the government of the Republic maintained the same forms which the assembly had claimed for it in the long controversy with the governor-general, and which have been sufficiently described.[1]

[PHILIP II]

[In a few paragraphs Motley gives one of the most striking of his numerous portraits of Philip II.]

It is now time to look in upon the elderly letter-writer in the Escorial, and see how he was playing his part in the drama.

His counsellors were very few. His chief advisers were rather like private secretaries than cabinet ministers; for Philip had been withdrawing more and more into seclusion and mystery as the webwork of his schemes multiplied and widened. He liked to do his work, assisted by a very few confidential servants. The Prince of Eboli, the famous Ruy Gomez, was dead. So was Cardinal Granvelle. So were Erasso and Delgado. His midnight council (*junta de noche*) for thus, from its original hour of assembling, and the air of secrecy in which it was enwrapped, it was habitually called—was a triumvirate. Don Juan de Idiaquez was chief secretary of state and of war;

[1] *History of the United Netherlands* (New York, 1860–1867), II, 342–346.

the Count de Chinchon was minister for the household, for Italian affairs, and for the kingdom of Aragon; Don Cristoval de Moura, the monarch's chief favorite, was at the head of the finance department, and administered the affairs of Portugal and Castile.

The president of the council of Italy, after Granvelle's death, was Quiroga, Cardinal of Toledo and inquisitor-general. Enormously long letters, in the King's name, were prepared chiefly by the two secretaries, Idiaquez and Moura. In their hands was the vast correspondence with Mendoza and Parma, and Olivarez at Rome, and with Mucio, in which all the stratagems for the subjugation of Protestant Europe were slowly and artistically contrived. Of the great conspiracy against human liberty, of which the Pope and Philip were the double head, this midnight triumvirate was the chief executive committee.

These innumerable despatches, signed by Philip, were not the emanations of his own mind. The King had a fixed purpose to subdue Protestantism and to conquer the world; but the plans for carrying the purpose into effect were developed by subtler and more comprehensive minds than his own. It was enough for him to ponder wearily over schemes which he was supposed to dictate, and to give himself the appearance of supervising what he scarcely comprehended. And his work of supervision was often confined to pettiest details. The handwriting of Spain and Italy at that day was beautiful, and in our modern eyes seems neither antiquated nor ungraceful. But Philip's scrawl was like that of a clown just admitted to a writing-school, and the whole margin of a fairly penned despatch, perhaps fifty pages long, laid before him for comment and signature by Idiaquez or Moura, would be sometimes covered with a few awkward sentences, which it was almost impossible to read, and which, when deciphered, were apt to reveal suggestions of astounding triviality.

Thus a most important despatch—in which the King, with his own hand, was supposed to be conveying secret intelligence to Mendoza concerning the Armada, together with minute directions for the regulation of Guise's conduct at the memorable epoch of the barricades—contained but a single comment from the monarch's own pen. "The Armada has been in Lisbon about a month—*quassi un mes*"—wrote the secretary. "There is but one *s* in *quasi*," said Philip.

Again, a despatch of Mendoza to the King contained the intelligence that Queen Elizabeth was, at the date of the letter, residing at St. James's. Philip, who had no objection to display his knowledge of English affairs—as became the man who had already been almost sovereign of England, and meant to be entirely so—supplied a piece of information in an apostille to this despatch. "St. James is a house of recreation," he said, "which was once a monastery. There is a park between it, and the palace which is called Huytal; but *why it is called Huytal*, I am sure I don't know." His researches in the English language had not enabled him to recognize the adjective and substantive out of which the abstruse compound White-Hall (*Huyt-al*) was formed.

On another occasion, a letter from England containing important intelligence concerning the number of soldiers enrolled in that country to resist the Spanish invasion, the quantity of gunpowder and various munitions collected, with other details of like nature, furnished besides with a bit of information of less vital interest. "In the windows of the Queen's presence-chamber they have discovered a *great quantity of lice*, all clustered together," said the writer.

Such a minute piece of statistics could not escape the microscopic eye of Philip. So, disregarding the soldiers and the gunpowder, he commented *only* on this last-mentioned clause of the letter; and he did it cautiously too, as a King surnamed the Prudent should:—

"But perhaps they were fleas," wrote Philip.[1]

[MAURICE OF NASSAU AND LEWIS WILLIAM]

[After the departure of Leicester from the Netherlands the military leadership in the seven provinces fell into the hands

[1] *History of the United Netherlands* (New York, 1860–1867), II, 458–461.

of the son of William of Orange, Maurice of Nassau, and his cousin, Lewis William. Of these two leaders Motley gives interesting pen pictures in the opening pages of the third volume of the *History of the United Netherlands*.]

At length the twig was becoming the tree—*tandem fit surculus arbor*—according to the device assumed by the son of William the Silent after his father's death.

The Netherlands had sore need of a practical soldier to contend with the scientific and professional tyrants against whom they had so long been struggling, and Maurice, although so young, was pre-eminently a practical man. He was no enthusiast; he was no poet. He was at that period certainly no politician. Not often at the age of twenty has a man devoted himself for years to pure mathematics for the purpose of saving his country. Yet this was Maurice's scheme. Four years long and more, when most other youths in his position and at that epoch would have been alternating between frivolous pleasures and brilliant exploits in the field, the young prince had spent laborious days and nights with the learned Simon Stevinus of Bruges. The scientific work which they composed in common, the credit of which the master assigned to the pupil, might have been more justly attributed perhaps to the professor than to the prince, but it is certain that Maurice was an apt scholar.

In that country, ever held in existence by main human force against the elements, the arts of engineering, hydrostatics, and kindred branches were of necessity much cultivated. It was reserved for the young mathematician to make them as potent against a human foe.

Moreover, there were symptoms that the military discipline, learning, and practical skill, which had almost made Spain the mistress of the world, were sinking into decay. Farnese, although still in the prime of life, was broken in health, and there seemed no one fit to take the place of himself and his lieutenants when they should be removed from the scene where they had played their parts so consummately. The army of the Netherlands was still to be created. Thus far the contest had been mainly carried on by domestic militia and foreign volunteers or hirelings. The trainbands of the cities were aided in their struggles against Spanish pikemen and artillerists, Italian and Albanian cavalry, by the German riders, whom every little potentate was anxious to sell to either combatant according to the highest bid, and by English mercenaries, whom the love of adventure or the hope of plunder sent forth under such well-seasoned captains as Williams and Morgan, Vere and the Norrises, Baskerville and Willoughby.

But a Dutch army there was none and Maurice had determined that at last a national force should be created. In this enterprise he was aided and guided by his cousin Lewis William, Stadholder of Friesland—the quaint, rugged little hero, young in years but almost a veteran in the wars of freedom, who was as genial and intellectual in council as he was reckless and impulsive in the field.

Lewis William had felt that the old military art was dying out and that there was nothing to take its place. He was a diligent student of antiquity. He had revived in the swamps of Friesland the old maneuvers, the quickness of wheeling, the strengthening, without breaking ranks or columns, by which the ancient Romans had performed so much excellent work in their day, and which seemed to have passed entirely into oblivion. Old colonels and rittmasters, who had never heard of Leo the Thracian nor the Macedonian phalanx, smiled and shrugged their shoulders as they listened to the questions of the young count, or gazed with profound astonishment at the eccentric evolutions to which he was accustoming his troops. From the heights of superior wisdom they looked down with pity upon these innovations on the good old battle order. They were accustomed to great solid squares of troops wheeling in one way, steadily, deliberately, all together, by one impulse and as one man. It was true that in narrow fields, and when the enemy was pressing, such stately evolutions often became impossible or ensured defeat; but when the little stadholder drilled his soldiers in small bodies of various shapes, teaching them to turn, advance, retreat, wheel in a variety of ways, sometimes in considerable masses, sometimes man by man, sending the fore-

most suddenly to the rear, or bringing the hindmost ranks to the
front, and began to attempt all this in narrow fields as well as
in wide ones, and when the enemy was in sight, men stood aghast
at his want of reverence, or laughed at him as a pedant. But
there came a day when they did not laugh, neither friends nor
enemies. Meantime the two cousins, who directed all the
military operations in the provinces, understood each other
thoroughly and proceeded to perfect their new system, to be
adopted at a later period by all civilized nations.

The regular army of the Netherlands was small in number
at that moment—not more than twenty thousand foot with two
thousand horse—but it was well disciplined, well equipped,
and, what was of great importance, regularly paid. Old cam-
paigners complained that in the halcyon days of paper enrol-
ments a captain could earn more out of his company than a
colonel now received for his whole regiment. The days when a
thousand men were paid for, with a couple of hundred in the
field, were passing away for the United Provinces and existed
only for Italians and Spaniards. While, therefore, mutiny on an
organized and extensive scale seemed almost the normal condition of the unpaid legions of Philip, the little army of Maurice
was becoming the model for Europe to imitate.[1]

[CAPTURE OF BREDA]

[The military struggle between Philip II and the seven Dutch
provinces was to a large extent a war of sieges—the investment
and defense of cities. Motley described many of these sieges
at great length. The capture of Breda illustrates his powers of
describing such military actions.]

The fair and pleasant city of Breda lies on the Merk, a slender
stream, navigable for small vessels, which finds its way to the
sea through the great canal of the Dintel. It had been the
property of the Princes of Orange, Barons of Breda, and had
passed with the other possessions of the family to the house of
Châlons-Nassau. Henry of Nassau had, half a century before,

[1] *History of the United Netherlands* (New York, 1860–1867), III, 2–5.

adorned and strengthened it by a splendid palace-fortress which, surrounded by a deep and double moat, thoroughly commanded the town. A garrison of five companies of Italian infantry and one of cavalry lay in this castle, which was under the command of Edward Lanzavecchia, governor both of Breda and of the neighboring Gertruydenberg.

Breda was an important strategical position. It was, moreover, the feudal superior of a large number of adjacent villages as well as of the cities Oosterhout, Steenbergen, and Rosendaal. It was obviously not more desirable for Maurice of Nassau to recover his patrimonial city than it was for the States-General to drive the Spaniards from so important a position.

In the month of February, 1590, Maurice, being then at the castle of Voorn in Zeeland, received a secret visit from a boatman, Adrian van der Berg by name, who lived at the village of Leur, eight or ten miles from Breda, and who had long been in the habit of supplying the castle with turf. In the absence of woods and coal mines, the habitual fuel of the country was furnished by those vast relics of the antediluvian forests which abounded in the still partially submerged soil. The skipper represented that his vessel had passed so often into and out of the castle as to be hardly liable to search by the guard on its entrance. He suggested a stratagem by which it might be possible to surprise the stronghold.

The prince approved of the scheme and immediately consulted with Barneveld. That statesman at once proposed, as a suitable man to carry out the daring venture, Captain Charles de Heraugiere, a nobleman of Cambray, who had been long in the service of the States, had distinguished himself at Sluys and on other occasions, but who had been implicated in Leicester's nefarious plot to gain possession of the city of Leyden a few years before. The Advocate expressed confidence that he would be grateful for so signal an opportunity of retrieving a somewhat damaged reputation. Heraugiere, who was with his company in Voorn at the moment, eagerly signified his desire to attempt the enterprise as soon as the matter was communicated to him; avowing the deepest devotion to the house of William the Silent and perfect willingness to sacrifice his life, if necessary, in its cause and that of the country. Philip Nassau, cousin of Prince Maurice and brother of Lewis William, governor of Gorcum, Dorcum, and Lowenstein Castle, and colonel of a regiment of cavalry, was also taken into the secret, as well as Count Hohenlo, President Van der Myle, and a few others; but a mystery was carefully spread and maintained over the undertaking.

Heraugiere selected sixty-eight men, on whose personal daring and patience he knew that he could rely, from the regiments of Philip Nassau and of Famars, governor of the neighboring city of Heusden, and from his own company. Besides himself, the officers to command the party were captains Logier and Fervet, and lieutenant Matthew Held. The names of such devoted soldiers deserve to be commemorated and are still freshly remembered by their countrymen.

On the 25th of February, Maurice and his staff went to Willemstad on the Isle of Klundert, it having been given out on his departure from the Hague that his destination was Dort. On the same night at about eleven o'clock, by the feeble light of a waning moon, Heraugiere and his band came to the Swertsenburg ferry, as agreed upon, to meet the boatman. They found neither him nor his vessel, and they wandered about half the night, very cold, very indignant, much perplexed. At last, on their way back, they came upon the skipper at the village of Terheyde, who made the extraordinary excuse that he had overslept himself and that he feared the plot had been discovered. It being too late to make any attempt that night, a meeting was arranged for the following evening. No suspicion of treachery occurred to any of the party, although it became obvious that the skipper had grown fainthearted. He did not come on the next night to the appointed place, but he sent two nephews, boatmen like himself, whom he described as daredevils.

On Monday night, the 26th of February, the seventy went on board the vessel, which was apparently filled with blocks of turf, and packed themselves closely in the hold. They moved slowly during a little time on their perilous voyage; for the winter wind, thick with fog and sleet, blew directly down the river, bringing along with it huge blocks of ice and scooping the water out of the dangerous shallows, so as to render the vessel at any moment liable to be stranded. At last the navigation became impossible and they came to a standstill. From Monday night till Thursday morning those seventy Hollanders lay packed like herrings in the hold of their little vessel, suffering from hunger, thirst, and deadly cold; yet not one of them attempted to escape or murmured a wish to abandon the enterprise. Even when the third morning dawned there was no better prospect of proceeding; for the remorseless east wind still blew a gale against them, and the shoals which beset their path had become more dangerous than ever. It was, however, absolutely necessary to recruit exhausted nature, unless the adventurers were to drop powerless on the threshold when they should at last arrive at their destination. In all secrecy they went ashore at a lonely castle called Nordam, where they remained to refresh themselves until about eleven at night, when one of the boatmen came to them with the intelligence that the wind had changed and was now blowing freshly in from the sea. Yet the voyage of a few leagues, on which they were embarked, lasted nearly two whole days longer. On Saturday afternoon they passed through the last sluice, and at about three o'clock the last boom was shut behind them. There was no retreat possible for them now. The seventy were to take the strong castle and city of Breda or to lay down their lives, every man of them. No quarter and short shrift—such was their certain destiny, should that half-crippled, half-frozen little band not succeed in their task before another sunrise.

They were now in the outer harbor and not far from the watergate which led into the inner castle haven. Presently an officer of the guard put off in a skiff and came on board the vessel. He held a little conversation with the two boatmen, observed that the castle was much in want of fuel, took a survey of the turf with which the ship was apparently laden, and then lounged into the little cabin. Here he was only separated by a sliding trapdoor from the interior of the vessel. Those inside could hear and see his every movement. Had there been a single cough or sneeze from within, the true character of the cargo, then making its way into the castle, would have been discovered and every man would within ten minutes have been butchered. But the officer, unsuspecting, soon took his departure, saying that he would send some men to warp the vessel into the castle dock.

Meantime, as the adventurers were making their way slowly towards the watergate, they struck upon a hidden obstruction in the river, and the deeply laden vessel sprang a leak. In a few minutes those inside were sitting up to their knees in water— a circumstance which scarcely improved their already sufficiently dismal condition. The boatmen vigorously plied the pumps to save the vessel from sinking outright; a party of Italian soldiers soon arrived on the shore, and in the course of a couple of hours they had laboriously dragged the concealed Hollanders into the inner harbor and made their vessel fast, close to the guardhouse of the castle.

And now a crowd of all sorts came on board. The winter nights had been long and fearfully cold, and there was almost a dearth of fuel both in town and fortress. A gang of laborers set to work discharging the turf from the vessel with such rapidity that the departing daylight began to shine in upon the prisoners much sooner than they wished. Moreover, the thorough wetting, to which after all their other inconveniences they had just been exposed in their narrow escape from foundering, had set the whole party sneezing and coughing. Never was a catarrh so sudden, so universal, or so ill-timed. Lieutenant Held, unable to control the violence of his cough, drew his dagger and eagerly implored his next neighbor to stab him to the heart, lest his infirmity should lead to the discovery of the whole party. But the calm and wary skipper, who stood on the deck, instantly commanded his companion to work at the pump with as much clatter as possible, assuring the persons present that the hold was nearly full of water. By this means the noise of the coughing was effectually drowned. Most thoroughly did the bold boatman deserve the title of daredevil, bestowed by his more fainthearted uncle. Calmly looking death in the face, he stood there quite at his ease, exchanging jokes with his old acquaintances, chaffering with the eager purchasers of peat, shouting most noisy and superfluous orders to the one man who composed his crew, doing his utmost, in short, to get rid of his customers and to keep enough of the turf on board to conceal the conspirators.

At last, when the case seemed almost desperate, he loudly declared that sufficient had been unladen for that evening and that it was too dark and he too tired for further work. So, giving a handful of stivers among the workmen, he bade them go ashore at once and have some beer, and come next morning for the rest of the cargo. Fortunately, they accepted his hospitable proposition and took their departure. Only the servant of the captain of the guard lingered behind, complaining that the turf was not as good as usual and that his master would never be satisfied with it.

"Ah!" returned the cool skipper, "*the best part of the cargo is underneath. This is expressly reserved for the captain. He is sure to get enough of it tomorrow.*"

Thus admonished, the servant departed and the boatman was left to himself. His companion had gone on shore with secret orders to make the best of his way to Prince Maurice, to inform him of the arrival of the ship within the fortress and of the important fact which they had just learned, that Governor Lanzavecchia, who had heard rumors of some projected enterprise and who suspected that the object aimed at was Gertruydenberg, had suddenly taken his departure for that city, leaving as his lieutenant his nephew Paolo, a raw lad quite incompetent to provide for the safety of Breda.

A little before midnight, Captain Heraugiere made a brief address to his comrades in the vessel, telling them that the hour for carrying out their undertaking had at length arrived. Retreat was impossible, defeat was certain death, only in complete victory lay their own safety and a great advantage for the commonwealth. It was an honor to them to be selected for such an enterprise. To show cowardice now would be an eternal shame for them, and he would be the man to strike dead with his own hand any traitor or poltroon. But if, as he doubted not, every one was prepared to do his duty, their success was assured, and he was himself ready to take the lead in confronting every danger.

He then divided the little band into two companies, one under himself to attack the main guardhouse, the other under Fervet to seize the arsenal of the fortress.

Noiselessly they stole out of the ship where they had so long been confined, and stood at last on the ground within the precincts of the castle. Heraugiere marched straight to the guardhouse.

"Who goes there?" cried a sentinel, hearing some movement in the darkness.

"A friend," replied the captain, seizing him by the throat, and commanding him, if he valued his life, to keep silence except when addressed and then to speak in a whisper.

"How many are there in the garrison?" muttered Heraugiere.

"Three hundred and fifty," whispered the sentinel.

"How many?" eagerly demanded the nearest followers, not hearing the reply.

"He says there are but fifty of them," said Heraugiere, prudently suppressing the three hundred, in order to encourage his comrades.

Quietly as they had made their approach, there was nevertheless a stir in the guardhouse. The captain of the watch sprang into the courtyard.

"Who goes there?" he demanded in his turn.

"A friend," again replied Heraugiere, striking him dead with a single blow as he spoke.

Others emerged with torches. Heraugiere was slightly wounded, but succeeded, after a brief struggle, in killing a second assailant. His followers set upon the watch who retreated into the guardhouse. Heraugiere commanded his men to fire through the doors and windows, and in a few minutes every one of the enemy lay dead.

It was not a moment for making prisoners or speaking of quarter. Meantime Fervet and his band had not been idle. The magazine-house of the castle was seized, its defenders slain. Young Lanzavecchia made a sally from the palace, was wounded and driven back together with a few of his adherents.

The rest of the garrison fled helter-skelter into the town. Never had the musketeers of Italy—for they all belonged to Spinola's famous Sicilian Legion—behaved so badly. They did not even take the precaution to destroy the bridge between the castle and the town as they fled panic-stricken before seventy Hollanders. Instead of encouraging the burghers to their support they spread dismay, as they ran, through every street.

Young Lanzavecchia, penned into a corner of the castle, began to parley; hoping for a rally before a surrender should be necessary. In the midst of the negotiation and a couple of hours before dawn, Hohenlo, duly apprised by the boatman, arrived with the vanguard of Maurice's troops before the field-gate of the fort. A vain attempt was made to force this portal open, but the winter's ice had fixed it fast. Hohenlo was obliged to batter down the palisade near the water-gate and enter by the same road through which the fatal turf-boat had passed.

Soon after he had marched into the town at the head of a strong detachment, Prince Maurice himself arrived in great haste, attended by Philip Nassau, the Admiral Justinus Nassau, Count Solms, Peter van der Does, and Sir Francis Vere, and followed by another body of picked troops; the musicians playing merrily that national air, then as now so dear to Netherlanders—

> "Wilhelmus van Nassouwen
> Ben ick van Duytsem bloed."

The fight was over. Some forty of the garrison had been killed, but not a man of the attacking party. The burgomaster sent a trumpet to the prince asking permission to come to the castle to arrange a capitulation; and before sunrise, the city and fortress of Breda had surrendered to the authority of the States-General and of his Excellency. [1]

[1] *History of the United Netherlands* (New York, 1860–1867), III, 6–14.

[THE NETHERLANDS IN 1590]

[The following pages give one of the most vivid and detailed of the many descriptions of conditions in the Netherlands. It describes the situation about 1590.]

Despite a quarter of a century of what is commonly termed civil war, the United Netherlands were prosperous and full of life. It was in the provinces which had seceded from the Union of Utrecht that there was silence as of the grave, destitution, slavery, abject submission to a foreign foe. The leaders in the movement which had brought about the scission of 1579—commonly called the "Reconciliation"—enjoyed military and civil posts under a foreign tyrant, but were poorly rewarded for subserviency in fighting against their own brethren by contumely on the part of their masters. As for the mass of the people it would be difficult to find a desolation more complete than that recorded of the "obedient" provinces. Even as six years before, wolves littered their whelps in deserted farmhouses, cane-brake and thicket usurped the place of cornfield and orchard, robbers swarmed on the highways once thronged by a most thriving population, nobles begged their bread in the streets of cities whose merchants once entertained emperors and whose wealth and traffic were the wonder of the world, while the Spanish viceroy formally permitted the land in the agricultural districts to be occupied and farmed by the first comer for his own benefit, until the vanished proprietors of the soil should make their reappearance.

"Administered without justice or policy," said a Netherlander who was intensely loyal to the king and a most uncompromising Catholic, "eaten up and abandoned for that purpose to the arbitrary will of foreigners who suck the substance and marrow of the land without benefit to the king, gnaw the obedient cities to the bones, and plunder the open defenseless country at their pleasure, it may be imagined how much satisfaction these provinces take in their condition. Commerce and trade have ceased in a country which traffic alone has peopled, for without it no human habitation could be more miserable and poor than our land."

Nothing could be more gloomy than the evils thus described by the Netherland statesman and soldier, except the remedy which he suggested. The obedient provinces, thus scourged and blasted for their obedience, were not advised to improve their condition by joining hands with their sister states, who had just constituted themselves by their noble resistance to royal and ecclesiastical tyranny into a free and powerful commonwealth. On the contrary, two great sources of regeneration and prosperity were indicated, but very different ones from those in which the Republic had sought and found her strength. In the first place, it was suggested as indispensable that the obedient provinces should have more Jesuits and more Friars. The mendicant orders should be summoned to renewed exertions, and the king should be requested to send seminary priests to every village in numbers proportionate to the population, who should go about from house to house, counting the children, and seeing that they learned their catechism if their parents did not teach them, and, even in case they did, examining whether it was done thoroughly and without deception.

In the second place it was laid down as important that the bishops should confirm no one who had not been sufficiently catechized. "And if the mendicant orders," said Champagny, "are not numerous enough for these catechizations, the Jesuits might charge themselves therewith, not more and not less than the said mendicants, some of each being deputed to each parish. To this end it would be well if his Majesty should obtain from the Pope a command to the Jesuits to this effect, since otherwise they might not be willing to comply. It should also be ordered that all Jesuits, natives of these provinces, should return hither, instead of wandering about in other regions as if their help were not so necessary here."

It was also recommended that the mendicant friars should turn their particular attention to Antwerp, and that one of them should preach in French, another in German, another in English, every day at the opening of the Exchange.

With these appliances it was thought that Antwerp would revive out of its ruins and, despite the blockade of its river, renew its ancient commercial glories. Founded on the substantial rocks of mendicancy and Jesuitism, it might again triumph over its rapidly rising rival, the heretic Amsterdam, which had no better basis for its grandeur than religious and political liberty, and uncontrolled access to the ocean.

Such were the aspirations of a distinguished and loyal Netherlander for the regeneration of his country. Such were his opinions as to the true sources of the wealth and greatness of nations. Can we wonder that the country fell to decay, or that this experienced statesman and brave soldier should himself, after not many years, seek to hide his dishonored head under the cowl of a monk?

The coast of the obedient provinces was thoroughly blockaded. The United Provinces commanded the sea, their cruisers, large and small, keeping diligent watch off every port and estuary of the Flemish coast, so that not a herring-boat could enter without their permission. Antwerp, when it fell into the hands of the Spaniard, sank for ever from its proud position. The city which Venetians but lately had confessed with a sigh to be superior in commercial grandeur to their own magnificent capital had ceased to be a seaport. Shut in from the ocean by Flushing—firmly held by an English garrison as one of the cautionary towns for the Queen's loan—her world-wide commerce withered before men's eyes. Her population was dwindling to not much more than half its former numbers, while Ghent, Bruges, and other cities were diminished by two-thirds.

On the other hand, the commerce and manufactures of the United Republic had enormously augmented. Its bitterest enemies bore witness to the sagacity and success by which its political affairs were administered, and to its vast superiority in this respect over the obedient provinces. "The rebels are not ignorant of our condition," said Champagny, "they are themselves governed with consummate wisdom, and they mock at those who submit themselves to the Duke of Parma. They are the more confirmed in their rebellion, when they see how many are thronging from us to them, complaining of such bad government, and that all take refuge in flight who can from the misery and famine which it has caused throughout these provinces!" The industrial population had flowed from the southern provinces into the north, in obedience to an irresistible law. The workers in iron, paper, silk, linen, lace, the makers of brocade, tapestry, and satin, as well as of all the coarser fabrics, had fled from the land of oppression to the land of liberty. Never in the history of civilization had there been a more rapid development of human industry than in Holland during these years of bloodiest warfare. The towns were filled to overflowing. Amsterdam multiplied in wealth and population as fast as Antwerp shrank. Almost as much might be said of Middelburg, Enkhuyzen, Horn, and many other cities. It is the epoch to which the greatest expansion of municipal architecture is traced. Warehouses, palaces, docks, arsenals, fortifications, dykes, splendid streets and suburbs, were constructed on every side, and still there was not room for the constantly increasing population, large numbers of which habitually dwelt in the shipping. For even of that narrow span of earth called the province of Holland, one-third was then interior water, divided into five considerable lakes, those of Haarlem, Schermer, Beemster, Waert, and Purmer. The sea was kept out by a magnificent system of dykes under the daily superintendence of a board of officers, called the dykegraves, while the rain-water, which might otherwise have drowned the soil thus painfully reclaimed, was pumped up by windmills and drained off through sluices opening and closing with the movement of the tides.

The province of Zeeland was one vast "polder." It was encircled by an outer dyke of forty Dutch, equal to one hundred and fifty English, miles in extent, and traversed by many interior barriers. The average cost of dyke-building was sixty florins the rod of twelve feet, or 84,000 florins the Dutch mile. The total cost of the Zeeland dykes was estimated at 3,360,000 florins, besides the annual repairs.

But it was on the sea that the Netherlanders were really at

home, and they always felt it in their power—as their last resource against foreign tyranny—to bury their land for ever in the ocean, and to seek a new country at the ends of the earth. It has always been difficult to doom to political or personal slavery a nation accustomed to maritime pursuits. Familiarity with the boundless expanse of ocean, and the habit of victoriously contending with the elements in their stormy strength, would seem to inspire a consciousness in mankind of human dignity and worth. With the exception of Spain, the chief seafaring nations of the world were already Protestant. The counter-league, which was to do battle so strenuously with the Holy Confederacy, was essentially a maritime league. "All the maritime heretics of the world, since heresy is best suited to navigators, will be banded together," said Champagny, "and then woe to the Spanish Indies, which England and Holland are already threatening."

The Netherlanders had been noted from earliest times for a free-spoken and independent personal demeanor. At this epoch they were taking the lead of the whole world in marine adventure. At least three thousand vessels of between one hundred and four hundred tons, besides innumerable doggers, busses, cromstevens, and similar craft used on the rivers and in fisheries, were to be found in the United Provinces, and one thousand, it was estimated, were annually built.

They traded to the Baltic regions for honey, wax, tallow, lumber, iron, turpentine, hemp. They brought from farthest Indies and from America all the fabrics of ancient civilization, all the newly discovered products of a virgin soil, and dispensed them among the less industrious nations of the earth. Enterprise, led on and accompanied by science, was already planning the boldest flights into the unknown yet made by mankind, and it will soon be necessary to direct attention to those famous arctic voyages, made by Hollanders in pursuit of the northwest passage to Cathay, in which as much heroism, audacity, and scientific intelligence were displayed as in later time have made so many men belonging to both branches of the Anglo-Saxon race illustrious. A people engaged in perennial conflict with a martial and sacerdotal despotism the most powerful in the world could yet spare enough from its superfluous energies to confront the dangers of the polar oceans, and to bring back treasures of science to enrich the world.

Such was the spirit of freedom. Inspired by its blessed influence this vigorous and inventive little commonwealth triumphed over all human, all physical obstacles in its path. It organized armies on new principles to drive the most famous legions of history from its soil. It built navies to help rescue, at critical moments, the cause of England, of Protestantism, of civil liberty, and even of French nationality. More than all, by its trade with its arch-enemy, the Republic constantly multiplied its resources for destroying his power and aggrandizing its own.

The war navy of the United Provinces was a regular force of one hundred ships—large at a period when a vessel of thirteen hundred tons was a monster—together with an indefinite number of smaller craft, which could be put into the public service on short notice. In those days of close quarters and light artillery a merchant ship was converted into a cruiser by a very simple process. The navy was a self-supporting one, for it was paid by the produce of convoy fees and licenses to trade. It must be confessed that a portion of these revenues savored much of blackmail to be levied on friend and foe; for the distinctions between freebooter, privateer, pirate, and legitimate sea-robber were not very closely drawn in those early days of seafaring.

Prince Maurice of Nassau was lord high admiral, but he was obliged to listen to the counsels of various provincial boards of admiralty, which often impeded his action and interfered with his schemes.

It cannot be denied that the inherent vice of the Netherland polity was already a tendency to decentralization and provincialism. The civil institutions of the country, in their main characteristics, have been frequently sketched in these pages. At this period they had entered almost completely into the forms which were destined to endure until the commonwealth fell in the great crash of the French Revolution. Their beneficial effects were more visible now—sustained and bound together as the nation was by the sense of a common danger, and by the consciousness of its daily developing strength—than at a later day when prosperity and luxury had blunted the fine instincts of patriotism.

The supreme power, after the deposition of Philip, and the refusal by France and by England to accept the sovereignty of the provinces, was definitely lodged in the States-General. But the States-General did not technically represent the people. Its members were not elected by the people. It was a body composed of delegates from each provincial assembly, of which there were now five—Holland, Zeeland, Friesland, Utrecht, and Gelderland. Each provincial assembly consisted again of delegates, not from the inhabitants of the provinces, but from the magistracies of the cities. Those magistracies, again, were not elected by the citizens. They elected themselves by renewing their own vacancies, and were, in short, immortal corporations. Thus, in final analysis, the supreme power was distributed and localized among the mayors and aldermen of a large number of cities, all independent alike of the people below and of any central power above.

It is true that the nobles, as a class, had a voice in the provincial and in the general assembly, both for themselves and as technical representatives of the smaller towns and of the rural population. But, as a matter of fact, the influence of this caste had of late years very rapidly diminished, through its decrease in numbers, and the far more rapid increase in wealth and power of the commercial and manufacturing classes. Individual nobles were constantly employed in the military, civil, and diplomatic service of the Republic, but their body had ceased to be a power. It had been the policy of William the Silent to increase the number of cities entitled to send deputies to the States; for it was among the cities that his resistance to the tyranny of Spain, and his efforts to obtain complete independence for his country, had been mainly supported. Many of the great nobles, as has been seen in these pages, denounced the liberator and took sides with the tyrant. Lamoral Egmont had walked to the scaffold to which Philip had condemned him, chanting a prayer for Philip's welfare. Egmont's eldest son was now foremost in the Spanish army, doing battle against his own country in behalf of the tyrant who had taken his father's life. Aremberg and Ligny, Aerschot, Chimay, Croy, Capres, Montigny, and most of the great patrician families of the Netherlands fought on the royal side.

The revolution which had saved the country from perdition and created the great Netherland Republic was a burgher revolution, and burgher statesmen now controlled the state. The burgher class of Europe is not the one that has been foremost in the revolutionary movements of history, or that has distinguished itself—especially in more modern times—by a passionate love of liberty. It is always easy to sneer at Hans Miller and Hans Baker, and at the country where such plebeians are powerful. Yet the burghers played a prominent part in the great drama which forms my theme, and there has rarely been seen a more solid or powerful type of their class than the burgher statesman, John of Olden-Barneveld, who, since the death of William the Silent and the departure of Lord Leicester, had mainly guided the destinies of Holland. Certainly no soldier nor statesman who ever measured intellects with that potent personage was apt to treat his genius otherwise than with profound respect.[1]

[IVRY]

[The battle of Ivry, a crucial event both for France and the Netherlands, illustrates very well the ability of Motley to describe a battle.]

The alarm proved to be a false one, but Henry lost no time in ordering his battle. His cavalry he divided in seven troops or squadrons. The first, forming the left wing, was a body of three hundred under Marshal d'Aumont, supported by two regiments of French infantry. Next, separated by a short interval, was another troop of three hundred under the Duke

[1] *History of the United Netherlands* (New York, 1860–1867), III, 21–29.

of Montpensier, supported by two other regiments of foot, one Swiss and one German. In front of Montpensier was Baron Biron the younger, at the head of still another body of three hundred. Two troops of cuirassiers, each four hundred strong, were on Biron's left, the one commanded by the Grand Prior of France, Charles d'Angoulême, the other by Monsieur de Givry. Between the Prior and Givry were six pieces of heavy artillery, while the battalia, formed of eight hundred horse in six squadrons, was commanded by the king in person, and covered on both sides by English and Swiss infantry, amounting to some four thousand in all. The right wing was under the charge of old Marshal Biron, and comprised three troops of horse, numbering one hundred and fifty each, two companies of German riders, and four regiments of French infantry. These numbers, which are probably given with as much accuracy as can be obtained, show a force of about three thousand horse and twelve thousand foot.

The Duke of Mayenne, seeing too late the advantage of position which he might have easily secured the day before, led his army forth with the early light, and arranged it in an order not very different from that adopted by the king, and within cannon-shot of his lines. The right wing under Marshal de la Châtre consisted of three regiments of French and one of Germans, supporting three regiments of Spanish lancers, two cornets of German riders under the Bastard of Brunswick, and four hundred cuirassiers. The battalia, which was composed of six hundred splendid cavalry, all noblemen of France, guarding the white banner of the Holy League, and supported by a column of three thousand Swiss and two thousand French infantry, was commanded by Mayenne in person, assisted by his half-brother, the Duke of Nemours. In front of the infantry was a battery of six cannon and three culverins. The left wing was commanded by Marshal de René, with six regiments of French and Lorrainers, two thousand Germans, six hundred French cuirassiers, and the mounted troopers of Count Egmont. It is probable that Mayenne's whole force, therefore, amounted to nearly four thousand cavalry and at least thirteen thousand foot.

Very different was the respective appearance of the two armies, so far, especially, as regarded the horsemen on both sides. Gay in their gilded armor and waving plumes, with silken scarves across their shoulders, and the fluttering favors of fair ladies on their arms or in their helmets, the brilliant champions of the Holy Catholic Confederacy clustered around the chieftains of the great house of Guise, impatient for the conflict. It was like a muster for a brilliant and chivalrous tournament. The Walloon and Flemish nobles, outrivalling even the self-confidence of their companions in arms, taunted them with their slowness. The impetuous Egmont, burning to eclipse the fame of his ill-fated father at Gravelines and St. Quentin in the same holy cause, urged on the battle with unseemly haste, loudly proclaiming that if the French were faint-hearted he would himself give a good account of the Navarrese prince without any assistance from them.

A cannon-shot away, the grim puritan nobles who had come forth from their mountain fastnesses to do battle for king and law and for the rights of conscience against the Holy League—men seasoned in a hundred battlefields, clad all in iron, with no dainty ornaments nor holiday luxury of warfare—knelt on the ground, smiting their mailed breasts with iron hands, invoking blessings on themselves and curses and confusion on their enemies in the coming conflict, and chanting a stern psalm of homage to the God of battles and of wrath. And Henry of France and Navarre, descendant of Lewis the Holy and of Hugh the Great, beloved chief of the Calvinist cavaliers, knelt among his heretic brethren, and prayed and chanted with them. But not the staunchest Huguenot of them all, not Duplessis, nor D'Aubigné, nor De la Noue with the iron arm, was more devoted on that day to crown and country than were such papist supporters of the rightful heir as had sworn to conquer the insolent foreigner on the soil of France or die.

When this brief prelude was over, Henry made an address to his soldiers, but its language has not been preserved. It is known, however, that he wore that day his famous snow-white plume, and that he ordered his soldiers, should his banner go down in the conflict, to follow wherever and as long as that plume should be seen waving on any part of the field. He had taken a position by which his troops had the sun and wind in their backs, so that the smoke rolled toward the enemy and the light shone in their eyes. The combat began with the play of artillery, which soon became so warm that Egmont, whose cavalry—suffering and galled—soon became impatient, ordered a charge. It was a most brilliant one. The heavy troopers of Flanders and Hainault, following their spirited chieftain, dashed upon old Marshal Biron, routing his cavalry, charging clean up to the Huguenot guns and sabering the cannoneers. The shock was square, solid, irresistible, and was followed up by the German riders under Eric of Brunswick, who charged upon the battalia of the royal army, where the king commanded in person.

There was a panic. The whole royal cavalry wavered, the supporting infantry recoiled, the day seemed lost before the battle was well begun. Yells of "Victory! Victory! up with the Holy League, down with the heretic Béarnese," resounded through the Catholic squadrons. The king and Marshal Biron, who were near each other, were furious with rage, but already doubtful of the result. They exerted themselves to rally the troops under their immediate command, and to reform the shattered ranks.

The German riders and French lancers, under Brunswick and Bassompierre, had, however, not done their work as thoroughly as Egmont had done. The ground was so miry and soft that in the brief space which separated the hostile lines they had not power to urge their horses to full speed. Throwing away their useless lances, they came on at a feeble canter, sword in hand, and were unable to make a very vigorous impression on the more heavily armed troopers opposed to them. Meeting with a firm resistance to their career, they wheeled, faltered a little and fell a short distance back. Many of the riders being of the Reformed religion, refused moreover to fire upon the Huguenots, and discharged their carbines in the air.

The king, whose glance on the battlefield was like inspiration, saw the blot and charged upon them in person with his whole battalia of cavalry. The veteran Biron followed hard upon the snow-white plume. The scene was changed, victory succeeded unto impending defeat, and the enemy was routed. The riders and cuirassiers, broken into a struggling heap of confusion, strewed the ground with their dead bodies, or carried dismay into the ranks of the infantry as they strove to escape. Brunswick went down in the *mêlée*, mortally wounded, as it was believed. Egmont renewing the charge at the head of his victorious Belgian troopers, fell dead with a musket-ball through his heart. The shattered German and Walloon cavalry, now pricked forward by the lances of their companions, under the passionate commands of Mayenne and Aumale, now falling back before the furious charges of the Huguenots, were completely overthrown and cut to pieces. Seven times did Henry of Navarre in person lead his troopers to the charge; but suddenly, in the midst of the din of battle and the cheers of victory, a message of despair went from lip to lip throughout the royal lines. The king had disappeared. He was killed, and the hopes of Protestantism and of France were fallen for ever with him. The white standard of his battalia had been seen floating wildly and purposelessly over the field; for his bannerman, Pot de Rhodes, a young noble of Dauphiny, wounded mortally in the head, with blood streaming over his face and blinding his sight, was utterly unable to control his horse, who galloped hither and thither at his own caprice, misleading many troopers who followed in his erratic career. A cavalier, armed in proof, and wearing the famous snow-white plume, after a hand-to-hand struggle with a veteran of Count Bossu's regiment, was seen to fall dead by the side of the bannerman. The Fleming, not used to boast, loudly asserted that he had slain the Béarnese, and the news spread rapidly over the battlefield. The defeated Confederates gained new courage, the victorious Royalists were beginning to waver, when suddenly, between the hostile lines, in the very midst of the battle, the king galloped forward, bareheaded, covered with blood and dust, but entirely unhurt. A wild shout of "*Vive le Roi!*" rang through the air. Cheerful as ever, he addressed a few encouraging words to his soldiers, with a smiling face, and again led a charge. It was all that was necessary to complete the victory. The enemy broke and ran away on every side in wildest confusion, followed by the royalist cavalry, who sabered them as they fled. The panic gained the foot-soldiers, who should have supported the cavalry, but had not been at all engaged in the action. The French infantry threw away their arms as they rushed from the field and sought refuge in the woods. The Walloons were so expeditious in the race, that they never stopped till they gained their own frontier. The day was hopelessly lost, and although Mayenne had conducted himself well in the early part of the day, it was certain that he was excelled by none in the celerity of his flight when the rout had fairly begun. Pausing to draw breath as he gained the wood, he was seen to deal blows with his own sword among the mob of fugitives, not that he might rally them to their flag and drive them back to another encounter, but because they encumbered his own retreat.

The Walloon carbineers, the German riders, and the French lancers, disputing as to the relative blame to be attached to each corps, began shooting and sabering each other, almost before they were out of the enemy's sight. Many were thus killed. The lansquenets were all put to the sword. The Swiss infantry were allowed to depart for their own country on pledging themselves not again to bear arms against Henry IV. It is probable that eight hundred of the leaguers were either killed on the battlefield or drowned in the swollen river in their retreat. About one-fourth of that number fell in the army of the king. It is certain that of the contingent from the obedient Netherlands, two hundred and seventy, including their distinguished general, lost their lives. The Bastard of Brunswick, crawling from beneath a heap of slain, escaped with life. Mayenne lost all his standards and all the baggage of his army, while the army itself was for a time hopelessly dissolved.[1]

[1] *History of the United Netherlands* (New York, 1860–1867), III, 51–57.

[MAURICE AND HIS ARMY]

[In the following pages Motley describes the military methods and the army created by Maurice of Nassau.]

The highest military office in the Netherlands was that of captain-general or supreme commander. This quality was from earliest times united to that of stadholder, who stood, as his title implied, in the place of the reigning sovereign, whether count, duke, king, or emperor. After the foundation of the Republic this dynastic form, like many others, remained, and thus Prince Maurice was at first only captain-general of Holland and Zeeland, and subsequently of Gelderland, Utrecht, and Overyssel, after he had been appointed stadholder of those three provinces in 1590 on the death of Count Nieuwenaar. However much in reality he was general-in-chief of the army, he never in all his life held the appointment of captain-general of the Union.

To obtain a captain's commission in the army, it was necessary to have served four years, while three years' service was the necessary preliminary to the post of lieutenant or ensign. Three candidates were presented by the province for each office, from whom the stadholder appointed one. The commissions, except those of the highest commanders, were made out in the name of the States-General, by advice and consent of the council of state. The oath of allegiance, exacted from soldiers as well as officers, mentioned the name of the particular province to which they belonged, as well as that of the States-General. It thus appears that, especially after Maurice's first and successful campaigns, the supreme authority over the army really belonged to the States-General, and that the powers of the state-council in this regard fell, in the course of four years, more and more into the background, and at last disappeared almost entirely. During the active period of the war, however, the effect of this revolution was in fact rather a greater concentration of military power than its dispersion, for the States-General meant simply the province of Holland. Holland was the Republic.

The organization of the infantry was very simple. The

tactical unit was the company. A temporary combination of several companies made a regiment, commanded by a colonel or lieutenant-colonel, but for such regiments there was no regular organization. Sometimes six or seven companies were thus combined, sometimes three times that number, but the strength of a force, however large, was always estimated by the number of companies, not of regiments.

The normal strength of an infantry company, at the beginning of Maurice's career, may be stated at one hundred and thirteen, commanded by one captain, one lieutenant, one ensign, and by the usual non-commissioned officers. Each company was composed of musketeers, harquebussiers, pikemen, halberdiers, and bucklermen. Long after portable firearms had come into use, the greater portion of foot-soldiers continued to be armed with pikes, until the introduction of the fixed bayonet enabled the musketeer to do likewise the duty of pikeman. Maurice was among the first to appreciate the advantage of portable firearms, and he accordingly increased the proportion of soldiers armed with the musket in his companies. In a company of a hundred and thirteen, including officers, he had sixty-four armed with firelocks to thirty carrying pikes and halberds. As before his time the proportion between the arms had been nearly even, he thus more than doubled the number of firearms.

Of these weapons there were two sorts, the musket and the harquebus. The musket was a long, heavy, unmanageable instrument. When fired it was placed upon an iron gaffle, or fork, which the soldier carried with him, and stuck before him into the ground. The bullets of the musket were twelve to the pound.

The harquebus—or hak-bus, "hook-gun," so called because of the hook in the front part of the barrel to give steadiness in firing—was much lighter, was discharged from the hand, and carried bullets of twenty-four to the pound. Both weapons had matchlocks.

The pike was eighteen feet long at least, and pikemen as well as halberdsmen carried rapiers.

There were three bucklermen to each company, introduced

by Maurice for the personal protection of the leader of the company. The prince was often attended by one himself, and, on at least one memorable occasion, was indebted to this shield for the preservation of his life.

The cavalry was divided into lancers and carabineers. The unit was the squadron, varying in number from sixty to one hundred and fifty, until the year 1591, when the regular complement of the squadron was fixed at one hundred and twenty.

As the use of cavalry on the battlefield at that day, or at least in the Netherlands, was not in rapidity of motion, nor in severity of shock—the attack usually taking place on a trot— Maurice gradually displaced the lance in favor of the carbine. His troopers thus became rather mounted infantry than regular cavalry.

The carbine was at least three feet long, with wheel-locks, and carried bullets of thirty to the pound.

The artillery was a peculiar organization. It was a guild of citizens, rather than a strictly military force like the cavalry and infantry. The arm had but just begun to develop itself, and it was cultivated as a special trade by the Guild of the Holy Barbara existing in all the principal cities. Thus a municipal artillery gradually organized itself, under the direction of the gun-masters (bus-meesters), who in secret labored at the perfection of their art, and who taught it to their apprentices and journeymen, as the principles of other crafts were conveyed by master to pupil. This system furnished a powerful element of defense at a period when every city had in great measure to provide for its own safety.

In the earlier campaigns of Maurice three kinds of artillery were used; the whole cannon (kartouw) of forty-eight pounds; the half-cannon, or twenty-four pounder, and the field-piece carrying a ball of twelve pounds. The two first were called battering pieces or siege-guns. All the guns were of bronze.

The length of the whole cannon was about twelve feet; its weight one hundred and fifty times that of the ball, or about seven thousand pounds. It was reckoned that the whole kartouw could fire from eighty to one hundred shots in an hour. Wet haircloths were used to cool the piece after every ten or twelve discharges. The usual charge was twenty pounds of powder.

The whole gun was drawn by thirty-one horses, the half cannon by twenty-three.

The field-piece required eleven horses but a regular field-artillery, as an integral part of the army, did not exist, and was introduced in much later times. In the greatest pitched battle ever fought by Maurice, that of Nieuport, he had but six field-pieces.

The prince also employed mortars in his sieges, from which were thrown grenades, hot shot, and stones; but no greater distance was reached than six hundred yards. Bombshells were not often used although they had been known for a century.

Before the days of Maurice a special education for engineers had never been contemplated. Persons who had privately acquired a knowledge of fortification and similar branches of the science were employed upon occasion, but regular corps of engineers there were none. The prince established a course of instruction in this profession at the University of Leyden, according to a system drawn up by the celebrated Stevinus.

Doubtless the most important innovation of the prince, and the one which required the most energy to enforce, was the use of the spade. His soldiers were jeered at by the enemy as mere boors and day laborers who were dishonoring themselves and their profession by the use of that implement instead of the sword. Such a novelty was a shock to all the military ideas of the age, and it was only the determination and vigor of the prince and of his cousin Lewis William that ultimately triumphed over the universal prejudice.

The pay of the common soldier varied from ten to twenty florins the month, but every miner had eighteen florins, and, when actually working in the mines, thirty florins monthly. Soldiers used in digging trenches received, over and above their regular pay, a daily wage of from ten to fifteen stivers, or nearly a shilling sterling.

Another most wholesome improvement made by the prince

was in the payment of his troops. The system prevailing in every European country at that day, by which governments were defrauded and soldiers starved, was most infamous. The soldiers were paid through the captain, who received the wages of a full company, when perhaps not one-third of the names on the muster-roll were living human beings. Accordingly two-thirds of all the money stuck to the officer's fingers, and it was not thought a disgrace to cheat the government by dressing and equipping for the day a set of ragamuffins, caught up in the streets for the purpose, and made to pass muster as regular soldiers.

These passe-volants, or scarecrows, were passed freely about from one company to another, and the indecency of the fraud was never thought a disgrace to the colors of the company.

Thus, in the Armada year, the Queen had demanded that a portion of her auxiliary force in the Netherlands should be sent to England. The States agreed that three thousand of these English troops, together with a few cavalry companies, should go, but stipulated that two thousand should remain in the provinces. The Queen accepted the proposal, but when the two thousand had been counted out, it appeared that there was scarcely a man left for the voyage to England. Yet every one of the English captains had claimed full pay for his company from her Majesty's exchequer.

Against this tide of peculation and corruption the strenuous Maurice set himself with heart and soul, and there is no doubt that to his reformation in this vital matter much of his military success was owing. It was impossible that roguery and venality should ever furnish a solid foundation for the martial science.[1]

[PHILIP II AND THE DUKE OF PARMA]

[Philip II was prevented from attaining the successful execution of his wide-reaching plans by the multiplicity of his interests. The effect of this situation on the conflict in the

[1] *History of the United Netherlands* (New York, 1860–1867), III, 93–99.

Netherlands is illustrated by the relations between Alexander Farnese and his sovereign.]

And thus through the whole of the two memorable campaigns made by Alexander in France, he never failed to give his master the most accurate pictures of the country, and an interior view of its politics; urging above all the absolute necessity of providing much more liberal supplies for the colossal adventure in which he was engaged. "Money and again money is what is required," he said. "The principal matter is to be accomplished with money, and the particular individuals must be bought with money. The good will of every French city must be bought with money. Mayenne must be humored. He is getting dissatisfied. Very probably he is intriguing with Béarn. Everybody is pursuing his private ends. Mayenne has never abandoned his own wish to be king, although he sees the difficulties in the way; and while he has not the power to do us as much good as is thought, it is certainly in his hands to do us a great deal of injury."

When his army was rapidly diminishing by disease, desertion, mutiny, and death, he vehemently and perpetually denounced the utter inadequacy of the King's means to his vast projects. He protested that he was not to blame for the ruin likely to come upon the whole enterprise. He had besought, remonstrated, reasoned with Philip—in vain. He assured his master that in the condition of weakness in which they found themselves, not very triumphant negotiations could be expected, but that he would do his best. "The Frenchmen," he said, "are getting tired of our disorders, and scandalized by our weakness, misery, and poverty. They disbelieve the possibility of being liberated through us."

He was also most diligent in setting before the king's eyes the dangerous condition of the obedient Netherlands, the poverty of the finances, the mutinous degeneration of the once magnificent Spanish army, the misery of the country, the ruin of the people, the discontent of the nobles, the rapid strides made by the republic, the vast improvement in its military organization, the rising fame of its young stadholder, the thrift of its exchequer, the rapid development of its commerce, the menacing aspect which it assumed towards all that was left of Spanish power in those regions.

Moreover, in the midst of the toils and anxieties of war-making and negotiation, he had found time to discover and to send to his master the left leg of the glorious apostle St. Philip, and the head of the glorious martyr St. Lawrence, to enrich his collection of relics; and it may be doubted whether these treasures were not as welcome to the king as would have been the news of a decisive victory.[1]

[RECALL AND DEATH OF THE DUKE OF PARMA]

[In spite of his ability and his fidelity to the interests of his master, Philip II decided to remove Alexander Farnese, Duke of Parma. The following passage describes, as Motley saw it, the dissimulation of Philip II in bringing about the dismissal of his able and faithful representative in the Netherlands.]

On the conclusion of his Rouen campaign he had returned to the Netherlands, almost immediately betaking himself to the waters of Spa. The Marquis de Cerralbo meanwhile had been superseded in his important secret mission by the Count of Fuentes, who received the same instructions as had been provided for the marquis.

But ere long it seemed to become unnecessary to push matters to extremities. Farnese, although nominally the governor, felt himself unequal to take the field against the vigorous young commander who was carrying everything before him in the north and east. Upon the Mansfelds was the responsibility for saving Steenwyk and Coeworden, and to the Mansfelds did Verdugo send piteously, but in vain, for efficient help. For the Mansfelds and other leading personages in the obedient Netherlands were mainly occupied at that time in annoying Farnese, calumniating his actions, laying obstacles in the way of his administration, military and civil, and bringing him into con-

[1] *History of the United Netherlands* (New York, 1860–1867), III, 214–216.

tempt with the populace. When the weary soldier—broken in
health, wounded and harassed with obtaining triumphs for his
master such as no other living man could have gained with the
means placed at his disposal—returned to drink the waters previously to setting forth anew upon the task of achieving the
impossible, he was made the mark of petty insults on the part
of both the Mansfelds. Neither of them paid their respects to
him, ill as he was, until four days after his arrival. When the
duke subsequently called a council, Count Peter refused to
attend it on account of having slept ill the night before. Champagny, who was one of the chief mischief-makers, had been
banished by Parma to his house in Burgundy. He became very
much alarmed, and was afraid of losing his head. He tried to
conciliate the duke, but finding it difficult he resolved to turn
monk, and so went to the convent of Capuchins, and begged
hard to be admitted a member. They refused him on account
of his age and infirmities. He tried a Franciscan monastery with
not much better success, and then obeyed orders and went to
his Burgundy mansion, having been assured by Farnese that
he was not to lose his head. Alexander was satisfied with that
arrangement, feeling sure, he said, that so soon as his back was
turned Champagny would come out of his convent before the
term of probation had expired, and begin to make mischief
again. A once valiant soldier, like Champagny, whose conduct
in the famous "fury of Antwerp" was so memorable, and whose
services both in field and cabinet had been so distinguished,
fallen so low as to be used as a tool by the Mansfelds against a
man like Farnese, and to be rejected as unfit company by Flemish friars, is not a cheerful spectacle to contemplate.

The walls of the Mansfeld house and gardens, too, were
decorated by Count Charles with caricatures, intending to illustrate the indignities put upon his father and himself. Among
others, one picture represented Count Peter lying tied hand
and foot, while people were throwing filth upon him; Count
Charles being portrayed as meantime being kicked away from
the command of a battery of cannon by De la Motte. It seemed
strange that the Mansfelds should make themselves thus elabo-

rately ridiculous, in order to irritate Farnese; but thus it was. There was so much stir about these works of art that Alexander transmitted copies of them to the king, whereupon Charles Mansfeld, being somewhat alarmed, endeavored to prove that they had been entirely misunderstood. The venerable personage lying on the ground, he explained, was not his father, but Socrates. He found it difficult, however, to account for the appearance of La Motte, with his one arm wanting and with artillery by his side, because, as Farnese justly remarked, artillery had not been invented in the time of Socrates nor was it recorded that the sage had lost an arm. . . .

Suffering from a badly healed wound, from water on the chest, degeneration of the heart, and gout in the limbs, dropsical, enfeebled, broken down into an old man before his time, Alexander still confronted disease and death with as heroic a front as he had ever manifested in the field to embattled Hollanders and Englishmen, or to the still more formidable array of learned pedants and diplomatists in the hall of negotiation. This wreck of a man was still fitter to lead armies and guide councils than any soldier or statesman that Philip could call into his service, yet the king's cruel hand was ready to stab the dying man in the dark.

Nothing could surpass the spirit with which the soldier was ready to do battle with his best friend, coming in the guise of an enemy. To the last moment, lifted into the saddle, he attended personally as usual to the details of his new campaign, and was dead before he would confess himself mortal. On the 3rd of December, 1592, in the city of Arras, he fainted after retiring at his usual hour to bed, and thus breathed his last.

According to the instructions in his last will, he was laid out barefoot in the robe and cowl of a Capuchin monk. Subsequently his remains were taken to Parma, and buried under the pavement of the little Franciscan church. A pompous funeral, in which the Italians and Spaniards quarrelled and came to blows for precedence, was celebrated in Brussels, and a statue of the hero was erected in the capitol at Rome.

The first soldier and most unscrupulous diplomatist of his age, he died when scarcely past his prime, a wearied, broken-hearted old man. His triumphs, military and civil, have been recorded in these pages, and his character has been elaborately portrayed. Were it possible to conceive of an Italian or Spaniard of illustrious birth in the sixteenth century, educated in the school of Machiavelli, at the feet of Philip, as anything but the supple slave of a master and the blind instrument of a church, one might for a moment regret that so many gifts of genius and valor had been thrown away, or at least lost to mankind. Could the light of truth ever pierce the atmosphere in which such men have their being; could the sad music of humanity ever penetrate to their ears; could visions of a world—on this earth or beyond it—not exclusively the property of kings and high-priests be revealed to them, one might lament that one so eminent among the sons of women had not been a great man. But it is a weakness to hanker for any possible connection between truth and Italian or Spanish statecraft of that day. The truth was not in it nor in him, and high above his heroic achievements, his fortitude, his sagacity, his chivalrous self-sacrifice, shines forth the baleful light of his perpetual falsehood.[1]

[PERSECUTION OF ANNA VAN DER HOVE]

[Motley seeks to rouse antagonism toward Philip II by giving such specific instances of his tyranny as the persecution of Anna van der Hove.]

Two maiden ladies lived on the north rampart of Antwerp. They had formerly professed the Protestant religion, and had been thrown into prison for that crime; but the fear of further persecution, human weakness, or perhaps sincere conviction, had caused them to renounce the error of their ways, and they now went to mass. But they had a maidservant, forty years of age, Anna van der Hove by name, who was staunch in that

[1] *History of the United Netherlands* (New York, 1860–1867), III, 221–225.

Reformed faith in which she had been born and bred. The Jesuits denounced this maidservant to the civil authority, and claimed her condemnation and execution under the edicts of 1540, decrees which everyone had supposed as obsolete as the statutes of Draco, which they had so entirely put to shame.

The sentence having been obtained from the docile and priest-ridden magistrates, Anna van der Hove was brought to Brussels and informed that she was at once to be buried alive. At the same time, the Jesuits told her that by converting herself to the Church, she might escape punishment.

When King Henry IV was summoned to renounce that same Huguenot faith, of which he was the political embodiment and the military champion, the candid man answered by the simple demand to be instructed. When the proper moment came, the instruction was accomplished by an archbishop with the rapidity of magic. Half an hour undid the work of half a lifetime. Thus expeditiously could religious conversion be effected when an earthly crown was its guerdon. The poor serving-maid was less open to conviction. In her simple fanaticism she talked of a crown, and saw it descending from Heaven on her poor forlorn head as the reward, not of apostasy, but of steadfastness. She asked her tormentors how they could expect her to abandon her religion for fear of death. She had read her Bible every day, she said, and had found nothing there of the pope or purgatory, masses, invocation of saints, or the absolution of sins except through the blood of the blessed Redeemer. She interfered with no one who thought differently; she quarrelled with no one's religious belief. She had prayed for enlightenment from Him, if she were in error, and the result was that she felt strengthened in her simplicity, and resolved to do nothing against her conscience. Rather than add this sin to the manifold ones committed by her, she preferred, she said, to die the death. So Anna van der Hove was led, one fine midsummer morning, to the hayfield outside of Brussels, between two Jesuits, followed by a number of a peculiar kind of monks called love-brothers. Those holy men goaded her as she went, telling her that she was the devil's carrion, and calling on her to repent at the last moment, and thus save her life and escape eternal damnation beside. But the poor soul had no ear for them, and cried out that, like Stephen, she saw the heavens opening, and the angels stooping down to conduct her far away from the power of the evil one. When they came to the hayfield they found the pit already dug, and the maidservant was ordered to descend into it. The executioner then covered her with earth up to the waist, and a last summons was made to her to renounce her errors. She refused, and then the earth was piled upon her, and the hangman jumped upon the grave till it was flattened and firm.[1]

[LAST ILLNESS AND DEATH OF PHILIP II]

[The last illness and death of Philip II gave Motley an opportunity to make a dramatic picture.]

Meantime, Philip II, who had been of delicate constitution all his life, and who had of late years been a confirmed valetudinarian, had been rapidly failing ever since the transfer of the Netherlands in May. Longing to be once more in his favorite retirement of the Escorial, he undertook the journey towards the beginning of June, and was carried thither from Madrid in a litter borne by servants, accomplishing the journey of seven leagues in six days.

When he reached the palace cloister, he was unable to stand. The gout, his lifelong companion, had of late so tortured him in the hands and feet that the mere touch of a linen sheet was painful to him. By the middle of July a low fever had attacked him, which rapidly reduced his strength. Moreover, a new and terrible symptom of the utter disintegration of his physical constitution had presented itself. Imposthumes, from which he had suffered on the breast and at the joints, had been opened after the usual ripening applications, and the result was not the hoped relief, but swarms of vermin, innumerable in quantities,

---

[1] *History of the United Netherlands* (New York, 1860–1867), III, 444–446.

and impossible to extirpate, which were thus generated and reproduced in the monarch's blood and flesh.

The details of the fearful disorder may have attraction for the pathologist, but have no especial interest for the general reader. Let it suffice, that no torture ever invented by Torquemada or Peter Titelman to serve the vengeance of Philip and his ancestors or the pope against the heretics of Italy or Flanders, could exceed in acuteness the agonies which the Most Catholic King was now called upon to endure. And not one of the long line of martyrs, who by decree of Charles or Philip had been strangled, beheaded, burned, or buried alive, ever faced a death of lingering torments with more perfect fortitude, or was sustained by more ecstatic visions of heavenly mercy, than was now the case with the great monarch of Spain.

That the grave-worms should do their office before soul and body were parted, was a torment such as the imagination of Dante might have invented for the lowest depths of his Inferno.

On the 22nd July, the king asked Dr. Mercado if his sickness was likely to have a fatal termination. The physician, not having the courage at once to give the only possible reply, found means to evade the question. On the 1st August his Majesty's confessor, father Diego de Yepes, after consultation with Mercado, announced to Philip that the only issue to his malady was death. Already he had been lying for ten days on his back, a mass of sores and corruption, scarcely able to move, and requiring four men to turn him in his bed.

He expressed the greatest satisfaction at the sincerity which had now been used, and in the gentlest and most benignant manner signified his thanks to them for thus removing all doubts from his mind, and for giving him information which it was of so much importance for his eternal welfare to possess.

His first thought was to request the papal nuncio, Gaetano, to despatch a special courier to Rome to request the pope's benediction. This was done, and it was destined that the blessing of his Holiness should arrive in time.

He next prepared himself to make a general confession, which lasted three days, father Diego having drawn up at his request a full and searching interrogatory. The confession may have been made the more simple, however, by the statement which he made to the priest, and subsequently repeated to the Infante his son, that in all his life he had never consciously done wrong to any one. If he had ever committed an act of injustice, it was unwittingly, or because he had been deceived in the circumstances. This internal conviction of general righteousness was of great advantage to him in the midst of his terrible sufferings, and accounted in great degree for the gentleness, thoughtfulness for others, and perfect benignity, which, according to the unanimous testimony of many witnesses, characterized his conduct during this whole sickness.

After he had completed his long general confession, the sacrament of the Lord's Supper was administered to him. Subsequently, the same rites were more briefly performed every few days.

His sufferings were horrible, but no saint could have manifested in them more gentle resignation or angelic patience. He moralized on the condition to which the greatest princes might thus be brought at last by the hand of God, and bade the prince observe well his father's present condition, in order that, when he too should be laid thus low, he might likewise be sustained by a conscience void of offense. He constantly thanked his assistants and nurses for their care, insisted upon their reposing themselves after their daily fatigues, and ordered others to relieve them in their task.

He derived infinite consolation from the many relics of saints, of which, as has been seen, he had made plentiful provision during his long reign. Especially a bone of St. Alban, presented to him by Clement VIII, in view of his present straits, was of great service. With this relic, and with the arm of St. Vincent of Ferrara, and the knee-bone of St. Sebastian, he daily rubbed his sores, keeping the sacred talismans ever in his sight on the altar, which was not far from his bed. He was much pleased when the priests and other bystanders assured him that the remains of these holy men would be of special efficacy to him, because he had cherished and worshipped them in times when misbelievers and heretics had treated them with disrespect.

On a sideboard in his chamber a human skull was placed, and upon this skull—in ghastly mockery of royalty, in truth, yet doubtless in the conviction that such an exhibition showed the superiority of anointed kings even over death—he ordered his servants to place a golden crown. And thus, during the whole of his long illness, the Antic held his state, while the poor mortal representative of absolute power lay living still, but slowly mouldering away.

With perfect composure, and with that minute attention to details which had characterized the king all his lifetime, and was now more evident than ever, he caused the provisions for his funeral obsequies to be read aloud one day by Juan Ruys de Velasco, in order that his children, his ministers, and the great officers of state who were daily in attendance upon him, might thoroughly learn their lesson before the time came for performing the ceremony.

"Having governed my kingdom for forty years," said he, "I now give it back, in the seventy-first year of my age, to God Almighty, to whom it belongs, recommending my soul into His blessed hands, that His Divine Majesty may do what He pleases therewith." . . .

As the days wore on he felt himself steadily sinking, and asked to receive extreme unction. As he had never seen that rite performed, he chose to rehearse it beforehand, and told Ruys de Velasco, who was in constant attendance upon him, to go for minute instructions on the subject to the Archbishop of Toledo. The sacrament having been duly administered, the king subsequently, on the 1st September, desired to receive it once more. The archbishop, fearing that the dying monarch's strength would be insufficient for the repetition of the function, informed him that the regulations of the Church required in such cases only a compliance with certain trifling forms, as the ceremony had been already once thoroughly carried out. But the king expressed himself as quite determined that the sacrament should be repeated in all its parts; that he should once more be anointed —to use the phrase of Brother Francis Neyen—with the oil which holy athletes require in their wrestle with death.

This was accordingly done in the presence of his son and daughter, and of his chief secretaries, Christopher de Moura and John de Idiaquez, besides the Counts Chinchon, Fuensalido, and several other conspicuous personages. He was especially desirous that his son should be present, in order that, when he too should come to die, he might not find himself, like his father, in ignorance of the manner in which this last sacrament was to be performed.

When it was finished he described himself as infinitely consoled, and as having derived even more happiness from the rite than he had dared to anticipate.

Thenceforth he protested that he would talk no more of the world's affairs. He had finished with all things below, and for the days or hours still remaining to him he would keep his heart exclusively fixed upon Heaven. Day by day, as he lay on his couch of unutterable and almost unexampled misery, his confessors and others read to him from religious works, while with perfect gentleness he would insist that one reader should relieve another, that none might be fatigued.

On the 11th September he dictated these words to Christopher de Moura, who was to take them to Diego de Yepes, the confessor:—

"Father Confessor, you are in the place of God, and I protest thus before His presence that I will do all that you declare necessary for my salvation. Thus upon you will be the responsibility for my omissions, because I am ready to do all."

Finding that the last hour was approaching, he informed Don Fernando de Toledo where he could find some candles of Our Lady of Montserrat, one of which he desired to keep in his hand at the supreme moment. He also directed Ruys de Velasco to take from a special shrine—which he had indicated to him six years before—a crucifix which the emperor his father had held upon his deathbed. All this was accomplished according to his wish.

He had already made arrangements for his funeral procession, and had subsequently provided all the details of his agony. It was now necessary to give orders as to the particulars of his burial.

He knew that decomposition had made such progress even while he was still living as to render embalming impossible. He accordingly instructed Don Christopher to see his body wrapped in a shroud just as it lay, and to cause it to be placed in a well-soldered metallic coffin already provided. The coffin of state, in which the leaden one was to be enclosed, was then brought into the chamber by his command, that he might see if it was entirely to his taste. Having examined it, he ordered that it should be lined with white satin and ornamented with gold nails and lacework. He also described a particular brocade of black and gold, to be found in the jewel-room, which he desired for the Pall.

Next morning he complained to Don Christopher that the sacrament of the Lord's Supper had not been administered to him for several days. It was urged that his strength was deemed insufficient, and that, as he had received that rite already four times during his illness, and extreme unction twice, it was thought that the additional fatigue might be spared him. But as the king insisted, the sacrament was once more performed and prayers were read. He said with great fervor many times, "*Pater, non mea voluntas, sed tua fiat.*" He listened, too, with much devotion to the Psalm, "As the hart panteth for the water-brooks"; and he spoke faintly at long intervals of the Magdalen, of the prodigal son, and of the paralytic.

When these devotional exercises had been concluded, father Diego expressed the hope to him that he might then pass away, for it would be a misfortune by temporary convalescence to fall from the exaltation of piety which he had then reached. The remark was heard by Philip with an expression of entire satisfaction.

That day both the Infanta and the prince came for the last

time to his bedside to receive his blessing. He tenderly expressed his regret to his daughter that he had not been permitted to witness her marriage, but charged her never to omit any exertion to augment and sustain the holy Roman Catholic religion in the Netherlands. It was in the interest of that holy Church alone that he had endowed her with those provinces, and he now urged it upon her with his dying breath to impress upon her future husband these his commands to both.

His two children took leave of him with tears and sobs. As the prince left the chamber he asked Don Christopher who it was that held the key to the treasury.

The secretary replied, "It is I, Sir." The prince demanded that he should give it into his hands. But Don Christopher excused himself, saying that it had been entrusted to him by the king, and that without his consent he could not part with it. Then the prince returned to the king's chamber, followed by the secretary, who narrated to the dying monarch what had taken place.

"You have done wrong," said Philip; whereupon Don Christopher, bowing to the earth, presented the key to the prince.

The king then feebly begged those about his bedside to repeat the dying words of our Saviour on the cross, in order that he might hear them and repeat them in his heart as his soul was taking flight.

His father's crucifix was placed in his hands, and he said distinctly, "I die like a good Catholic, in faith and obedience to the Holy Roman Church." Soon after these last words had been spoken, a paroxysm, followed by faintness, came over him, and he lay entirely still.

They had covered his face with a cloth, thinking that he had already expired, when he suddenly started, with great energy, opened his eyes, seized the crucifix again from the hand of Don Fernando de Toledo, kissed it, and fell back again into agony.

The archbishop and the other priests expressed the opinion that he must have had, not a paroxysm, but a celestial vision, for human powers would not have enabled him to arouse himself so quickly and so vigorously as he had done at that crisis.

He did not speak again, but lay unconsciously dying for some hours, and breathed his last at five in the morning of Sunday the 13th September.

His obsequies were celebrated according to the directions which he had so minutely given.[1]

[ESTIMATE OF PHILIP'S REIGN]

[The description of the death of Philip II was naturally followed by an estimate of the man and his reign.]

The Spanish monarchy in the reign of Philip II was not only the most considerable empire then existing, but probably the most powerful and extensive empire that had ever been known. Certainly never before had so great an agglomeration of distinct and separate sovereignties been the result of accident. For it was owing to a series of accidents—in the common acceptation of that term—that Philip governed so mighty a realm. According to the principle that vast tracts of the earth's surface, with the human beings feeding upon them, were transferable in fee-simple from one man or woman to another by marriage, inheritance, or gift, a heterogeneous collection of kingdoms, principalities, provinces, and wildernesses had been consolidated, without geographical continuity, into an artificial union—the populations differing from each other as much as human beings can differ, in race, language, institutions, and historical traditions, and resembling each other in little, save in being the property alike of the same fortunate individual.

Thus the dozen kingdoms of Spain, the seventeen provinces of the Netherlands, the kingdoms of the Two Sicilies, the duchy of Milan, and certain fortresses and districts of Tuscany, in Europe; the kingdom of Barbary, the coast of Guinea, and an indefinite and unmeasured expanse of other territory, in Africa; the controlling outposts and cities all along the coast of the two Indian peninsulas, with as much of the country as it seemed good to occupy, the straits and the great archipelagoes,

[1] *History of the United Netherlands* (New York, 1860–1867), III, 503–512.

so far as they had been visited by Europeans, in Asia; Peru, Brazil, Mexico, the Antilles—the whole recently discovered fourth quarter of the world in short, from the "Land of Fire" in the South to the frozen regions of the North—as much territory as the Spanish and Portuguese sea-captains could circumnavigate and the pope in the plenitude of his power and his generosity could bestow on his fortunate son, in America; all this enormous proportion of the habitable globe was the private property of Philip, who was the son of Charles, who was the son of Joanna, who was the daughter of Isabella, whose husband was Ferdinand. By what seems to us the most whimsical of political arrangements, the Papuan islander, the Calabrian peasant, the Amsterdam merchant, the semi-civilized Aztec, the Moor of Barbary, the Castilian grandee, the roving Comanche, the Guinea negro, the Indian Brahmin, found themselves—could they but have known it—fellow-citizens of one commonwealth. Statutes of family descent, aided by fraud, force, and chicane, had annexed the various European sovereignties to the crown of Spain; the genius of a Genoese sailor had given to it the New World, and more recently the conquest of Portugal, torn from hands not strong enough to defend the national independence, had vested in the same sovereignty those Oriental possessions which were due to the enterprise of Vasco da Gama, his comrades and successors. The voyager, setting forth from the Straits of Gibraltar, circumnavigating the African headlands and Cape Comorin, and sailing through the Molucca Channel and past the isles which bore the name of Philip in the Eastern Sea, gave the hand at last to his adventurous comrade, who, starting from the same point, and following westward in the track of Magellan and under the Southern Cross, coasted the shore of Patagonia, and threaded his path through unmapped and unnumbered clusters of islands in the Western Pacific; and during this spanning of the earth's whole circumference not an inch of land or water was traversed that was not the domain of Philip.

For the sea, too, was his as well as the dry land.

From Borneo to California the great ocean was but a Spanish

lake, as much the king's private property as his fishponds at the Escorial with their carp and perch. No subjects but his dared to navigate those sacred waters. Not a common highway of the world's commerce, but a private path for the gratification of one human being's vanity, had thus been laid out by the bold navigators of the sixteenth century.

It was for the Dutch rebels to try conclusions upon this point, as they had done upon so many others, with the master of the land and sea. The opening scenes therefore in the great career of maritime adventure and discovery by which these republicans were to make themselves famous will soon engage the reader's attention.

Thus the causes of what is called the greatness of Spain are not far to seek. Spain was not a nation, but a temporary and factitious conjunction of several nations, which it was impossible to fuse into a permanent whole, but over whose united resources a single monarch for a time disposed. And the very concentration of these vast and unlimited powers, fortuitous as it was, in this single hand, inspiring the individual, not unnaturally, with a consciousness of superhuman grandeur, impelled him to those frantic and puerile efforts to achieve the impossible which resulted in the downfall of Spain. The man who inherited so much material greatness believed himself capable of destroying the invisible but omnipotent spirit of religious and political liberty in the Netherlands, of trampling out the national existence of France and of England, and of annexing those realms to his empire. It has been my task to relate, with much minuteness, how miserably his efforts failed.

But his resources were great. All Italy was in his hands, with the single exception of the Venetian republic; for the Grand Duke of Florence and the so-called republic of Genoa were little more than his vassals, the pope was generally his other self, and the Duke of Savoy was his son-in-law. Thus his armies, numbering usually a hundred thousand men, were supplied from the best possible sources. The Italians were esteemed the best soldiers for siege, assault, light skirmishing. The German heavy troopers and arquebuseers were the most effective for open field-work, and these were to be purchased at reasonable prices and to indefinite amount from any of the three or four hundred petty sovereigns to whom what was called Germany belonged. The Sicilian and Neapolitan pikemen, the Milanese light-horse, belonged exclusively to Philip, and were used, year after year, for more than a generation of mankind, to fight battles in which they had no more interest than had their fellow-subjects in the Moluccas or in Mexico, but which constituted for them personally as lucrative a trade on the whole as was afforded them at that day by any branch of industry.

Silk, corn, wine, and oil were furnished in profusion from these favored regions, not that the inhabitants might enjoy life, and, by accumulating wealth, increase the stock of human comforts and contribute to intellectual and scientific advancement, but in order that the proprietor of the soil might feed those eternal armies ever swarming from the south to scatter desolation over the plains of France, Burgundy, Flanders, and Holland, and to make the crown of Spain and the office of the Holy Inquisition supreme over the world. From Naples and Sicily were derived in great plenty the best materials and conveniences for shipbuilding and marine equipment. The galleys and the galleyslaves furnished by these subject realms formed the principal part of the royal navy. From distant regions, a commerce which in Philip's days had become oceanic supplied the crown with as much revenue as could be expected in a period of gross ignorance as to the causes of the true grandeur and the true wealth of nations. Especially from the mines of Mexico came an annual average of ten or twelve millions of precious metals, of which the king took twenty-five per cent for himself.

It would be difficult and almost superfluous to indicate the various resources placed in the hands of this one personage, who thus controlled so large a portion of the earth. All that breathed or grew belonged to him, and most steadily was the stream of blood and treasure poured through the sieve of his perpetual war. His system was essentially a gigantic and perpetual levy of contributions in kind, and it is only in this vague and unsatisfactory manner that the revenues of his empire can be stated. A despot really keeps no accounts, nor needs to do so, for he is responsible to no man for the way in which he husbands or squanders his own. Moreover, the science of statistics had not a beginning of existence in those days, and the most common facts can hardly be obtained, even by approximation. The usual standard of value, the commodity which we call money—gold or silver—is well known to be at best a fallacious guide for estimating the comparative wealth of individuals or of nations at widely different epochs. The dollar of Philip's day was essentially the same bit of silver that it is in our time in Spain, Naples, Rome, or America, but even should an elaborate calculation be made as to the quantity of beef or bread or broadcloth to be obtained for that bit of silver in this or that place in the middle of the sixteenth century, the result, as compared with prices now prevalent, would show many remarkable discrepancies. Thus a bushel of wheat at Antwerp during Philip's reign might cost a quarter of a dollar, in average years, and there have been seasons in our own time when two bushels of wheat could have been bought for a quarter of a dollar in Illinois. Yet if, notwithstanding this, we should allow a tenfold value in exchange to the dollar of Philip's day, we should be surprised at the meagerness of his revenues, of his expenditures, and of the debts which at the close of his career brought him to bankruptcy, were the sums estimated in coin.

Thus his income was estimated by careful contemporary statesmen at what seemed to them the prodigious annual amount of sixteen millions of dollars. He carried on a vast war without interruption during the whole of his forty-three years' reign against the most wealthy and military nations of Christendom not recognizing his authority, and in so doing he is said to have expended a sum total of seven hundred millions of dollars—a statement which made men's hair stand on their heads. Yet the American Republic, during its civil war to repress the insurrection of the slaveholders, has spent nominally as large a sum as this every year; and the British Empire in time of profound

peace spends half as much annually. And even if we should
allow sixteen millions—a purely arbitrary supposition—as compared with our times, what are a hundred and sixty millions of
dollars, or thirty-three millions of pounds sterling as the whole
net revenue of the greatest empire that had ever existed in the
world, when compared with the accumulated treasures over
which civilized and industrious countries can now dispose?
Thus the power of levying men and materials in kind constituted
the chief part of the royal power and, in truth, very little revenue
in money was obtained from Milan or Naples, or from any of
the outlying European possessions of the crown.

Eight millions a year were estimated as the revenue from the
eight kingdoms incorporated under the general name of Castile,
while not more than six hundred thousand came from the three
kingdoms which constituted Aragon. The chief sources of
money receipts were a tax of ten per cent upon sales, paid by
the seller, called Alcabala, and the Almoxarifalgo, or tariff upon
both imports and exports. Besides these imposts he obtained
about eight hundred thousand dollars a year by selling to his
subjects the privilege of eating eggs upon fast-days, according
to the permission granted him by the pope in the bull called the
Cruzada. He received another annual million from the Sussidio
and the Excusado. The first was a permission originally given
by the popes to levy six hundred thousand dollars a year upon
ecclesiastical property for equipment of a hundred war-galleys
against the Saracens, but which had more recently established
itself as a regular tax to pay for naval hostilities against Dutch
and English heretics—a still more malignant species of unbelievers in the orthodox eyes of the period. The Excusado
was the right accorded to the king always to select from the
Church possessions a single benefice and to appropriate its
fruit—a levy commuted generally for four hundred thousand
dollars a year. Besides these regular sources of income, large
but irregular amounts of money were picked up by his Majesty
in small sums, through monks sent about the country simply as
beggars, under no special license, to collect alms from rich and
poor for sustaining the war against the infidels of England and

Holland. A certain Jesuit, Father Sicily by name, had been industrious enough at one period in preaching this crusade to accumulate more than a million and a half, so that a facetious courtier advised his sovereign to style himself thenceforth king, not of the two, but of the three Sicilies, in honor of the industrious priest.

It is worthy of remark that at different periods during Philip's reign, and especially towards its close, the whole of his regular revenue was pledged to pay the interest on his debts, save only the Sussidio and the Cruzada. Thus the master of the greatest empire of the earth had at times no income at his disposal except the alms he could solicit from his poorest subjects to maintain his warfare against foreign miscreants, the levy on the Church for war-galleys, and the proceeds of his permission to eat meat on Fridays. This sounds like an epigram, but it is a plain, incontestable fact.

Thus the revenues of his foreign dominions being nearly consumed by their necessary expenses, the measure of his positive wealth was to be found in the riches of Spain. But Spain at that day was not an opulent country. It was impossible that it should be rich, for nearly every law, according to which the prosperity of a country becomes progressive, was habitually violated. It is difficult to state even by approximation the amount of its population, but the kingdoms united under the crown of Castile were estimated by contemporaries to contain eight millions, while the kingdom of Portugal, together with those annexed to Aragon and the other provinces of the realm, must have numbered half as many. Here was a populous nation in a favored land, but the foundation of all wealth was sapped by a perverted moral sentiment.

Labor was esteemed dishonorable. The Spaniard, from highest to lowest, was proud, ignorant, and lazy. For a people endowed by nature with many noble qualities—courage, temperance, frugality, endurance, quickness of perception, a high sense of honor, a reverence for law—the course of the national history had proved as ingeniously bad a system of general education as could well be invented.

The eternal contests, century after century, upon the soil of Spain between the crescent and the cross, and the remembrance of the ancient days in which Oriental valor and genius had almost extirpated Germanic institutions and Christian faith from the peninsula, had inspired one great portion of the masses with a hatred, amounting almost to insanity, towards every form of religion except the Church of Rome, towards every race of mankind except the Goths and Vandals. Innate reverence for established authority had expanded into an intensity of religious emotion and into a fanaticism of loyalty which caused the anointed monarch leading true believers against infidels to be accepted as a god. The highest industrial and scientific civilization that had been exhibited upon Spanish territory was that of Moors and Jews. When in the course of time those races had been subjugated, massacred, or driven into exile, not only was Spain deprived of its highest intellectual culture and its most productive labor, but intelligence, science, and industry were accounted degrading, because the mark of inferior and detested peoples.

The sentiment of self-esteem, always a national characteristic, assumed an almost ludicrous shape. Not a ragged Biscayan muleteer, not a swineherd of Estremadura, that did not imagine himself a nobleman because he was not of African descent. Not a half-starved, ignorant brigand, gaining his living on the highways and byways by pilfering or assassination, that did not kneel on the church pavement and listen to orisons in an ancient tongue, of which he understood not a syllable, with a sentiment of Christian self-complacency to which Godfrey of Bouillon might have been a stranger. Especially those born towards the northern frontier, and therefore farthest removed from Moorish contamination, were proudest of the purity of their race. To be an Asturian or a Gallician, however bronzed by sun and wind, was to be furnished with positive proof against suspicion of Moorish blood; but the sentiment was universal throughout the peninsula.

It followed as a matter of course that labor of any kind was an impeachment against this gentility of descent. To work was the province of Moors, Jews, and other heretics; of the Marrani or accursed, miscreants and descendants of miscreants; of the Sanbeniti or infamous, wretches whose ancestors had been convicted by the Holy Inquisition of listening, however secretly, to the Holy Scriptures as expounded by other lips than those of Roman priests. And it is a remarkable illustration of this degradation of labor and of its results, that in the reign of Philip twenty-five thousand individuals of these dishonored and comparatively industrious classes, then computed at four millions in number in the Castilian kingdoms alone, had united in a society which made a formal offer to the king to pay him two thousand dollars a head if the name and privileges of hidalgo could be conferred upon them. Thus an inconsiderable number of this vilest and most abject population—oppressed by taxation which was levied exclusively upon the low, and from which not only the great nobles but mechanics and other hidalgos were exempt—had been able to earn and to lay by enough to offer the monarch fifty millions of dollars to purchase themselves out of semi-slavery into manhood, and yet found their offer rejected by an almost insolvent king. Nothing could exceed the idleness and the frivolity of the upper classes, as depicted by contemporary and not unfriendly observers. The nobles were as idle and as ignorant as their inferiors. They were not given to tourneys nor to the delights of the chase and table, but were fond of brilliant festivities, dancing, gambling, masquerading, love-making, and pompous exhibitions of equipages, furnitures, and dress. These diversions—together with the baiting of bulls and the burning of Protestants—made up their simple round of pleasures. When they went to the wars they scorned all positions but that of general, whether by land or sea, and as war is a trade which requires an apprenticeship, it is unnecessary to observe that these grandees were rarely able to command, having never learned to obey. The poorer Spaniards were most honorably employed perhaps—so far as their own mental development was concerned—when they were sent with pike and arquebus to fight heretics in France and Flanders. They became brave and indomitable soldiers when exported to the seat of war, and thus afforded proof—by strenuously doing the hardest physical work that human beings can be called upon to perform, campaigning year after year amid the ineffable deprivations, dangers, and sufferings which are the soldier's lot—that it was from no want of industry or capacity that the lower masses of Spaniards in that age were the idle, listless, dice-playing, begging, filching vagabonds into which cruel history and horrible institutions had converted them at home.

It is only necessary to recall these well-known facts to understand why one great element of production—human labor—was but meagerly supplied. It had been the deliberate policy of the government for ages to extirpate the industrious classes, and now that a great portion of Moors and Jews were exiles and outcasts, it was impossible to supply their place by native workmen. Even the mechanics, who condescended to work with their hands in the towns, looked down alike upon those who toiled in the field and upon those who attempted to grow rich by traffic. A locksmith or a wheelwright who could prove four descents of western blood called himself a son of somebody—a hidalgo—and despised the farmer and the merchant. And those very artisans were careful not to injure themselves by excessive industry, although not reluctant by exorbitant prices to acquire in one or two days what might seem a fair remuneration for a week, and to impress upon their customers that it was rather by way of favor that they were willing to serve them at all.

Labor being thus deficient, it is obvious that there could hardly have been a great accumulation, according to modern ideas, of capital. That other chief element of national wealth, which is the result of generations of labor and of abstinence, was accordingly not abundant. And even those accretions of capital, which in the course of centuries had been inevitable, were as clumsily and inadequately diffused as the most exquisite human perverseness could desire. If the object of civil and political institutions had been to produce the greatest ill to the greatest number, that object had been as nearly attained at last in Spain as human imperfection permits; the efforts of government and of custom coming powerfully to the aid of the historical evils already indicated.

It is superfluous to say that the land belonged not to those who lived upon it—but subject to the pre-eminent right of the crown—to a small selection of the human species. Moderate holdings, small farms, peasant proprietorships, were unknown. Any kind of terrestrial possession, in short, was as far beyond the reach of those men who held themselves so haughtily and esteemed themselves so inordinately, as were the mountains in the moon.

The great nobles—and of real grandees of Spain there were but forty-nine, although the number of titled families was much larger—owned all the country, except that vast portion of it which had reposed for ages in the dead-hand of the Church. The law of primogeniture, strictly enforced, tended with every generation to narrow the basis of society. Nearly every great estate was an entail, passing from eldest son to eldest son, until these were exhausted, in which case a daughter transferred the family possessions to a new house. Thus the capital of the country—meager at best in comparison with what it might have been, had industry been honored instead of being despised, had the most intelligent and most diligent classes been cherished rather than hunted to death or into obscure dens like vermin—was concentrated in very few hands. Not only was the accumulation less than it should have been, but the slenderness of its diffusion had nearly amounted to absolute stagnation. The few possessors of capital wasted their revenues in unproductive consumption. The millions of the needy never dreamed of the possibility of deriving benefit from the capital of the rich, nor would have condescended to employ it, nor known how to employ it, had its use in any form been vouchsafed to them. The surface of Spain, save only around the few royal residences, exhibited no splendor of architecture, whether in town or country, no wonders of agricultural or horticultural skill, no monuments of engineering and constructive genius in roads, bridges, docks, warehouses, and other ornamental and useful fabrics, or in any of the thousand ways in which man facilitates intercourse among his kind and subdues nature to his will.

Yet it can never be too often repeated that it is only the Spaniard of the sixteenth century, such as extraneous circumstances had made him, that is here depicted; that he, even like his posterity and his ancestors, had been endowed by Nature with some of her noblest gifts. Acuteness of intellect, wealth of imagination, heroic qualities of heart, and hand, and brain, rarely surpassed in any race, and manifested on a thousand battlefields, and in the triumphs of a magnificent and most original literature, had not been able to save a whole nation from the disaster and the degradation which the mere words Philip II and the Holy Inquisition suggest to every educated mind.

Nor is it necessary for my purpose to measure exactly the space which separated Spain from the other leading monarchies of the day. That the standard of civilization was a vastly higher one in England, Holland, or even France—torn as they all were with perpetual civil war—no thinker will probably deny; but as it is rather my purpose at this moment to exhibit the evils which may spring from a perfectly bad monarchical system, as administered by a perfectly bad king, I prefer not to wander at present from the country which was ruled for almost half a century by Philip II.

Besides the concentration of a great part of the capital of the country in a very small number of titled families, still another immense portion of the national wealth belonged, as already intimated, to the Church.

There were eleven archbishops, at the head of whom stood the Archbishop of Toledo, with the enormous annual revenue of three hundred thousand dollars. Next to him came the Archbishop of Seville, with one hundred and fifty thousand dollars yearly, while the income of the others varied from fifty thousand to twenty thousand dollars respectively.

There were sixty-two bishops, with annual incomes ranging from fifty thousand to six thousand dollars. The churches, also, of these various episcopates were as richly endowed as the great hierarchs themselves. But without fatiguing the reader with minute details, it is sufficient to say that one-third of the whole annual income of Spain and Portugal belonged to the ecclesiastical body. In return for this enormous proportion of the earth's fruits, thus placed by the caprice of destiny at their disposal, these holy men did very little work in the world. They fed their flocks neither with bread nor with spiritual food. They taught little, preached little, dispensed little in charity. Very few of the swarming millions of naked and hungry throughout the land were clothed or nourished out of these prodigious revenues of the Church. The constant and avowed care of those prelates was to increase their worldly possessions, to build up the fortunes of their respective families, to grow richer and richer at the expense of the people whom for centuries they had fleeced. Of gross crime, of public ostentatious immorality, such as had made the Roman priesthood of that and preceding ages loathsome in the sight of man and God, the Spanish church dignitaries were innocent. Avarice, greediness, and laziness were their characteristics. It is almost superfluous to say that, while the ecclesiastical princes were rolling in this almost fabulous wealth, the subordinate clergy, the mob of working priests, were needy, half-starved mendicants.

From this rapid survey of the condition of the peninsula it will seem less surprising than it might do at first glance that the revenue of the greatest monarch of the world was rated at the small amount—even after due allowance for the difference of general values between the sixteenth and nineteenth centuries—of sixteen millions of dollars. The King of Spain was powerful and redoubtable at home and abroad, because accident had placed the control of a variety of separate realms in his single hand. At the same time Spain was poor and weak, because she had lived for centuries in violation of the principles on which the wealth and strength of nations depend. Moreover, every one of those subject and violently annexed nations hated Spain with undying fervor, while an infernal policy—the leading characteristics of which were to sow dissensions among the nobles, to confiscate their property on all convenient occasions, and to bestow it upon Spaniards and other foreigners; to keep the discontented masses in poverty, but to deprive them of the power or disposition to unite with their superiors in rank in demonstrations against the crown—had sufficed to suppress any extensive revolt in the various Italian states united under Philip's scepter. Still more intense than the hatred of Italians was the animosity which was glowing in every Portuguese breast against the Spanish sway; while even the Aragonese were only held in subjection by terror, which, indeed, in one form or another, was the leading instrument of Philip's government.

It is hardly necessary to enlarge upon the regulations of Spain's foreign commerce; for it will be enough to repeat the phrase that in her eyes the great ocean from east to west was a Spanish lake, sacred to the ships of the king's subjects alone. With such a simple code of navigation coming in aid of the other causes which impoverished the land, it may be believed that the maritime traffic of the country would dwindle into the same exiguous proportions which characterized her general industry.

Moreover, it should never be forgotten that, although the various kingdoms of Spain were politically conjoined by their personal union under one despot, they were commercially distinct. A line of custom-houses separated each province from the rest, and made the various inhabitants of the peninsula practically strangers to each other. Thus there was less traffic between Castile, Biscay, and Aragon than there was between any one of them and remote foreign nations. The Biscayans, for example, could even import and export commodities to and from remote countries by sea, free of duty, while their merchandise to and from Castile was crushed by imposts. As this ingenious perversity of positive arrangements came to increase the negative inconveniences caused by the almost total absence of tolerable roads, canals, bridges, and other means of inter-communication, it may be imagined that internal traffic—the very lifeblood of every prosperous nation—was very nearly stagnant in Spain. As an inevitable result, the most thriving branch of national industry was that of the professional smuggler, who, in the pursuit of his vocation, did his best to aid government in sapping the wealth of the nation.

The whole accumulated capital of Spain, together with the land—in the general sense which includes not only the soil but the immovable property of a country—being thus exclusively owned by the crown, the Church, and a very small number of patrician families, while the supply of labor—owing to the special causes which had converted the masses of the people into paupers ashamed to work but not unwilling to beg or to rob—was incredibly small, it is obvious that, so long as the same causes continued in operation, the downfall of the country was a logical result from which there was no escape. Nothing but a general revolution of mind and hand against the prevalent system, nothing but some great destructive but regenerating catastrophe, could redeem the people.

And it is the condition of the people which ought always to be the prominent subject of interest to those who study the records of the Past. It is only by such study that we can derive instruction from history, and enable ourselves, however dimly and feebly, to cast the horoscope of younger nations. Human history, so far as it has been written, is at best a mere fragment; for the few centuries or year-thousands of which there is definite record are as nothing compared to the millions of unnumbered years during which man has perhaps walked the earth. It may be as practicable therefore to derive instruction from a minute examination in detail of a very limited period of time and space, and thus to deduce general rules for the infinite future, during which our species may be destined to inhabit this planet, as by a more extensive survey, which must however be at best a limited one. Men die, but Man is immortal, and it would be a sufficiently forlorn prospect for humanity if we were not able to discover causes in operation which would ultimately render the system of Philip II impossible in any part of the globe. Certainly, were it otherwise, the study of human history would be the most wearisome and unprofitable of all conceivable occupations. The festivities of courts, the magnificence of an aristocracy, the sayings and doings of monarchs and their servants, the dynastic wars, the solemn treaties, the Ossa upon Pelion of diplomatic and legislative rubbish by which, in the course of centuries, a few individuals or combinations of individuals have been able to obstruct the march of humanity, and have essayed to suspend the operation of elemental laws—all this contains but little solid food for grown human beings. The condition of the brave and quick-witted Spanish people in the latter half of the sixteenth century gives more matter for reflection and possible instruction.

. That science is the hope of the world, that ignorance is the real enslaver of mankind, and therefore the natural ally of every form of despotism, may be assumed as an axiom, and it was certainly the ignorance and superstition of the people upon which the Philippian policy was founded.

A vast mass, entirely uneducated, half fed, half clothed, unemployed, and reposing upon a still lower and denser stratum—the millions namely of the "accursed," of the Africans, and last and vilest of all, the "blessed" descendants of Spanish Protestants whom the Holy Office had branded with perpetual infamy because it had burned their progenitors—this was the People; and it was these paupers and outcasts, nearly the whole nation, that paid all the imposts of which the public revenue was composed. The great nobles, priests, and even the hidalgos, were exempt from taxation. Need more be said to indicate the inevitable ruin of both government and people?

And it was over such a people, and with institutions like these, that Philip II was permitted to rule during forty-three years. His power was absolute. With this single phrase one might as well dismiss any attempt at specification. He made war or peace at will with foreign nations. He had power of life and death over all his subjects. He had unlimited control of their worldly goods. As he claimed supreme jurisdiction over their religious opinions also, he was master of their minds, bodies, and estates. As a matter of course, he nominated and removed at will every executive functionary, every judge, every magistrate, every military or civil officer; and moreover, he not only selected, according to the license tacitly conceded to him by the pontiff, every archbishop, bishop, and other Church dignitary, but, through his great influence at Rome, he named most of the cardinals, and thus controlled the election of the popes. The whole machinery of society, political, ecclesiastical, military, was in his single hand. There was a show of provincial privilege here and there in different parts of Spain, but it was but the phantom of that ancient municipal liberty which it had been the especial care of his father and his great-grandfather to destroy. Most patiently did Philip, by his steady inactivity, bring about the decay of the last ruins of free institutions in the peninsula. The councils and legislative assemblies were convoked and then wearied out in waiting for that royal assent to the propositions and transactions, which was deferred intentionally, year after year, and never given. Thus the time of the deputies was consumed in accomplishing infinite nothing, until the moment arrived when the monarch, without any violent stroke of state, could feel safe in issuing decrees and pragmatic edicts; thus reducing the ancient legislative and consultative bodies to nullity, and substituting the will of an individual for a constitutional fabric. To criticize the expenses of government or to attempt interference with the increase of taxation became a sorry farce. The forms remained in certain provinces after the life had long since fled. Only in Aragon had the ancient privileges seemed to defy the absolute authority of the monarch; and it was reserved for Antonio Perez to be the cause of their final extirpation. The grinning skulls of the Chief Justice of that kingdom and of the boldest and noblest advocates and defenders of the national liberties, exposed for years in the market-place, with the record of their death-sentence attached, informed the Spaniards, in language which the most ignorant could read, that the crime of defending a remnant of human freedom and constitutional law was sure to draw down condign punishment. It was the last time in that age that even the ghost of extinct liberty was destined to revisit the soil of Spain. It mattered not that the immediate cause for pursuing Perez was his successful amour with the king's mistress, nor that the crime of which he was formally accused was the deadly offense of Calvinism, rather than his intrigue with the Eboli and his assassination of Escovedo; for it was in the natural and simple sequence of events that the last vestige of law or freedom should be obliterated wherever Philip could vindicate his sway. It must be admitted, too, that the king seized this occasion to strike a decisive blow with a promptness very different from his usual artistic sluggishness. Rarely has a more terrible epigram been spoken by man than the royal words which constituted the whole trial and sentence of the Chief Justice of Aragon, for the crime of defending the law of his country: "You will take John of Lanuza, and you will have his head cut off." This was the end of the magistrate and of the constitution which he had defended.

His power was unlimited. A man endowed with genius and virtue, and possessing the advantages of a consummate education, could have perhaps done little more than attempt to mitigate the general misery, and to remove some of its causes. For it is one of the most pernicious dogmas of the despotic system, and the one which the candid student of history soonest discovers to be false, that the masses of mankind are to look to any individual, however exalted by birth or intellect, for their redemption. Woe to the world if the nations are never to learn that their fate is and ought to be in their own hands; that their institutions, whether liberal or despotic, are the result of the national biography and of the national character, not the work of a few individuals whose names have been preserved by capricious Accident as heroes and legislators. Yet there is no doubt that, while comparatively powerless for good, the individual despot is capable of almost infinite mischief. There have been few men known to history who have been able to accomplish by their own exertions so vast an amount of evil as the king who had just died. If Philip possessed a single virtue it has eluded the conscientious research of the writer of these pages. If there are vices—as possibly there are—from which he was exempt, it is because it is not permitted to human nature to attain perfection even in evil. The only plausible explanation—for palliation there is none—of his infamous career is that the man really believed himself not a king but a god. He was placed so high above his fellow-creatures as, in good faith perhaps, to believe himself incapable of doing wrong; so that, whether indulging his passions or enforcing throughout the world his religious and political dogmas he was ever conscious of embodying divine inspirations and elemental laws. When providing for the assassination of a monarch, or commanding the massacre of a townful of Protestants; when trampling on every oath by which a human being can bind himself; when laying desolate with fire and sword, during more than a generation, the provinces which he had inherited as his private property, or in carefully maintaining the flames of civil war in foreign kingdoms which he hoped to acquire; while maintaining over all Christendom a gigantic system of bribery, corruption, and espionage, keeping the noblest names of England and Scotland on his pension-lists of traitors, and impoverishing his exchequer with the wages of iniquity paid in France to men of all degrees, from princes of blood like Guise and Mayenne down to the obscurest of country squires, he ever felt that these base or bloody deeds were not crimes, but the simple will of the godhead of which he was a portion. He never doubted that the extraordinary theological system which he spent his life in enforcing with fire and sword was right, for it was a part of himself. The Holy Inquisition, thoroughly established as it was in his ancestral Spain, was a portion of the regular working machinery by which his absolute kingship and his superhuman will expressed themselves. A tribunal which performed its functions with a celerity, certainty, and invisibility resembling the attributes of Omnipotence; which, like the pestilence, entered palace or hovel at will, and which smote the wretch guilty or suspected of heresy with a precision against which no human ingenuity or sympathy could guard—such an institution could not but be dear to his heart. It was inevitable that the extension and perpetuation of what he deemed its blessings throughout his dominions should be his settled purpose. Spain was governed by an established terrorism. It is a mistake to suppose that Philip was essentially beloved in his native land, or that his religious and political system was heartily accepted because consonant to the national character. On the contrary, as has been shown, a very large proportion of the inhabitants were either secretly false to the Catholic faith, or descended at least from those who had expiated their hostility to it with their lives. But the Grand Inquisitor was almost as awful a personage as the king or the pope. His familiars were in every village and at every fireside, and from their fangs there was no escape. Millions of Spaniards would have rebelled against the crown or accepted the Reformed religion, had they not been perfectly certain of being burned or hanged at the slightest movement in such a direction. The popular force in the course of the political combinations of centuries seemed at last to have been eliminated. The nobles, exempt from taxation, which crushed the people to the earth, were the enemies rather than the chieftains and champions of the lower classes in any possible struggle with a crown to which they were united by ties of interest as well as of affection, while the great churchmen, too, were the immediate dependents and of course the firm supporters of the king. Thus, the people, without natural leaders, without organization, and themselves divided into two mutually hostile sections, were opposed by every force in the state. Crown, nobility, and clergy; all the wealth and all that there was of learning, were banded together to suppress the democratic principle. But even this would hardly have sufficed to extinguish every spark of liberty, had it not been for the potent machinery of the Inquisition; nor could that perfection of terrorism have become an established institution but for the extraordinary mixture of pride and superstition of which the national character had been, in the course of the national history, compounded. The Spanish portion of the people hated the nobles, whose petty exactions and oppressions were always visible; but they had a reverential fear of the unseen monarch, as the representative both of the great unsullied Christian nation to which the meanest individual was proud to belong, and of the God of wrath who had decreed the extermination of all unbelievers. The "accursed" portion of the people were sufficiently disloyal at heart, but were too much crushed by oppression and contempt to imagine themselves men. As to the Netherlanders, they did not fight originally for independence. It was not until after a quarter of a century of fighting that they ever thought of renouncing their allegiance to Philip. They fought to protect themselves against being taxed by the king without the consent of those constitutional assemblies which he had sworn to maintain, and to save themselves and their children from being burned alive if they dared to read the Bible. Independence followed after nearly a half-century of fighting, but it would never have been obtained, or perhaps demanded, had those grievances of the people been redressed.

Of this perfect despotism Philip was thus the sole administrator. Certainly he looked upon his mission with seriousness, and was industrious in performing his royal functions. But this earnestness and seriousness were, in truth, his darkest vices; for the most frivolous voluptuary that ever wore a crown would never have compassed a thousandth part of the evil which was Philip's lifework. It was because he was a believer in himself, and in what he called his religion, that he was enabled to perpetrate such a long catalogue of crimes. When an humble malefactor is brought before an ordinary court of justice, it is not often, in any age or country, that he escapes the pillory or the gallows because, from his own point of view, his actions, instead of being criminal, have been commendable, and because the multitude and continuity of his offenses prove him to have been sincere. And because anointed monarchs are amenable to no human tribunal, save to that terrible assize which the People, bursting its chain from time to time in the course of the ages, sets up for the trial of its oppressors, and which is called Revolution, it is the more important for the great interests of humanity that before the judgment-seat of History a crown should be no protection to its wearer. There is no plea to the jurisdiction of history, if history be true to itself.

As for the royal criminal called Philip II, his life is his arraignment, and these volumes will have been written in vain if a specification is now required.

Homicide such as was hardly ever compassed before by one human being was committed by Philip when in the famous edict of 1568 he sentenced every man, woman, and child in the Netherlands to death. That the whole of this population, three millions or more, were not positively destroyed was because no human energy could suffice to execute the diabolical decree. But Alva, toiling hard, accomplished much of this murderous work. By the aid of the Council of Blood, and of the sheriffs and executioners of the Holy Inquisition, he was able sometimes to put eight hundred human beings to death in a single week for the crimes of Protestantism or of opulence, and at the end of half a dozen years he could boast of having strangled, drowned, burned, or beheaded somewhat more than eighteen thousand of his fellow-creatures. These were some of the non-combatant victims; for of the tens of thousands who perished during his administration alone, in siege and battle, no statistical record has been preserved.

In face of such wholesale crimes, of these forty years of blood-shed, it is superfluous to refer to such isolated misdeeds as his repeated attempts to procure the assassination of the Prince of Orange, crowned at last by the success of Balthazar Gérard, nor to his persistent efforts to poison the Queen of England; for the enunciation of all these murders or attempts at murder would require a repetition of the story which it has been one of the main purposes of these volumes to recite.

For indeed it seems like mere railing to specify his crimes. Their very magnitude and unbroken continuity, together with their impunity, give them almost the appearance of inevitable phenomena. The horrible monotony of his career stupefies the mind until it is ready to accept the principle of evil as the fundamental law of the world.

His robberies, like his murders, were colossal. The vast system of confiscation set up in the Netherlands was sufficient to reduce unnumbered innocent families to beggary, although powerless to break the spirit of civil and religious liberty or to pay the expenses of subjugating a people. Not often in the world's history have so many thousand individuals been plundered by a foreign tyrant for no crime, save that they were rich enough to be worth robbing. For it can never be too often repeated that those confiscations and extortions were perpetrated upon Catholics as well as Protestants, monarchists as well as rebels; the possession of property making proof of orthodoxy or of loyalty well-nigh impossible.

Falsehood was the great basis of the king's character, which perhaps derives its chief importance, as a political and psychological study, from this very fact. It has been shown throughout the whole course of this history, by the evidence of his most secret correspondence, that he was false, most of all, to those to whom he gave what he called his heart. Granvelle, Alva, Don John, Alexander Farnese, all those, in short, who were deepest in his confidence experienced in succession his entire perfidy, while each in turn was sacrificed to his master's sleepless suspicion. The pope himself was often as much the dupe of the Catholic monarch's faithlessness as the vilest heretic had ever been. Could the great schoolmaster of iniquity for the sovereigns and politicians of the South have lived to witness the practice of the monarch who had most laid to heart the precepts of "The Prince," he would have felt that he had not written in vain, and that his great paragon of successful falsehood, Ferdinand of Aragon, had been surpassed by the great-grandson. For the ideal perfection of perfidy, foreshadowed by the philosopher who died in the year of Philip's birth, was thoroughly embodied at last by this potentate. Certainly Nicholas Machiavelli could have hoped for no more docile pupil. That all men are vile, that they are liars, scoundrels, poltroons, and idiots alike, ever ready to deceive and yet easily to be duped, and that he only is fit to be king who excels his kind in the arts of deception—by this great maxim of the Florentine, Philip was ever guided. And those well-known texts of hypocrisy, strewn by the same hand, had surely not fallen on stony ground when received into Philip's royal soul:

"Often it is necessary, in order to maintain power, to act contrary to faith, contrary to charity, contrary to humanity, contrary to religion. . . . A Prince ought therefore to have great care that from his mouth nothing should ever come that is not filled with those five qualities, and that to see and hear him he should appear all piety, all faith, all integrity, all humanity, all religion. And nothing is more necessary than to seem to have this last-mentioned quality. . . . Every one sees what you seem, few perceive what you are."

Surely this handbook of cant had been Philip's _vade mecum_ through his life's pilgrimage.

It is at least a consolation to reflect that a career controlled by such principles came to an ignominious close. Had the mental capacity of this sovereign been equal to his criminal intent, even greater woe might have befallen the world. But his intellect was less than mediocre. His passion for the bureau, his slavery to routine, his puerile ambition personally to superintend details which could have been a thousand times better administered by subordinates, proclaimed every day the narrowness of his mind. His diligence in reading, writing, and commenting upon despatches may excite admiration only where there has been no opportunity of judging of his labors by personal inspection. Those familiar with the dreary displays of his penmanship must admit that such work could have been at least as well done by a copying clerk of average capacity. His ministers were men of respectable ability, but he imagined himself, as he advanced in life, far superior to any counsellor that he could possibly select, and was accustomed to consider himself the first statesman in the world.

His reign was a thorough and disgraceful failure. Its opening scene was the treaty of Cateau-Cambrésis, by which a triumph over France had been achieved for him by the able generals and statesmen of his father, so humiliating and complete as to make every French soldier or politician gnash his teeth. Its conclusion was the treaty of Vervins with the same power, by which the tables were completely turned, and which was as utterly disgraceful to Spain as that of Cateau-Cambrésis had been to France. He had spent his life in fighting with the spirit of the age—that invincible power of which he had not the faintest conception—while the utter want of adaptation of his means to his ends often bordered, not on the ludicrous, but the insane.

He attempted to reduce the free Netherlands to slavery and to papacy. Before his death they had expanded into an independent republic, with a policy founded upon religious toleration and the rights of man. He had endeavored all his life to exclude the Béarnese from his heritage and to place himself or his daughter on the vacant throne; before his death Henry IV was the most powerful and popular sovereign that had ever reigned in France. He had sought to invade and to conquer England, and to dethrone and assassinate its queen. But the queen outwitted, outgeneraled, and outlived him; English soldiers and sailors, assisted by their Dutch comrades in arms, accomplished on the shores of Spain what the Invincible Armada had in vain essayed against England and Holland; while England, following thenceforth the opposite system to that of absolutism and the Inquisition, became, after centuries of struggles towards the right, the most powerful, prosperous, and enlightened kingdom in the world.

His exchequer, so full when he ascended the throne as to excite the awe of contemporary financiers, was reduced before his death to a net income of some four millions of dollars. His armies, which had been the wonder of the age in the earlier period of his reign for discipline, courage, and every quality on which military efficiency depends, were in his later years a horde of starving, rebellious brigands, more formidable to their commanders than to the foe. Mutiny was the only organized military institution that was left in his dominions, while the Spanish Inquisition, which it was the fell purpose of his life from youth upwards to establish over the world, became a loathsome and impossible nuisance everywhere but in its natal soil.

If there be such a thing as historical evidence, then is Philip II convicted before the tribunal of impartial posterity of every crime charged in his indictment. He lived seventy-one years and three months, he reigned forty-three years. He endured the martyrdom of his last illness with the heroism of a saint, and died in the certainty of immortal bliss as the reward of his life of evil.[1]

[COMMERCE OF THE NETHERLANDS ABOUT 1600]

[Motley gives this picture of the commerce of the United Netherlands, the economic foundation of the country, toward the close of the sixteenth century.]

During a great portion of Philip's reign the Netherlanders, despite their rebellion, had been permitted to trade with Spain. A spectacle had thus been presented of a vigorous traffic between two mighty belligerents, who derived from their intercourse with each other the means of more thoroughly carrying on their mutual hostilities. The war fed their commerce, and commerce fed their war. The great maritime discoveries at the close of the fifteenth century had inured quite as much to the benefit of the Flemings and Hollanders as to that of the Spaniards and Portuguese, to whom they were originally due. Antwerp and subsequently Amsterdam had thriven on the great revolution of the Indian trade which Vasco da Gama's voyage around the Cape had effected. The nations of the Baltic and of farthest Ind now exchanged their products on a more extensive scale and with a wider sweep across the earth than when the mistress of the Adriatic alone held the keys of Asiatic commerce. The haughty but intelligent oligarchy of shopkeepers, which had grown so rich and attained so eminent a political position from its magnificent monopoly, already saw the sources of its grandeur drying up before its eyes, now that the world's trade—for the first time in human history—had become oceanic.

In Holland, long since denuded of forests, were great markets of timber, whither shipbuilders and architects came from all parts of the world to gather the utensils for their craft. There,

[1] *History of the United Netherlands* (New York, 1860–1867), III, 514–543.

too, where scarcely a pebble had been deposited in the course of the geological transformations of our planet, were great artificial quarries of granite, and marble, and basalt. Wheat was almost as rare a product of the soil as cinnamon, yet the granaries of Christendom, and the Oriental magazines of spices and drugs, were found chiefly on that barren spot of earth. There was the great international mart where the Osterling, the Turk, the Hindoo, the Atlantic and the Mediterranean traders stored their wares and negotiated their exchanges; while the curious and highly-prized products of Netherland skill—broadcloths, tapestries, brocades, laces, substantial fustians, magnificent damasks, finest linens—increased the mass of visible wealth piled mountains high upon that extraordinary soil which produced nothing and teemed with everything.

After the incorporation of Portugal with Spain, however, many obstacles were thrown in the way of the trade from the Netherlands to Lisbon and the Spanish ports. Loud and bitter were the railings uttered, as we know, by the English sovereign and her statesmen against the nefarious traffic which the Dutch Republic persisted in carrying on with the common enemy. But it is very certain that although the Spanish armadas would have found it comparatively difficult to equip themselves without the tar and the timber, the cordage, the stores, and the biscuits furnished by the Hollanders, the rebellious commonwealth, if excluded from the world's commerce, in which it had learned to play so controlling a part, must have ceased to exist. For without foreign navigation the independent Republic was an inconceivable idea. Not only would it have been incapable of continuing the struggle with the greatest monarch in the world, but it might as well have buried itself once and forever beneath the waves from which it had scarcely emerged. Commerce and Holland were simply synonymous terms. Its morsel of territory was but the wharf to which the republic was occasionally moored; its home was in every ocean and over all the world. Nowhere had there ever existed before so large a proportion of population that was essentially maritime. They were born sailors—men and women alike—and numerous were the children who had never set foot on the shore. At the period now treated of the Republic had three times as many ships and sailors as any one nation in the world. Compared with modern times, and especially with the gigantic commercial strides of the two great Anglo-Saxon families, the statistics both of population and of maritime commerce in that famous and most vigorous epoch would seem sufficiently meager. Yet there is no doubt that in the relative estimate of forces then in activity it would be difficult to exaggerate the naval power of the young commonwealth. When therefore, towards the close of Philip II's reign, it became necessary to renounce the carrying trade with Spain and Portugal, by which the communication with India and China was effected, or else to submit to the confiscation of Dutch ships in Spanish ports, and the confinement of Dutch sailors in the dungeons of the Inquisition, a more serious dilemma was presented to the statesmen of the Netherlands than they had ever been called upon to solve.[1]

[EXPANSION OF COMMERCE WITH THE EAST]

[Motley did not neglect the expansion of Dutch commerce into the East Indies and the Far East. The next three passages give some account of the beginnings of this commercial intercourse.]

The Hollanders as a nation had never been engaged in the direct trade around the Cape of Good Hope. Fortunately, however, at this crisis in their commercial destiny there was a single Hollander who had thoroughly learned the lesson which it was so necessary that all his countrymen should now be taught. Few men of that period deserve a more kindly and more honorable remembrance by posterity for their contributions to science and the progress of civilization than John Huygen van Linschoten, son of a plain burgher of West Friesland. Having always felt a strong impulse to study foreign history and distant nations and customs, he resolved at the early age of seventeen

[1] *History of the United Netherlands* (New York, 1860–1867), III, 544–546.

"to absent himself from his fatherland, and from the conversation of friends and relatives," in order to gratify this inclination for self-improvement. After a residence of two years in Lisbon he departed for India in the suite of the Archbishop of Goa, and remained in the East for nearly thirteen years. Diligently examining all the strange phenomena which came under his observation and patiently recording the results of his researches day by day and year by year, he amassed a fund of information which he modestly intended for the entertainment of his friends when he should return to his native country. It was his wish that "without stirring from their firesides or counting-houses" they might participate with him in the gratification and instruction to be derived from looking upon a world then so strange, and for Europeans still so new. He described the manners and customs, the laws, the religions, the social and political institutions, of the ancient races who dwelt in either peninsula of India. He studied the natural history, the botany, the geography of all the regions which he visited. Especially the products which formed the material of a great traffic, the system of culture, the means of transportation, and the course of commerce, were examined by him with minuteness, accuracy, and breadth of vision. He was neither a trader nor a sailor, but a man of letters, a scientific and professional traveller. But it was obvious when he returned, rich with the spoils of Oriental study during thirteen years of life, that the results of his researches were worthy of a wider circulation than that which he had originally contemplated. His work was given to the public in the year 1596, and was studied with avidity not only by men of science but by merchants and seafarers. He also added to the record of his Indian experiences a practical manual for navigators. He described the course of the voyage from Lisbon to the East, the currents, the trade-winds and monsoons, the harbors, the islands, the shoals, the sunken rocks and dangerous quicksands, and he accompanied his work with various maps and charts, both general and special, of land and water, rarely delineated before his day, as well as by various astronomical and mathematical calculations. Already a countryman of his own, Wagenaer of Zeeland, had laid the mariners of the world under special obligation by a manual which came into such universal use that for centuries afterwards the sailors of England and of other countries called their indispensable *vade mecum* a Wagenaer. But in that textbook but little information was afforded to Eastern voyagers, because, before the enterprise of Linschoten, little was known of the Orient except to the Portuguese and Spaniards, by whom nothing was communicated.[1]

But it was not in Europe nor in Christendom alone, during that twilight epoch of declining absolutism, regal and sacerdotal, and the coming glimmer of freedom, religious and commercial, that the contrast between the old and new civilizations was exhibiting itself.

The same fishermen and fighting men, whom we have but lately seen sailing forth from Zeeland and Friesland to confront the dangers of either pole, were now contending in the Indian seas with the Portuguese monopolists of the tropics.

A century long, the generosity of the Roman pontiff in bestowing upon others what was not his property had guaranteed to the nation of Vasco da Gama one half at least of the valuable possessions which maritime genius, unflinching valor, and boundless cruelty had won and kept. But the spirit of change was abroad in the world. Potentates and merchants under the equator had been sedulously taught that there were no other white men on the planet but the Portuguese and their conquerors the Spaniards, and that the Dutch—of whom they had recently heard, and the portrait of whose great military chieftain they had seen after the news of the Nieuport battle had made the circuit of the earth—were a mere mob of pirates and savages inhabiting the obscurest of dens. They were soon, however, to be enabled to judge for themselves as to the power and the merits of the various competitors for their trade.

Early in this year Andreas Hurtado de Mendoza with a stately

[1] *History of the United Netherlands* (New York, 1860–1867), III, 546–548.

fleet of galleons and smaller vessels, more than five-and-twenty in all, was on his way towards the island of Java to inflict summary vengeance upon those Oriental rulers who had dared to trade with men forbidden by his Catholic Majesty and the Pope.

The city of Bantam was the first spot marked out for destruction, and it so happened that a Dutch skipper, Wolfert Hermann by name, commanding five trading vessels, in which were three hundred men, had just arrived in those seas to continue the illicit commerce which had aroused the ire of the Portuguese. His whole force both of men and of guns was far inferior to that of the flagship alone of Mendoza. But he resolved to make manifest to the Indians that the Batavians were not disposed to relinquish their promising commercial relations with them, nor to turn their backs upon their newly found friends in the hour of danger. To the profound astonishment of the Portuguese admiral, the Dutchman, with his five little trading ships, made an attack on the pompous armada, intending to avert chastisement from the king of Bantam. It was not possible for Wolfert to cope at close quarters with his immensely superior adversary, but his skill and nautical experience enabled him to play at what was then considered long bowls with extraordinary effect. The greater lightness and mobility of his vessels made them more than a match, in this kind of encounter, for the clumsy, top-heavy, and sluggish marine castles in which Spain and Portugal then went forth to battle on the ocean. It seems almost like the irony of history, and yet it is the literal fact, that the Dutch galiot of that day—hardly changed in two and a half centuries since—"the bull-browed galiot butting through the stream,"—was then the model clipper, conspicuous among all ships for its rapid-sailing qualities and ease of handling. So much has the world moved, on sea and shore, since those simple but heroic days. And thus Wolfert's swift-going galiots circled round and round the awkward, ponderous, and much-puzzled Portuguese fleet, until by well-directed shots and skilful manoeuvring they had sunk several ships, taken two, run others into the shallows, and, at last, put the whole to confusion. After several days of such fighting,

Admiral Mendoza fairly turned his back upon his insignificant opponent, and abandoned his projects upon Java. Bearing away for the Island of Amboina with the remainder of his fleet, he laid waste several of its villages and odoriferous spice-fields, while Wolfert and his companions entered Bantam in triumph, and were hailed as deliverers. And thus on the extreme western verge of this magnificent island was founded the first trading settlement of the Batavian Republic in the archipelago of the equator—the foundation-stone of a great commercial empire which was to encircle the earth. Not many years later, at the distance of a dozen leagues from Bantam, a congenial swamp was fortunately discovered in a land whose volcanic peaks rose two miles into the air, and here a town duly laid out with canals and bridges, and trim gardens and stagnant pools, was baptized by the ancient and well-beloved name of Good Meadow, or Batavia, which it bears to this day.

Meantime Wolfert Hermann was not the only Hollander cruising in those seas able to convince the Oriental mind that all Europeans save the Portuguese were not pirates and savages and that friendly intercourse with other foreigners might be as profitable as slavery to the Spanish crown.

Captain Nek made treaties of amity and commerce with the potentates of Ternate, Tidore, and other Molucca islands. The King of Kandy, on the Island of Ceylon, lord of the odoriferous fields of cassia which perfume those tropical seas, was glad to learn how to exchange the spices of the equator for the thousand fabrics and products of western civilization which found their great emporium in Holland. Jacob Heemskerk, too, who had so lately astonished the world by his exploits and discoveries during his famous winter in Nova Zembla, was now seeking adventures and carrying the flag and fame of the republic along the Indian and Chinese coasts. The King of Johore, on the Malayan peninsula, entered into friendly relations with him, being well pleased, like so many of those petty rulers, to obtain protection against the Portuguese whom he had so long hated and feared. He informed Heemskerk of the arrival in the straits of Malacca of an immense Lisbon carrack, laden with pearls and spices, brocades and precious stones, on its way to Europe, and suggested an attack. It is true that the roving Hollander merely commanded a couple of the smallest galiots with about a hundred and thirty men in the two. But when was Jacob Heemskerk ever known to shrink from an encounter —whether from single-handed combat with a polar bear, or from leading a forlorn hope against a Spanish fort, or from assailing a Portuguese armada? The carrack, more than one thousand tons burden, carried seventeen guns, and at least eight times as many men as he commanded. Nevertheless, after a combat of but brief duration Heemskerk was master of the carrack. He spared the lives of his seven hundred prisoners, and set them on shore before they should have time to discover to what a handful of Dutchmen they had surrendered. Then dividing about a million florins' worth of booty among his men, who doubtless found such cruising among the spice-islands more attractive than wintering at the North Pole, he sailed in the carrack for Macao, where he found no difficulty in convincing the authorities of the Celestial Empire that the friendship of the Dutch Republic was worth cultivating. There was soon to be work in other regions for the hardy Hollander —such as was to make the name of Heemskerk a word to conjure with down to the latest posterity. Meantime he returned to his own country to take part in the great industrial movements which were to make this year an epoch in commercial history.

The conquerors of Mendoza and deliverers of Bantam had, however, not paused in their work. From Java they sailed to Banda, and on those volcanic islands of nutmegs and cloves made, in the name of their commonwealth, a treaty with its republican antipodes. For there was no king to be found in that particular archipelago, and the two republics, the Oriental and the Germanic, dealt with each other with direct and becoming simplicity. Their convention was in accordance with the commercial ideas of the day, which assumed monopoly as the true basis of national prosperity. It was agreed that none but Dutchmen should ever purchase the nutmegs of Banda, and that neither nation should harbor refugees from the other. Other articles, however, showed how much farther the practice of political and religious liberty had advanced than had any theory of commercial freedom. It was settled that each nation should judge its own citizens according to its own laws, that neither should interfere by force with the other in regard to religious matters, but that God should be judge over them all. Here at least was progress beyond the system according to which the Holy Inquisition furnished the only enginery of civilization. The guardianship assumed by Holland over these children of the sun was at least an improvement on the tyranny which roasted them alive if they rejected religious dogmas which they could not comprehend, and which proclaimed with fire, sword, and gibbet that the Omnipotent especially forbade the nutmeg trade to all but the subjects of the Most Catholic king.

In Atsgen, or Achin, chief city of Sumatra, a treaty was likewise made with the government of the place, and it was arranged that the king of Atsgen should send over an embassy to the distant but friendly Republic. Thus he might judge whether the Hollanders were enemies of all the world, as had been represented to him, or only of Spain; whether their knowledge of the arts and sciences, and their position among the Western nations entitled them to respect, and made their friendship desirable; or whether they were only worthy of the contempt which their royal and aristocratic enemies delighted to heap upon their heads. The envoys sailed from Sumatra on board the same little fleet which, under the command of Wolfert Hermann, had already done such signal service, and on their way to Europe they had an opportunity of seeing how these republican sailors could deal with their enemies on the ocean.[1]

Nor are we to forget how very recently, and even dimly, the idea of freedom in commerce had dawned upon nations the

[1] *History of the United Netherlands* (New York, 1860–1867), IV, 105–110.

freest of all in polity and religion. Certainly the vices and shortcomings of the commercial system now inaugurated by the Republic may be justly charged in great part to the epoch, while her vast share in the expanding and upward movement which civilization, under the auspices of self-government, self-help, political freedom, free thought, and unshackled science, was then to undertake—nevermore, perhaps, to be permanently checked—must be justly ascribed to herself.

It was considered accordingly that the existence of so many private companies and copartnerships trading to the East was injurious to the interests of commerce. Merchants arriving at the different Indian ports would often find that their own countrymen had been too quick for them, and that other fleets had got the wind out of their sails, that the eastern markets had been stripped, and that prices had gone up to a ruinous height, while on the other hand, in the Dutch cities, nutmegs and cinnamon, brocades and indigo, were as plentiful as red herrings. It was hardly to be expected at that day to find this very triumph of successful traffic considered otherwise than as a grave misfortune, demanding interference on the part of the only free Government then existing in the world. That already free competition and individual enterprise had made such progress in enriching the Hollanders and the Javanese respectively with a superfluity of useful or agreeable things, brought from the farthest ends of the earth, seemed to the eyes of that day a condition of things likely to end in a general catastrophe. With a simplicity amazing only to those who are inclined to be vain of a superior wisdom—not their own but that of their wisest contemporaries—one of the chief reasons for establishing the East India Company was stated to be the necessity of providing against low prices of Oriental productions in Europe.

But national instinct is often wiser than what is supposed to be high national statesmanship, and there can be no doubt that the true foundation of the East India Company was the simple recognition of an iron necessity. Every merchant in Holland knew full well that the Portuguese and Spaniards could never be driven out of their commercial strongholds under the equator, except by a concentration of the private strength and wealth of the mercantile community. The government had enough on its hands in disputing inch by inch, at so prodigious an expenditure of blood and treasure, the meager territory with which nature had endowed the little commonwealth. Private organization, self-help, union of individual purses and individual brains, were to conquer an empire at the antipodes, if it were to be won at all. By so doing, the wealth of the nation and its power to maintain the great conflict with the spirit of the past might be indefinitely increased, and the resources of Spanish despotism proportionally diminished. It was not to be expected of Jacob Heemskerk, Wolfert Hermann, or Joris van Spilberg, indomitable skippers though they were, that each, acting on his own responsibility or on that of his supercargo, would succeed every day in conquering a whole Spanish fleet and dividing a million or two of prize-money among a few dozen sailors. Better things even than this might be done by wholesome and practical concentration on a more extended scale.

So the States-General granted a patent or charter to one great company with what, for the time, was an enormous paid-up capital, in order that the India trade might be made secure and the Spaniards steadily confronted in what they had considered their most impregnable possessions. All former trading companies were invited to merge themselves in the Universal East India Company, which, for twenty-one years, should alone have the right to trade to the east of the Cape of Good Hope and to sail through the Straits of Magellan.

The charter had been signed on 20th March, 1602, and was mainly to the following effect:

The company was to pay twenty-five thousand florins to the States-General for its privilege. The whole capital was to be six million six hundred thousand florins. The chamber of Amsterdam was to have one half of the whole interest, the chamber of Zeeland one fourth; the chambers of the Meuse, namely, Delft, Rotterdam, and the north quarter, that is to say,

Hoorn and Enkhuizen, each a sixteenth. All the chambers were to be governed by the directors then serving, who, however, were to be allowed to die out, down to the number of twenty for Amsterdam, twelve for Zeeland, and seven for each of the other chambers. To fill a vacancy occurring among the directors, the remaining members of the board were to nominate three candidates, from whom the estates of the province should choose one. Each director was obliged to have an interest in the company amounting to at least six thousand florins, except the directors for Hoorn and Enkhuizen, of whom only three thousand should be required. The general assembly of these chambers should consist of seventeen directors, eight for Amsterdam, and four for Zeeland, two for the Meuse, and two for the north quarter; the seventeenth being added by turns from the chambers of Zeeland, the Meuse, and the north quarter. This assembly was to be held six years at Amsterdam, and then two years in Zeeland. The ships were always to return to the port from which they had sailed. All the inhabitants of the provinces had the right, within a certain time, to take shares in the company. Any province or city subscribing for forty thousand florins or upwards might appoint an agent to look after its affairs.

The Company might make treaties with the Indian powers, in the name of the States-General of the United Netherlands or of the supreme authorities of the same, might build fortresses, appoint generals, and levy troops, provided such troops took oaths of fidelity to the States, or to the supreme authority, and to the Company. No ships, artillery, or other munitions of war belonging to the Company were to be used in service of the country without permission of the Company. The admiralty was to have a certain proportion of the prizes conquered from the enemy.

The directors should not be liable in property or person for the debts of the Company. The generals of fleets returning home were to make reports on the state of India to the States.

Notification of the union of all India companies with this

great corporation was duly sent to the fleets cruising in those regions, where it arrived in the course of the year 1603.

Meantime the first fleet of the Company, consisting of fourteen vessels under command of Admiral Wybrand van Warwyk, sailed before the end of 1602, and was followed towards the close of 1603 by thirteen other ships, under Stephen van der Hagen.

The equipment of these two fleets cost two million two hundred thousand florins.[1]

[SPAIN IN 1607]

[Motley gives the following picture of Spain in 1607.]

Spain was still superstitiously regarded as the leading power of the world, although foiled in all its fantastic and gigantic schemes. It was still supposed, according to current dogma, to share with the Ottoman Empire the dominion of the earth. A series of fortunate marriages having united many of the richest and fairest portions of Europe under a single scepter, it was popularly believed in a period when men were not much given as yet to examine very deeply the principles of human governments or the causes of national greatness, that an aggregation of powers which had resulted from preposterous laws of succession really constituted a mighty empire, founded by genius and valor.

The Spanish people, endowed with an acute and exuberant genius, which had exhibited itself in many paths of literature, science, and art; with a singular aptitude for military adventure, organization, and achievement; with a great variety, in short, of splendid and ennobling qualities; had been, for a long succession of years, accursed with almost the very worst political institutions known to history. The depth of their misery and of their degradation was hardly yet known to themselves, and this was perhaps the most hideous proof of the tyranny of which they had been the victims. To the outward world, the hollow fabric,

[1] *History of the United Netherlands* (New York, 1860–1867), **IV,** 132–135.

out of which the whole pith and strength had been slowly gnawed away, was imposing and majestic still. But the priest, the soldier, and the courtier had been busy too long, and had done their work too thoroughly, to leave much hope of arresting the universal decay.

Nor did there seem any probability that the attempt would be made.

It is always difficult to reform wide-spread abuses, even when they are acknowledged to exist, but when gigantic vices are proudly pointed to as the noblest of institutions and as the very foundations of the state, there seems nothing for the patriot to long for but the deluge.

It was acknowledged that the Spanish population—having a very large admixture of those races which, because not Catholic at heart, were stigmatized as miscreants, heretics, pagans, and, generally, as accursed—was by nature singularly prone to religious innovation. Had it not been for the Holy Inquisition, it was the opinion of acute and thoughtful observers in the beginning of the seventeenth century, that the infamous heresies of Luther, Calvin, and the rest would have long before taken possession of the land. To that most blessed establishment it was owing that Spain had not polluted itself in the filth and ordure of the Reformation, and had been spared the horrible fate which had befallen large portions of Germany, France, Britain, and other barbarous northern nations. It was conscientiously and thankfully believed in Spain, two centuries ago, that the state had been saved from political and moral ruin by the admirable machine which detected heretics with unerring accuracy, burned them when detected, and consigned their descendants to political incapacity and social infamy to the remotest generation.

As the awful consequences of religious freedom, men pointed with a shudder to the condition of nations already speeding on the road to ruin, from which the two peninsulas at least had been saved. Yet the British empire, with the American republic still an embryo in its bosom, France, North Germany, and other great powers, had hardly then begun their headlong career.

Whether the road of religious liberty was leading exactly to political ruin, the coming centuries were to judge.[1]

Spain at this epoch had probably less than twelve millions of inhabitants, although the statistics of those days cannot be relied upon with accuracy. The whole revenue of the state was nominally sixteen or seventeen millions of dollars, but the greater portion of that income was pledged for many coming years to the merchants of Genoa. All the little royal devices for increasing the budget by debasing the coin of the realm, by issuing millions of copper tokens, by lowering the promised rate of interest on government loans, by formally repudiating both interest and principal, had been tried, both in this and the preceding reign, with the usual success. An inconvertible paper currency, stimulating industry and improving morals by converting beneficent commerce into baleful gambling—that fatal invention did not then exist. Meantime, the legitimate trader and innocent citizen were harassed, and the general public endangered, as much as the limited machinery of the epoch permitted.

The available, unpledged revenue of the kingdom hardly amounted to five millions of dollars a year. The regular annual income of the church was at least six millions. The whole personal property of the nation was estimated—in a very clumsy and unsatisfactory way, no doubt—at sixty millions of dollars. Thus the income of the priesthood was ten per cent of the whole funded estate of the country, and at least a million a year more than the income of the Government. Could a more biting epigram be made upon the condition to which the nation had been reduced?

Labor was more degraded than ever. The industrious classes, if such could be said to exist, were esteemed every day more and more infamous. Merchants, shopkeepers, mechanics, were reptiles, as vilely esteemed as Jews, Moors, Protestants, or Pagans. Acquiring wealth by any kind of production was dis-

[1] *History of the United Netherlands* (New York, 1860–1867), IV, 330–332.

honorable. A grandee who should permit himself to sell the wool from his boundless sheep-walks disgraced his caste, and was accounted as low as a merchant. To create was the business of slaves and miscreants; to destroy was the distinguishing attribute of Christians and nobles. To cheat, to pick, and to steal, on the most minute and the most gigantic scale—these were also among the dearest privileges of the exalted classes. No merchandise was polluting save the produce of honest industry. To sell places in church and state, the army, the navy, and the sacred tribunals of law; to take bribes from rich and poor, high and low, in sums infinitesimal or enormous; to pillage the exchequer in every imaginable form; to dispose of titles of honour, orders of chivalry, posts in municipal council, at auction; to barter influence, audiences, official interviews against money cynically paid down in rascal counters—all this was esteemed consistent with patrician dignity.

The ministers, ecclesiastics, and those about court, obtaining a monopoly of such trade, left the business of production and circulation to their inferiors, while, as has already been sufficiently indicated, religious fanaticism and a pride of race, which nearly amounted to idiocy, had generated a scorn for labor even among the lowest orders. As a natural consequence, commerce and the mechanical arts fell almost exclusively into the hands of foreigners—Italians, English, and French—who resorted in yearly increasing numbers to Spain for the purpose of enriching themselves by the industry which the natives despised.

The capital thus acquired was at regular intervals removed from the country to other lands, where wealth resulting from traffic or manufactures was not accounted infamous.

Moreover, as the soil of the country was held by a few great proprietors—an immense portion in the dead-hand of an insatiate and ever-grasping church, and much of the remainder in vast entailed estates—it was nearly impossible for the masses of the people to become owners of any portion of the land. To be an agricultural day-laborer at less than a beggar's wage could hardly be a tempting pursuit for a proud and indolent race. It was no wonder, therefore, that the business of the brigand, the smuggler, the professional mendicant became from year to year more attractive and more overdone; while an ever-thickening swarm of priests, friars, and nuns of every order, engendered out of a corrupt and decaying society, increasing the general indolence, immorality, and unproductive consumption, and frightfully diminishing the productive force of the country, fed like locusts upon what was left in the unhappy land. "To shirk labor, infinite numbers become priests and friars," said a good Catholic, in the year 1608.

Before the end of the reign of Philip III the peninsula, which might have been the granary of the world, did not produce food enough for its own population. Corn became a regular article of import into Spain, and would have come in larger quantities than it did had the industry of the country furnished sufficient material to exchange for necessary food.

And as if it had been an object of ambition with the priests and courtiers who then ruled a noble country to make at exactly this epoch the most startling manifestation of human fatuity that the world had ever seen, it was now resolved by government to expel by armed force nearly the whole stock of intelligent and experienced labor, agricultural and mechanical, from the country. It is unnecessary to dwell long upon an event which, if it were not so familiarly known to mankind, would seem almost incredible. But the expulsion of the Moors is, alas! no exaggerated and imaginary satire, but a monument of wickedness and insanity such as is not often seen in human history.

Already, in the very first years of the century, John Ribera, Archbishop of Valencia, had recommended and urged the scheme.

It was too gigantic a project to be carried into execution at once, but it was slowly matured by the aid of other ecclesiastics. At last there were indications, both human and divine, that the expulsion of these miscreants could no longer be deferred. It was rumoured and believed that a general conspiracy existed among the Moors to rise upon the government, to institute a general massacre, and, with the assistance of their allies and relatives on the Barbary coast, to re-establish the empire of the infidels.

A convoy of eighty ass-loads of oil on the way to Madrid had halted at a wayside inn. A few flasks were stolen, and those who consumed it were made sick. Some of the thieves even died, or were said to have died, in consequence. Instantly the rumor flew from mouth to mouth, from town to town, that the royal family, the court, the whole capital, all Spain, were to be poisoned with that oil. If such were the scheme it was certainly a less ingenious one than the famous plot by which the Spanish government was suspected but a few years before to have so nearly succeeded in blowing the king, peers, and commons of England into the air.

The proof of Moorish guilt was deemed all-sufficient, especially as it was supported by supernatural evidence of the most portentous and convincing kind. For several days together a dark cloud, tinged with blood-red, had been seen to hang over Valencia.

In the neighborhood of Daroca, a din of drums and trumpets and the clang of arms had been heard in the sky, just as a procession went out of a monastery.

At Valencia the image of the Virgin had shed tears. In another place her statue had been discovered in a state of profuse perspiration.

What more conclusive indications could be required as to the guilt of the Moors? What other means devised for saving crown, church, and kingdom from destruction but to expel the whole mass of unbelievers from the soil which they had too long profaned?

Archbishop Ribera was fully sustained by the Archbishop of Toledo, and the whole ecclesiastical body received energetic support from government.

Ribera had solemnly announced that the Moors were so greedy of money, so determined to keep it, and so occupied with pursuits most apt for acquiring it, that they had come to be the sponge of Spanish wealth. The best proof of this, continued the reverend sage, was that, inhabiting in general poor little villages and sterile tracts of country, paying to the lords of the manor one third of the crops, and being overladen with special taxes imposed only upon them, they nevertheless became rich, while the Christians, cultivating the most fertile land, were in abject poverty.

It seems almost incredible that this should not be satire. Certainly the most delicate irony could not portray the vicious institutions under which the magnificent territory and noble people of Spain were thus doomed to ruin more subtly and forcibly than was done by the honest brutality of this church-man. The careful tillage; the beautiful system of irrigation by aqueduct and canal; the scientific processes by which these "accursed" had caused the wilderness to bloom with cotton, sugar, and every kind of fruit and grain; the untiring industry, exquisite ingenuity, and cultivated taste by which the merchants, manufacturers, and mechanics, guilty of a darker complexion than that of the peninsular Goths, had enriched their native land with splendid fabrics in cloth, paper, leather, silk, tapestry, and by so doing had acquired fortunes for themselves, despite iniquitous taxation, religious persecution, and social contumely —all these were crimes against a race of idlers, steeped to the lips in sloth which imagined itself to be pride.

The industrious, the intelligent, the wealthy, were denounced as criminals, and hunted to death or into exile as vermin, while the Lermas, the Ucedas, and the rest of the brood of cormo-rants, settled more thickly than ever around their prey.

Meantime, government declared that the piece of four mara-vedis should be worth eight maravedis; the piece of two maravedis being fixed at four. Thus the specie of the kingdom was to be doubled, and by means of this enlightened legislation, Spain, after destroying agriculture, commerce, and manufacture, was to maintain great armies and navies, and establish universal monarchy.

This measure, which a wiser churchman than Ribera, Cardinal Richelieu, afterwards declared the most audacious and barbarous ever recorded by history, was carried out with great regularity of organization. It was ordained that the Moors should be collected at three indicated points, whence they were not to move on pain of death, until duly escorted by troops to the ports of embarkation. The children under the age of four years were retained, of course without their parents, from whom they were forever separated. With admirable forethought, too, the priests took measures, as they supposed, that the arts of refining sugar, irrigating the rice-fields, constructing canals and aqueducts, besides many other useful branches of agricultural and mechanical business, should not die out with the intellectual, accomplished, and industrious race, alone competent to practise them, which was now sent forth to die. A very small number, not more than six in each hundred, were accordingly reserved to instruct other inhabitants of Spain in those useful arts which they were now more than ever encouraged to despise.

Five hundred thousand full-grown human beings, as energetic, ingenious, accomplished as any then existing in the world, were thus thrust forth into the deserts beyond sea, as if Spain had been overstocked with skilled labor, and as if its native production had already outgrown the world's power of consumption.

Had an equal number of mendicant monks, with the two archbishops who had contrived this deed at their head, been exported instead of the Moors, the future of Spain might have been a more fortunate one than it was likely to prove. The event was in itself perhaps of temporary advantage to the Dutch Republic, as the poverty and general misery, aggravated by this disastrous policy, rendered the acknowledgment of the States' independence by Spain almost a matter of necessity.

It is superfluous to enter into any farther disquisition as to the various branches of the royal revenue. They remained essentially the same as during the preceding reign, and have been elaborately set forth in a previous chapter. The gradual drying up of resources in all the wide-spread and heterogeneous territories subject to the Spanish scepter is the striking phenomenon of the present epoch. The distribution of such wealth as was still created followed the same laws which had long prevailed, while the decay and national paralysis, of which the prognostics could hardly be mistaken, were a natural result of the system.

The six archbishops had now grown to eleven, and still received gigantic revenues; the income of the Archbishop of Toledo, including the fund of one hundred thousand destined for repairing the cathedral, being estimated at three hundred thousand dollars a year, that of the Archbishop of Seville and the others varying from one hundred and fifty thousand dollars to fifty thousand. The sixty-three bishops perhaps averaged fifty thousand a year each, and there were eight more in Italy.

The commanderies of chivalry, two hundred at least in number, were likewise enormously profitable. Some of them were worth thirty thousand a year; the aggregate annual value being from one-and-a-half to two millions, and all in Lerma's gift, upon his own terms.

Chivalry, that noblest of ideals, without which, in some shape or another, the world would be a desert and a sty; which included within itself many of the noblest virtues which can adorn mankind—generosity, self-denial, chastity, frugality, patience, protection to the feeble, the down-trodden, and the oppressed; the love of daring adventure, devotion to a pure religion and a lofty purpose, most admirably pathetic, even when in the eyes of the vulgar most fantastic—had been the proudest and most poetical of Spanish characteristics, never to be entirely uprooted from the national heart.

Alas! what was there in the commanderies of Calatrava, Alcantara, Santiago and all the rest of those knightly orders, as then existing, to respond to the noble sentiments on which all were supposed to be founded? Institutions for making money, for pillaging the poor of their hard-earned pittance, trafficked in by greedy ministers and needy courtiers with a shamelessness which had long ceased to blush at vices however gross, at venality however mean.

Venality was in truth the prominent characteristic of the Spanish polity at this epoch. Everything political or ecclesiastical, from highest to lowest, was matter of merchandise.

It was the autocrat, governing king and kingdom, who disposed of episcopal miters, cardinals' hats, commanders' crosses, the offices of regidores or municipal magistrates in all the cities, farmings of revenues, collectorships of taxes, at prices fixed by himself.

It was never known that the pope refused to confirm the ecclesiastical nominations which were made by the Spanish court.

The nuncius had the privilege of dispensing the small cures from thirty dollars a year downwards, of which the number was enormous. Many of these were capable, in careful hands, of becoming ten times as valuable as their nominal estimate, and the business in them became in consequence very extensive and lucrative. They were often disposed of for the benefit of servants and the hangers-on of noble families, to laymen, to women, children, to babes unborn.

When such was the most thriving industry in the land, was it wonderful that the poor of high and low degree were anxious in ever-increasing swarms to effect their entrance into convent, monastery, and church, and that trade, agriculture, and manufactures languished?

The foreign polity of the court remained as it had been established by Philip II.

Its maxims were very simple. To do unto your neighbor all possible harm, and to foster the greatness of Spain by sowing discord and maintaining civil war in all other nations, was the fundamental precept. To bribe and corrupt the servants of other potentates, to maintain a regular paid body of adherents in foreign lands, ever ready to engage in schemes of assassination, conspiracy, sedition, and rebellion against the legitimate authority, to make mankind miserable, so far as it was in the power of human force or craft to produce wretchedness, were objects still faithfully pursued. They had not yet led to the entire destruction of other realms and their submission to the single scepter of Spain, nor had they developed the resources, material or moral, of a mighty empire so thoroughly as might have been done perhaps by a less insidious policy but they had never been abandoned.

It was a steady object of policy to keep such potentates of Italy as were not already under the dominion of the Spanish crown in a state of internecine feud with each other and of virtual dependence on the powerful kingdom. The same policy pursued in France, of fomenting civil war by subsidy, force, and chicane during a long succession of years in order to reduce that magnificent realm under the scepter of Philip, has been described in detail. The chronic rebellion of Ireland against the English crown had been assisted and inflamed in every possible mode, the system being considered as entirely justified by the aid and comfort afforded by the queen to the Dutch rebels.

It was a natural result of the system according to which kingdoms and provinces with the populations dwelling therein were transferable like real estate by means of marriage-settlements, entails, and testaments, that the proprietorship of most of the great realms in Christendom was matter of fierce legal dispute. Lawsuits, which in chancery could last for centuries before a settlement of the various claims was made, might have infinitely enriched the gentlemen of the long robe and reduced all the parties to beggary, had there been any tribunal but the battle-field to decide among the august litigants. Thus the King of Great Britain claimed the legal proprietorship and sovereignty of Brittany, Normandy, Anjou, Gascony, Calais, and Boulogne in France, besides the whole kingdom by right of conquest. The French king claimed to be rightful heir of Castile, Biscay, Guipuscoa, Aragon, Navarre, nearly all the Spanish peninsula in short, including the whole of Portugal and the Balearic Islands to boot. The King of Spain claimed, as we have seen often enough, not only Brittany but all France as his lawful inheritance. Such was the virtue of the prevalent doctrine of proprietorship. Every potentate was defrauded of his rights, and every potentate was a criminal usurper. As for the people, it would have excited a smile of superior wisdom on regal, legal, or sacerdotal lips, had it been suggested that by any possibility the governed could have a voice or a thought in regard to the rulers whom God in His grace had raised up to be their proprietors and masters.

The army of Spain was sunk far below the standard at which it had been kept when it seemed fit to conquer and govern the world. Neither by Spain nor Italy could those audacious, disciplined, and obedient legions be furnished, at which the enemies of the mighty despot trembled from one extremity of earth to the other. Peculation, bankruptcy, and mutiny had done their work at last. We have recently had occasion to observe the conduct of the veterans in Flanders at critical epochs. At this moment seventy thousand soldiers were on the muster- and pay-roll of the army serving in those provinces, while not thirty thousand men existed in the flesh.

The navy was sunk to fifteen or twenty old galleys, battered, dismantled, unseaworthy, and a few armed ships for convoying the East and West Indiamen to and from their destinations.

The general poverty was so great that it was often absolutely impossible to purchase food for the royal household. "If you ask me," said a cool observer, "how this great show of empire is maintained, when the funds are so small, I answer that it is done by not paying at all." The Government was shamelessly, hopelessly bankrupt. The noble band of courtiers were growing enormously rich. The state was a carcase which unclean vultures were picking to the bones.[1]

[PHILIP III]

[Philip II was succeeded by his son, Philip III. In a few pages Motley gives a picture of this inglorious successor of the more famous father.]

The nominal sovereign, Philip III, was thirty years of age. A very little man, with pink cheeks, flaxen hair, and yellow beard, with a melancholy expression of eye, and protruding under lip and jaw, he was now comparatively alert and vigorous in constitution, although for the first seven years of his life it had been doubtful whether he would live from week to week. He had been afflicted during that period with a chronic itch or

---

[1] *History of the United Netherlands* (New York, 1860–1867), IV, 333–344.

leprosy, which had undermined his strength, but which had almost entirely disappeared as he advanced in life.

He was below mediocrity in mind, and had received scarcely any education. He had been taught to utter a few phrases, more or less intelligible, in French, Italian, and Flemish, but was quite incapable of sustaining a conversation in either of those languages. When a child, he had learned and subsequently forgotten the rudiments of the Latin grammar.

These acquirements, together with the catechism and the offices of the Church made up his whole stock of erudition. That he was devout as a monk of the Middle Ages, conforming daily and hourly to religious ceremonies, need scarcely be stated. It was not probable that the son of Philip II would be a delinquent to church observances. He was not deficient in courage, rode well, was fond of hunting, kept close to the staghounds, and confronted, spear in hand, the wild-boar with coolness and success. He was fond of tennis, but his especial passion and chief accomplishment was dancing. He liked to be praised for his proficiency in this art, and was never happier than when gravely leading out the queen or his daughter, then four or five years of age—for he never danced with any one else —to perform a stately bolero.

He never drank wine, but, on the other hand, was an enormous eater; so that, like his father in youth, he was perpetually suffering from stomach-ache as the effect of his gluttony. He was devotedly attached to his queen, and had never known, nor hardly looked at, any other woman. He had no vice but gambling, in which he indulged to a great extent, very often sitting up all night at cards. This passion of the king's was much encouraged by Lerma, for obvious reasons. Philip had been known to lose thirty thousand dollars at a sitting, and always to some one of the family or dependents of the duke, who of course divided with them the spoils. At one time the Count of Pelbes, nephew of Lerma, had won two hundred thousand dollars in a very few nights from his sovereign.

For the rest, Philip had few peculiarities or foibles. He was not revengeful, nor arrogant, nor malignant. He was kind and affectionate to his wife and children, and did his best to be obedient to the Duke of Lerma. Occasionally he liked to grant audiences, but there were few to request them. It was ridiculous and pathetic at the same time to see the poor king, as was very frequently the case, standing at a solemn green table till his little legs were tired, waiting to transact business with applicants who never came; while ushers, chamberlains, and valets were rushing up and down the corridors, bawling for all persons so disposed to come and have an audience of their monarch. Meantime the doors of the great duke's apartments in the same palace would be beleaguered by an army of courtiers, envoys, and contractors, who had paid solid gold for admission, and who were often sent away grumbling and despairing without entering the sacred precincts.

As time wore on, the king, too much rebuked for attempting to meddle in state affairs, became solitary and almost morose, moping about in the woods by himself, losing satisfaction in his little dancing and ball-playing diversions, but never forgetting his affection for the queen nor the hours for his four daily substantial repasts of meats and pastry. It would be unnecessary and almost cruel to dwell so long upon a picture of what was after all not much better than human imbecility, were it not that humanity is a more sacred thing than royalty. A satire upon such an embodiment of kingship is impossible, the simple and truthful characteristics being more effective than fiction or exaggeration. It would be unjust to exhume a private character after the lapse of two centuries merely to excite derision, but if history be not powerless to instruct, it certainly cannot be unprofitable to ponder the merits of a system which, after bestowing upon the world forty-three years of Philip the tyrant, had now followed them up with a decade of Philip the simpleton.

In one respect the reigning sovereign was in advance of his age. In his devotion to the Madonna he claimed the same miraculous origin for her mother as for herself. When the prayer, "*O Sancta Maria sine labe originali concepta*," was chanted, he would exclaim with emotion that the words embodied his devoutest aspirations. He had frequent interviews with doctors of divinity on the subject, and instructed many bishops to urge upon the pope the necessity of proclaiming the virginity of the Virgin's mother. Could he secure this darling object of his ambition, he professed himself ready to make a pilgrimage on foot to Rome. The pilgrimage was never made, for it may well be imagined that Lerma would forbid any such adventurous scheme. Meantime the duke continued to govern the empire and to fill his coffers, and the king to shoot rabbits.[1]

[SUMMARY]

[Motley concludes his account of the Dutch struggle for independence with a summary that reveals his point of view and his conclusions.]

Forty-three years had passed since the memorable April morning in which the great nobles of the Netherlands presented their "Request" to the Regent Margaret at Brussels.

They had requested that the holy Spanish Inquisition might not be established on their soil to the suppression of all their political and religious institutions.

The war which those high-born "Beggars" had then kindled, little knowing what they were doing, had now come to a close, and the successor of Philip II, instead of planting the Inquisition in the provinces, had recognized them as an independent, sovereign, Protestant republic.

In the ratification which he had just signed of the treaty of truce the Most Catholic King had in his turn made a Request. He had asked the States-General to deal kindly with their Catholic subjects.

That request was not answered with the axe and fagot; with the avenging sword of mercenary legions. On the contrary, it was destined to be granted. The world had gained something in forty-three years. It had at least begun to learn that the hangman is not the most appropriate teacher of religion.

[1] *History of the United Netherlands* (New York, 1860–1867), IV, 355–358.

During the period of apparent chaos with which this history of the great revolt had been occupied, there had in truth been a great reorganization, a perfected new birth. The republic had once more appeared in the world.

Its main characteristics have been indicated in the course of the narrative, for it was a polity which gradually unfolded itself out of the decay and change of previous organisms.

It was, as it were, in their own despite and unwittingly that the United Provinces became a republic at all.

In vain, after originally declaring their independence of the ancient tyrant, had they attempted to annex themselves to France and to England. The sovereignty had been spurned. The magnificent prize which France for centuries since has so persistently coveted, and the attainment of which has been a cardinal point of her perpetual policy—the Low Countries and the banks of the Rhine—was deliberately laid at her feet, and as deliberately refused.

It was the secret hope of the present monarch to repair the loss which the kingdom had suffered through the imbecility of his two immediate predecessors. But a great nation cannot with impunity permit itself to be despotically governed for thirty years by lunatics. It was not for the Béarnese, with all his valor, his wit, and his duplicity, to obtain the prize which Charles IX and Henry III had thrown away. Yet to make himself sovereign of the Netherlands was his guiding but most secret thought during all the wearisome and tortuous negotiations which preceded the truce; nor did he abandon the great hope with the signature of the treaty of 1609. Maurice of Nassau, too, was a formidable rival to Henry. The stadholder-prince was no republican. He was a good patriot, a noble soldier, an honest man. But his father had been offered the sovereignty of Holland and Zeeland, and the pistol of Balthazar Gérard had alone, in all human probability, prevented the great prince from becoming constitutional monarch of all the Netherlands, Batavian and Belgic.

Maurice himself asserted that not only had he been offered a million of dollars, and large estates besides in Germany, if he would leave the provinces to their fate, but that the archdukes had offered, would he join his fortunes with theirs, to place him in a higher position over all the Netherlands than he had ever enjoyed in the United Provinces, and that they had even unequivocally offered him the sovereignty over the whole land.

Maurice was a man of truth, and we have no right to dispute the accuracy of the extraordinary statement. He must, however, have reflected upon the offer once made by the Prince of Darkness from the mountain top, and have asked himself by what machinery the archdukes proposed to place him in possession of such a kingdom.

There had, however, been serious question among leading Dutch statesmen of making him constitutional, hereditary monarch of the United Netherlands. As late as 1602 a secret conference was held at the house of Olden-Barneveld, in which the Advocate had himself urged the claims of the prince to the sovereignty, and reminded his guests that the signed and sealed documents—with the concurrence of the Amsterdam municipality alone lacking—by which William the Silent had been invited to assume the crown were still in the possession of his son.

Nothing came of these deliberations. It was agreed that to stir in the matter at that moment would be premature, and that the pursuit by Maurice of the monarchy in the circumstances then existing would not only overburden him with expense, but make him a more conspicuous mark than ever for the assassin. It is certain that the prince manifested no undue anxiety at any period in regard to those transactions.

Subsequently, as Olden-Barneveld's personal power increased, and as the negotiations for peace became more and more likely to prove successful, the Advocate lost all relish for placing his great rival on a throne. The whole project, with the documents and secret schemes therewith connected, became mere alms for oblivion. Barneveld himself, although of comparatively humble birth and station, was likely with time to exercise more real power in the state than either Henry or Maurice; and thus while there were three individuals who in different ways aspired to supreme power, the Republic, notwithstanding, asserted and established itself.

Freedom of government and freedom of religion were, on the whole, assisted by this triple antagonism. The prince, as soon as war was over, hated the Advocate and his daily increasing power more and more. He allied himself more closely than ever with the Gomarites and the clerical party in general, and did his best to inflame the persecuting spirit, already existing in the provinces, against the Catholics and the later sects of Protestants.

Jeannin warned him that "by thus howling with the priests" he would be suspected of more desperately ambitious designs than he perhaps really cherished.

On the other hand Barneveld was accused of a willingness to wink at the introduction, privately and quietly, of the Roman Catholic worship. That this was the deadliest of sins, there was no doubt whatever in the minds of his revilers. When it was added that he was suspected of the Arminian leprosy, and that he could tolerate the thought that a virtuous man or woman, not predestined from all time for salvation, could possibly find the way to heaven, language becomes powerless to stigmatize his depravity. Whatever the punishment impending over his head in this world or the next, it is certain that the cause of human freedom was not destined on the whole to lose ground through the lifework of Barneveld.

A champion of liberties rather than of liberty, he defended his fatherland with heart and soul against the stranger; yet the government of that fatherland was, in his judgment, to be transferred from the hand of the foreigner, not to the self-governing people, but to the provincial corporations. For the People he had no respect, and perhaps little affection. He often spoke of popular rights with contempt. Of popular sovereignty he had no conception. His patriotism, like his ambition, was provincial. Yet his perceptions as to eternal necessity in all healthy governments taught him that comprehensible relations between the state and the population were needful to the very existence of a free commonwealth. The United Provinces, he maintained, were not a republic, but a league of seven provinces very loosely hung together, a mere provisional organization for which it was not then possible to substitute anything better. He expressed this opinion with deep regret, just as the war of independence was closing, and added his conviction that, without some well-ordered government, no republic could stand.

Yet, as time wore on, the Advocate was destined to acquiesce more and more in this defective constitution. A settled theory there was none, and it would have been difficult legally and historically to establish the central sovereignty of the States-General as matter of right.

Thus Barneveld, who was anything but a democrat, became, almost unwittingly, the champion of the least venerable or imposing of all forms of aristocracy—an oligarchy of traders who imagined themselves patricians. Corporate rights, not popular liberty, seemed, in his view, the precious gains made by such a prodigious expenditure of time, money, and blood. Although such acquisitions were practically a vast addition to the stock of human freedom then existing in the world, yet torrents of blood and millions of treasure were to be wasted in the coming centuries before mankind was to convince itself that a republic is only to be made powerful and perpetual by placing itself upon the basis of popular right rather than on that of municipal privilege.

The singular docility of the Dutch people, combined with the simplicity, honesty, and practical sagacity of the earlier burgher patricians, made the defects of the system tolerable for a longer period than might have been expected; nor was it until theological dissensions had gathered to such intensity as to set the whole commonwealth aflame that the grave defects in the political structure could be fairly estimated.

It would be anticipating a dark chapter in the history of the United Provinces were the reader's attention now to be called to those fearful convulsions. The greatest reserve is therefore necessary at present in alluding to the subject.

It was not to be expected that an imperious, energetic but somewhat limited nature like that of Barneveld should at the epoch thoroughly comprehend the meaning of religious freedom. William the Silent alone seems to have risen to that height. A conscientious Calvinist himself, the father of his country would have been glad to see Protestant and Papist, Lutheran, Presbyterian, and Anabaptist living together in harmony and political equality. This was not to be. The soul of the immortal prince could not inspire the hearts of his contemporaries. That Barneveld was disposed to a breadth of religious sympathy unusual in those days seems certain. It was inevitable, too, that the mild doctrines of Arminius should be more in harmony with such a character than were the fierce dogmas of Calvin. But the struggle, either to force Arminianism upon the Church which considered itself the established one in the Netherlands, or to expel the Calvinists from it, had not yet begun; although the seeds of religious persecution of Protestants by Protestants had already been sown broadcast.

The day was not far distant when the very Calvinists, to whom, more than to any other class of men, the political liberties of Holland, England, and America are due, were to be hunted out of churches into farmhouses, suburban hovels, and canal-boats by the arm of provincial sovereignty and in the name of state-rights, as pitilessly as the early reformers had been driven out of cathedrals in the name of emperor and pope; and when even those refuges for conscientious worship were to be denied by the dominant sect. And the day was to come, too, when the Calvinists regaining ascendency in their turn, were to hunt the heterodox as they had themselves been hunted; and this, at the very moment when their fellow Calvinists of England were driven by the Church of that kingdom into the American wilderness.

Toleration—that intolerable term of insult to all who love liberty—had not yet been discovered. It had scarcely occurred to Arminian or Presbyterian that civil authority and ecclesiastical doctrine could be divorced from each other. As the individual sovereignty of the seven states established itself more and more securely, the right of provincial power to dictate religious dogmas, and to superintend the popular conscience, was exercised with a placid arrogance which papal infallibility could scarcely exceed. The alternation was only between the sects, each in its turn becoming orthodox, and therefore persecuting. The lessened intensity of persecution however, which priesthood and authority were now allowed to exercise, marked the gains secured.

Yet while we censure—as we have a right to do from the point of view which we have gained after centuries—the crimes committed by bigotry against liberty, we should be false to our faith in human progress did we not acknowledge our debt of gratitude to the hot gospellers of Holland and England.

The doctrine of predestination, the consciousness of being chosen soldiers of Christ, inspired those Puritans, who founded the commonwealths of England, of Holland, and of America, with a contempt of toil, danger, and death which enabled them to accomplish things almost supernatural.

No uncouthness of phraseology, no unlovely austerity of deportment, could, except to vulgar minds, make that sublime enthusiasm ridiculous, which on either side the ocean ever confronted tyranny with dauntless front, and welcomed death on battlefield, scaffold, or rack with perfect composure.

The early Puritan at least believed. The very intensity of his belief made him—all unconsciously to himself, and narrowed as was his view of his position—the great instrument by which the widest human liberty was to be gained for all mankind.

The elected favorite of the King of kings feared the power of no earthly king. Accepting in rapture the decrees of a supernatural tyranny, he rose on mighty wings above the reach of human wrath. Prostrating himself before a God of vengeance, of jealousy, and of injustice, he naturally imitated the attributes which he believed to be divine. It was inevitable, therefore, that Barneveld, and those who thought with him, when they should attempt to force the children of Belial into the company of the elect and to drive the faithful out of their own churches, should be detested as bitterly as papists had ever been.

Had Barneveld's intellect been broad enough to imagine in a great republic the separation of church and state, he would deserve a tenderer sympathy, but he would have been far in advance of his age. It is not cheerful to see so powerful an intellect and so patriotic a character daring to entrust the relations between man and his Maker to the decree of a trading corporation. But alas! the world was to wait for centuries until it should learn that the state can best defend religion by letting it alone, and that the political arm is apt to wither with palsy when it attempts to control the human conscience.

It is not entirely the commonwealth of the United Netherlands that is of importance in the epoch which I have endeavored to illustrate. History can have neither value nor charm for those who are not impressed with a conviction of its continuity.

More than ever during the period which we call modern history has this idea of the continuousness of our race, and especially of the inhabitants of Europe and America, become almost oppressive to the imagination. There is a sense of immortality even upon earth when we see the succession of heritages in the domains of science, of intellectual and material wealth by which mankind, generation after generation, is enriching itself.

If this progress be a dream, if mankind be describing a limited circle instead of advancing towards the infinite, then no study can be more contemptible than the study of history.

Few strides more gigantic have been taken in the march of humanity than those by which a parcel of outlying provinces in the north of Europe exchanged slavery to a foreign despotism and to the Holy Inquisition for the position of a self-governing commonwealth, in the front rank of contemporary powers, and in many respects the foremost of the world. It is impossible to calculate the amount of benefit rendered to civilization by the example of the Dutch Republic. It has been a model which has been imitated, in many respects, by great nations. It has even been valuable in its very defects; indicating to the patient observer many errors most important to avoid.

Therefore, had the little Republic sunk for ever in the sea so soon as the treaty of peace had been signed at Antwerp, its career would have been prolific of good for all succeeding time.

Exactly at the moment when a splendid but decaying despotism, founded upon wrong—upon oppression of the human body and the immortal soul, upon slavery, in short, of the worst kind—was awaking from its insane dream of universal empire to a consciousness of its own decay, the new Republic was recognized among the nations.

It would hardly be incorrect to describe the Holland of the beginning of the seventeenth century as the exact reverse of Spain. In the commonwealth labor was most honorable; in the kingdom it was vile. In the North to be idle was accounted and punished as a crime. In the Southern peninsula, to be contaminated with mechanical, mercantile, commercial, manufacturing pursuits, was to be accursed. Labor was for slaves, and at last the mere spectacle of labor became so offensive that even the slaves were expelled from the land. To work was as degrading in the south as to beg or to steal was esteemed unworthy of humanity in the north. To think a man's thought upon high matters of religion and government, and through a thousand errors to pursue the truth, with the aid of the Most High and with the best use of human reason, was a privilege secured by the commonwealth at the expense of two generations of continuous bloodshed. To lie fettered, soul and body, at the feet of authority wielded by a priesthood in its last stage of corruption, and monarchy almost reduced to imbecility, was the lot of the chivalrous, genial, but much-oppressed Spaniard.

The pictures painted of the Republic by shrewd and caustic observers, not inclined by nature or craft to portray freedom in too engaging colors, seem, when contrasted with those revealed of Spain, almost like enthusiastic fantasies of an ideal commonwealth.

During the last twenty years of the great war the material prosperity of the Netherlands had wonderfully increased. They had become the first commercial nation in the world. They had acquired the supremacy of the seas. The population of Amsterdam had in twenty years increased from seventy thousand to a hundred and thirty thousand, and was destined to be again more than doubled in the coming decade. The population of

Antwerp had sunk almost as rapidly as that of its rival had increased; having lessened by fifty thousand during the same period. The commercial capital of the obedient provinces, having already lost much of its famous traffic by the great changes in the commercial current of the world, was unable to compete with the cities of the United Provinces in the vast trade which the geographical discoveries of the preceding century had opened to civilization. Freedom of thought and action were denied, and without such liberty it was impossible for oceanic commerce to thrive. Moreover, the possession by the Hollanders of the Scheldt forts below Antwerp, and of Flushing at the river's mouth, suffocated the ancient city, and would of itself have been sufficient to paralyze all its efforts.

In Antwerp the exchange, where once thousands of the great merchants of the earth held their daily financial parliament, now echoed to the solitary footfall of the passing stranger. Ships lay rotting at the quays, brambles grew in the commercial streets. In Amsterdam the city had been enlarged by two-thirds, and those who swarmed thither to seek their fortunes could not wait for the streets to be laid out and houses to be built, but established themselves in the environs, building themselves hovels and temporary residences, although certain to find their encampments swept away with the steady expanse of the city. As much land as could be covered by a man's foot was worth a ducat in gold.

In every branch of human industry these republicans took the lead. On that scrap of solid ground, rescued by human energy from the ocean, were the most fertile pastures in the world. On those pastures grazed the most famous cattle in the world. An ox often weighed more than two thousand pounds. The cows produced two and three calves at a time, the sheep four and five lambs. In a single village four thousand kine were counted. Butter and cheese were exported to the annual value of a million, salted provisions to an incredible extent. The farmers were industrious, thriving, and independent. It is an amusing illustration of the agricultural thrift and republican simplicity of this people that on one occasion a farmer proposed to Prince Maurice that he should marry his daughter, promising with her a dowry of a hundred thousand florins.

The mechanical ingenuity of the Netherlanders, already celebrated by Julius Caesar and by Tacitus, had lost nothing of its ancient fame. The contemporary world confessed that in many fabrics the Hollanders were at the head of mankind. Dutch linen, manufactured of the flax grown on their own fields or imported from the obedient provinces, was esteemed a fitting present for kings to make and to receive. The name of the country had passed into the literature of England as synonymous with the delicate fabric itself. The Venetians confessed themselves equalled, if not outdone, by the crystal workers and sugar refiners of the northern republic. The tapestries of Arras—the name of which Walloon city had become a household word of luxury in all modern languages—were now transplanted to the soil of freedom, more congenial to the advancement of art. Brocades of the precious metals; splendid satins and velvets; serges and homely fustians; laces of thread and silk; the finer and coarser manufactures of clay and porcelain; iron, steel, and all useful fabrics for the building and outfitting of ships; substantial broadcloths manufactured of wool imported from Scotland—all this was but a portion of the industrial production of the provinces.

They supplied the deficiency of coal, not then an article readily obtained by commerce, with other remains of antediluvian forests long since buried in the sea, and now recovered from its depths and made useful and portable by untiring industry. Peat was not only the fuel for the fireside, but for the extensive fabrics of the country, and its advantages so much excited the admiration of the Venetian envoys that they sent home samples of it, in the hope that the lagunes of Venice might prove as prolific of this indispensable article as the polders of Holland.

But the foundation of the national wealth, the source of the apparently fabulous power by which the Republic had at last overthrown her gigantic antagonist, was the ocean. The Republic was sea-born and sea-sustained.

She had nearly one hundred thousand sailors, and three thousand ships. The sailors were the boldest, the best disciplined, and the most experienced in the world, whether for peaceable seafaring or ocean warfare. The ships were capable of furnishing from out of their number in time of need the most numerous and the best appointed navy then known to mankind.

The Republic had the carrying trade for all nations. Feeling its very existence dependent upon commerce, it had strode centuries in advance of the contemporary world in the liberation of trade. But two or three per cent *ad valorem* was levied upon imports; foreign goods however being subject, as well as internal products, to heavy imposts in the way of both direct and indirect taxation.

Every article of necessity or luxury known was to be purchased in profusion and at reasonable prices in the warehouses of Holland.

A swarm of river vessels and flyboats were coming daily through the rivers of Germany, France, and the Netherlands, laden with the agricultural products and the choice manufactures of central and western Europe. Wine and oil, and delicate fabrics in thread and wool, came from France, but no silks, velvets, nor satins; for the great Sully had succeeded in persuading his master that the white mulberry would not grow in his kingdom, and that silk manufactures were an impossible dream for France. Nearly a thousand ships were constantly employed in the Baltic trade. The forests of Holland were almost as extensive as those which grew on Norwegian hills, but they were submerged. The foundation of a single mansion required a grove, and wood was extensively used in the superstructure. The houses, built of a framework of substantial timber, and filled in with brick or rubble, were raised almost as rapidly as tents, during the prodigious expansion of industry towards the end of the war. From the realms of the Osterlings, or shores of the Baltic, came daily fleets laden with wheat and other grains, so that even in time of famine the granaries of the Republic were overflowing, and ready to dispense the material of life to the outer world.

Eight hundred vessels of lesser size but compact build were perpetually fishing for herrings on the northern coasts. These hardy mariners, the militia of the sea, who had learned in their life of hardship and daring the art of destroying Spanish and Portuguese armadas, and confronting the dangers of either pole, passed a long season on the deep. Commercial voyagers as well as fishermen, they salted their fish as soon as taken from the sea, and transported them to the various ports of Europe, thus reducing their herrings into specie before their return, and proving that a fishery in such hands was worth more than the mines of Mexico and Peru.

It is customary to speak of the natural resources of a country as furnishing a guarantee of material prosperity. But here was a republic almost without natural resources, which had yet supplied by human intelligence and thrift what a niggard nature had denied. Spain was overflowing with unlimited treasure, and had possessed half the world in fee; and Spain was bankrupt, decaying, sinking into universal pauperism. Holland, with freedom of thought, of commerce, of speech, of action, placed itself, by intellectual power alone, in the front rank of civilization.

From Cathay, from the tropical coasts of Africa, and from farthest Ind, came every drug, spice, or plant, every valuable jewel, every costly fabric, that human ingenuity had discovered or created. The Spaniards, maintaining a frail tenure upon a portion of those prolific regions, gathered their spice harvests at the point of the sword, and were frequently unable to prevent their northern rivals from ravaging such fields as they had not yet been able to appropriate.

Certainly this conduct of the Hollanders was barbarism and supreme selfishness, if judged by the sounder political economy of our time. Yet it should never be forgotten that the contest between Spain and Holland in those distant regions, as everywhere else, was war to the knife between superstition and freedom, between the spirits of progress and of dogma. Hard blows and foul blows were struck in such a fight, and humanity, although gaining at last immense results, had much to suffer and much to learn ere the day was won.

But Spain was nearly beaten out of those eastern regions, and the very fact that the naval supremacy of the Republic placed her ancient tyrant at her mercy was the main reason for Spain to conclude the treaty of truce. Lest she should lose the India trade entirely, Spain consented to the treaty article by which, without mentioning the word, she conceded the thing. It was almost pathetic to witness, as we have witnessed, this despotism in its dotage, mumbling so long over the formal concession to her conqueror of a portion of that India trade which would have been entirely wrested from herself had the war continued. And of this Spain was at heart entirely convinced. Thus the Portuguese, once the lords and master, as they had been the European discoverers, of those prolific regions and of the ocean highways which led to them, now came with docility to the Republic which they had once affected to despise, and purchased the cloves and the allspice, the nutmegs and the cinnamon, of which they had held the monopoly; or waited with patience until the untiring Hollanders should bring the precious wares to the peninsular ports.

A Dutch Indiaman would make her voyage to the antipodes and her return in less time than was spent by a Portuguese or a Spaniard in the outward voyage. To accomplish such an enterprise in two years was accounted a wonder of rapidity, and when it is remembered that inland navigation through France by canal and river from the North Sea to the Mediterranean was considered both speedier and safer, because the sea voyage between the same points might last four or five months, it must be admitted that two years occupied in passing from one end of the earth to the other and back again might well seem a miracle.

The Republic was among the wealthiest and the most powerful of organized states. Her population might be estimated at three millions and a half, about equal to that of England at the same period. But she was richer than England. Nowhere in the world was so large a production in proportion to the numbers of a people. Nowhere were so few unproductive consumers. Every one was at work. Vagabonds, idlers, and do-nothings, such as must be in every community, were caught up by the authorities and made to earn their bread. The devil's pillow, idleness, was smoothed for no portion of the population.

There were no beggars, few paupers, no insolently luxurious and ostentatiously idle class. The modesty, thrift, and simple elegance of the housekeeping, even among the wealthy, was noted by travellers with surprise. It will be remembered with how much amused wonder, followed by something like contempt, the magnificent household of Spinola, during his embassy at The Hague, was surveyed by the honest burghers of Holland. The authorities showed their wisdom in permitting the absurd exhibition, as an example of what should be shunned, in spite of grave remonstrances from many of the citizens. Drunken helotism is not the only form of erring humanity capable of reading lessons to a republic.

There had been monasteries, convents, ecclesiastical establishments of all kinds in the country, before the great war between Holland and the Inquisition. These had, as a matter of course, been confiscated as the strife went on. The buildings, farms, and funds, once the property of the Church, had not, however, been seized upon, as in other Protestant lands, by rapacious monarchs, and distributed among great nobles according to royal caprice. Monarchs might give the revenue of a suppressed convent to a cook, as reward for a successful pudding; the surface of Britain and the continent might be covered with abbeys and monasteries now converted into lordly palaces—passing thus from the dead hand of the Church into the idle and unproductive palm of the noble; but the ancient ecclesiastical establishments of the free Netherlands were changed into eleemosynary institutions, admirably organized and administered with wisdom and economy, where orphans of the poor, widows of those slain in the battles for freedom by land and sea, and the aged and the infirm, who had deserved well of the republic in the days of their strength, were educated or cherished at the expense of the public, thus endowed from the spoils of the Church.

In Spain monasteries upon monasteries were rising day by

day, as if there were not yet receptacles enough for monks and priests, while thousands upon thousands of Spaniards were pressing into the ranks of the priesthood, and almost forcing themselves into monasteries, that they might be privileged to beg, because ashamed to work. In the United Netherlands the confiscated convents, with their revenues, were appropriated for the good of those who were too young or too old to labor, and too poor to maintain themselves without work. Need men look further than to this simple fact to learn why Spain was decaying while the Republic was rising?

The ordinary budget of the United Provinces was about equal to that of England, varying not much from four millions of florins, or four hundred thousand pounds. But the extraordinary revenue was comparatively without limits, and there had been years, during the war, when the citizens had taxed themselves as high as fifty per cent on each individual income, and doubled the receipts of the exchequer. The budget was proposed once a year by the council of state, and voted by the States-General, who assigned the quota of each province; that of Holland being always one-half of the whole, that of Zeeland sixteen per cent, and that of the other five of course in lesser proportions. The revenue was collected in the separate provinces, one-third of the whole being retained for provincial expenses, and the balance paid into the general treasury. There was a public debt, the annual interest of which amounted to 200,000 florins. During the war, money had been borrowed at as high a rate as thirty-six per cent, but at the conclusion of hostilities the states could borrow at six per cent, and the whole debt was funded on that basis. Taxation was enormously heavy, but patriotism caused it to be borne with cheerfulness, and productive industry made it comparatively light. Rents were charged twenty-five per cent. A hundred per cent was levied upon beer, wine, meat, salt, spirits. Other articles of necessity and luxury were almost as severely taxed. It is not easy to enumerate the tax-list, scarcely anything foreign or domestic being exempted, while the grave error was often committed of taxing the same article, in different forms, four, five, and six times.

The people virtually taxed themselves, although the superstition concerning the state, as something distinct from and superior to the people, was to linger long and work infinite mischief among those seven republics which were never destined to be welded theoretically and legally into a union. The sacredness of corporations had succeeded, in a measure, to the divinity which hedges kings. Nevertheless, those corporations were so numerous as to be effectively open to a far larger proportion of the population than, in those days, had ever dreamed before of participating in the government. The magistracies were in general unpaid and little coveted, being regarded as a burden and a responsibility rather than an object of ambition. The jurisconsults, called pensionaries, who assisted the municipal authorities, received, however, a modest salary, never exceeding 1500 florins a year.

These numerous bodies, provincial and municipal, elected themselves by supplying their own vacancies. The magistrates were appointed by the stadholder, on a double or triple nomination from the municipal board. This was not impartial suffrage nor manhood suffrage. The germ of a hateful burgher-oligarchy was in the system, but, as compared with Spain, where municipal magistracies were sold by the crown at public auction; or with France, where every office in church, law, magistrature, or court was an object of merchandise disposed of in open market, the system was purity itself, and marked a great advance in the science of government.

It should never be forgotten, moreover, that while the presidents and judges of the highest judicature in other civilized lands were at the mercy of an irresponsible sovereign, and held office—even although it had been paid for in solid specie—at his pleasure, the supreme justices of the high courts of appeal at the Hague were nominated by a senate, and confirmed by a stadholder, and that they exercised their functions for life, or so long as they conducted themselves virtuously in their high office—*quamdiu se bene gesserint.*

If one of the great objects of a civilized community is to secure to all men their own—*ut sua tenerent*—surely it must be admitted that the Republic was in advance of all contemporary states in the laying down of this vital principle, the independence of judges.

As to the army and navy of the United Provinces, enough has been said, in earlier chapters of these volumes, to indicate the improvements introduced by Prince Maurice, and now carried to the highest point of perfection ever attained in that period. There is no doubt whatever, that for discipline, experience, equipment, effectiveness of movement, and general organization, the army of the Republic was the model army of Europe. It amounted to but thirty thousand infantry and two thousand five hundred cavalry, but this number was a large one for a standing army at the beginning of the seventeenth century. It was composed of a variety of materials, Hollanders, Walloons, Flemings, Scotch, English, Irish, Germans, but all welded together into a machine of perfect regularity. The private footsoldier received twelve florins for a so-called month of forty-two days, the drummer and corporal eighteen, the lieutenant fifty-two, and the captain one hundred and fifty florins. Prompt payment was made every week. Obedience was implicit; mutiny, such as was of periodical recurrence in the archduke's army, entirely unknown. The slightest theft was punished with the gallows, and there was therefore no thieving.

The most accurate and critical observers confessed, almost against their will, that no army in Europe could compare with the troops of the States. As to the famous regiments of Sicily, and the ancient legions of Naples and Milan, a distinguished Venetian envoy, who had seen all the camps and courts of Christendom, and was certainly not disposed to overrate the Hollanders at the expense of the Italians, if any rivalry between them had been possible, declared that every private soldier in the Republic was fit to be a captain in any Italian army; while, on the other hand, there was scarcely an Italian captain who would be accepted as a private in any company of the States. So low had the once-famous soldiery of Alva, Don John, and Alexander Farnese descended.

The cavalry of the Republic was even more perfectly organized than was the infantry. "I want words to describe its perfection," said Contarini. The pay was very high and very prompt. A captain received four hundred florins a month (of forty-two days), a lieutenant one hundred and eighty florins, and other officers and privates in proportion. These rates would be very high in our own day. When allowance is made for the difference in the value of money at the respective epochs, the salaries are prodigious; but the thrifty Republic found its account in paying well and paying regularly the champions on whom so much depended, and by whom such splendid services had been rendered.

While the soldiers in the pay of Queen Elizabeth were crawling to her palace gates to die of starvation before her eyes; while the veterans of Spain and of Italy had organized themselves into a permanent military, mutinous republic, on the soil of the so-called obedient Netherlands, because they were left by their masters without clothing or food; the cavalry and infantry of the Dutch commonwealth, thanks to the organizing spirit and the wholesome thrift of the burgher authorities, were contented, obedient, well fed, well clothed, and well paid; devoted to their Government, and ever ready to die in its defense.

Nor was it only on the regular army that reliance was placed. On the contrary, every able-bodied man in the country was liable to be called upon to serve, at any moment, in the militia. All were trained to arms, and provided with arms, and there had been years during this perpetual war in which one man out of three of the whole male population was ready to be mustered at any moment into the field.

Even more could be said in praise of the navy than has been stated of the armies of the republic; for the contemporary accounts of foreigners, and of foreigners who were apt to be satirical, rather than enthusiastic, when describing the institutions, leading personages, and customs of other countries, seemed ever to speak of the United Provinces in terms of eulogy. In commerce, as in war, the naval supremacy of the republic was indisputable. It was easy for the States to place two thousand vessels of war in commission, if necessary, of tonnage varying from four hundred to twelve hundred tons, to man them with the hardiest and boldest sailors in the world, and to despatch them with promptness to any quarter of the globe.

It was recognised as nearly impossible to compel a war-vessel of the Republic to surrender. Hardly an instance was on her naval record of submission, even to far superior force, while it was filled with the tragic but heroic histories of commanders who had blown their ships, with every man on board, into the air, rather than strike their flag. Such was the character, and such the capacity of the sea-born Republic.

That Republic had serious and radical defects, but the design remained to be imitated and improved upon centuries after-wards. The history of the rise and progress of the Dutch Re-public is a leading chapter in the history of human liberty.

The great misfortune of the commonwealth of the United Provinces, next to the slenderness of its geographical propor-tions, was the fact that it was without a center and without a head, and therefore not a nation capable of unlimited vitality. There were seven states. Each claimed to be sovereign. The pretension on the part of several of them was ridiculous. Overyssel, for example, contributed two and three-quarters per cent of the general budget. It was a swamp of twelve hundred square miles in extent, with some heath-spots interspersed, and it numbered perhaps a hundred thousand inhabitants. The doughty Count of Emden alone could have swallowed up such sovereignty, have annexed all the buckwheat patches and cran-berry marshes of Overyssel to his own meager territories, and nobody the wiser.

Zeeland, as we have seen, was disposed at a critical moment to set up its independent sovereignty. Zeeland, far more im-portant than Overyssel, had a revenue of perhaps five hundred thousand dollars,—rather a slender budget for an independent republic, wedged in as it was by the most powerful empires of the earth, and half drowned by the ocean, from which it had scarcely emerged.

There was therefore no popular representation, and on the

other hand no executive head. As sovereignty must be exercised in some way, however, in all living commonwealths, and as a low degree of vitality was certainly not the defect of those bustling provinces, the supreme function had now fallen into the hands of Holland.

While William the Silent lived, the management of war, foreign affairs, and finance, for the revolted provinces, was in his control. He was aided by two council boards, but the circumstances of history and the character of the man had invested him with an inevitable dictatorship.

After his death, at least after Leicester's time, the powers of the state-council, the head of which, Prince Maurice, was almost always absent at the wars, fell into comparative disuse. The great functions of the confederacy passed into the possession of the States-General. That body now came to sit permanently at The Hague. The number of its members, deputies from the seven provinces—envoys from those seven immortal and soulless sovereigns—was not large. The extraordinary assembly held at Bergen-op-Zoom for confirmation of the truce was estimated by Bentivoglio at eight hundred. Bentivoglio, who was on the spot, being then nuncius at Brussels, ought to have been able to count them, yet it is very certain that the number was grossly exaggerated.

At any rate the usual assembly at the Hague rarely amounted to one hundred members. The presidency was changed once a week, the envoy of each province taking his turn as chairman.

Olden-Barneveld, as member for Holland, was always present in the diet. As Advocate-General of the leading province, and keeper of its great seal, more especially as possessor of the governing intellect of the whole commonwealth, he led the administration of Holland, and as the estates of Holland contributed more than half of the whole budget of the confederacy, it was a natural consequence of the actual supremacy of that province, and of the vast legal and political experience of the Advocate, that Holland should govern the confederacy, and that Barneveld should govern Holland.

The States-General remained virtually supreme, receiving

envoys from all the great powers, sending abroad their diplomatic representatives, to whom the title and rank of ambassador was freely accorded, and dealing in a decorous and dignified way with all European affairs. The ability of the republican statesmen was as fully recognized all over the earth, as was the genius of their generals and great naval commanders.

The People did not exist; but this was merely because, in theory, the People had not been invented. It was exactly because there was a People—an energetic and intelligent People—that the Republic was possible.

No scheme had yet been devised for laying down in primary assemblies a fundamental national law, for distributing the various functions of governmental power among selected servants, for appointing representatives according to population or property, and for holding all trustees responsible at reasonable intervals to the nation itself.

Thus government was involved, fold within fold, in successive and concentric municipal layers. The States-General were the outer husk, of which the separate town-council was the kernel or bulb. Yet the number of these executive and legislative boards was so large, and the whole population comparatively so slender, as to cause the original inconveniences from so incomplete a system to be rather theoretic than practical. In point of fact, almost as large a variety of individuals served the state as would perhaps have been the case under a more philosophically arranged democracy. The difficulty was rather in obtaining a candidate for the post than in distributing the posts among candidates.

Men were occupied with their own affairs. In proportion to their numbers they were more productive of wealth than any other nation then existing. An excellent reason why the people were so well governed, so productive, and so enterprising was the simple fact that they were an educated people. There was hardly a Netherlander—man, woman, or child—that could not read and write. The school was the common property of the people, paid for among the municipal expenses. In the cities, as well as in the rural districts, there were not only common schools but classical schools. In the burgher families it was rare to find boys who had not been taught Latin, or girls unacquainted with French. Capacity to write and speak several modern languages was very common, and there were many individuals in every city, neither professors nor pedants, who had made remarkable progress in science and classical literature. The position, too, of women in the commonwealth proved a high degree of civilization. They are described as virtuous, well-educated, energetic, sovereigns in their households, and accustomed to direct all the business at home. "It would be ridiculous," said Donato, "to see a man occupying himself with domestic housekeeping. The women do it all, and command absolutely." The Hollanders, so rebellious against church and king, accepted with meekness the despotism of woman.

The great movement of emancipation from political and ecclesiastical tyranny had brought with it a general advancement of the human intellect. The foundation of the Leyden university in memory of the heroism displayed by the burghers during the siege was as noble a monument as had ever been raised by a free people jealous of its fame. And the scientific luster of the university well sustained the nobility of its origin. The proudest nation on earth might be more proud of a seat of learning, founded thus amidst carnage and tears, whence so much of profound learning and brilliant literature had already been diffused. The classical labor of Joseph Scaliger; Heinsius, father and son; the elder Dousa, almost as famous with his pen in Latin poetry as his sword had made him in the vernacular chronicle; of Dousa the son, whom Grotius called "the crown and flower of all good learning, too soon snatched away by envious death, than whom no man more skilled in poetry, more consummate in acquaintance with ancient science and literature, had ever lived"; of Hugo Grotius himself, who at the age of fifteen had taken his doctor's degree at Leyden, who as a member of Olden-Barneveld's important legation to France and England very soon afterwards had excited the astonishment of Henry IV and Elizabeth, who had already distinguished himself by editions of classic poets, and by original poems and dramas in Latin, and was already, although but twenty-six years of age, laying the foundation of that magnificent reputation as a jurist, a philosopher, a historian, and a statesman, which was to be one of the enduring glories of humanity—all these were the precious possessions of the high school of Leyden.

The still more modern university of Franeker, founded amid the din of perpetual warfare in Friesland, could at least boast the name of Arminius, whose theological writings and whose expansive views were destined to exert such influence over his contemporaries and posterity.[1]

The very necessities of its geographical position had forced it to pre-eminence in hydraulics and hydrostatics. It had learned to transform water into dry land with a perfection attained by no nation before or since. The wonders of its submarine horticulture were the despair of all gardeners in the world.

And as in this gentlest of arts, so also in the dread science of war, the Republic had been the instructor of mankind. The youthful Maurice and his cousin Lewis William had so restored and improved the decayed intelligence of antique strategy, that the greybeards of Europe became docile pupils in their school. The mathematical teacher of Prince Maurice amazed the contemporary world with his combinations and mechanical inventions; the flying chariots of Simon Stevinus seeming products of magical art.

Yet the character of the Dutch intellect was averse to sorcery. The small but mighty nation, which had emancipated itself from the tyranny of Philip and of the Holy Inquisition, was foremost to shake off the fetters of superstition. Out of Holland came the first voice to rebuke one of the hideous delusions of the age. While grave magistrates and sages of other lands were exorcising the devil by murdering his supposed victims, John Wier, a physician of Grave, boldly denounced the demon which had taken possession, not of the wizards, but of the judges.

The age was lunatic and sick, and it was fitting that the race

[1] *History of the United Netherlands* (New York, 1860–1867), IV, 542–568.

which had done so much for the physical and intellectual emancipation of the world, should have been the first to apply a remedy for this monstrous madness. Englishmen and their descendants were drowning and hanging witches in New England long after John Wier had rebuked and denounced the belief in witchcraft.

It was a Zeelander, too, who placed the instrument in the hand of Galileo by which that daring genius traced the movements of the universe, and who, by another wondrous invention, enabled future discoverers to study the infinite life which lies all around us, hidden not by its remoteness but its minuteness. Zacharias Jansens of Middelburg, in 1590, invented both the telescope and the microscope.

The wonder-man of Alkmaar, Cornelius Drebbel, who performed such astounding feats for the amusement of Rudolph of Germany and James of Britain, is also supposed to have invented the thermometer and the barometer. But this claim has been disputed. The inventions of Jansens are proved.

Willebrord Snellius, mathematical professor of Leyden, introduced the true method of measuring the degrees of longitude and latitude, and Huygens, who had seen his manuscripts, asserted that Snellius had invented, before Descartes, the doctrine of refraction.

But it was especially to that noble band of heroes and martyrs, the great navigators and geographical discoverers of the Republic, that science is above all indebted.

Nothing is more sublime in human story than the endurance and audacity with which those pioneers of the sixteenth and seventeenth centuries confronted the nameless horrors of either pole, in the interests of commerce, and for the direct purpose of enlarging the bounds of the human intellect.

The achievements, the sufferings, and the triumphs of Barentz and Cordes, Heemskerk, Van der Hagen, and many others, have been slightly indicated in these pages. The contributions to botany, mineralogy, geometry, geography, and zoölogy, of Linschoten, Plancius, Wagenaar, and Houtmann, and so many other explorers of pole and tropic, can hardly be overrated.

The Netherlanders had wrung their original fatherland out of the grasp of the ocean. They had confronted for centuries the wrath of that ancient tyrant, ever ready to seize the prey of which he had been defrauded.

They had waged fiercer and more perpetual battle with a tyranny more cruel than the tempest, with an ancient superstition more hungry than the sea. It was inevitable that a race, thus invigorated by the ocean, cradled to freedom by their conflicts with its power, and hardened almost to invincibility by their struggle against human despotism, should be foremost among the nations in the development of political, religious, and commercial freedom.[1]

[1] *History of the United Netherlands* (New York, 1860–1867), IV, 569–571.

From THE LIFE AND DEATH OF JOHN OF BARNEVELD

[GENERAL ESTIMATE OF JOHN OF BARNEVELD]

[In the opening pages of *The Life and Death of John of Barneveld* the author gives his estimate of the central character of the work.]

There is no doubt whatever that John of Barneveld, Advocate and Seal Keeper of the little province of Holland during forty years of as troubled and fertile an epoch as any in human history, was second to none of his contemporary statesmen. Yet the singular constitution and historical position of the Republic whose destinies he guided and the peculiar and abnormal office which he held combined to cast a veil over his individuality. The ever-teeming brain, the restless almost omnipresent hand, the fertile pen, the eloquent and ready tongue, were seen, heard, and obeyed by the great European public, by the monarchs, statesmen, and warriors of the time, at many critical moments of history, but it was not John of Barneveld that spoke to the world. Those "high and puissant Lords, my masters the States-General" personified the young but already majestic Republic. Dignified, draped, and concealed by that overshadowing title the informing and master spirit performed its never-ending task.

Those who study the enormous masses of original papers in the archives of the country will be amazed to find how the penmanship, most difficult to decipher, of the Advocate meets them at every turn. Letters to monarchs, generals, ambassadors, resolutions of councils, of sovereign assemblies, of trading corporations, of great Indian companies, legal and historical disquisitions of great depth and length on questions agitating Europe, constitutional arguments, drafts of treaties among the leading powers of the world, instructions to great commissions, plans for European campaigns, vast combinations covering the world, alliances of empire, scientific expeditions and discoveries —papers such as these, covered now with the satirical dust of centuries, written in the small, crabbed, exasperating characters which make Barneveld's handwriting almost cryptographic, were once, when fairly engrossed and sealed with the great seal of the haughty burgher-aristocracy, the documents which occupied the close attention of the cabinets of Christendom.

It is not unfrequent to find four or five important despatches compressed almost in miniature upon one sheet of gigantic foolscap. It is also curious to find each one of these rough drafts conscientiously beginning in the statesman's own hand with the elaborate phrases of compliment belonging to the epoch such as "Noble, strenuous, severe, highly honourable, very learned, very discreet, and very wise masters," and ending with "May the Lord God Almighty eternally preserve you and hold you in His holy keeping in this world and forever"—decorations which one might have thought it safe to leave to be filled in by the secretary or copying clerk.

Thus there have been few men at any period whose lives have been more closely identical than his with a national history. There have been few great men in any history whose names have become less familiar to the world, and lived less in the mouths of posterity. Yet there can be no doubt that if William the Silent was the founder of the independence of the United Provinces Barneveld was the founder of the commonwealth itself. He had never the opportunity, perhaps he might have never had the capacity, to make such prodigious sacrifices in the cause of country as the great prince had done. But he had served his country strenuously from youth to old age with an abiding sense of duty, a steadiness of purpose, a broad vision, a firm grasp, and an opulence of resource such as not one of his compatriots could even pretend to rival.

Had that country of which he was so long the first citizen maintained until our own day the same proportionate position among the empires of Christendom as it held in the seventeenth century, the name of John of Barneveld would have perhaps been as familiar to all men as it is at this moment to nearly every inhabitant of the Netherlands. Even now political passion is almost as ready to flame forth either in ardent affection or enthusiastic hatred as if two centuries and a half had not elapsed since his death. His name is so typical of a party, a polity, and a faith, so indelibly associated with a great historical cataclysm, as to render it difficult even for the grave, the conscientious, the learned, the patriotic of his own compatriots to speak of him with absolute impartiality.[1]

[THE ISSUE IN THE CIVIL STRUGGLE]

[In the following passage Motley states the fundamental issue, as he saw it, in the struggle which rent the United Netherlands during the period of the truce.]

At about the same period the great question of Church and State, which Barneveld had always felt to be among the vital problems of the age, and on which his opinions were most decided, came up for partial solution. It would have been too much to expect the opinion of any statesman to be so much in advance of his time as to favor religious equality. Toleration of various creeds, including the Roman Catholic, so far as abstinence from inquisition into consciences and private parlors could be called toleration, was secured, and that was a considerable step in advance of the practice of the sixteenth century. Burning, hanging, and burying alive of culprits guilty of another creed than the dominant one had become obsolete. But there was an established creed—the Reformed religion, founded on the Netherland Confession and the Heidelberg Catechism. And there was one established principle then considered throughout Europe the grand result of the Reformation, "*Cujus regio ejus religio*," which was in reality as impudent an invasion of human right as any heaven-born dogma of infallibility. The sovereign of a country, having appropriated the revenues of the ancient church, prescribed his own creed to his subjects. In the royal conscience were included the million consciences of his sub-

[1] *The Life and Death of John of Barneveld* (London, 1874), I, 1-4.

jects. The inevitable result in a country like the Netherlands, without a personal sovereign, was a struggle between the new church and the civil government for mastery. And at this period, and always in Barneveld's opinion, the question of dogma was subordinate to that of church government. That there should be no authority over the King had been settled in England. Henry VIII, Elizabeth, and afterwards James, having become popes in their own realm, had no great hostility to, but rather an affection for, ancient dogma and splendid ceremonial. But in the seven provinces, even as in France, Germany, and Switzerland, the reform where it had been effected at all had been more thorough, and there was little left of Popish pomp or aristocratic hierarchy. Nothing could be severer than the simplicity of the Reformed Church, nothing more imperious than its dogma, nothing more infallible than its creed. It was the true religion, and there was none other. But to whom belonged the ecclesiastical edifices, the splendid old minsters in the cities—raised by the people's confiding piety and the purchased remission of their sins in a bygone age—and the humbler but beautiful parish churches in every town and village? To the state, said Barneveld, speaking for government; to the community represented by the states of the provinces, the magistracies of the cities and municipalities. To the church itself, the one true church represented by its elders, and deacons, and preachers, was the reply.

And to whom belonged the right of prescribing laws and ordinances of public worship, of appointing preachers, church servants, schoolmasters, sextons? To the Holy Ghost inspiring the Class and the Synod, said the Church.

To the civil authority, said the magistrates, by which the churches are maintained, and the salaries of the ecclesiastics paid. The states of Holland are as sovereign as the kings of England or Denmark, the electors of Saxony or Brandenburg, the magistrates of Zürich or Basel or other Swiss cantons. "*Cujus regio ejus religio.*"

In 1590 there was a compromise under the guidance of Barneveld. It was agreed that an appointing board should be established composed of civil functionaries and church officials in equal numbers. Thus should the interests of religion and of education be maintained.

The compromise was successful enough during the war. External pressure kept down theological passion, and there were as yet few symptoms of schism in the dominant church. But there was to come a time when the struggle between church and government was to break forth with an intensity and to rage to an extent which no man at that moment could imagine.[1]

[GROWING TENSION BETWEEN JOHN AND MAURICE]

[The religious issue gradually brought the two principal Dutch leaders, John of Olden-Barneveld and Maurice of Nassau, into conflict. In a few pages Motley attempted to explain the growing tension between the two men.]

During the war Maurice had been, with exception of Henry IV, the most considerable personage in Europe. He was surrounded with that visible atmosphere of power the poison of which it is so difficult to resist, and through the golden haze of which a mortal seems to dilate for the vulgar eye into the supernatural. The attention of Christendom was perpetually fixed upon him. Nothing like his sieges, his encampments, his military discipline, his scientific campaigning had been seen before in modern Europe. The youthful aristocracy from all countries thronged to his camp to learn the game of war, for he had restored by diligent study of the ancients much that was noble in that pursuit, and had elevated into an art that which had long since degenerated into a system of butchery, marauding, and rapine. And he had fought with signal success and unquestionable heroism the most important and most brilliant pitched battle of the age. He was a central figure of the current history of Europe. Pagan nations looked up to him as one of the leading sovereigns of Christendom. The Emperor of Japan addressed him as his brother monarch, assured him that his

[1] *The Life and Death of John of Barneveld* (London, 1874), I, 15-17.

subjects trading to that distant empire should be welcomed and protected, and expressed himself ashamed that so great a prince, whose name and fame had spread through the world, should send his subjects to visit a country so distant and unknown, and offer its emperor a friendship which he was unconscious of deserving.

He had been a commander of armies and a chief among men since he came to man's estate, and he was now in the very vigour of life, in his forty-second year. Of Imperial descent and closely connected by blood or alliance with many of the most illustrious of reigning houses, the acknowledged master of the most royal and noble of all sciences, he was of the stuff of which kings were made, and belonged by what was then accounted right divine to the family of kings. His father's death had alone prevented his elevation to the throne of Holland, and such possession of half the sovereignty of the United Netherlands would probably have expanded into dominion over all the seven, with a not fantastic possibility of uniting the ten still obedient provinces into a single realm. Such a kingdom would have been more populous and far wealthier than contemporary Great Britain and Ireland. Maurice, then a student at Leyden, was too young at that crisis, and his powers too undeveloped to justify any serious attempt to place him in his father's place.

The Netherlands drifted into a confederacy of aristocratic republics, not because they could not get a king, foreign or native. The documents regarding the offer of the sovereign countship to William remained in the possession of Maurice, and a few years before the peace there had been a private meeting of leading personages, of which Barneveld was the promoter and chief spokesman, to take into consideration the propriety and possibility of conferring that sovereignty upon the son which had virtually belonged to the father. The obstacles were deemed so numerous, and especially the scheme seemed so fraught with danger to Maurice, that it was reluctantly abandoned by his best friends, among whom unquestionably was the Advocate.

There was no reason whatever why the now successful and mature soldier, to whom the country was under such vast obligations, should not aspire to the sovereignty. The provinces had not pledged themselves to republicanism, but rather to monarchy, and the crown, although secretly coveted by Henry IV, could by no possibility now be conferred on any other man than Maurice. It was no impeachment on his character that he should nourish thoughts in which there was nothing criminal.

But the peace negotiations had opened a chasm. It was obvious enough that Barneveld having now so long exercised great powers, and become as it were the chief magistrate of an important commonwealth, would not be so friendly as formerly to its conversion into a monarchy and to the elevation of the great soldier to its throne. The Advocate had even been sounded, cautiously and secretly, so men believed, by the princess-dowager, Louise de Coligny, widow of William the Silent, as to the feasibility of procuring the sovereignty for Maurice. She had done this at the instigation of Maurice, who had expressed his belief that the favorable influence of the Advocate would make success certain and who had represented to her that, as he was himself resolved never to marry, the inheritance after his death would fall to her son Frederic Henry. The princess, who was of a most amiable disposition, adored her son. Devoted to the house of Nassau and a great admirer of its chief, she had a long interview with Barneveld, in which she urged the scheme upon his attention without in all probability revealing that she had come to him at the solicitation of Maurice.

The Advocate spoke to her with frankness and out of the depths of his heart. He professed an ardent attachment to her family, a profound reverence for the virtues, sacrifices, and achievements of her lamented husband, and a warm desire to do everything to further the interests of the son who had proved himself so worthy of his parentage.

But he proved to her that Maurice, in seeking the sovereignty, was seeking his ruin. The Hollanders, he said, like to be persuaded and not forced. Having triumphantly shaken off the yoke of a powerful king, they would scarcely consent now to accept the rule of any personal sovereign. The desire to save themselves from the claws of Spain had led them formerly to offer the dominion over them to various potentates. Now that they had achieved peace and independence and were delivered from the fears of Spanish ferocity and French intrigue, they shuddered at the dangers from royal hands out of which they had at last escaped. He believed that they would be capable of tearing in pieces any one who might make the desired proposition. After all, he urged, Maurice was a hundred times more fortunate as he was than if he should succeed in desires so opposed to his own good. This splendor of sovereignty was a false glare which would lead him to a precipice. He had now the power of a sovereign without the envy which ever followed it. Having essentially such power, he ought, like his father, to despise an empty name, which would only make him hated. For it was well known that William the Silent had only yielded to much solicitation, agreeing to accept that which then seemed desirable for the country's good but to him was more than indifferent.

Maurice was captain-general and admiral-general of five provinces. He appointed to governments and to all military office. He had a share of appointment to the magistracies. He had the same advantages and the same authority as had been enjoyed in the Netherlands by the ancient sovereign counts, by the dukes of Burgundy, by Emperor Charles V himself.

Every one now was in favor of increasing his pensions, his salaries, his material splendor. Should he succeed in seizing the sovereignty, men would envy him even to the ribbons of his pages' and his lackeys' shoes. He turned to the annals of Holland and showed the princess that there had hardly been a sovereign count against whom his subjects had not revolted, marching generally into the very courtyard of the palace at the Hague in order to take his life.

Convinced by this reasoning, Louise de Coligny had at once changed her mind, and subsequently besought her stepson to

give up a project sure to be fatal to his welfare, his peace of
mind, and the good of the country. Maurice listened to her
coldly, gave little heed to the Advocate's logic, and hated him
in his heart from that day forth.[1]

[THE RELIGIOUS ISSUE]

[The following pages describe the development of the religious issue into an open schism.]

The doctrine of predestination in its sternest and strictest
sense had long been the prevailing one in the Reformed Church
of the revolted Netherlands, as in those of Scotland, France,
Geneva, and the Palatinate. No doubt up to the period of the
truce a majority had acquiesced in that dogma and its results,
although there had always been many preachers to advocate
publicly a milder creed. It was not until the appointment of
Jacob Arminius to the professorship of theology at Leyden,
in the place of Francis Junius, in the year 1603, that a danger of
schism in the Church seemed impending. Then rose the great
Gomarus in his wrath, and with all the powers of splendid
eloquence, profound learning, and the intense bigotry of conviction, denounced the horrible heresy. Conferences between
the two before the court of Holland, theological tournaments
between six champions on a side, gallantly led by their respective chieftains, followed, with the usual result of confirming
both parties in the conviction that to each alone belonged
exclusively the truth.

The original influence of Arminius had however been so
great that when the preachers of Holland had been severally
called on by a synod to sign the Heidelberg Catechism, many
of them refused. Here was open heresy and revolt. It was
time for the true church to vindicate its authority. The great
war with Spain had been made, so it was urged and honestly
believed, not against the Inquisition, not to prevent Netherlanders from being burned and buried alive by the old true
church, not in defense of ancient charters, constitutions, and

[1] *The Life and Death of John of Barneveld* (London, 1874), I, 23–27.

privileges—the precious result of centuries of popular resistance to despotic force—not to maintain an amount of civil liberty and local self-government larger in extent than any then existing in the world, not to assert equality of religion for all men, but simply to establish the true religion, the one church, the only possible creed; the creed and church of Calvin.

It is perfectly certain that the living fire which glowed in the veins of those hot gospellers had added intense enthusiasm to the war spirit throughout that immense struggle. It is quite possible that without that enthusiasm the war might not have been carried on to its successful end. But it is equally certain that Catholics, Lutherans, Baptists, and devotees of many other creeds, had taken part in the conflict in defence both of hearth and altar, and that without that aid the independence of the provinces would never have been secured.

Yet before the war was ended the arrogance of the Reformed priesthood had begun to dig a chasm. Men who with William the Silent and Barneveld had indulged in the vision of religious equality as a possible result of so much fighting against the Holy Inquisition were perhaps to be disappointed.

Preachers under the influence of the gentle Arminius having dared to refuse signing the creed were to be dealt with. It was time to pass from censure to action. Heresy must be trampled down. The churches called for a national synod, and they did this as by divine right. "My Lords the States-General must observe," they said, "that this assembly now demanded is not a human institution but an ordinance of the Holy Ghost in its community, not depending upon any man's authority, but proceeding from God to the community." They complained that the true church was allowed to act only through the civil government, and was thus placed at a disadvantage compared even with Catholics and other sects, whose proceedings were winked at. "Thus the true church suffered from its apparent and public freedom, and hostile sects gained by secret connivance."

A crisis was fast approaching. The one church claimed infallibility and superiority to the civil power. The Holy Ghost was placed in direct, ostentatious opposition to My Lords the States-General. . It was for Netherlanders to decide whether, after having shaken off the Holy Inquisition, and subjected the old true church to the public authority, they were now to submit to the imperious claims of the new true church.

There were hundreds of links connecting the church with the state. In that day a divorce between the two was hardly possible or conceivable. The system of Congregationalism so successfully put into practice soon afterwards in the wilderness of New England, and to which so much of American freedom political as well as religious is due, was not easy to adopt in an old country like the Netherlands. Splendid churches and cathedrals, the legal possession of which would be contended for by rival sects, could scarcely be replaced by temporary structures of lath and plaster, or by humble back parlors of mechanics' shops. There were questions of property of complicated nature. Not only the states and the communities claimed in rivalry the ownership of church property, but many private families could show ancient advowsons and other claims to present or to patronize, derived from imperial or ducal charters.

So long as there could be liberty of opinion within the church upon points not necessarily vital, open schism could be avoided, by which the cause of Protestantism throughout Europe must be weakened, while at the same time subordination of the priesthood to the civil authority would be maintained. But if the Holy Ghost, through the assembled clergy, were to dictate an iron formulary to which all must conform, to make laws for church government which every citizen must obey, and to appoint preachers and schoolmasters from whom alone old and young could receive illumination and instruction religious or lay, a theocracy would be established which no enlightened statesman could tolerate.

The States-General agreed to the synod, but imposed a condition that there should be a revision of creed and catechism. This was thundered down with one blast. The condition implied a possibility that the vile heresy of Arminius might be correct. An unconditional synod was demanded. The Heidelberg Catechism and Netherland Creed were sacred, infallible, not to be touched. The answer of the government, through the mouth of Barneveld, was that "to My Lords the States-General, as the foster-fathers and protectors of the churches, every right belonged."

Thus far the States-General under the leadership of the Advocate were unanimous. The victory remained with state against church. But very soon after the truce had been established, and men had liberty to devote themselves to peaceful pursuits, the ecclesiastical trumpet again sounded far and wide, and contending priests and laymen rushed madly to the fray. The Remonstrance and Contra-Remonstrance, and the appointment of Conrad Vorstius, a more abominable heretic than Arminius, to the vacant chair of Arminius—a step which drove Gomarus and the Gomarites to frenzy, although Gomarus and Vorstius remained private and intimate friends to the last—are matters briefly to be mentioned on a later page.

Thus to the four chief actors in the politico-religious drama, soon to be enacted as an interlude to an eighty years' war, were assigned parts at first sight inconsistent with their private convictions. The King of France, who had often abjured his religion, and was now the best of Catholics, was denounced ferociously in every Catholic pulpit in Christendom as secretly an apostate again, and the open protector of heretics and rebels. But the cheerful Henry troubled himself less than he perhaps had cause to do with these thunderblasts. Besides, as we shall soon see, he had other objects political and personal to sway his opinions.

James the ex-Calvinist, crypto-Arminian, pseudo-Papist, and avowed Puritan-hater, was girding on his armor to annihilate Arminians and to defend and protect Puritans in Holland, while swearing that in England he would pepper them and harry them and hang them and that he would even like to bury them alive.

Barneveld, who turned his eyes, as much as in such an inflammatory age it was possible, from subtle points of theology, and relied on his great-grandfather's motto of humility, *"Nil scire tutissima fides,"* was perhaps nearer to the dogma of the dominant Reformed Church than he knew, although always the consistent and strenuous champion of the civil authority over church as well as state.

Maurice was no theologian. He was a steady churchgoer, and his favorite divine, the preacher at his court chapel, was none other than Uytenbogaert. The very man who was instantly to be the champion of the Arminians, the author of the Remonstrance, the counsellor and comrade of Barneveld and Grotius, was now sneered at by the Gomarites as the "Court Trumpeter." The preacher was not destined to change his opinions. Perhaps the Prince might alter. But Maurice then paid no heed to the great point at issue, about which all the Netherlanders were to take each other by the throat—absolute predestination. He knew that the Advocate had refused to listen to his stepmother's suggestion as to his obtaining the sovereignty. "He knew nothing of predestination," he was wont to say, "whether it was green, or whether it was blue. He only knew that his pipe and the Advocate's were not likely to make music together." This much of predestination he did know, that if the Advocate and his friends were to come to open conflict with the prince of Orange-Nassau, the conqueror of Nieuport, it was predestined to go hard with the Advocate and his friends.[1]

[ISSUES AND PARTISANS IN THE CIVIL STRUGGLE]

[In spite of the delicate diplomatic situation that called for a united front the theologians continued their quarrel and split the nation into two warring camps. They precipitated an open struggle by the formulation of their different points of view into definite statements. Thenceforth the Remonstrants and the Contra-Remonstrants struggled for control of the country. The succeeding passages explain the issues involved and the partisans of the two conflicting points of view.]

[1] *The Life and Death of John of Barneveld* (London, 1874), I, 40–45.

Meantime the preachers who were disciples of Arminius had in a private assembly drawn up what was called a Remonstrance, addressed to the states of Holland, and defending themselves from the reproach that they were seeking change in the divine service and desirous of creating tumult and schism.

This Remonstrance, set forth by the pen of the famous Uytenbogaert, whom Gomarus called the Court Trumpeter, because for a long time he had been Prince Maurice's favorite preacher, was placed in the hands of Barneveld, for delivery to the states of Holland. Thenceforth the Arminians were called Remonstrants.

The Hague Conference followed, six preachers on a side, and the states of Holland exhorted to fraternal compromise. Until further notice, they decreed that no man should be required to believe more than had been laid down in the Five Points.

Before the conference, however, the Gomarite preachers had drawn up a Contra-Remonstrance of Seven Points in opposition to the Remonstrants' five.

They demanded the holding of a national synod to settle the difference between these Five and Seven Points, or the sending of them to foreign universities for arbitration, a mutual promise being given by the contending parties to abide by the decision.

Thus much it has been necessary to state concerning what in the seventeenth century was called the platform of the two great parties: a term which has been perpetuated in our own country, and is familiar to all the world in the nineteenth.

There shall be no more setting forth of these subtle and finely wrought abstractions in our pages. We aspire not to the lofty heights of theological and supernatural contemplation, where the atmosphere becomes too rarefied for ordinary constitutions. Rather we attempt an objective and level survey of remarkable phenomena manifesting themselves on the earth; direct or secondary emanations from those distant spheres.

For in those days, and in that land especially, theology and politics were one. It may be questioned at least whether this practical fusion of elements, which may with more safety to the commonwealth be kept separate, did not tend quite as much to lower and contaminate the religious sentiments as to elevate the political idea. To mix habitually the solemn phraseology which men love to reserve for their highest and most sacred needs with the familiar slang of politics and trade seems to our generation not a very desirable proceeding.

The aroma of doubly distilled and highly sublimated dogma is more difficult to catch than to comprehend the broader and more practical distinctions of everyday party strife.

King James was furious at the thought that common men—the vulgar, the people in short—should dare to discuss deep problems of divinity which, as he confessed, had puzzled even his royal mind. Barneveld modestly disclaimed the power of seeing with absolute clearness into things beyond the reach of the human intellect. But the honest Netherlanders were not abashed by thunder from the royal pulpit, nor perplexed by hesitations which darkened the soul of the great Advocate.

In burghers' mansions, peasants' cottages, mechanics' backparlors, on board herring smacks, canal boats, and East Indiamen; in shops, counting-rooms, farmyards, guardrooms, alehouses; on the exchange, in the tennis-court, on the mall; at banquets, at burials, christenings, or bridals; wherever and whenever human creatures met each other, there was ever to be found the fierce wrangle of Remonstrant and Contra-Remonstrant, the hissing of red-hot theological rhetoric, the pelting of hostile texts. The blacksmith's iron cooled on the anvil, the tinker dropped a kettle half mended, the broker left a bargain unclinched, the Scheveningen fisherman in his wooden shoes forgot the cracks in his pinkie, while each paused to hold high converse with friend or foe on fate, free will, or absolute foreknowledge; losing himself in wandering mazes whence there was no issue. Province against province, city against city, family against family; it was one vast scene of bickering, denunciation, heartburnings, mutual excommunication and hatred.

Alas! a generation of mankind before, men had stood banded together to resist, with all the might that comes from union, the fell spirit of the Holy Inquisition, which was dooming all who had wandered from the ancient fold or resisted foreign tyranny to the axe, the faggot, the living grave. There had been small leisure then for men who fought for fatherland, and for comparative liberty of conscience, to tear each others' characters in pieces, and to indulge in mutual hatreds and loathing on the question of predestination.

As a rule the population, especially of the humbler classes, and a great majority of the preachers were Contra-Remonstrant; the magistrates, the burgher patricians, were Remonstrant. In Holland the controlling influence was Remonstrant; but Amsterdam and four or five other cities of that province held to the opposite doctrine. These cities formed therefore a small minority in the States Assembly of Holland sustained by a large majority in the States-General. The province of Utrecht was almost unanimously Remonstrant. The five other provinces were decidedly Contra-Remonstrant.

It is obvious therefore that the influence of Barneveld, hitherto so all-controlling in the States-General, and which rested on the complete submission of the states of Holland to his will, was tottering. The battle-line between Church and State was now drawn up; and it was at the same time a battle between the union and the principles of state sovereignty.

It had long since been declared through the mouth of the Advocate, but in a solemn state manifesto, that My Lords the States-General were the foster-fathers and the natural protectors of the church, to whom supreme authority in church matters belonged.

The Contra-Remonstrants, on the other hand, maintained that all the various churches made up one indivisible church, seated above the states, whether provincial or general, and governed by the Holy Ghost acting directly upon the congregations.

As the schism grew deeper and the States-General receded from the position which they had taken up under the lead of the Advocate, the scene was changed. A majority of the provinces being Contra-Remonstrant, and therefore in favor of a national synod, the States-General as a body were of necessity for the synod.

It was felt by the clergy that, if many churches existed, they would all remain subject to the civil authority. The power of the priesthood would thus sink before that of the burgher aristocracy. There must be one church—the Church of Geneva and Heidelberg—if that theocracy which the Gomarites meant to establish was not to vanish as a dream. It was founded on divine right, and knew no chief magistrate but the Holy Ghost. A few years before the States-General had agreed to a national synod, but with a condition that there should be revision of the Netherland Confession and the Heidelberg Catechism. Against this the orthodox infallibilists had protested and thundered, because it was an admission that the vile Arminian heresy might perhaps be declared correct. It was now however a matter of certainty that the States-General would cease to oppose the unconditional synod, because the majority sided with the priesthood.

The magistrates of Leyden had not long before opposed the demand for a synod on the ground that the war against Spain was not undertaken to maintain one sect; that men of various sects and creeds had fought with equal valor against the common foe; that religious compulsion was hateful, and that no synod had a right to claim Netherlanders as slaves.

To thoughtful politicians like Barneveld, Hugo Grotius, and men who acted with them, that seemed a doctrine fraught with danger to the state, by which mankind were not regarded as saved or doomed according to belief or deeds, but as individuals divided from all eternity into two classes which could never be united, but must ever mutually regard each other as enemies.

And like enemies Netherlanders were indeed beginning to regard each other. The men who, banded like brothers, had so heroically fought for two generations long for liberty against an almost superhuman despotism, now howling and jeering against each other like demons, seemed determined to bring the very name of liberty into contempt.

Where the Remonstrants were in the ascendant, they excited

the hatred and disgust of the orthodox by their overbearing determination to carry their Five Points. A broker in Rotterdam of the Contra-Remonstrant persuasion, being about to take a wife, swore he had rather be married by a pig than a parson. For this sparkling epigram he was punished by the Remonstrant magistracy with loss of his citizenship for a year and the right to practice his trade for life. A casuistical tinker, expressing himself violently in the same city against the Five Points, and disrespectfully towards the magistrates for tolerating them, was banished from the town. A printer in the neighborhood, disgusted with these and similar efforts of tyranny on the part of the dominant party, thrust a couple of lines of doggerel into the lottery:

"In name of the Prince of Orange, I ask once and again,
  What difference between the Inquisition of Rotterdam and
    Spain?"

For this poetical effort the printer was sentenced to forfeit the prize that he had drawn in the lottery, and to be kept in prison on bread and water for a fortnight.

Certainly such punishments were hardly as severe as being beheaded or burned or buried alive, as would have been the lot of tinkers and printers and brokers who opposed the established church in the days of Alva, but the demon of intolerance, although its fangs were drawn, still survived, and had taken possession of both parties in the Reformed Church. For it was the Remonstrants who had possession of the churches at Rotterdam, and the printer's distich is valuable as pointing out that the name of Orange was beginning to identify itself with the Contra-Remonstrant faction. At this time, on the other hand, the gabble that Barneveld had been bought by Spanish gold, and was about to sell his country to Spain, became louder than a whisper. Men were not ashamed, from theological hatred, to utter such senseless calumnies against a venerable statesman whose long life had been devoted to the cause of his country's independence and to the death struggle with Spain.

As if, because a man admitted the possibility of all his fellow-creatures being saved from damnation through repentance and the grace of God, he must inevitably be a traitor to his country and a pensionary of her deadliest foe!

And where the Contra-Remonstrants held possession of the churches and the city governments, acts of tyranny which did not then seem ridiculous were of everyday occurrence. Clergymen, suspected of the Five Points, were driven out of the pulpits with bludgeons or assailed with brickbats at the church door. At Amsterdam, Simon Goulart, for preaching the doctrine of universal salvation and for disputing the eternal damnation of young children, was forbidden thenceforth to preach at all.

But it was at The Hague that the schism in religion and politics first fatally widened itself. Henry Rosaeus, an eloquent divine, disgusted with his colleague Uytenbogaert, refused all communion with him, and was in consequence suspended. Excluded from the Great Church, where he had formerly ministered, he preached every Sunday at Ryswyk, two or three miles distant. Seven hundred Contra-Remonstrants of The Hague followed their beloved pastor, and, as the roads to Ryswyk were muddy and sloppy in winter, acquired the unsavory nickname of the "Mud Beggars." The vulgarity of heart which suggested the appellation does not inspire today great sympathy with the Remonstrant party, even if one were inclined to admit, what is not the fact, that they represented the cause of religious equality. For even the illustrious Grotius was at that very moment repudiating the notion that there could be two religions in one state. "Difference in public worship," he said, "was in kingdoms pernicious, but in free commonwealths in the highest degree destructive."

It was the struggle between church and state for supremacy over the whole body politic. "The Reformation," said Grotius, "was not brought about by synods, but by kings, princes, and magistrates." It was the same eternal story, the same terrible two-edged weapon, *"Cujus regio ejus religio,"* found in the arsenal of the first Reformers, and in every politico-religious arsenal of history.

"By an eternal decree of God," said Gomarus in accordance

with Calvin, "it has been fixed who are to be saved and who damned. By His decree some are drawn to faith and godliness, and, being drawn, can never fall away. God leaves all the rest in the general corruption of human nature and their own misdeeds."

"God has from eternity made this distinction in the fallen human race," said Arminius, "that He pardons those who desist from their sins and put their faith in Christ, and will give them eternal life, but will punish those who remain impenitent. Moreover, it is pleasanter to God that all men should repent, and, coming to knowledge of truth, remain therein, but He compels none."

This was the vital difference of dogma. And it was because they could hold no communion with those who believed in the efficacy of repentance that Rosaeus and his followers had seceded to Ryswyk, and the Reformed Church had been torn into two very unequal parts. But it is difficult to believe that out of this arid field of controversy so plentiful a harvest of hatred and civil convulsion could have ripened. More practical than the insoluble problems, whether repentance could effect salvation, and whether dead infants were hopelessly damned, was the question who should rule both church and state.

There could be but one church. On that Remonstrants and Contra-Remonstrants were agreed. But should the Five Points or the Seven Points obtain the mastery? Should the framework of hammered iron, the Confession and Catechism, be maintained in all its rigidity around the sheepfold, or should the disciples of the arch-heretic Arminius, the salvation-mongers, be permitted to prowl within it?

Was Barneveld, who had the Reformed religion (so men told each other), and who believed in nothing, to continue dictator of the whole Republic through his influence over one province, prescribing its religious dogmas and laying down its laws; or had not the time come for the States-General to vindicate the rights of the church, and to crush for ever the pernicious principle of state sovereignty and burgher oligarchy?

The abyss was wide and deep, and the wild waves were

raging more madly every hour. The Advocate, anxious and troubled, but undismayed, did his best in the terrible emergency. He conferred with Prince Maurice on the subject of the Ryswyk secession, and men said that he sought to impress upon him, as chief of the military forces, the necessity of putting down religious schism with the armed hand.

The prince had not yet taken a decided position. He was still under the influence of John Uytenbogaert, who with Arminius and the Advocate made up the fateful three from whom deadly disasters were deemed to have come upon the commonwealth. He wished to remain neutral. But no man can be neutral in civil contentions threatening the life of the body politic any more than the heart can be indifferent if the human frame is sawn in two.

"I am a soldier," said Maurice, "not a divine. These are matters of theology which I don't understand, and about which I don't trouble myself."

On another occasion he is reported to have said, "I know nothing of predestination, whether it is green or whether it is blue; but I do know that the Advocate's pipe and mine will never play the same tune."

It was not long before he fully comprehended the part which he must necessarily play. To say that he was indifferent to religious matters was as ridiculous as to make a like charge against Barneveld. Both were religious men. It would have been almost impossible to find an irreligious character in that country, certainly not among its highest-placed and leading minds. Maurice had strong intellectual powers. He was a regular attendant on divine worship, and was accustomed to hear daily religious discussions. To avoid them indeed, he would have been obliged not only to fly his country, but to leave Europe. He had a profound reverence for the memory of his father, Calbo y Calbanista, as William the Silent had called himself. But the great prince had died before these fierce disputes had torn the bosom of the Reformed Church, and while Reformers still were brethren. But if Maurice were a religious man, he was also a keen politician; a less capable politician, however, than a soldier, for he was confessedly the first captain of his age. He was not rapid in his conceptions, but he was sure in the end to comprehend his opportunity. The church, the people, the Union—the sacerdotal, the democratic, and the national element—united under a name so potent to conjure with as the name of Orange-Nassau, was stronger than any other possible combination. Instinctively and logically therefore the stadholder found himself the chieftain of the Contra-Remonstrant party, and without the necessity of an apostasy such as had been required of his great contemporary to make himself master of France.

The power of Barneveld and his partisans was now put to a severe strain. His efforts to bring back the Hague seceders were powerless. The influence of Uytenbogaert over the stadholder steadily diminished. He prayed to be relieved from his post in the Great Church of The Hague, especially objecting to serve with a Contra-Remonstrant preacher whom Maurice wished to officiate there in place of the seceding Rosaeus. But the stadholder refused to let him go, fearing his influence in other places. "There is stuff in him," said Maurice, "to outweigh half a dozen Contra-Remonstrant preachers." Everywhere in Holland the opponents of the Five Points refused to go to the churches, and set up tabernacles for themselves in barns, outhouses, canal-boats. And the authorities in town and village nailed up the barn-doors, and dispersed the canal-boat congregations, while the populace pelted them with stones. The seceders appealed to the stadholder, pleading that at least they ought to be allowed to hear the word of God as they understood it without being forced into churches where they were obliged to hear Arminian blasphemy. At least their barns might be left them. "Barns," said Maurice, "barns and outhouses! Are we to preach in barns? The churches belong to us, and we mean to have them too."

Not long afterwards the stadholder, clapping his hand on his sword hilt, observed that these differences could only be settled by force of arms. An ominous remark and a dreary comment on the forty years' war against the Inquisition.

And the same scenes that were enacting in Holland were going on in Overyssel and Friesland and Groningen; but with a difference. Here it was the Five Points men who were driven into secession, whose barns were nailed up, and whose preachers were mobbed. A lugubrious spectacle, but less painful certainly than the hangings and drownings and burnings alive in the previous century to prevent secession from the indivisible church.

It is certain that stadholders and all other magistrates ever since the establishment of independence were sworn to maintain the Reformed religion and to prevent a public divine worship under any other form. It is equally certain that by the 13th article of the Act of Union—the organic law of the confederation made at Utrecht in 1579—each province reserved for itself full control of religious questions. It would indeed seem almost unimaginable in a country where not only every province, but every city, every municipal board, was so jealous of its local privileges and traditional rights that the absolute disposition over the highest, gravest, and most difficult questions that can inspire and perplex humanity should be left to a general government, and one moreover which had scarcely come into existence.

Yet into this entirely illogical position the commonwealth was steadily drifting. The cause was simple enough. The states of Holland, as already observed, were Remonstrant by a large majority. The States-General were Contra-Remonstrant by a still greater majority. The Church, rigidly attached to the Confession and Catechism, and refusing all change except through decree of a synod to be called by the general government which it controlled, represented the national idea. It thus identified itself with the Republic, and was in sympathy with a large majority of the population.

Logic, law, historical tradition were on the side of the Advocate and the states'-right party. The instinct of national self-preservation, repudiating the narrow and destructive doctrine of provincial sovereignty, were on the side of the States-General and the church.[1]

[1] *The Life and Death of John of Barneveld* (London, 1874), I, 336–348.

[TRIAL, SENTENCING, AND EXECUTION OF JOHN]

[In the contest of personalities and principles which tore the United Netherlands almost asunder, Maurice of Nassau and the Contra-Remonstrants finally triumphed. Their victory resulted in the trial, the sentencing, and the execution of John of Olden-Barneveld, the leader of the Remonstrants. The next three passages describe these three events.]

It would be a thankless and tedious task to wander through the wilderness of interrogatories and answers, extending over three months of time, which stood in the place of a trial. The defence of Barneveld was his own history, and that I have attempted to give in the preceding pages. A great part of the accusation was deduced from his private and official correspondence, and it is for this reason that I have laid such copious extracts from it before the reader. No man except the judges and the States-General had access to those letters, and it was easy therefore, if needful, to give them a false coloring. It is only very recently that they have been seen at all, and they have never been published from that day to this.

Out of the confused mass of documents appertaining to the trial, a few generalizations can be made which show the nature of the attack upon him. He was accused of having permitted Arminius to infuse new opinions into the University of Leyden, and of having subsequently defended the appointment of Vorstius to the same place. He had opposed the national synod. He had made drafts of letters for the King of Great Britain to sign, recommending mutual toleration on the five disputed points regarding predestination. He was the author of the famous Sharp Resolution. He had recommended the enlistment by the provinces and towns of Waartgelders, or mercenaries. He had maintained that those mercenaries as well as the regular troops were bound in time of peace to be obedient and faithful, not only to the generality and the stadholders, but to the magistrates of the cities and provinces where they were employed, and to the states by whom they were paid. He had sent to Leyden, warning the authorities of the approach of the prince. He had encouraged all the proceedings at Utrecht, writing a letter to the secretary of that province advising a watch to be kept at the city gates as well as in the river, and ordering his letter when read to be burned. He had received presents from foreign potentates. He had attempted to damage the character of his Excellency the Prince by declaring on various occasions that he aspired to the sovereignty of the country. He had held a ciphered correspondence on the subject with foreign ministers of the Republic. He had given great offence to the King of Great Britain by soliciting from him other letters in the sense of those which his Majesty had written in 1613, advising moderation and mutual toleration. He had not brought to condign punishment the author of *The Balance*, a pamphlet in which an oration of the English ambassador had been criticized, and aspersions made on the Order of the Garter. He had opposed the formation of the West India Company. He had said many years before to Nicolas van Berk that the Provinces had better return to the dominion of Spain. And in general, all his proceedings had tended to put the Provinces into a "blood-bath."

There was however no accusation that he had received bribes from the enemy or held traitorous communication with him, or that he had committed any act of high treason.

His private letters to Caron and to the ambassadors in Paris, with which the reader has been made familiar, had thus been ransacked to find treasonable matter, but the result was meagre in spite of the minute and microscopic analysis instituted to detect traces of poison in them. . . .

The testimony of Nicolas van Berk was, at any rate, more direct.

On the 21st December, 1618, the burgomaster testified that the Advocate had once declared to him that the differences in regard to divine worship were not so great but that they might be easily composed; asking him at the same time "whether it would not be better that we should submit ourselves again to the King of Spain." Barneveld had also referred, so said Van

Berk, to the conduct of the Spanish king towards those who had helped him to the kingdom of Portugal. The Burgomaster was unable, however, to specify the date, year, or month in which the Advocate had held this language. He remembered only that the conversation occurred when Barneveld was living on the Spui at The Hague, and that having been let into the house through the hall on the side of the vestibule, he had been conducted by the Advocate down a small staircase into the office. . . .

Always instructive to his judges as he swept at will through the record of nearly half a century of momentous European history, in which he was himself a conspicuous figure, or expounding the ancient laws and customs of the country with a wealth and accuracy of illustration which testified to the strength of his memory, he seemed rather like a sage expounding law and history to a class of pupils than a criminal defending himself before a bench of commissioners. Moved occasionally from his austere simplicity, the majestic old man rose to a strain of indignant eloquence which might have shaken the hall of a vast assembly and found echo in the hearts of a thousand hearers as he denounced their petty insults or ignoble insinuations; glaring like a caged lion at his tormentors, who had often shrunk before him when free, and now attempted to drown his voice by contradictions, interruptions, threats, and unmeaning howls.[1]

With an effrontery which did not lack ingenuity, Barneveld's defence was called by the commissioners his confession, and was formally registered as such in the process and the sentence; while the fact that he had not been stretched upon the rack during his trial, nor kept in chains for the eight months of his imprisonment, were complacently mentioned as proofs of exceptionable indulgence.

"Whereas the prisoner John of Barneveld," said the sentence, "without being put to the torture and without fetters of iron, has confessed . . . to having perturbed religion, greatly afflicted

[1] *The Life and Death of John of Barneveld* (London, 1874), II, 319–324.

the church of God, and carried into practice exorbitant and
pernicious maxims of state . . . inculcating by himself and accomplices that each province had the right to regulate religious
affairs within its own territory, and that other provinces were
not to concern themselves therewith"—therefore and for many
other reasons he merited punishment.

He had instigated a protest by vote of three provinces against
the national synod. He had despised the salutary advice of
many princes and notable personages. He had obtained from
the King of Great Britain certain letters furthering his own
opinions, the drafts of which he had himself suggested, and
corrected and sent over to the states' ambassador in London,
and when written out, signed, and addressed by the King to the
States-General, had delivered them without stating how they
had been procured.

Afterwards he had attempted to get other letters of a similar
nature from the king, and not succeeding had defamed his
Majesty as being a cause of the troubles in the provinces. He
had permitted unsound theologians to be appointed to church
offices, and had employed such functionaries in political affairs
as were most likely to be the instruments of his own purposes.
He had not prevented vigorous decrees from being enforced
in several places against those of the true religion. He had
made them odious by calling them Puritans, foreigners, and
"Flanderizers," although the United Provinces had solemnly
pledged to each other their lives, fortunes, and blood by various
conventions, to some of which the prisoner was himself a party,
to maintain the Reformed, Evangelical religion only, and to
suffer no change in it to be made forevermore.

In order to carry out his design and perturb the political
state of the provinces he had drawn up and caused to be enacted
the Sharp Resolution of 4th August, 1617. He had thus nullified
the ordinary course of justice. He had stimulated the magistrates to disobedience, and advised them to strengthen themselves with freshly enlisted military companies. He had suggested new-fangled oaths for the soldiers, authorizing them to
refuse obedience to the States-General and his Excellency. He

had especially stimulated the proceedings at Utrecht. When it was understood that the prince was to pass through Utrecht, the states of that province, not without the prisoner's knowledge, had addressed a letter to his Excellency, requesting him not to pass through their city. He had written a letter to Ledenberg suggesting that good watch should be held at the town gates and up and down the river Lek. He had desired that Ledenberg having read that letter should burn it. He had interfered with the cashiering of the mercenaries at Utrecht. He had said that such cashiering without the consent of the states of that province was an act of force which would justify resistance by force.

Although those States had sent commissioners to concert measures with the Prince for that purpose, he had advised them to conceal their instructions until his own plan for the disbandment could be carried out. At a secret meeting in the house of Tressel, clerk of the States-General, between Grotius, Hoogerbeets, and other accomplices, it was decided that this advice should be taken. Report accordingly was made to the prisoner. He had advised them to continue in their opposition to the national synod.

He had sought to calumniate and blacken his Excellency by saying that he aspired to the sovereignty of the provinces. He had received intelligence on that subject from abroad in ciphered letters.

He had of his own accord rejected a certain proposed, notable alliance of the utmost importance to this Republic.

He had received from foreign potentates various large sums of money and other presents.

All "these proceedings tended to put the city of Utrecht into a blood-bath, and likewise to bring the whole country and the person of his Excellency into the uttermost danger."

This is the substance of the sentence, amplified by repetitions and exasperating tautology into thirty or forty pages.[1]

But it was not to a merrymaking that the soldiers were marching and the citizens thronging so eagerly from every

[1] *The Life and Death of John of Barneveld* (London, 1874), II, 356–359.

street and alley towards the castle. By four o'clock the Outer and Inner Courts had been lined with detachments of the prince's guard and companies of other regiments to the number of 1200 men. Occupying the northeastern side of the court rose the grim, time-worn front of the ancient hall, consisting of one tall pyramidal gable of ancient grey brickwork flanked with two tall slender towers, the whole with the lancet-shaped windows and severe style of the twelfth century, excepting a rose-window in the centre with the decorated mullions of a somewhat later period.

In front of the lower window, with its Gothic archway hastily converted into a door, a shapeless platform of rough, unhewn planks had that night been rudely patched together. This was the scaffold. A slight railing around it served to protect it from the crowd, and a heap of coarse sand had been thrown upon it. A squalid, unclean box of unplaned boards, originally prepared as a coffin for a Frenchman—who some time before had been condemned to death for murdering the son of Goswyn Meurskens, a Hague tavern-keeper, but pardoned by the stadholder—lay on the scaffold. It was recognized from having been left for a long time, half forgotten, at the public execution-place of The Hague.

Upon this coffin now sat two common soldiers of ruffianly aspect, playing at dice, betting whether the Lord or the Devil would get the soul of Barneveld. Many a foul and ribald jest at the expense of the prisoner was exchanged between these gamblers, some of their comrades, and a few townsmen who were grouped about at that early hour. The horrible libels, caricatures, and calumnies which had been circulated, exhibited, and sung in all the streets for so many months had at last thoroughly poisoned the minds of the vulgar against the fallen statesman.

The great mass of the spectators had forced their way by daybreak into the hall itself to hear the sentence, so that the Inner Courtyard had remained comparatively empty.

At last, at half past nine o'clock, a shout arose, "There he comes! There he comes!" and the populace flowed out from the hall of judgment into the courtyard like a tidal wave.

In an instant the Binnenhof was filled with more than three thousand spectators.

The old statesman, leaning on his staff, walked out upon the scaffold and calmly surveyed the scene. Lifting his eyes to Heaven, he was heard to murmur, "O God! what does man come to!" Then he said bitterly once more: "This, then, is the reward of forty years' service to the state!"

La Motte, who attended him, said fervently: "It is no longer time to think of this. Let us prepare your coming before God."

"Is there no cushion or stool to kneel upon?" said Barneveld, looking around him.

The provost said he would send for one, but the old man knelt at once on the bare planks. His servant, who waited upon him as calmly and composedly as if he had been serving him at dinner, held him by the arm. It was remarked that neither master nor man, true stoics and Hollanders both, shed a single tear upon the scaffold.

La Motte prayed for a quarter of an hour, the Advocate remaining on his knees.

He then rose and said to John Franken, "See that he does not come near me," pointing to the executioner who stood in the background grasping his long double-handed sword. Barneveld then rapidly unbuttoned his doublet with his own hands and the valet helped him off with it. "Make haste! Make haste!" said his master.

The statesman then came forward and said in a loud, firm voice to the people:

"Men, do not believe that I am a traitor to the country. I have ever acted uprightly and loyally as a good patriot, and as such I shall die."

The crowd was perfectly silent.

He then took his cap from John Franken, drew it over his eyes, and went forward towards the sand, saying:

"Christ shall be my guide. O Lord, my heavenly Father, receive my spirit."

As he was about to kneel with his face to the south, the provost said:

"My lord will be pleased to move to the other side, not where the sun is in his face."

He knelt accordingly with his face towards his own house. The servant took farewell of him, and Barneveld said to the executioner:

"Be quick about it.   Be quick."

The executioner then struck his head off at a single blow.

Many persons from the crowd now sprang, in spite of all opposition, upon the scaffold and dipped their handkerchiefs in his blood, cut wet splinters from the boards, or grubbed up the sand that was steeped in it; driving many bargains afterwards for these relics to be treasured, with various feelings of sorrow, joy, and glutted or expiated vengeance.[1]

[1] *The Life and Death of John of Barneveld* (London, 1874), II, 385–388.